MONUMENTS, EMPIRES, AND RESISTANCE

From 1550 to 1850, the Araucanian polity in southern Chile was a center of political resistance to the intruding Spanish empire. In this book, Tom D. Dillehay examines the resistance strategies of the Araucanians and how they incorporated Andean knowledge and used mounds and other sacred monuments to reorganize their political and cultural life in order to unite against the Spanish. Drawing on anthropological research conducted over three decades, Dillehay focuses on the development of leadership, shamanism, ritual landscapes, and power relations, and on how healing ceremonies performed at actively used mounds today give meaning to the past and reveal the social and cosmological principles by which the Araucanians have organized their society. His study combines recent developments in social theory with the archaeological, ethnographic, and historical records. Both theoretically and empirically informed, this book is a fascinating account of an indigenous ethnic group that successfully resisted outsiders for more than three centuries and flourished under these conditions.

Monuments, Empires, and Resistance is an indispensable text for all archaeologists interested in the social, ideological, and demographic processes that construct and maintain mound building and mound worship in the past. This book details for the first time ethnographic ritual narratives that reveal the kin relations between mounds and living shamans. Dillehay illuminates these complex processes and the changing consciousness of the people who built and live with the mounds.

Tom D. Dillehay is Distinguished Professor and Chair of Anthropology at Vanderbilt University. He has conducted extensive anthropological research in Peru, Chile, and the United States. He has published extensively in both English and Spanish. He is the author of several books, including *The Settlement of the Americas: A New Prehistory*, and the editor of *Tombs for Living: Andean Mortuary Practices* and has been a visiting professor at more than fifteen universities worldwide.

CAMBRIDGE STUDIES IN ARCHAEOLOGY

Cambridge Studies in Archaeology aims to showcase the very best in contemporary archaeological scholarship. Reflecting the wide diversity and vigour of archaeology as an intellectual discipline, the series covers all regions of the world and embraces all major theoretical and methodological approaches. Designed to be empirically grounded and theoretically aware, and including both single-authored and collaborative volumes, the series is arranged around four highlighted strands:

- Prehistory
- Classical Archaeology
- Medieval Archaeology
- Historical Archaeology

Titles in series

The Archaeology of Class in Urban America
Stephen A. Mrozowski
Archaeology, Society, and Identity in Modern Japan
Koji Mizoguchi
Death and Memory in Early Medieval Britain
Howard Williams

MONUMENTS, EMPIRES, AND RESISTANCE

THE ARAUCANIAN POLITY AND RITUAL NARRATIVES

TOM D. DILLEHAY

Vanderbilt University

CAMBRIDGE
UNIVERSITY PRESS

CAMBRIDGE UNIVERSITY PRESS
Cambridge, New York, Melbourne, Madrid, Cape Town, Singapore, São Paulo

Cambridge University Press
32 Avenue of the Americas, New York, NY 10013-2473, USA

www.cambridge.org
Information on this title: www.cambridge.org/9780521872621

First published 2007

Printed in the United States of America

A catalog record for this publication is available from the British Library.

Library of Congress Cataloging in Publication Data
Dillehay, Tom D.
Monuments, empires, and resistance : the Araucanian polity and ritual narratives /
Tom D. Dillehay.
p.   cm. – (Cambridge studies in archaeology)
Includes bibliographical references and index.
ISBN-13: 978-0-521-87262-1 (hardback)
ISBN-10: 0-521-87262-6 (hardback)
1. Mapuche Indians – History.   2. Mapuche Indians – Wars.   3. Mapuche Indians – Social life and
customs.   4. Mounds – Chile – Araucanma.   5. Spain – Colonies – America.   6. Araucanma
(Chile) – History.   7. Araucanma (Chile) – Social life and customs.   8. Chile – History –
1565–1810.   I. Title.   II. Series.
F3126.D57   2007
983′.0049872 – dc22   2006027844

ISBN   978-0-521-87262-1 hardback

DEDICATED TO THE LATE AMÉRICO GORDON STECKEL

CONTENTS

FIGURES

PREFACE

Much of the data in this book come in the form of archaeological research, ethnohistorical documentation, and ethnographical recordings and observations. For more than thirty years, I have participated in many different ritual ceremonies and other events in many different Araucanian, or Mapuche, communities, always examining the living behavior from the perspective of their spatial, material, and symbolic correlates. The Mapuche are not partial to interviews and prefer a non-interventionist style of fieldwork where they offered information when they thought that my colleagues and I were ready to receive it or needed to be corrected. My language skills in Mapundungun are barely sufficient for understanding the conversation at hand during daily life but certainly not proficient to understand the often archaic intonations and nuances of shamanic speech and chant in ceremony. Most interviews and rituals were tape recorded when we were given permission. A native speaker, Maria Catrileo, translated the tapes from Mapundungun to Spanish. For much of the material, I assisted in the translation of many words and phrases, now having become somewhat proficient in the ritual language. The majority of the Spanish texts, especially those from the early chroniclers, were translated by Patricia Netherly. Others were translated by other colleagues and by me. Netherly also edited these translations in order to derive a similar style.

Although the research themes examined in these pages encompass several centuries and primarily one river valley, the impetus for this book comes from my experiences in almost all parts of the Araucanian territory. Much of this research was carried out in a time when a different Chile existed. Today, people arrive to ski on the high slopes of the Andes, to bathe in the hundreds of thermal baths flowing from the Andean foothills, and to enjoy good seafood and wine. I know and have a deep passion for this Chile. But there was another Chile, one engulfed in political turmoil and ruled by the Pinochet dictatorship (see Ensalaco 2000) when I began my studies in early 1975. It was a time of *toque de queda* (curfew) when the side of the street you walked on identified the side of political life you affiliated with and when people disappeared and were never heard from again.

During these years in the mid to late 1970s, I was writing my dissertation and teaching first at the Pontíficia Universidad Católica de Temuco and later at the Universidad Austral de Chile. I still am a professor at the latter institution.

In the late 1970s and throughout the 1980s during the Pinochet regime, I occasionally witnessed unpleasant conflicts between the military and some Mapuche communities over land and resources. I have commented both privately and publicly about some of these experiences. In addition to stories and tales about mounds and other themes of historical and archaeological interest, informants told me about *desaparecidos* and armed conflicts. Therefore, I have not listed all informants I worked with over the past three decades in accordance with their wishes, in order to protect those who confided in me during the years of my research and to prevent the use of informant knowledge beyond the anthropological community.

This book has benefited from its long gestation. Parts of it were begun in the mid-1990s, initially supported by the Banco Interamericano de Desarrollo, Fulbright Commission, National Geographic Society, Pontíficia Universidad Católica de Temuco, and Universidad Austral de Chile; later by the Heinz Foundation, John Simon Memorial Guggenheim Foundation, Vanderbilt University, and National Science Foundation; and always by the University of Kentucky. I would like to thank numerous colleagues over the years for their help as sounding boards and valuable sources of information: José Saavedra, Patricio Sanzana, Arturo Rojas, Gaston Sepulveda, Mario Pino, Teresa Durán, Leonor Adan, Rolf Foerster, Carlos Ocampo, Ana Mariella Bacigalupo, Hans Gundermann, René San Martin, Ximena Navarro, Alejandro Saavedra, Maria Ester Grebe, José Manuel Zavala, Raul Ortiz, Gerson Levy, Tim Earle, Ian Hodder, Richard Bradley, David Pollack, Gwynn Henderson, William Adams, and Kenneth Hirth. Special gratitude is given to the late Alberto Medina, an ethnohistorian and professor at the Universidad de Chile and to the late Américo Gordon, who was a good archaeologist, a connoisseur of Mapuche culture, and a dear friend. Américo and I spent many informative days together in the field and had many relaxed conversations in his home in Temuco. This book is dedicated to him.

There are countless people who have worked closely with me in the field since I first went to Chile: Mario Pino, José Saavedra, Patricio Sanzana, Gaston Sepulveda, Américo Gordon, Ximena Navarro, Arturo Rojas, and René San Martin. All of these colleagues are good friends. We have spent many enjoyable times in the field. Also included in this group are hundreds of Mapuche workers and informants from many different areas in south-central Chile and students from various universities worldwide. Comments on a draft of this manuscript by Patricia Netherly, José Bengoa, Norman Yoffee, José Manuel Zavala, and Gerardo Ardila helped me strengthen the final version. José Saavedra and Arturo Rojas provided comments on the ethnography chapters, and José Manuel Zavala read and reviewed the ethnohistory chapter. Ashley Colby Parrott and Paige Silcox provided excellent technical support. Special thanks also are extended to four anonymous readers for Cambridge University Press, who provided invaluable comments and suggestions. I also would like to thank Simon Whitmore and Beatrice Rehl at Cambridge University Press, for all of their help and encouragement. Thanks also are extended to Mary Paden and Lee A. Young for their editorial advice. A special gratitude is extended to José Saavedra who has spent more time in the field with me in Chile than anyone else listed here. José collected a substantial portion of the ethnographic data with me. He has been a loyal friend and colleague. I also thank my wife, Dana Nelson, for her invaluable support, advice, and companionship. Lastly, to thank the Mapuche seems somewhat lame, as without them this book could not have been written. Their patience, encouragement, influence, and friendship not only affected me while I lived in and have continued to carry out research in Chile but have taught me the importance of indigenous struggles and of questioning received anthropological wisdom.

INTRODUCTION

This book is about *living, interactive* mounds and other monuments that were built between the thirteenth and nineteenth centuries by the Araucanians, or Mapuche, of south-central Chile and that are still in ritual use today by a few indigenous communities (Fig. 1). Mounds, or *kuel* (*cuel*) in the native language, are perceived by people as living kindred who participate in public ceremony, converse with priestly shamans about the well-being and future of the community, and thus have powerful influence over people. The oldest *kuel* are archaeological sites associated with the rise of dynastic late pre-Hispanic patrilineages that rapidly developed into the early historic Araucanian "*estado*," or polity, referenced by the first Spanish in the region. (In sixteenth-century Spanish, *estado* means an organized political condition and not necessarily the "state" level of society we recognize in the scholarly literature today.) This polity successfully resisted European intrusion longer than any indigenous society in American history until it was finally defeated by the Chilean army in the mid-1890s. The Araucanians were not conquered and influenced by the Spanish the way other Native American groups were. Instead, after initial sporadic contact in the latter half of the sixteenth century, they were outside of the authority of the Spanish and defeated and drove them out of their territory for nearly 300 years from the late 1500s to the late 1800s. In this process, the Araucanians established a formal military frontier and sovereign territory recognized by the Spanish Crown. One of the first and strongest political resistances along the frontier was located in the Purén and Lumaco Valley of south-central Chile, where the oldest and most elaborate mound cultures are found and where this study is primarily situated. The presence of these mounds reflects the relatively high level of social complexity and political power in the valley during the period of study.

The type of complex Araucanian society I refer to in the study area initially consisted of many small and a few large "chiefdom" mound-building communities in late pre-Hispanic times. These communities probably had kin relationships established with many outside settlements, with the confirmation of bonds between them taking place in the form of political alliances, marriage exchanges,

1

and regular feasts and ceremonies. The archaeological and early historical records show a wide array of crisscrossing, overlapping, and intersecting distributions of goods, ideas, and peoples – the reflection of individual and community networks over wide regions, transcending differences in environment, economic specialization, and political organization (Dillehay 1976, 1990a). Any forms of social and political differentiation seem to have been weakly to moderately developed, with kin-based rulers; there apparently were no formally sanctioned institutions of power. Later, in times of unrest and social upheaval when sporadic contacts with the Spanish first occurred in the mid-1550s, multilevel settlement hierarchies of dominant centers and subordinate communities emerged. Also developed was the importance of larger and more elaborate public ceremonial architecture, with mound complexes constructed as instruments of social power as well as religious institutions. In this early contact period, new kinds of leaders emerged from large patrilineages that had access to favorable agricultural resources and large kin-related labor for defense against outsiders and for public projects. Further expansion of power was pursued through the manipulation of indigenous community institutions, in the form of the sponsorship of large multilineage feasts and other events, in return for portions of the community labor pool. The ability to extract these tributes was greatly enhanced when embedded in reorganized indigenous concepts of communal ideology, religion, and ancestry worship, many of which were already Andean in principle and some of which were probably adopted and enhanced from the Inka. There is no doubt that Araucanian leaders increased their authority as a result of contact with the Inka and Spanish empires, built on existing Araucanian (and Andean) principles of organization by incorporating some Inka ideas to reorganize larger groups of people, and thus used indigenous forms of power and authority, in new and different ways, to resist outsiders and to further develop their own society.

The role of mounds and other monuments within the formation of the Araucanian polity has meaning with regard to political power and varying forms of traditional leadership and authority, agency and power, identity and memory, sacred landscape and ceremony, institutionalized shamanic spiritualism and healing, rules of intergroup compatriotism, low-intensity warfare, and settlement nucleation and agricultural intensity. Above all, the mounds are related to the establishment of an indigenous anticolonial social order that resisted invasions for more than three years. This new order was founded on indigenous organizational principles and comprised confederated patrilineal groups. These groups employed mounded ceremonial landscapes in selected areas to politically unite a previously decentralized population of dispersed patrilineages and to set the Araucanians on a course toward polity formation, sovereignty, and control of their own destiny. In this book, I attempt to relate the historical trajectory of these developments to the creation and use of mounds and to changes in the spatial arrangements and scale of mound complexes.

1. General view of the *Rehueñichikuel* mound (black arrow) complex in Butarincón built on the modified hilltop which has been deliberately leveled to form a ritual platform or *ñichi* (white arrows). The flat plaza area around the mound is the present-day *nguillatun* ceremonial field.

Recent anthropological theory has stressed the importance of analyzing the changing organizational transformations in social and political relations as the product of colonialism and of culture contact and interaction between societies. The early colonial history of the Araucanians and their relationship with external societies centers on five basic issues that will reoccur throughout this book.

1. Political and religious organizations: On what basis did the Araucanians form and maintain a new social order and polity that united regional social, religious, and political organizations to resist outsiders (e.g., Allen 1999; Comaroff 1998; Cooper 2005; Smith 2003)?

2. Local spheres of interaction and recruitment: What was the relationship between local populations of stable lineages and lineages displaced by armed conflict? How did lineages employ certain forms of tactical and strategical organization in special settings to increase their power and to achieve higher forms of social order (*sensu* Wolf 1999)?

3. Recruitment and expansion: How did local lineages expand their power through commensal ritual feasting (Dietler 1996) and the recruitment, adoption, and annexation of other groups?

4. Imagined or utopic polity of resistance: How did Araucanian leaders envision and construct a new social order on the basis of traditional and new principles of organization (e.g., Anderson 1983; Cooper 2005; Marin 1984)?

5. Archaeological expressions of these interactions and organizations: What were the material and spatial signatures, especially mound building, of a new order and polity formation?

The anthropological data gathered on the Araucanians are extensive enough to answer these questions and allow us to interpret their polity on its own terms. But the test of any question is in its application. Those presented here should explain the data in a coherent fashion so that a nonspecialist can understand the flow of events and changing formations, while allowing the specialist to test them further against the total body of historical information.

Over the past thirty years, I have carried out archaeological, ethnographical, and ethnohistorical research on these themes, focusing primarily on five issues: (1) tracing the historical development of mound building from its inception in the twelfth to thirteenth centuries and how social complexity initially developed in the study area; (2) examining how the leaders of large patrilineages created new and reorganized traditional institutions by tactically recruiting fragmented lineages and incorporating them into their own groups through ceremonial feasting and by annexation of neighboring groups to expand their base of military and political power; (3) elucidating the symbolic and cultural landscape meaning of Araucanian monuments and ceremonialism and the role of priestly shamans as mediators between the spiritual and living worlds in recent times; (4) studying how the identity and power of the Araucanians were expanded by incorporating elements of the Andean and Inka models of state authority and organizational power; and (5) how Araucanian polity, compatriotism, and territory were formed to resist outsiders. The approach to these themes is through the Purén and Lumaco Valley, which contains more than 300 mounds, several of which comprise large complexes overlooking expansive marshes, or *ciénegas*, and are associated with extensive domestic sites, agricultural systems, and occasionally hilltop defenses. Being the first known mound complexes in the southern Andes and the only place in the Araucania (southern Araucanian populations living between the Bio Bio and Rio Bueno rivers) where mound-related rituals still are practiced, Purén and Lumaco are unique in their anthropology and in their availability to study where a mound-building society developed and spread. This analysis combines the hard data of archaeology, ethnohistory, and ethnography to produce identifiable social, cultural, and demographic patterns and to infer the meaning of these patterns.

This study is unprecedented in the anthropological examination of mound-building societies, because two lengthy ritual narratives between shamans and communally active, living mounds recorded during ethnographic healing ceremonies are linked analytically to the archaeological and textual evidence to provide rich and insightful details of the wider social, ideological, spatial, and historical contexts of mound worship and its meaning to the people who built them. (The reader is encouraged to carefully examine the richly textured details of the full narratives in Appendix 1 for insights into the role and meaning of shamanism and of the social interactions between mounds, sacred landscapes, and people. Also revealed is the Andean influence in Araucanian culture.) This analysis reveals how the narratives and the metaphors in rituals performed at sacred places are important performative and oral traditions that give meaning to the past and reveal the social and cosmological principles by which the Araucanians have guided their ways of life and organized themselves to successfully defend themselves against outsiders. My provisional conclusion is that the Araucanian society of the sixteenth to nineteenth centuries was a cultural system with social principles and practices that were directed by a deeply embedded cosmological framework. This framework was and still is characterized by historical continuity in the metaphors that support the social institutions and ritual practices that permeated and, in many ways, still permeate all cultural activities and knit the society together (*sensu* Sekaquaptewa and Washburn 2004). I show how many of these same principles and pressures that are expressed metaphorically in the shaman's ritual narratives are also metaphorically, spatially, and materially represented in the archaeological and early written records. The messages that I want to leave with readers are that mounds are human-like, can act in both good and bad ways, and may need placatory rituals to regenerate their gestures of benevolence toward local communities. Mounds also have multiple characters as places of burial, abodes of dead shamans, memorials to ancestry and genealogy, status markers for lineage leaders, loci of ceremony, feasting and political power, and cosmological media. Thus, mounds are socially constructed and inscribed with meaning by people, but, on the other hand, once they are built and engaged in public ritual, they also organize people's responses and patterns of interaction. As one anonymous reviewer of the book remarked, "it is this multivalency that extracts the mounds from their mute archaeology and enables us to see them as the Araucanians do, as essentially alive."

The core of Araucanian cosmology focuses on practices that link the living with their ancestors and deities and that employ past knowledge to guide present and future behavior. (I consider ideology here as an epistemology or concept of the way people know their world. Cosmology organizes this knowledge and teaches it to people through repetitive ceremonial practices.) One way of communicating these practices is through ritual performances participated in by the entire community. Healing rituals at mounds are oral and performative acts that express all of the cosmological principles that have long guided the political actions and religious thoughts of the Araucanians. The consistent continuity in form, function, and meaning of narrative histories and metaphors and of many other cultural patterns permits me, through a direct historical approach that employs archaeology, ethnohistory, and ethnography, to reliably extend our interpretation of the past at least back to the fifteenth and seventeenth centuries, depending on the specific theme of study. Many of the archaeological patterns express the same or similar metaphorical constructions that have been uncovered in ethnography and ethnohistory, because they convey similar ideas and interpretations that have been shared by past and present communities in the study area for the past few centuries (see Chapters 2 and 3). By first understanding the principles of organization and cosmologies that governed how these communities have lived, a better understanding is attained of how mounds, the spaces between and around them, and other artifacts are the material and spatial correlates of those conceptual principles. I also attempt to recover a past that is the Araucanian ethnographic view of their past as preserved in ritual, oral tradition, public ceremony, and their understandings of the mounded landscapes that surround them.

I have learned that Araucanian mounds cannot be adequately explained by just the conventional and narrowly focused approaches of political economy, culture ecology, landscape anthropology, hermeneutics, phenomenology, and others. As explained in Chapter 2, this study requires a convergence of key aspects of these approaches to derive a historical, material, and cognitive perspective. By presenting a variety of interdisciplinary data and by combining these approaches, this analysis hopefully provides the opportunity to add to the archaeological discourse on different trajectories of social complexity, to bring a different perspective to studies of historical process and meaning, and to contemplate how we think about social power, structure and agency, identity and memory, and interaction and what they meant in crafting polities. The Araucanian case reveals the articulation of ritual, social, and knowledge power as primary variables in the construction and expansion of regional political organization, the role and meaning of religious landscapes in forming and sustaining emergent corporate structures, and the forms of resistance to outside contact that guided the form and organization of new social orders and power relations. I view this case being particularly significant to archaeologists analyzing social organizations characterized by recursive monumental landscapes and artifact styles and by regional polities coalescing to form larger and cooperative (or competitive) geopolitical entities. From a technical perspective, this case also reveals the types of perishable artifacts and ceremonial spaces that may be associated with mounds but rarely preserved in the archaeological record.

Archaeologists have long considered monuments to represent the conspicuous landmarks and registers of past social relations; have recognized many patterns in mounds, *menhirs*, *tumuli*, *cursus*, barrows, and other culturally constructed edifices; and have proposed several different functions and meanings, at the regional and global scales, to explain their recurrence in time and space. Two basic approaches can be identified in the scholarly study of these registers. One focuses on functionalism and structuralism that has generally given emphasis to culture history, political economy, symbolism, and cultural materialism (cf. Bradley 1998; Dillehay 1990a; Knight 1989; Smith 1990; Squier and Davis 1997); the other owes a debt to poststructuralism and centers on ideology, symbolism, and meaning (cf. Bradley 2000; Dillehay 1999; Lewis et al. 1998; Scarre 2002a; Thomas 1995; Tilley 1994). These two perspectives are usually set against each other as competing explanations for the same phenomena. In contrast, both are relevant and necessary components of any full explanation or understanding of monuments – they deal with different but equally relevant dimensions of the same phenomena and with different aspects of society in which their material expressions are conspicuously absent or present. In addition, both perspectives have espoused simplistic and sophisticated notions of the archaeological records of mounds, and how we can learn from them, as well as limiting the scope of model-building toward archaeological inference and meaning. However, these oppositions are largely of our own creation, and are not inherent in past human behaviors. Our perpetuation of such contrasts in the archaeological study of mounds guarantees that we will never approach more than a partial understanding of the phenomena we are trying to explain. I thus hope to offer more than a partial understanding of the Araucanian mounds by presenting a holistic and direct historical approach to them and by occasionally relating this understanding to mound-building societies of other periods and in other parts of the world. In this regard, students of past mound builders such as the Adena, Hopewell, Fort Ancient, and Hohokam cultures in the United States, various Formative cultures of Central America and South America, and the Mesolithic and Neolithic cultures of Europe should find this analysis useful for comprehending the specific behavioral frameworks and intricate social interactions that produced polities and sacred landscapes and for relating these practices to physical and symbolic evidence. Archaeologists interested in secondary state formation should be interested in the transformative processes by which the Araucanians were influenced by certain Andean and Inka principles of political and religious organization to develop a more effective and expansive regional polity.

On a global level, archaeologists have attributed an important role in the early development of social and political complexity to public monuments and especially to ceremonial centers (Grove 1981; Milner 2004; Pauketat 2004). While extremely variable in form and scale as well as the range of activities associated with them, these centers are thought to represent the architectural foci of communal practices and interactions, and through these, the production and reproduction of authority structures and social stratification. Several integrative venues have been identified with public monuments, including the regulation of competitive ritual feasting for retainers, the manipulation of religious and exotic symbols, the elaboration of new production techniques, the facilitation of trade and exchange of exotic goods, and the proliferation of other outside interactions (e.g., Brumfiel 1987; Clark and Blake 1994; Helms 1979; Parker 2006; Stanish 2003). Early monuments also are seen as regional nodes of intense interaction engaged in the construction of ever-wider political and ideational landscapes (e.g., Bradley 1998;

Lane 2001). Archaeologists are learning that the intrinsic features characteristic of diverse local landscapes both informed the settings selected for the construction of monuments and played a role in determining their form and visual appearance. Also realized is that the interpretative experiences past peoples had with different monuments and altered landscapes probably related to the changing meanings and effective relationships derived from them. In short, many different approaches have recently converged to place the study of early monuments within broader regional and intellectual contexts in order to reflect on the changing consciousness of the people who built them. As revealed throughout this book, several of these approaches have influenced my thinking on Araucanian mounds.

Also influencing my approach to the study of form and meaning of the Araucanian mounds is the monumental architecture of various Formative societies in South America. Although distinct in different parts of the continent, the general forms range from small earthen mounds and ritual stone enclosures dating from 7000 to 600 years ago in both the Andes and the eastern tropical lowlands of Amazonia to large U-shaped ceremonial structures dating between 4500 and 500 years ago in Peru. In scale, coastal and highland Peru, southern Ecuador, and northern Bolivia exhibit the largest and earliest monuments (Burger 1992). By 4000 years ago some monumental ceremonial centers on the north coast of Peru had permanent populations while others probably served as periodic pilgrimage centers. Similar but later patterns are observed in the south-central Andes of Bolivia, north Chile, and northwest Argentina. In the eastern lowlands of southeast Brazil and north Uruguay, early mound-building societies characterized by a village lifestyle have been dated as far back as 4000 years ago. Regardless of their time, place, and form, most archaeologists view Formative monuments as built landscapes associated with autonomous, territorial groupings organized on the level of ranked societies (Janusek 2004; Stanish 2003), stratified multicommunity polities, competitive peer-polities, or incipient states (cf. Haas et al. 2005; Shady and Leyva 2002). Although the political, economic, and religious importance of monuments and how they first developed in South America have been studied, little attention has been given to how they were modified and experienced to suit the changing needs of past societies and to how people interacted with them. I hope to shed some light on these themes in this study.

Lastly, in addition to recovering social knowledge and meaning, this book is concerned with situating the history of the Araucanians within a broader project of challenging official written histories about these people. I am critical of existing models of Araucanian history as largely a unilateral process of Spanish contact and colonial state expansion (which never developed because the Araucanians were first colonized by the Chileans, not the Spanish) and of Araucanian social complexity as a corresponding amalgamation of scattered ethnic populations that defended themselves against outside intrusion (see Chapters 1 and 3). In this analysis, the emergence of a regional Araucanian confederacy during the sixteenth to eighteenth centuries was not merely a passive indigenous response to changing contexts of power in the present-day territory of Chile but a hyperactive process of building a powerful political community and an indigenous "socially engineered utopic" society (*sensu* Marin 1984; see Chapter 1) that already had begun to organize itself as an expansive, disruptive geopolitical force by the mid-1550s. (In using the term utopic, I do not refer to crisis cults, revitalization movements, or millenarian events, which are associated with indigenous social protests and reactions to outsiders and to radical change in the distribution of wealth, power, and status once Spanish colonial rule had been established in other regions of Latin America [see Bernard 1994; Scott 1985; Stern 1987]. These movements did not take place in south-central Chile before the late 1900s.) This utopic process was rooted in traditional Araucanian and Andean forms of constructing different social hierarchies of religious communities, large agricultural communities, and secular and priestly shamanic powers and of conceptualizing the future place of non-Araucanians in the world. Although this process involved resistance to external realities, the Araucanians showed openness to exotic knowledge and often reached to outsiders, including the Spanish, in search of new insights and conceptual models (see Alvaro 1971; Bengoa 2003; Boccara 1999; Villalobos et al. 1982; Villalobos and Pinto 1985).

Araucanian history thus provided a model not only for resistance and social order among the indigenous peoples of south-central Chile but also a blueprint for encoding and acting on changing geopolitical and interethnic relations along a Spanish frontier. Whereas the official history of the Araucanians (as written by outsiders) often has failed to perceive their geographic and political knowledge through the imposition of Spanish-based cartographies, I hope to counteract some of this bias through exploring the emergence of the Araucanian polity as an active process of producing local histories and creating new cultural and political spaces. Construction of this polity was a contested arena of struggle over regional representations and traditional authenticities, with different ethnic and other groups manifesting their changing identities through continuity and change within historically shaped indigenous political and religious structures, which were constructions materially expressed in the mounded landscapes under study here. That is, the Araucanians were social and cultural actors who endeavored to control their own destiny by altering their ideologies and ways of life to manipulate space and time to build a new "utopic" or imagined social order to both resist outsiders and expand their geopolitical power. This is not to deny the violence and institutionalized effort first by the Inka and later by the Spanish and Chileans to conquer these people, the full impact of historic disruptions on the Araucanians, and the prolonged resistance of the Araucanians to these efforts. (I discuss the impact of Spanish contact and the social, economic, and demographic adjustments made by the Araucanians to it throughout the book [also see Dillehay 1995, 2003]). But through the analysis of local indigenous histories like those in the Purén and

Lumaco Valley in the sixteenth and seventeenth centuries, this study partly aims to reveal local native strategies for responding to outside contact, for defeating the Spanish, and for creating a *longue durée* of resistance. In this sense, I wish to make it clear that I do not pretend that the history of Purén and Lumaco is also the history of all areas within the Araucania. However, it is an important history that defines much of the early resistance to the Spanish and that addresses the previously neglected indigenous mound cultures of the south Andes.

Given these concerns, I suspect that this book will not be well received by some historians, particularly those purists that believe in the absolute author-ity of the written word in early texts for interpretation of the early historic period. Since focusing my earlier dissertation research on the archaeological and ethnographic verification/falsification of sixteenth-century documents in Peru, I have had problems with historical studies that minimally consider the results of archaeological and ethnographic research and specifically of the direct historical approach. Each of these subdisciplines has its strengths and weaknesses but the latter can often be reduced by combining as many different approaches as possible to understand a phenomenon and to reduce ambiguity (Dillehay 2003). Unfor-tunately, this has not always been the case in Araucanian studies. My primary concern with these studies is that many historians of Araucanian society need to more actively problematize their textual sources – that is, treat the texts as problems to be mulled over rather than pristine representations of an antecedent reality to be reconstructed. The good historians have always done this to some degree, but perhaps not with the obsessive energy that characterizes certain vari-eties of deconstructive postmodernist thinking in the human sciences. To date, most interpretations of the early historic Araucanians have been derived from tex-tualized viewpoints. However, we should be more prepared to admit that what historical actors do not write in their texts is often just as telling as what they do write. The case in point here is the scarcity of early textual evidence on the mound-building practices present in one of the most celebrated and commented areas of the Spanish conquest in Chile – the Purén and Lumaco Valley. In convey-ing motives, meanings, or even the most straightforward descriptions of this and other areas, the early texts distort (or simply follow their own internal logic) or tell only part of the story, and other important explanatory elements may lie just under the surface of those texts or beyond the barriers of consciousness, percep-tion, or language. One of the implications following this is the fragmentation of causal statements in the texts. So what actors tell us about themselves and about the phenomena they observe in early texts, or what other actors or observers tell us about them, may very well be true, it may not only be true. The intent here is not to single out historians for criticism. As discussed in Chapter 3, archaeology and ethnography also distort data and tell only part of the story, but I believe that the distortions and partial stories told by each discipline can be revealed and the strengths of each can be enhanced by combining various approaches to shed multiple and hopefully complementary dialogues on both similar and dissimilar problems.

THEMATIC ORGANIZATION OF THE BOOK

Having set out the objectives of this book and the general idea of Araucanian mounds and polities in this introduction, I briefly outline its organization. This is a work of data presentation and interpretation, with most chapters representing a broad range of theoretical perspectives, methods, and data sets. The book is divided into two parts. Part 1 has six chapters dealing with selected previous literature on monuments and complex societies in general and with presentation of the ethnohistorical, ethnographic, and archaeological data. Part 1 is concerned with critical questions that arise in the effort to imbue historiography with ethnographical and archaeological insight. Part 2 contains three chapters that treat the meaning and significance of the data in both the local and global contexts of complex societies.

In Part 1, Chapter 1 discusses the historical and social problems under analysis in this book and the specific kinds of interdisciplinary data employed to study them. It also presents the primary concepts guiding this analysis. Chapter 2 provides a discussion of the models and concepts in the literature on monuments, emergent social complexity, memory, identity and power, landscape, and other issues that are relevant to the objectives of this book. Chapter 3 presents synoptic aspects of Araucanian archaeology and ethnohistory related to the kind of society that built mounds. In this chapter, I mainly turn to an ethnohistorical analysis of Araucanian society at the time of victory and prolonged resistance to the Spanish. Although this chapter is given primarily to the written sources, ethnohistorical data are presented throughout the book to build bridges between the ethnographic and archaeological records. Chapters 4 to 6 are mainly the presentation of descriptive and patterned data. Chapter 4 provides a general discussion of Araucanian religion, ideology, and sense of history. This chapter is important for defining the spatial and temporal dimensions of cosmology, public ceremony, and their integration with ancestral history and for initially placing the multiple roles and meanings of mounds and other monuments within these dimensions. Chapter 5 discusses the present-day ethnographic setting and meaning of mounds or *kuel* and mound complexes based largely on two long ritual dialogues between shamans and "living" mounds. The dialogues reveal the interchanging identities between the shamans and the mounds, and how mounds relate to community practices and destinies. The shamans' relations to the mounds in this chapter set the stage for interpreting much of the subsequent ethnohistorical, ethnoarchaeological, and archaeological data. In Chapter 6, I examine the archaeology of the type, location, and role of mounds and mound complexes in the cultural and bounded geography of the Purén and Lumaco Valley. The archaeological data are not presented in detail such that all artifact types, stratigraphy, and settlement patterns are analyzed. Such an analysis is ongoing and also would require a much lengthier treatise than a single chapter. The intent of this chapter is to interpret what is known of the mound networks in the valley as they are reconstructed from the combined data bases. In this chapter, I also show that mounds and ceremonial fields are more than static localities and archaeological sites; they culturally configure a topographically defined model of politico–religious organization, which was employed by the Araucanians to more fully integrate communities in times of periodic warfare and to show them how to become active, contributing compatriots within the new social order of the confederated polity.

In Part 2, Chapters 7 to 9 are analytical and interpretative. Chapter 7 studies the religious and political organization of mounds and mound networks as they relate to recruitment by lineage leaders of fragmented lineages defeated in warfare and to annexed neighboring areas. This chapter also examines the important political relations between shamans, leaders, feasting, and other encounters. Chapter 8 turns to the political organization and meaning of the larger political territorial units (i.e., *ayllarehue* and *butanmapu*) and how they relate to mounded landscapes, to the Araucanian polity, and to the Purén and Lumaco Valley. Chapter 9 draws out the broader meaning of mounds and sketches their relevance to Araucanian society as a whole and to the archaeological understanding of social complexity, sacred landscapes, memory and identity, compatriotism, and polity-formation. Part 2 is followed by two appendices presenting the two long ritual narratives and a list of the radiocarbon and thermoluminescence dates for relevant mound and other sites.

Finally, although this book is not given primarily to a broad comparative analysis of prehistoric monuments, all chapters after Chapter 2 provide occasional discussion of some of the archaeological correlates of mound building and mound use and of the kind of society that built and used mounds. Although I present a considerable amount of information on mound forms, functions, meanings, and chronologies and link them with the ethnographic and ethnohistorical data, I do not provide detailed settlement pattern, economic, internal site, and artifact analyses. Rather than a text focused on archaeological artifacts and sites, it treats the broader social, historical, and ideological contexts in which they were and still are produced and given meaning, the choices made by mound and site producers within a larger social system, and the interpretation of the material record by living producers.

PART ONE

PROSPECTS AND PATTERNS

ONE:

PURPOSES, SETTINGS, AND

DEFINITIONS

In a short time the Spanish conquered the three powerful empires of the American hemisphere, those of Peru, Mexico, and Bogotá, but the hundred and ninety years that have elapsed since the beginning of this conquest have not sufficed to end it with the subjugation of the Araucanians. Nor has the vast expenditure of fifty million pesos and more than 25,000 recruits, nor the effusion of blood that has been spilled done so, even though in the past century the King declared this war to be equal to those of Spain, Flanders, and Italy. Today the Araucanians possess the fairest portion of Chile from the Bio Bio River to the Straits of Chiloé, a hundred and fifty leagues stretching between the Cordillera and the sea. In the whole of this area the Spanish hold nothing but the fortified towns of Arauco and Valdivia: the Indians live in independence and enjoyment of their coveted liberty.

> Córdoba y Figueroa [1861] 1942, II: 29; translated by and quoted in Padden 1993:88.

What faculty or genius did the Araucanians possess which enabled them to succeed so brilliantly where other indigenous American cultures had failed? The Araucanians, under this external pressure [Spanish intrusion] turned inward upon themselves and developed their own corresponding [political and religious] forms to a point of equal resistive strength.

> Padden 1993:71.

This is old business, walking slowly over the land and the *kuel* with an appreciation of their needs and of their immediacy to the human senses and form, with knowledge of the history that lies in them and the history that they tell, and in anticipation of the history yet to come. *Kuel* are our kindred spirits. They teach us; we learn how to

2. Large *TrenTrenkuel* mound (black arrow) situated on a modified *ñichi* platform (white arrows) in Isla de Katrileo and Butarincón.

> live and how to work with them. *Rehuekuel* are places where a family
> of mounds lives and where people learn how to live with them
>
> the late shaman Cármen Curín, Huilinco, Chile, 1994.

These quotes from a Spanish chronicler, a modern historian, and an Araucanian shaman encapsulate several of the issues addressed in this book. *Kuel* in the Mapuche, or what the first Spaniards called Araucanian, language means a socially built mound where ancestral spirits reside, important people are occasionally buried, and public rituals are performed (Fig. 1). In the Purén and Lumaco Valley, the ancient term *rehuekuel* (*reguakuel*) refers to sacred knolls and hilltops that are artificially leveled, where one or several *kuel* are located and where large-scale *nguillatun* (fertility) and other public ceremonies are sponsored by multiple patrilineages (Fig. 2). (*Rehuekuel* is an ancient concept provided by two knowledgeable and now deceased shamans or *machi*, Cármen and Fabiana, and by elders who lived in Lumaco and ritually interacted with mounds. The term still is used in ritual today by two living *machi*: Lucinda and Juanita.) *Ñichi* is the culturally leveled surface, or hilltop platform, on which mounds are erected. *Ayllarehue* (*aillarehue*) is a related group of *rehuekuel* in a bounded geographic area. *Ayllarehue* literally means nine *rehue* or lineages and figuratively implies a noble and sacred landscape that is politically divided. Each *kuel*, *rehuekuel*, and *ayllarehue* has its own name and history. The fact that each is named and that the names are recalled and used by living shamans (*machi*) and lineage members tells us of the importance of these sacred features to the Araucanian people today. Each *kuel* is composed of *reñinmapu*, which are the artificially prepared soil layers that make up the mounds and which represent ritual offerings to important ancestors

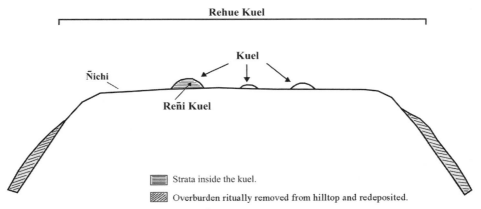

3. Schematic representation of the Araucanian terms for mound (*kuel*), the modified *ñichi* or platform the *kuel* is built on (note the leveled top surface of the hill and the overburden or topsoil removed and tossed downslope on the hillsides to produce a symmetrical form), and the individual soil layers (*reñinkuel*). The total complex is called *rehuekuel*.

and deities (Fig. 3). These features reflect the intersection of Araucanian history, geography, ideology, and political organization and provide guidance in the anthropological interpretation and meaning of the mound-worshipping society that developed in the south Andes in late pre-Hispanic times and survives to the present day.

From an archaeological perspective, the mounded landscape of the Araucanians represents (1) single, isolated mounds, or *kuel*, which are the tombs of important leaders and are associated with nearby domestic sites, and (2) *rehuekuel* complexes defined by two or more related mounds built on top of *ñichi* platforms and associated with nearby domestic sites and occasionally agricultural features and fortresses. A *rehuekuel* and its associated sites collectively represent a single large site complex that is spatially planned and socially integrated. As culturally built monuments, these complexes range between one and ten ha in size. More than three hundred *kuel* are recorded in the Purén and Lumaco Valley, a remote area located on the eastern slopes of the Pacific coastal Nahuelbuta cordillera in south-central Chile (Fig. 4). *Kuel* in the valley are radiocarbon dated between approximately 1200 and 1900. *Kuel* also are found in other valleys in the Araucanian region, but appear to date slightly later. At least nine *rehuekuel* complexes are present in the Purén and Lumaco Valley (see Chapter 6). They are contemporaneous, dating from at least 1500 to 1700. *Rehuekuel* appear infrequently in other valleys. The continued use and spatial stability of *kuel* and *rehuekuel* over this period reflect the general social and political stability of local patrilineal communities in Purén and Lumaco, despite sporadic low-intensity warfare with the Spanish. Based on ethnohistorical and ethnographic records, we know that *rehuekuel* were the places where elaborate ritual ceremonies and commensal feasts were performed, as they are today in a few localities in the valley. That is, some *rehuekuel* are still used for large-scale public gatherings such as the *nguillatun* fertility ceremony when hundreds of people come together to propitiate the ancestors and deities, to exchange goods, and to reaffirm political alliances.

As presented in the Introduction, I will investigate how and why mounded landscapes of the Araucanians were defined and transformed by historical events, how they emerged as organizational nodes and symbols of victory and resistance, and how they represent a socially materialized form of history built across the land. Although the Araucanians were relatively conservative and materially inconspicuous until the Spanish contact period, in the 1550s they suddenly were thrust into a new world of awareness – one of immediate survivability. They quickly became aware of the need for a newly built social landscape associated with a new politico–religious order and a new form of government and compatriotism to facilitate their survival. Although they had built earthen mounds prior to the arrival of the Spanish, they constructed larger and more structurally complex ones in the Spanish-contact period that glorified the ideology of ancestral cosmological principles, victory and resistance, and deity-worship from whom patrilineages derived most of their authority and guidance. During this period, a sacred political loyalty and an emergent ethnic nationalism and intercommunity compatriotism were materially etched upon the landscape in the form of *kuel* and *rehuekuel*. This fostered traditional religious and social structures to facilitate the institutionalization of new social meanings and values of the new form of government – a confederated and sovereign polity of dynastic patrilineages – that united the Araucanians to produce a widespread anticolonial movement and to not only defeat the Spanish but keep them out of their territory. Particularly significant are the means by which ordinary lineages became members or compatriots of the broader Araucanian society as local kinship systems became less important and the overarching polity was built. Compatriotism was largely bound to and dependent on ancestor worship, glorified death in battle, elite-sponsored ritual feasting, and recruitment of defeated and fragmented lineages. Resistance to the Spanish in conjunction with rapid wholesale reorganization of the society, restructuration of a guiding cosmology, appropriation of certain Inka organizational elements that were grafted to existing Araucanian and Andean forms, and shamanic and priestly communication with the spirit world of the ancestors provided much of the impetus and context for increased social complexity, mound architecture, ethnic survival, and polity formation.

In 1978, I encountered the social memory and fading ceremonial acts of mound building, mound ritual, and ancestry worship in Purén and Lumaco, where the staunchest center of sixteenth- and seventeenth-century political resistance to the Spanish was located, where the oldest, largest, and most numerous *kuel* and *rehuekuel* are found, and where this study is concentrated. The valley is full of these memorial places, which are pivotal in providing a sense of place, history, and identity to the present-day Araucanians. Memories tied to warfare with the Spanish and Chileans and to lineage genealogy are spatialized in these

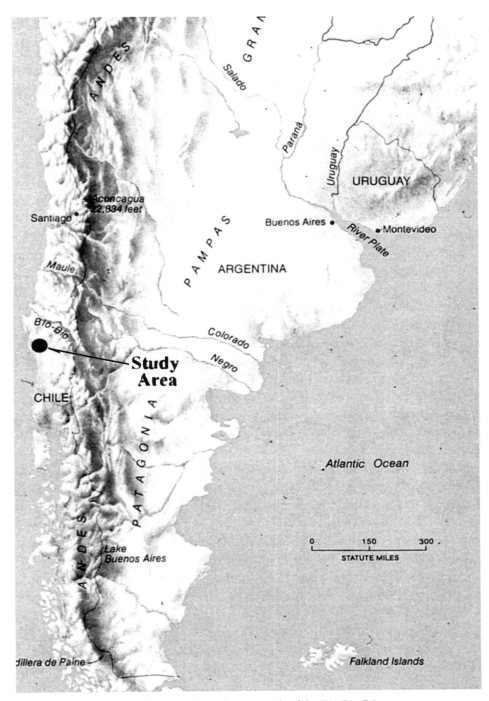

4. Map showing the study area south of the Bio Bio River.

places. *Kuel* still have special social meanings that not only maintain the relationship between the living and their ancestors but also between living consanguinally related patrilineages. The ancestors are omnipresent in popular memory and constantly invoked in political identity and geographical space. One only needs to walk the landscape in the company of shamans like *machi* Cármen to realize that the ancestors still have a strong presence, their historical traces being incorporated into sacred places like *kuel* and volcanoes. The *kuel* and the *ñichi* platforms, upon which they are built, are said to take their form from the volcanoes of the Andean mountain chain, which are visible to the east of the valley and where *Pillan*, the great ancestral deity spirit, resides. Although most *kuel* and other sacred places are no longer used for political and religious purposes as they once were, they are respected as old but living memorials and lineage members that dominate the landscape and still interact with priestly shamans, or *machi*, in ritual ceremony to communicate with individual deity spirits and as portals for ancestors to move back and forth between the upper world of the deities and the middle world of the living during ritual. In many ways, the use and meaning of *kuel* and *rehuekuel* today are continuous with what emerged in late pre-Hispanic times and especially in the 1550s when the Araucanians fiercely defended their lands against outside intrusion.

When I began my study of Araucanian mounds in the late 1970s, I viewed them as temporally static archaeological sites that once served as burial or ceremonial mounds (Dillehay 1985a). Although I describe the physical, spatial, and functional aspects of these mounds in later chapters, I have learned that they are not just culturally built objects whose interiors were used to bury important people and whose exteriors served for cosmological reflection, political theatre, public ritual, and shamanic agency. Ethnographic research has taught me that they are all of these and more, which becomes evident to the reader in Chapter 5, where I present the ritual dialogues between shamans and living mounds in public healing ceremonies. These dialogues reveal that *kuel* (1) are places where performative rituals occur that teach the cosmological principles that have guided the political actions and religious thoughts of the Araucanians, (2) are material expressions of the cosmological metaphors that are instruments of the cultural forces and central tools that create social and ethnic identities, (3) are sources of knowledge and teaching that are dynamic participants in making and storing local history, and (4) are kindred spirits that interact with priestly shamans and form part of a kin network of mounds that actively engaged in stewarding local communities and in linking powerful deities and ancestors to the living. In mimicking human kinship structure, each *kuel* has a name and is a member of a local mound kinship network that is genealogically related to a local patrilineage. To the present-day Araucanians in Purén and Lumaco, *kuel* are alive, familial, ethereal, and discursive like the human spirit – they are anthropomorphic and require attention like humans. Hence, *kuel* do not just represent archaeological sites for study and local places of historical significance and political identity, but anthropomorphic entities that impart permanency and express human feelings and needs.

Treating *kuel* and *rehuekuel* strictly as archaeological sites has the effect of denying the historically and culturally specific situations in which they invoked and foreclosed reflection on the purposes, agents, identities, subjects, and objects imputed on particular occasions. For this reason, I consider mounds and other sacred landscapes as sources of traditional knowledge and the use of this knowledge in a range of situated ritual, political, and social practices (Dillehay 1990a, 1995, 1999, 2002). So participation in ritual at *kuel* and *rehuekuel* situates different uses of knowledge and identities, instead of postulating them as temporally static objects, and highlights the consequences of such uses. Treating mounds as these kinds of practices articulates well with how the Araucanians have publicly represented their own knowledge and identity to themselves and how they dealt with their increasingly frequent encounters with the outside world over the past several centuries. Today, the Mapuche shamans do not speak of the mounds as objects, but of knowing and remembering them as active kindred spirits and as acts of kin-related agents. Considering mounds as situated agents of public practices requires revising some of our archaeological presuppositions about these kinds of monuments. As seen throughout this study, they are active participants and agents in society that have their own social identities and create their own memories of humankind and history.

We also see in the following chapters that the kindred spirits of dead leaders and shamans living in *kuel* are revered by local communities who constantly have to learn how to interact ritually with them, learn from them, and use them to their benefit, as revealed in the quote by the shaman Curín at the beginning of this chapter and by the ritual dialogues presented in Chapter 5. If communities fail to revere the mounds and to give them ritual offerings of food and drink, they run the risk of the mounds turning against them and bringing them ill-will. Constructive interaction with the spirits residing in mounds and learning from their life experiences provide communities with therapeutic relief, political savvy, and historical meaning. That savvy and meaning relate to what the shamans call *ñauchi* and to what I have termed *mound literacy*:

> We can say that those lineages manipulating chiefly burials at public places [*kuel*] to inaugurate a new chief and actively change (or even maintain) the structure and direction of social events were *mound literate*, so to speak.... Mounds and mound-related rituals had (and still have) a life beyond the theme of death and burial; they were memorabilia and ceremonial places actively used and, through the death of a leader and the reconstruction of alliances by new leaders, [they] actively restructured who participated in ceremony. Mound politics culturally transformed social structure as death did political structure.

Thus mound literacy – knowing how to use mounds socially to maintain the status quo or to bring change for one's lineage – became
as much of a prerequisite for the political conduct and networking
of a group as did technological literacy (weapons, irrigation systems)
and economic literacy (monetary exchange, resource values). Each of
these devices demanded a special way of human [religious and politi-
cal] interaction in Mapuche society, and, for the archaeologist, a special
way of perceiving the archaeological record. (Dillehay 1995:305)

In the following chapters, I argue that the Araucanian leaders (e.g., *ülmen,
toqui, apo-ülmen, lonko*) and priestly shamans (*machi*) of the late pre-Hispanic and
early Hispanic period learned how to interact with and learn from the *kuel* in order
to link community goals to ancestral history, to establish a new identity, and to
reorganize themselves through guiding cosmological principles to become active
compatriots in a new social order. *Mound literacy* and ritual participation *with*
and not just *at* mounds were special forms of religious belief, social interaction,
and group compatriotism educated in ancestral ways (*admapu*) and in knowing
the political usages of public ceremony. Mound literacy was, in effect, a social
contract between *kuel*, deities, ancestors, and the living community that enabled
a new kind of society to develop and to resist outside intrusion.

Mounded landscapes and mound literacy also are pivotal in providing the
Araucanians in the Purén and Lumaco Valley (and other valleys where they were
built) with a sense of place, agency, identity, and belonging. This does not imply
that nonliterates and non–mound builders are not empowered with identity and
agency. Rather, those populations in the region not having built and worshipped
mounds generally did and do not exhibit the same kinds of social organization
and military success and thus, for the early historic period under consideration
here, did not have the special agency and identity associated with the history and
spirituality of mounded landscapes. Nowhere is the importance of this connection
between people, land, history, genealogy, spirituality, and membership in a new
society more evident than in the *nguillatun* fields, *kuel*, and *rehuekuel* in Purén and
Lumaco. Today, all that remains of most *rehuekuel* are conical mounds covered in
grass and associated with old *nguillatun* and *palin* (ball game) fields and sacred altars
(*llangi-llangi*). Although *kuel* are no longer widely used for religious ritual as they
once were, they still mark the presence of deities and ancestors in the landscape
and the successful victories and resistance the Araucanians had against outsiders.
As each decade passes, however, fewer communities interact ritually with *kuel*
and fewer people remember the names of mounds and the relationships between
them and the populations that once used them.

Set in this context, *kuel* and *rehuekuel* are an important chapter in the history
of Araucanian political and religious organization, one that is mainly rooted in
local knowledge and its Spanish contact transformations. Although the function

and meaning of monuments changed during the wars with the Spanish and Chilean armies, the resiliency of the Araucanians played a key role in the perpetuation, development, and memory of mounds and ancestors and in the spiritual cohesiveness of the society at large. The Araucanians have undergone considerable cultural change since they were conquered at the turn of the twentieth century. Nevertheless, many aspects of the traditional religious system remain intact in a few areas. The intactness permits closer insight into the system and the type of society that produced mounded landscapes through an anthropological and archaeological analysis. Of particular interest in this study is how much of the present-day and ethnohistorical knowledge of *kuel* and *rehuekuel* extends to the archaeological past and to the archaeological correlates associated with cosmological principles of organization, mound literacy, and polity formation.

Although this study is about mounds and polity formation, it is equally about places where pronounced social complexity first developed and materialized in the kinds of anthropological records analyzed here. It also is about the Purén and Lumaco Valley, which was known to the first Spanish in south-central Chile as "*Purén indómito*," unconquerable Purén. Not only were the people of this valley the designated center and leader of the frontier fighters in the Araucania, but they were the direct descendants of the first pre-Hispanic mound builders in the region. In commenting on the historical role of Purén, the Chilean historian Bengoa notes that:

> Asi como habia patrullas de conquistadores que asolaban el territorio "campeando," también, comienzan a haber grupos indígenas que dedican toda su energía a guerrear, emboscar, asaltar y dañar al enemigo. Pareciera que el primer y más importante grupo que dio lugar a este nuevo "ejército fronterizo," el de Purén, conocidos sus integrantes como Puréninos y que ostentaran su fama de guerreros a lo largo de la historia. Son ellos quienes descubren el campamento del gobernador Oñez de Loyola, lo atacan y le dan muerte. Es el segundo gobernador de Chile que cae en la Araucanía. Se produce el alzamiento generalizado y los españoles son expulsados al norte del Bio Bio, prácticamente por dos siglos y medio. (Bengoa 2003:309)

> Just as there were patrols of conquerors that were ravaging the territory [Purén], there began to be groups of indians that dedicated all their energy to fighting, ambushing, attacking and doing damage to the enemy. It would appear that the first and most important group which gave rise to this new "army of the frontier" was that of Purén, whose members were known as *Puréninos* and whose fame as warriors is manifest throughout history. They were the ones who discovered the camp of the governor Oñez de Loyola, attacked it and killed him. He

was the second governor of Chile who fell in Araucania. The general uprising followed and the Spanish were expelled to north of the Bio Bio for almost two and a half centuries. (Bengoa 2003: 309)

This book interprets the political and cultural legacy of Purén from the combined perspective of these records.

For the purpose of providing provisional conclusions and the types of information and patterns derived from different sources, I present a synopsis of the ethnographic, ethnohistorical, and archaeological records and the conjunctive implications of these different but complementary approaches. As revealed in the individual chapters on these records, there are historical continuities in the form, use, and meaning of indigenous knowledges, principles of organization, and spatial and material practices. In some cases, we can trace similar organizations and agencies through time and determine if, how, and why they changed.

SETTING THE HISTORICAL BACKGROUND: FIFTEENTH TO SEVENTEENTH CENTURIES

At the beginning of the fifteenth century, the Inka created one of the largest empires ever to develop in the preindustrial world. At its climax, the empire extended 4,300 km from central Chile to the present-day border of Colombia and Ecuador, an area that was united without the use of animal transportation (llamas and alpacas were used as cargo carriers). The empire was integrated as much by a system of economic redistribution as by military force or political organization. The basic unit of all Inka organization was the traditional central Andean social structure, the *ayllu*, which was a lineage-based community. The *ayllu* was highly self-sufficient and integrated by common territory and by complex interrelationships of social and economic reciprocity. Each *ayllu* had its own leader. Most *ayllu* were united into larger polities and confederacies for trade and defense. Many Inka governmental structures and practices were modeled after the *ayllu*. For example, the system of corporate labor for the construction of public projects was an outgrowth of the traditional *ayllu* collective labor patterns. In effect, one of the greatest accomplishments of the Inka was to integrate a wide diversity of existing *ayllu* (and other social) units to form the geographically vast state system (see Morris 1972; Zuidema 1977), a pattern somewhat reminiscent of the later and geographically smaller Araucanian polity, which coalesced multiple local lineages or *rehue* and regionally allied *ayllarehue* units.

Through military conquest and negotiated incorporation, the Inka integrated different kinds of societies into the empire. State expansion constantly produced different types of frontiers with different groups, which led to different kinds of frontier situations and provoked different political and economic responses to the state. Some groups surrendered peacefully, while others fiercely resisted Inka colonialism (D'Altroy 2003; Patterson 1987; Pease 1987). Others abandoned their home territories altogether and moved to distant neighboring areas where they were isolated from state intervention. Others simply established trade and social relations with the Inka and maintained their autonomy and independence. The kinds of relationship formed with the Inka largely depended on the state itself, which was more interested in some areas than others. In the early 1550s, the Spanish conquered the Inka and extended their empire to the central Andes.

The sixteenth-century efforts of Spain and other western European powers to extend their empires overseas into the Americas led to a frontier-state expansion and confrontation among vastly different cultures. Colliding with each other and with powerful indigenous societies, the Spanish established the most extensive empire in the New World. The outcome shaped the destiny of America, Spain, and the world. The age of the Spanish in the Americas began in the 1490s, as part of a new world order. For the Spanish in the New World, many factors determined success and failure: geography, timing, natural resources, climate, leadership, technology, a trained military, bureaucracy, and religion all played roles. The earliest ventures of exploration, contact, and conquest had dramatic immediate impacts; survival required sustained adaptive measures on the part of all peoples involved. Among those impacts were the disappearance of traditional American indigenous society in many areas, and the making of what we call today the Hispanic–American and other cultural traditions.

Of special interest to the Spanish was the size of the indigenous populations and their own economic, social, political, and religious institutions. The Spanish, unlike the English and French, faced large, densely populated indigenous civilizations with complex institutions, particularly those of the Aztec, Maya, and Inka. Resistance of America's native peoples to Spanish institutions as well as to the Spanish presence in general was a consistent fact. Prolonged, successful resistance seems more characteristic of those regions inhabited by semisedentary to nomadic people who were not centrally organized or who could not be centrally controlled. There were exceptions, however, with some complex societies, such as the Maya, the Navajo, and the Araucanians, successfully sustaining their resistance over a long period of time. Highly centralized state systems such as the Aztec and Inka succumbed more quickly to the Spanish armies.

In effect, both Inka and Spanish colonialism produced lasting demographic, economic, and political repercussions. Throughout the history of both the Inka and Spanish empires refugees escaped from the domination of their lands, and military and other personnel deserted the state armies and resided with populations located in remote areas beyond the state frontier. Changing empire relations in frontier zones fostered many contradictions and opportunities not only for the Inka and Spanish, but for local populations as well. In fear of these powerful outsiders, both intact and fragmented local populations often developed new alliances and formerly independent groups integrated into new political organizations to defend their lands.

The Araucanians, as other Andean societies, were subjected to the expansionistic and integrative tendencies of these great empires, as they conquered and moved through central Chile and produced a domino effect of shifting formal and informal frontiers that also impacted populations residing in distant neighboring lands (see Dillehay and Netherly 1988; Hyslop 1984), including south-central Chile. These effects created different kinds of frontier contact situations between state personnel and Araucanian populations. These situations often produced more cultural, ethnic, and racial mixing than developed in more politically controlled areas of the state. They not only provided occasions for military conflict but also opportunities for the exchange of ideas, goods, and peoples and for the further development of some indigenous populations such as the Araucanians.

We can provide a brief historical synopsis of the Araucanians. Genetic and linguistic evidence suggests that they are related to Tupi-Guarani and other language groups in the southern tropical lowlands of eastern South America (e.g., Croese 1985; Key 1978, 1979; Latcham 1924; Sans 2000). We do not yet know how this affinity was established. As discussed in Chapters 3 and 6, the archaeological record indicates strong pre-Hispanic affinities with central and south-central Andean cultures on both sides of the Andean cordillera. The Araucanian's historic homeland originally consisted of central and south-central Chile, although today they are confined to the cool, temperate rainforest and mountains of the latter area, which begins at the Bio Bio River and ends at the Isle of Chiloé (Fig. 4). The homeland of the Araucanians contained five indigenous linguistic families: the Promaos, Pircunche, Pehuenche, Mapuche, and Huilliche. In early historic times they were collectively called *reche* (see Bengoa 1985, 2003; Boccara 1998, 1999; Cooper 1946; Zapater 1973, 1974, 1978, 1992), *aucas* (a Quechua word meaning wild savages), and Araucanos (southern people) or Araucanians in English. Boccara (1999:427) distinguishes between the Araucanos of the Arauco area, which includes the territory designated as the "*estado*" by Ercilla ([1569] 1982), and the *reche* residing between the Itata and the Tolten rivers. Since the late nineteenth century, the different terms were narrowed down to refer to the surviving southern Araucanians – the Mapuche – who lived between the military frontiers established at the Bio Bio and Rio Bueno rivers and who resisted outside occupation until the 1890s. Araucanians residing north of the Bio Bio in central Chile were conquered first by the Inka and then by the Spanish and later blended within Chilean society. The Mapuche, who number between eight hundred thousand and one million today, are the largest indigenous group in southern South America. They were and still are a patrilineal, patrilocal, bilateral inheritance, and virilocal society that lives in dispersed communities or *reducciones*. In the anthropological literature, the Araucanians are best known as mixed economists of piñon collectors in the highlands and fisherfolk, hunters, gatherers, and horticulturalists in the central valley and along the Pacific coast. I refer to the past indigenous peoples of the Purén and Lumaco area as the Araucanos or Araucanians in this study, because they lived within the boundaries of the Arauco area. When I discuss the contemporary population, I call them Mapuche, the name they prefer today.

For centuries prior to Spanish contact, the Araucanians had moved around, migrating from one valley to another, probably looking for new economic opportunities, and defending themselves against outsiders or against each other. Each community often fought with its neighbors over land, women, and resources, as suggested by the early written records (e.g., Bengoa 2003; Guevara 1913:232; Rosales [1674] 1989:903) and by the presence of hilltop fortresses that may have been built in late pre-Hispanic times (Guevara 1913:232, 593; León 1986). We also know that periodic relocations often involved the fusion of two or more previously separated lineage communities (Bengoa 1985, 2003; Dillehay 1995; see Chapter 7). As discussed in later chapters, the larger more demographically stable communities seem to have become magnets that gained more population as they recruited and incorporated smaller or defeated communities. These larger communities were often relocated near isolated defensible hilltops with steep slopes and wetlands, or *ciénegas*, below, such as those in the Purén and Lumaco Valley. This settlement shift was probably adopted for increased agricultural production near rich wetlands and for defensive purposes as armed conflict increased among the Araucanians themselves and later with the Spanish. By at least the 1300s to 1400s, Araucanians south of the Bio Bio River had begun combining into larger communities and building mounds in such fertile river valleys as Purén-Lumaco, Chol-Chol, Imperial, Cautín, and Toltén.

From the mid-1550s on, the Spanish arrived sporadically on the coast and through the central valley, looking for trading partners, new political dominions, and gold. The Spanish immediately recognized the importance of creating and maintaining an infrastructure – roads, harbors, and forts – along the frontiers to facilitate the exploration of minerals and other products and to attempt to politically control the Araucanians. This infrastructure eventually formed the military frontier for the Araucanians along the Bio Bio in the north and the Rio Bueno in the south and caused a shift in populations from one area to another. As noted earlier, coincident with the Spanish contact were complex Araucanian social developments such as intensification of mound building, demographic restructuring, heightened political authority, and often drastic reorganization of traditional institutions especially in frontier areas like Purén and Lumaco where much of the defense of the territory was organized. There was also intense competition over limited riverine and coastal resources despite the richness of the southern lands. Some populations were forced to move into safe areas placing greater population pressure on stable lineage communities. This in turn often led to increased feuding and, in cases of recruitment and incorporation, eventually to greater social complexity and polity formation (see Chapters 3, 7, 8). Such was the case in Purén, Lumaco, Angol, Tucupel, and other areas located along the Bio Bio frontier of the southern Araucanians.

SCHOLARLY RESEARCH

So far, symbolic and historical landscape studies have predominated in my anthropological scholarship about Araucanian mounds (see Dillehay 1990c, 1999). The strength of symbolic studies derives from their attention to cultural meaning and localized experiences of contemporary public ceremony at *rehuekuel* and *kuel* sites, but they offer few insights into the diachronic history and transformation of mounds and rituals or the influence of extra-local political forces on them. These studies are useful for understanding how symbols have changed partly in response to social change and partly by guiding social change. The historical research has provided insight into specific political and economic events at specific times and in specific places. It also has suggestive value for local and regional geopolitical processes and for correlating names and places with ethnographic and archaeological observations. Historical studies also have attracted a few Chilean scholars who have not systematically researched the archaeological past but who have provided shorter historical notices within larger works dedicated to ethnographic issues, for instance, mortuary practices and religious beliefs (e.g., Latcham 1924, 1928a, 1928b). Although limited by its broad chronologies and by generally poor preservation of cultural remains, archaeology has been useful for recording mounds, domestic sites, fortresses, cemeteries, and other locales. Abbreviated research by Latcham and other archaeologists on small mounds located burial practice within a broad religious context while concerning themselves less with mounds as a dimension of social life and religio-political experience. This research has enhanced our understanding of the chronology and function of mound sites and our ability to relate the archaeological and ethnographical records. I have followed these leads but through archaeological research have placed the origin of mound building in the thirteenth to fifteenth centuries and related its later development to the successful anticolonial resistance of the Araucanians in the sixteenth and seventeenth centuries.

The Archaeology of Mound Building

Although small burial mounds were mentioned before in Chilean archaeology, little systematic work had been done on them prior to our research (see Chapter 6). The available scholarship for the most part seemed far removed from the few living Mapuche who still used mounds in ceremony, and failed to engage the larger questions crucial to understanding them. It seemed to me that there was substantial unfinished archaeological business, much of which corresponded closely to our lack of understanding of the relation between mounds, history, landscape, religion, and political ideology. In 1978, I began study of the *kuel* mounds with an interest in broad questions surrounding their chronology, size, location, content and organization, and religious meaning, which I later learned was a matter not only of technological and economic change but of deeply contested social and ideological shifts from the sixteenth to eighteenth centuries that resulted from the Araucanian Wars. We now know from archaeological research that the construction of *kuel* began in this southern Andean region at least between the twelfth and fourteenth centuries and continued into the late twentieth century. In the 1990s, I decided to work not just on the chronology, location, and organization of mounds, but on the circumstances and principles of social and organizational changes among the Araucanian populations producing them. I also attempted to relate these concerns with broader issues in the archaeology and anthropology of early complex societies, landscape studies, and mound building.

Archaeology provides the linking data to employ the direct historical approach and to develop a more precise chronology and a means of evaluating conflicting hypotheses between various records. Although the written texts provide substantial information on the general course of historical events and on the sociopolitical transformations in important religious and political centers (i.e., Purén-Lumaco), we have not had a good understanding of the material and spatial correlates of these changes and how archaeology enhances, contradicts, and/or confirms the ethnohistorical and ethnographical registers. Unfortunately, until recently, little systematic archaeological research has been carried out in south-central Chile, which has seriously constrained researcher's ability to test various historical models against independent archaeological data. The present investigation has begun to address the need for more thorough archaeological research through a synthesis of regional survey and excavation in the Purén and Lumaco Valley.

The archaeological profiles collected so far from the valley both contradict and verify some of the presently constructed models of sociocultural development at the time of Spanish contact based on textual evidence. For instance, although some chroniclers mention mound building, the large mound complexes in Purén and Lumaco are not discussed by the chroniclers. This indicates a serious gap in the written records. On the other hand, there is a wealth of textual information on Araucanian religious and ceremonial practices that suggests remarkable similarity to those inferred from the archaeological record and still performed today. The archaeology also indicates an explosive buildup of mound and domestic sites between 1500 and 1700, heavy population fragmentation and displacement between 1550 and 1800, and the rise of complex polities in certain areas that correspond geographically and toponimically with those mentioned in the texts (Inostraza 1991; Quiroga [1690] 1979; Rosales [1674] 1989). Both sources suggest a developed polity leadership structure that organized different networks of social, military, and ritual power, a semicentralized to centralized religious system, and a controlled agricultural economy that was of a markedly different organizational order from that found before 1550.

In specific consideration of the importance of these findings to broader issues in archaeology, the opportunity to examine the kind of live social behavior and ideological constructs that produced *kuel* and other monuments is of substantial importance to understanding past mound-building societies and social formation processes. Although describing site formation processes are not a specific aim of this book, I provide an example of how kinship patterns and history in the form of ancestral relations are manifested in an ideologically construed space–time continuum to determine the physical formation, organization and maintenance of monuments and their relation to other features in the archaeological record. I also realize how certain interrelated materialistic and ideological characteristics may combine to regularly condition and sustain (1) the context and the form of social use patterns at mound sites, and (2) the type of site patterning observed by archaeologists. However, more detailed archaeological and ethnoarchaeological work on *kuel* and other types of religious architectural sites and more ethnographic research on the relationships between ideology, spatial behavior, and kinship need to be studied before we can systematically consider all factors that differentially conditioned the long-term range use, maintenance, and abandonment of these sites by successive lineage generations and the social and political meaning of those sites in social transformative terms. More attention also needs to be given to the political economy of mound building, particularly in regard to agricultural intensification in the form of terraces, canals, raised fields, and other features and to the appearance of formal leadership, settlement hierarchy, and polity. These topics are the primary subject of a forthcoming volume on the archaeology of the mounds.

Ethnohistory and the Araucanian Estado

In contrast to the core areas of the Spanish Empire, the southern Araucanians were much less impacted by contact with the European world. Unable to defeat them and preoccupied with the control and administration of many other regions throughout the continent, the Spanish decided to employ a sporadic defensive stance and established formal frontiers between the Araucanians and themselves. In fact, the Spanish signed a royal treaty in 1643 that recognized the sovereignty of the Araucanian nation between the Bio Bio and Rio Bueno rivers. Although other indigenous societies in Latin America also were successful in resisting Spanish control, they did not survive or flourish the way the southern Araucanians did over a period of nearly three hundred fifty years. The Araucanian case thus shows that frontier contact engendered rapid inventiveness and expansiveness rather than culture demise. For scholarly research, the drawback to this success was less contact between the Araucanians and Spanish personnel, which resulted in significantly less historical documentation on the indigenous culture and society in comparison to areas such as Peru, Mexico, Bolivia, Brazil, and the Caribbean. The positive side of prolonged resistance and cultural continuity is the integrity of certain religious orders and social organizations, which have allowed me to apply a critical direct historical approach to this study.

The historical narratives available to us for the Araucanians are those contained in the documents written by Spanish soldiers, clergymen, and bureaucrats in the years following contact with the Araucanians, beginning in 1550 (see Chapter 3 for more details). Early written records indicate that in their long struggle with outsiders, the Araucanians underwent social, economic, religious, and political changes, with some groups defeated and fragmented and others developed into a powerful polity of confederated dynastic patrilineages (*lov, lof*) (e.g., Bengoa 1985, 2003; Dillehay 1990a, 1995, 2002; Krumm 1971; Rosales [1674] 1989). The leaders of these lineages negotiated ideological, military, economic (*sensu* Earle 1997), and tactical and organizational venues (Wolf 1999) of power to restructure traditional social and cultural forces to form the Araucanian "*estado*" in the Purén, Lumaco, Arauco, and Tucapel region of the Nahualbuta mountains along the coast (Ercilla [1569] 1982; A. Medina 1978; Padden 1993; Fig. 4). This polity became the stronghold of Araucanian resistance between 1550 and 1700 (Dillehay 1990a, 1999; Rosales [1674] 1989; Villalobos and Pinto 1985) and had lasting political and spiritual effects on resisting populations throughout the Araucania until the early twenty-first century. In the late seventeenth century, the *estado* expanded eastward from Andean mountain passes into Argentina and was second only to the Inka empire in terms of its geopolitical expanse (Fig. 5) and cultural influence in South America (e.g., León 1991; Mandrini 1984, 1992; Mandrini and Ortelli 2002; Nacuzzi 1998; Villalobos et al. 1982).

Most Chilean scholars believe that the pre-Hispanic Araucanians were living in dispersed communities and were uncentralized hunters and gatherers, which accounted for the inability of the Inka and Spanish to defeat them (see Chapter 3). However, Pedro de Valdivia ([1555] 1960), the first conquistador in the region, refers to the high density of the population residing in the Imperial Valley south of Purén in terms of "unas casas estaban casi encima de otras" (some houses are almost on top of others). An uncentralized political structure implies that each isolated population had to be defeated and controlled individually, thus making it impossible to conquer the Araucanians. However, if decentralization was a preventive factor, then how did the Inka and the Spanish conquer so many decentralized and dispersed hunter–gatherer societies in other places and not the Araucanians? More to the point, how could Araucanian hunters and gatherers have organized themselves so effectively to have culturally influenced and politically controlled extensive areas of the southern cone in the 1700s and 1800s? Writing in 1673, the Spanish priest Rosales ([1674] 1989: 114) rhetorically asked why the Spanish who were able to defeat the Aztec and the Inka could not conquer the southern Araucanians. The answer is that the southern Araucanians had a well-organized political system, a productive environment, a high population density in some areas, and a designated fighting population located along the northern Bio Bio frontier – the Purén and Lumaco Valley – which was supported logistically and economically by an interior population of stable agriculturalists. As surmised by Bengoa (2003: see Chapters 13–15):

> En resumen, vemos una sociedad indigena repartida en una zona de frontera, defendida por grupos [p. j. Purén] que pasan en armas permanentemente y una zona interior que ha logrado volver a un sistema de vida creciente y relativamente tranqullo y que los apoya. Incluso los grupos armados, al parecer, tenian responsabilidades sobre diversas partes de la frontera. . . . (Bengoa 2003:423)

> In sum, we see an indigenous society spread out along a frontier, defended by groups [e.g., Purén] that are permanently at arms and an interior zone that had managed to return [after the wars in the late 1500s] to a flourishing and relatively tranquil way of life and which supported them. Further, it seems, the armed groups were responsible for different parts of the frontier. . . . (Bengoa 2003:423)

In reference to Purén in the late 1500s, Bengoa mentions the defeat of the Spaniard Don Luis and his soldiers by the "*Puréninos*" (people of Purén) in the hills of Butapichón (Butarincón) near Lumaco, who were the "guardians of the frontier," and the complementary relations between frontier and interior populations.

> Pero desde lo alto de los cerros Butapichón y los *Puréninos*, guardianes fronterizos, lo [Don Luis who was the Spaniard of the troops] estaban esperando. Dicen que eran unos tres mil los que se le vinieron encima. Les arrebataron los ganados y liberaron a todos los prisioneros y a Don Luis le costó el cargo. (Bengoa 2003:426)

> But from the heights of the Butapichcón hills and [sic] the *Puréninos*, guardians of the frontier, were waiting for him [Don Luis who was the Spaniard commanding the troops]. They say there were some three thousand [warriors] who attacked him. They seized the livestock and freed all the prisoners and cost Don Luis his command. (Bengoa 2003:426)

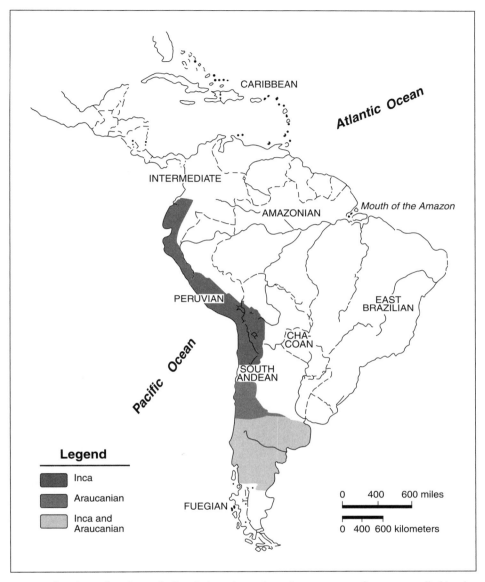

5. Map showing cultural areas in South America and maximum extent of areas controlled by the Inka state (ca. 1400–1515) and by the Araucanian polity (ca. 1600–1800).

As noted earlier, the largest and densest *rehuekuel* complexes and agricultural villages are located in Purén, especially in the Butarincón or Butapichcón area.

We do not yet understand from the written records the highest level of political organization achieved by the Araucanians, which seemingly fluctuated between a constantly expanding polity headed by a confederation of patrilineal leaders to a group-oriented, centralized polity comprised four territorial divisions directed by paramount rulers. In his study of the early documents, the modern historian Padden reasons that:

> The existence of a skilled and effective [Araucanian] military force bespeaks the presence of a comparable political organization under whose genius it is formed and directed. . . . Centralization of a politico-military authority was achieved to a point where successful resistance was possible, but did not develop to a state where the Spanish could defeat and usurp it. (Padden 1993:78)

Alonso Ercilla and other chroniclers writing in the sixteenth and seventeenth centuries compared the organizational and military capability of the Araucanians to that of an *estado*. By most standards, the Araucanians attained a geopolitical scale and a level of organizational complexity that could be associated with an incipient state expansion (cf. Agnew 1999; Claessen 2000; León 1999; A. Medina 1978). However, while some aspects are state-like (e.g., large territory, multitiered hierarchy, centralized politico-religious network, centralized provision of public goods and services), other features represent horizontal and heterarchical consensus within a polity of confederated traditional leaders, in which distinct corporate segments maintained various degrees of autonomy (Boccara 1999; Dillehay 1995). (The use of heterarchy here considers social and economic interactions among a network of relatively independent communities while still recognizing hierarchical rankings that are based on a number of criteria [cf. Crumley 1995].) Thus, although the Araucanian society lacked many institutions and infrastructures of a state-like system (e.g., capital city, formal tax system), its expansion into most of Argentina in the eighteenth century (Fig. 6), its successful 350-year anticolonialism, and its strong cultural influence in the southern cone of South America extended it beyond the normal capacity of confederated patrilineal leaders to a wider polity organization, which I call a *confederated regional polity* in this study.

Crucial to understanding the successful anticolonialism and polity-formation of the Araucanians was the struggle of patrilineage-agents (i.e., leaders, shamans, priests, military personnel, and others) to impose a higher, more centralized level of political and economic order and a new social organization for politically strategic ends (Boccara 1999; Dillehay 2002). The initial emergence of incipient agriculture and petty mound building between 1200 and 1500 was related to population growth, social emulation, competitive feasting, and differential power relations between lineages in highly fertile, circumscribed valleys (Dillehay 1976, 1981, 1990c, 1992a; 1999, 2002). Between 1500 and 1600, the explosive development of mound complexes and extensive lineage agricultural villages in Purén and Lumaco and, to a lesser extent, other valleys in south-central Chile represents a major settlement and political shift (Fig. 7). These

6. Map showing the maximum extent of the early Araucanian or Mapuche polity in the sixteenth century and the location of the various indigenous ethnic groups in Argentina that later came under Araucanian influence in the seventeenth to nineteenth centuries (after Jones 1999).

localities became important nodes of population nucleation, settlement hierarchy, politico–religious centralization, societal reorganization, and polity-formation. I argue that the development of this polity is specifically related to the tactical, structural, and organizational power (*sensu* Wolf 1999) of ruling agents who drastically and rapidly reorganized the society at a higher sociopolitical level by recruiting groups fragmented by warfare along the Araucanian–Spanish frontier and by incorporating them into their lineages (or ranked lineages under them) through public feasting at *rehuekuel* complexes (Dillehay 1990a, 1995), and by geographical expansion by means of the annexation of neighboring lineage territories and of secondary mound building in them. These strategies permitted leaders to increase the size of their lineages, to provide them with more warriors, to solidify their internal coherence, to expand their geopolitical reach, and to politically unify and confederate among themselves. Both the written and archaeological records suggest that leadership power geographically shifted from one dynastic lineage to another as leaders cyclically gained and lost power. Shamanic ceremonies and the employment of sacred knowledge and cosmological principles also were important in uniting different groups and in legitimizing rulers' power. Not all of these transformations occurred evenly in Araucanian territory or everywhere but only in strategic locations, which were favorable to geopolitical defense, sustainable population nucleation, and intensive agriculture, and where some local lineages were victorious and sustained long-term resistance to outsiders. As discussed in later chapters, these strategies of emergent complexity and polity formation are inferred primarily from historic texts, which present dated and named events, the size and movement of specific lineages, competitive recruiting and annexing by lineage leaders, cyclical rise and fall of patrilineages, interlineage alliances, conflicts with the Spanish, and named and dated locations of patrilineage residential areas and *rehuekuel* complexes, especially in the Purén-Lumaco area (e.g., Bibar [1555] 1966; Góngora de Marmolejo [1575] 1960; Núñez de Pineda [1673] 2003; Quiroga [1690] 1979; Rosales [1674] 1989).

In sum, we can infer from the written records that the end result of these processes was the emergence of a more complex framework of political and religious authority that restructured the institutionalized sociopolitical, economic, and religious organizations of the Araucanians from small peer-polities before 1500 to a polity of confederated patrilineal lineages by 1600. At the time of Spanish contact around 1550, the socioeconomic organization of places like Purén and Lumaco was already becoming complex (see Boccara 1999:434–36), probably as a result of indirect or direct contact with the Inka (Dillehay and Gordon 1988; see Chapter 3), with ruling patrilineages (*lov, lof*) organized into a polity (Boccara 1999; Leiva 1984; Montecino 1980), building more and larger mounds (Dillehay 1985a, 1990a, 2002), and occasionally annexing adjacent groups. Between 1550 and 1650, it can be estimated that the powerful lineages in Purén and Lumaco had between 4,000 and 6,000 people, which were some of the largest recorded for

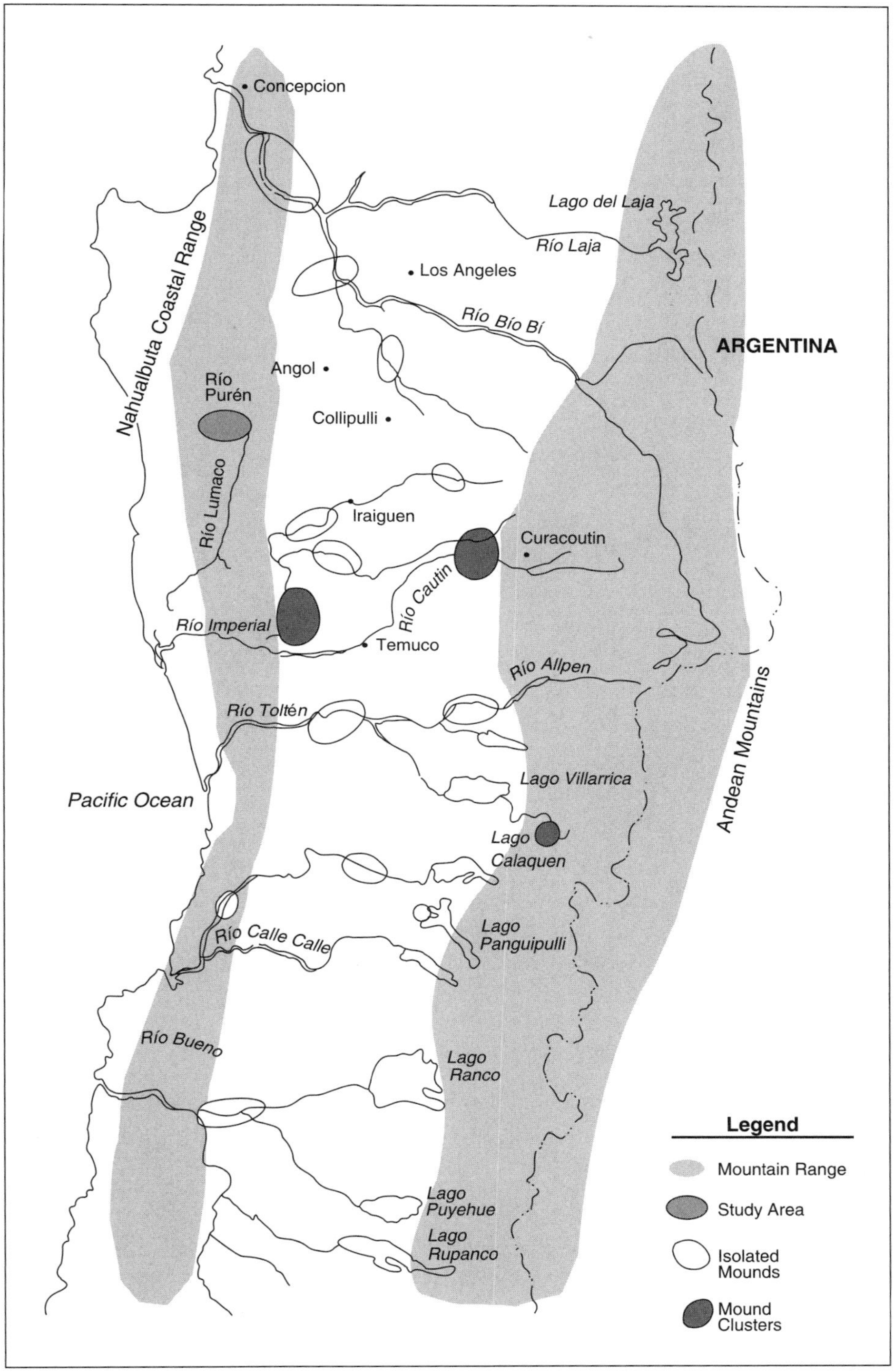
Concepcion
Lago del Laja
Río Laja
Los Angeles
Nahualbuta Coastal Range
Río Bío Bí
ARGENTINA
Angol
Río Purén
Collipulli
Río Lumaco
Iraiguen
Curacoutin
Río Cautin
Río Imperial
Temuco
Río Allpen
Río Toltén
Andean Mountains
Lago Villarrica
Pacific Ocean
Lago Calaquen
Lago Panguipulli
Río Calle Calle
Río Bueno
Lago Ranco
Legend
Mountain Range
Study Area
Isolated Mounds
Mound Clusters
Lago Puyehue
Lago Rupanco

7. Geographical distribution of isolated and clustered mound cultures where emergent complexity developed between approximately 1200 and 1700 in the Araucania region of south-central Chile.

the Araucanian region, even after initial population loss due to European diseases (Inostraza 1991). The valley apparently grew between 6,000 and 10,000 people between 1700 and 1800. This larger population was the result of a rich, productive environment, the recruitment and annexation of outside lineages, minimal impact by disease, population nucleation and stability, and reorganization of the society, all of which partly led to increased social complexity in the valley and to its rise as a center of Araucanian resistance. The written texts also suggest that competitive lineage leaders, with their intensive and escalating monopolies of recruitment and feasting, were primarily the products of the centralizing effect of increased conflict on a previously uncentralized confederation of loosely knitted patrilineages. Eventually, several dynastic lineages in the late 1500s united at a higher level of politico-religious order to defend themselves and to engage in an even larger-scale politico-religious organization – the *ayllarehue* that comprised several local *rehues* or *lof* patrilineages. In the early 1600s, an even larger, more efficient geopolitical organization was formed, the *butanmapus (futanmapus, butamapus, utanmapus)*, which were made up of three (and later four) proximal territories (Rosales [1674] 1989: 1026–1027), each comprising numerous *ayllarehue*. Each *butanmapu* covered about 4500 km^2 and was ruled by a *guen-toqui* leader with a hierarchy of lesser rulers (cf. Boccara 1999; Dillehay 2002; León 1991; A. Medina 1978). All of this relates to emerging yet centralizing divisions in the geo-ideological organization of the Araucanian territory and to identifying and defining boundaries and successive movements within the region. I hope to demonstrate that Araucanian, Andean, and Inka principles of organization were combined to achieve these changes. Because of sporadic contact with the Spanish, the Araucanians also began to adopt certain advantageous European traits (e.g., horse, other domesticated animals, crops), which eventually facilitated their ability to successfully combat the Spanish and to improve their economy.

Ethnography and Sacred Geographies

Over the past three decades, I have gained considerable information about Araucanian mounds, which has resulted in several publications about their function, history, and meaning (Dillehay 1985a, 1990b, 1992a, 1995, 1999, 2002). In these publications, I have discussed my prior ethnographic and ethnohistorical understanding of mound burial and how it relates to the political succession of patrilineal leaders, to relations between the living and the dead, to territorial boundaries and ritual landscapes, and to the sustainability of dynastic patrilineages. I surmised that:

> Temporal segregation through political eschatologies and cosmologies, as continually manifested in monumental burials, was a powerful means of creating and maintaining lineage distinction, recounting achievement of ancestors, and recording social history. As such, the

distribution of mounds in space is the same as the distribution of the historical behavior of lineages in time. Hence, a special pattern of mound burials is interchangeable with a temporal or historical pattern of lineage history. (Dillehay 1995:305)

I also have published several articles about the spatial, material, social, and religious organization of mounds and large-scale ceremonial fields and how this information can be used to study mound building and to establish archaeological correlates for principles of spatial and social organization. (Dillehay 1990a, 1990b, 1995: see Chapters 3 and 4 for more complete discussion of Mapuche ethnography)

The ethnographic information about *kuel* was derived from on-site examination of mounds with local informants, from the memory of *machi* and elders who know how mounds have been used in the past and today and what is said about their meaning in oral folklore, and from my participation in healing and other ceremonies at actively used *kuel* sites. The ethnographic research has led me to also consider a phenomenological approach to the meaning of mounds and the relation between sacred geographies and polities (Bradley 1998; Thomas 1995; Tilley 1994). This approach has given me the opportunity to view the spiritual and therapeutic significance of mounded landscapes from the perspective of living shamans and other ritual leaders (*nguillatufe*) who look to public ceremony at *rehuekuel* and *kuel* sites to reflect on broader societal issues, to predict certain aspects of the future, and to build social harmony by telling ancestral stories and by linking them to powerful forces in the ethereal world above. The most valuable information comes from the lengthy orations by two *machi* during public *nguillatun, illetun,* and *dahatun* healing ceremonies at actively used *kuel*, when the shamans speak and the ritual audience interacts with the mounds. One mound, called *Hualonkokuel*, was sick and had turned against the local community for not giving it offerings and medicine. This required a healing ceremony to cure the sick *kuel* and to mend relations between it and the community. The other case involved my excavation of the largest and most powerful *kuel* in the region – *TrenTrenkuel*. (*TrenTrenkuel* had developed a reputation for its power in resolving conflicts, ameliorating misfortunes due to sorcery, and advising on important community affairs. It also harmed communities if they did not worship it, and give it offerings.) Local communities and national Mapuche organizations had granted us permission to excavate the mound with local Mapuche residents. In order to commission our work, shamans performed a solacing ceremony to prevent *TrenTrenkuel* from being upset by the proposed work and from bringing ill-will to us and to local communities. The ritual orations that I recorded during these ceremonies reveal the intimate relationships between the *machi*, the *kuel*, and the kindred spirits housed inside the mound and also the *machi's* role as mediator between the *kuel* and local communities (see Chapter 5).

I also have learned from ethnographic and ethnoarchaeological research that Araucanian monumentalism is more than a single archaeological mound or group of *rehuekuel* mounds built on modified *ñichi* hilltops. It is an organizing concept or principle related to sacred landscapes and their networks of bounded topographies defined by the location of sacred mountains and hills, mounds, and ceremonial fields and trails that serve as ancestral reference nodes in time and space. That is, the Araucanians understand *kuel* and *rehuekuel* as members of a vertically – and horizontally – layered network of social relations between the living and their ancestors and deities. This network is defined metaphorically by a proliferating kinship network of new son:daughter and brother:sister mounds through which history is made, recorded, and perpetuated across the landscape (Dillehay 1990a, 1999). Participation in public ceremony rekindles these linkages and provides solace and tranquility. It is a concept and an activity that unites *kuel* and *rehuekuel* (and in the past *ayllarehue*) and other features into a dynamic system of human interaction. Araucanian monumentalism is thus symbolically interactive, socially integrative, topographically bounded, and experientially holistic and meaningful. As noted earlier, these monuments become memorials and historical places that are designed and intended to communicate lasting and effective meaning. They are endowed with the spirits of important ancestors that are of special consequences and meanings to past, present, and future generations. As such, *kuel* and *rehuekuel* as monuments impart value, home place, and ancestry to the cultural landscape (Dillehay 2002), from which the Araucanians derive inspiration and cultural identity.

UNITING THE ARCHAEOLOGICAL AND TEXTUAL PAST AND THE ETHNOGRAPHIC PRESENT

Most newly formed polities or complex societies are characterized by two parallel and interrelated organizational trends: an expanded social network for sharing production and political activities, and the development of more institutionalized mechanisms for integrating different communities as a whole with their natural and historical landscapes (Dillehay 1999). In studying these trends in the Araucanian case, we cannot limit ourselves only to sources and objects of political and economic comparison between social, settlement, and subsistence patterns. We also need a perspective that considers the social and historical relations between people, their ideology and religion, their memories, experiences, meanings, and identities, their culture material world, and their natural environments, which permits us to link the past and present through combined ethnographic, ethnohistorical, and archaeological analyses. Social and symbolic interaction approaches provide one set of the conceptual tools to make linkages between the social and natural environments and between the past and present.

The symbolic interactionist Herbert Blumer expressed the relationships that different groups have with their social and natural environment in the following manner:

> Humans are seen as living in a world of meaningful objects.... This world is socially produced in that the meanings are fabricated through the process of social interaction. Thus, different groups come to develop different worlds – and these worlds change as the objects that compose them change in meaning.... To identify and understand the life of a group it is necessary to identify its world of objects...in terms of the meanings objects have for the members of the group.... Within this framework, some elements of the natural environment – land, rivers, mountains, forests – are socially produced in the sense that the meanings these elements have to people transform the elements into meaningful symbolic landscapes through social and cultural experiences.... Once transformed, elements of the natural environment become symbols that convey meaning to the group. In this manner, special features of the natural environment are absorbed into the life of the group through shared symbols and meanings. (Blumer 1969:238–239)

To the Araucanians, the meanings of landscape, ancestors, future generations, and sovereignty are not representations of any one meaning at different levels of inclusiveness. Rather, they bear relationship to each other as components of a framework of ethnic sovereignty. None of these component meanings is more or less important; they interact with each other, and together comprise the conceptual framework through which participant patrilineages interpreted and generated increased religio-political action. This ideological interpretative and participatory framework shifted with respect to the relations between the living and their ancestors, the cosmological world, the increased role of warfare, warrior status, and large nucleated settlements for defense (see Chapter 3). Although contact with the Inka and the Spanish also produced changes, many of the traditional ideological constructs were not eliminated but altered and expanded creatively in various ways. The "objects" or sacred landscapes of the *kuel* and *rehuekuel* used to represent meanings also changed over time. The power of any single *kuel* or *rehuekuel* complex was derived from its reference to an entire set of meanings and to each other. That is, each was related to the other as component sectors of the broader *ayllarehue* political organization, which was comprised of multiple *rehuekuel* and *kuel* that were continually created, absorbed, and interrelated within the broader conceptual framework. This organization allowed for flexibility in responding to various instances of what may be essentially the same basic participation at different locations and times in places like Purén and Lumaco and their neighboring areas. By studying this framework, we gain insight into some but not all of the Araucanian's ideology of the past.

As I study later, the Araucanian's religious ideology is associated with a cognitive map or imagery of sacred routes and places in the study area, which can be described as a symbolic infra-organization that connects historically meaningful landscapes and spiritual locations of the real physical world and the spiritual or esoteric worlds, that is, other regions or levels of the cosmos. The map is part of geographical teachings and cosmological knowledge, which includes mythical journeys (the powerful naming process of geographical places during shamanistic or *machi* rituals or other religious feasts, for instance) and a complex network of physical pathways that connect different *kuel* and *rehuekuel* in the Purén and Lumaco Valley and facilitate social order. These pathways also are linked to strategic resources (i.e., gold, silver, stones, waterfalls) for political and economic purposes and pass through lands, marshes, rivers, creeks, and lagoons. It is this combination of land and water routes that gave (and still gives) the Araucanians ways to develop strategies of physical resistance, economic development, and social order. As discussed in Chapter 6, the use and meaning of these routes are reminiscent of Inka *ceque* lines and dreamlines, which were employed to connect sacred places across the landscape with living communities and with the cosmological world above in order to create a legitimate state history and practice.

Taken together, *kuel* and *rehuekuel* form a social and aesthetic physical arrangement of spaces, pathways, meanings, and objects that keep alive the memories of those individuals and lineages that make Araucanian history. As aesthetic objects or artifacts arranged in *rehuekuel*, mounds help to create an ongoing meaning and effective social order (*sensu* Bradley 1998; Pollard 2001; Pollard and Ruggles 2001) beyond the fleeting and chaotic experiences of daily life. The appropriation and maintenance of ancient *kuel*, ceremonial fields, and shrines across the landscape are largely structured by ancient Andean and Araucanian principles and by contemporary expectation and participation in ceremonies held at these sacred places. Memories are inscribed on the land in the names that have become historic and lived places. Each *kuel* is named and each encompasses linked social and physical differences. Like the landscape as a whole vis-a-vis the larger territory, the *kuel* represent geographically reconstituted social meanings and genealogies. The Araucanians are not obliged to maintain these monuments; they want to preserve them and they need them to record and remember their ancestors and their history. Because mounds and other sacred features across the landscape endure as places and rituals, the Araucanians are thus consciously made to confront the important experiences that are a part of their history. These experiences are memorized in oral prayers, stories, songs, and narrative rituals and symbolized in mounds, wooden statues, and other objects that showcase the large dynastic patrilineages who held land and who have mattered in the political events that make up Araucanian history. These memories also record the fragmented populations who moved into the study area from other areas, the various occupations they practiced, and the activities they pursued.

Most of our current knowledge of *kuel* and other sacred places derives from living priestly shamans (*machi*) who administer public ritual ceremonies held at them, who know the meaning and the history of the mounds as they are preserved in ceremony and memory, and who visualize the history etched across the landscape. Shamanism, ancestors, and the spirit world of the Araucanians lie at the center of this study as much as landscape, agency, identity, and memory, because the meaning of landscape is not just physical but is itself bound up with a causality that embraces both visible and invisible phenomena. *Kuel* as visible archaeological and ethnographical mounds are easy to detect and study. But the spiritual-matter, ancestral meaning, and metaphorical implication of *kuel* are invisible and constitute a fundamental part of the experience of past and present Araucanian reality.

The response of most archaeologists when confronted with evidence pertaining to shamanism, ancestors, and the spirit world is either to avoid it because of its metaphysical complications and its material and spatial invisibility, or to overemphasize its importance so that they become a reductionist tool, replacing ecological, economic, cultural, or social determinism as yet another ultimate explanatory device. Here, I attempt to resist that reduction in the name of a more holistic understanding of Araucanian mounds and their linkage to the natural and spiritual world. A holistic approach to these relations renders symbolic, ecological, spiritual, experiential, and material understandings complementary rather than competing. In these understandings, the natural environment is transformed by human action, meaning it is a cultural and historical product. It also is an objective, external, spiritual, and physical order. For the Araucanians, the invisible spirit world is a reality that provides the means of understanding their lives and their relations with death, history, identity, ancestry, compatriotism, and landscape (e.g., Dillehay 1990a, 1990b, c; Bacigalupo 2001). Through dreams, visions, and ritual experiences, spirits provide those possessing priestly shamanic skills with the analytical tools that they need for explanation of the world and for the teaching of this explanation through metaphorical expression in oral narratives, prayers, tales, songs, and dances, in mental dreams and visions, and in material mounds, textiles, and other artifacts.

This book approaches the invisible spirit world from the perspective of shamanic practitioners as mediators between lineage rulers, the population at large, the ancestors, the spirit world, and the *kuel* and *rehuekuel* as sacred texts or geographies. To make the spirit world understandable to people, shamanic spiritual practice and belief have spatial location and have time dimensions and material manifestations. Shamans' relationships with the spirit world and the political implications of their thoughts and activities provide a context in which both Araucanians and non-Araucanians can appreciate the complexities and intricacies of existence. Relating the visible and invisible worlds of the shamans to specific archaeological contexts has largely been lacking (see Atkinson 1992; Price 2001), because few ethnographic studies and even fewer ethnoarchaeologies have examined the spatial and material correlates of these aspects. Interpreting the Araucanian *kuel* thus requires understanding the logic of the nexus – shamanism, agency, history, memory, identity, landscape, and the social reorganization that the *kuel* encapsulate. In doing this, I take the Araucanian worldview and its material, symbolic, and spatial correlates as the linking points between these entities (see Chapter 4). I also consider how symbols and metaphors in rituals transmit cosmological knowledge, what they mean, how they embody information about principles of organization, how they are used to organize the society, and how they are presented in other visual formats, such as mounds, textiles, and other artifact designs. I trace the temporal lines of these objects in expanding their spatio-temporal notion of reality, and in linking their experiential present to the past, future, and the afterlife. As revealed later, to the Araucanians, the universe is a multiplicity of intersecting social spheres with different conditions of temporality, constantly shifting and changing, but with permanently fixed or static locations – the *kuel*, the *rehuekuel*, and the *nguillatun* fields.

Shamanism (and priesthood) was and still is an institutionalized political and spiritual form in Araucanian society. The shamanic political structure was and is grounded on both an extensive network of political relations with other peoples and the shared religious systems that are divided into layered ancestral and living histories (see Bacigalupo 1995, 1996, 1998, 2001, 2004a, 2004b, 2005; Dillehay 1990a, 1990c; Foerster 1993; Foerster and Gundermann 1996; Titiev 1951). Each history consists of a corpus of ritual narratives (stories, myths, chants, songs, prayers, etc.), ritual knowledges, rites and feasts and comprises a wide variety of ideological-symbolic and practical codes. These codes teach important knowledge that has been associated with ancestors and with supreme beings, and has influenced and oriented the Araucanians' strategies to face events and situations of their ritual and secular lives. In this manner both the historical or ancestral interpretation and the living representation of the world, natural beings, society, and humankind are closely related to the Araucanians' system of ancient beliefs. Mythic narratives and oral histories are thus two complementary genres that influence one another; through these methods the Araucanians narrate, tell, and interpret their historical processes of change. Most of all, however, the ancestors came to their world to teach people all of their sacred ritual powers. These powers or teachings are learned by people during public rituals.

As a final introductory comment on shamanism, from my perspective, I find that the anthropological literature on shamanism is heavily biased toward curing, trances, and medical aspects, toward characterization of what are supposedly general symbols or ecstatic techniques, and toward the shaman as a singular ritual practitioner (cf. Atkinson 1992; Balzer 1990; Eliade 1972; Fuerst 1974; Pentikainen 1998; Price 2001; Vitebsky 1995). Although I consider these aspects of Araucanian shamans, I also view them and other ritual specialists as political actors, mediators, and even disruptors of historically constituted social relations between secular leaders and the public at large and between indigenous communities and outsiders (Dillehay 1985a). Shamans not only develop strategies to confront unequal and hierarchical power relationships within the society today and within the Spanish colonial system in the past, but they also are models of traditional ways for constructing and interpreting ethnic and political identities and for creating and interpreting the effective meaning of aesthetic sacred landscapes.

Furthermore, I have been following the ethnographic literature on the Mapuche in referring to *machi* as shamans (e.g., Bacigalupo 1999, 2004 a–d; Faron 1964; Foerster and Gundermann 1996). As evidenced in the early documents and in the contemporary society, *machi* not only heal the sick but are leaders of group rituals, bearers and interpreters of sacred knowledge and history, and perform a variety of political and public ceremonial roles that extend beyond the traditional healing and spiritual activities of shamans to include those of ritual priests (or *nguillatufe* in the native language; see Faron 1964). Further, their power is not just derived from a divine calling but from prolonged study of the supernatural world and Araucanian cosmology. As discussed in Chapters 4 and 7, given the expanded role of *machi* in the historic and contemporary society, it is perhaps more appropriate to refer to some *machi* as priestly shamans rather than just shamans. This is particularly the case with the shamans in Lumaco and Purén who are noted for their wide-ranging power, political prowess, and knowledge of and relations with the esoteric world. Thus, when I use the term *machi* and shaman, they both refer to a wider priestly shamanic role focused on medicinal healing and, invariably, spiritual healing and political action.

THE UTOPIC POLITY

Throughout the above discussion, I have alluded to the polity constructed by the Araucanians and to the aspired or "utopic" lifeway and social community that leaders were attempting to build in the sixteenth to eighteenth centuries. I will now define what I mean by these terms and by this allusion by employing a modified version of Johnson and Earle's definition of "regional polity" to the Araucanian model of political and religious organization and by extending it with Marin's concept of "utopic social engineering." According to Johnson and Earle, regional polities

> arise out of formerly fragmented local groups ... in which warfare between groups is endemic but becomes directed toward conquest and incorporation rather than toward the exclusion of defeated groups from their land. Economic strategies ... notably irrigation agriculture

and external trade, provide opportunities for elite investment and control, which are used to extract surplus production from the subsistence economy to finance the chiefdom's operations. As the regional integration of the polity proceeds, clearly defined offices of leadership emerge at the local and regional levels and are occupied by members of a hereditary elite... Ceremonies legitimize the leadership and control of the ruling elite. (Johnson and Earle 1987:21)

Archaeologically, chiefdoms succeed the simpler community organization of early Neolithic society. With chiefdoms we see the beginnings of truly large-scale constructions, such as the mound groups of the Olmec... and of the Mississippian, the ziggurats of the Ubaid, and the henges and cursus of the Wessex chiefdoms. These early monuments testify unambiguously both to the central organization of a large labor force and to the function of a site as a regional ceremonial and political center. (Johnson and Earle 1987:210)

Although functional and structural in its approach, this definition is useful for relating the variables of warfare, fragmentation and displacement of groups, regional integration, territorial expansion, legitimizing ceremonies, and religious and political centers in the Araucanian polity. Rather than external trade at the outset of the polity, the Araucanians relied on intensive agriculture, adoption of fragmented groups, support from nonwarring groups, and later raiding to "finance" their cause against the Spanish. Required for the Araucanian case is an expansion of this definition to include the concept of "socially engineered *utopic* space" as paraphrased from the geographer Marin (1984, 1992).

Utopic space does not imply the presence of "utopia communities" but to wider social practices whereby a society's concept of utopia is expressed spatially, materially, and, I add, aesthetically. Marin refers to this kind of utopics as "spatial play." In today's world, spatial play is represented in urban planning, landscape gardening, and civic building. In these expressions of utopics, there is a "modernizing utopics" set into action in which future-oriented notions of order, control, improvement, development or even resistance are manifested through planned social spaces and the practices associated with them. What makes these spaces utopic practices is their importance in relation to other places or spaces against which they are compared and related. Certain places are more amenable to "utopic play" or "engineering of social space" and landscape than others. Once built and socially engineered, these places become important nodes in a network of aesthetic social spaces that express varying degrees of connectivity, centrality, and influence within that setting of relations. There also is a distinct time frame that is related with these sites. Although these places may utilize past or present forms of architecture and built landscape – they are oriented to the future, or to a sense of something new, rather than to the present or the past. It is the focus on order, newness, and the future that gives utopic places a different status. These places achieve this status only when perceived as sites where distinct spatial practices occur (*sensu* Foucault 1984; Hetherington 1997). According to Marin, the utopic purpose is to transform these new places into "obligatory places of passage" that order and legitimize a new social network and social practice. I see agency having meaning in this utopic play when communities negotiate the particular place and circumstance of new sites or spaces to establish a new social order. Tactical or strategic power (*sensu* Wolf 1999), in turn, is derived from producing and regulating the activities and outcomes in these newly defined utopic settings. Of further significance is the aesthetic arrangement of architecture, roads, canals, and other landscape features in this new social space, which collectively give it local identity, historical meaning, and familiarity and thus practical effectiveness (see later discussion).

A modified perspective of utopic spatial play is central to the idea of Araucanian polity formation and mound literacy, but is not limited to the social engineering and construction of places like *kuel* and *rehuekuel* alone. As described earlier, the Araucanian polity grew over time through newly organized and intensified flows of people, resources, and ideas; through the unification of ritual networks; through multilineage fragmentation, recruitment, annexation, and nucleation in certain areas; through growing participation in politics; through the expansion of a standardized ideology, cosmology, and religion that celebrated the new collectivities and the widening of channels of communication; through military training and the establishment of codes of law; through the division of new norms of compatriotism relevant to the expanding political society; and through the elaboration and proliferation of these features. All of these had spatial, material, aesthetic, and temporal expression in *kuel*, *rehuekuel*, and other landscape features.

I also argued earlier that *kuel* and *rehuekuel* should be seen as spaces out of which a process of resistance generated by outside intrusion lead to the generation of the conditions to establish and to give direction to the new political order of desired action and organization. I stated that *kuel* and *rehuekuel* came to express a special materialized idea (and imagined *sensu* Anderson 1983) of social and religious "utopia" through the notion of introducing religious and political places and processes that helped to create a better organized society that could defend itself against outsiders. These places collectively expressed a sense of utopia not only concerned with the spatial aspects of religious and social engineering but its temporal aspect too. As well as providing a sense of how a polity should be organized, this order also helped to express a new sense of social time that came into acceptance through the scheduling of seasonal battles, regular political meetings, and designated ceremonial gatherings. I do not refer to the process of instilling ceremonial scheduling within the society, although it certainly achieved this in practice (Dillehay 1990c). Rather, I refer to its role in becoming an obligatory point of passage for a discourse of interlineage tactical organization that led to the *idea* of the Araucanian society organized and united as it moved forward in historical time and to the materialization of this idea in mounded landscapes. Further, my argument is that over the course of the sixteenth and seventeenth centuries we see that ideas of improvement, which started out as part of a discourse of localized patrilineal spaces and landscapes, also became part of a discourse of historical time as well. That shift occurred primarily through regularized schedules of public ceremony and mandatory political meetings at *kuel* and *rehuekuel*.

In this book, I combine the concepts of regional polity and utopics to refer to the Araucanian polity as a politically and religiously materialized "utopic" organization or *utopic polity*. *Kuel* and *rehuekuel* were sites of variable engineering and testaments to this utopic expression of social ordering through new forms of spatial, material, and aesthetic arrangements. The utopics of this new order turned up almost everywhere in the Purén and Lumaco society – mounds, canals, roads, terraces – anywhere social aspirations that focused on creating a better-organized society in the immediate future that could constantly be spatially engineered. In particular, the *rehuekuel* came to be seen as a way in which the newly organized society in the valley, represented in particular by sacred and domestic places at particular times, could be improved not only in terms of the use of natural resources and in comparison with other places in the region but also in comparison with its own ancestral past. That is, the ultimate purpose of *rehuekuel* and the scheduling of public ceremonies at them was to contextualize collateral processes in space and time. Individual leaders and communities used the conjunction of time and space in public ceremony (see Chapter 4) as resources to fashion particular obligatory ritual paths from one *rehuekuel* to another in the valley, a trajectory or movement that spanned the daily to the yearly and even the lifetime scales. In turn, these paths interacted with larger time–space projects across the valley and region to achieve similar goals. By taking into account the relationship between obligatory paths and desired or utopic outcomes, it is possible to determine the cumulative time–space prism of *kuel* and *rehuekuel* networks in the valley. In this regard, the valley must be seen as a ceremonial kaleidoscope of scheduled and synchronized meetings across a socially engineered *utopic landscape*. When these were organized to coordinate across the landscape and not performed at the same time, greater social complexity was reached for the present and for the future.

For the purpose of this study, something is missing in Marin's notion of socially engineered places. This is the aesthetic appeal that these places have on public audiences and what the political effectiveness is of the arrangement of individual mounds in *rehuekuel*. As discussed in later chapters, the Araucanians curated and enlarged the landscapes around *rehuekuel* to make them (1) aesthetically pleasing to the attending deities and ancestors and to the living ritual audiences and (2) architecturally and spatially legible to people who were accustomed to viewing and being around similar but smaller and less numerous design features in public ceremony. In studying the megalithic monuments of Great Britain, Pollard (2001:314–316; cf. Pollard and Ruggles 2001 and Bradley's [1998, 2000] "ritualization process") refers to the aesthetics of artifact deposition and to the perception of effectiveness that "intimately related to [the] effort and care expended upon the appropriate section, arrangement, and burial of things." He believes that the placement of individual artifacts may not have inspired an aesthetic sense, but the collective association and spatial arrangement of several objects and the construction of several monuments together in the same space imparts an "aesthetic effectiveness," which may relate to the identity of places, the negotiated values and obligations of groups, and the character of personhoods. In effect, depositional arrangements are "performative in that they draw on inventive constructs of material resources that employed [and suggested] notions of correct actions" (*sensu* Thomas 1991; Pollard 2001:316). Consideration of the aesthetics of effectiveness thus extends beyond the functional–structural meaning of utopically negotiated spaces to the cogency of places such as different *kuel* and *rehuekuel* and their individual locations, construction plans of these architectural features, viewsheds to and from them, the histories of these places, and the practices in bringing about change and reordering society. The utopic vision of the Araucanian society is expressed in the totality of the constructed architectural ideology of the valley landscape, not just the artifact and site levels. Taken together, the construction of mounds on the *ñichi* platforms of *rehuekuel* in topographically unique settings that can be viewed from afar and, in turn, can see in the distance to other *rehuekuel*, the immediate spatial layout of several *kuel* in *rehuekuel* (see maps in Chapter 6), and the ritual practice at *rehuekuel* all depict a "creative play, or bricolage" (*sensu* Thomas 1991), of effective social compatriotism and political solidarity between struggling populations within the wider Araucanian cause. We see later that some *rehuekuel* occupy more aesthetically majestic topographic settings and are situated in places that produced more social histories than others, which, for the Araucanians, imbues them with reverence, drama, sensuality, deep history, and acknowledgment (cf. Cohen 1981; Kus 1989; Smith 2000, 2003). Also important are the way these settings are perceived at night under a full moon, the milky way, and other constellations or by torch and other artificial lighting used during ceremonies. In effect, the aesthetically designed landscape, whether observed during the daytime or nighttime, appealed to the divine world of the deities and ancestors in the sky above the earth's surface and embedded it within the daily activities of the living.

Also missing in the above concepts is an element of social therapy associated with utopic and aesthetic effective landscapes, whereby people aggregate at places like *rehuekeul* not only for religious and political reasons but to receive wisdom and solace, to heal the emotional wounds of warfare and death, and to look to the future for hope and restitution just as they do today. That is, ceremonies and healing rituals at mounds and *nguillatun* fields (as revealed in Chapter 5 in the two ritual narratives at the "living" mounds) provide a therapeutic discourse that comforts communities and gives them the opportunity to steer themselves via participation in public rituals through tough circumstances of their own internal changes and contradictions. In the past, these may have included tendencies toward increased hierarchy and heterarchy as opposed to previous commitments to decentralized and autonomous communities as they changed in response to new circumstances. They also may have involved ethnic and patrilineal boundary maintenance as groups moved more toward regional integration, and the incorporation of new symbol systems and metaphorical cosmologies designed to accommodate the assimilation of fragmented groups. Particularly important were rituals of misfortune and healing, which were performed at times of crisis, including the onset of ill health, natural disasters, defeat in battle, and loss of crops. These rituals were intended not only to heal individuals and the society at large but *kuel* as well during difficult times. Specifically, they functioned in four ways changing the physiological and social status of communities: (1) psychologically, to lessen anxiety and to produce catharsis; (2) socially, to expose and then heal conflicts and to recreate values; (3) protectively, to guard people against physical and mental dangers; and (4) ideologically, to constantly remind people of ancestral knowledge and history and of the pragmatic principles of their cosmological organization. Today, people receive a therapeutic or healing aesthetic from participation in public ritual ceremonies, from walking through them, and from viewing them from across the valley.

We can determine from these discussions that the collective grouping of *kuel, rehuekuel*, domestic villages, cemeteries, and other sites in settings like the Purén and Lumaco Valley provides a set of integrated places that are dynamic social and cosmological creations. They demonstrate remarkable continuity and change through their connected life histories. It is thus difficult to separate analytically a single locality as an archaeological or ethnographic site from the others, because each site is often embedded in broader temporal frames and was part of a wider scheme that historically united sequent instances of communities that are still in the minds, identities, and interactions of the people who structured them and whose existence they structured. As discussed in Chapters 4 and 6, *kuel, rehuekuel*, cemeteries, and domestic sites were and are laid out in integrated community patterns with these schemes in mind, not that each was necessarily planned according to a wide valley design, but they were locally placed with respect to each other in terms of the principles of cosmology, patrilineal history, natural resources, awareness of the upper and lower worlds, the cardinal directions, and historical and sacred places. In other words, communities were structured by pliable and durable material, historical, and spatial conditions.

In this book, I refer to this type of integrated ritual and domestic community minimally comprising a *kuel* or *rehuekuel*, a cemetery, and a domestic site, which were collectively oriented in terms of cosmological spatial referents, as a *cosmunity*.

Just as some sites have location specified by resources, social, and/or military boundaries, these sites are often placed next to water and agricultural fields for biological sustenance and to hilltops for defense. But they also have location defined by cosmological reference to the upper and lower worlds and to historical monuments such as sacred mountains, waterfalls, lakes, and ancestral mounds and ceremonial fields, thus making them a cosmological community.

EPILOGUE

This introductory account of Araucanian mounds and histories serves for the time being to indicate the broad features of the subject and to suggest the empirical and thematic foci that are adopted for the more detailed picture presented in the following chapters. I focus on the idea of *kuel* and *rehuekuel* as aesthetic monuments, time lines, memorials, identities, and architectural ideologies that reveal how the social landscape was developed as part of a new polity, and how traditional secular leaders and priestly shamans inhabited sacred spaces, inscribed values to such spaces, and articulated ideological systems within the broader society. Shamans are especially important figures, because they are the social brokers (and at times disruptors) between the population at large, rulers, ancestors, spiritual figures, and deities. Equally important are secular rulers as lineage agents who had utopic visions of a new social order and who negotiated between different groups in times of warfare and peace to deliberately alter the sociopolitical organization and historical course of the Araucanian society. Drawing attention to the historical and ideological Andean and Araucanian ideas behind these landscape memorials and their architectural forms, I trace the temporal lines these monuments chart in the creation of an aesthetically ritualized landscape and in linking the present to the pre-Hispanic and Hispanic past. In this sense, the *kuel* connected various worlds of the Araucanians, from places like the Purén and Lumaco Valley through to the larger Araucanian region itself, to the wider political and historical environment in which they lie.

Although this book broadens our empirical base and conceptual understanding of the late developing and little-known Araucanian polity that once dominated southern South America, I do not want to lose sight of the value this case has for understanding wider anthropological problems of emergent social complexity, monumentalism, landscape, memory and identity, agency, and anticolonialism. Archaeological studies of social differentiation and political centralization of pre-state societies have led to a consideration of polities and the economic, political, and ideological conditions that created and sustained them. Such societies have taken many forms (e.g., intermediate societies, chiefdoms, tribes), and they are not inevitable developments from egalitarian precursors. They should not be viewed as a stage through which each region passed. Nonetheless, they appeared in many parts of the world in later prehistoric times with important common characteristics: differences in access to status, power, and wealth, elaborate monuments, differentiation among settlements, changes in subsistence, feasting, and other transformations as the social order changed from one of household groups competing on a relatively level playing field to institutionalized differences between groups. Most of these forms are barely known due to little archaeological research on them, poor preservation of their buried record, and no written or ethnographic accounts of them. One exception is the Araucanian case which provides a rich, detailed corpus of ethnographic, ethnohistorical, and archaeological material relevant to understanding a newly formed complex society in which central leadership authority, often of a military nature, was paired with a ceremonial power structure that was segmentary and situationally heterarchical and hierarchical, as well as patrilineage groups in which considerable complexity was achieved through cyclical recruitment, annexation, and feasting. However, the rise of the Araucanian polity was not just related to centralized religio-political power in *kuel* and *rehuekuel* and increased cooperation for defense and competition for fragmented groups, but to a marked *reorganizational shift* that was orchestrated by confederated patrilineages. This shift produced new spaces for agency and identity that was constantly negotiated and ritually enacted to bring about a higher order of social cohesion and resistance to outsiders. The distribution of religio-political power and the way it was tactically and strategically organized in Araucanian and Andean terms, among several consensually confederated entities (i.e., individual rulers, patrilineages, *ayllarehue* ceremonial groups, *butanmapu*) is believed to be the primary Araucanian strategy that successfully resisted the consolidation of power by outsiders for more than three centuries.

TWO:

SHAPING ANALOGICAL AND CONCEPTUAL PERSPECTIVES

The patterns of Araucanian historical expression that I study find their origins in the late pre-Hispanic period and their transformative influences in the contact and colonial periods. I believe that Araucanian leaders, who reforged the nature of religious, demographic, and sociopolitical order to resist and defeat outsiders, used existing traditions and organizational structures and borrowed several ideological constructs from the Inka state to fashion a new geopolitical and religious model of society relevant to their day and needs. Of particular interest is how different aggregates and organizations of Araucanians, operating on diverse territorial and institutional levels, were drawn into more extensive religious and political units (e.g., *ayllarehue, butanmapu*) only to be reshuffled and repositioned into alternative arrangements (e.g., Fine 1984). It is the transformative process by which this new order matured in the form of a confederated regional polity, the selective archaism it practiced in adopting certain Inka (i.e., Andean) principles of organization to centralize politically the anticolonialism and emergent nationalism and ethnicity of the Araucanians that halted the Spanish empire in south-central Chile, and the involved conditioning and determining variables that interest me, as well as their changing expressions in the archaeological, ethnohistorical, and ethnographic records.

Colonialism is widely recognized as an institution that produced enduring hierarchies of subjects and knowledges – the colonizer and the colonized, the civilized and the primitive, the scientific and the superstitious, and the developed and the underdeveloped (Boccara 2000; Comaroff 1998; Cooper 2005; Prakash 1995; Stein 2005; Stocking 1987). The scholarship in different disciplines has made us all too aware that such dichotomies often reduce complex differences and interactions to the binary logic of we/they and self/other relations and colonial power. For many scholars, colonialism implies that the European colonizer transformed the colonized into primarily a political and economic dependent, with the relation leading to major cultural change and syncretism, to underdevelopment of the latter, and to depopulation by exposure to new diseases and armed conflict (Alcock et al. 2001; Bengoa 2003; Boccara 1999; Dobyns 1983; Gosden 2004;

Kicza 1993; Ramenofsky 1988). As a result of these transformations, traditional indigenous structures usually come into view only after they have been analyzed through a colonial "eyeglass." However, these structures and the histories of their transformations often are covered over flimsily by scholars and can be recovered through in-depth analyses. There also are several accounts of the resistance of the colonized, but few treatments of their successful resistance as analytical events or even archaeological expressions. There exist descriptions of these successes, but their conceptions are frequently treated as glorified myths and military histories for anthropologists to decode and interpret. While there are accounts of Western dominations, we have yet to fully recognize other histories of indigenous agency, knowledge, or victory in the colonial past.

While most indigenous groups in the Americas were transformed rapidly by colonialism, it did not exist at the outset of contact between the Araucanians and the Spanish and later was minimal until the late eighteenth century. The Araucanian's defeat of the Spanish at the beginning of the seventeenth century and their anticolonialism transgressed the interethnic internal polarities of south-central Chile as it politically articulated a stressed population. The Spanish recognized that the first Araucanians they encountered south of the Bio Bio River formed a viable political unity – the *estado* – and that they constituted a territorial national essence opposed to that of the Spanish colonizers (see Chapter 3). But the creation of this unity required the invocation of difference, of symbolic and physical defiance, and of the creation of a new society and utopic order. These assertions were not merely polemical responses to the Spanish invaders; instead, there are hints that the late sixteenth and early seventeenth century Araucanians underscored the necessity of tactical and strategic organizational planning and the production of a sacred landscape to both symbolize and materialize utopic planning for the long-term success of the polity's unity. Thus, I believe that the demand for a newly ordered geopolitical territory (e.g., *ayllarehue* and *butanmapu* units) was partially anchored symbolically in appeals to a "distant" Inka empire, and the unity of the ethnic Araucanian subject was partially forged in the historical spaces of the previous achievements, differences, and conflicts of the Inka and of their own ancestors and deities. But if Araucanian nationalism achieved part of its authority from the transgression of Inka (and Andean) political symbolism, it also announced its own process of emergence during this period (see Chapters 3 and 8). It normalized and contained its own space of internal differences that it invoked in performing the polity's unity. I argue that this process first arose at the intersection of political, social, and cultural differences internal to the Araucanian population and sought to negotiate a confederated regional unity that became the prolonged force of resistance and anticolonialism. It is in this respect that the present volume hopefully moves beyond marking the contradictions and impasses in the scholarly treatment of Araucanian resistance (cf. Bacigalupo 2004a–2004c; Bengoa 1985, 1998, 2003; Boccara 1999; Dillehay 1995; Leiva 1977, 1984; León 1999; Maítus

1914; Quiroga [1690] 1979; Tesillo [1647] 1911; Villalobos and Pinto 1985; Villalobos et al. 1982) to proceed to the sacred landscape, social agency, memory, and identity of anticolonialism expressed in the anthropological record.

Before presenting the interdisciplinary details of these events and processes, I consider ways to place them within a broader analogical, explanatory, and conceptual context. As noted in Chapter 1, the appearance of mound building and polity formation among the Araucanians cannot be adequately explained by just the approaches of political economy, cultural materialism, poststructuralism, and others. In recent years, there has been a shift away from environmental and technological determinants toward a greater understanding of history and of the social and symbolic use of space – that is, an understanding of human agency, historical process, identity, memory and power, landscape modification, and organizational modeling (Kroskrity 2000; Stewart and Strathern 2005). Needed here are several approaches drawn from anthropology and other fields to holistically study these issues through interlinked analogical sets of information. In Chapter 1, I discussed Marin's concept of utopics as a model of socially engineered space and place. Presented next are other concepts and understandings that also have influenced my thinking in applying analogical reasoning to link different data bases and ideas.

The reader may be perplexed at my eclectic conceptual coverage and by some of the juxtapositions of various concepts. The intention is to recognize the multiplicity of Araucanian experiences through time and space; to relativize those experiences and to recognize that they are part of a historical process and therefore continually open to change; and to permit an exploration of the ways in which the Araucanians, differently engaged and differently empowered, appropriated and contested their landscapes. In order to derive the function, not just the meaning and effectiveness, of an artifact or place, a functional–structural approach must be applied, though it has its limits as other approaches do. For example, political economy studies are useful for comprehending prestige goods and emergent leadership but are inadequate for linking landscape and religion. Symbolic studies provide insight into the latter linkage but have not yet fully incorporated history, kinship, and ecology. Phenomenology is important for studying the possible meanings assigned by social groups to objects and places but does little to explain political economy. Analyses of agency, identity, memory, and symbols generally also have been useful for providing fresh insights into social processes, but they have involved little serious methodological design and little hard evidence to back up postulations. These and other approaches also have said little about the sphere of community life that makes a society, about the ascribed rules of practice of compatriotism and citizenship within a society, and about the processes and institutions that united and fragmented it. Although my study adapts ideas from these various approaches and broadly from processualism and constructivism, it draws on mixtures of functionalism, structuralism, and historical or practice-oriented anthropology. Within this mixture, it also may seem to the reader that I view culture as conservative, cultural institutions as real, belief systems as monothetic, and history limited by structure, but this is not the case. I recognize that these and many other elements are dimensions of an ever-changing field of social relations, but ones that often transform slowly over the course of the two centuries under study here.

ANALOGICAL REASONING

In archaeology, most analogical reasoning is associated with ethnographic analogy (e.g., Hodder 1999; Wylie 1982). Wylie has defined two kinds of analogies: the comparison of forms and the study of causal relationships between variables in similar and dissimilar contexts. Analogies have suggestive value to archaeologists for expanding their range of interpretative possibilities, particularly in regard to artifact form, function, and meaning and to the organization of activities, and for supporting their behavioral arguments. Archaeologists usually muster several ethnographic case studies to show how similar the past record is to one or more documented ethnographic cases. Also used is the direct historical approach for tracing social similarities and differences from one generation to another within the same cultural stock and context. Constructing comparisons and inferring causal relationships on the basis of similarities and dissimilarities are more reasonable in the direct historical approach, because there is a greater possibility of constancy in the function, context, and meaning of similar and related variables. In these cases, the key to analogical reasoning is grouping together societies that are deemed comparable by the investigator. As Hodder (1999:47) has noted, "the argument has to evaluate whether the contexts are similar enough to allow the transfer" of knowledge from one cultural setting to another. The problem is that we cannot always know that the same artifacts in the same contexts have the same functions and meanings. Crucial to making a successful analogical argument is to demonstrate that "things are done similarly, that people respond similarly to similar situations" in similar bounded contexts.

Archaeologists have had difficulties recovering the culturally specific meanings encoded in material culture by a particular society. We will likely never know the past human agency that was responsible for creating the meanings, which are transmitted by the archaeological record into our present-day world. Those meanings are objectified by the archaeological attempt to understand what others meant by creating particular forms of material patterning in the past. In recent years, a greater effort has been placed on attempting to define the material and spatial correlates of those meanings. This task is easier when the archaeological context is late in time and can be linked directly to ethnohistorical and ethnographical accounts in the same area. This is the case with the Araucanians whereby we have direct spatial, temporal, and ethnic continuities from the past to the present that are connected by archaeology, ethnohistory, and ethnography beginning in the fifteenth century, if not earlier, and ending in the present day. Whichever record offers information about the Araucanians' past and particularly about the specific research problems related to the emergence of mound building and polity formation, it must be either falsified or verified through analogical reasoning – that is, an argument has to be made to explain the function, context, and meaning of a particular artifact, social structure, settlement pattern, or religious expression. This implies searching for the symbolic, spatial, and/or material correlates of statements made in the ethnohistorical and ethnographic records, or the reverse, looking for observations and statements in the living or written records that help to explain the meanings, continuities, and discontinuities of the observed patterns in the archaeological record. This comes to the suggestive value of analogical reasoning and to the degree of social and cultural change the Araucanians have undergone over the past several centuries.

Contemporary ethnographers and historical linguists such as Faron (1964), Stuchlik (1976), Montecino (1980), Leiva (1977), Croese (1985), Key (1978, 1979) and others have recognized the minimal impact of European contact on the Araucanians or Mapuche. Louis Faron was one of the first modern ethnographers to study Mapuche culture change and the impact of outside invaders. He understood the ideological and religious foundations of the twentieth-century Mapuche society perhaps more than other scholars. Although his fieldwork was carried out in the 1950s, many of his observations and interpretations are consistent with those of other observers of the Mapuche. In commenting on cultural continuity, he stated that:

> In spite of these socially disruptive forces, the Mapuche have maintained a great measure of cultural and social integrity. These forces have not caused traditional Mapuche life to disappear: rather their effect has been to weld Mapuche society into a more complex structure than existed in prereservation times. (Faron 1964:1)

> In prereservation times, a major form of local unification was large religious congregations, which brought together multiple lineage groups to propitiate the authenticity of lineage ancestors, to deify mythical ancestors, to give reverence to a multitude of gods, and to pray for victory in war. Although to a lesser extent today, there still is a "chain of congregational units [patrilineages] overlapping on their peripheries, which binds together the total Mapuche society in a single expression of religious morality." (Faron 1964:214)

Writing in the 1970s, another anthropologist, Milan Stuchlik (1976), commented that:

> A rather vague process called acculturation – which is often used to explain ongoing changes in a simple society exposed to contact with a more developed one – cannot be satisfactorily used here. In the first place contact between the Mapuche and Spanish (later Chileans) was limited predominantly to war and eventually to commerce; war, if anything, led to the strengthening of the corporate ties within and between groups. In the second place, over the last hundred years acculturation has consisted mostly of the gradual entrance of consumer goods into the reservations. There is certainly nothing which can account for the organizational changes which have occurred in the Mapuche society.... Mapuche society suffered arbitrary interference through the process of the foundation of reservations [in the early twentieth century]. The steps directly taken by the Chilean government were relatively few, and were seemingly related only to some aspects of the future existence of the Mapuche within the Chilean state.... (Stuchlik 1976:202)

In referring to changes within the Araucanian society that many previous scholars (e.g., Guevara 1929:392) had attributed to traits borrowed from the Spanish in the sixteenth and seventeenth centuries, another social anthropologist, Sonia Montecino (1980:85, 93), produced an insightful master's thesis on early historical cultural and social changes. Her comments on certain organizational aspects of this period are worth citing.

> Reorganización que conduce al fortalecimiento y dominancia de unas esferas sobre otras, a saber, la política-militar se yergue sobre las demás, y esto no como producción de las "prestaciones" de la sociedad española, sino como respuesta al dominio y conquista de su territorio, respuesta hecha con la plena injerencia de las "armazones" propias al sistema social mapuche. En otras palabras, los principios de cooperación y dispersión territorial no son afectados ni transformados por la Guerra, por el contrario, son ellos que guían y dinamizan la reorganización y la puesta en marcha del proceso de readecuación interno de la sociedad durante el largo período de tiempo que hemos venido relatando. (Montecino 1980:85)

> Reorganization which led to the strengthening and dominance of some spheres over others, for example, the political-military

dominated the rest, and this was not a product of "borrowing" from Spanish society, rather it was a response to the domination and conquest of their territory, a response made fully within the "framework" of the Mapuche social system. In other words, the principles of cooperation and territorial dispersion were neither affected nor transformed by the War, on the contrary, they guided and energized the reorganization and the initiation of the process of internal adjustment in the society. (Montecino 1980:85)

En el plano ideológico se mantuvieron las mismas creencias, persistiendo el antiquo sistema de ideas frente al rol de los antepasados. El influjo de los misioneros se deja sentir en un nivel mas que nada formal expresado en las prácticas bautismales a que eran sometidos los niños, prácticas que se convirtieron en acciones puramente "conciliadoras" por parte de los mapuches frente a las exigencias constantes de los sacerdotes. Chamanes y curanderos prosiguen siendo estamentos encargados de mediatizar ante de los pillanes y el grupo, ejerciendo labores de adivinación y curación respectivamente. (Montecino 1980:93)

[The Araucanians] maintained the same beliefs on the ideological level, persisting in the ancient system of ideas about the role of the ancestors. The influence of the missionaries was felt only on a formal level, expressed in the baptism of children, a conciliatory practice on the part of the Mapuche in the face of the constant pressure of the priests. The shamans and healers continued as the groups charged with the responsibility to mediate between the *pillanes* and the society by means of divination and healing respectively. (Montecino 1980:93)

More recently, the contemporary historian, Arturo Leiva (1977), wrote in another compelling thesis that:

No existe ningún testimonio terminante de los cronistas y otros autores – a no ser opiniones y deseos – que probara fehacientemente la introducción del cristianismo entre los indios. Sino la mayoría coincide en observar que el rechazo al catolicismo fue tajante y casi total. (Leiva 1977:16)

There exists no conclusive testimony of the chroniclers or other authors – other than opinions and wishes – that reliably proves the introduction of Christianity to the Indians. However, the majority agree that the rejection of Catholicism was emphatic and almost total. (Leiva 1977:16)

And writing in 1985, the historical linguist Robert Croese states that:

> Mapuche society continues to function as it has for many years with
> its own religious observances, social structure and language. Though
> there exists a surface socio-economic integration with Chilean society
> and widespread bilingualism, most of the Mapuche on reservations are
> by no means bi-cultural. (Croese 1985:786)

The Araucanians have undoubtedly undergone considerable changes over
the past four centuries and cannot just be taken as a minimally modified indigenous
society. However, Stuchlik is correct in noting that contact between the Spanish
and the Araucanians was intermittent and focused primarily on sporadic armed
conflict, mainly along the frontier zone, and later on long-distance raiding and
trading into Argentina. Minimal contact allowed many traditional aspects of the
religious, ideological, and social organization of the Araucanians to continue or to
restructure themselves in terms of indigenous rather than European principles of
organization. Even later, during the early *reduccion* period in the twentieth century,
the Chilean government essentially took a hands-off policy toward the Araucanians except in cases of conflict with European colonists. As Stuchlik, Montecino,
and others imply, nothing that is notably colonial or European explains the organizational changes experienced by the Araucanians over the past few centuries.
These changes were mainly created and regulated by the Araucanians themselves,
as Padden (1993) and others (see also Dillehay 1999, 2002) have argued. That
is, until recent modern times the Araucanians primarily maintained themselves
precisely through their own self-generated reconstruction and accommodation
(*sensu* Sahlins 1985); their indigenous structure maintained itself by changing
itself. However, since the early 1990s, some Araucanians have changed because
of significantly modernization, evangelism, and new indigenous laws designed
to exploit the natural resources on their lands (Anonymous 1993; Bengoa 1985;
Faiola 1999; Millaman 1993). These changes have largely been directed by government laws, nongovermental organizations, and other nonindigenous organizations, which have resulted in more rapid culture change and incorporation into
Chilean society. I point out these distinctions because we need to be aware of
the differences between indigenous principles of organization restructured by the
Araucanians and hybrid principles later partially formed by European colonialism
and modernization (Dillehay 2002; A. Saavedra 2002).

In returning to analogical reasoning, we thus cannot always assume strict
culture continuity and persistence in all aspects of society, even in timeless traditional societies of direct historical continuity such as the Araucanians. A premise
of this study is that the Araucanians instituted major social, demographic, and
ideological changes in the sixteenth through the eighteenth centuries to establish
territorial sovereignty and to form a new order. Although influenced by outside

pressures and institutions, these changes were "self-generated reconstructions and accommodations" guided by indigenous principles of organization. As noted in the Introduction and in Chapter 1 and explained below, there are easily recognizable continuities in several spatial, material, and symbolic patterns observed in the archaeological, ethnohistorical, and ethnographic records that allow us to reliably connect important principles of organization, historical processes, and social meanings across time and space.

For instance, my colleagues and I have compared contemporary artifacts and their spatial and temporal patterns with those recovered archaeologically, working from the present back through time as far as possible (e.g., Adán and Alvarado 1999; Adán and Mera 1997; Castro and Adán 2001; Dillehay 1976, 1990a–1990c, 1999, 2002, 2004; Gordon 1992; Navarro and Adan 1999). In other words, we have applied a classic direct historical approach. Although successful in some cases, such as women-specific *ketru metawe* pottery vessels that were used for similar purposes in seventeenth century written accounts and today (Dillehay and Gordon 1979), this approach has limitation. This method works only so long as a given artifact assemblage or social structure remains coherent or retains its original meaning. This is not always the case. For example, in the past the indigenous *palin* played in the *nguillatun* field was a warrior's game related to glorification and success in battle, but today it has little meaning other than gaming competition among different lineage communities. However, both the past and present *palin* games have produced similar material and spatial traits in *nguillatun* fields, which need to be recognized in reconstructing the form and meaning of ceremonial spaces. Missing is the warlike setting today in the field (see Chapter 4).

Furthermore, there are *rehuekuel* located on *ñichi* platforms where the Mapuche still conduct *nguillatun* ceremonies and carry out administrative meetings (*cahuin*) in the Purén and Lumaco Valley. Three such places are *Ñachekuel, TrenTrenkuel,* and *Hualonkokuel,* where I have attended ceremonies and meetings. In these places, *chicha* (*muday, mudai*) is consumed, animals are sacrificed, *palin* is played, and religio-political meetings are held between several communities. The fields are generally characterized by U- or circular-shaped structures where participants cook, eat, and reside for several days. The central plaza has an altar or *llangi-llangi* pole positioned near one to two *kuel* where the primary ritual and dance activities take place (see Chapter 4). We have excavated similar places throughout the valley and dated them between the fourteenth and nineteenth centuries (Dillehay, forthcoming). The patterning of activity areas, postholes, hearths, broken vessels, and food remains in these places is similar to that of lineage structures, artifact scatters, and activity areas found in modern-day *nguillatun* fields. Similar localities and functions also are described and referred to as *borracheras, alihuenes, cahuines,* and *nguillatun* or *rehuetun* ceremonies by several early chroniclers (e.g., Rosales [1674] 1989; Núñez de Pineda [1673] 2003: see Chapter 6) writing about Purén and nearby areas, so we can confidently rely on a certain degree of continuity in the content, structure, and meaning of these places (see Chapters 3 and 4).

Similar continuity can be said of the use of *kuel* and *rehuekuel* by present-day *machi* and local communities who see them as their guardian kindred spirits and use them as oracle shrines to converse with ancestors and deities, to mediate conflicts between malefic spirits residing in the mounds and the living, and to predict, if not influence, future events. Furthermore, both the historic and ethnographic accounts have observed activities such as animal sacrifice and the burning of cinnamon (*foye*) on the top of mounds as sacrificial offerings to important figures. Archaeological evidence for these activities has been excavated from buried surfaces within the mounds and in off-mound task specific activity areas in sites of the Purén and Lumaco Valley (Dillehay 2003). Because there is a high degree of correspondence in the form and location among many ethnographic, ethnohistorical, and archaeological patterns such as these, because the geographical areas involved in the written records are often the same in Lumaco and Purén, and because a good case can be made for the continuity of certain religious, ideological, and social practices in this area from the late archaeological past to the present day, we can argue by analogy that the memory and current use of *kuel, rehuekuel, nguillatun* fields, and other features in the study approximate those of the past two to four hundred years.

These same similar conditions are not always met in studying the domestic settlement pattern. In the past there were both highly aggregated and extensive agricultural villages associated with agricultural terraces, fortresses, cemeteries, and *rehuekuel*. The aggregated settlement form corresponded to a higher level of sociopolitical organization, which was lost at the end of the nineteenth century when the *reduccion* system was imposed. In some areas, there is continuity in family and lineage community patterns whereby historically stable lineages still live near and respect traditional spacing orders with regard to closely placed *rehuekuel*, cemeteries, and old agricultural features and fortresses once used by their ancestors, as evidenced by written records (see Chapters 3–5) and by oral tradition (see Chapter 6). However, in a few areas this ordering has been altered greatly and now follows a pattern adapted to the population pressures of living on the *reducciones*.

Because these same conditions are obviously not fulfilled in all artifact, community, and landscape cases in the study area, other means of linking the Araucanian past and present are necessary. One means is ethnoarchaeology, which we have conducted for the past thirty years to study the analogy between highly specific features of the past and present (e.g., household sizes and location, burial patterns, pottery types) and the roles of changing kinship and social organization in decision-making about settlement location and internal site structure and to understand the relationships between ceremonial landscapes, diffused leadership, exchange systems, and their material and symbolic expressions (Dillehay 1990c,

1992a–1992c, 1995, 1999). These organizational and locational similarities reflect commonalties in the way domestic and ritual spaces were and still are organized under conditions dictated by aspects of the political and religious system, whether it be the past or present. Although the impetus of change and the meaning of this organization have altered over the centuries, we still can associate certain spatial structures with certain triggering variables, such as increased outside political influence (whether historic Spanish or modern Chilean), shrinking agricultural land, population movement and pressure, fusion and fission of ritual kin groups, and so forth. Thus, it is the social network rather than meaning content – organizational structure rather than culture – that are projected back into the past. The ethnoarchaeology often acts as a bridging approach between archaeology and ethnography to formulate suggestions concerning the variables that are likely to be structuring the data to particular political, demographic, religious, and economic contexts, and, at the very least, points to questions that need to be answered before interpretation of more complex issues such as social and religious arrangements can begin. The ethnoarchaeological approach also has guided the methodology and interpretation of the ethnohistorical data.

We also have conducted ethnography among many different communities throughout the Araucania, seeking information about a wide range of topics specific to the past and observing the individual and collective use of materials, knowledges, spaces, symbols, and places. We have learned that people have different sources of knowledge made available to them according to occupation, traditional education, class, gender, wealth, age, and the ways in which their life histories are spread out across space and intersect with those of others. This indicates that they are differentially positioned in power and identity relationships, such as *machi* and *lonko* leaders, to retain knowledge of the past. This suggests that power and knowledge are deeply intertwined, and these forms of positioning constrain and enable one's emergence as a particular kind of person. This creates considerable diversity among informants and extra caution among those of us gathering informant data. We also have learned that informant's memory of the old ways is often partial and fragmented. Yet, there are elder *machi, lonko, weupin,* and others who provide tales of the military feats and deaths of such famous rulers as Anganamón, Pelantaro, and Lientur who lived in the sixteenth, seventeenth, and eighteenth centuries (see Chapter 7). These tales generally correspond with the information given by chroniclers dating to the same period, thus further indicating the validity of the memory for several centuries back in time.

In addition to sociocultural, organizational, spatial, and temporal overlap and interdisciplinary complementarity, a successful analog depends on other variables, for instance, comparability of environment and cultural complexity. That is, we cannot use all written records on the agricultural Araucanians of the central valley to examine the hunters and gatherers of the Andeans highlands and coast and vice versa. In some areas, such as Purén-Lumaco, Chol-Chol, and

Villarrica, cultural complexity was much greater in the past and increased after contact; in other areas such as Nacimiento, Boroa, and Quele, complexity likely decreased in the seventeenth and eighteenth centuries due to depopulation, settlement abandonment, and other sociocultural changes, thus making it difficult to compare them with the former areas where the core of the polity under study here lasted well into the early nineteenth century (Bengoa 1985, 2003; see Chapters 3 and 2).

Another reliable means of linking the past and the present is oral tradition. Cultures without written records use oral and visual means to preserve tradition (Finnegan 1984). The use of oral tradition as a reliable source of information about past cultures generally has been avoided by archaeologists because their research designs and methodologies typically focus on visible landscapes and artifacts and because the symbolic codes of oral data are often esoteric and elusive. Oral traditions have generally been treated as invisible, sacred, or mental domains and thus difficult to or unavailable for study by nonmembers of the culture. As Sekaquaptewa and Washburn (2004; cf. Mason 2000) have shown in their study of metaphors in Hopi ritual songs, oral traditions can reflect ancient cosmological principles and other practices and, in turn, show how these same principles are manifested in symbols, spaces, and artifacts.

In the same sense as the ritual songs of the Hopi, shamanic narratives and informant's memory about the Araucanian mounds express stories, songs, and passages that are visual and spatial metaphors for the past and present fundamental relationships in the culture that are oral traditions that embody evidence that is highly informative about the personification of *kuel* in history and in the culture identity of the Araucanians and especially about their cosmological principles. Based on the content, theme, and structure of these narratives and memories, which address spatial, material, and symbolic patterns that usually can be reliably traced as far back as the sixteenth century, we can apply the direct historical approach because these systems have time depth in meaning and continuity in their use from the ethnographic present to the historic period and to the pre-Hispanic past. The Araucanian ritual ceremonies are performed by all members of participating communities. Members sing and dance, exchange gifts, sacrifice animals, listen to sacred messages from the *lonko* leaders, shamans, deities, and ancestors, and pray to the deities and ancestors. By repeatedly engaging in ceremony, people remember the messages and their meanings and histories, and are inspired and motivated by them.

It is important to make clear that the Araucanian shamans' and the people's views of the past 400 years are generally preserved, both metaphorically in oral tradition and referentially in the material (or archaeological) and landscape records. For example, it is constantly referenced in shamanic ritual narratives at mounds today that the Araucanians will "defeat their opponents ten times" (*Marichiwew*; see Appendix 1). Informants report that this message refers to the defeat of the

Spanish and Chilean armies, which demonstrate that indigenous communities in Purén and Lumaco still strongly adhere to past events in their history and to the way they defended themselves against outsiders (see Chapter 5). Successive generations of shamans have used this and other messages in different contexts and combinations to communicate particular and general experiences and concepts of the Araucanians. As shown in the two mound rituals discussed in Chapter 5 (also see Appendix 1), what varies in ceremony are the combined words, phrases, and messages used by the shamans to express different historical events and guiding principles. Change in the content and structure of rituals has obviously occurred; and shamans have changed the details of the narratives to fit the specific contexts and special situations of each lineage history. Nonetheless, the messages are representative of specific *kuel* and specific moments in a long tradition of the ritual recollective memory of histories and cosmologies that is consciously shared and verbally expressed both in and out of ceremonies. The reenactment of public ritual at the same *kuel* and *rehuekuel* and the metaphorical reference to these places and to their significance to the Araucanians assure their permanent place in history and their remembrance. The Araucanians participating in these ceremonies are fully conscious of the spatial and material referents and the metaphors and the messages referencing them. Once again, what Sekaquaptewa and Washburn (2004) describe for the spiritual benefits the Hopi people receive from ritual is similar for the Araucanians.

> The ritual forms that accompany songs in public performance are the primary ways in which the Hopi people experience the power and importance of the beliefs and reciprocal behaviors that are shared and practiced by all as they carry out their communal and ceremonial obligations. Indeed, the awe-inspiring drama and intensity of feeling projected in these performances instill such respect that the words of the *katsinas* ring in the minds of the Hopi well beyond the day of the performance as they sing the songs out loud while carrying out activities in their daily lives. In this way, over time, the constant character of these metaphorical song words and phrases reinforces both the ceremonial and communal spheres and insures that this belief system will not be easily forgotten. In effect the repetitive character of oral and visual traditions has the effect of law by consistently outlining a standard of behavior that everyone in the community must follow. This is the nature of the communication process in cultures without writing. These are the elements that form Hopi oral tradition. (Washburn 2003; Sekaquaptewa and Washburn 2004:462)

I return to what I stated in Chapter 1: We have to think beyond the image that mounds are static artifacts and consider them as metaphors of larger concepts fundamental to Araucanian practices and historical principles that have guided and continue to guide the Araucanian's lives. In this regard, mound building and mound worship must be comprehended not only with regard to their meaning within the immediate complex of performance featuring ritual, prayer, dance, and associated objects and images – but also as they relate to the yearly schedule of ritual events, certain sacred places, leadership roles, and to other community activities that collectively advance the philosophical ideas underlying the Araucanian lifeway.

In sum, what makes the Araucanian case suitable for analogical interpretation is the degree of cultural continuity between the contemporary society and the early Hispanic past. Yet, caution is necessary because there are known historic and present-day changes in the way of life that make it difficult to always employ the direct historical approach and draw analogies between the two. Some of these changes are the scalar effects of a fluctuating population and the increased presence of mounds and associated domestic sites and what this means in terms of intergroup political, economic, and religious organization. Thus, analogical interpretation and the direct historical approach are working hypotheses to be tested archaeologically, ethnohistorically, and ethnographically, if continuities in form and function have meaning and are correct. The more correspondences that are found between the records, and the more strictly the specific attributes identified refer to a particular kind of feature – in this case various activities related to mound building and mound worship, mound literacy and to polity formation – the stronger the analogical interpretation.

CONCEPTS USEFUL TO UNDERSTANDING THE ARAUCANIAN CASE

Until recently, traditional approaches to the study of social change frequently have neglected issues of social creation, manipulation, and meaning that have become important as we continue to inject concepts of agency, practice, structuration, and interaction into our models of the past (cf. Blanton 2001; Blanton et al. 1996; Brumfiel 1994; Jones 1999; Saitta 1994). As noted by Yaeger and Canuto (2002:6): "The interactionalist perspective focuses our attention on the relationship between the interactions that occur in a given space and the sense of shared identity that both fosters and is fostered by these interactions . . . every community contains an irreducible and historically contingent dimension, an insight derived from both the historical development and interactionalist paradigms." Interactionalist approaches ask how people created communities and other social institutions through their relationships. It has been practice theory that has emphasized interaction most strongly, positioning individual practice as the locus for the production of the patterned processes that create and recreate society (Bourdieu

1977, 1994; Giddens 1976, 1984). Instead of seeing the community as the basis for social interaction and reproduction, a practice or agent-oriented approach views all social institutions, including the community, as socially constituted (cf. Anderson 1983). This perspective does not ignore spatial and material conditions, but views them as constitutive of the structures and agents that pattern practice (Allen 1999; Bourdieu 1977; Dobres and Robb 2000).

Concepts of agency view the actions and boundaries of political organizations not just demarcated by centralized control but by integrated networks or spheres of everyday social practices; that is, by the interactions between agents and the structures within which they exist and which they create (Allen 1999; Archer 1988; Latour 1986; Mann 1984). (Agency is not just confined to leaders but involves nonelites as well.) Agents require knowledge of the structure or traditions of the society within which they operate, and a social position within the society that allows them to exercise knowledge to bring about change vis-à-vis local structural conditions (e.g., technologies, material goods, symbolic orders) and principles (*sensu* Barrett 1990, 2000). Social, religious, and political organizations are aspects of the structural principles of a society and knowledge of the workings of organizations can be used to bring change. Applying this knowledge and practicing it to bring about change in both the structural conditions and principles give the acts of agency historical significance. That is, society exists as the result of prior conditions and this gives history a prominent role in shaping social formations and identities and the practices constituting them. To structure something thus gives it identity. For instance, the Araucanian war itself acted as an agent in structuring both the indigenous and Spanish societies and their respective identities. Further, some defeated patrilineages acted as their own agents in defining their own identities within the structural conditions of the war either by assimilating into more stable groups or by remaining unstable and fragmented for political and economic reasons (see Chapters 3 and 7).

While recent studies have advanced our understanding of the role of agents in interactional settings and in the emergence of complexity and how they consciously developed strategies for manipulating traditions and structures, they often too narrowly focus on individual or group power strategies (i.e., Blanton et al. 1996) that neglect the historical contingencies, organizational variability, institutional settings, and patterned processes that create and recreate society (cf. Flannery 1999). Most agency approaches actively have discouraged the deification of social institutions like the community or ceremonial groupings like the *rehuekuel* and *ayllarehue* by emphasizing how individual actors competently manipulated their place within multiple social contexts, which were in turn contingent on agent's practices (see Barrett 2001; Dobres and Robb 2000). As a social grouping, the *rehuekuel* was a traditional ceremonial-civic center that brought together several patrilineage communities for ancestor worship, gift exchange, alliance-building, and polity-formation. It was an institution that both structured the practices of its members within special places and time frames and was structured by these practices. Rulers, shamans, and kinsmen acting as agents for their patrilineages also worked within the structure and practice of ceremonies and other traditional practices at *rehuekuel* to achieve their political goals. Araucanian warfare and agency also changed the concept of the community by redefining interaction through the recruitment of fragmented lineages with similar structures, situations, and histories and by co-opting those lineages to participate in hierarchically structured ceremonies, military campaigns, and other public events. This process fitted with traditional spatial structures such as residential and *cahuin* (political meetings) sites, and thus was not a structural adjustment but a structural overlay, or imbrication, shared by patrilineages. Knowing that Araucanian leaders manipulated power, agency still was an important part of social interaction because individual leaders and other lineage members employed knowledge and power to determine the nature, location, flow, and outcome of interaction.

According to agency theory, there are different scales and different spaces of power relations that "permeate and structurate" the legitimacy and regulation of various spatially defined social units, such as households, villages, communities, states, and other spatialized entities (*sensu* Fuerst 2002; cf. Massey 1993, 2000). Two complementary and coterminous types of practice construct power in space, according to agency theory. One is *leveraging* or the employment of agency "over" space; the other is *empowering* or the use of agency "in" space (Agnew 1999). Associated with these two types of agency are four types of power. Two of these involve the empowerment of individuals through their experiences and talents and their ability to transform social interactions and transactions within particular settings (Cohen 1979:873, 875; Wolf 1984:586). A third type is "tactical or organizational power," defined by Wolf (1999:5) as power that "controls the contexts in which people exhibit their capabilities and interact with others. This sense calls attention to the instrumentalities through which individuals or groups direct or circumscribe the actions of others within determinate settings," such as political reunions, religious gatherings, and sporting events. A related venue is structural power: "power manifest [itself] in relationships that not only operates within settings and domains but also organizes and orchestrates the settings themselves, and that specifies the distribution and direction of energy flows." This venue establishes the basic distinctions between the organizers of feasts and public events, for example, and those who respond to the directives of the organizers. This also constitutes power "to deploy and allocate social power" (cf. Lefebvre 1991; Smith 2003). A fourth mode is the power of capital to aggregate and allocate labor (cf. Saitta 1994, agency and surplus labor). Foucault (1984:428) defines this mode as the ability "to structure the possible field of action of others." The third and fourth modes of power primarily involve the leveraging of social space.

When in power, the authority of Araucanian leaders rested not just on military, ideological, and economic venues and new political and economic roles created by widespread conflict but particularly on the contingency of "tactical, organizational, and structural powers," which was used by some leaders to create new forms of cultural organization to solidify and enhance the political position of their lineage and their allied lineages (see Chapters 7 and 8). To paraphrase Wolf, this is power that controlled the religious and political contexts in which individuals and lineages (1) employed their knowledges, (2) exhibited their interactive skills with others, and (3) organized and directed the institutional contexts and public settings within which interactions occurred. Leaders were not the only agents of power. Priestly shamans and common lineage kinsmen also wielded considerable social agency and power, as demonstrated in several cases presented in Chapters 3, 5, and 7.

More specifically, we can infer from early Spanish texts that certain leaders (i.e., Anganamón, Pelantaro, Peletan, Auipuavilo, Lientur, and Butapichón) in the Purén-Lumaco area (e.g., cited throughout Núñez de Pineda [1673] 2003; Quiroga [1690] 1979; Rosales [1674] 1989 and other sources; see Chapters 3 and 7) imposed a new strategist or tactical organization that established the contexts, or settings, which led to competitive leadership for recruiting defeated refugee populations and for annexing neighboring lineages. These and other individuals were great leaders (*guen-toqui, toqui, apo-ulmen*) who were highly skilled in tactical warfare (cf. Boccara 1998, 1999; Casanova 1989; Zavala 2000; Zavala 2005, 2006), in the organizational incorporation of fragmented lineages into their own more stable lineages through recruitment and annexation, and in establishing and controlling the specific politico–religious settings at *rehuekuel* localities where alliances were made and celebrated. The adoption of other lineages fragmented in warfare apparently served to increase the social complexity of the recruiting patrilineage and the labor force for communal projects (e.g., agricultural production, construction of *kuel* and *rehuekuel* for interlineage feasting) and for success in warfare. The annexation of neighboring lineages involved control of their lands and labor pool and sometimes the construction of small-scale *rehuekuel* for feasting in these annexed areas. As a result, powerful lineage rulers transformed their neighbors into extensions of themselves (Dillehay 1999, 2002). In short, the organizational model of rulers suggested by the texts is control of repetitive ceremonial and commensal feasting at *rehuekuel*, both in their home territories and in annexed lands. Leaders' control of ceremonial feasting partly defined their power and their capacity to fuel a larger network of ranked fragmented but incorporated lineages under them and to build their military fecundity and corporate labor pool. (Recruited and annexed lineages became lower ranking members of the recruiting lineage, which also created more hierarchical levels within it. See Chapter 7.) Thus, in my opinion, the emergence of an organized and expansionistic confederacy of patrilineage leaders was not linked just to warfare so much as it was to the creation of opportunities (*sensu* Claessen 2000) for these leaders to recruit new personnel and territories, to expand lineage populations, and to operate within a stratified leadership of war leaders, warriors, and priestly shamans. As seen later, much of this recruitment was done through ritual feasting, which served many social purposes, establishing political alliances for war and marriage, mobilizing labor, creating political power and economic advantages, and redistributing wealth (see Dietler and Hayden 2001; Kertzer 1988).

This latter point is important because several Chilean historians have emphasized the social prestige allotted to Araucanian warriors, or *konas*, during the Spanish wars and how it became a meaningful and influential force in reshaping a more cohesive and organized force of resistance and in developing into a *modus operandi* for the members of warring lineages that organized their public ceremonies and ritual games, competitiveness, and alliance-building around the social recognition given to brave deeds and glory in battle. Quotes from contemporary historians (Boccara 1999; Leiva 1977; also see Bengoa 2003; Montecino 1980) demonstrate these points.

> Nos parece en cambio que entre los araucanos el apoyo psicológico y cultural a la incorporación de préstamos militares, deriva del rol que la sociedad asignaba a los guerreros y del hecho que las acciones famosas eran el principal mecanismo para adquirir prestigio ... Quizás la palabra más ajustada para definir a estos guerreros araucanos – los konas –, sea la de "campeones." La competencia por sobresalir brinda la pauta para entender toda su conducta y en ella se expresa el interés predominante de la sociedad araucana: ser nombrado ... la acción militar no está tomada como un fin en sí misma, sino se la usa al interior de la sociedad. En pocas palabras, la milicia no tiene intereses propios, sino que expresa los de todos los araucanos, participen o no participen en ella: tal es su mayor fuerza.... No puede llamar la atención entonces que estos "campeones," los soldados se pusieran rápidamente en acción al ver aparecer los conquistadors españoles que amenazaban aplastarlos y exterminarlos como capa social. Y a la vez que la sociedad los apoyara incondicionalmente, puesto que el soldado expreso a las ambiciones de todos. (Leiva 1977:162–63)

I believe, on the other hand, that the psychological and cultural support for the incorporation of military borrowing among the Araucanians derives from the role that the society assigned to the warriors and the fact that renowned deeds were the principal mechanism for acquiring prestige.... Perhaps the best word to describe these Araucanian warriors – the *konas* – would be "champions." The competition to excel offers a model for understanding all their behavior and in it the predominant interest of Araucanian society – to be renowned ... military action is not taken as an end in itself, but is used within the society.

In brief, warfare does not have its own interests, but rather expresses those of all Araucanians, whether or not they participate in it; this is its greatest strength. . . . Thus, it is not surprising that these "champions," the warriors, quickly went into action at the appearance of the Spanish conquistadores who threatened to wipe them out and eliminate them as a social category. And at the same time, the society supported them unconditionally since the warrior expressed the aspirations of everyone. (Leiva 1977:162–63)

la imagen del guerrero ideal se percibía en todas las facetas de la vida social reche: en el espiritu de los juegos (el palín, o chueca, representaba una verdadera propedéutica de la guerra), en la educación de los jóvenes al estilo esparciata, y en el prestigio de los guerreros que se destacaban durante el combate al buscar la lucha individual. (Boccara 1999:435–436)

the image of the ideal warrior could be seen in all the facets of *reche* social life: in the spirit of the games (*palin* or *chueca* was a true preparation for war), in the education of youths in Spartan fashion, and in the prestige of the warriors who distinguished themselves in war by seeking individual combat. (Boccara 1999:435–436)

We see from these passages not only the important role of religion and ideology in the socialization of warriors and in their ritual preparation for battle and the celebration of victory but also the wider social niche and power structure produced by warriors and by the ways in which they were revered by the society at large. Achieved warriors were granted special consumptive privileges during celebration feasts and great social prestige (see Chapters 3, 7, and 8). Following their military victory over their enemies, warriors often refocused their tactical powers by defining an area of "peace" or social order within their own society, creating political power within that space to keep the peace, and supporting the development of a warrior ideology that further rationalized a new social order and power structure (Keeley 1996; cf. Otterbein 1973:947). This in turn increased the authoritative presence of the Araucanian "military class" and stratified the political system more than warfare *per se*. In this regard, I agree with Claessen's (2000) view that increased complexity may be related less to warfare and more to the emergence of warrior strata within stratified societies. That is, warfare did not necessarily *cause* the formation of the Araucanian polity, as Carneiro (1970) might argue in this case. Rather it fostered the setting which permitted *toqui* war leaders and their warriors to realize their ambitions to achieve social status and leadership in the community at large (*sensu* Claessen 2000). It also consolidated the tactical power of leaders and warriors into a *bona fide* warrior social "class."

Other processes of emergent complexity characterize the Araucanian polity. Normally, "chiefdoms" undergo cycling between simple and more complex socioeconomic forms (Anderson 1994:9, 1996; Flannery 1999:5) in their ascent to higher forms of power and authority. In building on the insights of others (e.g., Wright 1984), Flannery suggests that particularly able leaders, or chiefs, surpassed the limits of cycling in three ways: by demanding increased production from their subjects, by improving their subjects' production through technology, or by finding new subjects to add to the production under leader's control. This first option requires territorial expansion as ambitious leaders attempt to extend their power beyond areas that they could personally oversee. Because a leader can directly control only the area within a short distance from his residence, territorial expansion forces him to delegate governing authority over distant parts of the new territory to others (Flannery 1999:15). Thus, territorial expansion plays a key role in state formation by necessitating a hierarchy of administrators and a specialized form of government that is qualitatively and quantitatively different. (See Blitz [1999], Hally [1996], and Spencer [1993] for a critique of the cycling model. They view it as reflecting the rise and fall of simple chiefdoms or the demographic fission and fusion of the same chiefly communities rather than cyclical flux between different socioeconomic levels of complexity.)

Ethnohistoric records show that most Araucanian populations cycled between different levels of social complexity and, in a few areas such as Purén, Lumaco, Tucupel and Arauco, achieved a higher-order interregional, confederated level of organization the Spanish called the "*estado*" (see Chapters 1 and 3). In these areas, the limits of cycling were surpassed by success in warfare, by recruiting and annexing others, by adopting new technologies, and by increasing economic production in fertile valleys in order to support more nucleated populations (Bibar [1555] 1966; Caravallo y Goyeneche [1796] 1876; Dillehay 2002; Molina 1788, 1795; Ovalle [1646] 2003; P. Valdivia [1545] 1960; see Chapters 3 and 7). Important leaders from Purén-Lumaco constantly led organizational movements across the entire Araucanian territory to form new or to restructure old lineages at higher levels of sociopolitical articulation where there was previously social disintegration due to warfare, disease, population displacement, and fragmentation of lineages (see Chapter 7). Although cycling was typical throughout the territory, only a few valleys ever sustained power over a prolonged period by apparently rotating rulers' authority through regionally allied patrilineages (i.e., *ayllarehue*) located at related *rehuekuel* in certain circumscribed areas rather than permanently losing it and being dominated by a distant or neighboring lineage. Textual and archaeological evidence suggests that few single patrilineages ever sustained power for more than 50 to 100 years. Lineages in Purén-Lumaco were one of the most successful in this regard; they remained a powerful dynastic political force for an estimated 200 years or more (Bengoa 2003:Chapters 12–15; Dillehay 1990a, 1990c). The demise of patrilineages resulted from the death of leaders, from the inability of their successors to sustain power, and/or from the defeat and fragmentation of their lineages (e.g., Dillehay 1990a–1990c; Núñez de Pineda [1673] 2003; Olaverría [1594] 1852; Ovalle [1646] 2003).

Despite the rise of several dynastic patrilineages, the early development of a confederated Araucanian polity, and its later expansion into vast areas of Argentina, they never evolved into a formally centralized state system. While certain centralized pan-Araucanian features emerged in the context of the early sixteenth-century *butanmapu* structure, these did not constitute a fully integrated political hierarchy. Instead, the Araucanian society was characterized by a system of competing patrilineage segments that provided the framework of a religio-political structure in which a centralized administrative organization was sporadically and situationally present. It was an easy and fluid variety of patrilineal populations that cyclically moved back and forth from lineage to village headship to regional polity and *toqui* warlord. Depending upon the situation, the structure ranged from simple to complex polities to the larger confederated polity. As discussed below and in later chapters, besides its political history and anticolonialism, what makes this polity interesting from an anthropological view is its utopic, spiritually therapeutic, and aesthetic properties and landscape features.

Lastly, the Andean and Inka influence on the organizational development of the Araucanian polity leads us to a brief consideration of secondary "state" formation processes (Price 1978) and archaism (see Chapter 3). The Araucanian polity involved a transformation from sociopolitical systems based primarily on kinship to one based on hierarchical group rulership. Price has pointed out that the development of secondary states involves nomothetic processes – the influence of more advanced or superordinate external states that introduce causative variables that are not found in more independent state formations. This development occurs directly through the expansion or influence of an existing state into areas that did not previously have a state-level organization or through the historical successor of preexisting states. In the Araucanian case, it is not yet known whether direct or indirect models of Inka provincial administration were introduced. Either venue had the minimal effect of providing a model of an alternative form of social, religious, and political organization. As discussed later, there is no hard evidence to suggest that the Inka ever attempted to consciously restructure the southern Araucanians into a state. However, the presence of the Inka in the northern Araucanian territory and their probable interaction with southern populations would have had ramifications on the latter in subtler ways. It is these possible indirect processes of suggesting social stratification, expanded cosmological views, and trends toward greater monumentalism and geopolitical restructuring that have the greatest utility in explaining secondary polity formation in the south-central Andes. In Chapters 3 and 7, I attempt to delineate the external context and internal dynamics of this formation, arguing that the southern Araucanian polity partly emerged by emulating and internalizing certain elements of the Inka state (cf. Dillehay and Gordon 1988; Medina 1978; Silva 1983) into the tactical organizational structure of the society. However, the Araucanian polity was not a copycat of the Inka model. Rather, it was a hybrid model formed primarily by the Araucanians themselves, with only moderate influences from the Inka and earlier Andean (and possibly Amazonian) societies. The historian Leiva recognizes the transformations within Araucanian society that were developed internally by following traditional principles of organization and those imitated from outsiders.

> La sociedad araucana inmediatamente posterior a la invasión española, es para nosotros un caso de sociedad que cambia más por crecimiento interno, que por imitación externa.... Por último, los araucanos logran encontrar la norma dinámica para organizar su sociedad: la guerra. (Leiva 1977:159)

> For us, Araucanian society immediately after the Spanish invasion is a case of a society changing more by internal growth than by external imitation.... Finally, the Araucanians found the dynamic means to organize themselves – the warfare. (Leiva 1977:159)

Imitation of the historical past is conceptually defined as archaism, which is:

> the imitation of something old in order to promote illusions of continuity or revival of past institutions and practices ... These revivals occur frequently during periods of class and state formation, when people are making their own histories as existing social orders are actively being decomposed and reconstituted. (Patterson 2004:292)

Fragmentation and reordering of society in a period of new social development fit the Araucanian case. As discussed in Chapter 3, several social units (i.e., *lov, cahuin, rehue, ayllarehue,* and *butanmapu*) were transformed or created to reorder the political cartography and the design of the social structure of the emerging Araucanian polity. The Araucanians promoted polity-building through the incorporation of fragmented communities, the elaboration of geopolitical technologies of governance of increasingly larger and mixed residential populations, and the forging of a national culture and identity among ethnically heterogenous groups from the coast, the central valley, and the Andes of south-central Chile (see Chapters 7–9). The stock of hybrid symbols, cultural traditions, organizational principles, historical mythologies, and ideological cultures sculpted by Araucanian leaders in the sixteenth and seventeenth centuries was commonly supplied by the dominant patrilineages within the region, especially those from the northern frontier areas of Purén, Lumaco, Tucapel, Catiray, and Arauco, who may have received direct or indirect impetus from the Inka state. Irrespective of the date and means of Inka influence and Araucanian archaism, the Araucanians were a population that already had operated within certain Andean principles of social and ideological organization, which thus were legible to and congruent with Inka ways of political and religious administration and which presumably made emulation of some Inka ways easier.

APPROACHES TO SPACE, PLACE, AND LANDSCAPE

How did the Araucanians perceive and imbue mounds with meaning and symbolism, how did they experience their world, how did they move between mounds and other sites, how did they organize mounds according to their social, cosmological, and knowledge schemes, and how was mound literacy used as a political, spiritual, and religious mechanism to build a new social order? These questions lead to certain themes developed in the literature on space, place, landscape, sacredness, and monuments (e.g., Ashmore and Knapp 1999; Hirsch and O'Hanlon 1995; Keith and Pile 1993; Miller 1995; Pearson and Richards 1994; Sheldrake 2001).

In recent years, studies of the relationship between social meaning and space have taken different but interrelated avenues of inquiry. Some major concerns have been how land useable within the cultural potential (topography) interposes social and cultural boundaries, how society models space and utilizes it to control the relationship of individuals, and how adaptation to space is a fundamental part of learning to interact with others (e.g., Levine 1997; Ley 1981). There also has been a strong emphasis on space as a public communication medium for organizing and regulating the flow of knowledge (e.g., Benko and Strohmayer 1997; Czarniawska-Joerges 1990; Soja 1996; Turner 1990). Where the sources of knowledge are located, how that knowledge is formed and shared, how it is learned, and how it is related to behavior and cognitive maps and rules, how spatial agency operates, and by what processes it changes are important questions of consideration for understanding mound literacy, polity-formation, the meaning given to socially constructed space (see Chapters 4 and 5).

Archaeological studies show that mounds were used for the burial of important people, mortuary rituals, religious ceremonies, for elite residence and public display of power, and for boundary markers between groups (e.g., Bradley 1998, 2000; Milner 2004; Smith 2003; Tilley 1994). Other approaches integrate mounds with the location, form and meaning of natural landforms (e.g., rock formations, lakes) in local settings (see Blagg 1986; Bradley 2000). These settings attracted socially built monuments and provided meaningful locations whereby nature, society, and culture blended together or one became an extension of the other.

Monuments are thus often envisioned as features that mimic natural forms or were built on them to represent the natural extension of culture out of nature. Other studies consider the visual awareness of people in specific physical settings and how mounds relate to "vanished landforms," such as places where animals gathered seasonally or forests once existed. Others examine how the grammar of the architectural design of monuments can be decoded within schemes of social interaction (e.g., Lewis, Stout, and Wesson 1998). A more intangible model has been proposed by Tilley (1994) who argues that people perceive their world as meaningful and that agreed understandings are negotiated from social interactions. Meanings then become part of daily routine and certain social strategies are formalized within local schemes of knowledge and experience that are practiced in special places. Tilley refers to these places as "numinous landscapes" that are given special cosmological and mythical powers and meanings (cf. Bradley 1998, 2000; Pollard 2001; Pollard and Ruggles 2001; Scarre 2002a; Thomas 1991).

These and other studies suggest that social spaces and special places like mounds are created out of the vast intricacies, the complexities, and the interlocking and noninterlocking networks of social relations, belief systems, and shared meanings constructed across the natural environment at every scale from local to regional (Dillehay 1999; Mitchell 1994; Schama 1996; Van Dyke and Alcock 2003). Place and landscape are thus socially constructed from lived spaces. Spatially contextualized economies, politics, and cultures invent and inscribe places and landscapes with ethical, symbolic, spiritual, and aesthetic meanings. Space, then, is not a static and passive template of social existence, but an active, constitutive force of society's composition and construction. Space and spatiality become complex and articulated material, cultural, symbolic, and discursive formations that structure and are simultaneously structured by historical changes (e.g., Lane 2001; Thrift 1988, 1989, 1998; Thrift and Pred 1981; Tuan 1974a, 1974b, 1976, 1977), memories (Bradley 2000; Carruthers 1990; Connerton 1989; Kaulicke 2001; Van Dyke and Alcock 2003), and identities (Abercrombie and Longhurst 1998; Bondi 1993; Janusek 2004; Malkki 1992; Pred 1983, 1990; Taussig 1991).

Much like other Andean people (e.g., Isbell 1978; Urton 1990; Zuidema 1964, 1990), the Araucanians commonly make symbolic comparisons between humans, social groups, and special natural features, spaces, and places. Andeans employ their historical comprehension of mountains, rivers, and animals to understand themselves and their changing relationship with the natural environment. People also draw on this comprehension to formulate ideas about their society and its place in history and on the landscape. Special purpose and meaning are assigned to historic monuments and sacred landscapes. Araucanians relate them to ethnic history and memory, identity and ideology, social interaction and political complexity, ritual, and knowledge about spaces, places, and aesthetics. Particularly relevant are sacred spaces and geographies.

Sacred space does not exist naturally, but is assigned sanctity and defines, limits, and characterizes it through culture (Lane 2001; Pred 1990). Tuan elaborates that "the true meaning of 'sacred' goes beyond stereo images of temples and shrines, because at the level of experience sacred phenomena are those that stand out from the commonplace" (Tuan 1976:45). He puts emphasis on qualities such as separateness, otherworldliness, orderliness, and wholeness in defining what is sacred. Sacred space is sharply discriminated from the nonsacred or profane world around it. Eliade (1959, 1961) has explored how ordinary (profane) space is converted into a holy or sacred one. He suggests that such a conversion reflects the spiritual characteristics associated with both the physical features and the deeper, abstract implications delimiting a particular site as sacred space. Many religions, particularly historic ones, have designated certain places in the natural world as sacred and have worshipped them as the dwellings of supernatural elements and celestial figures. These places have divine association, either as homes of gods or as gods in themselves (Blagg 1986; Koss-Chioino and Hefner 2006), or as special places associated with healing the sick and with predicting the future.

Ritual Healing Narratives and Recollective Memories

Also of special interest to this study are illness narratives that tell how life's problems are created, controlled, and made meaningful. They also inform about cultural values and about social relations (Helman 1994; Kleinman 1988). In other words, when sick people relate their experience of illness, they often reveal more than the "facts" of the illness itself. They place the illness in the context of their life history and the values of the society in which they live (Brody 1987; Feierman and Janzen 1991; Gopal 1988). These values for the Araucanian society are revealed in the narratives presented in Chapter 5 and Appendix 1, whereby a *machi* shaman converses with a sick patient — in this case, a "sick" *kuel* that is the son of a powerful deity spirit. These narratives show that the shaman's medical system is experienced not just as the discursive, analytical prose of a medicinal person or *machi*, but also as the narratives or sagas of historical illness occurrences in the society at large, as expressed through the ill-effects of the maligned *kuel* on the living people. The narratives dictate episodes that cut to varying depths across the normal flow of life of the people, across values and cosmological principles of how to live, and across the past and present. To discover the broader social meaning attached to the *kuel's* illness and what it represents to people, it is important to pay attention to the sacred language the *machi* and the *kuel* (who also speaks) use in the narratives. Particular use of this language is applied to explore meanings that have reference to different arenas of ritual, history, politics, identities, memories, and worldview experiences and to the meaning of the *kuel* as part of the setting for shamanic and symbolic healing interactions. These narratives intricately present the way Araucanian shamans employ mound literacy (*nauchi*) to relate the natural, spatial, and social worlds. Also revealed is the tension between good and evil forces in the world and how it is reconciled through ritual interaction with *kuel*, the objects of local memories and identities. Ultimately, the narratives unfold these memories to socially unite the *kuel*, deities, ancestors, and living in order to collectively make "prudent" decisions about the future.

In studying the importance of Araucanian memory and symbolic healing in uniting the past and present, I primarily follow the thinking of Carruthers (1990; cf. Golden 2005; Van Dyke and Alcock 2003). She states:

> Prudence is knowing how to do what is good or bad, a knowledge which in turn depends upon past experience, because we can only judge of the future by what is past. Memory can be considered in two ways, as the storage capability of the brain, or as the recollective process. As the store of what is past, memory is the nurse and engenderer of prudence and so a part thereof. As the process of recollection, memory is a habit; recollection is a natural function which can be strengthened through training and practice. This makes it truly necessary for prudence to exist. (Carruthers 1990:70)

Carruthers (1990:259–260) sees memory as a "social institution," as a modality that fosters the growth and development of symbol-systems. Symbols, in turn, are public and social and must be recognized and remembered in order to operate within a society. Symbols, images, and special places work to store memory and to recollect memory and past experience. To her, knowledge and sound decision-making depend upon past experience, because societies can only judge of the future what they know of their past. In a similar vein, "Memories are not primarily about revisiting the past but about defining the present and managing the future of individuals and groups within meaningful, yet shifting, contexts. Thus, the control of memory and the objects of memory is an important component of power" (Lillios 2003:1E46).

I am interested in knowing how the Araucanian knew what was good and bad and how to make correct decisions as newly formed compatriots for the good of their local community and the wider confederated polity. I argue that this involved a "recollective process" of past or ancestral experience, and how it was employed to know the difference between good and bad and to make "prudent" decisions through practice in public meetings and ceremonies. The collective symbols, images, and special places of *kuel*, *rehuekuel*, and *nguillatun* sites worked (and still work) together to remind people of their ascribed duties and responsibilities not only to the past – the ancestors and the deities – but to the present and future generations as they continually formed a new social order and became compatriots within it, as citizens do within newly developed states.

The Araucanians have encoded identity and memory in dances with costumes representing ancient symbols and beings and in regularly scheduled political, healing, and other rituals. They have inscribed the past in sacred artifacts: lifelike ancestor shrines, trophy heads of enemies and masks with human faces to commemorate victories. They have created short historical narratives for the edification of youth. At major ceremonies and events, specialists (*weupife, weupin*) recite history and perform ballads of the deeds of famous *toqui* leaders, warriors and ancestors. The most important recitals are associated with mortuary rituals and the honors given to great war leaders. These methods of memory-building accompany ideas of the past as parallel realities into which the Araucanians could enter by ritual means, retrieving powerful ancestral knowledge to build a new identity and to influence the future.

In the sixteenth and seventeenth centuries, important to this new identity was the increased adoption of fragmented groups into stable political settings. This process entailed a committment to both old and new ways of acting as responsible members or compatriots of the society at large, which I refer to as *ascriptive compatriotism*. My underlying notion of ascriptive compatriotism involves ascribed duties, rights, and actions of individuals that were crafted by political elites and expected of newly adopted or mixed peoples to meet the basic political imperatives of a new social order or polity in this case. Leaders needed a society of newly mixed people that imagined themselves in ways that made leadership by those leaders appropriate. These needs drove leaders to employ ideologies and traditional ways that fostered the requisite sense of belonging and security. In return, leaders promised security and resources in times of stress. Specifically, ascriptive compatriotism within this order was mainly defined with respect to social structure, religion, and tradition or *admapu* (customary rules and laws), which was perpetuated by recollective memory of ancestral ways in public ritual and everyday practices (cf. Whitehouse and Laidlaw 2004). At the outset, it pertained to formal kinship in a patrilineage (*lov, lof*) and eventually to the larger non-kin, mixed political units of the *ayllarehue* and *butanmapu*. While the protocols of compatriotism probably varied according to region, its ordering premise must have been that ruling patrilineage elites and their followers identified themselves with the ideology of ancestors and deities.

In sum, I see the historic Araucanian society as one using landscape and newly defined spaces and places to aggregate the power of memories, ceremonial flows, agency, and new community structures and organizational networks in times of low-intensity warfare with outsiders to both unite and to spiritually solace people. Spaces containing ancestral mounds, cemeteries, and habitation sites flowed together and continually across the landscape to connect history to people, to their memories and identities, and to particular topographic places (i.e., *rehuekuel*, fortresses) where public rituals were performed and important decisions made. The interactive flow between Araucanians and their physical environments passed through specific topographic locations on the sacred landscape where these elements historically conjoined. The nexus of this interaction was the *kuel* and *rehuekuel*, which have specific spatial, political, and numinous agency.

CONCLUSION

I have attempted to develop an interconceptual approach that offers a heuristic analysis of mound literacy, mound worship, and polity formation in times of periodic warfare and restructuring of society. This approach tries to explain the enactment of power by formal political and religious leaders, focusing on the reorganizational activities and power of flows that were typical of many patrilineages in the study area. In these areas, symbolic ritual action, narrative, memory, and power relationships stood in dialectical relationship to one another, confirming and reproducing the new order that served to resolve the Araucanians' continuous struggles to culturally survive. Another objective is to render the contemporary, subjective experience of the sacred landscape as an integral part of the historical processes that have been shaped, and are somewhat continuing to shape, the social environment and especially the historical identity of the past and present Araucanians.

THREE:

ARAUCANIAN PREHISTORY
AND HISTORY: OLD BIASES
AND NEW VIEWS

Historically, from pre-Columbian times to the present, all of Latin America passed through colonial and frontier stages of kaleidoscopic variety, each shaped by a particular combination of physical and human environments. Some regions within Latin America experienced several types of colonial politics, ranging from total defeat and decimation of the indigenous population in the Caribbean to passive mutualism and peaceful change in most of Paraguay to strong, prolonged resistance to all outsiders in south-central Chile. These experiences led to many transformations along geopolitical frontiers, where different modes of organizing societies competed with one another. It was the power of colonial frontiers to transform cultures as well as themselves that give them special interest (Comaroff 1998; Cooper 2005). In some places the actions of frontier peoples transformed political and economic institutions well beyond the frontier itself, contributing to national cultures and shaping a people's understanding of their identity. Larger historical processes also shaped the lives of frontier peoples, often as a result of decisions made by policymakers in distant centers of political, economic, or cultural power such as Spain and Portugal. Relatively peaceful accommodation and mutual acculturation characterized Spanish–Indian relations along some frontiers; a state of ongoing, low-intensity warfare typified other frontiers (Ribeiro 1973). One of those war zones was the Araucanian–Spanish frontier, which was the longest standing and most resistant political frontier in American colonial history.

For at least the last 600 years various frontier experiences shaped the history, identity, and character of the Araucanians and their institutions (Bengoa 2003; Boccara 1998, 1999; Cooper 1946; Eliade 1961; Errazuriz 1912; Olivares [1594] 1864; Thayer 1908, 1917; Valderrama 1927; Villalobos et al. 1982). First were pre-Hispanic groups from north-central Chile and the eastern side of the Andes in Argentina who engaged in trade and exchange and sporadic armed conflict (Latcham 1924, 1928a, 1928b; Menghin 1962). Next were the Inka who conquered the northern Araucanians in central Chile and established a military frontier at the Maele River (e.g., Cieza de León 1945) and who must have had intermittent social and economic contact with the southern Araucanians living south of the Bio Bio political frontier (Fig. 4). Afterward, there were the Spanish and Chileans who did not defeat the southerners until the 1890s. Today, the region between the Bio Bio and Toltén Rivers is still called "*La Frontera*" in reference to the historic military frontiers between the Spanish and the Araucanians.

As presented earlier, the Araucanians resisted outside encroachment successfully because they restructured their society to socially and politically adapt imaginatively to the Inka, Spanish, and Chilean invasions, to the fighting techniques of their adversaries, and to eventually thrive economically from the frontier situation. If frontier conditions promoted inventiveness and progress, then the case of the Araucanians shows that colonial frontiers engendered inventiveness among peoples encroached upon as well as the encroachers (Villalobos and Pinto 1985; Villalobos et al. 1982; Jones 1999). Unable to defeat the southern Araucanians by means of offensive punitive, the Spanish adopted an essentially retreat and defend posture, as did the Chileans until they developed an effective military and governmental system that finally defeated the Araucanians.

Today, approximately 450,000 Araucanians or Mapuche reside in the humid temperate forest and mountains of *La Frontera*. An additional 400,000 live in urban areas scattered throughout central and southern Chile. Since the early twentieth century, the Araucanians have been semi-integrated into the Chilean society through mandatory concentration in *reducciones*. As a result, the indigenous population has undergone social and cultural change, but aspects of their traditional lifeway have survived, particularly their social structure, ideology, religion, and land use patterns.

Little is known of the late pre-Hispanic and early Hispanic periods. Until recently the archaeological and ethnohistorical evidence suggested that most Araucanians lived in scattered, loosely confederated agricultural communities operating under rulers with a kinship-based structure of authority prior to the Spanish (Dillehay 1976, 1981, 1999). They had a mixed economy with regional variations that largely depended upon the type of environment (i.e., coast, central valley, mountains). Farming was usually the primary food-producing activity in the central valley, though hunting, fishing, and plant gathering also contributed to the diet (Dillehay 1976; Aldunate 1989, 1996). Most areas never reached a centralized authoritative network in late pre-Hispanic times, but were headed by formal rulers or *toqui* warchiefs during periods of military conflict. In times of peace, *ülmen* and *lonko* held respectable, but informal leadership roles. A few areas achieved even higher sociopolitical levels in late pre-Hispanic and Hispanic times due to several social and historical factors.

The best evidence for late pre-Hispanic complex societies is archaeological, as indicated by the presence of mound sites, ancient ceremonial fields, differential grave goods with human skeletons, large and, at times, dense agricultural settlements and terraces, raised agricultural fields, and hilltop fortresses in Purén-Lumaco and other areas. The labor involved in constructing the mounds and fields was considerable, and the guiding hand of centralized political leaders in their construction is evident. Other evidence for these societies is the distinctly rank-sized distribution of large and small settlements associated with these features (Dillehay 1999). The political complexity of some Araucanian populations around 1550 was clearly recognized by the first Spaniards who called the conflicted region between the Bio Bio and Toltén rivers "*el estado*" (Ercilla [1569] 1982; J. Medina [1852] 1952, 1953; Olaverría [1594] 1844–71; see Chapter 1). This is where Araucanian resistance was strongest and developed at a higher political and economic level.

The 350-year interval between 1550 and 1900 was a time of rapid change for the Araucanians. Although early Spanish documentation is available for most parts of the region (cf. Bengoa 1985, 2003; Guevara 1913; Inostraza 1991; Latcham 1924; Montecino 1980; Núñez de Pineda [1673] 2003; Olavarría [1594] 1844–71; Padden 1993; Quiroga [1690] 1979; Villalobos et al. 1982), this record is sketchy, has many gaps, and is often difficult to reconcile with geographical, archaeological, and ethnographical data. Nonetheless, several major political and demographic transformations can be derived from the early documents. The Spanish kept elaborate records that not only documented military campaigns and the social and economic transformations occurring along the Araucanian frontier, but also detailed aspects of traditional Araucanian society (e.g., Acosta [1590] 1894; Bibar [1555] 1966; Boccara 1999; Ercilla [1569] 1982; Gay 1852; Góngora y Marmolejo [1575] 1960; Guevara 1913; Loyola [1620] 1908; Mariño de Lobera [1594] 1960; González de Nájera [1614] 1971; Núñez de Pineda [1673] 2003; Oña [1596] 1975; Ovalle [1646] 2003; Oviedo [1626] 1964; Quiroga [1690] 1979; Rosales [1674] 1989; Tesillo [1647] 1911; P. de Valdivia [1555] 1861; Zapater 1973). The known archaeological record is not as bountiful as the written record. Nonetheless, increased work in the region over the past thirty years allows us to sketch the long-term history of the region's indigenous settlement and of its ascent to an expanding regional polity that initially had its organizational roots in the "*estado*" region as early as 1200 to 1400.

In this chapter, I summarize the findings of archeological research over the past few decades and highlight the various themes in the scholarly historical record of the Araucanians that relate to the broader objectives of this book, with the intent of elaborating on them in later chapters. Although this chapter presents the primary historical evidence for these objectives, I provide more collaborating written records as I discuss the ethnographic and archeological evidence in Chapters 4, 5, and 6 and elaborate on interpretative themes in Part 2 of this book. Although this study has thoroughly searched the published chroniclers for information on mounds, indigenous leaders, ceremonial spaces, and related themes, it has not carried out a detailed analysis on these topics in the Archivo General de Indios in Seville, Spain. This work is currently underway by José Manuel Zavala, a Chilean ethnohistorian, who is collaborating with the author in the study of the Purén and Lumaco Valley.

PREVIOUS IDEAS ABOUT ARAUCANIAN HISTORY AND IDENTITY

I begin by commenting briefly on the more important Spanish chroniclers and on how they have been perceived and used by scholars. The only historical narratives available to us for the Araucanians are those contained in the documents written by Spanish soldiers, clergymen, and bureaucrats in the years following the Spanish contact with the Araucanians, beginning in the 1530s in central Chile and in the 1550s in south-central Chile. Unlike other regions conquered by the Spanish, fewer chroniclers are available on the Araucanians because there was no sustained contact with Araucanians south of the Bio Bio River and because many years often passed between Spanish efforts to penetrate the region. Nevertheless, through the study of the information in the chroniclers pertaining to the history of the Araucanians, a diverse scholarly tradition of interpretation has built up over the years since the late nineteenth century.

Two of the earliest chroniclers in south-central Chile were Pedro de Valdivia, the first Spanish conquistador in charge of the military campaigns in the south, and Jeronimo Bibar, who was one of the first priests in the region. Both were in the region in the 1550s and wrote several documents which contain useful descriptive passages of the Araucanians. For this study, Bibar is more valuable because he viewed the Araucanian culture from the perspective of a clergyman and provided more details into rituals and cultural practices. Another early writer was Góngora Marmelejo, who was a soldier accompanying Pedro de Valdivia in 1550. His first-hand observation of armed skirmishes between the Spanish and the Araucanians is important. His accounts are dependable. Miguel de Olaverría also was a soldier in the early military campaigns. He wrote his memoirs in 1594, and is generally considered to be reliable and accurate. Pedro Mariño de Lobera also was a soldier who came to Chile in 1551. Much of his historical account of the Spanish experience in Chile was later rewritten by Jesuit priests who often distorted his original notes and rendered them less useful to modern scholars. Nonetheless, Mariño de Lobera offers some detailed insights into the indigenous culture that coincide with those of other early writers. Two others writing in the middle to late 1500s were Alonso de Ercilla y Zuñiga and Pedro de Oña, both of whom often overstated and glorified Spanish activity in the region. These two chroniclers have less to offer in understanding early Araucanian culture. In the early 1600s, González de Nájera was an experienced military man who provides invaluable detailed descriptions of the Araucanians. In the mid-1600s, Francisco Núñez de Pineda y Bascuñan was a military man who was captured and held captive for many months among the Araucanians. Although he published a lengthy report of his captivity and experiences with the Araucanians, it is burdened with repetitive commentary on Spanish policy and polemics. However, there are invaluable passages that describe Araucanian military, religious, and cultural traits, especially in areas near Purén and Lumaco, which make his account particularly important to this study. Other chroniclers observing the Araucanians in the middle to late 1600s were Diego de Rosales and Geronimo Quiroga, the first a clergyman and the second a soldier. These two are perhaps most important, especially Rosales, because they spent considerable time in the Purén and Lumaco region and had first-hand knowledge of the land, the people, and their history. Among early writers, useful information is also contained in the works of assorted officials, clergymen, and travelers. In the seventeenth century, two other notable observers are Luis de Valdivia ([1606] 1887) and Alonso Ovalle ([1646] 1888); in the eighteenth and nineteenth centuries, there are Victor Caravallo y Goyeneche ([1796] 1876) and J. Molina (1795).

Based on their research on these and other chroniclers and on unpublished archives, the current scholarly perspective of Araucanian history by historians and anthropologists using the written texts can be divided into three general groups. Some scholars uncritically follow the traditional interpretation of Araucanian history as presented in the Spanish chroniclers (see Chapter 2; e.g., Amunategui 1909; Barros Arana 1884, 1909; Córdoba y Figueroa [1861] 1942; Encina 1950; Errázuriz 1912; Guevara 1908, 1913, 1929; Jara 1971; Jufre y Aguila 1896; Luigi 1957; J. Medina [1852] 1952; Villalobos and Pinto 1985; Zapater 1973). For them the Araucanians never emerged from an advanced hunter-gather to incipient horticultural level of society until they united to defend themselves against the Spanish. The second group examines history from the interactions of broader segments of the Araucanian, Inka, and Spanish societies (e.g., Aldunate 1996; Bengoa 1985, 2003; Dillehay 1976; Dillehay and Gordon 1988; Espejo 1967; Latcham 1924, 1928a, 1928b; Leiva 1977, 1982; Montecino 1980; Solís 1990; Villalobos et al. 1982). These scholars see development through time as a result of local and nonlocal transformations of social, economic, and religious institutions, with advances toward social complexity in late pre-Hispanic times. The third group of researchers suggests that the chroniclers should not always be read as direct or literal representations of the past (e.g., Bengoa 2003; Boccara 1998, 1999; Cordero 2001; Dillehay 1990c; Foerster and Gundermann 1996; Jones 1999; Mandrini 1992; Robles 1942; Silva and Téllez 1995; Truetler 1958; Zavala 2000). These researchers believe that the oral traditions of the Spanish chroniclers are often distorted by western notions of historicity and by self-interested representations of Araucanian history and identity presented by various indigenous inhabitants. These scholars have rejected literal interpretation of the chroniclers as a valid means of understanding late pre-Hispanic social development and argue in favor of developing new and more interdisciplinary approaches to the study of the past. In sum, some sources provide acute observations and others are biased.

In this study, I do not carry out a detailed historiographic and ethnohistoric analysis of the published and unpublished texts on the Araucanains. My academic training is not specifically in these areas, although I have several years of experience in working with early texts to apply the direct historical approach to the study of Andean culture and society. As noted in Chapter 1, my interest employs selected passages from chroniclers that are relevant to the themes under study here and that provide material and spatial correlates to test and to complement the archaeological and ethnographic records and vice versa.

I also am interested in how historians and anthropologists have traditionally constructed Araucanian cultural identity on the basis of partial or incomplete knowledge of their culture history and in the identity politics resulting from this partial knowledge. How this identity is constructed and who is doing the construction have been issues that have been debated for decades (Bacigalupo 2004a; Bengoa 1985, 2003; Boccara 1999; Dillehay 2003; Faiola 1999; Marimán 1998, 2003) and will continue for more to come. Historically, there have been several major areas of conflict between the Araucanians and the Chileans that have influenced this debate. The most contested relate to indigenous land rights and laws. Others relate to the perception of the Araucanians from a historical viewpoint that sees them as a recent amalgamation of different ethnic groups who colonized the region during the colonial wars (e.g., Cooper 1946; Faron 1964; Latcham 1928a, 1928b; Medina [1852] 1952; Padden 1993; Silva and Téllez 1995; Stuchlik 1976; Zapater 1973), implying that this is a historical process of migration no different from the Inka, Spanish and Chilean ones, and that the Araucanian identity is associated with this same process. This perception also views the Araucanians as never having achieved a high level of cultural development similar to the better known Aymara, Atacameños, and other indigenous groups residing to the north. By having become more developed as a result of their resistance to and adoption of traits from outsiders, the Araucanians are viewed as progressing for the first time in their history as a result of contact with the Spanish. That is, in the absence of detailed historical and archaeological records for the late pre-Hispanic period, most scholars believe that some military success of the Araucanians is attributed to the Inka *yanacona* who accompanied the first Spanish to the south and later defected to the southern populations (e.g., Cooper 1946; Silva 1983; Silva and Téllez 1995; Villalobos et al. 1982; Zapater 1973). Most scholars also envision all Araucanian culture, in both its past and present forms as a single rather culturally homogenous entity (albeit comprising several regional ethnic variants: Promaucos, Pehuenche, Pircunche, Huilliche, and Mapuche) that never developed beyond a hunter–gatherer level in most places to a petty horticultural tribe in other places without formal political leadership (cf. Zapater 1973; Guarda 1986;

Aldunate 1989, 1996; Boccara 1999). A few scholars have recognized the Araucanians attaining some degree of political centralization and hierarchy during the
historic period, but again this is largely attributed to a defense against European
intrusion or to indirect Inka influence (e.g., Aldunate 1989, 1996; Boccara 1999;
Cooper 1946; Guarda 1986; Latcham 1924; Leiva 1977, 1984; León 1986, 1991,
1999; Menghin 1962; Silva 1983; Titiev 1951; Zapater 1973). These and other
historians often recast the Araucanian's prolonged resistance as an element of
national Chilean character, as observed by Padden (1993:71).

> Historians have been prone to avail themselves of superficially reason-
> able explanations: most cite the numerical superiority of the Indians:
> some blame the forest because it hampered the functions of the Spanish
> cavalry; others stress the overly long lines of supply from Peru, coupled
> with a chronic lack of viceregal interest. These factors are joined to a
> common belief that the Araucanians simply adopted the Spanish forms
> and techniques of war, making up in numbers what they lacked in skill.
> Chilean historians, especially since the nineteenth century when their
> homeland fought for independence from Spain, have quite happily
> viewed the historical record as a proof of Araucanian hence mestizo
> thence Chilean bravery and love of freedom. (Padden 1993:71)

This viewpoint has been seen by some present-day Mapuche as a further means of
domination and the colonial dispossession of their historical identity (Anonymous
1993; Marimán 2003; Millaman 1993).

As typifies all such generalizations many previous reconstructions of early
Araucanian history are composed of fiction and facts mixed with interpolations
from sparse archival data and colored by biased nationalistic projections. Because
so little archaeological evidence has been produced until recently and because
the area under discussion became almost at once a zone of perpetual conflict, the
work of the Spanish religious orders, traders, and other observers did not develop
as it did with the military chronicles. Consequently, most of our information
concerning Araucanian life during the first century of contact is derived from
chronicles and histories of the war in which brief glimpses of indigenous life all
too infrequently appear. There are added limitations. The chroniclers were seldom
efficient observers. In matters of simple fact they tend to be trustworthy, but when
the fact becomes interpretative, they invariably failed to grasp the human thought
and action that lay behind it. This leads us to recognition of a neglected factor –
the complexity of early Araucanian society. Too many reconstructions of the
Araucanians have assigned cultural forms found in later and better documented
periods to earlier periods wherein documentation is not generously provided (see
Chapter 2). With disregard for the depth of time, elements often have been taken
from documentary sources of the late colonial period and placed side by side in a

synchronic mosaic with the late pre-Hispanic and early Historic period. At best, this type of reconstruction is a loose abstraction of Araucanian society, and like any abstraction, it is essentially incomplete. Nowhere does it give a realistic hint of the social complexity of early Araucanian society, especially in politically more organized areas like Purén and Lumaco.

Examples of early texts describing the level of organization of the Araucanians that are uncritically accepted by scholars are provided below. Writing in the late sixteenth century, the chronicler of González de Nájera states that:

> No tienen los indios ciudades, villas o lugares para su habitación, ni fuertes, ni otro género de fortaleza fuera de la gran Ciénaga de Purén, que lo es por naturaleza y ayudada de ellos por arte. Rehusan el congregarse en pueblos, por razón de que se dan venenos unos a otros, y así tienen divididas y apartadas sus habitaciones en diversos valles, que no es de poca importancia para la dificultad de su conquista, donde gozan habitaciones alegres y deleitosas. (González de Nájera [1614] 1971:48)

> The Indians do not have cities, towns or dwelling places, nor forts nor any kind of fortification apart from the great Marsh of Purén, which exists naturally through nature and is assisted by their skill. They refuse to gather into towns, because they poison each other, and thus they have their dwellings separated and distant [from one another] in different valleys, which is not unimportant as a difficulty for their defeat, where they enjoy pleasant and delightful dwellings. (González de Nájera [1614] 1971:48)

In the early 1600s, Rosales observed that:

> NO TIENEN REY, gobernador, ni cabeza, a quien reconozcan, y den obediencia, como a señor supremo, los indios Chilenos.... (Rosales [1674] 1989:136)

> The Chilean Indians have neither king, nor governor, nor leader, whom they recognize, and obey as a supreme lord.... (Rosales [1674] 1989:136)

Historians writing in the nineteenth and twentieth centuries followed these descriptions.

> Al arribo de los españoles al territorio araucano vivían entonces las familias agrupadas en rancherías pequeñas. Todas estas aldeillas constable de un número reducido de habitaciones circulares y de otras

formas, que pocas veces excedian de 50.... Estas rancherías de parientes ocupaban un solo lugar, que se extendía en proporción al número de individuos. Era un grupo local. A cierta distancia de un grupo i en distintas direcciones se hallaban radicados otros, con la separación a veces de algún accidente de terreno. Era una serie de familias que ocupaban una zona. Los parientes del grupo local constituían, pues, una pequeña comunidad autónoma que reconocía un solo jefe...El conjunto de zona fue una simple confederación de grupos, los cuales teniendo cada cual un jefe a su cabeza, se consideraban unidos por comunidad de razas o de intereses y se coligaban a menudo para prestarse mutual atención. (Guevara 1925:284–87)

When the Spanish came into the territory of the Araucanians, at that time the families were living clustered in small rural settlements. All these villages had a small number of dwellings, round or of other shapes, which were rarely more than 50.... These settlements of kinsmen were in one location and increased in size according to the number of people. It was a local group. Some distance away from a given group and in different directions, others had settled, sometimes separated by accidents of terrain. It [the settlement] was made up of a number of families who occupied an area. The kin of the local group constituted a small autonomous community which recognized a single chief.... The regional aggregation was a simple confederation of groups, each one having a chief at its head, [;] they considered themselves united by the community of race or interest and they came together frequently to render each other mutual assistance. (Guevara 1925:284–87)

More recently, Boccara alludes to the absence of a formal political authority in late pre-Hispanic and early Hispanic times and then recognizes the later development of more formal and larger political structures (i.e., *ayllarehue* and *butanmapu*), which he primarily attributes to responsive transformations made by the *Reche* or Araucanians in times of war with the Spanish. He also recognizes the influence of *a priori* indigenous political structures in these transformations.

Como un gran número de poblaciones encontradas por los conquistadores en las márgenes de los grandes imperios inca y méxica, así como en las Amazonas, los reche [the earliest term applied by the Spanish to the Indians living in the Araucania] fueron calificados de pueblo "sin Rey, sin fe, sin ley." El término empleado de manera recurrente para designar a la organización de esos grupos situados en la frontera sur del Tawantinsuyu era el de *behetría*. La característica principal de la distribución espacial de esos grupos era la dispersión; su organización

sociopolítica era acéfala, esto es, caracterizada por la ausencia de obe-
diencia a una figura política, la del jefe, dotada de los medios para
ejercer su autoridad. (Boccara 1999:427)

Like many of the populations encountered by the conquistadors at the
frontiers of the great Inca and Mexica empires, and in Amazonia, the
reche [the earliest term applied by the Spanish to the Indians living in
the Araucania] were considered a people "without King, without faith,
without law." The term used repeatedly to describe the organization
of those groups located on the southern frontier of Tawantinsuyu was
behetria [meaning a free settlement whose occupants had the right to
elect their own leader]. The principal characteristic of the settlement
pattern of these groups was dispersal; their sociopolitical organization
was acephalous, that is, characterized by the absence of obedience to
a political figure, a chief, who had the means to exercize his authority.
(Boccara 1999:427)

Uno de los cambios notables en la estructura sociopolítica y territorial
reche fue justamente la institucionalización de los *ayllarehue* y de los
futamapu, que de unidades temporarias prehispánicas que funcionaban
en períodos de guerra pasaran a ser agregados permanentes al sistema
colonial tardío dotados de representantes políticos propios.... Por lo
tanto, esa guerra de resistencia traía fundamentalmente consigo la transformación de la sociedad, era esencialmente vector de aculturación.
(Boccara 1999:434)

One of the noteworthy changes in *reche* sociopolitical and territorial
structure was precisely the institutionalization of the *ayllarehue* and the
futamapu, which from temporary units in prehispanic times became
permanent political associations in the late colonial system with their
own political representatives.... Thus, the war of resistance brought
with it the fundamental transformation of society, it was essentially a
vector of acculturation. (Boccara 1999:434)

There is no doubt that the wars with the Spanish (and Inka) left their political mark
and influence on the Araucanians in the form of military strategy, domestic crops
and animals, and technology, but this influence was mainly adopted and structured
through indigenous institutions and principles of organization, as discussed in
Chapter 2.

In sum, despite the occasional scholarly admittance of sporadic political
centralization in response to the Araucanian Wars with the Spanish and of different historical events linked with different populations, there remains a constant,

attending message for others to receive: the Araucanians never emerged in pre-European times to the levels of autonomous sociocultural complexity observed elsewhere in the Americas, and they were not culturally differentiated as a total population. Political hierarchy and cultural pluralism are infrequently in the discourse of Araucanian identity, something that poses a challenge to the empirical basis for constructing this identity and to the accuracy of previous constructions. In recent years, there has been a more complete reconstruction of Araucanian social history and a new construction of Araucanian identity, one that includes more of the archaeological record and of a critical approach to the historical record, and one that more fully recognizes the local, the historical plurality or cultural diversity of the Araucanians, and the autonomous political hierarchy they attained in late pre-European times.

Presented below is a synthesis of the archeological patterning and interpretation of mounds in the Araucania region and of the origins of the Araucanian culture. This is followed by a brief presentation of passages from selected chroniclers that describe various types of political units and leaders during the late pre-Hispanic and early Hispanic periods. Next is a more detailed presentation of accounts specific to the study area and to topographical, burial, mound, and ceremonial themes, which are occasionally related to archeological and ethnographic observations in order to reveal cultural continuity. The passages are not arranged chronologically, except in cases demonstrating the utility of the direct historical approach.

Archaeological Voices

Over the past twenty-five years several archaeologists have amassed a substantial quantity of new archaeological data from south-central Chile to shed new light on the pre-Hispanic development and hybridity of Araucanian culture history.

Initial archaeological work inventoried sites in the Araucanian region (e.g., Berdichewski and Calvo 1973; Bullock 1955; Latcham 1928a, 1928b; Menghin 1962). Many of the sites studied were indigenous cemeteries for which Latcham (1928a–1928c) and others developed a ceramic typology. During the 1950s, especially with the work of Menghin (1962), archeologists established a more detailed pre-Hispanic chronology with many small-scale excavations. More systematic work on cemeteries began in the late 1960s and early 1970s with excavations by Gordon (1975, 1978, 1984) and others (Hajduk 1978, 1986). These studies revealed social differentiation among the late pre-Hispanic and post-Hispanic people as evidenced by the presence of elaborate grave goods associated with tombs or human skeletons and little or no goods with others.

In Chile, small earthen "*tumuli*" had previously been reported from the Valles Transversalles in central Chile and the Araucanian region (Cornely 1956;

Iribarren 1964; Latcham 1928a, 1928b; Mostny 1971:107–133). Archaeologists associated the *tumuli* with advanced hunters and gatherers and ceramic horti-culturalists, which I have classified as late Andean Formative societies (Dille-hay 1981, 1990a). In this area the *tumuli* first appeared with the Molle culture (500–1000), while farther south in central Chile they were late pre-Inka in age. Based on the scant chronological information available on ceramics associated with *tumuli* first mentioned by Latcham (1928a) in Angol, Tirua, Curacautín, and Victoria in the Araucania, it can be estimated that mound burial began in the late pre-Hispanic era and, as my recent research has shown, has lasted into the modern-day period (Dillehay 1985a, 1995).

The *tumuli* vary in size, form, number, and type of burials, and contain single and multiple individuals. Individuals interred in mounds were considered to be important "elite" figures or families (Latcham 1924, 1928a, 1928b). Individuals or families of less importance were usually placed in community cemeteries, and although they may be interred with status objects, the tomb normally exhibited no special or conspicuous architecture like that of the mounds. Although a high density of *tumuli* was recorded at some sites (10–30), generally one or a small number of *tumuli* were found. No large mounds that might classify as adminis-trative or residential platform sites had been found in central Chile. Most tumuli south of the Bio Bio River, mentioned before our archeological work in Purén and Lumaco, were small like those in central Chile, and ranging in size from 8 to 15 m in diameter and from 1 to 3 m in height (Latcham 1924).

My archaeological research in the Araucanian region began in the mid-1970s and carried out settlement pattern and subsistence studies in various areas. I have focused more on the ethnoarchaeology of old and contemporary *nguillatun* fields, isolated *kuel*, and *rehuekuel* complexes (Dillehay 1976, 1981, 1992b, 1992c, 1995, 1999, 2003). In working with various colleagues, I have sought to unite archaeological, ethnohistorical, linguistic, and ethnographic data to study the origins and developments of the Araucanian culture, especially in the Purén and Lumaco Valley.

Since the early 1990s, previous research has been augmented by several environmental archaeological projects and basic research (e.g., Mera and García 2002; Navarro and Adán 1999; Quiroz and Sánchez 1997). These studies com-bined with earlier perspectives on settlement, economy, and social organization and with more radiocarbon dated archeological sites have provided more data on the long-term developmental trajectory of proto-Araucanian and Araucanian societies.

To summarize this trajectory, from the long Archaic or preceramic period, beginning around 7000 B.C. and lasting until about 400–500, nomadic hunters and gatherers probably ruled the land. Sometime between 500 and 1200, during the Formative or early ceramic agricultural period, small and scattered settlements existed, suggesting the presence of relatively egalitarian mixed economies of hunters, gatherers, and gardeners generally associated with the Pitrén ceramic style. Sometime between 1000 and 1500, the south-central region received strong cultural influences from agriculturalists in central Chile and western Argentina (Dillehay 1992a–1992c; Latcham 1928a, 1928b; Menghin 1962). During this period, the subsistence economy was based on hunting and gathering, fishing and collecting shellfish, slash and burn horticulture, or any combination of these activities, depending on whether people lived in the mountains, the central valley, or the coast. At the same time, more complex, autonomously developed small polities appeared in a few valleys and developed further during the contact and colonial periods. Associated with these changes was a new agricultural base, which included the likely presence of several domesticated plants (e.g., corn, quinoa, chili peppers, beans, squash), polished stone axes, elaborate ceramic containers, agricultural settlements and defensive sites, and early mound building represented by single isolated mounds or groups of two to three mounds associated with domestic sites. Multiple mounds forming planned *rehuekuel* complexes begin to appear by at least 1500 (Dillehay 1992c). The proto-Araucanians probably had their cultural beginnings in the twelfth to thirteenth century with the El Vergel and Tirua ceramic styles located in the Arauco region south of the Bio Bio River. Some proto-Araucanian populations looked to the strategic location and enclosed nature of circumscribed valleys, such as Purén, Lumaco, Angol, and Liucura, for the construction of larger mound and ceremonial field complexes at key nodes of communication and control. By 1200, if not earlier, the agricultural economy in parts of the Araucania supported a modest population of farmers. The early historic data suggest distinct Andean and local characteristics, which may reflect older cultural patterns from northern Chile and south coastal Peru and from Bolivia and Argentina. In the middle 1500s and early 1600s, several localities intensified agricultural and trading activity and planned and assumed leadership of a widespread resistance movement against the Spanish invaders (Dillehay 2002). Two of these localities, the Villarrica–Pucón and the Purén and Lumaco Valleys, contain the largest known mound groups in the region. Some areas generally suffered population loss and/or displacement during the conquest and colonial periods and thus lost cultural complexity rather than gained it as a result of European conquest and colonialism.

First Mound Encounters

I first became aware of the presence of mounds in south-central Chile in 1976 when the late Américo Gordon and I visited burial mounds near Los Sauces, a small town located about 25 km north of Lumaco. It was not until 1978 that I visited mounds near Lumaco when Gaston Sepulveda, a linguist, showed me two small ones built in Rucalleco and Isla de Katrileo. One mound was located in an old *nguillatun* field that was known and still used by a local shaman during ceremonies. It was during this visit that I learned the Araucanian word for mounds – *kuel* (*cuel*). At the time I thought that all *kuel* in Lumaco were abandoned archaeological sites like all other mounds I had seen before. Upon returning to the area in 1981 with Patricio Sanzana, an archaeologist, I first realized that these mounds still have special use and meaning to the local communities. Informants said the *kuel* were used as "maps" or "nodes" to orient pedestrians passing through the area and to demarcate geographical "lines" between local families (Dillehay 1985b, 1990a). In 1983, Gordon and I returned on several occasions to interview *machi* and elders about the historic and contemporary function of these mounds. During these visits, we saw two small, 1.5-m and 2-m high mounds that were not present in 1981: they were new mounds. The mounds were called *pichikuel*, or "boy" mounds, because they were young brothers (*pichipeñi*) and had not yet matured according to informants. We also were told that they were the offspring mounds of older (*kuifilkuel*) and larger *kuel*, indicating kinship affinities between them.

Over the years, I have gained valuable anthropological information about *kuel*, which have resulted in several publications about their function, history, and meaning. From an archaeological perspective, the mounds are monuments defined by pre-Hispanic origins, specific topographic locations, restricted distribution, relatively standarized sizes, and a ceremonially landscaped architectural complex. This landscape is bounded on low hilltop promontories that have been deliberately modified into *terra pleins* with flat tops and beveled sides, upon which the primary mound and usually smaller ones are constructed (Fig. 8). As noted in Chapter 1, informants in Purén-Lumaco have told us that a large multimound complex is called *rehuekuel*; individual mounds are referred to as *kuel*; and the modified *terra plein* or surface platform on which the mound(s) are built is called *ñichi*. The individual soil layers comprising them are called *reñimapu* (the center of the earth).

There are certain types of topographic settings where *kuel* are located and where the surrounding terrain and neighboring *kuel* can be seen. Most mound complexes are located along first-order streams where two or more secondary streams come together to form a marshy drainage basin at the base of a long hill range. Most individual mounds are usually situated on low spurs or promontories, usually at their highest point, overlooking a valley floor. The promontories are not always well-defined but are often located between mountain passes or large isolated hills. Other mound groups are defined variously by streams, slopes, or other topographic features (Fig. 9). Some mounds, usually the smaller ones, occur in isolation. Individual mounds range in size from 5 to 40 m in diameter and from 1 to 18 m in height (Fig. 10). Most mounds are conical, though both elliptical and round ones also occur. A few platform mounds exist.

8. General view of the *Maicoyakuel* (black arrow), its *ñichi* platform (white arrows), and the *ciénega* in the Purén Valley.

9. Actively used *nguillatun* field at *Hualonkokuel* showing the shaman's *rehue* pole (foreground to the left) and the "sick" mound (arrow) that needed curing by the shaman (see Chapter 5 and Appendix 1 ritual narrative of the *Hualonkokuel*).

Since 1980, our archaeological surveys have located more than 600 *kuel* in several river valleys but primarily in the Purén-Lumaco drainage. *Rehuekuel* mound complexes have been found in only the Purén-Lumaco and Liucura valleys, which are located in low precordillera passes along the eastern flanks of the coastal mountain range and along the western slopes of the Andean chain, respectively. These are primary passes from the Pacific coast to the interior valley (Purén-Lumaco) and from the interior valley of Chile to the Argentine pampa (Liucura) (see Fig. 4). Both areas are composed of several subgroups made up of 3 to 50 mounds. The single largest and densest complex is located at Butarincón at the confluence of the Purén and Lumaco rivers. Isolated and smaller mound complexes are located along several other river drainages in south-central Chile.

All *kuel* and *rehuekuel* in the Purén and Lumaco Valley share a number of common traits: (1) traversed by at least one foot trail linking different community lands; (2) provide imposing views of the valley below and of other *kuel* and *rehuekuel* in the distance; (3) usually situated on a *ñichi* ceremonial platform; (4) constructed of earth though stones occasionally have been used in interior architectural features; (5) associated with late pre-Hispanic, historic, or contemporary (i.e., thirteenth to twentieth centuries) artifacts; and (6) after named by local *machi*. Twenty-eight *kuel* are located inside ancient and, in four localities, still used *nguillatun* fields (see Chapter 6).

Archaeological Evidence for the Origins of Araucanian Culture

This is not the place to provide a lengthy discussion of the origins of the Araucanian culture. However, it is necessary to establish some sources of the fundamental principles of organization upon which the society was restructured in the sixteenth and seventeenth centuries. There are external traits in the Araucanian culture that are pre-Inka Andean and probably eastern tropical lowland (Dillehay 1990b; Latcham 1928a, 1928b; Menghin 1962). Andean and some Amazonian influences are suggested in the dual spatial and political organization of Araucanian political and religious space, in the art and iconography of ceramics, wooden statues, and textiles, and in myths, tales, and legends (Casamiquela 1960; Dillehay 1992b, 1998; González 1998; Latcham 1924). The dual nature of Araucanian social organization and religious traits, including the employment of felines and other carnivorous animals (i.e., snakes, raptorial birds) in myths and in iconography (see Chapter 4 and discussion below on Inka influence), are typical Andean and tropical patterns (Casamiquela 1960; Dillehay 1999; Menghin 1962). Complementary opposition also is expressed in ritual symbolism. For instance, during public rituals, several oppositions are present: women on the left, men on the right; two *lonko* administrators or headmen; two wings to the U-shaped *nguillatun* field; double spout jars; and dual opposing figures in textile and ceramic design motifs (see Chapter 4 and Dillehay 1990c). Furthermore, the traditional

10. Aerial view of the actively used *Rehueñichikuel* mound showing its leveled *ñichi* and ceremonial plaza where *nguillatun* take place, the *rehuekuel*, and borrow pits for mound construction. Note the nearby archaeological domestic site in the background.

numbering system is divided into 2s, 4s, 8s, 12s, 16s, and so on and uses the decimal system, which are typical Andean and Amazonian features. Triads also exist just as predominantly as dyads in Andean, Amazonian, and Araucanian ceremony and kinship structure. The *nguillatun* is administered by three lineages, which is called a *trokinche* (Dillehay 1995). Dualism appears when the three lineages divide into a binary opposition of two. The *nguillatin* field also has three elements, the two wings and the base. Today, public feasts are traditionally headed by three powerful figures: the *machi*, the *lonko*, and the *nguillatufe*, a pattern which also exists in the chroniclers but with different names for the three categorical leaders (see later discussion). There also are polychrome ceramic styles in the study area (e.g., Tirua, El Vergel, and Valdivia; see later discussion) that exhibit pre-Hispanic Andean and probable Inka influences in vessel forms and in the color and design of decorative motifs (see discussions by Aldunate 1989; Dillehay 1990a; González 1998; Latcham 1928a). The Tirua and El Vergel styles are dated by radiocarbon means to the late pre-Hispanic era (ca. 1200–1500), and suggest contact with Andean groups farther north in central and northern Chile (e.g., Molle, Aconcagua, Llolleo, and possibly Diaguita) and probably west-central Argentina (i.e., Mendoza and San Juan areas). Dates for the Valdivia pottery style vary considerably from terminal pre-Hispanic to early colonial times. These late local styles were influenced by cultures in central Chile between 500 and 1000 (e.g., Molle and Llolleo cultures). The late pre-Hispanic Araucanian archaeological culture seems to be a hybridization of local cultures, central Chilean cultures, and various cultures from the eastern flanks of the Andes in west-central Argentina, all of which invariably expressed Andean and probably Amazonian influences.

It is difficult to distinguish between Inka and earlier non-Inka Andean influences in the Araucanian culture. More northerly pre-Inka Andean influences in south-central Chile began at least 1000 to 1500 years ago in the form of the Pitrén culture. As discussed next, the presence of Inka pottery forms and design motifs in Araucanian ceramics and of Inka loan words, stories about the Inka ruler Atahualpa, and other traits suggest an "Inka Andean" influence as well, one that probably began in the early sixteenth century and lasted no more than a few decades. Although the Andean and Inka influences are more conspicuous archaeologically, linguistically, and ethnographically, only linguistic and genetic records reliably indicate contacts with Amazonian groups, particularly the Arawak (Croese 1985; Payne and Croese n.d.), the Bolivian Tacanan (Key 1978, 1979), and especially Guarani (Acuna et al. 2003; Carnese 1996; Casamiquela 1960; Goicoechea et al. 2000; Haas 1985; Kaufman et al. 1998; Sans 2000). The chronology and means of this contact is not known.

Becoming Andean: Andean, Inka, and Araucanian Interaction

In this section, I am interested in the Inka influence on the Araucanians. Several recent historians (e.g., Leiva 1977, 1984; León 1999; Padden 1993; Silva 1983) have recognized the organizational changes that took place within Araucanian society during the sixteenth century and invariably have attributed them to preexisting organizations simply intensified at the moment of contact with the Inka and later with the Spanish and to emulating certain structural orders of these outsiders to reorganize themselves for territorial defense. *Toqui* war leaders and possibly ritual priests and/or shamans (e.g., *hechicero, boquivoye, boquibuye*) were the main articulators of anticolonial transformation and the leaders of the Araucanian polity movement in the late sixteenth century and throughout the seventeenth and eighteenth centuries. For *toqui*, polity seemingly represented a political and military pilgrimage – an expansion of consciousness beyond the confines of small-patrilineage kin-based communities in which they may have began their military lives toward the ever larger geopolitical units of the *rehuekuel, ayllarehue,* and *butanmapu* communities. Although conclusive hard evidence is presently lacking, I believe that their imaginings of a prospective Araucanian polity was predicated on importing and internalizing certain Andean, Inka, and Spanish ideas of "state" and "citizenship." However, as stated earlier, I do not want to reduce the Araucanian polity to a mere imitation of a (modular) Inka organization. Rather, I believe that their ambition was to fashion a polity that was nonetheless politically and organizationally legible to the Spanish, which meant a state-like population of prolonged resistance and emerging national and ethnic consciousness (cf. Leiva 1977; Boccara 1998, 1999; Zavala 2000) – one the Spanish had encountered previously in Andean areas farther north. Boccara recognizes a similar response of the Araucanians to contact and conflict with outsiders:

> las tentativas de conquista y colonización del centro-sur de Chile produjeron un efecto que podríamos llamar "perverso," en el sentido de efecto no querido o no esperado: el nacimiento de una nueva entidad identidad étnica: los mapuche [a través de la guerra a la maloca y al comercio]. (Boccara 1999:440)

> the attempts to subdue and colonize south-central Chile produced what we might call a "perverse" effect in the sense of an unwanted or unexpected result: the birth of a new unit of ethnic identity: the mapuche [brought about by warfare, raiding and commerce]. (Boccara 1999:440)

To explain further, northern Araucanian populations from central Chile were conquered and culturally absorbed by the Inka in the late 1400s, as evidenced by ethnohistorical evidence and the presence of numerous Inka fortresses, ceramics, and other traits at local indigenous settlements (e.g., Hyslop 1984; Stehberg 1976). In this region, the Inka were engaged in gold, silver, and copper mining, extraction of human labor for state projects, and production of agricultural and other food produce. Many early chroniclers and thus most traditional scholarly thinking have the Inka empire stopping at the Cachapoal River in central Chile, which is located approximately 100 km south of Santiago and where the southernmost Inka fortresses were built (Stehberg 1976). However, there are a few reliable accounts from the first chroniclers that the Inka might have reached the Bio Bio River prior to the Spanish invasion. When the first conquistador, Pedro de Valdivia ([1555] 1955:46), arrived in the vicinity of the Bio Bio River, he remarked that the Araucanians: "Llamannos a nosotros Ingas y a nuestros caballos heques Ingas, que queire decir ovejas de Ingas." (They called us Ingas [Inka] and our horses the llama of the Ingas.) Writing in 1594, Olaverría ([1594] 1852) also noted that the Inka reached the Bio Bio and were defeated there by the Araucanians (see Bibar [1555] 1966 for a similar account). Góngora Marmolejo ([1575] 1960) and González de Nájera ([1614] 1971) writing in 1589 and 1601–07, respectively, also claimed that the Inka reached this river. Commenting several decades later, Rosales ([1674] 1989:339) stated that the Inka arrived near Concepción in the mouth of the Bio Bio and penetrated further south to the Imperial River (Fig. 4) before the Spanish conquest. These accounts of a pre-Hispanic

Inka presence in the south have largely been dismissed by contemporary scholars, because most historians and archaeologists uncritically accept the southernmost military presence of the Inka at the Maele River, as evidenced by some early texts and by the presence of state fortresses (see Silva 1983; Stehberg 1976). However, as discussed previously (see Dillehay and Gordon 1988), I view a dual Inka presence in central and south-central Chile: a formal military frontier at the Maele River and an informal cultural boundary of Inka trading, exploratory activity, and perhaps sporadic military action that extended to the Bio Bio and possibly farther south (Fig. 11). Alconini (2004) has found that this dual frontier model also explains the Inka presence in the Chiriguano frontier region of south-central Argentina.

Based on early written records, the historians Mason (1961:126–127) and Zapater (1974:27–30) also believe that the Inka explored and/or attempted to conquer lands south of the Maele River but could not defeat the southern Araucanians, and thus established their formal frontier at the former. Zapater (1978) also suggests that the Bio Bio was first established as a military frontier between the Inka and the Araucanians, which later facilitated its defense and its formal designation as "*La Frontera*" between the Spanish and the Araucanians. León (1986:88–100) has studied Inka rebellions against the Spanish in the 1540s before the first conquistador, Pedro de Valdivia, tried to conquer the south in 1550. He suggests that some Inka personnel (e.g., *yanacona*) and local indigenous groups, who had been conquered by the former and thus knew their ways, had escaped and moved south from central Chile after they had been defeated by the Spanish. In the 1540s or earlier, these groups might have mixed with the southern Araucanians and taught them Inka organizational tactics. On the other hand, Padden (1993) does not believe that the Inka could have influenced the southern groups, because the Inka state collapsed before the rise of the Araucanian *estado*. However, Padden does not consider the possibility that the Inka reached the Bio Bio before the Spanish arrival or that Inka personnel and other groups enculturated into the ways of the Inka escaped from the Spanish to live with southern populations. (The chroniclers often mention *yanacona* among the southern Araucanians, but it is not certain whether they refer to indigenous people brought to Chile by the Inka and later the Spanish or to all Indians living north of the Bio Bio. Thus, the ethnicities and political affiliations of the *yanacona* are not known.) Of further interest is the quadripartite division of the Araucanian concepts of *estado* and *butanmapu*, both of which were composed of four units. The earlier *estado* was comprised of four territories or *ayllarehue* divided into four cardinal directions: Arauco to the northeast, Tucupel to the southeast, Catiray to the northwest, and Purén to the southeast (Zavala 2005, 2006). The later *butanmapu* polity also was structured in four cardinal territories. Writing in 1606, Luis de Valdivia ([1606] 1887:46–47) describes a ranked dual division of land in the Araucanian *regua*, or multiple patrilineage community, that

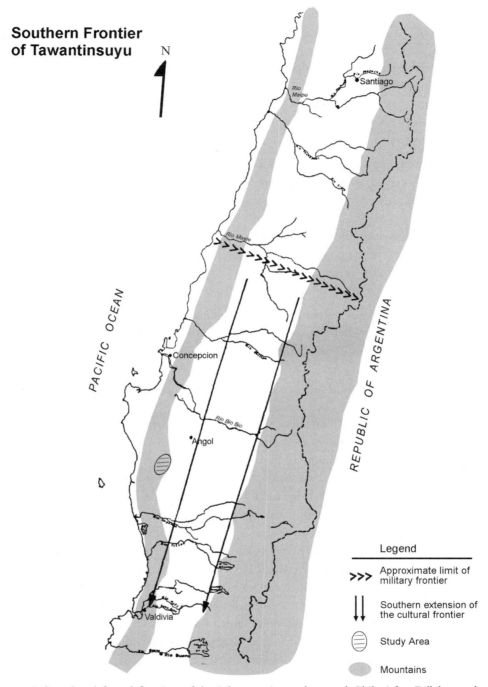

11. Informal and formal frontiers of the Inka state in south-central Chile (after Dillehay and Gordon 1988).

is similar to the Inka's ranked *hanan* and *hurin* moiety system for dividing the two halves of an *ayllu* population (*sensu* Zavala 2006).

> Cada regua se divide en dos mitades que cada una llaman llacahuyn, que quiere dezir la mitad de la población y quando la una mitad es de gente mas principal que la otra la llaman suigal[¿?] que quiere dezir cabeza y rey, y á la otra llaman huenchu_ [¿?] ue [sic] quiere dezir como gente ydalga.

> En cada mitad destas ay un Indio muy principal que llaman butaülmen que quiere dezir señor mas principal de aquella mitad.... (ANCH, M.V.M, Vol. 279, fs. 46–47: quoted in Zavala 2006)

> Each *regua* is divided into two halves, each one called *llacahuyn*, which means half of the population, and when one half has people who rank higher than the other, it is called *suigal* [?] which means head and king, and the other they call *huenchu* which means gentlefolk.

> In each of these halves there is a high-ranking indian whom they call *butaülmen* which means the highest-ranking lord of that half.... (ANCH, M.V.M, Vol. 279, ff. 46–47: quoted in Zavala 2006)

Not known is whether this quadripartite and dual divisioning is an earlier Andean or later Inka pattern.

Unfortunately, little archaeological research has been carried out between the Maele and Bio Bio rivers and none has focused on Inka archaeology. Nor has any Inka activity been convincingly established south of the Bio Bio, although there is ceramic and possibly architectural evidence to suggest contact prior to or at the time of the Spanish invasion (see Chapter 6). Inka design motifs and vessel forms (i.e., arybulli, kero drinking mugs, plates, jars, and statues) appear in the late Tirua and El Vergel pottery styles located in the Arauco region and in the later Valdivia style found between the Bio Bio and Rio Bueno rivers (Fig. 12). These styles are radiocarbon dated between 1450 and 1600 and are primarily found in burial contexts (Aldunate 1989; Dillehay 1990a). However, given the two standard deviation of the dates, it is difficult to determine whether Inka influence was terminal pre-Hispanic or early Hispanic. The widespread presence of these traits in the Araucanian region, however, may suggests a terminal Hispanic origin (cf. Dillehay and Gordon 1988; Guevara 1925; Latcham 1928a; J. Medina [1852] 1952; A. Medina 1978).

Besides the archaeological and ethnohistorical records, several ethnographic studies have described the presence of Inka social, religious, linguistic, and symbolic traits in contemporary Araucanian society (e.g., Augusta 1934; Catrileo

12. Polychrome ceramics types from south Chile showing probable Inka influence: a. El Vergel. b. Tirua. c. Valdivia. El Vergel and Tirua date approximately between 1300 and 1600. Valdivia dates between 1500 and 1700. d. Arybullus from a cemetery near Purén. e. Inka-like drinking vessel. (a, b, c, and e are courtesy of the Museo Van de Maele de Historia y Antropologia, Universidad Austral de Chile; d is courtesy of Juan Alquiman, Elicura).

1998; Febres [1765] 1882; Latcham 1924; A. Medina 1978; Menghin 1962; Silva 1983; Uhle 1909). This evidence suggests that some Araucanian leaders may have identified with aspects of Inka political organization and symbols of authority which were embodied in *kero* drinking vessels, religious codes, and other features (Dillehay and Gordon 1988). We know that the Araucanian concept of reciprocal labor arrangements between kin groups, or *mingaco*, is derived from the Quechua term *minga*. Other Inka (or Quechua) influence is in the Araucanian word for sun, *antu*, which stems from the Quechua word for sun, *inti*. There also is the *Mareupuante* cult (meaning the son of the sun in Mapudungun) to the son of the sun, which is remarkably similar to the Inka cult to *Inti's* son (A. Medina 1978; Uhle 1909). Even the Araucanian word for foreigner (*huinca*) is derived from the Inka, as Bengoa (2003) notes.

La expansión incaica deber haber tenido una importancia política fundamental en la sociedad de los antiguos mapuches, la que por primera vez conoció a un grupo de extranjeros organizados que tenían por objeto instalarse, dominar la población y ponerla a trabajar mediante el sistema de mitas o mitayos que utilizaba el sistema incaico. No es por casualidad que pareciera que de esa experiencia surge la voz *huinca*, que había derivado de *pu inca*, esto es, los Incas en *mapudungu*. (Bengoa 2003:39–40)

The Inca expansion must have had a fundamental political importance in ancient Mapuche society, which for the first time encountered a group of organized foreigners whose objective was to establish themselves, dominate the population and put it to work by means of the system of *mitas* or *mitayos* used in the Inca system. It would seem that it is not by chance that from this experience emerged the word *huinca*, which was derived from *pu inca*, that is the Incas in *mapudungu*. (Bengoa 2003:39–40)

Linguists have not yet established the origin of the Araucanian word for shaman, *machi*. However, informants in Purén and Lumaco, including shamans, say the word means healer, medicine person, or communicator with the ancestors. It is possible that *machi* comes from the Quechua word *malqui* (linguist Gaston Sepulveda, personal communication, 1987), which means sacred ancestors, ancestor, or to be in contact with or the ability to transform oneself into an ancestor. Doyle (1988:103–104; cited in Moore 1996:125) has studied the concept of *malqui* in seventeenth and eighteenth century Peru and related it to *machay*, the special burial places of ancestors. She states that "The actual burial place of the sacred ancectors and their decendants, the *machay* was where the ritual and ceremonies in honor of them took place. The *machay* constituted a sacred space due to its sacralization by the *malquis* and by the rituals performed there. In this sense, *machays* should be considered to some extent as ceremonial centers." She also notes that the burial places were flat areas where groups met to carry out rituals related to *machay* worship. In Moore's (1996:125) study of the architecture of Andean ritual, he draws on Doyle's work to make several distinctions between *malqui* and oracles, stating that the "*Malquis* were honored with sacrifices of chicha, llama blood, and guinea pigs; oracles were honored with gold and fine cloth. *Malquis* were worshipped by ayllus; oracles cross-cut kin and ethnic boundaries . . . *malquis* were seen and oracles were not."

The concept of *machay* is similar to the sacred place and meaning of the Araucanian *rehuekuel*, where the mortuary rituals of important dead rulers and the construction of their mounded tombs took place. In ceremonies performed at *rehuekuel*, the deceased leaders become sacred ancestors and their burial mounds and built *ñichi*, or *terra pleins*, are converted to oracles and *nguillatun* fields, where animal sacrifices and offerings of blood, *chicha*, and other items occur. In essence, *rehuekuel* are shrines, oracles, and ceremonial centers. They are places where local kin or patrilineages worship and make offerings to their ancestors and where *machi* interact with important ancestors and receive power from predicting events through the *kuel* oracle where the kindred spirits reside. Fictive kin, newly recruited kin, and non-kin pilgrims or guests from other ethnic groups also participate in ceremonies at *rehuekuel* rituals. In short, the similarities between *rehuekuel* and *machay* are considerable enough to suggest that both may have been derived from fundamental Andean principles and cosmological orders.

Moore (1996:126–127) further believes that Andean oracles were special places that produced interactive networks between rulers and sacred ancestors, "were active forces who were consulted via their priests," and were important politically by regulating public discourse and political decisions. Oracles were personified and seen as having kinship relations similar to those of humans. An example is the diaspora oracles of the powerful pre-Inka shrine at the coastal site of Pachacamac in Peru. These oracles were the kin affiliates of the shrine and were geographically dispersed on the central coast and in the central highlands (see Duviols 1967:34; Rostowrowski 1983). When the Inka conquered the coast, they continued using some of these shrines for state functions. In describing the importance of Inka shrines to Andean political discourse, MacCormack states that:

> Oracular shrines both great and small bounded in the Andes; their principal role was to legitimate political power by establishing and articulating consensus. In the course of doing this, the oracular shrines also predicted the future. Because such predictions were capable of generating either support or dissent at times of political uncertainty, they were taken most seriously and were carefully remembered. (MacCormack 1991:59)

> The religion that existed among these people was most carefully observed and comprised many ceremonies and sacrifices, because people were devoted to such things. Lords and Incas in particular held frequent converse with huacas and houses of religion and communicated to everyone else that they approximated more closely to the gods they adored than did other people, and that they knew the future. The principal means whereby they held all other people in subjection was this profession of observing their religion and worship. (MacCormack 1991:159)

Of additional significance is the sacrifice of animals to oracles and the gifts of gold and other special offerings made to them when the oracles correctly predicted future events. When their predictions were wrong, gold and other gifts were withdrawn from them (cf. Pizarro [1571] 1921:209–210; Moore 1996:127). There also is a parallel between proper ritual and natural well-being, and how violation of this principle led to disasters, such as flooding and droughts (see Moore 1996:178–179).

These latter concerns are the same themes of the *Hualonkokuel* and *Tren-Trenkuel* ritual narratives presented in Chapter 5 and Appendix 1 and of most public ceremonies carried out in the past and present by Araucanians. In the *Hualonkokuel* ritual, the *machi* chides the local community for not making proper prayer and offerings to the kindred spirits of the *kuel*, which resulted in the sickness of the *kuel* and in its threat to retaliate against the community by carrying out malicious acts against it. In the narrative at *TrenTrenkuel*, a *machi* asks not to avenge the archaeological work being carried out in the area. Both narratives express the need for consensus between the *kuel*, the ancestors, and the living and open expressions of dissent or support for community actions.

Equally, the patterns mentioned by Moore and MacCormack are found in ceremonies described by chroniclers for past ceremonies and in *nguillatun* ceremonies performed at *rehuekuel* today. In the Purén and Lumaco Valley, the personification of *kuel* and *rehuekuel* is reflected by expressing relationships between them in human kinship terms. This also is similar to the study of Rostworowski de Díez Canseco (1983), a Peruvian ethnohistorian, on *huaca* (pyramids) that were the sons and daughters of the great oracle at Pachacamac. These *huaca* formed brother and sister relationships across the outlying territories they occupied, a pattern similar to that described by Mapuche informants for secondary *kuel* positioned around *TrenTrenkuel*, the largest and most important *kuel* in the Purén and Lumaco Valley (see Dillehay 1999 and Chapter 5). All other *kuel* in the valley are the sons and daughters of *TrenTrenkuel*. Furthermore, *kuel* intervene in public discourse and politics and are both feared and revered for their contacts with the great dieties and ancestors in the upper world and for their ability to predict the future, another pattern similar to Andean oracles. Also important is that the *kuel* are given special offerings of "gold," *chicha*, and other gifts and animals are sacrificed on top of them. Gifts and objects of gold are commonly associated with healing rituals held at misaligned *kuel*. In times of duress, when active *kuel* make erroneous judgments or maliciously overreact to the lack of prayer and offerings, local communities may treat them badly and refuse to make future offerings to them.

Another similarity between the Inka and the Araucanians may be the *ushnu*, a sacred pillar or structure built in the open plazas and ceremonial spaces of Inka settlements (see Hyslop 1984; Moore 1996:132–136). *Ushnu* are dedicated to the observation and worship of the sun. Major Inka settlements were always accessed by four roads that departed to and from the four cardinal directions and converged at the *ushnu* in the central plaza. As reported in Chapter 7, we have located a sacred place located on top of an old volcano that overlooks the Purén and Lumaco Valley and was used by shamans in the immediate past. This place is called *Wenucolla*, which means the great stairway to the upper world of the deities and ancestors (Fig. 13). The most conspicuous and centrally located structure on top of *Wenucolla* is called *usnan* in Mapudungun and said to relate to the *miñchemapu* underworld and to imaginary lines that extend from the hill to distant *rehuekuel*. This is a small rectangular stone structure that has a flat elevated platform facing the east (Fig. 14). We have recorded more than 400 other stone structures and terraces built around the top of *Wenucolla* and facing in all cardinal directions (Fig. 15). Local *machi* say that the structures are *deumerupu*, meaning a large built place that has roads or lines radiating in all directions from it. Located along these lines are *kuel*, *rehuekuel*, and other sacred places in the valley. Stone architecture is rare in Araucanian archaeology, suggesting that *Wenucolla* may have received its impetus from non-Araucanians, perhaps the Inka. In some ways, *Wenucolla* reminds me of the Inka *ceque* system, which is made up of imaginary lines, roads, and sectioned lands that radiate in the cardinal directions from the Inka capital of Cuzco and pass through numerous sanctuaries and *huacas* (shrines) in the surrounding countryside. Are the *usnan* and associated stone structures at *Wenucolla* local versions of the Inka *ushnu* or shrine in the Inka *ceque* system, respectively? Is the word *usnan* derived from *ushnu*?

Public ceremonies carried out at *Wenucolla* and at *rehuekuel* in the valley today are regularly characterized by sacrificing one black and one white sheep (referred to as *cheuque* in the past, which means llama) tied to *rehue* posts placed in the center of *nguillatun* ceremonial plazas. The sacrifical blood of the animals is combined with salt, chile pepper, corn chica, or *muday* or *chicha*, hot water, quinoa, and wheat or corn floor and then fed to *kuel* to nourish them. The mixture is called *melquen* in Mapundungun. During these ceremonies, *machi* shamans climb the *rehue* post, which is wrapped in cinnamon (*foye*) and other sacred branches, to pour blood on it, to communicate with the deities and ancestors above, and to make offerings to the *kuel* and deities. Afterward, the meat of the sacrificed animals is consumed by all ceremonial participants. Similar ceremonial practices are described by chroniclers observing the Araucanians in the sixteenth and seventeenth centuries (see below and Chapter 4). These rituals also are remarkably similar an Andean ceremony described in 1560 by an Augustinian priest who attended a ritual ceremony in honor of Ataguju, the major diety of Huamachuco in the northern highlands of Peru.

> To adore and honor this false Trinity [Ataguju] they have great patios [*corrales*] . . . and inside the patio they place posts to make their fiestas and in the middle they set a post and wrap it with straw and anoint

a

b

13. a. Location of the sacred *Wenucolla* mountain. b. Closeup of *Wenucolla* where an archaeological site is characterized by numerous stone structures (arrows) and an *"usnan"* located on its summit. See Chapter 6.

14. The *"usnan"* located in the central plaza on the summit of *Wenucolla*. It measures about 4 by 7 m in size and has a 1.5-m high platform or table on the east end.

it . . . and the man who is going to sacrifice climbs up the post dressed in white garments and they kill a guinea pig and offer the blood to Ataguju and he eats the meat; and others kill alpacas and pour the blood on the post and they eat the meat . . . at the foot of these posts the chief priest would mix *chicha* [maize beer] and *zaco-zaco* is a little maize flour mixed in hot water – and with that make a communal meal . . . for all the huacas and this said Ataguju eats. (Augustinians 1865 [1560]:14–15, translated by and quoted in Moore 1996:134–135)

To provide more commonalities between the Araucanians and the Inka, Andean rituals often connect warfare with agricultural fertility (Zuidema 1985: 1990) just as the *nguillatun* ceremony does for the Araucanians. A major concern in Andean ritual is productivity, fecundity, and order, which emphasizes the availability of water, the welfare of animals and crops, and the prevention of entropy (see Isbell 1978; Rostworowski 1983; Urton 1999; Wachtel 1971; Zuidema 1964). The *nguillatun* and other Araucanian rituals are expressions to abate decay and defeat and to insure continuance of order and culture by insuring reproductivity and social order. Further, Zuidema (1964, 1990) specifically relates water, ancestors, and the underworld with the Inka concept of *amaru* (snake). The Araucanian

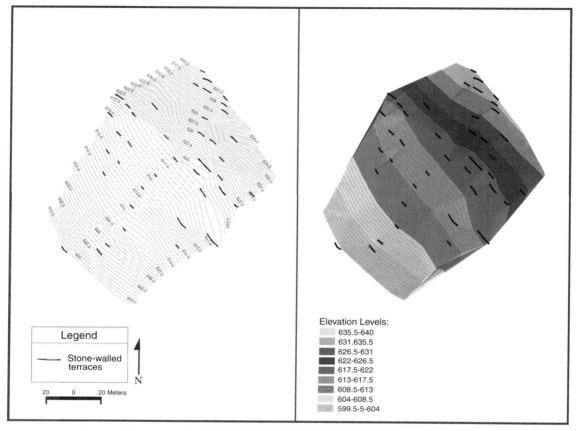

15. Sector of the sacred stone-walled terraces on the southwest slopes of *Wenucolla* mountain.

snake, or *filu*, also is associated with ancestors and the *miñchemapu* underworld. In the Araucanian origin story, the battle between two snakes, *Tren-Tren* and *Kai-Kai*, to save or destroy humanity is centered on the violent movement of water and on the growth of hills (i.e., *kuel*; see Chapter 4). In Cuzco, the canal system of the Inka intersects below the Temple of the Sun, where the mummies of the nobility were housed. Informants in Lumaco report that small tunnels pass through and under some *kuel* to carry water and the blood of sacrificed animals and to renourish the spirit of the dead ancestor buried inside. The water and blood mixture passes through the evil *miñchemapu* underworld as it travels to the *Wenumapu* upperworld where important ancestral spirits and deities reside. All of these practices take place publicly and are viewed by ritual participants and by the ancestors. In Inka society, rituals of regeneration and renewal also are performed within view of ancestral burial grounds. There are other ritual correspondences between the Inka (or Andeans) and the Araucanians: for example, the sacrifice of black and white animals during ritual; planting the ritual plaza of the *nguillatun*

16. A sacred *rehue* pole with a sheepskin draped across the top.

with the remains left in the bottom of *metawe* ceramic pots which are used to prepare corn beer or *mudai*; and ritual acts of sexual reversals related to procreating and regeneration (see Isbell 1978:207 for Andean versions of these rituals). To the Araucanians, black sheep, which represent females and the moon, are sacrificed to protect the people from the dark underworld of *miñchemapu*. White sheep, which represent males and the sun, are dedicated to the good upper world. Another similarity is the use of puma heads and skins worn by important elderly men during rituals and by Inka royalty during public feasts (Zuidema 1985). A common Araucanian pattern is to drape a sheep head and skin over the *lonko* or secular leader during the *nguillatun* ceremony and to place it over the top of the sacred *rehue* pole after ritual (Fig. 16). The skin stays atop the *rehue* for a year until the next *nguillatun* to protect the community from evil spirits. Informants in Lumaco report that in the past their grandfathers draped puma heads and skins over *rehue*; this practice stopped decades ago when puma disappeared in the area (see Rosales [1674] 1989:1336 for a discussion of the importance of the feline skin). Several chroniclers also mention the use of the *khuipu* (knotted-string counting device) in the 1500s and 1600s by southern Araucanians (see below and Bengoa 2003:34–40). González de Nájera, living in the Araucania in the early 1600s, describes a messenger and a *khuipu*.

> se debió de encaminar el mens[a]jero a esta casa, a quien hospedaron, por ser tarde aquella noche, con todo agasajo, dándole de cenar, de beber y en qué dormir, acomodándose con el apersevido; y al amanecer pasó adelante con su flecha o carta citatoria dejando en un hilo grueso de lana ocho ñudos que era el término y plaso d ocho días, que en el último y al fin de ellos había de estar en los altos de Eloy –que es un cerro alto que está en medio de sus parcialidades–, y ser parte comediada para los unos y los otros aplazados. (Núñez de Pineda [1673] 2003:120)

> the messenger had to travel to this house because it was late that night, where he was given lodging with all courtesy, and given food and drink and a place to sleep, settling him with things provided, and at dawn he went on with his arrow or sign of convocation, leaving behind a thick strand of woolen yarn with eight knots, which marked the span and period of eight days at the end of which they had to be on the heights of Eloy – which is a high hill in the midst of their lineages – and is a favored place for one and the other group summoned. (Núñez de Pineda [1673] 2003:120)

Today, in Purén and Lumaco elders still refer to the "*quipan*" in Mapudungun, or *khuipu*, which was used by ancient *huinca* (outsiders) to count crops, days, people, and other entities. In the ritual narratives presented in Appendix 1, *machi* Juanita mentions the use of knotted strings in reference to the ancient use of the *khuipu* (see Appendix 1:XXXIII:2).

Perhaps most significant is that local communities in Purén and Lumaco still tell stories about Atahualpa, one of the last Inka lords, and how he once came to their area to warn the Araucanians of the pending arrival of the Spanish. To briefly recount the tale, Antonio Painequeo of Butarincón, Lumaco, stated that there was an old *lonko* (leader) called Atahualpa who was the lord of gold. When the Spanish entered, Atahualpa was asked by the Mapuche to travel north to speak with the Spanish on their behalf. Atahualpa complied and asked the Spanish not to spill Mapuche blood. Another informant, Pedro Cheuque, said that when the famous *toqui* war chief, Colo Colo, ruled the lands [seventeenth century], Atahualpa possessed powerful mirrors. Atahualpa knew that the Mapuche had gold, which they carried in small pouches hanging from their belts. The Mapuche exchanged the gold for the mirrors. When Pedro de Valdivia arrived in the region, he told Atahualpa to give him all of the gold, because it belonged to his king in Spain. Atahualpa then killed Valdivia. Cheuque further reported that the Mapuche had to be careful with Atahualpa, because he was the principal leader of the *huinca* (Inka); in other words, he was like Colo Colo to the Araucanians. Other informants (Segundo Huircaleo, Emelina Cheuque, Filomena Cheuque) state that the lord of gold, Atahualpa, had a baston and a crown. They claim that Atahualpa passed through the Purén Valley prior to the arrival of the Spanish. They said that Atahualpa was a great leader whom you could not face and look into his eyes. (In the Inka state, it was taboo to look directly at the lords.) His clothing was made of solid gold. They also say that when Atahualpa's head was cut off (it's not stated who beheaded him), it was discovered that it too was made of pure gold. When the head was severed, seven states [nations] fell out, meaning Atahualpa's seven territories had been defeated. In ancient times, informants report that the gold was like rocks in the nearby mountains. During the night of the San Juan feast, the Mapuche still build fires which represent the gold of Atahualpa and the defeat of his seven territories. Other informants state that the Inka taught the Mapuche how to look for and to appreciate gold.

We asked our informants if they knew anything about the Inka state. They were unaware of it except for the Atahualpa story and the foreign people called *huinca* long ago. (Other more acculturated Mapuche often know about Atahualpa through the Chilean education system.) To informants, it seems that the Spanish quest for gold led to the downfall of Atahualpa and to the seven states under his control. We know from the chroniclers that Atahualpa never traveled to Chile, but it is possible that *yanacona*, other state personnel, or northern Araucanains who escaped from the Inka or Spanish told tales of this lord, of his pursuit of gold, and of his eventual death. It is not known when and how this tale reached the Purén and Lumaco Valley and whether it reflects direct or indirect contact between the Inka and the valley in terminal pre-Hispanic times or later. We have asked several Mapuche informants in communities outside of the Purén and Lumaco if they knew of Atahualpa and the Inka and few did.

Of further importance is the mention of rich gold mines south of the Bio Bio River and in Purén by several chroniclers writing between 1551 and 1563 (e.g., P. de Valdivia [1555] 1960; Mariño de Lobera [1595] 1960; Góngora Marmolejo [1575] 1862; mentioned later by Núñez de Pineda [1673] 2003:132 and Rosales [1674] 1989). Núñez de Pineda states that:

> [el gobernador Valdivia] tenia grande opinión de cudicioso y avariento, y entre las reparticiones que hizo de las *regües* – que son "parcialida-des" – se quedó con sinco o seis de las más opulentas de indios y de minas de oro conocidas; por cuya causa cargó la mano en los tributos, que fueron intolerables. (Núñez de Pineda [1673] 2003 I:116)

[Governor Valdivia] had a great reputation for greed and avarice, and in the distribution which he made of the *regües* – which are "*parcialidades*" [lineages] – he kept for himself five or six of the wealthiest in Indians and known gold mines, for this reason he had a heavy hand with the tributes, which were intolerable. (Núñez de Pineda [1673] 2003 I:116)

Although no archaeological evidence has yet been found to document Araucanian gold mining and the use of gold in the pre-Hispanic era, it is possible that the Inka were mining in the Nahualbuta range west of Purén prior to the Spanish invasion (see Chapter 3). In the late 1500s, the Spanish mined gold in several localities in the region during periods of peace or when they successfully defended themselves against the Araucanians. If not for the Inka exploiting gold in the area, then how did the Spanish find the gold mines so quickly when they first entered the south (Dillehay and Gordon 1988)?

In summary, I have presented a synopsis of various material styles, social and political organizations, cosmological beliefs, and ritual practices that reveal Andean and Inka influences in the late pre-Hispanic and early Hispanic Araucanian society south of the Bio Bio River. It is known that Andean influence existed in the region prior to the Inka state. Not known is how much Inka influence was imposed directly or indirectly upon populations living south of the river, and if this influence occurred before or after the Spanish conquest. During both the Inka and Spanish invasions, it is likely that some northern Araucanians from central Chile were displaced southwardly and mixed with southern groups, thus establishing a long "informal frontier" between the Maele and Bio Bio rivers (Dillehay and Gordon 1988). There also is the possibility that Inka design motifs on late El Vergel, Tirua, and Valdivia ceramic styles and other artifacts in the south were derived from *yanacona* who first accompanied the Inka and then the Spanish to the south and who deserted the causes of both to fight on the side of the southern Araucanians. Given continuous contacts between the northern and southern Araucanians, it also is plausible that the former escaped to the south and taught Inka ways to the latter and/or that the latter observed them first-hand on visits to the north. More research on these topics will likely reveal a combination of these and other scenarios to explain Inka influence farther south. Whatever the means and dates of contact between the Inka and southern groups, mutual intelligibility in their Andean organizational structures must have facilitated the adoption of certain Inka ways in Purén, Lumaco, Arauco, Tucapel, and other areas where large and politically complex populations lived and where the mound cultures were concentrated. This intelligibility and the presence of dense populations, gold, and other minerals probably attracted the Inka.

Regardless of the chronology, context, and nature of interaction between the Inka and the southern Araucanians (see Chapters 7 and 8), opportunities must have existed for the latter (1) to emulate Inka principles of organized warfare, administered public ceremony, recruitment and incorporation of defeated and fragmented groups, construction of large-scale monuments, and employment of religious symbols expressive of these activities, and (2) to appropriate Inka identity through the consumption of goods, symbols, institutions, and infrastructures. If this was the case, the purpose of appropriation probably was not just symbolic but tactical and organizational. Further, the Inka way of doing things was not just a symbolic expression but, I argue, a venue of power deliberately emulated by some Araucanian leaders to provide a continuous flow and structured organization of goods, ideas, and peoples to defend their territory. Because these imports emerged in the early Spanish period under conditions of stigmatized warfare, I also hypothesize that emulation was an attempt to define power via the accumulation of symbols of power already recognized by the Spanish in their previous encounters with the Inka in other areas. That is, the southern Araucanians did not develop an Inka identity; they developed an identity with Inka accomplishment as a powerful state society that the Spanish knew. Araucanian interest in Inka sacred spaces, imaginary lines, aesthetic pyramid or *huaca* designs, symbols of power, and organizational knowledge may have been a matter of reinforcing local models of utopic polity-formation, tactical and organizational political power, and their materiality and performative display in public monuments and religious feasts by unconsciously extending or keeping alive the official Inka state history. Even if the Araucanians were more directly influenced by the Inka than we know, the way in which the former used it to more effectively develop a polity and to establish a social vision or target to strive toward was congruent and legible with their own ideologies, cosmologies, and political circumstances, which already were Andean in form and practice.

Ethnohistorical Voice

Before proceeding to coverage of relevant themes in the early texts on the Purén and Lumaco Valley, I discuss the meaning of key Araucanian social and political terms. In Chapter 1, I referred to several terms mentioned by chroniclers and modern-day scholars that describe social units and political organizations in the sixteenth through eighteenth centuries. Although there is no consensual agreement on the precise meaning of these terms in the scholarly literature, I present their most accepted understanding in the literature and to informants in Purén and Lumaco today. All social units have spatial connotations that refer to political or religious gatherings (see Bengoa 2003; Foerster and Gundermann 1996; Krumm 1971:90; Ñanculef 1990; see Chapter 4).

The basic social unit was the *quinelob, lob, lebo, lof,* or *lov* which were several united households that formed a community of large, dispersed extended patrilineal families (Krumm 1971). Mariño de Lobera ([1594] 1960) describes the *lov* as a "*parcialidad*" or lineage with 400 people. He also notes that a *rehuenor lebo* comprises several lineages. The *cahuin* (*caguin, cabbie*) is one or more patrilineage(s) and a large meeting, where political decisions are made and feasting and dancing occur (cf. Núñez de Pineda [1673] 2003:523; Krumm 1971). In 1606, Luis de Valdivia ([1606] 1887:46–48) indicates that *cahuin* is "a gathering or *regua*, where the indians dwell" and *cahuintú* is "the drinking feast." Ovalle ([1646] 2003:396) refers to a *rehuetun* as a ceremony among members of a *regua* (*rehue*) that takes place in times of peace. Latcham (1924:132) also thought that the *rehue* was a *cahuin*. Bengoa (2003:160–161) views the *cahuin* as the reunion of several *rehue* or lineages. A *rehue* (*rehua, regua*) also is described as one or several patrilineages (cf. Núñez de Pineda [1673] 2003:593; Ovalle [1646] 2003:395; Saavedra 1870:164) headed by a principal ruler or "*cacique*," but also as a meeting place (Bibar [1555] 1966:160; Rosales [1674] 1989: Chapter 25, 147). *Rehue* also is mentioned as a priestly personage, but this simply may be a role related to the *machi* and to her use of the *rehue* pole in ritual (see later discussion). Boccara (1999) interprets the *lebo* or *lov* as a lineage and the *rehue* as its ceremonial space.

At this point, it can be seen that the meanings of these terms overlap considerably: *lov, rehue,* and *cahuin* invariably relate to one or more patrilineages and *rehue* and *cahuin* imply a ceremonial gathering and meeting place of multiple lineages. The *lov* or *lof* seems to be a spatially defined community of dispersed households of multiple extended families of one or more patrilineages. The *rehue* (*regua*) comprises several spatially contiguous *lov* communities that are related through intermarriage and through a shared *rehuekuel* (*cahuintú?*) ceremonial place, such as those described in the Purén and Lumaco Valley. There is a concensus among chroniclers and scholars that *ayllarehue* (*allirehue*) were nine *rehue* allied geopolitically and religiously. The *butanmapu* comprised multiple *ayllarehue* residing in three and later four large, confederated geopolitical divisions that were initially organized in the early 1600s (e.g., Núñez de Pineda [1673] 2003:629) and fully developed by the late 1700s. These divisions were located between the Bio Bio and Rio Bueno rivers and represent the maximum level of geopolitical development. Collectively, the *lov, rehue, ayllarehue,* and *butanmapu* represent a telescopic political and territorial organization of similar social and ritual units designed to situationally shrink or expand, respectively, to meet different political and economic demands.

The historical meaning of these terms to informants in the Purén and Lumaco area generally agrees with those previously described. They view the *lov* corresponding to a group of extended families making up two to three patrilineages living in a spatially designated area like a community or *reduccion*. An example is in the community of Rukalleco near Lumaco where four patrilineal extended families (Marileo, Colipi, Huircaleo, Mariman) reside together. Traditionally, each *lov* in the study area occupied between 10,000 and 20,000 ha, although today community lands have shrunk between 400 and 1,000 ha. Each *lov* has its own *nguillatun* ceremonial field and individual *kuel*. To the informants, *cahuin* refers to a religious and political meeting of one or more *lov* where a *machi* may be present but does not conduct a ceremony. The meetings are administered by secular *lonko* or headmen and generally held at *nguillatun* fields. When a *machi* is present, she is asked to give a prayer to bless the meeting and to legitimize the word of the *lonko*. *Rehue* has two meanings. First, it refers to the sacred pole or *axis mundi* and *imago mundi* of the *machi* that is located in the plaza of a *nguillatun* ceremonial field (see Chapter 5). Second, it was and still is a sociopolitical organization and a ritual congregation of several contiguously residing patrilineal *lov* communities, such as Butarincón, Isla Katrileo, and San Genaro near Lumaco. Traditionally, *rehue* communities occupied between 80,000 and 120,000 ha and had their own *rehuekuel* field where multiple mounds are located and where larger intercommunity *nguillatun* ceremonies were held. Today, the hectares are between 2,000 and 15,000. Ceremonies are administered by a principal *lonko*. (Informants report that the founding rulers of the principal patrilineages are buried in the largest mounds in a *rehuekuel*. These primary mounds also are places where the kindred spirits of dead *machi* reside. See the ritual narratives analyzed in Chapter 5.) Informants also say that in historic times, some *rehue* gatherings (*cahuin*?) were large and attended by hundreds of *toqui* and *ülmen* rulers and their relatives and allies, particularly in Lolonko near Purén and in Butarincón where the largest and most numerous *rehuekuel* are located. (In 1698, Redrado [1775] was at a large political gathering in the Purén Valley, where 800 caciques met to form the first three divisions of the *butanmapu*.) Although the *ayllarehue* and *butanmapu* disappeared at the end of the nineteenth century, they still exist in the memory of elders in the study area. *Ayllarehue* are interpreted as old political and religious unions made up of several *rehue* from multiple and geographically proximal valleys. They say that the Purén and Lumaco Valley *ayllarehue* was one of the first formed by the Araucanians to resist the Spanish. (Informants are proudly aware that the Purén and Lumaco Valley was a military, political, and religious seat of power in the past and still serves as a strong political voice among the Mapuche today. This valley also has the highest number of practicing shamans in Chile.) *Butanmapu* means a large territorial gathering of allied *ayllarehue*.

Several different types of leaders are described in late sixteenth and early seventeenth century texts: *genvoye, apuülmen, guecubus, gentoqui, toqui, ülmen,* and *heuipife* or *weipife*. Although the sacred and secular roles of these rulers are difficult to separate, most seem to be associated with nonreligious activities, especially the *gen-toqui* and *toqui* who were military commanders. *Genvoye* was a lineage head. *Apoülmen* was the principal ruler of several related lineages (e.g., Rosales [1674] 1989). *Guecubus* were powerful *ülmen* who were great leaders (Ovalle [1646] 2003:473). *Ülmen* ruled multilineage communities. Today, *ülmen* usually attain prestige through economic dealings, and *lonko* are community leaders. *Weupife* (*weupufe, weupin, heuipife*) was an important orator who wielded certain political skills. In concept, most of these positions were inherited but they also could be acquired, especially an achieved leader in war who became a *toqui* (see Chapter 7).

In regard to sacred leadership roles, *machi, hechicero, reñi, boquivoye (huecubuye, boquibuye)* and *nguillatufe* are mentioned most often. In the middle 1600s, Núñez de Pineda states that:

> se usaban en todas nuestras parcialidades unos *huecubuyes*, que llaman *renis*, como entre vosotros los sacerdotes; estos andaban vestidos de unas mantas largas, con los cabellos largos . . . estos acostumbr[a]n estar separados del concurso de las gentes, y por tiempos no ser comunicados, y en diversas montañas divididos, adonde tenían unas cuevas lóbregas en que consultaban al *Pillan* [un dios] – que es el demonio –, a quien conosen por dios los *hechiceros* y endemoniados *machis* – que son 'médicos.' (Núñez de Pineda [1673] 2003:737)

> there were *huecubuyes* in all our lineages [*parcialidades*], whom they call *renis*, like priests among you; these used to wear long mantles, with long hair . . . they used to live apart from most people and at times to be without communication on different distant mountains, where they used to have dens in caves where they consulted *Pillan* –who is the devil – who is considered god by the *sorcerers* and devil-possessed *machis* – who are "healers." (Núñez de Pineda [1673] 2003:737)

Huecubuye (reñi, boquivoye) were powerful ritual leaders who determined whether leaders and their warriors should engage in war and where and when it took place (e.g., Rosales [1674] 1989:168). *Machi* were shamans or healers (cf. Núñez de Pineda [1673] 2003:624; Rosales [1674] 1989; Ovalle [1646] 2003:472). Ovalle ([1646] 2003) refers to *machi* as "*machi weye,*" which is similar to the term "*voye, boqui, buye,*" meaning cinnamon tree, *foye,* and implying a degree of ritual leadership as well (Núñez de Pineda ([1673] 1973:107) states that the *machi* and the *hueye* are the same figure). As described above and in Chapter 4, the *axis mundi* or sacred stairway of the *machi* into the upper world of the deities is the *rehue,* which is partly made of cinnamon branches, suggesting that the terms *rehue, boqui, weye,* and *boye* perhaps have overlapping meanings, or are different terms associated with the sacred pole and the *machi.* Another important figure is the *regue (rehue),* which Núñez de Pineda ([1673] 2003:42) describes in a priest-like role. Once again, the *rehue* is related to sacred roles, places, and gatherings. (I suspect that the *reñi* and *rehue* are different phonetic versions of the same word and thus have similar meanings.) Today, the *nguillatufe* is a ritual priest who makes contact between the living and ancestral worlds. Although the early chroniclers usually ascribe different roles to *machi*, *hechicero* (a Spanish term used to describe demonic medicine men), and *boquibuye*, there apparently was considerable overlap between these sacred figures, with each having leadership roles.

Not enough descriptive information is available in the chroniclers to clarify the individual and overlapping roles of these leaders and how and why they changed names and functions. It is likely that over the past few centuries *machi* have increasingly combined various functions of the *hechicero* and *boquivoye* (or *fokeweye*). In the past and present, clergymen of western denominations often accuse *machi* of working for the devil and for overseeing pagan rituals. Ancient *hechicero* and *boquivoye* also were accused of representing the "*demonio*" (devil) and referenced as powerful religious figures who sacrificed captured soldiers and led the people in "pagan" cults (see Núñez de Pineda [1673] 1973:107; Ovalle [1646] 1888; L. de Valdivia [1606] 1887).

In the twentieth century, *machi* may have a more publicly politicized role than they had in the past. Faron (1964) and Bengoa (2003:16–17) believe this is related to the demise of the *nguillatufe*, or ritual priest, in public ceremonies (cf. Dillehay 1985b; Bacigalupo 2004a). It is possible that the traditional role of the *nguillatufe* changed when the Araucanians were pacified in the late 1800s. It also is possible that before *machi* became institutionalized public personas in the twentieth century, they had coalesced the functions and powers of both shamans and ritual priests. The fact that shamans control so much esoteric knowledge and the public contexts, where this knowledge is employed to link the living and the dead and to maintain intergroup solidarity, gives them the agency to manipulate a wide range of religious and political affairs.

Today, in Purén and Lumaco, *machi*, *nguillatufe*, and *weipife* refer to shamans, ritual priests and keepers of the word or history, respectively, although older more powerful *machi* have both shamanic and priestly roles (see Chapter 4). The only ancient terms known by informants for these figures are *boquivoye* and *reñi*. Both refer to ancient *machi* but in different ways: the former to *machi* who used the power of the cinnamon or *foye* tree, as they do today, and the latter to *machi* who enter into the interior of *kuel* or mounds. (In Mapundungun, *reñimapu* means the earth inside and is the term used by informants to refer to the interior earth layers of *kuel*. See Chapter 5.) Given the above comments on *machi* in the early historic texts and the *machi's* association with public ritual, the cinnamon tree, *rehue*, *reñi*, and healing, I view them as having had and still possessing roles that extend well beyond just healing the sick to conducting public ceremonies, to making important decisions about community policy, to conferring with *lonko* and other secular leaders, to serving as the keepers of sacred knowledge, and to acting the primary mediator between the living and the ancestors and deities in the upper *Wenumapu* world (see narratives in Chapter 5). I thus refer to *machi* in this study as priestly shamans.

TEXTUAL EVIDENCE FROM THE PURÉN AND LUMACO VALLEY: As reported earlier, in the mid-1500s and early 1600s several localities planned and assumed leadership of the resistance movement against the Spanish and later Chilean invaders. Among these localities, Purén, Lumaco, Tucapel, and Arauco (see Chapter 1) developed into the primary centers of resistance with formally recognized borders and their own hierarchical leadership (Boccara 1999; Dillehay 2002; León 1991, 1999; Padden 1993; Villalobos et al. 1982; Zapater 1978; Zavala 2000). In 1569, Ercilla ([1569] 1982) referred to these localities as the *"estado,"* which is roughly equivalent to the modern-day concept of polity. In 1670, Rosales ([1674] 1989:434) called this area the *"Reino de Arauco"* (Kingdom of Arauco). In commenting on the *estado,* the modern historian Padden notes that:

> The center of anti-Spanish unity was founded in what the Spanish termed *"el estado."* [At first] this was a geographic expression signifying the area that Valdivia held in personal *encomienda.* It was these Indians, particularly those of Arauco, Tucapel, and Purén, who planned and carried out the revolt of 1553, and who assumed leadership of the resistance movement. After the first few years of bitter warfare the Spaniards began to imbue the term *"estado"* with political connotations, hence Don Alonso de Ercilla's image of *"el estado indomito"* was much more than a flight of poetic fancy. (Padden 1993:78)

The most comprehensive analysis of the application of the term *estado* to the Araucanians is by the Chilean historian A. Medina (1978:144) who writes that:

> La palabra estado en Ercilla y los cronistas adquiere una significada precisión donde va envuelta la idea general sobre tal término aceptada en esa época: el territorio dominado por algún principe, monarca o soberano, por un jefe de súbditos, por un señor de vasallos o de siervos; señor que por sus títulos y derechos adquiría a veces notable preeminencia. (Medina 1978:144)

> The word *state* in Ercilla and the chroniclers adheres to a precise understanding that relates to the general idea of an accepted term during this period: the dominate territory based on some principle, monarchy, or sovereignty, based on a chief of subjects, based on a lord of vassals or servants; a lord who by entitlement and rights adheres to a notable permanence. (Medina 1978:144)

Medina cites several chroniclers in estimating the geographical size of the *estado* between 25 and 30 leagues long and 8 and 10 leagues wide (a league is 5,572 m long or approximately 5.6 km) and to its location in Arauco, Tucapel, Lebu, and

Purén (Fig. 17). This establishes the western border of the *estado* roughly along the Pacific coast from present day Lebu and the delta of the Bio Bio southward to Tirua and the delta of the Imperial River and the eastern border along the eastern flanks of the Nahualbuta mountain range from Yumbel and Angol to Nueva Imperial.

An important organizational aspect of the *estado* is described by Olaverría in the 1590s.

> Toda la tierra referida del *estado* e indios de ella están repartidos en cinco allareguas, que la allaregua es una junta y concurso de nueve parcialidades, la gente de las cuales por naturaleza y continuo ejercicio en las armas es tan arrogante, feroz e inquieta y tan inclinados a la Guerra que conocidamente se ve ser su elemento y que la quieren y apetecen. (Olaverría [1594] 1852:20)

> All of the land referred to as the *state* and the Indians in it are divided into five *allareguas*, which is a *unified* group of nine lineages or *levos* whose people are by nature and by their continued armed conduct are so arrogant, fierce and restless and so inclined toward War that they knowingly see it as their element and that they want it and crave it. (Olaverría [1594] 1852:20)

Olavarría's description of the "*allareguas*," or *ayllarehue*, and the nine lineages that compose each of them may correspond with the nine major mound or *rehuekuel* complexes defined archeologically in the Purén and Lumaco Valley, which he and other chroniclers describe as one of the five *allaregues* of the *estado*. Informants in the valley report that each major lineage in the past had its own *rehuekuel* (see Chapter 6), perhaps suggesting that the latter may be a spatial and material expression of the *ayllarehue* level of political organization. The largest and earliest known agricultural villages and terraces, and extensive hilltop fortresses with multiple moats and palisades in the valley are located near these complexes, indicating a hierarchically arranged socioeconomical system and an increasingly marked settlement pattern with artificial earthworks aimed toward a higher political order and defensive system (Dillehay 1999, 2003). Radiocarbon dates and ceramic styles place these features between the fourteenth and eighteenth centuries (see Appendix 2). Although I have not carried out systematic archaeological research in the other areas of the *estado*, I have found similar but less developed mound complexes in them and in a few places along the Cautín and Toltén rivers. These complexes either do not occur in valleys outside of the *estado*, or they are present in dispersed and low densities and associated with smaller settlements, suggesting less cultural development and political centralization (Dillehay 1995, 1999).

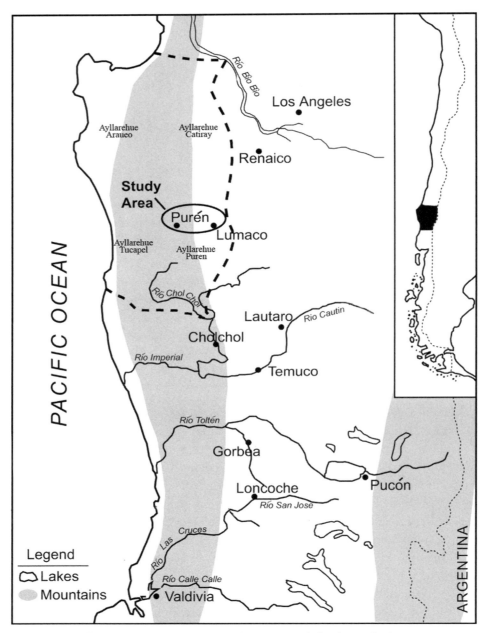

17. Location of the Araucanian "*Estado*" (dashed lines) and the four *ayllarehue* comprising it around 1600.

The resistant military role played by Purén and Lumaco in particular is revealed in the writings of early chroniclers. Commenting in the early 1600s, Rosales ([1674] 1989:572) noted it as the "*Prouincia indómita*" or "unconquerable

18. The impenetrable wetlands or *ciénega* of Purén in the winter.

Province," where the indigenous population resided in and around a vast network of highly productive and geographically formidable wetlands, or *ciénegas*, that protected it from the Spanish armies (Fig. 18). In several passages below, each of which offers a different insight into the setting, Rosales, Tesillo, Quiroga, and others describe the distinct geography of the valley that was conducive to defense of the Araucanians and to the important role played by Purén and Lumaco and their paramount leaders (i.e., Anganamón, Nabalburi, Pelantaro) in the defeat of and resistance to the Spanish.

> Arrimasse a Ilicura el decantado Valle de Purén, donde esta la más celebrada laguna deste Reyno, por auer sido el receptáculo, y inexpugnable castillo, y fortaleza de los más ferozes, y sangrientos indios desta guerra: y que antiguamente, solo estubieron veinte y quatro horas de paz, y siempre an sustentado porfiadamente la guerra fortalecidos en su laguna, y los pantanos, que como muralla la rodean. (Rosales [1674] 1989:223)

> The broad Valley of Purén where is found the most famous lake in this Kingdom, because it was the holding and impregnable castle and fortress of the fiercest and most bloody indians of this war and who formerly were only at peace for twenty-four hours at a time and who always stubbornly kept on making war, fortified in their lake and in the swamps which surround it like a wall. (Rosales [1674] 1989:223)

> la principal defensa de estos indios de Purén era esta ciénega: y sin duda la causa más eficaz porque se juzgaban por indomables. A esta

ciénega dábamos nombre de Rochela, a imitación de la de Francia, donde los franceses piensan o lo deben de soñar que han de fundar con formidable imperio de tierra y de mar los designios de su república, así entre estos rebeldes chilenos, esta ciénega o esta Rochela de Purén era su mayor y más principal asilo. (Tesillo [1647] 1911:22–23; cited in Bengoa 2003:428)

this swamp was the principal defense of these indians of Purén: and doubtless the most solid reason they were considered indomitable. We gave the name of Rochelle to this swamp, after the one in France, where the French think or must dream that they will fullfil the designs of their nation with formidable rule over land and sea, thus among these Chilean rebels, this swamp or this Rochelle of Purén was their greatest and most important refuge. (Tesillo [1647] 1911:22–23; cited in Bengoa 2003:428)

Los Indios de Purén que sintieron venir a los Españoles se metieron en la Ciénega, y aunque corrió toda la tierra el Gobernador no halló ni un alma, y viéndose señor de la campaña, taló las sementeras quemó las casas y hizo el daño, que pudo, y después intentó entrar a vuscar los Indios, en la fortaleza de su ciénega; mas fue en vano, porque aunque echó algunas canoas, por los brazos de aqua, no siruió; sino de que se le ahogassen tres soldados, con que se voluió, por entrar ya el imbierno. (Rosales [1674] 1989:518)

The Indians of Purén [when] they realized the Spanish were coming, entered into the marsh and although the Governor found not a soul in all the land and seeing he was successful in the campaign, cut down the crops, burned the houses and did what damage he could, and afterward he tried to enter the swamp to seek out the indians, within the vastness of their swamp, but it was in vain because although he launched several canoes into the open channels, it was for naught, except that three soldiers were drowned, at which point he withdrew, to return again in the winter. (Rosales [1674] 1989:518)

Purén que era el gran Coco de la Guerra. (Rosales [1674] 1989:585)

Purén was the great head of the war. (Rosales [1674] 1989:585)

Los más famosos capitanes, a los cuales ha durado más tiempo el mando el respeto que les han tenido los indios, han sido aquellos que antes fueron nuestros prisioneros o que sirvieron a nuestros españoles, como ha sido Anganamón, Pelantaro, Nabalburi y Longotegua, que eran todo su gobierno en mi tiempo. (González de Nájera [1614] 1889:97–98; cited in Bengoa 2003:311)

The most renowned captains, those who have retained command [and] the respect of the Indians the longest, have been those who previously were our prisoners or who served our Spanish forces, such as Anganamón, Pelantaro, Nabalburi and Longotegua, who were up their government in my time. (González de Nájera [1614] 1889:97–98; cited in Bengoa 2003:311)

Anganamón [un cacique podoroso de Purén] aesperando, en los campos de Tabón con dos embocadas de seis mil Indios, los más valientes, y animosos de la tierra, quales eran los de Purén, y Lumaco. (Rosales [1674] 1989:729)

Anganamón [a powerful local chief from Purén] was waiting in the fields of Tabon with two groups of six thousand indians, the bravest and most daring in the land, which were those from Purén and Lumaco. (Rosales [1674] 1989:729)

What made the Purén and Lumaco Valley so formidable was not just the fierceness of its warriors and its political and religious organization, but the geography of its huge marsh system that expanded into a vast lake and winter fortress (see additional quotes in Chapter 1). The wetland ecology also was important for its rich soils, which produced some of the best crops in the south. Located around and overlooking these wetlands are the ancient sacred oracles – the *kuel* and *rehuekuel* – agricultural villages, fortresses, cemeteries, and other sites studied here (Fig. 19). (Today, the valley is well known for producing some of the largest and tastiest potatoes in Chile. Araucanian communities living adjacent to the marshes still seasonally grow crops along the shorelines in traditional ways described by the early chroniclers. For example, see Rosales [1674] 1989:620, 626, 678 for descriptions of agricultural fields in the Purén area and Chapter 6.)

Several chroniclers mention specific places in the valley where battles took place between the Spanish and local groups, often providing detailed accounts of the number of warriors and residents killed, of the movement and names of Araucanian groups defeated elsewhere and recruited into the valley by local leaders, of the names and locations of oracles important to pan-Araucanian divinations, of famed local lineage rulers, of communities and agricultural fields burned and sacked by the Spanish, and of defensive sites (e.g., Quiroga [1690] 1979: 232; cf. Rosales [1674] 1989 and Ovalle [1646] 2003:392 who present detailed descriptions of the Purén and Lumaco Valley). We know from written records that settlement stability occurred in the valley for most of the time period under study, although dispersion and loss of lives often resulted from intermittent battles with the Spanish (see Chapter 7), as noted by Rosales below.

> Pero en todo el valle de Purén, ni en su ciénega, hallaron, ni aun cenizas del antigua fuego. Porque todos los Indios de dos aquella prouincia acosados, y amedrentados de las armas Españolas se avían metido la tierra adentro, desamparando la suya por mal segura, siendo antes el fuerte más inexpugnable. Cosa sin duda digna de notar, aver sido la ciénega de Purén y su Prouincia la que todos los reveldes tenian por sagrado como parte que juzgaban incontrastable. . . . Despoblado hemos la sierra de Purén, que ya no ay gente en la ciénega. Porque era la ciénega de Purén el sagrado de todos los foragidos. (Rosales [1674] 1989:1090)

> But in all the valley of Purén they found [nothing] neither in its marsh nor the ashes of the former fire. Because all the indians of the province, attacked and harassed by Spanish arms, had moved inland, abandoning their place for undefendable lands though formerly it was an unconquerable fortress. The swamp of Purén and its hinterland were something worthy of note which all the rebels considered sacred as a place which could not be taken. . . . We found the highlands of Purén depopulated, for there are now no people in the marsh. Because the marsh of Purén was the holy place of all the rebels. (Rosales [1674] 1989:1090)

Collectively, this information allows us to reconstruct the political and demographic organization of the valley's inhabitants and to compare it with oral traditions (see Chapters 4 and 5) and with the archeological record (see Chapter 6).

POLITICAL AND DEMOGRAPHIC CONFIGURATIONS

By the mid- to late 1500s, a series of major demographic and social changes were underway in the Araucania. During this period, communities were organized into the ruling patrilineages of different river valleys (Bengoa 2003; Dillehay 1995; Guevarra 1913). Although some multilineage communities may have been fairly large with 5,000 to 10,000 people, they may not have been strongly institutionalized except in times of war. We know from the written records that localized organizational movements in the late sixteenth to early seventeenth centuries consisted of the formation of new and expanded patrilineages, where in some areas there was previously social disintegration due to defeat in warfare with

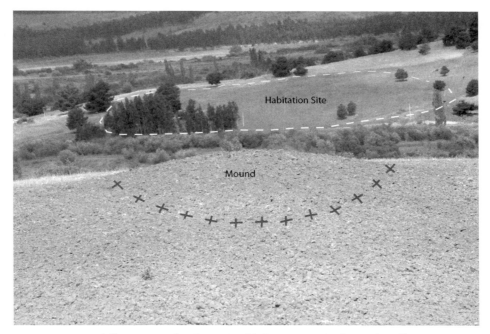

19. A hillcrest mound and associated habitation site in the Purén Valley.

Araucanian enemies or with the Spanish, population displacement, consequent fragmentation, and occasionally disease. As a result of these circumstances, strong to weak separations existed between many indigenous rulers and their followers, except in times of armed conflict when *toqui* and *gentoqui* war leaders ruled with wider geopolitical authority (cf. Bengoa 2003; Boccara 1999:434–36). Secular leadership roles were usually inherited, although the holding of office by these leaders during periods of warfare was justified by warrior prowess and alliance building, and in the nineteenth century, by control of long-distance trade networks. Several chroniclers mention that two powerful leaders in the Purén area, Anganamón and Pelantaro, ruled over several thousand warriors and had alliances with other rulers that extended two to three hundred kilometers to the south (e.g., Rosales [1674] 1989:690, 696, 703). The historian Bengoa summarizes the period.

> Una tercera generación de caciques condujo la guerra entre el 1560 y el 80 (50). Fue un tiempo de guerra casi permanente. Los españoles eran pocos y trataban de hacer trabajar a los mapuches por la fuerza de las armas; había guerras, batallas, masacres. Los españoles sembraban el temor en las rucas y territorios mapuches. Muchos indígenas huyeron hacia las montañas o a poblar tierras del interior, donde aun no se aventuraban los invasores. (Bengoa 1985:31)

A third generation of caciques led the war between 1560 and 1580. It was a time of almost constant warfare. The Spanish were few and tried to oblige the Mapuche to work by force of arms; there were wars, battles, massacres. The Spanish fostered fear in Mapuche dwellings and territories. Many indians fled to the mountains or to settle lands in the interior, where the invaders still did not venture. (Bengoa 1985:31)

In the following account, Bengoa cites Quiroga, a Spanish soldier writing about the fluctuating size and displacement of local indigenous populations in the mid-1600s. Quiroga observes that prior to the Spanish arrival the Araucanians lived in larger, more nucleated settlements composed of hundreds and possibly thousands of families, but due to warfare they dispersed into smaller communities. This patterning also is inferred from the archaeology of the Purén and Lumaco Valley, which shows that large and permanent agricultural populations existed in late pre-Hispanic times and occasionally in historic times (see Chapter 6).

viven estos indios derramados por montes y valles, retirados los unos de los otros, y este modo de vivir es proporcionado al modo de mantenerse . . . y como nunca tuvieron pueblos, así nunca se han reducido a ellos hasta hoy, ni es fácil reducirlos y reformar esta costumbre antigua, pues ninguna razón de conveniencia podrá persuadirlos a mudar la forma del gobierno en que nacieron y se enseñaron. En la antigüedad vivían derramados en grandes vegas y dilatadas valles, y aun en los montes, *según demuestran las faldas y las cumbres labradas para los sembrados y estaban más juntos y unidos que en el tiempo presente porque había cien mil familias en muchas partes donde hoy no se hallan cien familias*; y así como en tierra desocupada están muchas leguas apartadas unas parcialidades de otras, asimismo los indios de ellas, cada uno en su rincón o quebrada; y esto les sirve de estar más espaciosos, y asímismo de estar más defendidos de las invasiones de nuestras armas, pues no es fácil acometer a muchos juntos ni apresar a los que están separados, porque cada cual tiene en su rancho la huida puesta para el bosque, de calidad que al menor rumor se ocultan como los animales en sus cuevas. (Quiroga [1690] 1979; cited in Bengoa 2003:178)

these indians live scattered over hills and valleys, distant from each other and this way of life is congruent with their means of subsistence . . . and since they never had towns, thus they have never been gathered into such until now, nor is it easy to gather them and change this ancient custom, since no reason of convenience can persuade them to change the form of government into which they were born and are accustomed. Formerly they lived scattered on wide river bottoms and broad valleys, and even in the mountains, as the slopes and summits modified for cultivated fields indicate and they were closer together and more united than at the present time because there were one hundred thousand families in many places where today there are not one hundred families, and, as if it were uninhabited land, the lineages are separated from each other by many leagues and the Indians in them, each one in his distant place or valley; and this enables them to occupy greater areas and in like manner to be better defended against our armed invasions, since it is difficult to attack many together or to take prisoner those who are so widely separated, because each one has on his property a path for flight into the forest, so that at the least rumor they hide themselves like animals in their lairs. (Quiroga [1690] 1979; cited in Bengoa 2003:178)

Depopulation, population movement, and amalgamation took place for reasons other than warfare, fragmentation, and dispersion. The abandonment of some areas, and subsequent amalgamations of survivors in continuing or new settlements, also was related to a response to depopulation from European-introduced epidemic diseases (see Chapter 7). Bengoa (2003) has estimated up to a 30 percent decline among some defeated northern Araucanian populations during the early historical period due to disease. I suspect that populations located south of the Bio Bio frontier probably suffered less loss, because they were more isolated from contact with the Spanish. Nonetheless, disease also must have led to a general decline in the political complexity of some southern areas due to abandonment and depopulation. In other areas, where groups were coalescing, complexity may have increased, as occurred in Purén and Lumaco as a more organized response to the Spanish invasion and because they already had the organizational infrastructure and tactical know-how to advance quicker. Yet, even where disease may have played a significant role in sociocultural change, we cannot entirely determine how the change was played out socially and demographially. For example, the spread of disease may have brought about the abandonment of some areas, but other social and political factors (e.g., warfare, recruitment, annexation) may have had a greater influence on where survivors moved and joined other groups and what the political outcome was from this greater aggregation. The chroniclers P. de Valdivia ([1555] 1978:39), Bibar ([1555] 1966:205), Mariño de Lobera ([1594] 1865:49–50, 69–70), and Góngora de Marmolejo ([1575] 1960:152) refer to high mortality rates in many areas brought about by both armed conflict and European diseases. Once again, Bengoa (1985:31) summarizes the chronicler's descriptions of the social impact of European diseases on the Araucanians.

Esos años [ca. 1558] surgió la primera gran peste de tifus, de los mapuches llamaron chavalongo. Se dice en las crónicas que habría muerto un 30 por ciento de la población indígena, lo que representaría alrededor de trescientas mil personas. Eı año 63, esto eso, cinco años más tarde, sobrevino la peste de viruela, que asoló a la población indígena, muriendo un quinto de ella, lo que equivale a unas 100 mil personas aproximadamente (46). Estas pestes afectaron principalmente a los picunches o mapuches del norte del Bío-Bío, que tenían más contactos con los españoles. En el valle Central de Chile quedó muy poca población aborigen; las pestes los diezmaron y muchos otros arrancaron a la zona sur a defenderse junto a los mapuches, Pero también murieron muchos mapuches del sur; se cuenta que en medio de las batallas se producían vómitos y muertes por el chavalongo. (Bengoa 1985:47)

During those years [ca. 1558] there was a severe typhus epidemic, which the Mapuche called *chavalongo*. The chroniclers state that about 30 per cent of the indian population died, which would have been some three hundred thousand persons. In [15]63, some five years later, there was an epidemic of smallpox which afflicted the indigenous population, killing about a fifth of them, which would come to approximately one hundred thousand people. These epidemics mainly affected the Picunche or Mapuche north of the Bío-Bío, who had more contact with the Spanish. Very few aboriginal inhabitants remained in the Central Valley of Chile; they had been decimated by epidemics and many had pulled up roots and gone south to defend themselves alongside the Mapuche. However, many Mapuche in the south also died; it is said that in the midst of the fighting, the *chavalongo* caused vomiting and death. (Bengoa 1985:47)

The major effect of widespread conflict and disease was the fragmentation and dissolution of patrilineal kin-groups in many areas and the search for new lands and new allies by those groups. These groups were often recruited by powerful lineage leaders such as those in Purén and Lumaco to increase their own group size, which also had been decimated by warfare, and to increase their labor force for communal projects (e.g., agricultural production, ceremonialism, other public works, mound construction). Leaders also expanded their territory by annexing neighboring groups by the process of territorial segmentation (see Chapter 7). We can infer from early texts that the annexation of neighbors operated in terms of the replication of similar ceremonial systems across adjacent lineage territories, whereby rulers transformed their neighbors into extensions of themselves. Thus, control of recruitment, annexation, and associated ceremonial feasting defined the increased power of leaders in some areas, and their capacity to fuel the network of kinship alliances and intergroup exchange, their military fecundity, and their authority and control over recruits. In addition to alliance building through these mechanisms, several extended families (*lov*) and patrilineages (*rehue*) in the late 1500s to the early 1700s united at a higher level of order to defend themselves and to engage in public ceremony. This higher level of multi-*rehue* organization was the *ayllarehue*, several of which came together in the latter half of the fifteenth century to form the feared *estado*. *Ayllarehue* were headed by powerful *apoülmen* who were, at the same time, *ülmen* of the most powerful *rehue* in the *ayllarehue* (Boccara 1999:453–457). Later, in the seventeenth century the *ayllarehue* united on an even larger geopolitical scale to form the interregional *butanmapu* organization, which was comprised of three and later four territorial divisions to defend the whole Araucania territory.

Of further interest are Boccara's comments on the recruitment, inculcation, and socialization of new members brought into the order of the *butanmapu* organization, on the influence of Spanish colonial order on this organization, and on the formal spatial placement of leaders and participants at its meetings. This same spatial formality exists today at *nguillatun*, *cahuin*, *palin*, and other public events, as discussed in Chapters 4, 5, 7, and 8.

> Vemos aquí que la formación de esta nueva unidad sociopolitica macroregional [futamapu] fue acompañada por el surgimiento de un nuevo sentimiento identitario que transcendía al simple grupo local antes constituído por el rehue . . . ofrecemos un ejemplo de como una institución o un dispositivo de poder colonial (el parlamento general) pudo influir tanto sobre los mecanismos politicos como sobre la conciencia de los indígenas. . . . A un nivel puramente formal, la realización regular de parlamentos obligaba a cada grupo a elegir individuos para representarlo hacia afuera de la comunidad. Además, cada furamapu debia elegir solamente a un representante, lo que contribuía aun más a la concentración del poder político y a la dinámica de la delegación de poder. Los parlamentos se con- virtieron en una reunión política obligatoria para todos los caciques de la Araucanía . . . los diferentes grupos que participaban en el parlamento general eran clasificados y repartidos en el espacio de manera rígida, creando así también una visión entre los mapuche de su espacio sociopolítico. Se asignaba un lugar propio a cada *futamapu* y las parcialidades, llamadas *sueltas*, debían ser necesariamente integradas a esta nueva representación y organización del espacio. Cada uno de los representantes indígenas debía encontrar su sitio y permanecer en él. La construcción de un espacio político ordenado según distritos claramente delimitados era concomitante a la inculcación de estructuras cognitivas y a la difusión de una norma

jurídico-política sin las cuales toda armonia entre el orden objetivo de las cosas y el orden subjetivo de las conciencias hubiese sido imposible. (Boccara 1999:458–60)

We see here that the formation of this new macroregional sociopolitical entity [*futumapu*] was accompanied by the upswelling of a new sentiment of identity which transcended the simple local group formerly constituted by the *rehue* . . . we offer an example of how colonial institution or colonial power structure (the general assembly [or *parlamento*] could influence both political practice and indigenous awareness. . . . At a purely formal level, holding regular assembly [*parlamento*] required each group to elect individuals to represent it outside the community. Moreover, each *futamapu* had to elect only one representative, which contributed still further to the concentration of political power and to the dynamic of the delegation of power. The assemblies [*parlamentos*] became a political meeting obligatory for all the caciques of Araucania . . . the different groups which participated in the general assembly [*parlamento*] were classified and distributed in space in a rigid fashion, thus creating among the Mapuche a vision of their sociopolitical space. Each *futamapu* was assigned its own place and the groups [*parcialidades* or *ayllarewes*] called unaffiliated were necessarily integrated into this new representation and organization of space. Each one of the indigenous representatives had to find his place and remain within it. The elaboration of a political space ordered by clearly delimited districts was concomitant with the inculcation of cognitive structures and the diffusion of a legal-political norm without which all harmony between the objective order of things and the subjective order of consciousness would have been impossible. (Boccara 1999: 458–60)

León (1999:136–37), a Chilean historian, refers to another Araucanian political unit, the *coyan*, that developed among *lonko* leaders in the 1700s to make a peace pact with the Spanish to end the war. Although he views the *coyan* as the closest unit to a state level of organization achieved by the Araucanians, other contemporary historians do not even mention it.

Padden's comments on the power and changing geopolitical structure of these political organizations are worth quoting.

The existence of a skilled and effective military force bespeaks the presence of a comparable political organization under whose genius it is formed and directed. In the development of Araucanian political organization the chronicles indicate two major forces at work: the geo-graphical particularism in which the Araucanians traditionally lived and a counterforce provoked by the presence of the enemy and inclin-ing towards Araucanian unity. Throughout the first century of con-quest ancient localism clashed with incipient nationalism. This conflict produced a political ambivalence which in itself contributed heavily to the cause of Araucanian independence. Centralization of politico-military authority was achieved to a point where successful resistance was possible, but did not develop to a state where the Spaniards could defeat and usurp it. (Padden 1993:78)

By 1594, according to Olaverría, the *estado* claimed suzerainty over all of the *allareguas* from the Bio-Bio to the Imperial River, and was held in dread by all of the Indians as far south as Osorno. The *estado* was so feared and respected, he said, that Indians in the extreme south would break the peace when the chiefs of the *estado* so desired. . . . Nevertheless, the chiefs never succeeded in gaining effective suzerainty, even for purposes of war. Authority continued to be local, rather than central, and cooperation was most often found in the realm of diplomacy.

   With the turn of the century a more precise political and military division was created by the Araucanians. The region between the Bio-Bio and Tolten rivers was divided into three longitudinal strips called *butanmapos*, each made up of various *allirewes [allareguas]*: they were the sub-Andean range, the central valley, and the coastal strip. Each *butan-mapo* had clearly defined limits and jurisdictions: each had, at least in time of war, a principal chief, or *toque* [with a hierarchy of lesser chiefs representing outlying areas]. It was customary for the chiefs to debate plans for war in a parliamentary junta in which the three territories were represented. Strategy was agreed upon by common consent. . . . The relationship between the local chiefs and territorial *toques* is not clear, but it seems likely that military power was held both to qualify and to assure authority. When disagreement occurred between *toques*, war between territories could and did sometimes develop. (Padden 1993:79)

Not included in Padden's discussion of these political units is the role of patrilin-eages as represented by their *toqui* and other secular leaders. On a regional level, the political organization of the Araucanians was the replication of local-level, patrilineage-based politics at ever-higher levels of incorporation (i.e., *lov, rehue, ayllarehue, butanmapus, coyan*). The patrilineage (*rehue*) was at the core of both the economy and politics. Differences between wealth and power within these lineages must have enabled certain individuals to claim leadership roles; they regulated conflict within the group and organized it for defense or aggression against enemies. Growth of larger units must have been an attempt by ambitious leaders to combine ever-greater numbers of groups under their control or representation. This process eventually resulted in the Araucanian creation of the broader tripartite and later quadripartite *butanmapu* (*futamapu*) system in the mid-seventeenth century (cf. Bengoa 2003:27) and possibly the *coyan*. An objective of this geopolitical system was to create a landscape of heterarchically ranked *ayllarehue* (see Chapters 7 and 8), all bound to the Araucanian cause, enabling a history of patrilineage royalty and dependents to be read through the material traces of cultural and visual effects (e.g., *kuel, rehuekuel*). The relative rank and geographic position of the *ayllarehue* members of this system and its earlier expression in the so-called *estado* was to defend the territory against outside invaders, but this seems not to have always been the case and alliances were constructed and broken in all directions, including with the Spanish. These different levels of organization also developed new identities associated with different orders and symmetries of political meetings, plans, and cultural spaces.

Although warfare with the Spanish was periodic and generally of a low intensity, feuding existed regularly among various Araucanian populations in late pre-Hispanic and early Hispanic times, with the taking of prisoners (as sacrificial victims or as slaves) being an important objective. Public feasts and political gatherings were numerous and often involved human sacrifice of captives. Speakers at these events appealed to the deity *Pillan* for victory in battle and for many captives. To return with captives or the heads of enemies was glorious and gave prestige to warriors. Rituals with fictive battles and with the *palin* warrior's games were important for organizing the relations between different patrilineages (*rehue*) and multilineage communties within *ayllarehue* and for establishing individual and familty social status. Armed conflict provided warriors with the opportunity to gain the highest social status by proving their worth in real battle and by incorporating the Spanish "other" into increased identity and exchange, as argued by Boccara.

> Así, la guerra se dibuja también como una institución que estructuraba las relaciones entre las diversas unidades sociales de los ayllarehue. La lucha para la captura de trofeos guerreros... ponía en movimiento una verdadera dinámica de don/contra-don entre los diversos rehue de un solo ayllarehue. Un lebo que había capturado a un enemigo lo enviaba, vivo o muerto, a otro lebo con el fin de obligarlo a que le devolviera el don. Por eso, el lebo que recibía un trofeo de guerra se veía obligado a entrar en la dinámica guerrera para capturar a un enemigo, decapitarlo y mandar su cabeza al lebo donador, cerrando

así, por lo menos temporariamente, el ciclo de la deuda. (Boccara 2000:457)

Thus, war also can be seen as an institution that structured the relationships between the different social units of the *ayllarehue*. The struggle for the capture of trophies of war...set in motion a true dynamic of gift/counter-gift between the diverse *rehue* of a single *ayllarehue*. A *lebo* which had captured an enemy sent him, dead or alive, to another *lebo* in order to obligate them to return the gift. For this reason, the *lebo* which had received a war trophy was obliged to enter the war dynamic to capture an enemy, decapitate him and send the head to the donor *lebo*, thus closing the cycle of debt, at least temporarily. (Boccara 2000:457)

[La Guerra Reche] Jugaba un papel fundamental en la elaboración de la identidad propia y en la producción del "sí-mismo" y del "otro." En efecto, la Guerra reche era una verdedera Guerra de captación de la diferencia, de construcción del "sí-mismo" en un movimiento de apertura canibal hacia el "otro". Todo lo que se hacía en las prácticas y representaciones de la guerra tendía a la asimilación de las cualidades del enemigo; asi, durante el combate los guerreros hacían todo lo possible para capturar un objeto que simbolizara al otro. De vuelta de la expedición, los guerreros y úlmen se vestían como españoles en un significativo movimiento de identificación con sus contrincantes. Pero es seguramente en el trabajo ritual realizado sobre el cuerpo del cautivo que se percibe de la manera más clara ese afán de digerir al otro, aunque no todos los cautivos eran "buenos para comer." El cuerpo que servía para los rituales de antropofagia era el de un enemigo famoso y valiente. En tal caso el cautivo era decapitado y su cabeza empleada como recipiente-trofeo para las ceremonial guerreras. Se confeccionaban flautas de los huesos de las piernas y una especie de gorra guerrera de las quijadas y la piel de la cara. (Boccara 2000:438)

[The *Reche* War] played an important role in the elaboration of a self-identity and the creation of a sense of "self" and "other." Indeed, the *Reche* War was a war of seizing the difference, of creating the "self" in a cannibal movement of opening toward the "other." Everything that was done in the conduct and representation of the war led to the assimilation of characteristics of the enemy; thus during combat the warriors did everything possible to capture an object which symbolized the other. On their return from the campaign, the warriors and *ülmen* dressed like Spaniards in a significant movement of identification with their opponents. However, it is surely in the ritual treatment of the body of the captive that this desire to consume the other can be most clearly seen although not all the captives were "good to eat." The body used in the rituals of cannibalism was that of a famous and courageous enemy. In this case the captive was beheaded and his head used as a trophy vessel for the war rituals. Flutes were made from the leg bones and a sort of war cap was made from the jaws and the skin of the face. (Boccara 2000:438)

In the mid-1600s, Rosales refers to Lientur, a *toqui* war leader from Purén, who invited his people and his allies from distant areas to participate in large feasts to celebrate victories in battle and to sacrifice captives. The sponsorship of feasts and human sacrifice must have given much social prestige to hosting leaders.

> y por rumores de que Lientur [después de derrotar la ciudad de Chillan] revoluía, tubo toda la gente junta, y en arma, hasta que se supo cómo avía llegado a su tierra y celebrado la victoria con grandes fiestas y borracheras...y tienen por una de sus mayores fiestas el matar un Español en sus borracheras, y cantar Victoria con su cabeza, y comerle el corazón. (Rosales [1674] 1989:1039)

> and because of rumors that Lientur (after defeating the city of Chillan] was returning, he had all the people together and at arms until they learned that he had arrived in his country and celebrated the victory with great feasts and drinking parties . . . and they considered it one of their greatest celebrations to kill a Spaniard in their drunken feasts and to sing the victory with his head and to eat his heart. (Rosales [1674] 1989:1039)

> que en la plaza de sus borracheras tenían desmochados, en uno de los cuales tenían puesta por triunfo la cabeza del desgraciado Capitán Antón Sánchez. (Rosales [1674] 1989:842)

> in the field where they held their drinking feasts, they had trophy heads [displayed] and in one of these as a sign of victory they had put the head of the unfortunate Captain Anton Sanchez. (Rosales [1674] 1989:842)

In the mid-1600s, Quiroga ([1686] 1979) notes that allies were invited to sacrifice captives at feasts.

> Los prisioneros sirven para celebrar sus juntas y borracheras, sacrificándolos en honor de sus triunfos, y de su valor, y así hacen una grande junta en que convocan a todos los caciques de unas y otras parcialidades; y presentes en concurso grande, sacan el corazón al mísero cautivo antes de quitarle la vida.... (Quiroga [1686] 1979: 29)

> The prisoners are used as sacrifices in honor of their victories and their valor in the celebration of their feasts and drinking parties and thus they hold a great gathering in which they call all the caciques of one and another lineages and when they are in a great multitude, they take out the heart of the unfortunate captive while he is still alive.... (Quiroga [1686] 1979: 29)

The exchanges between lineages spurred a greater interest in the consumption of the other or exotic – in this case goods, emblems, and Spanish captives and trophy heads (see Rosales [1674] 1989:684–688) – and later gave the Araucanians the symbolic and social capacity to incorporate even more conspicuous goods. Thus, what began as indigenous symbols and Spanish trophy head and dress became a broader material economy in the late 1700s. From the late 1700s onward with the increased acquisition of the horse, the Araucanians more frequently raided long distances north of the Bio Bio River and into Argentina, which shifted the political economy in some areas from a farming subsistence to commercialization and a prestige good economy (Araya 1999; Canals Frau 1946; Jones 1999; León 1991; Mandrini 1984; Nacuzzi 1998; Palermo 1986; Villalobos et al. 1982; Villalobos and Pinto 1985; Zapater 1973). This resulted in the assertion of a new local and regional polity extending into Argentina and stemming from the accumulation of capital and wealth. Beginning in the mid-eighteenth century, various Araucanian groups established territorial rights and hierarchies and competed over trading rights with the Europeans and even more extensive raiding and marauding into Argentina.

Between the sixteenth and eighteenth centuries, lineage-based communities were turned into defensive settlements and later into maurauding groups. During this period, people were separated from their home lands, and the Spanish armies drove some people into exile and ransacked the land. Subsequently, I submit that some leaders sought to reassemble a new kind of setting (*sensu* Wolf 1999) – a restructured "people place" and "social space" – by resettling the region with their own people or with refugees who were depopulated and homeless. In the Purén and Lumaco Valley, these settings probably were the multimound *rehuekuel* of multiple lineages and the social spaces were the multi-*rehue ayllarehue*, both of which were associated with continuous land, history, and ancestors. In the process, some leaders hoped to transform a power that was based on violent conquest into legitimate and traditional authority. In assembling a new kind of people place at *rehuekuel*, the Araucanians drew on traditional and Andean institutions of leadership, priestly shamanism, ancestor cults, fertility rites, and trophy head-taking to establish social prestige and social cohesion. But it was clearly the threat of warfare that spurred a greater sense of unity and purpose among the Araucanians and developed pan-regional ideas of an ethnic nationalism. Leiva (1977) comments that:

> Los araucanos de ese tiempo nos parecen también un caso de desen-volvimiento de 1a cultura a partir del espiritu national: la resistencia a la dominación y la autosuficiencia. Vemos además que entre los arau-canos se despertaron intereses crecientemente nacionales de una man-era intensa y desconocida antes. Tenemos así una prueba de la tenaci-dad del vínculo, de las cualidades culturales con el suelo, de lo que llama Kroeber, "la facultad a un mismo tiempo absorbente y resistente de una cultura" que, durante muchos años, por más que se difunden préstamos culturales a su interior, logra conversarse como algo propio. Por último, los araucanos logran encontrar la norma dinámica para organizar su sociedad: la guerra. (Leiva 1977:160)

> The Araucanians of that time appear to us as a case of the development of a culture beginning with a national spirit: the resistence to domina-tion and self-sufficiency. Moreover, we see that there arose among the Araucanians an increasingly intense and previously unknown national interest. Thus we have proof of the tenacity of the linkage of cultural ties with the land, of what Kroeber calls "the capacity of a culture to absorb and resist at the same time," which, over many years, for all that cultural borrowings diffuse into the interior, became its own. In the end, the Araucanians succeeded in finding the dynamic prin-ciple to organize their society: warfare. (Leiva 1977:160)

To conclude this section, the written texts suggests that competitive lineage leaders, with their intensive and escalating monopolies of recruitment and feasting, were products of the centralizing effect of increased conflict. As discussed later, this is collaborated by the archaeology (see Chapter 6), which suggests (1) an explosive buildup of mound, feasting, domestic, and defensive sites and the rise of the *estado*, (2) heavy population fragmentation and displacement in some areas, (3) the appearance of supra-local *ayllarehue* and patrilineage polities, and the eventual development of a new social order and the regional Araucanian polity between 1550 and 1650 (see above discussions and Chapter 1). The order had an aesthetic appeal and a utopic vision of accomplishment, history, and nationhood. These developments occurred primarily in places like Purén and Lumaco, which were the prototype systems for things to come in other areas. These places were aesthetically spatialized and materialized in the *kuel* and *rehuekuel* under study here.

LINKING KUEL ARCHAEOLOGY, ETHNOHISTORY, AND ETHNOGRAPHY

In drawing on documentary and archaeological records, we can understand better the temporal, terminological, and functional relationships between mound building – a socially engineered utopic landscape – and its aesthetics, leadership and *kuel* burial, ancestor worship, and *rehuekuel* from the sixteenth to nineteenth century. Several Spanish chroniclers and foreign travelers have described the burial settings of important leaders and how mounds were constructed physically and socially. Particularly important are the passages by Bibar and Rosales, who observed ceremonies in the mid-1500s and mid-1600s, respectively. Rosales associates *regua* (*regue, rehue* or *rewe*) ceremonial areas on high hills with interlineage political meetings, warrior games, leader's burial in mounds, the placement of wooden ancestral statues on their tombs, and ritual feasting. His descriptions of the *regua* place where these different but related activities came together and where ritual priests (*boquibuye*) lived are remarkably similar to the *nguillatun* ceremonies performed on the *ñichi* platforms of *rehuekuel* ceremonial centers by *machi* today. Described next are the textual descriptions of key chroniclers that reveal continuity in the form and function of *kuel* and in the rituals associated with them from the present-day ethnographic record to the ethnohistorical and archaeological records.

Writing in the middle of the sixteenth century, Bibar ([1555] 1966) states that:

> Ciertas veces del año se ajuntan en una parte que ellos tienen senalado para aquel efecto que se llama <u>regua</u>, que es tanto como decir "parte donde se ayuntan"...este ayuntamiento es para averiguar pleitos y muertes y alli se casan y beben largo.... Y todo aquello que alli se acuerda y hace es guardado y tenido y no quebrantado. Estando alli todos juntos estos principales, pide cada uno su justicia. Si tienen Guerra con otro señor todos estos cabis y señores son obligados a salir con sus armas y gente a favorecer aquella parcialidad según y como allí se ordena...y allí venden y compran los días aquel cabildo y junta dura.... (Bibar [1555] 1966:160, [*sic*]: cited in Montecino 1980:31])

> At certain times of the year they come together in a place which they have set aside for that purpose which is called *regua*, which is to say

"place where they meet"... this gathering is to hear complaints and deaths and there they marry and drink long... and all that which is agreed and done is kept and held and not broken. When all these chiefs are there together, each one asks for justice [for his claim]. If they are at war with another chief, all these *cabis* and chiefs are required to come out with arms and men to support that group as they are ordered... and there they sell and buy during the days that councils and meetings lasts.... (Bibar [1555] 1966:160, [*sic*] cited in Montecino 1980:31)

In the following century, Rosales describes similar public ceremonies and the burial of important leaders on "*regue*" hilltops where ritual games were played and feasts were performed to honor the dead.

Los Indios de Arauco, y amigos antiguos, viendo las inquietudes, que podían causer estos quentos, y deseosos de hazer de su parte alguna diligencia, por conseruar en nuestra amistad, los indios de Purén, y de la Costa, trazaron de hazer una inuención, que solo de tarde en tarde la hazen, y es entre ellos un gran sacramento, y medio efficaz, para conseruar las pazes. Que es, hazer Boquibuyes, que es un género de sacerdotes... los quales tratan de la paz, y visten hábito differente, abitan en una montaña, que tienen para este propósito, que llaman Regue, y es como su conuento donde se recogen.... Y el tiempo, que son religiosos, no puede ninguno tomar las armas de sus soldados, ni auer guerra.... Lo que al presente haze para el intento es, que los Araucanos conuidaron a los de Purén, que nunca avían estado de paz, sino quando más veinte, y quatro horas. Y ahora la abáan abrazado con veras, y para que perseuerassen en ella algun tiempo, y se fuessen afficionando, les digeron, que hiziessen Boquibuyes, que ellos también los harían, y concertándose, eligieron los Caciques más principales de una, y otra Prouincia, que para el officio sacerdotal, no admite esta gente personas plebeyas (Rosales [1674] 1989:1154).

The indians of Arauco and their long-time allies seeing the restlessness that these tales were causing, and wanting to undertake a task so as to retain our friendship, the indians of Purén and the coast undertook to hold a ceremony that they only hold from time to time, which is considered a great ceremony and a very effective means for keeping the peace. This is the installation of *Boquibuyes*, who are a kind of priest... these make peace, and wear different dress, they live on a hill, which they have for this purpose which they call *regue* and it is like a convent where they stay.... and while they are priests none can

take up the weapons of their warriors, nor make war. . . . What was
pertinent for this effort was that the Araucanos invited those from
Purén, who had never made peace or only for twenty-four hours. . . .
And now they have truly embraced it, and so they may keep it for some
time and come to value it, they told them to designate *Boquibuyes* and
that they would also do this, and coming to agreement, they elected
the highest-ranking chiefs from one Province and the other, for these
people do not allow commoners to hold priestly office. (Rosales [1674]
1989:1154)

Pero los caciques y indios nobles, para que su memoria quede para
siempre, se hacen enterrar en los cerros más altos y en los lugares donde
se juntan a jugar a la chueca o en los regues, que son los lugares donde
se juntan a tratar las cosas de importancia, que son como los lugares de el cabildo, y como allí se hacen las borracheras, y las fiestas
principales, la parentela va antes de beber, a derramar en su sepultura
cada uno un jarro de chicha, brindándole para que beba y se halle en
la fiesta. (Rosales [1674] 1989:164)

But the caciques and noble indians, so that their memory should
endure forever, have themselves interred on the highest hills and in
places where they gather to play *chueca* [*palin*] or in the *regues* which
are the places where they gather to consider matters of importance,
which are like the places where the *cabildo* [council] meets, and there
they also hold the drinking parties and the principal feasts, the kindred
before beginning the drinking, goes to his [the dead chief's] tomb, each
one pouring a jar of chicha onto the tomb, offering it to him so that
he may drink and take part in the feast. (Rosales [1674] 1989:164)

Observing in the 1640s and writing later, Quiroga ([1690] 1979) describes a similar
hilltop burial for a ruler and the placement of a mound on top of his tomb.

entierran [los caciques] en el campo en un cerro alto. . . . Luego le
entran dentro y le ponen sus mujeres carne llega a la otra parte de la
Cordillera, que en su sentir es la otra vidon, y sobre el cuerpo levantan
un gran montón de piedras y tierra porque no vuelva salir y yerre el
camino del dentro del mundo. . . . (Quiroga [1690] 1979:293)

They bury [the *caciques*] on a high hill in the countryside. . . . They
later bury the body and their wives place meat [for the journey] to
the other side of the cordillera, which in their reckoning is the other
life, and they place a large mound of stones and earth over the body
so that it should not come out again and wander on the road from the
world within [below]. . . . (Quiroga [1690] 1979:293)

20. A nineteenth century cemetery site showing *chemamüll* and a *machi*. Courtesy of the Biblioteca Nacional de Chile.

Revealed in these passages is the spatial and social importance of *rehue* as isolated hilltop places where important ritual feasts, political meetings, and games (*palin*) were performed by relatives, friends, allies, and lineages associated with important ancestors and deities in the upper world and where the *boquibuye* (*boquivoye*, *machi?*), who ritually administer the feasts, reside. Oral tradition in Purén and Lumaco points to the *rehuekuel* located on high, flat *ñichi* hilltops overlooking the valley floor as those places described in the texts where important leaders were buried, where *cahuins* and various feasts (e.g., *nguillatun*) were and still are carried out by their descendents, and, in a few places, where *machi* still reside and perform the same rituals as the *boquibuye* once did. One of the most powerful and knowledgeable *machi* in the valley was Cármen who died a few years ago and who was quoted at the outset of Chapter 1. She lived on top of a sacred hill where she performed *nguillatun* in a *rehuekuel* that had a *rehue* pole and a small *kuel*. Today, *machi* not only refer to *rehue* as the stepped *llangi llangi* (i.e., *axis mundi* and *imago mundi*), which they climb to ascend to and descend from the upper world of the deities, but also to the *rehuekuel* or old *nguillatun* fields where mounds were built on *ñichi* hilltops and where ceremonies were performed. They say that interred in the mounds are principal *toqui* war leaders and *lonko* whose tombs are seen, remembered, and revered by the living. They also report that the ritual consumption of *mudai* by the living and the placement of wooden ancestral statues, or *chemamüll*, at the mounds sustain the link between sacred landscapes, distant sightings to them, and multilineage identities and memories (Fig. 20). *Chemamüll*

21. An ancient unnamed *kuel* (mound) and low *rehuekuel* (platform and ceremonial field) used until the early twentieth century for *nguillatun* ceremonies near Pucón in the Andean cordillera about 180 km southeast of Purén. Informants say that the *nguillatun* site was selected for ceremonies because it had a *kuifilkuel* (old mound) on it. The human figure standing to the left provides a scale.

still exist in traditional areas and stand in *nguillatun* fields and other sacred areas as monuments to important lineage ancestors. As mentioned in Chapter 1, today, several old *kuel* and *rehuekuel* are still used as *nguillatun* fields in the Araucanian region (Fig. 21: also see Chapters 4–6).

In referring to ancient ceremonies in the 1640s, Núñez de Pineda describes a feast he attended whereby the lineage leaders danced and drank on various levels of an "*andamio*," a term employed by seventeenth century Spanish to describe an artificial platform and possible mound. Later, during the feast, he was taken to the highest level of the platform so everyone could see him as the captive. Núñez de Pineda also states that the structure measured several meters in height. His description of this elevated artificial platform may the earliest reference to a ritual associated with a *kuel*.

> Asentaronse todos a la vista de los que estaban cantando y bailando en las gradas y escaleras del andamio. Tenian por delante los seis tinajones referidos; y levantose el cacique con un criado, y fuelos repartiendo a los recién venidos.... El cacique Huirumanque, advertido de otros que le asistían, dijo a Maulicán, que me rogase, que subiese arriba a

la grada más alta del andamio...llegó el cacique y otros cuatro de ellos a donde yo estaba con mis compañeros y el viejo Llancareu, repartiendo la chichi que nos habian traído, y con amorosas razones y corteses súplicas me pidio que le hiciese favor de subir a la última grada del andamio.... En este me puso el cacique en la primera grada, que estaría del suelo una vara, y había sobre ella otras cinco gradas, a distancia de tres cuartas poco más o menos las unas de las otras. (Núñez de Pineda [1673] 2003:524–525)

Everyone sat in sight of those who were singing and dancing on the steps and terraces of the structure. In front of them were the six large jars already mentioned, and the *cacique* stood up with an assistant, and distributed them among the recently arrived.... The *cacique* Huiru-manque, alerted by others who were assisting him, told Maulican to entreat me to climb up to the highest level of the mound. The *cacique* came to where I was with my companions and the ancient Llancareu, distributing the *chicha* which they had brought us, and with friendly reasoning and courteous requests, he asked me to go up to the highest level of the structure.... At this, the *cacique* set me on the first level which was about a *vara* above the ground and there were five other levels above it, with about three *cuartas* [one fourth of a vara] separating them. (Núñez de Pineda [1673] 2003:524–525)

This is an interesting account because commoners who are invited to drink *chicha* or to consume a sacrificed animal near or on a mound today are allowed to stand only at the base of the *kuel* or to step onto its lowest or middle levels, which usually are defined by the first turn of an ascending footpath used by the *machi* to reach the top of the mound. In a 1987, I was invited by an officiating *machi* at a *nguillatun* ceremony to drink *chicha* at the base of a mound in *Ñachekuel*, a *rehuekuel* and *nguillatun* field located near Lumaco (Fig. 22). The base was about 80 cm above the level of the *ñichi* platform and about 2 m below the top of the mound. In Núñez de Pineda's description, if each of the six levels of the *andamio* was approximately a "*vara*" high, which is a little less than a meter in height, then the structure would have been at least 6 m in height. Although we do not know for certain that Núñez de Pineda's *andamio* was a *kuel* or mound, we can say with certainty that he described an artificial platform structure used for public ceremony and by exclusive persons.

In comparison, Bengoa (2003) interprets the same description of the *andamio* mentioned by Núñez de Pineda as wooden "*tablones*" or planks which formed a wooden scaffolding-like dance platform. (In modern Spanish, *andamio* means scaffolding.) In fairness to Bengoa, at the time of his writing he was not familiar with *kuel* in the archeological record and thus did not consider the possibility

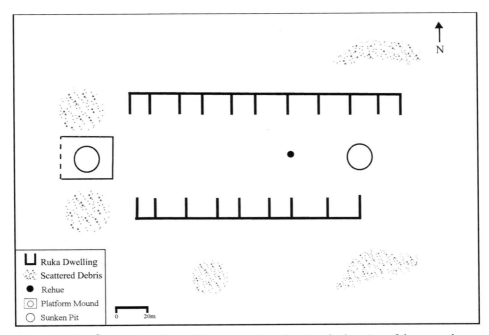

22. Plan of the Ñachekuel nguillatun field in Rucalleco showing the location of the mound on a small ñichi platform, the rehue, the seating areas of participants along the two opposing side of the field, and a sunken pit to bury trash during ceremony.

of the *andamio* being an earthen structure with wooden statues, for instance. The wooden planks mentioned in the quote may refer to *chemamüll* (wooden ancestral figures placed on the top of the graves of leaders buried in mounds; see Moesbach 1936:405 and Rosales above and below). Described below by Rosales is the placement of wooden statues, which he calls "*cruces*," on the graves of dead rulers (see Fig. 20).

> En sus cementerios plantan cruces en las tumbas de sus caciques; en los parlamentos o tratados que sé hacen con ellos, exigen tambien que se les plante la cruz en memoria de lo sucedido, y mientras la ven, guardan fidelilad y respeto. (Rosales [1674] 1989:27)

> They place crosses on the tombs of their *caciques*, during the assemblies they hold with them, they also demand that a cross be erected in memory of what occurred, and for as long as/while they can see it they remain faithful and respectful. (Rosales [1674] 1989:27)

It is possible that Núñez de Pineda's description of the wooden platform structure is correct and that he substituted the only conceptual term (*andamio*) he knew in seventeenth century Spanish to describe an elevated artificial structure. Curiously, he is the only chronicler or traveler ever to describe this type of structure. Other chroniclers mention *monticulos*, *cerritos*, or *piramides* to refer to artificial structures. Writing in the 1640s and in the vicinity of Purén, Núñez de Pineda also describes the social events accompanying the funerary or *awn (awün)* rite of a leader's son and then his participation in a feasting ritual on and around a "*cerro levantado*" or an artificial mound.

> ... el primer que echó tierra sobre el sepulcro fue su padre [del hijo muerto], con cuya acción se levantó otro alarido como los pasados, y entre todos los dolientes y convidados cubrieron el hoyo en un momento y sobre él formaron un cerro levantado en buena proporción, el cual se divisaba desde la casa muy a gusto y de algunos leguas se Señoreaba mejor.... Después de acaba esta acción, se sentaron a la redonda del cerillo y pusieron todos las botijas de chicha de la propia suerte en orden, y como había mas de doscientos almas, brevemente las despacharon. (Núñez de Pineda [1673] 1973:187–191)

> ... the first to place earth on the tomb was his father [of his dead son], at which act there arose another cry of grief like the ones before, and between all the mourners and their guests the tomb was covered in a moment and over it was placed a good sized mound, which could be easily seen from the house and it was prominent from several leagues away.... After completing this ceremony, they sat down all around the base of the mound and placed their jars of *chicha* in proper order according to their group, and since there were more than two hundred souls, they smashed them in short order. (Núñez de Pineda [1673] 1973:187–191)

Today, in many traditional areas the Mapuche still place drinking vessels containing *chicha* around the tomb of an important leader and smash others over his mounded grave. When translating the Mapudungun used in ritual to Spanish, informants also use the term "*despachar*," which means that the *chicha* vessels are raised above the drinkers head and smashed over the grave. Further, based on ethnoarchaeological studies in the study area (Dillehay n.d.), we can suggest that Núñez de Pineda's description of placing vessels in "proper order" refers to the social rank of the 200 souls who probably are the relatives and friends of the deceased (see Chapter 5). Today, in funerary rites, the highest ranking relatives of the deceased (i.e., fathers, mothers, sons, wives, daughters, and brothers) locate their drinking vessels closest to the head and shoulders of the deceased in his/her grave. The vessels of people of lesser rank are arranged in concentric rings farther away from the body. Food, drink, and tobacco are stored in these latter containers. Also important in this passage is mention of the preeminent position of the mound built over the dead son's grave and how it could easily be seen from several leagues away. As discussed in Chapters 5 and 6, the visual sighting of mounds and the clearing and preparation of *rehuekuel* landscapes is significant for cross-valley participation of multiple lineages in public ceremony.

Núñez de Pineda also describes a feast that he attended with Anganamón, a powerful leader who resided in the Purén Valley, which took place around a plaza and a palisaded space. Of particular interest is his observation of a specific seating arrangement for each lineage, a pattern that still occurs today in *nguillatun* and other ceremonies and again reminds us of the "proper" spatial placement of drinking vessels.

> Después de haber brindado a todos los caciques y hombres principales, Anganamón con los suyos cogió la delantera y dió principio a nuestra marcha, a quien atropados yen el cuerpo fuimos siguiendo sus pasos, hasta llegar al sitio en que habíamos de asistir, inmediato al palenque y andamio de el baile. Alli nos asentamos en unos tapetes los que éramos de nuestra parcialidad, adonde trajeron luego una oveja de la tierra, que sería a modo de camello. (Núñez de Pineda [1673] 2003:522)

> After toasting all the *caciques* and principal men, Anganamón took the lead with his men and began our march, and mustered in a company, we followed his footsteps until we arrived at the place next to the palisade and mound for the dance where we were to attend [the ceremonies]. There we sat on woven reed mats which belonged to our lineage [*parcialidad*], where they then brought a llama [lit. sheep of the land], which was like a kind of camelid. (Núñez de Pineda [1673] 2003:522)

In the 1700s, Molina (1788) also describes a leader's burial in the form of a mound or pyramid and the placement of *chicha* vessels on the tomb.

> ...lo entierran con caballo y se despiden con mucho llanto...y después volver a cubrir de tierra y de piedras, en forma pirámidal, sobre la qual derraman chichi en abundancia. (Molina 1788:91)

> ...they bury him with his horse and they say farewell with much weeping...and afterwards [the tomb] is covered again with earth and stones in the form of a pyramid over which they pour abundant *chicha*. (Molina 1788:91)

In an account from the late 1800s, Coña (1973:395–415) mentions the elaborate and well-attended burial of a *lonko* ruler whose grave was covered by a mound. Offerings were placed in the tomb, and a wooden pole with his image on it was erected on top of the grave. Coña also notes the number of days a large group of relatives and friends spent in rituals and other social events to sustain social ties and obligations between them, the dead leader, and lineage ancestors.

> Aprovisionado el difunto, vuelven a tapar la canoa y erígen un túmulo de tierra encima. El palo con la figura (del finado) lo plantan a la cabecera del sepultado.... Terminado el túmulo, empieza a platicar un cacique. (Coña 1973:412)

> Once the deceased was supplied [with food and drink], they covered the canoe again and erected an earthen mound on top of it. The pole with the image (of the deceased) was placed at the head of the burial.... When the mound was finished a chief began to speak. (Coña 1973: 412)

> En el cementerio, el cadáver fue depositado sobre el suelo, se le colocaron al lado sus armas, algunos choclos y varios cántaros de chichi y aguardiente. Luego cada uno de los presentes le hizo un saludo de despidad, deseánoloe [sic for deseándole] buen viaje, y se cubrió el cuerpo con piedras, hasta formar una pirámide, sobre el cual se puso una sencilla cruz de madera. (Coña 1973:441)

> In the cemetery, the deceased was placed on the ground, his weapons, some corn cobs, and several jars of *chicha* and *aguardiente* were placed beside him. Then every one of those present bade him farewell, wishing him a good journey, and the body was covered with stones to form a pyramid, above which was placed a simple wooden cross. (Coña 1973:441)

Observing Mapuche burial practices in the late 1800s and early 1900s and commenting on the observations of early chroniclers, Guevara (1925:47–48) writes about the construction of a ruler's burial mound on a hilltop, the offerings made to the nearby *rehue*, and the burial of commoners in other places.

> Cuando llegaron los españoles i aun después de la conquista, las tumbas de los caciques se colocaban en los cerros o en lugares destinados a las reuniones, donde se hallaba plantado el *rehue* para que recibieran la chicha i los comestibles que les ofendaban sus descendientes. E1 resto de los individuos que no investían autoridad debieron ser depositados en sitios o faldas vecinas, más o menos apartados, a juzgar por los restos de pedernal, de alfareria y huesos que se han encontrado en algunos parades. Se llamaban estos enterramientos *puullil* (de *puulli*, loma, palabra anticuada). Con anterioridad a la conquista española, los

cadáveres no recibían propiamente sepultura sino que eran colocados sobre el suelo i cubiertos de tierra i piedras hasta formar una especie de tumulo. Envolvíanlos en cuero o cortezas de arboles. A esta costumbre sucedió la de sepultar los muertos en hoyos muy superfiales, sobre los cuales se aggregaba el montículo. (Guevara 1925:47–48)

When the Spanish arrived and even after the conquest, the tombs of the *caciques* were placed on the hills or in places set aside for the assemblies, where the *rehue* were set up so they would receive the *chicha* and food that their descendants offered them. The rest of the people who were not invested with authority were buried in nearby places or hillsides, more or less isolated, to judge by the remains of flint, pottery, and bone which have been found in some spots. These burials were called *puullil* (an ancient term for hill). Before the Spanish conquest, the bodies were not actually buried, but were placed on the ground and covered with earth and rocks until a kind of mound was formed. The dead were wrapped in leather or tree bark. This custom was followed by that of burying the dead in very shallow graves over which a mound was built. (Guevara 1925:47–48)

Also writing in the late 1800s and early 1900s was Housse (1939), who notes that:

Los Araucanos limitaron antíguamente la costumbre inca de construir encima una pirámide [tumulo] de piedras destrabadas por los que derramaban chorros de chicha. . . . (Housse 1939:320)

In the past, the Araucanians practiced the Inca custom of constructing a pyramid of broken rocks [over the tomb] over which they poured streams of *chicha*. . . . (Housse 1939:320)

Un año después del entierro, los antiguos mapuches volvieron al cementerio, degollaban sobre la tumba varias ovejas, de modo que la tierra se emparara en sangre, postrera pitanza del fallecido. Después, con un jarro de chicha en mano, rodeaban la sepultura hablando al difunto, haciéndole saber cómo se le echaba aún de menos, contándole los sucesos de los doce meses pasados, y acabando por derramar la bebida . . . A continuación enterraban algunas provisiones nuevas, encendían una hoguerilla y se alejaban dejando ya para siempre al muerto consigo mismo. (Housse 1939:320, 333)

One year after the burial, the ancient Mapuche returned to the cemetery, sacrificing various llamas over the tomb, so that the earth was saturated with blood, the final ration of the deceased. Afterwards, with a jar of chicha in hand, they circled the mound speaking to the deceased, telling him how much they missed him, telling him what had happened during during the past twelve months, and finishing by pouring the drink [of *chicha* over the tomb]. . . . Afterward, they buried some new provisions, lit a small fire and left, leaving the deceased alone forever. . . . (Housse 1939:320, 333)

In addition to the above accounts, Treutler (1958), Joseph (1930), and others provide details on the practice of mound construction and how consanguinally related Mapuche and close allies participated in funeral and postinternment rites held by the living at mounded graves a year or more after the death of important figures. Beginning with Bibar and Rosales in the mid-1550s and mid-1600s, respectively, and ending with the latter passages, collectively these observers reveal a 350-year continuity in form, function, and meaning of mound location and construction, rulers' burial, animal sacrifice, *chicha* consumption, grave offerings, and relations between the living and the dead.

Last, although several different types of rituals are described by the chroniclers, the most important to this study is the *nguillatun* fertility ceremony, which is first mentioned by Núñez de Pineda ([1673] 2003:639) in the mid-seventeenth century. He refers to it as the *Gnapitun* or great "fiestas y bailes" (feasts and dances). His description of the public ritual performed at this ceremony is remarkably similar to present day *nguillatun* ceremonies (c.f. Núñez de Pineda [1673] 2003:523–532 and Chapter 4).

I have participated in ceremonies at several *palin* and *nguillatun* fields that are located in *rehuekuel* and built around *kuel*, two of which are *Hualonkokuel* and *Ñachekuel* (see Chapters 5 and 6). Local informants at these ceremonies believe these fields date back at least 300 hundred years. The radiocarbon dates that we have excavated from five *nguillatun* fields in the valley and the diagnostic ceramics collected from them and other fields chronologically place them between the thirteenth to twentieth centuries We also have excavated off-mound areas in the *rehuekuel* and found rows of postholes and hearths similar to those observed today in *nguillatun* fields, suggesting continuity in form and function of these feasting localities (Dillehay 2004, 2005, 2006). The same continuity has been recorded in the size and form of the *ruca* house (Fig. 23) in archaeological and present-day domestic sites.

CONCLUSIONS

From discussion of the archaeology of south-central Chile and from the sample of early testimonies presented above, it is clear that mound building and the use

23. A thatched *ruca* house of a family in Lumaco.

of public ritual space at *awün*, *rehuekuel*, and *nguillatun* fields in various forms was practiced in the Araucania before and after the beginning of the sixteenth century. Based on continuities in the form, place, and function of *rehue*, *kuel*, and *rehuekuel*, there is no doubt that the term *rehue* refers to both the patrilineage unit and to the sacred place where leaders of the patrilineage were buried and where their decendants and their relatives and guests practice public ceremonies (e.g., *lukutun*, *nguillatun*; see Chapter 4). In addition to mound building, *chicha* consumption, vessel smashing over graves and mounds, and camelid sacrifice are distinctly Andean in practice and symbolism. Participation in these practices provided the occasions to learn mound literacy and to demonstrate proper mound treatment and responsible compatriotism in the community.

The relative popularity of mound building remains unclear and the precise forms it took cannot be linked ethnographically to any specific parts of the region beyond Purén and Lumaco, although archaeological mounds and ethnohistoric descriptions are present in many other areas. Most important are the types of mound burial, building, and worship described in the above passages for Purén and Lumaco, which were seldom mentioned by other European contemporaries for other areas, suggesting they were not especially prevalent in all areas during certain periods or absent altogether. There also is no doubt that mound building and mound worship was a more widespread practice throughout the Araucanian area than it is in the twentieth century. However, their archaeological occurrence in low densities in most other areas tells us that it was not only a selective ceremonial practice for a few privileged rulers, but also a custom restricted to certain population segments or perhaps not yet developed by others. Colleagues and I have discovered that informants in areas beyond Purén and Lumaco have rarely heard of the terms *kuel* and *rehuekuel*, implying that mound building and mound worship were not well developed traditions in some areas and/or that they are lost and forgotten practices.

FOUR:

IMBRICATING SOCIAL, MATERIAL,

METAPHORICAL, AND

SPIRITUAL WORLDS

Although the Araucanians were relatively conservative and materially inconspicuous until the Spanish conquest, they suddenly were thrust into a new
world of awareness in the mid-1500s – one of survival. They rapidly became aware
of the need for a new societal organization and a new built landscape to resist
Spanish invasion. In some areas, this need was partly engendered by the frequency
and repetition of mound building and by the public ceremonies, larger agricultural communities, and institutions that accompanied these acts. Today, memories
and knowledge of these events saturate the landscape; they are inscribed spatially
on the land in the architectural ideology of *kuel* and *rehuekuel* and in the names
that have become historic and lived places. Memories also record the successes of
dynastic patrilineages and the fragmented populations who moved in, the occupations that they practiced, the activities they pursued, and the roles they played
in reconstituted settings. Thus, like the landscape as a whole, *kuel* and *rehuekuel*
represent geographically reconstituted social meanings, genealogies, memories,
compatriotism, and shared political identities.

Yet, the landscape is more than just identities and memorial places that
define and are defined by history. It also is a network of bounded pathways of
social interaction defined by the movement of people between and practices at
the locations of these places and of the sacred mountains and hills, *nguillatun* fields,
and residential sites. All of these elements serve as reference nodes in time and
in space (see Chapters 5 and 6). It was the motion or movement of people that
united valley-long *kuel* and *rehuekuel* into a dynamic system of human interaction
and experience. This "landscape in motion" (*sensu* Sahlins 1985) was symbolically interactive, socially integrative, spatially bounded, temporally extended, and
functionally holistic. Analogously, the Araucanians understand *kuel* and *rehuekuel*
as members of a vertically – and horizontally – layered network of social relations
between the living and their ancestors, which is a microcosmic representation of
the larger vertically and horizontally structured ethereal world of ancestors and

deities (Faron 1964; Dillehay 1990c). According to informants, this network is defined metaphorically by a proliferating kinship network of new son:daughter and brother:sister mounds through which history is made, recorded, and perpetuated across the countryside (Dillehay 1999; see kin relations between communities and mounds in Chapter 5 and Appendix 1). It is through incorporation into this participatory network that *kuel* and *rehuekuel* became aesthetic memorials and historic places that were designed to communicate lasting meaning and to effect political order. These places are endowed with the spirits of important ancestors and the deities that are of special consequences and meanings to past, present, and future generations (Dillehay 1990c). Although *kuel* are no longer used for religious ritual and political purpose as widely as they once were, they are respected as living memorials that still serve as portals for the shamans, ancestors, and deities to descend from the upper world to the earth and as special aesthetically pleasing and therapeutic healing localities. It is for these reasons that I refer to *kuel*, *rehuekuel*, *nguillatun* fields, and other sacred places as integrative elements of the *cosmunity* that relate the past, present, and future of the Araucanian's physical, spiritual, and social worlds.

To understand the fluidity and survivability of people and history across this landscape and the materiality and spirituality of *kuel* and *rehuekuel*, we must understand Araucanian religion, ancestral knowledge, healing practice, and sacred space. It is the symbolic overlay of the living and ancestral worlds together in the same mounded localities to form a locally unified cosmological and political community, or *cosmunity*, that is fundamentally important to explaining Araucanian mound literacy and polity-formation. *Kuel* relate to the spatial classification and organization of knowledge sources and how they are administered and utilized in the world of the living through congregational ritual (see Faron 1964). Space is specifically singled out here because all knowledge and behavior in Araucanian society must have locational reference in one of two culturally defined spatial worlds: the ideologically construed image of the sacred ancestral world and the natural topography and ecosystem in which live social action takes place. Described and analyzed below are the relations and structures of these two worlds, how ancestral knowledge is regulated in ceremony, and where the two worlds connect the past and present. This functional–structural classification is important to an understanding of the location, meaning, design, and spatial layout of *kuel*, *rehuelkuel*, *nguillatun* fields, and domestic and cemetery sites.

Most of the ethnographic data presented below have been collected by the author over the past thirty years in more than twenty different areas in the coast, central valley, and Andean mountains. It is complemented by reference to ethnographies published by others. Given the strong continuities in traditional religion and ideology that are expressed over the past three to four hundred years in the study area, these data are invaluable for linking the archeological and ethnohistorical records and thus the past and present and especially for contextualizng mound building and mound worship within broader social and historical processes. Lastly, the analysis in this chapter is deliberately focused on straightforward description of the function, structure, history, and meaning of Mapuche cosmology and religion in order to identify important spatial, temporal, and symbolic patterns. This knowledge is employed in later chapters to study agency, identity, memory, and polity.

ANCESTRAL KNOWLEDGE AND TRADITION

Perhaps more than any other scholar, Faron recognized the importance of ancestral knowledge to the Araucanians and how it indicates the collective social behavior of the live membership as examined in his classic study of their religion, *Hawks of the Sun*.

> I have tried to show specifically that in Mapuche society there is . . . a complementarity between the ideological system and the structure of social action. The relatedness of belief and action makes for a continuing balance among the several segments of the total social structure, and constitutes the rules of Mapuche society and their expression. (Faron 1964:194)

To Faron, the Mapuche or Araucanian world was primarily ordered and maintained by a "moral conviction" that unites the living and the dead. He viewed morality as a religious form of constant opposition of good and evil forces that influences the institutionalized behavior of the living.

> All behavior is in concordance with the moral order which permeates society, aberrant behavior being defined in relation to departure from this code. . . . This moral code is in turn anchored to the relationship which exists between the living and the dead, the rights and duties which exist between them in the context of Mapuche religious lore. (Faron 1964:10)

> Morality cannot be understood apart from supernatural sanctions and the nature of the continuum between the living and the dead – both authentic and mythical ancestor-gods – in the framework of lineal and congregational (multilineal) units of population. All traditional rights and duties are supernaturally sanctioned, and conflicts, arising mostly from contacts with non-Mapuche are handled with reference to these traditional moral sanctions. Customary law (*admapu*) is a fundamentally supernatural concept, sanctioned by supernatural forces

emanating from the very ancestors considered to have devised, supplemented, and adhered to the rules of Mapuche society. We do these things because our ancestors did them and because our fathers and grandfathers told us that they are right. These words are the gist of all answers to the anthropologists' questions about belief and customary activity. (Faron 1964:10–11)

These traditional ideas and beliefs in the moral order of Araucanian religion, as emanated from ancestral experiences and as maintained in the continuous relationship between ancestors and the living, are sources of information about customary norms and laws that are learned, influenced, and modified by symbolic communication in and inference from the real-world behavioral experiences of the living, including political and ceremonial participation. The Araucanians thus regard ancestral history, and the types of good and bad experiences contained in it, as an important part of their culture that gives them direction and a sense of right or wrong in their own world. Simply put, *admapu* and its teachings show the Araucanians the ancestral way to behave and how to act as proper members of society.

SPACE AND RELIGION AS KNOWLEDGE

To the Araucanians, space (in whatever form it may take) is a fundamental conjunction between their coded version of the visible, live world on the earth's surface (*mapu* or *Nag Mapu*) and the ideologically architectured, invisible ethereal world of knowledge-bearing "cosmological" surfaces or planes (*Wenumapu* and *miñchemapu* and *ilonagmapu*) where different good and evil ancestral spirits, deities, and lesser figures reside. The Araucanians believe that their ancestors represent the whole history of their culture, and thus are the sources of knowledge for human thought and action (Faron 1964; Alonqueo 1979). Each level of the ethereal world is based on different principles, each with its proper place in the life of the community and the ordering of the cosmos, and they alternate in the cycle of rituals and in the influence they have on human affairs.

Knowledge of and communication with the ethereal world are locally based, bounded, and secret. They are focused primarily on local mountains and other sacred localities, which are the sources of power and fertility, the embodiment of the remote ancestors and deities, and the guardians of local communities. Although this world may be identified in terms of particular places, it also contains pan-Araucanian features. For example, the local mountains in the Purén and Lumaco Valley form part of an encompassing regional landscape hierarchy at the apex of which are the highest peaks of the Nahualbuta coastal range (e.g., *Wenucolla*) and the volcanoes in the Andean range to the east where *Pillan*, a supreme deity, lives.

In ritual ceremony at the *nguillatun* field the ethereal and physical worlds become one contracted and unified ethereal–physical topography that represents a diagrammatic intersection of introspection on ancestral knowledge and its culturally construed meaning and use in live society. In this sense, the Araucanians consider earthly human ritual behavior as a synchronic time frame that reinforces the relationship between ancestral knowledge stored in the ethereal world and brought to social and ideological use in the live world. Henceforth, the key to understanding the classification and use of knowledge sources both in ethereal and physical space is to examine the relationship between the ancestral world and the living world, and how this relationship is structured in ideology and religion and in *kuel, rehuekuel*, and *nguillatun* sites. *Kuel* and *nguillatun* fields are the primary architectural referents through which these relations are played out vis-à-vis *machi, nguillatufe, weupin* or *weupife*, ancestral spirits, and public ceremony. A secondary concern is how knowledge, once it has been formed from whatever source and for whatever purpose, is culturally organized and socially applied for continuity in the world of the living.

In sum, Araucanian history is a concentration of ancestral knowledge that strives for continuity. Ancestral knowledge and experience are brought into the life experiences of the living society at large through myth, narrative tales, symbolism, and public ceremony. Knowledge is continually stored, identified, and materialized in the form of *kuel, rehuekuel*, and other sacred landscapes and of wooden statues and other artifacts. Historical narratives are considered an essential part of the education of Araucanian children, by which they learn the past and how to become proper members of society (e.g., Titiev 1951). In this regard, continuity and its materialized landscape contribute to producing a collective identity for all lineage members. In the past and present, this goes hand in hand with the project of a more integrated political organization, a greater centralization of identity, and an increased sense of communal solidarity.

ILLNESS, DEATH, AND THERAPEUTIC PLACES

Malefaction, illness, death, and healing have mental, spiritual, and moral components that are often difficult to separate out (see Citarella 1995). These components cannot always be distinguished from other aspects of daily life such as religion, economy, and politics. Although these issues may seem esoteric and unobtainable in the past, they have their behavioral expression in the curing practices and ritual ceremonies of *machi* and (less so) *nguillatufe*, their spatial location in the *rehuekuel* and *nguillatun* fields (*nguillatuhue*), and their material expressions in the *kuel* and ritual paraphernalia used by shamans. Places such as *rehuekuel* and *nguillatuhue* are associated primarily with ideology, ritual ceremony, social harmony, and commensal feasting (*sensu* Dietler 1996; Dietler and Hayden 2001), but also with suffering and healing (*sensu* Blagg 1986; Gallagher 1993; Kalipeni and Zeleza 1999; Lane 2001; Swan 1990, 1991; Turner 1973). These are therapeutic places in times of loss and suffering that are located in the ideological and religious practices of the Araucanians.

These relations are important because when we look at the effects of increased contact between the Spanish and the Araucanians from the perspective of increased illness and death resulting from warfare and disease (see Chapter 3 and 7), the alleviation of physiological symptoms and suffering as a human condition becomes important. Increased mortality rates in the contact period must have raised serious questions among early Araucanian populations about the meaning of wider issues such as life and death, what caused misfortune in general, what is evil, what is dangerous, and what can be done about it. Alleviation comes from understanding illness and death and from confronting the perceived sources of suffering in public ritual performed by specialized shamans.

To the Araucanians today, "bad deaths" come from accidents, illnesses, and sorcery attacks (see Faron 1964; Citarella 1995). "Good deaths" result from dying of natural causes in old age or from death in battle. Illness, disease, and bad death increase the role of shamans to explain these occurrences, to cure greater numbers of sick people, and to deal with death and with new relations between the living and the dead. In order to prevent bad death, the Araucanians had and still have a complicated procedure of curing rituals performed by *machi* that protects the spirit of a sick person from immediate dangers and communities from hostile forces (*kalku, weupufe*). This is why *machi* so often had and have power across extensive areas, including the political arena: they understand these issues and deal with them through public ritual and event (Dillehay 1985b). It is the spatiality and meaning of these understandings at *kuel* and *rehuekuel* that are of interest to this study.

ANCESTORS AND DEITIES

Araucanian ideology consists of a pantheon of deities, ancestral figures (both authentic and mythical), good and evil forces, and other less important beings that are hierarchically nested in an ideologically conceived time and space framework. Although there are pan-Araucanian religious forms, there is considerable local and regional variation in the different sets of figures that are deified and propitiated, particularly when it comes to patrilineage-specific beliefs and sanctions. Most variation is expressed in terms of the emphasis that is placed on local sets of deities and on animalistic forms that certain zoomorphic figures may take. Faron (1964:1–20) credits much of this variation to "social nature," meaning that each network of multilineage participation in ceremony brings in authentic ancestors and spirits of local importance but within a "framework of great cultural homogeneity." I concur with Faron's reasoning, and add that variability in local socially expressed figures is also attributed to regional differences in the economy and in the ecological trophic order (or hierarchical food chain) of plant and animal communities from which the nomenclature and the community organization of both the living and the ancestors are metaphorically drawn (Dillehay 1990a; Alonqueo 1979). I explain this order in a later section.

As creators and owners of all animals, plants, mountains and people, the major deities *Ngenechen* and *Pillan* are the most powerful. *Ngenechen* resides in the upper level of *Wenumapu*, although he has representatives such as *kuel* and other elements placed on *Nag Mapu* or earth among the people. According to local informants, *Pillan* resides in a *millaruca* or house of gold in the Andean volcanoes and in their microcosmic form – the *kuel* – in *Nag Mapu* space. In some written texts and in some present-day communities, these two deities appear to be the same, as noted by Latcham (1924:78): "Practically all of the attributes described for *Pillan* are embellished by the modern *Ngubnechen* [*Ngenechen*] and vice versa." In most *nguillatun* I have attended in Purén and Lumaco, *Pillan* and *Ngenechen* are addressed equally, with the former more in the context of ancestors and the latter more in regard to the upper *Wenumapu* world. In the past, *Pillan* is said to have been associated with *kona* (warriors) and with the spirits of important warlords in the study area (i.e., Pelantaro, Lientur, Colípi, Lautaro, Anganamón). This connection also was recorded by J. Medina, who wrote that "...in the *nguillatun*, people pray to Mareupuanti (the son of the Sun), who represents the souls of the warriors killed in battle who live with *Pillan* in the upper world" (J. Medina [1852] 1952: LXX). These warriors also are powerful *cona* ancestors that still interact with the living in *Nag Mapu* space.

The Araucanians trace their culture history to two types of ancestors: authentic and mythical ancestors (e.g., Faron 1964). Authentic ancestors (*kuifiche*) are traced through direct descent lines and are propitiated in *nguillatun*, *awün*, or *awn* (funeral), *kueltun* (the ritual act of capping the *kuel* with individual soil layers that are offerings to the ancestors and deities; see Dillehay 1985a, 1995), and other ceremonies and during private prayers. (*Winkulkuelchetue*, on the other hand, refers to the physical act of building a mound and not to the placement of individual soil layers). They act as intercessors before the major deities, *Ngenechen* (*Ngunechen, Ngnechen*) and *Pillan*, and play a minor role to less important deities and spirits. Mythical ancestors (*antüpainamko*), on the other hand, cannot be directly traced through a particular genealogical line and thus are considered pan-Araucanian. These ancestors are mentioned in creation myths and ritual beliefs held by most Araucanians. Mythical ancestors generally are more powerful than authentic ancestors, because the former have spent more time in *Wenumapu* space and once were more important figures (e.g., *toqui* war leaders) in the living world.

In my opinion, the difference between these two types of ancestors is primarily a function of time and of their status in the genealogy of lineages. That is, the mythical ancestors are much older and their formal line of descent has been lost or forgotten in the oral kinship records of any one patrilineage. As a result, they are affiliated with regional enclaves of multiple interrelated lineages (e.g., *ayllarehue*; see Chapters 1 and 3).

The loss of mythical ancestors in the genealogical record of individual lineages also is accounted for by population displacement and lineage mixing resulting from warfare and population fragmentation over the past few centuries and simply by memory loss in lineages. The authentic ancestors, on the other hand, are more recent in time and are remembered in the direct line of descent. Cultural homogeneity in Araucanian religion is best characterized by interregional belief in genealogically lost mythical ancestors that are most often and most strongly propitiated during large multilineage public ceremonies or *rehue* (Faron 1964; Citarella 1995:104). By being unattached to a particular kinship network these figures serve to obligate a much wider audience and provide a common reference for religious unification (see Chapter 7). On the other hand, authentic ancestors with specific lineage affiliation still occupy major places in the religious beliefs of local lineages. I suspect that in times of past warfare, when the *ayllarehue* and *butan-mapu* political alliances were intact, both ancestral types played more important roles in building interlineage relations.

The living believe that the proper care of ancestors and deities through ritual veneration, worship, and tomb maintenance can insure health and fertility (Faron 1964; Citarella 1995). Most rituals are structured to securely place ancestors into the good *Wenumapu* world and to maintain proper relations between the living and the dead. If this placement is not secured and if these relations are not maintained in proper ceremonies at *nguillatue*, *kuel*, and other sacred places, the living face complicated and protracted challenges ranging from sorcery and malevolence to defeat in warfare and politics (see Chapters 5 and 6). People believe that ancestors may oppose or encourage marriage, or intervene in political and economic decisions related to agriculture and politics. Moreover, ancestors are considered sources of blessing and guarantors of human and agricultural fertility. They may assist those who survive them to solve practical and emotional problems, providing encouragement and counsel in dreams and visions. Recurrent rituals are thus necessary, informants explain, because ancestors and ancestral spirits intervene in human lives and relationships. In ritual, the ancestral spirits are directly embodied in the living kin and the *kuel*. (In Purén and Lumaco, *kuel* are most identified with the mythical ancestors who speak through them to the living.) Here, the power and reproductive capacity of the dead are transmitted directly to the living and to those participating in ritual ceremony at *kuel* and other sacred places. But ancestors also may use their power in more coercive and menacing ways. If not worshipped and given offerings, such as the case of the sick *Hualonkokuel* discussed in Chapter 5, ancestral spirits may cause problems or withdraw their support of the living.

CONJUNCTION OF ETHEREAL AND PHYSICAL SPACES

As noted before, the Araucanians classify space in two forms – ethereal space and physical space – to organize their epistemological ordering of the world. It is during ceremony that the primary knowledge sources, the animals, the deities, the ancestors and the living, come together in one spatially ordered event of the ethereal and live physical worlds. Grebe, Pacheco, and Segura (1972) have demonstrated the vertically spaced "cosmovision" or ethereal world (see also Dillehay 1990a). They described it in terms of a "spatial hierarchy" of vertically ordered planes where the living, ancestors, deities, and other figures, as well as the good and evil forces, reside. Figure 24 shows a graphic conceptualization of these planes and their association with important figures. Ethereal space comprises the vertically arranged "surfaces" of the upper *Wenumapu* good world and of the lower *miñchemapu* evil world. The physical world of the earth's surface (*Nag Mapu* or *mapu*) is an intervening level, where the visible ecological elements, including humans, interact within a horizontal framework defined by the four cardinal directions. Each surface is occupied by different deities, ancestors, and spirits. The upper four planes of the central column are associated with good deities, ancestors, and spirits and are collectively referred to as the *Wenumapu* world. The nomenclature and role of characters that reside in the quadri-tiered *Wenumapu* space are equated with specific natural elements of the basic ecological trophic order in the region (see later discussion). Directly below the *Wenumapu* is located the *ankawenu* (also *ranginwenu*), translated literally to mean halfway between the *Nag Mapu* and *Wenumapu* planes. *Ankawenu* is an evil place (*weupufe*) controlled by the *kalku* (sorcerers). Informants in Lumaco report that it is the visible sky of *ankawenu* directly above the earth's surface where evil birds fly during the day and night. (In Purén and Lumaco, everyday knowledge of the living world, generally associated with daylight, is distinguished from esoteric knowledge, which is associated primarily with darkness, and the ability to speak with spirits under the moonlight.) Next is *Nag Mapu*, where the living reside. Another evil plane, the *miñchemapu*, lies under the *Nag Mapu* surface. This is where the dead are buried and eventually tested by both good and evil forces as they attempt to make their ascent into the *Wenumapu* levels above.

Machi in Lumaco have revealed that each vertical level also has a horizontal dimension oriented by the four cardinal directions. Each direction represents a lesser degree of good, moving counterclockwise from the east to the north (Fig. 25). The vertical surfaces intersect one another through the east–west direction. Ancestors move back and forth between the *Wenumapu* and *Nag Mapu* worlds

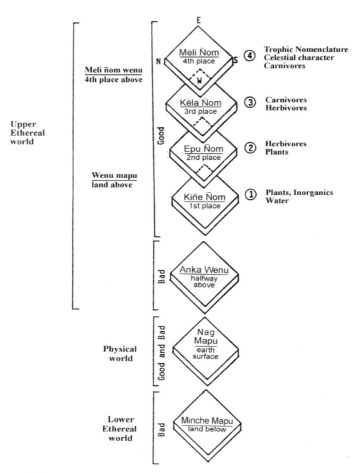

24. Schematic of the upper, middle, and lower planes of the Araucanian cosmological world mentioned throughout the text.

by a spiral ascent and descent through the good and evil sectors of the four vertical planes. The use of horizontal space in the living *Nag Mapu* world manifests an alternate pattern. During public ceremony in *nguillatun* fields, dance movements, social events, and food exchange between members of different lineages follow a counterclockwise movement from east (very good) and north (evil) to west (very evil) and south (good).

There is also a temporal scale represented in the vertical and horizontal dimensions. The older creation myths are primarily associated with *melinom* (fourth surface) of the *Wenumapu* space. The mythical ancestors are located in the *kelanom* (third) and *epunom* (fourth) levels and the younger authentic ancestors are positioned in the *epunom* and *keninom* levels. That is, the earliest or oldest ancestral events are associated with the most distant and higher levels of the ethereal world, while the most recent occurrences are correlated with the lower two levels or those

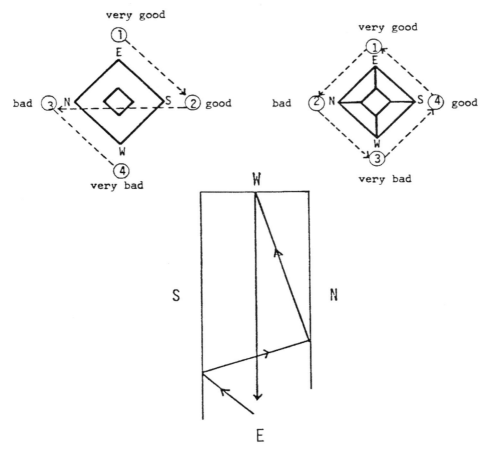

25. Schematic of the cardinal directions on the good and bad planes of the cosmological world (top two figures) and the zigzag movement of dance and ritual exchange in the U-shaped *nguillatun* ceremony (lower figure).

closest to the living *Nag Mapu* world. Only important ancestors, such as famous *toqui* war leaders and *ülmen* reside in the upper *melinom* and *kelanom* levels. The name of the "social soil" or individual layers comprising the artificially constructed mounds by kin during *kueltun* capping ceremonies are called *reñinmapu, melimapu, kelamapu,* and *miñchemapu* (Fig. 26: cf. Fig. 3), respectively, meaning the earth of the center or heart, the upper levels, the middle levels, and the lower levels of the mound (see discussion below and Chapter 6). As discussed in Chapters 5 and 6, one purpose of mound building and mound worship is to transform a dead leader from an authentic to a mythical ancestor by physically and metaphysically elevating his spirit into the upper and most powerful levels of the *Wenumapu* world where he later can better assist the living. A second purpose is that the acts of procuring, placing, and compacting the social soil layers in mounds are ritual offerings to the deities and ancestors.

Ceremonial space in the *nguillatun* and *kueltun* ceremonies is the intersecting loci of both worlds, integrating all vertical levels and horizontal dimensions through ritual thought and action. Ceremonial myths, narrative tales, and songs contain characters of the ethereal surfaces and structurally relate their interaction with one another according to their position along the vertical scale of ethereal space. Ceremony in *Nag Mapu* space also is an arena of conflicting good and evil forces that can affect the outcome of human behavior. However, the social and natural environment of *Nag Mapu* space is not merely a point of friction between good and evil forces. It is also a culturally defined framework of interaction between the living and the original sources of knowledge and power – that is, the animals and the ancestors. Traditional communities are constantly updating and refining their information on the world at large through their role in the natural environment. Death is one way this is done. When a person dies, he/she becomes an authentic ancestor and carries his/her recent life experiences into the upper ethereal world. (As noted above, more important ancestors eventually become powerful mythical ancestors who reside in higher levels.)

The Araucanians interpret the location and directional movement of the ancestors in *Wenumapu* space and the living in *Nag Mapu* space as a corrective measure that obligates the living and the dead to be aware of ever-occurring evil situations in the world. Constant encounters with evil, which include contact with outsiders, reinforce the relationship between the living and their ancestors and maintain the integrity of the society. Elders in Purén and Lumaco inform that this was particularly important in times of war when lineages were fragmented and moved and affiliated with others (see Chapters 3 and 7).

Machi reach the upper *Wenumapu* by climbing the "great stairway to heaven" – the *wenufutapurem*. Informants report that in microcosmic form, prepared floors and offerings were once placed on top of the *kuel* during past ceremonies, and were later capped over and are now buried or layered inside them (i.e., *reñinmapu*). These layers are used by the spirit of the interred deceased to ascend through the different planes of the upper world (see Chapters 5 and 6). By way of the interceding *machi* in ritual ceremony, the live membership of the *Nag Mapu* world has access to and control of the multiple sources of knowledge contained in the past experiences of all ancestors and figures, whether good or evil, residing on all planes. The ancestors of the ethereal world do not actively use this information; they only store it by residence in these spaces and are brought into the life experiences of *Nag Mapu* space through myth, oration, prayer, and invocation by the *machi* and occasionally the *nguillatufe* (both a ritual and secular leader).

Also important is the concept of *rehue* (*rewe*), which refers not only to the sacred pole or stepped ladder of the *machi* shamans, which carries them into the *Wenumapu* world, but also to the religious organization of a specified group of patrilineal families (e.g., *lov, lebo, lof*) united in a designated sacred place that is connected to good forces and spirits (see Chapter 3 and Foerster and Gundermann

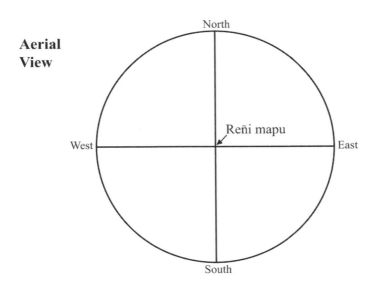

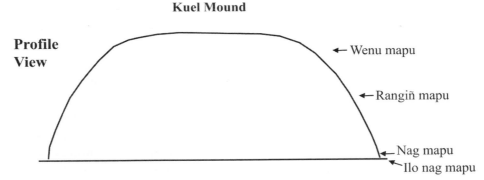

26. Schematic aerial view of the cardinal direction of the quadripartite internal division of space within circular *kuel* mounds (upper figure) and the names assigned by informants to the different vertical planes or levels of the profile view of *kuel* (lower figure).

1996; Citarella 1995:104–105). In Purén and Lumaco, *rehue* or *rehuekuel* also refers to the *ñichi*, or *terra plein*, where one or several *kuel* are located and where *nguillatun* and other rituals were performed by individual lineages and *ayllarehue* in the past and, in some places, still continue.

As noted the vertical layers of Araucanian cosmology are conceptualized onto horizontal space through the delineation of boundaries between each of the layers and their subzones. The focal point of these layers is *Nag Mapu* where the living and the dead interact on the earth's surface (see Fig. 24), and where this interaction is expressed in ritual and symbolically on the shaman's *kultrun*. Shamans mediate between these levels. The organization of space is thus conceived of segmentally and concentrically like a web, with compacted and duplicated segments spreading and growing in size outwardly from the community.

Kuel are located on the living Nag Mapu or mapu surface, are mediated by shamans, and also are vertically and concentrically segmented like a web in rehuekuel space (Fig. 26). According to shamans, kuel are divided into four cardinal quarters much like the kultrun (see later discussion). The internal strata of kuel represent different episodes of parental and ritual contact between the ancestral spirits residing inside and the living that benefit from and pay homage to kuel. As noted, each stratum composed of the kuel is considered "social soil" that is placed by consanguinal relatives of the deceased buried inside (Dillehay 1985a). In other words, the layered social soils and prepared floors in kuel metaphorically represent the continuity of relations between the living and the dead in time and space. Also spatially ordered are areas around and between kuel, where kueltun and nguillatun ceremonies take place (see Chapter 5 where the machi in the TrenTrenkuel narrative directs the ritual audience to cardinal points around the mound). In this space, each family and lineage has a permanently assigned seating place that corresponds with the cardinal position of its household location in the larger community pattern. For instance, a family located east of a kuel is seated in the east end of the nguillatun field, a family residing to the west is located in the west side, and so forth. As explained later and in Chapters 5 and 6, these designated spaces and their associated material remains are reliable correlates for linking the archaeological, ethnohistorical, and ethnographic records.

Machi state that the apex of the conical-shaped mounds is smaller than the base that covers the tomb of a dead ruler, because at the time of death the deceased's kinship network is large, with more people placing soil on and around the grave. As time passes, the network shrinks in size as the dead leader's spirit ascends toward and into the Wenumapu world and as his kinsmen marry outside of the community, die, and/or disperse. (From a practical viewpoint, the cone shape also is a function of the vertical stacking of earth, which also must take this form to maintain structural integrity.) Thus, over time fewer kinsmen exist to participate in mound-capping ceremonies, which results in smaller amounts of soil placed on the tomb through time. In contrasts, there are a few rectangular-shaped, non-burial platform mounds that date to the early historic period and that are larger than the conical mounds and reportedly once associated with inter-valley multilineage congregations (e.g., ayllarehue?). Although presently not well understood, it may be that the transformation from conical to rectangular mounds indicates a corresponding shift from local patrilineage-based to multilineage-based organizations. According to informants, a structure with four clearly defined sides is required for representation of the multiple lineages residing in all directions. The rectangular form also is said to accommodate larger groupings of politically allied lineages and to architecturally demarcate the four cardinal directions of allied lineages in public ceremony. Today, the only actively used rectangular-shaped sacred space is the nguillatun fields in some areas. In the Purén and Lumaco Valley, many used fields are located in old rehuekuel sites on hilltops overlooking the valley floor. These places are depicted in Figures 1, 2, 8–10, 21–22, in the following figures, and in the *rehuekuel* sites discussed in Chapter 6.

MACHI SHAMANS: MEDIATORS OF ANCESTRAL KNOWLEDGE AND HEALING EXPERIENCE

Machi have undergone initiation into esoteric knowledge, often precipitated through dreams, and developed by learning from an already established *machi*. In particular, *machi* are healers as well as diviners, and they are central to the performance of any ritual that involves the ancestors, mountains, the sun, the moon, agricultural fertility, and other phenomena. *Machi's* knowledge of the world is an intelligent understanding grounded in his or her experience of the deities and ancestors in the ethereal world and of the animals and other creatures of the natural world. In this regard, *machi* are media for knowledge that comes from and goes to those worlds, rather than being themselves the repository of knowledge. Knowledge concerning the past and the therapeutic healing of society thus are functions of ideology and religious and political authority. Supporting this authority is the *machi's* focus on central places of performative healing ritual's (*dahatun, illepun*) – the *kuel* and *rehuekuel*.

Today and probably in the past, *machi* know the esoteric knowledge of the upper world more than anyone else, which partially leads me to refer to them as priestly shamans (see Chapters 1 and 3). I suspect that in the past, *weupin* (special orators) and *nguillatufe*, both of whom are mentioned as ritual performers by the chroniclers (see Chapter 3 and Bengoa 2003:16–17; Faron 1964:124–127; Foerster and Gundermann 1996), had more sacred knowledge than they do today. (In most areas, where *machi* are available today, *weupin* and *nguillatufe* perform only occasionally or rarely. In the highlands where intensive agriculture is not practiced, *machi* are replaced by *lonko* and *nguillatufe*.) Faron (1964:105) claims that when *machi* rule over ceremony, it is more a shamanistic ritual than when *nguillatufe* preside. He believes that the latter are more priestly and deal more with the supernatural world than shamans do. This has not been my experience with the *machi*, especially those in Lumaco. Generally, *machi* interpret *admapu* or traditional laws, redefine traditions, and hold much more spiritual and moral judiciary authority over the community than other leaders, including *nguillatufe*. Admittedly, some *machi* are strictly healers, but others act as both shamans and ritual priests in ceremony and have extensive knowledge of the ancestral and cosmological worlds, as revealed throughout the works of several investigators (Bacigalupo 1995, 1996, 1998, 2001, 2002, 2004a–2004d; Citarella 1995:197–264; Cooper 1946; Dillehay 1985a, 1999, 2003; Eulogio 1911, 1912; Foerster 1993; Foerster and Gunderman 1996; Housse 1939; Latcham 1924; Métraux 1942;

Moesbach 1936; San Martín 1976; Titiev 1951) and throughout this book (especially Chapter 5). Faron's observations may have been biased by concentrating most of his research in moderately acculturated areas near Temuco, where *machi* have lost considerable spiritual prowess in the cosmological world as a result of a strong Christian presence and turned more toward healing as a survival vocation. Further, I have interviewed several *nguillatufe* and *weupin* who report that *machi* possess extensive knowledge of the other, or *Wenumapu*, supernatural world, especially shamans from more traditionally religious areas like Purén and Lumaco. Today, communication with and travel to "other worlds" is almost exclusively the domain of *machi*. *Nguillatufe* and *weupin* generally know history and local lineage genealogies better than *machi* and have historical relations with the ancestors and gods. However, their knowledge of and ability to communicate with figures in the *Wenumapu* world is restricted. Lastly, the fact that *machi* in the Purén and Lumaco Valley perform ceremonies at oracle *kuel* and that the spirits of both live and dead shamans reside in them suggest a form of priestly shamanism, which apparently is not the case in other areas today and perhaps the same in the past.

Núñez de Pineda ([1673] 2003:121) referred to *huecubuye* or *boquivoye* as *reñis* who were *sacerdotes* or ritual priests to the Spanish (see Chapter 3). In Mapundungun, the prefix *reñi* is particularly significant, because it is the term used by *machi* to refer to the center of *kuel* (*reñimapu* or individual soil layers inside mounds). As described in the ritual narrative at *TrenTrenkuel* in Chapter 5, when the *machi* transports the living ritual congregation (including the author) inside the *kuel* to observe activities there, she refers to its central area as *reñi* and, more importantly, to herself as a *reñis* – the one who has the power to see inside the mound and to transport herself and others inside it. The capacity of shamans to do this is another reason why I believe that *machi* were both powerful healers and probably the *huecubuye* or *boquivoye* ritual priests referred to in the past (cf. Bacigalupo 1999, 2004a, 2004b; Rosales [1674] 1989:1154; see Chapter 3 and earlier discussion).

Machi gain their power from *newen* (*ngen* or nature spirits that offer their powers to *machi*), from mastery over animals, from their ability to cure, and from their communication with ancestors and deities in *Wenumapu* space. *Fileu* or *machi pullu*, which literally means the ones who have knowledge, refers to the *machi's* spirits and to her powers, which are activated through ritual (see Bacigalupo 1996 and 2004a–2004d). *Pullu* is inherited from ancient *machi* (see the next chapter for ritual narratives between the *machi* and *kuel* and between the *machi* and her *pullu*.) *Machi* obtain esoteric knowledge and wisdom from their *pullu*, which accompanies them through their travels in *Wenumapu* space. Both dead and live *machi* have *fileu* or *machi pullu*. *Fileu* also refers to the physical embodiment of the *machi's* spirit, usually human, that resides inside a *kuel*. *Machi* renew kindred ties with their spirits through ritual at their personal *kuel*. In Lumaco, the renewal of spiritual ties at *kuel* is called *ngeikurrewenkueltun*.

The "invisible" or spiritual world of *Wenumapu* is a real place for the *machi* as is the visible world. Most forms of contact between *machi* and the spirit world are through dreams, rhythmic drumming and chanting, and entering a trance. *Miyaya* or *chamico* (*Datura stramonium*) often is used to create an altered state of consciousness (*kuymin*) to divine the future. Dreams and visions are important for *machi* to make decisions (cf. Bacigalupo 1996). Dreams and visions also provide entry into the *Wenumapu* world of the spirits by enabling the *machi's* spirit to leave the body and travel freely. In Lumaco and Purén, the visions of *machi* are more powerful when they take place at or inside *kuel* where their *pullu* spirits reside. During ceremonies at *kuel*, *machi* have the ability to enter inside mounds to converse with their *pullu* spirits. Machi informants report that *konkulpullukuel* means to enter the *kuel* to be with the living spirit or *machi pullu* living inside.

Bacigalupo's studies show that *machi* performed spiritual warfare against the Spanish and still do today against the Chileans (Bacigalupo 1998, 2001, 2004a–2004d; see Chapter 5). In the past, *machi* divined the locations of the Spanish and predicted the outcomes of battle by performing magic against them (see also Rosales [1674] 1989:155–161). *Machi* also invoked the sun, moon, and the planets during military divination to gain power to cure the wounded and to defeat intruders (Ercilla y Zuniga [1569] 1982: 45, 147; Oña [1596] 1975:15, 21; cited in Bacigalupo 2004a). In the same way that priests and shamans did in the past, *machi* today still employ political ritual to defend local communities (see Dillehay 1985b; Citarella 1995:222–26). To quote Bacigalupo,

> Today, Mapuche spiritual warfare against enemy spirits is no longer a political tool but has become an essential component in the ritual healing of bodies and communities. *Machi* kill evil *wekufe* spirits using spiritual warfare during exorcisms performed at all healing (*machitun* [*dajatun*]), initation (*Ngeikurrewen*), and collective fertily (*nguillatun*) rituals. (Bacigalupo 1998) *Machi* warfare ideologies have also remained part of *chueca*, or ritual war games in which *machi* give *pulluam* (spiritual power gained from ancestral spirits) and herbal remedies to players to grant them the strength, valor, and power needed to win.... (Bacigalupo 2004a:499)

Female *machi* use political functions as ritual orators in collective *nguillatun* rituals to bring fertility and abundance to the communities. They also have begun performing a contemporary version of colonial *machi weye's* spiritual *warfare*. They become "warrior *machi*" and draw on ancestral warriors to combat forestry companies who have taken their land, and they draw on their knowledge to rally for cultural rights and political autonomy from the state. In healing rituals they kill *wekuefe* [*weupufe*] spirits that threaten the bodies of their patients or their communities. (Bacigalupo 2004a:520–1)

As shown in Chapter 5 and Appendix 1, shamans repeat several phrases in ritual ceremonies that invoke memories in past and present times when the Mapuche have defended themselves against outsiders. As noted earlier, one commonly employed term is "*Marichiwew*," meaning we will conquer them (the Spanish and Chileans) ten times over and over again. This word is shouted loudly and assertively by the entire ritual congregation to provoke "recollective memory" and solidarity.

In typical Andean fashion, the Araucanians encode their history of struggle and success in their geographies and in their rituals, so that past meets present in the sacred terrain of the *kuel* and *nguillatun* fields in ceremony. However, history encoded in physical geography does more than carry important historical referents as media to preserve recollective memory; it also structures the manner in which these facts are conceptualized, remembered, and organized into a temporal framework. Mountains, hills, imposing trees, caves, streams, falls, and rapids that are associated with invisible entities (*cherufe*) and thus have become objects of veneration or fear are usually natural objects that are outside the cycle of mundane social transformations. These ingredients are used by powerful *machi* to perform rituals and invoke and appease gods and counteract *kalku* or evil. In many areas, the *machi* assign sanctity to certain portions of their natural landscape and regard them as worthy of devotion, loyalty, dignity, and worship. Some natural objects and their surroundings are personified in gods, deities, and spirits and such ecological features are believed to emanate power. Specifically, there are spirits of forests, trees, soils, rocks, springs, rivers, lakes, and many other natural things. Spirits also have their abode in volcanoes, hills, rock formations, mountains, and other physical landscapes. In the Purén and Lumaco area, there are a number of recognized territorial spirit shrines that are located at various natural phenomena, including caves, mountains, large rocks, and waterfalls, some of which are also believed to be inhabited by *kalku* and require performative healing rituals to extract the evil forces.

I will not examine in detail the ritual healing practices of *machi* and the different methods they use to help their patients (see Bacigalupo 2004a, 2004b; Citarella 1995:109–334). Pertinent to this study is simply the distinction of three types of *machi*: (1) the healer who cures the sick; (2) the teacher who introduces shamanistic knowledge and skills to young apprentices; and (3) the shamanic priest who serves as the main ritual intercessor before the gods, the *kuel* as spirit companions, the ancestors, and the living rulers and who administers sacred acts during public ceremonies (*nguillatufe* can also play this role). The methods employed by these specialists consist of ways by which the divided visible and invisible worlds are temporarily unified in ceremony at *kueltun* and *nguillatun* in order to establish communication between the different worlds and effect cures and to combat visible and invisible evil forces.

For the *machi*, healing rites (*dahatun*) are events by which species, spirits, and humans relate to ensure the health and continuity of the community. During periods of sickness and death, a person and the community as a whole facing life-threatening dangers can only be combated by means of shamanic techniques. Shamanic knowledge of curing resides with *machi*, who are recognized as having the capacity to diagnose and cure certain sicknesses using smoke, herbal medicines, and chants, the latter of which are learned over time and sung at the patient. Special words are chanted to gain a particular objective, as seen in the narratives of Chapter 5 and Appendix 1. They also can be used to cure, to increase growth, or to practice sorcery. They are learned from others but also contain much knowledge drawn from dreams, personal experience, ancestors, and *fileu pullu* spirits.

As part of their healing practice, *machi* gather the relatives of the patient before a sacred place (*kuel*, shrine) and publicly expose previously hidden social tensions. The personification of such objects as wooden statues (*chemamüll*), mountains, and rock outcrops in the physical environment and the intuitive rapport which *machi* establish with their natural landscape are the ways in which the local ecology becomes clothed with divine qualities still displayed in many communities. In some cases, these natural shrines are accentuated by the construction of people-made shrines, such as Piedra Santa near Lumaco, where *machi* once gathered annually to worship and to exchange knowledge. *Kuel* are of the greatest significance, because they represent the hidden forces on which *machi* draw their power and survival as shown in the *Hualonkokuel* and *TrenTrenkuel* dialogues presented in the next chapter.

CONCEPTS OF TIME, SPACE, CREATION NARRATIVES, AND KNOWLEDGE

Harcha (1977) has analyzed the concept of tradition or history from the Araucanian perspective. She specifically examined the cultural mechanisms and social channels through which "aspects of the past" (*kuifirapandungu*), including customary rules and laws, are brought to bear on behavior in the world of the living. According to Harcha, the Araucanians have no formal concept of absolute time or history, but only an idea of the succession of ancestrally related events from past to present and anticipation of the future. This is also important for understanding the spatial succession of *kuel* stratigraphy and the layout of mounds, because the stacked soil layers placed by the living to build them constitute (1) the cyclical time of history, (2) the successive generations of gatherings between the living and dead, and (3) the vertical ethereal world of the deities and ancestors.

Several social intercessors regulate the use of history in the live world. In ritual ceremony, the *machi* and *nguillatufe* provide this service. The *weupin* is mediator during the *awün* rite and also at birth and marriage ceremonies. *Weupin* also is a sociopolitical orator who relates local history. Another is the *ngutramkam* who converses during social occasions about the good forces, the achievements and knowledge of the ancestors, the things people think about doing, and the events to take place in the future. Tales (*epeus*) about animals, death and evil spirits, forms of entertainment (*kuneos*), and songs (*ilkatun*) are other oral devices used to teach the customary laws and beliefs to the young. Whoever the intercessor may be and for whatever ritual or social occasion he or she participates, there is always a competitive sense of display of knowledge about information contained in the ethereal world of the ancestors, how it is to be used in the world of the living, and what it means with respect to ancestry and history. Traditional social prestige today is best gained from the ability of one to use his knowledge of ancestral history to make good decisions for the good of the community.

Harcha's study also found that time, and the succession of events that comprise it, must have location, whether it be in the diachronic world of the mythical and authentic ancestors or in the synchronic world of the living in *Nag Mapu* space. In either case, however, past or present time is always classified according to spatially structured ritual behavior in the world of the living. To the Araucanians, living in the physical world is merely considered as one ongoing behavioral position along a successive continuum of past and present episodes defined by the historical events of these ancestors and by the passage of recently deceased ones into the ethereal world. *Machi* informants say that the internally segmented social earth of *kuel* must be seen in a similar manner, whereby the soil layers and prepared floors inside mounds represent a continuous upward flow of social history, or behavior, from the *Nag Mapu* surface of the mound and the living to the *Wenumapu* upper world of the ancestors and deities who protect the living.

Behavior in the live world is taken over by ritual participation to introspect on ancestral ways in the ethereal world. Thus, behavior is, in essence, a way of "doing ancestral things" by a living body in the physical world. Space, on the other hand, is a metaphor of locating the "doing" while it is being done along this temporal continuum of events. In this sense, all behavior must have time–space order. Thus, social and spatial order in the living world is patterned after that in the ancestral world, whose organization was learned originally from the plants and animals of the physical world. That is, the animals taught the ancestors what the physical world, or *Nag Mapu*, is like and how to organize themselves in it socially, spatially, and temporally. An elder *nguillatufe* once informed us that:

> Nosotros sabemos lo que hacen los animales y lo que son las necesidades de los ciervos, de los peces, de la aves, y de los otros animales. Ha estado solamente poco tiempo en esta tierra el chileno y el sabe muy poco

sobre los animales y las plantas. Nosotros vivimos aquí por miles de años y los animales nos enseñaron hace muchos años atrás. Nuestros antepasados cazaron a los animales y nos pasaron su conocimiento de familia a familia. (Antonio Alcaman, Mehuin, Provincial de Valdivia: cited in Dillehay and Gordon 1979:306)

We know what the animals do and the needs of the deer, fish, birds, and other animals. The Chileans have only been here for a short time in this land, and they know very little about the plants and animals. We have lived here for thousands of years, and the animals have taught us and we passed their knowledge from family to family. (Antonio Alcaman, Mehuin, Provincial de Valdivia: cited in Dillehay and Gordon 1977:306)

Ancestral spirits, deities, animals, and other figures enter into the everyday experiences of life through stories and other narrations, religious beliefs, and ritual participation. In particular, ancestors may take the form of anthropomorphic figures which are often symbolized by iconographic motives on certain textiles, pottery vessels, clay figurines, carved wooden masks, and dolls made of cloth or straw. These objects may be used during group ceremonies or during special family social occasions such as visits by leaders of related lineages who live at a distance or the birth of a child. These same objects serve as archeological indicators in tombs and domestic sites of ancestor representation and worship and certain kin relations. For example, Figure 27 shows a female and male *chemamüll*, which serve to demarcate lineage space and to represent the ancestors in living space. In the Purén Valley, elder informants of Ipinco state that the land located between *kuel* and between sacred hills and mountains is protected by standing ancestral men and women who are always depicted by two wooden *chemamüll* ancestor statues placed in or near *nguillatun* fields. Ancestors also appear in the form of protective animal spirits and visible animals, such as the hawks (*antüpainamko*) referred to by Faron (1964) in the title of his book on Mapuche religion. Rosales mentions the use of similar wooden statues as memory devices to remind the people of historical events and important warriors killed in battle (see Rosales [1674] 1989:120–140).

En sus cementerios plantan cruces en las tumbas de sus caciques; en los parlamentos o tratados que se hacen con ellos, exigen también que se les plante la cruz en memoria de lo sucedido, y mientras la yen, guardan fidelilad y respeto. (Rosales [1674] 1989:27)

In their cemeteries, they place crosses on the tombs of their *caciques*, during meetings they hold with them, they also demand that a cross be erected in memory of what occurred, and for as long as/while they can see it they remain faithful and reverent. (Rosales [1674] 1989:27)

Important to understanding the relations between Araucanians and animal spirits is the creation story, which has significant meaning to the relation between good and evil forces, people and their ancestors, natural hills and artificial *kuel*, and *kuel* and bodies of water (e.g., marshes and lakes). The story describes a great flood produced by an evil underworld snake, *Kai Kai*. Coming to rescue the humans from disaster are hills (*winkul*) that rise out of the floodwaters to provide a safe haven for people and animals. Living inside the hills is a benevolent snake called *Tren Tren*, who defeats *Kai Kai* in an epic battle. After their rescue, the people built artificial hills (the *kuel* in Purén and Lumaco) that take the form and name of *Tren Tren*, where special dedicatory ceremonies were and still are performed to propitiate the gods and to worship *Pillan* and the ancestral spirits. Today, each community or *lof* has a *Tren Tren* (*Ten Ten*) hill and a *Kai Kai* (*Cai-Cai*) hill, which usually are distinct, isolated physical features.

One of the earliest and most reliable observers of early Araucanian religion was Rosales who lived in the region during the 1620s and who first documented the original myth that is similar to one that I collected in the Purén Valley in 1985 and another that Bengoa (1985:9–10) recorded in the area in the 1980s.

Yellos que tienen muy creído que quando salió el mar y anegó la tierra antíguamente, sin saber quando . . . se escaparon algunos Indios en las cimas de unos montes altos que llaman *Tenten*, que los tienen por cosa sagrada. Y en todas las Prouincias ay algún Tenten y cerro de grande veneración, por tener creído que en él se salvaron sus antepassados del Dilubio general. Y están a la mira, para saber si hay otro dilubio, acogerse a él; para escapar de el peligro, perssuadidos a que en él tienen su sagrado para la occasión; prevención que pretendieron los descendientes de Noé, quando fabricaron la torre de Babel. . . . En la cumbre de cada uno de estos montes altos llamados Tenten, dizen, que habita una culebra de el mismo nombre, que sin duda es el Demonio, que los habla, y que antes que saliesse el mar, les dixo: lo que avía de succeder, y que se acogiessen al sagrado de aquel monte, que en el se librarían y el los ampararía. . . . Fingen también que avía otra Culebra en la sierra y en los lugares baxos llamada Caicai-Vilu, y otros dizen que en esos mismos cerros: y que esta era enemiga de la otra culebra Tenten y assimismo enemiga de los hombres, y para acabarlos hizo salir el mar, y con su inundacion quiso cubrir y anegar el cerro Tenten y a la culebra de su nombre, y assi mismo a los hombres, que se acogiessen a su amparo, y trepassen a su cumbre. Y compitiendo las dos culebras Tenten y Caicai, esta hazía subir el mar, y aquella hazía levantar el

27. Wooden *chemamüll* ancestral statues. Male figure is on the left and the female on the right. The two stepped-levels on top of the male's head represent the upper half of the stepped-diamond icon of authority depicted on the *makun* of *lonko* (see Fig. 38).

cerro de la tierra y sobrepujar al mar tanto quanto se lebantaban sus aguas. Y que lo que succedió a los Indios, quando el mar comenzó a salir y inundar la tierra, fue que todos a gran priessa se acogieron al Tenten, subiendo a porfía a lo alto y llebando cada uno consigo sus hijos y mugeres y la comida que con la prisa y la turbación podían cargar. . . . Y la otra culebra, que era como cosa diuina, que amparaba a los hombres y a los animales en lo alto de su monte, diziendo Tenten, hazía, que el monte se suspendiesse sobre las aquas, y en esta porfía subió tanto que llega hasta el sol. Los hombres que estaban en el Tenten se abrassaban con sus ardores, y aunque se cubrían con callanas y tiestos, la fuerza de el sol por estar tan cercanos a él, los quitó a muchos la vida y peló a otros, y de ay dizen que proceden los calvos. . . . Y que haziéndolo assí, se fueron disminuyendo las aguas y voluiendo a vajar el mar. Y al passo, que las aguas iban vaxando, a esse passo iba también vajando el monte Tenten; hasta que se assentó en su propio lugar. Y diciendo entonzes la culebra *Ten, ten*, quedaron ella y el monte con ese nombre de Tenten célebre y de grande religión entre los indios. . . . (Rosales [1674] 1989:27–29).

And they believe deeply that formerly, when the sea rose and invaded the land, they do not know when . . . some Indians escaped on the tops of high mountains which they call *Tenten* and consider sacred.

And in all the Provinces there is a *Tenten* and a mountain which is greatly venerated because they believe their ancestors were saved there from the general Flood. And they are on watch, ready should there be another flood, to withdraw there to escape the danger, persuaded that in their holy place they will have protection in the event, as did the descendents of Noah when they built the Tower of Babel.... They say that at the top of each of these high mountains called *Tenten* there lives a serpent with the same name, which is undoubtedly the Devil who speaks to them, and before the sea rose, it told them what was to happen and to take refuge in the sacred part of that mountain, that they would be safe there and he would protect them.... They also imagine that there was another Serpent in the land and in the low places called *Caicai-Vilu*, and others say on those same mountains, and that this one was the enemy of the other serpent *Tenten* and also an enemy of mankind, and in order to destroy them it caused the sea to rise and it wanted to cover and drown the *Tenten* mountain, and the serpent with the same name, and also the men who had put themselves under its protection and climbed to its summit. And as the two serpents, *Tenten* and *Caicai* competed, the latter causing the sea to rise and the former raising the mountain above the land as the waters rose. And what happened to the Indians, when the sea began to rise and invade the land, was that all in great haste sought refuge on *Tenten*, climbing steadily to the high part, each one taking with him his children and women and the food which, with the haste and confusion, they could carry.... And the other serpent, which was like a divine thing, which protected mankind and animals high up on its mountain, saying "*Tenten*," caused the mountain to be suspended above the waters, and in this enterprise it rose until it reached the sun. The men who were on *Tenten* were burned by its [sun] heat, although they covered themselves with pottery vessels and sherds, the strength of the sun, because they were so close to it, took the lives of many and the hair of others, and from this they say baldness comes.... And proceeding thus, the waters receded and the sea was lowered. And at the same time, as the waters were receding, the mountain *Tenten* was lowered at the same rate until it was seated in its proper place. And then the serpent saying, "*Tenten*," it and the mountain kept this name of *Tenten*, famous and greatly venerated among the indians.... (Rosales [1674] 1989:27–29)

According to shamans in Lumaco today, the tops of all *Tren Tren* hills were flattened in ancient times by the heavy weight of the large number of people and animals living on them to escape the floods in the origin story. These flattened

28. View of the *TrenTrenkuel* mound in Butarincón. Note the flattened used area on top and the footpaths passing over and around the mound that are used by local lineage communities.

areas are the *ñichi* platforms where mounds were built, such as *TrenTrenkuel*, the highest, most powerful, and largest *kuel* in the study area (Fig. 28). Located approximately 400 m northeast of *TrenTrenkuel* is a smaller mound called *KaiKaikuel* and *Pinuñichikuel*, (see Chapter 5) and across the Lumaco River and to the southeast of *TrenTrenkuel* is another smaller *kuel* also called *KaiKaikuel* (Fig. 29), which is identified with evil forces and *kalku* or sorcerers today. These *kuel* are said to represent the places in the valley where the battles occurred between the two snakes, *Tren Tren* and *Kai Kai*, in the origin story. All Mapuche *lov* or communities in the valley have *Tren Tren* and *Kai Kai* hills.

I should note that Faron (1964:75–79) interpreted the origin story as a struggle between the good and bad forces in life. I generally agree with him, but also view the story as the cultural production of nature and alliance-building between powerful totem-like creatures and the Araucanians. It also reflects social networks and other cultural phenomena and the use of relations between natural species and land to encode patterns of the historical relations among social groups and natural phenomenon, with *Tren Tren* adopting the role of mediator of the Araucanians.

Tren Tren, *Kai Kai*, *antüpainamko* (hawks of the sun), and other animal spirits also are depicted in Araucanian dreams, visions, stories, and symbols to metaphorically represent history and social relations. Various Andean scholars have discovered that animal imagery and metaphor function as an image of social history and social hierarchy (see Isbell 1978 and Urton 1985), which ultimately relates to the totality of social reproduction. As Urton has commented:

> As long as social groups and their interrelations are considered to be the primary motivation in human-animal metaphors, the metaphors will ultimately be intelligible only in relation to the patterns of inter-action which obtain at formal levels of organization, such as systems of alliance, descent, residence, and so on; that is, they will concern the formal, idealized institutions, structures, and practices by which society as a whole reproduces and validates itself within the public domain. The question then becomes, how does this relate to the formation of human social identity and the human (individual) construction of metaphors? (Urton 1985:4–5)

In the Araucanian case, these relationships are symbolically represented in animal form in ritual, stories, iconography, and the various systems of shamanism, curing practices, notions of death and cosmology discussed above and below. Yet, only those animals clearly linked within local ecological trophic orders ranging from carnivores at the top and insects and plants at the bottom are related to imagery and metaphor. These orders incorporate elements that participate closely with the productive contexts of the human world, such as bodies of water and celestial figures. The linkage between the Araucanians and their knowledge about and with the natural world also affects the designated spatiality of lineages and families in public ceremony, where they make metaphorical comparisons between their social and spatial positions in society and the trophic position of animals in the natural world. That is, the symbolic position of higher status lineages with metaphorical surnames of powerful celestial figures and carnivores (i.e., puma, eagle, hawk, jaguar, snake) is traditionally manifested in the spatial layout of the *nguillatun* and other public ceremonies (see Dillehay 1990c and below). As discussed earlier, knowledge about and mastery over these animals and about the social trophic orders they represent in public ceremony provide *machi* with power unavailable to others in the society.

THE CEREMONIAL MEETING OF *WENUMAPU* AND *NAG MAPU* WORLDS

Public ceremonies most dramatically represent the ideological and religious con-junction of the upper and lower worlds, of the living and their ancestors, and of kindred relationships between *kuel*. In ceremony, all planes of these two worlds are metaphorically collapsed into one spatially compacted event where deities and ancestors interact with the living on the earthly *Nag Mapu* plane. It is during

29. View of the *Kai Kai* hill located across valley from *Tren Trenkuel* (see Fig. 49). Note the series of small mounds on the ridge. Arrow points to the primary mound, or *winkul*, of *Kai Kai*.

ceremony when the greatest variation in ritual belief and behavior occurs on a local level, although a pantheon of major figures also are propitiated. There are various types of ceremony for different social occasions and all involve the concept of a "relationship of mutual dependence between the living and their ancestors" (Faron 1964:211). The degree of public importance and the size of the congregation are related to the function and meaning of ritual and to the level of social participation (e.g., family, sublineage, lineage, multiple lineage). For instance, a *rukatun*, the building of a new house, includes participation of related families while a *machitun*, the initiation of a new shaman, consists of family members, local elders, and *machi* of various lineages. A wide public level of participation takes place at the *awün*, *kueltun*, and *winkulkueltun* rituals, which usually include members of multiple lineages, and at the *nguillatun*, which is the largest public functioning congregation.

A major difference between these rites is that the *nguillatun* addresses a pan-Araucanian group of mythical ancestors and deities and works to maintain the presence of authentic ancestors in the *Wenumapu* world. The *awün* and *winkulkueltun* are more lineage specific and serve to escort the recently deceased into the *Wenumapu* world. The *awün* also orientates the authentic ancestors of specific local lineages to particular planes in the ethereal world. The *kueltun* is designed to assure their continued ascent into the upper world. Although different in content and purpose, these rites are inseparable in their general intent and purpose: as recognized by Faron, all center on maintenance of the relationship between the living and the ancestors and on negotiating time and space to structure history to desired outcomes.

The *nguillatun* ceremony is especially important because most *kuel* and *rehuekuel* are associated with old *nguillatuhue* fields (places where *nguillatun* ceremonies occur) in the Purén and Lumaco Valley. Faron (1964), Casamiquela (1960), Dillehay (1990c) and others (Alonqueo 1979; Foerster 1993) have noted previously that the *nguillatun* provides opportunity for the Mapuche to state their needs to the ancestors and gods, to publicly manifest interlineage marriage alliances, and in the past, to pray for victory in war. They pray for other things too: good health, the general conquest of good over evil, an abundance of crops and animals, and good weather. Today, the emphasis is on agricultural success, but in times of general duress or disaster from floods or earthquakes, the latter concerns are given prominence.

To understand the relationship of these ceremonies to concepts of time and space, I examine the following points: (1) the differences and similarities between them, (2) the conjunction of the vertically arranged ethereal space and the horizontally bounded physical space in ceremony, (3) how the settlement and community patterns of interrelated lineages reflect the interwoven relationship between the ecological trophic order and social structure of the ancestral world, and (4) how the socio-spatial structure of ritual behavior in the live *Nag Mapu* world models that of *Wenumapu* space. These same conjunctions and intersections of space and social relations take place at *kuel* and particularly at the larger and more complex *rehuekuel*, where multiple lineages unite for religious and political purposes.

I have studied these different ceremonies in variable social and ecological contexts, and have observed substantial variation in specific ritual belief on a local level (e.g., different minor deities and local authentic ancestors). But there also is a pan–Araucanian spatial, belief, and activity structure in ceremony followed by all communities. To illustrate my points here, I present one ritual community, Cherquenco, in the Province of Malleco, to exemplify the spatial and symbolic patterns I have observed at numerous ceremonies in other places.

Awün *(Awn)*

The funeral rite is the most direct and dramatic relationship between the living and the immediate dead. Faron contrasts the *awn* and the *nguillatun*.

> *Awn* is specifically geared to the safe passage of the recently released spirits (of the deceased) to the afterworld (*wenu mapu*), whereas *nillatun* is at least partly geared to keeping them there. And *nillatun* is a fertility

rite designed to exploit the obligation of these ancestors for the welfare of the living. *Awn* is more immediately concerned with authentic ancestors, *nillatun* more with mythical, regional deities, and *nenechen*. But the two ceremonies are more than merely complementary, they are duplicatory rites based on a common moral ideology. They are both also concerned with mitigating the influence of evil spirits on the living and the dead with the dispersion of evil spirits from the ceremonial field. (Faron 1964:108)

Although there are many aspects of the *awn* rite that are of interest, only one, the *weupin* (orations of burial ceremony) is elaborated here. Elder male mourners give discourse over the corpse. The *weupin* typically begins by making reference to supreme gods, mythical ancestral figures and spirits, and prays for the soul of the deceased by describing the nature of the sojourn that the dead will take as he transforms into an authentic ancestor. Near the end of the oration, the *weupin* traces the genealogy of the deceased "to the last remembered [authentic] ancestor of his patrilineage and extols the virtues of the principal male members on each generation back to the [authentic or mythical] founder" (Faron 1964:89). Also mentioned are the obligations of the ancestors to watch over the living as well as the spirit of the corpse (*layen*). The oration terminates with complimentary words about the deceased. As time passes, the spirit of the deceased eventually moves into the ethereal world and becomes the "last remembered [authentic] ancestor of the lineage." Once the transfer has occurred the deceased integrates his knowledge of the world of the living with past knowledge and history stored in the ethereal world of the mythical and other authentic ancestors.

I have no information on the factors determining whether or not the spirit actually becomes an *antüpainamko* (hawk of the sun) and how many years this process takes. Informants report that some spirits do not make it into the upper world, because they become the disciples of evil forces (*weupufe, weupife*). It is likely that continued contact between the spirit and the living in properly conducted and continuous ceremonies influences the outcome of the ultimate placement of the deceased (see Chapter 5). I also have been told that once the spirit achieves an authentic ancestral position, it first resides in the lower planes of *Wenumapu* space and, if it represents an important leader or other person, then transcends to the third and fourth levels as time passes, at which point it becomes a mythical ancestor. Informants say that continued *kueltun* soil cappings at burial mounds is the only way to help lift the spirit of an important deceased leader to make its way into the higher planes.

Burial in mounds is not the only form of bodily interment. In pre-Hispanic and Hispanic times the corpses of common people and offerings to them were placed in large urns or dugout canoes. In the late nineteenth century, the Araucanians turned to lining the grave with planks or logs and in most recent times to wooden coffins (Gordon 1975, 1978). In both the past and present, communal cemeteries are located on the most accessible ground in the community, usually on a lower hill slope below the domestic space of the living and above a creek, lake, or other body of water (see Chapter 6). Elevation of the burial spot above water places the spirit of the deceased closer to ancestors residing in *Wenumapu* space and makes it less susceptible to the influences of evil forces in the lower *miñchemapu* world. We have discovered that the majority of the historical cemeteries in the Purén and Lumaco Valley are located between domestic sites and bodies of water.

Winkulkueltun and *Kueltun*

Winkulkueltun is the rite of building the mound at the moment of interment of a deceased leader. That is, earth is piled on the grave of the deceased by relatives, friends, and allies to form a *kuel* (see Chapters 3 and 6). Every year after his death the lineage membership returns to the burial spot and places another layer of social soil or *reñimapu*; see Dillehay 1995) over the tomb, adding height and volume to the *kuel*.

Two once powerful and now deceased *machi*, Cármen and Fabiana, state that the act of recapping or placing more soil layers is a renovation ritual that reaffirms the bond between the deceased and the living. Informants also claim that each layer placed on the mounded grave corresponds to lifting the spirit of the corpse to a higher ethereal plane. The number of earth layers not only physically elevates the spirit and places it closer to *Wenumapu* space, but also symbolically correlates with the number of vertical planes and subplanes it passes through to reach the upper world. It is the successive vertical construction of *kuel* through the continued relationship between the dead and the living of interrelated lineages at the burial ground that ensures the spirit of the deceased a better chance to enter the upper ancestral world.

Nguillatun

The *nguillatun* is an agricultural fertility ritual usually held in the pre- and postharvest seasons. As Faron states above, the *nguillatun* also is designed to keep the ancestral spirits in the upper world. There is no exact ritual calendar, although the rite is usually performed around a full or crescent moon, at which time the fertility-bestowing god and goddess of the moon (*kuyenfucha* and *kushe*, respectively) are receptive to human prayer and sacrificial offerings. The ceremonies are planned by *machi*, elders (*ülmen, lonko*), and occasionally *nguillatufe*. Traditionally, three interrelated lineages (*trokinche*) cyclically rotate the obligatory responsibility of hosting the event (Dillehay 1995). Lineages external to the hosts are also invited. (*Nguillatun* administered by *machi* are generally absent in the cordillera

30. *Nguillatun* ceremony near Lumaco in 1981 that was attended by ca. 1,500 people. The animals in the foreground are slaughtered for consumption during the four-day event.

where little agriculture is practiced.) Played at most *nguillatun* is *palin*, which is a ball game enacted between competing lineages and mentioned often by chroniclers (see Chapter 3). Today, *palin* is ritually equivalent to battle; the members of competing teams are engaged in "war games" to prepare warriors, or players, for battle. (*Palin* is similar to the central Andean *tinku*, which also is a ritual war game among other things.)

The Cherquenco Nguillatun

The Cherquenco *nguillatun* is administered by three host lineages (*trokinche*) each year, with responsibility of holding the event revolving from one unit to the other every year. Each host keeps a permanent sacred field, the *nguillatuhue*, which is located on the communal land of the lineage *lonko*. Informants say that the field is sacred, never plowed, and always located in a flat area adjacent to or overlooking a body of water (creek, river, or lagoon). The size of fields varies according to the number of families that comprise the hosts and the invited units. I have observed as few as eighty individuals (e.g., the Quetrahue community in Lumaco) and as many as five thousand people (e.g., the Huilio community near Teodoro Schmidt) attending *nguillatun* in different areas. Today, the average number is between 200 and 600. In the past, the chroniclers describe this ceremony being attended by several thousand people (Fig. 30; see Chapter 3 and quotes below from chroniclers). In the 1600s, Núñez de Pineda [1673] 2003:101) states that some *junta* ceremonies had twenty thousand attendants.

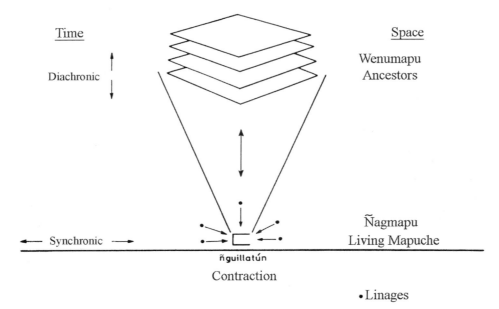

31. Schematic of the *nguillatun* field (lower rectangle with opening to the east) on the earth's surface (*Nag Mapu*), the lineages living around the field, and its contracted representation of four planes in the upper world (*Wenumapu*) and of the location of synchronic and diachronic time of the living and the ancestors.

The layout of the field is a semicircle or rectangular U-form with the opening to the east (Fig. 31; see Chapter 6 for archaeological description of ancient *nguillatun* fields.) Elders from Purén, Lumaco, and Los Sauces state that the U-form is the bodily profile of *nahual*, the stripped "*tigre*" or jaguar (*Felis onca*), with the base of the U being the body and the two sides representing the legs (Dillehay 1978, 1980, 1998). Others claim that the field reflects the filled-in rectangular sides of the southern cross (when mentally imagined). Although I have never been told that the *nguillatuhue* (or *nahualtue*, as referred to in this case) is both the jaguar and the southern cross, there may be a connection in that the feline is considered by the Araucanians to be the most dominant carnivore in all spaces and is capable of flying into the upper world and escorting the descent and ascent of ancestors and *machi* (cf. Zapater 1978:170). The intervening portal of entry and exit from and to the field and the *Wenumapu* world is the southern cross at the higher level and the open end of the U-form at the lower level. If a *kuel* is present in the field, then the flat top of its surface serves as the entry and exit point (Fig. 32: see also Fig. 25).

As mentioned earlier, much Araucanian knowledge was learned from the animals long ago. Informants in Purén and Lumaco relate that their ancestors used the seasonally fixed spatial configuration of the southern cross (and other

32. *Ñachekuel* mound showing the spiraling footpath used by shamans during ceremony to move from the central plaza in the *nguillatun* field to the top of the mound where the ancestors and deities enter and exit during ceremony. Note the two stakes on top where one black and one white sheep were sacrificial animals. Today, people still refer to the sacrificed animals as *cheque*, meaning "*oveja de la tierra*" or camelids (see also Figs. 52 and 53). The mound is ca. 2.5 m high.

stellar forms) above the earth to model the layout of multilineages in the *nguillatun* field. The cross is rectangular in form and has cardinal positions which parallel those of the ceremonial field. That is, the southern cross and the ceremonial field are one continuously flowing vertical space from the lower upper world (*ankawenu*) to the middle world (*Nag Mapu*). The form of these two bodies is an ideologically conceived reverse trapezoid with the southern cross representing the wider and upper side of the figure and the *nguillatuhue* field the lower and smaller base (see Fig. 25). In other words, it is a continuous flow of expanded (upper) and contracted (lower) spaces defined by similarity in their rectangular form. This configuration can also be considered a binary opposite, whereby the cross is an expanded version of the *nguillatuhue* field in upper space and the field is a contracted cross in lower space. Again, this vertically continuous corridor of space is the entering and exiting thresholds for ancestors and *machi* as they move up and down the vertically stacked cosmological planes in ceremony. As the supreme protector and organizer of this corridor, the feline in the form of the *nguillatuhue* field accompanies ancestors and *machi* during their travels. (As shown in the next chapter, this same corridor is used by shamans in communicating with deities during their dialogues with the sick *Hualonkokuel* and when the living ritual congregation ascends the sides of *Tren Trenkuel*.) It is the *ankawenu*

33. Individual *rucas* or family seating places and associated hearths (in front) in the *nguillatun* field as shown in the seasonally abandoned Repocura field.

world and its evil influences that initially test the validity, strength, and integrity of the relationship between the living and the spirits of the deceased that pass through it when moving to and from the *Wenumapu* world.

Internal Layout and Activity Structure of Nguillatun Space

The U-shaped layout of the field is formed by an alignment of individual family spaces constructed of poles and branches (Fig. 33) and by the *rehue* pole or *axis mundi* in the central plaza (Fig. 34). These spaces are built by each extended family of the participating host lineages. Each lineage and its families occupy a permanently designated seating area along one side of the U-shaped field. Located in the center of the field is the *rehue* pole. The seating arrangement of ceremonial participants with respect to the pole is important for understanding the intersection of *Nag Mapu* and *Wenumapu* space in the *nguillatun* and the relation between *kuel* in the valley. Living space in the *Nag Mapu* world is vertically structured from the domestic site at the lowest level of a hillside to the local cemetery at the intermediate level to the *rehuekuel* at the highest level or hilltop (see Chapter 6). This verticality also represents the ascent from the *Nag Mapu* level to the *Wenumapu* level.

The seating pattern is a contracted reflection of the actual multilineage settlement pattern of the host community. That is, those families and lineages located in the northern sector of the community sit along the north side of the

34. View of a *rehue* pole in the central plaza of a *nguillatun* field in the Andean cordillera east of Lumaco (courtesy of Arturo Rojas).

U-form, while those from the western sector locate along the west side and so on. The east end of the field is always open and bounded by a creek, marsh, or other body of water. No one occupies the grounds between the east opening and the creek, because it is the entry and exit way of the ancestral spirits from *Wenumapu*.

There also occurs a reverse dualism in the cardinal direction of ancestral entry to and exit from the above ethereal planes as opposed to the field. In passing from one vertical plane to another ancestors enter an ethereal plane through the west corner and exit through the east corner while entry to and exit from the horizontal ceremonial field is the opposite from east to west (see Fig. 25 for the direction of movement through the planes). During ceremony, the ancestors are called into the field by the *machi*. The spirits first enter through the east end of the lower ecological elements, and then move up the ecological nomenclature to the west end of the higher-order elements where the *lonko*, *machi*, and other important figures are seated (see Figs. 22, 35, and 41 for the layout of the field). The reverse occurs in *Wenumapu* space where the spirits enter into the *Nag Mapu* world by descending the four vertical planes from the highest trophic order to the lowest. Once again, the spirits pass from the east corner to the west corner of each plane repeating this pattern from one level to another. *Machi* report that the same spatial directions are followed around *kuel* when earth layers are placed on them during *kueltun* capping ceremonies; that is, ritual participants dance in a counterclockwise direction around the base of the mound, placing the individual basket loads of earth on the mound in the same direction.

Individual families are also seated in the *nguillatun* in accordance with the lineage community pattern. That is, each designated family area is a contracted side-by-side neighbor arrangement reflective of their location relative to the wider lineage and family settlement pattern. Figure 35 shows these patterns both on the lineage and family levels. The same spatiality of kinship patterns is applied to all other ceremonies and public events.

SPATIALITY OF RITUAL INTERCESSORS: *NGUILLATUFE* AND *MACHI*

The *nguillatufe*, the leader whose main role in many areas today is secular administration of the *nguillatun* (if a *machi* is conducting the service) and who usually is a *lonko*, works from the upper center of the ceremonial field near the west end. The *machi* directs services around the *rehue*, or *llangi llangi*, center pole where sacrificial animals, food, and *mudai* (*chicha*) are offered to deities and ancestors arriving from the *Wenumapu* (Fig. 36). The *llangi llangi* is flanked by several sacred plants – most of which are medicinal herbs and the sacred cinnamon tree or *foye* (*Drimys winters*). The vertical pole is the *machi's* altar used in staging communication with the ancestors above and directing ritual. The central placement of the vertical pole in the horizontal field signifies the intersection of the *Wenumapu* and *Nag Mapu* worlds.

The *rehue* pole takes various forms, ranging from an uncut pole to a cut-stepped pole with sculptured and painted faces and crossed-hands (Fig. 37). Crossed hands are a common feature on *chemamüll*. Shaman informants report that crossed hands represent permanent kinship, political, and ritual alliances between neighboring and distant lineages seated across from each other in *nguillatun* fields. Uncrossed hands also appear on *rehue* and *chemamüll*, and are said to represent different lineages with ephemeral ritual and kinship relations. Uncrossed hands are usually depicted by placement of one hand over the heart and the other over the stomach. Both crossed and uncrossed hands may point downward toward the earth or upward toward the sky. Upward-pointed hands reflect lineages with genealogical ties to high ranking and long-established regional ancestors in the *Wenumapu* world. Downward-facing hands reflect lineages with ties to local ancestors in the *Nag Mapu* world or the living earth's surface. (Cross hands also are common design motifs on stone sculptures and other artifacts at ceremonial sites of some Formative cultures in the Andes.)

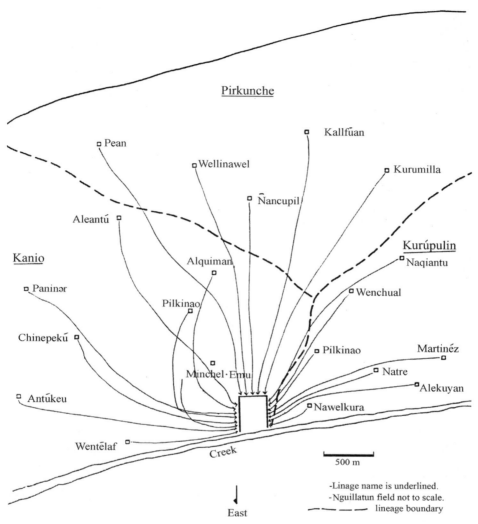

Pirkunche

Kallfüan

Pean

Wellinawel

Kurumilla

Ñancupil

Aleantú

Kurúpulin

Kanio

Alquiman

Naqiantu

Paninər

Wenchual

Pilkinao

Chinepekú

Pilkinao

Martinéz

Natre

Minchel·Emu

Alekuyan

Antúkeu

Nawelkura

Wentélaf

Creek

500 m

-Linage name is underlined.
-Nguillatun field not to scale.
— — — — lineage boundary

East

35. Spatial layout of the *nguillatun* field near Cherquenco, Malleco. Note the spatial correspondence between named families and their spatially contracted seating arrangement in the ceremonial field. Named lineage lands are underlined.

The stepped pole has four to eight steps that correspond to the vertical planes of the ethereal world. The number of steps depends upon the ritual knowledge and spiritual power of the *machi* conducting the ceremony. The least knowledgeable *machi* communicate with ancestors on the first or lowest ethereal plane of *Wenumapu* space. More powerful and knowledgeable *machi* contact the higher planes. *Rehue* are changed every four years. Old poles are buried facing east in a *menuco* (sacred body of water), which is a *rehue* cemetery.

As discussed later in Chapters 5 and 7, these spatial and symbolic relations are important to understand the flow of similar relations between *rehuekuel* sites,

36. View of a *rehue* pole in a *nguillatun* field that is associated with planted *foye* or cinnamon branches, *chicha* vessels, baskets of food, and other offerings during ceremony. Male dancers are chasing evil forces (*weupufe*) from the altar area.

37. Painted faces on *rehue chemamüll* in a *nguillatun* field near Cherquenco. The two figures represent male (right) and female (left) ancestral figures. Cross-hands, a common feature on *chemamüll*, are believed to represent the kinship ties between different lineages seated across from each other in the *nguillatun* field.

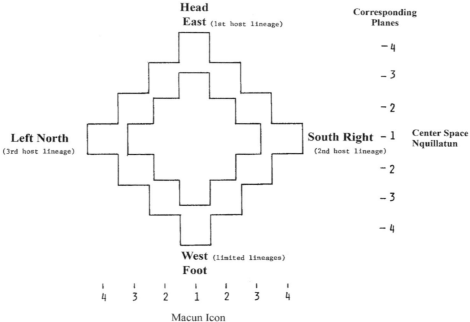

Head
East (1st host lineage)

Corresponding
Planes

– 4

– 3

– 2

Left North
(3rd host lineage)

South Right – 1
(2nd host lineage)

Center Space
Nquillatun

– 2

– 3

– 4

West (limited lineages)
Foot

4 3 2 1 2 3 4

Macun Icon

38. Stepped diamond motif on the *makun* ponchos of secular *lonko* leaders (upper photo). Cardinal directions of the motif, location of four lineages hosting a *nguillatun* and their place on the poncho, and the corresponding different cosmological planes represented by the vertical spacing of the motif (lower figure). Compare with Fig. 24.

where past ceremonies were cycled in a reciprocal zigzag pattern back and forth across the valley from one *rehuekuel* to another to unite the valley-long population during times of conflict and stress.

Iconographic Symbols of Ritual Spaces

The *lonko* or *nguillatufe* acts as a secular intercessor between the living, their ancestors, and the deities residing on the four ethereal planes. The spatially of these relations is symbolically depicted on his poncho or *makun* (Fig. 38). During ceremony, the *lonko* wears the *makun*, which exhibits an iconographic design in the form of a telescopic series of stepped or serrated geometric diamonds. This icon represents both sacred and secular authority. The stepped series is conceived as the ethereal planes of *Wenumapu* depicted in Figure 24 and a symbolic contraction of the settlement pattern of participating lineages and families. Each four-stepped side of the diamond also corresponds to the four-year ritual cycle of the *nguillatun* for each host lineage that resides in a different cardinal direction of the community. The open center area of the icon, which is either a smaller inset diamond pattern or a circle, symbolizes the central plaza of the *nguillatun* field.

Specifically, when viewed from a horizontal perspective, the four corners of the diamond motif correspond to the four cardinal directions of ethereal and living space, with the east at the top (or pointing toward the head of the wearer), the west at the bottom, the north at the left side, and the south at the right side. Each host lineage resides in a specific cardinal direction of living or *Nag Mapu* space and microcosmically corresponds to one of the four corners on the stepped diamond. When seen from a vertical perspective, the steps correspond to the vertical planes of the *Wenumapu* world. The host lineage is located on the fourth-highest plane or the top or east corner of the motif; the remaining three units correspond to the three lower surfaces of the motif, with the invited lineages related to the fourth and lowest plane. In short, each diamond quadrant and its stepped side represent a hierarchical configuration of the actual settlement pattern of each participating lineage and family in the *nguillatun*. Each lineage and its geographical location in *Nag Mapu* space are symbolically mirrored in the horizontal diamond icon while lineage affiliation with local mythical and authentic ancestors is correlated with the telescopic vertical layout of the total design motif. The symbolic role and communal position of a lineage along the vertical series of diamond motif planes shifts up or down the stepped icon according to the rotating role of the host lineage during ceremony.

The *machi* also is associated with a geometric design but one in the form of a cross on the *kultrun* (drum) (Fig. 39). Although there are stylistic variations of the cross on drums, the basic form depicts both ethereal space (vertical lines) and *Nag Mapu* space (horizontal lines) with the intersecting point representative of the *nguillatun* field where the live membership communicates with deities and

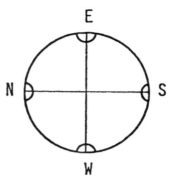

39. Schematic aerial representation of cardinal directions on the *kultrun* or drum of the *machi* shaman.

40. *Machi* playing the *kultrun* prior to climbing the *rehue* pole. Notice the *chicha* vessels on the *rehue* steps.

ancestors. When using the drum as a sounding signal to call forth and communicate with deities in *Wenumapu* space, the *machi* holds the instrument upright with the top of the cross (the east corner) pointed to the east (Fig. 40). When addressing the living participants in the ceremonial field, she beats it horizontally.

Since the *machi* is the primary ritual mediator who communicates with figures on all planes of the ethereal world, including the lower *miñchemapu*, the cross icon on the *kultrun* is not restricted to local lineages and to the upper surfaces like the motif design worn by the *nguillatufe*. The drum icon encompasses all lineages of *Nag Mapu* and *Wenumapu* space.

In essence, the icons associated with the *machi* and the *nguillatufe* are condensed physical spaces of their different levels of ritual knowledge and of the different ritual audiences they administer. The major difference between these two intercessors, as reflected in their roles and thus their associated iconographic motifs, is that the *nguillatufe* is bounded to the four consanguinal lineages participating in ceremony and is capable of communicating only with local deities and with direct or authentic ancestors of those lineages, all of whom are located in a particular area of ethereal space. The *machi*, on the other hand, are affiliated with a particular lineage but their services extend to many non-consanguinally related lineages, and they have the knowledge and flexibility to interact with or counterpose all ethereal forces, including evil ones influenced by the *kalku*. Thus, their range in the physical and ethereal world is much broader and their power is stronger.

Natural Symbolism and Ecological Trophic Order

In addition to the socio-spatial patterning of lineages in the *nguillatun*, there is a symbolic ecological structure reflected in the meaning and order of familial nomenclature along the U-shaped field. Figure 41 shows a literal translation of the names outlined in the Cherquenco field shown in Figure 35. Moving from the west or the base of the U-form down the wings to the east end, familial nomenclature takes the common names of specific natural elements (e.g., celestial characters, carnivores, herbivores, plants, rocks) of the regional ecological trophic order. That is, the highest ecological forms, the carnivores, occupy the west end or the top side of the field, while in ranked order below are the herbivorous animals and then plants and inorganic elements. Nomenclature order in the horizontal field parallels that of the ecological order outlined in the four vertical planes of *Wenumapu* space. Thus, there is a homologous structure in that the patterned trophic relations between ecological characters of the lineage-family nomenclature in the field mirror the relations between corresponding parts in the four planes of *Wenumapu* space.

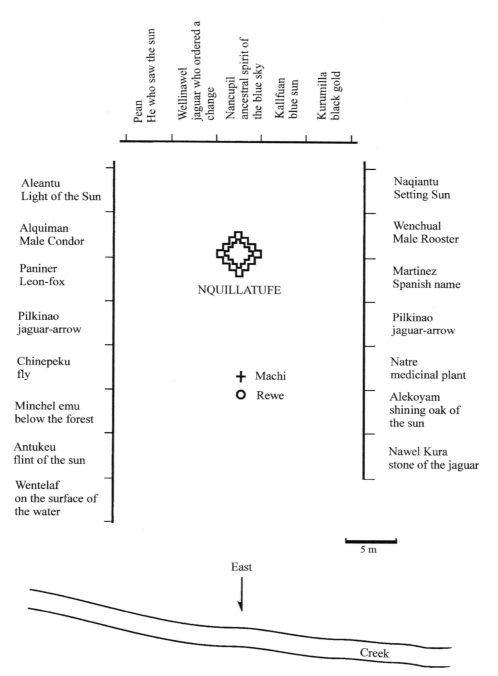

Pean
He who saw the sun

Wellinawel
jaguar who ordered a
change

Nancupil
ancestral spirit of
the blue sky

Kallfuan
blue sun

Kurumilla
black gold

Aleantu
Light of the Sun

Alquiman
Male Condor

Paniner
Leon-fox

Pilkinao
jaguar-arrow

Chinepeku
fly

Minchel emu
below the forest

Antukeu
flint of the sun

Wentelaf
on the surface of
the water

NQUILLATUFE

+ Machi
O Rewe

Naqiantu
Setting Sun

Wenchual
Male Rooster

Martinez
Spanish name

Pilkinao
jaguar-arrow

Natre
medicinal plant

Alekoyam
shining oak of
the sun

Nawel Kura
stone of the jaguar

5 m

East

Creek

41. Schematic of the settlement and seating pattern of named (Mapundungun and its meaning in English) families and lineages in the Cherquenco *nguillatun* field. Note the ecological trophic order of elements extending from the top or closed base to the lower or open end of the U-shaped field.

The importance of family names and the symbolic power especially given to carnivore terms is revealed by several Spanish chroniclers, including González de Nájera and Bibar.

> Presumen entre ellos de linajes o descendencias, y de apellidos, porque hay casas que se nombran del sol, otras de leones, raposas, ranas y cosas semejantes, de que hay parentelas que se agrupan y favorecen en sus disensiones y bandos. Y es tanto lo que se precian destos apellidos, que solo les falta usar de escudos de sus armas. (González de Nájera [1614] 1971:46)

> They assume among themselves lineages or descent and surnames, because there are houses named for the sun, others for lions, vixens, frogs and similar things, in which there are kindred which are gathered together and favored in their quarrels and factions. And these names are so highly regarded that all that is lacking is to use them as coats of arms. (González de Nájera [1614] 1971:46)

> A las puertas de sus casas, tienen dos palos, y arriba en la cabeza del palo tienen hecho del mesmo palo una águila; otras tienen gatos, y otras tienen zorro; otras tienen tigres y esto tienen por grandeza de gente noble. (Bibar [1555] 1966: 156)

> They place two poles at the doors of their houses and at the top of the pole there is an eagle carved from the same pole, and others have felines, and others have foxes; others have tigers and this is a sign of rank of the nobility. (Bibar [1555] 1966: 156)

In Figure 41, families whose names follow the lower elements of the ecological order are always located near the creek along the east end of the field. (There are exceptions to this rule, but only when the name has a double meaning that includes a higher carnivorous element, in which case the carnivore name is followed first.) Heading to the west or ascending the arms of the field, the higher ranking ecological elements are found. (Water is not only a lower element in the ecology but also the lower end of the vertical *Wenumapu* world.)

Further, the formal exchange of foodstuffs and the orientation of social contact between individual families of different lineages follows a diamond-like zigzag directional pattern from the east end to the south wing to the north wing and finally to the west end where the direction is reversed back to the east (see Fig. 25). This zigzag movement by the living also is said to be a horizontal *Nag Mapu* version of the different vertical planes of *Wenumapu* space where the ancestors reside, ascend, and descend in a zigzag back and forth pattern from one corner to another on each plane.

In sum, informants explain that the *nguillatun* field is physically and metaphorically structured to accommodate the relationship between the living members of *Nag Mapu* space and the ancestors and deities of *Wenumapu* space. The living participate in ceremony through ritual belief and behavior while the ancestors and deities are brought into ceremonial participation by *machi*, and are located subsequently in the field according to the socio-spatial structure of lineage nomenclature. They also construe the hierarchical patterning of ecological nomenclature in familial seating as a horizontally collapsed inversion (similar to the relationship between the *nawelhualtue* field and the southern cross) of the vertical *Wenumapu* world. The horizontal dimension of the ceremonial field represents the socio-ecological relationships between living members in the *Nag Mapu* world while the hierarchical layout and metaphorical structure of the ecological order in familial nomenclature, albeit horizontally arranged in ceremonial behavior and space, depict the vertical *Wenumapu* world. Moreover, it is the hierarchical order of ecological characters in familial nomenclature that metaphorically represents the primary and secondary sources of knowledge – that is, the animals and the ancestors, respectively. It is this order coupled with the designated space of families at the *nguillatun* that entails a ritually construed diagrammatic "succession of events" (or temporal history) or relationships between the animals, the ancestors, and the living. The *nguillatun* ceremony is thus only a synchronic spatial moment of history and of the formation of *Nag Mapu* and *Wenumapu* space. Narration, ritual prayers, and spatial relations between the living and the ancestors as represented in the total metaphorical layout of the event obligate all participants to fulfill their responsibilities to one another in anticipation of future events.

Further, all rites contain time (*kuifirapandungu*) as a spatialized succession of ancestral and living events. The contraction of the *Wenumapu* planes into the physical and metaphorical configuration of the *nguillatun* and all other ceremonies symbolizes a condensed diachronic time frame in which the total integrative history of the Araucanians is spatialized in one ritual episode of mutual obligations between the living and the dead. During the ceremony, space and time provide a set of bounded thresholds through which the intersection of the upper *Wenumapu* and *Nag Mapu* worlds meet. The most important aspect of this intersection of the two worlds is the socio-spatial order or succession of ritual events and of the propitiation of the trophically arranged ancestors and deities.

As for the *awn* rite, the direct relationship between the spirit of the deceased and his affiliated lineage does not relate to history throughout time and space. The attempt of the rite is rather a lineage directed expansion of the temporal-spatial context of the deceased so as to cautiously escort the spirit up the ethereal planes into the *Wenumapu* ancestral world. This expansion is achieved by the lineage through the successively annual addition of space or soil layers to the mounded tomb or *kuel*. Thus, the *awn* expands time and space to rejuvenate information in the ancestral world by sending updated experiences (those of the deceased) into the ethereal world. It is, on the other hand, the *nguillatun* that contracts the total time–space framework of history in order to utilize past ancestral knowledge.

Continuity from Past to Present in *Rehue*, *Kuel*, *Rehuekuel*, and *Nguillatun* Fields

The early sixteenth through seventeenth century chroniclers observed several ceremonies that correspond to the present-day *winkulkueltun*, *kueltun*, and *nguillatun* ceremonies, with the exception of human sacrifice and warfare, which are no longer practiced. (However, in response to an earthquake in 1972, shamans near the coast of Puerto Saavedra sacrificed a young boy to appease the deities for no further destruction. See Tierney 1989.) In observing Araucanian prayers for victory in battle and celebrations of victory, the chroniclers recorded several ceremonies named in Mapundungun, including *reguetun*, *guicha-boqui*, *boqui*, *cahuin*, *allihuene*, *ngatun*, *gnapitun*, *nguillatun*, and so forth. They also mentioned ceremonial gatherings as *junta*, *bebederos*, and *borracheras* in Spanish, meaning council meetings and drunken occasions, respectively. The Spanish also referred to some ceremonies as "consistorios y palacios de ayuntamientos" (town halls and palaces of town councils) (González de Nájera [1614] 1971:64), where dancing and drinking took place. Both secular (*toqui*) and sacred leaders (*boquibuyes*, *machi*) are mentioned as well the spatial layout and functions of ceremonial and political gatherings (e.g., González de Nájera [1614] 1971:120; Núñez de Pineda [1673] 2003:523–532). Observing in the mid-1500s, Bibar documents a ceremony similar to the *nguillatun* and refers to *lebo* (*lof*) social units and witches (*boquibuyes*, *machi?*) who speak with the devil.

> Esta junta dura quince y veinte dias y allí beben y se embriagan. En toda esta provincia se usa esto. En cada lebo son muy grandes hechiceros, hablan con el demonio. (Bibar [1555] 1966:160–61)

> This gathering lasts fifteen or twenty days and there they drink and become drunk. This is the custom throughout the province. In each *lebo* there are great witches who speak with the devil. (Bibar [1555] 1966:160–61)

Documenting in the early 1600s, Luis de Valdivia ([1606] 1887:433) briefly referred to a *reguetun* that is similar to a *nguillatun*. The description of a ceremony by Rosales ([1674] 1989) in the mid-1600s also is similar to the *nguillatun*. He states that it has a central altar made of the *foye* (cinnamon tree), a circular field, *chicha* consumption, exchange of marriage partners, sacrificial camelids or "*ovejas de la tierra*," and nonlocal invited allies. The first mention of the term *nguillatun*, or *gnapitun*, is by Núñez de Pineda in the mid-1600s.

> Aquella noche estaba dispuesto el baile y el regocijo que acostumbran en sus cavas y en el trabajo de sus sementeras... los demás *caciques* se acomodaron con las otras [mujeres] que venían en su compañía y empesaron a bailar con ellas de las manos; y, a persuaciones del Quilalebo, su padre, y de los demás principales ansianos, hice lo propio, habiendo antes de esto brindádonos las mosas, que es lo que acostumbran las solteras cuando quieren que las correspondan los que no tienen mujeres o cuando quieren hacer alguna lisonja a los *casiques* viejos; y de esta suerte suelen casarse en estas fiestas y bailes, que llaman ellos *gnapitun*. (Núñez de Pineda [1673] 2003:639)

> That night was given dance and joy which are customs in their communities and in working their agricultural fields... the other *caciques* arranged themselves with the other [women] who came with them and they began to dance with them hand in hand; and persuaded by Quilalebo, his father, and by other old principal [chiefs], I did the proper thing, before having done this the young women toasted us, which is a custom for unmarried women when they want to meet with men who have no women or when they want to flatter the old *casiques*; and if they are lucky they will marry during these feasts and dances, which they call *gnapitun*. (Núñez de Pineda [1673] 2003:639)

This quote also shows that these events were not just ceremonies but places where wares were traded, women were exchanged, justice served, and public affairs administered. These are the same functions described by elders in Purén and Lumaco for old *nguillatun* rituals at *rehuekuel*, which were varying combinations of *allihuene* feasts (see Bengoa 2003:29, 30, 101, 115) and *cahuin* political meetings. Whatever name they are given, most of the great festivals observed by the chroniclers appear to be *nguillatun*-like events attended by several thousand people. Núñez de Pineda ([1673] 2003:101) reports that some feasts were attended by as many as twenty thousand people. Quiroga mentions ceremonies having seven to eight thousand "souls."

> Celebran en partes señaladas, alegres y frescos... porque unas parcialidades convidan a otras y se ajuntan siete u ocho mil almas.... (Quiroga [1690] 1979:22)

They celebrate in designated places, pleasant and cool . . . because some lineages invite others and seven or eight thousand souls come together. (Quiroga [1690] 1979:22)

In their early descriptions of *guicha-boqui* ceremonies in the Purén Valley, both Rosales and Núñez de Pineda describe the *boquibuye* and *machi* who administered ceremony as being demonic and priestly and having great power (see Chapter 3 and quotes above). Rosales also identifies the *hechicero*, whom he describes as working with the devil, and the *machi*, who was a medicine person and healer (see Chapters 3 and 4). As described below, some *hechicero* were even powerful enough to make *toqui* warlords accountable for the deaths of important warriors and for the mistakes they made in battle. Núñez de Pineda's reference below to *machi* sacrificing animals, blowing smoke, and burning cinnamon trees also can be used to describe the same ritual and healing practices of *machi* today in the Purén and Lumaco Valley. *Machi* informants in Lumaco say that the smoke in past rituals carried the spirits of the dead warriors to the *Wenumapu* world where they became *antüpainamko* (ancestor spirits) (cf. Rosales [1674] 1989:163).

> los machis, que son los curanderos o médicos, es muy ordinario atribuir a esto el achaque y enfermedad del doliente, haciendo notables demostraciones de esto en las curas que hacen con sus yerbas . . . que algunos de estos machis tienen fama y opinión de hechiceros. . . . (Rosales [1674] 1989:347)

> the *machi*, who are healers or doctors, it is customary to attribute to this complaint and illness of the patient, providing notable evidence of this in the cures they bring about with their herbs . . . that some of these *machi* are renowned as and considered to be witches. . . . (Rosales [1674] 1989:347)

> Mientras andan los soldados en la Guerra, están los Hechizeros consultando al demonio sobre el succcesso de los suyos, incensando con tabaco a las tierras de el enemigo, I haziendo sus inuocaciones. . . . En aviendo algún mal successo, le echan la culpa al Toqui general, que convocó los soldados, para la guerra, y ha de pagar las muertes con chichi, i ouexas de la tierra, y con hazer otra suerte buena. (Rosales [1674] 1989:135)

> While the soldiers are at War, the witchdoctors consult the devil about the success of their [warriors], blowing tobacco [smoke] toward the lands of the enemy and making their invocations. . . . When there is a bad outcome, they blame the highest-ranking *Toqui* who called up the soldiers for the war and who must pay for the deaths with *chicha*

and sheep of the land [camelids] and make another good outcome. . . . (Rosales [1674] 1989:135)

los maches, que son curanderos, como entre nosotros médicos; que estos consultan al demonio, el cual se apodera de ellos cuando curan; de la suerte que lo llaman sacrificando un carnero, y con el humo del tabaco echándole de la boca incensan las ramas del canelo que hincan a la vista del enfermo. (Núñez de Pineda [1673] 2003:95)

the *maches* [*machi*], who are healers, as our physicians are among us; they consult the devil, who gives them power when they cure; when they call on him by sacrificing a camelid [*carnero*], and with the tobacco smoke they blow out through their mouths, they incense the branches of the cinnamon tree that is placed within sight of the sick one. (Núñez de Pineda [1673] 2003:95).

Along similar lines, Rosales ([1674] 1989:1154) states that the houses of the *machi* were located on a mountain or "convent" called a "*regue*" (*rehue*), which are places of feasting and burying rulers (cf. Bibar [1555] 1966:156; González de Nájera [1614] 1971:50). This description corresponds closely with the most important *machi* today who have their *rehue* and houses on high sacred hills above the valley floor. In some cases, these hills are the same ancient *rehuekuel* and *nguillatun* fields under study here and which have been continuously used for centuries.

y los Toquis generales, o los caciques más principales suelen conuocar la tierra para estas fiestas. Y en unas tienen, además de los bailes, sos entremeses, en que sacan figures differentes: y en otras truecan los trages hombres y mugeres. A otras fiestas conuocan: que llaman Guicha-boqui, en que ponen un arbol en medio del cerco, y de el pendientes quarto maromas adornadas con lana de differentes colores: de que estan assidos, para baylar todos los parientes de el que haze la fiesta, que como es el señor de la tierra; haze reseña de toda la gente noble que ay en ella. . . . Y sobre el árbol, que siempre es el canelo, para todas las fiestas, se pone el hijo del cacique o Toqui general, que haze la fiestas . . . y muy adornado de llancas, y piedras, el cual cuenta toda la gente noble. . . . Refiriendo las personas principales, que han muerto de su linage en aquellos años pasados, y dando el parabién a los presentes de que esten viuos. . . . La fiesta más solemne es, la que hazen los Boquibuyes que son los sacerdotes de el Demonio, para salir de su encerramiento, y dexar el hábito. Que para ella, no solo conuidan a los parientes, que les traigan chicha, y carne: sino los amigos; de muy lexos, que no tienen obligación a estas cargos, les obligan a que les traigan ouexas de la tierra, que son las más estimadas. Y aunque en otras borracheras, no las suelen matar: sino una, o otra por el aprecio, que de ellas hazen. Pero en esta borrachera matan todas las qua trahen los *Cullas*, fue assí llaman a estos amigos. Y ay grande fiesta y baile, que dura diez o doze dias. (Rosales [1674] 1989:141–142.)

And the head *toquis* or the highest-ranking *caciques* ordinarily summon everyone in the land to these feasts. And during some of these they have, in addition to their dances, their entertainments in which they represent different figures and in others men and women exchange clothing. They also hold other feasts called *Guicha-boqui* in which they set up a tree in the center of the circle of poles with four [ropes] hanging from it adorned with different colored wool yarn which are held so that all the relatives of the one offering the feast may dance who, since he is the lord of the land, calls forth all the nobility who live therein. . . . And in the top of the tree which is always a cinnamon tree at all the feasts they place the son of the highest-ranking *cacique* or *toqui* who sponsors the feast . . . and he is adorned with lances and stones as all the nobility tell it. . . . Referring to the high-ranking personages from their lineage who have died in past years and giving their blessing to the living who are present. . . . The most solemn feast is the one convoked by the *boquibuyes*, who are the priests of the Devil, may they leave their prison and abandon their habit. For this [feast] they not only summon their relatives to bring them *chicha* and meat but also [they call on] their allies from far away who are not obligated to this service and require from them sheep of the land [camelids] which are the most greatly esteemed. And although at other drinking feasts, they only kill one or another [camelid] because of the esteem they have for them. But at this drinking feast they kill all [the animals], the *Cullas*, as they call these friends, bring them. And there is a great feast and dance which lasts ten or twelve days. (Rosales [1674] 1989:141–142)

As noted by Montecino, several chroniclers associate the *regua* (*rehue*, *regue*) with a designated religious and political meeting place that also is similar to the *nguillatun* and *rehuekuel* where both ceremony and chiefly burial in mounds are brought together in the same place.

Ciertas veces del ano se ajuntan en una parte que ellos tienen señalado para aquel efecto que se llama *regua*, que es tanto como decir "parte donde se ayuntan" . . . este ayuntamiento es para averiguar pleitos y muertes y allí se casan y beben largo. . . . Y todo aquello que allí se acuerda y hace es guardado y tenido y no quebrantado. Estando allí

todos juntos estos principales, pide cada uno su justicia. Si tienen
Guerra con otro señor todos estos *cabis* y señores son obligados a salir
con sus armas y gente a favorecer aquella parcialidad según y como
allí se ordena . . . y allí venden y compran los días aquel cabildo y junta
dura. (Bibar [1555] 1966:160 [*sic*], cited in Montecino 1980:31)

At certain times of the year they come together in a place which
they have set aside for that purpose which is called *regua*, which is to
say "place where they meet" . . . this gathering is to hear complaints
and deaths and there they marry and drink long . . . and all that which
is agreed and done is kept and held and not broken. When all these
chiefs are there together, each one asks for justice [for his claim]. If they
are at war with another chief, all these *cabis* and chiefs are required to
present themselves with arms and men to support that group as they are
ordered . . . and there they sell and buy during the days that parliament
and meeting lasts. (Bibar [1555] 1966:160 [*sic*], cited in Montecino
1980)

Below, Núñez de Pineda adds that the enclosed field (*lepum*) of ceremonies
had a central altar (*llangollango*) where the *rehue* (*regue*) pole was placed. He also
gives the size of the central area of the *lepum* as 15 to 20 *varas* long and 5 to 6
varas wide, which is similar in size to *llangi llangi* areas today. In both the past
and present, the *llangi llangi* is comprised of *rehue* poles made of cinnamon (*foye*)
branches and is the place where food, *chicha*, and sacrificial animals (and humans
in the past) were offered to the deities and ancestors.

en el centro del lepum. . . . Se encerraba con ramas o cañas plantadas
de trecho en trecho, un espacio rectangular de unos 15 a 20 varas de
largo por 5 o 6 de ancho, dejando abierto uno de sus extremos. Dentro
de este espacio sagrado, llamado llangoll o llangollongo, se elevaba el
rehue propiamente dicho, que se componía de una especie de ramada
de unos dos metros y medio de alto, que formaba el verdadero altar.
Se llama llangiull y constituye una especie de mesa alto sobre la cual se
colocan las ofrendas y sacrificios. (Núñez de Pineda [1673] 1973:67)

in the middle of the *lepum* . . . a rectangular space of some 15 to 20
varas long and 5 or 6 *varas* wide is enclosed with branches or canes
planted at intervals, leaving one of the ends open. Within this sacred
space, called *llangoll* or *llango llongo*, was raised the *rehue* itself, which
was made up of a kind of *ramada* [or structure of branches] some two
and a half *vara* high which was the true altar. It is called *llanguill* and
was a kind of high table on which the offerings and sacrifices were
placed. (Núñez de Pineda [1673] 1973:67)

Several chroniclers also state that ceremonial places were special spaces and aesthetically lined with "*deformabas*" (deformed?) trees like "galleries and parks" (Bengoa 2003:93, 109). González de Nájera mentions that ceremonial fields "seem to be forests that were made or created for this affect, with little circulation and with high, deformed trees" (González de Nájera [1614] 1971:91). Elder informants in Lumaco told us that in the past the foot trails leading to old *nguillatun* fields were lined with large oak trees and that some mounds were flanked by sacred oak trees. Today, the largest mound in the *Rapahuekuel* complex is characterized by ten large oaks symmetrically placed around its base (see Chapter 6). (Growth rings counted in a core taken from one oak showed that the trees were planted more than 200 years ago.) Another large mound is called *Maicoyakuel*, which means a mound with ten oak trees. Local informants report that this mound once had many oaks planted around its base, but that they were cut down twenty to thirty years ago. Other informants state that another mound complex, *Rehueñichikuel* (Fig. 42), was stripped of most of its forest growth in the 1960s, so ceremonies could be seen from across the river (also see Chapter 3 and Núñez de Pineda ([1673] 1973:187–193). Only a few tall trees were left standing for an aesthetic effect. González de Nájera describes a similar setting in early 1600s.

> Y como en ninguna cosa ponen estos bárbaros más cuidado que en las pertenencias a su beber, tienen en los más amenos y apacibles campos, dispuestos particulares lugares para celebrar otras diferentes borracheras...que son unos bosques que parecen hechos o criados para tal efecto, de poco circuito y de altísimo y deformes árboles, lugares a los que comúnmente llaman los nuestros bebederos, por ser dedicados particularmente para beber los indios en ellos, donde como en consistorios o palacios de ayuntamientos, los caciques (y capitanes) en tales borracheras tienen sus consejos y determinaciones en las cosas de gobiernote la guerra, como tratar rebeliones, paces, jornadas o otras empresas. Cosa que causa maravilla, que para los negocios que les son de importancia se juntan en ocasiones de tanta embriaguez a determinarlos y que lo resuelvan tan a su provecho como lo hacen de que nos da testimonio el gobierno que ha tanto tiempo los conserva en su defensa. (González de Nájera [1614] 1971:48–54; see Bengoa 2003:112–13)

> And there is nothing in which these barbarians take more care than in the things relating to their drinking, they have designated special places in the most pleasant and peaceful fields to celebrate other different drinking feasts... which are several groves which appear to be made or cultivated for this purpose, of small circumference with very tall, strangely-shaped trees, places which our people commonly call

42. View of *Rehueñichikuel* ceremonial field in 1984 showing the forest cover cut back in order to view *nguillatun* ceremonies from across the river. Contrast this view with Figure 1 taken in 2002: the mound is presently blocked by the trees located on the left side of the photo. Black arrows point to *kuel* mounds: the central mound is flanked by two smaller mounds located on two low modified knolls. White arrows show the extension of the *ñichi* platform of *Rehueñichikuel*.

drinking places [*bebederos*] because they are where, in particular, the Indians engage in drinking, where, at these drinking feasts, as in consistories or palaces of council, the *caciques* (and captains) hold their councils and make decisions on matters of government, the war, how to deal with rebellions, peace, military expeditions or other undertakings. A thing which causes amazement, that to conduct business of such importance to them they meet on occasions of so much drunkenness to settle them and to resolve them so much to their benefit as they do to which the government they keep for their defense bears witness. (González de Nájera [1614] 1971:48–54; see Bengoa 2003:112–13)

Collectively, these quotes leave no doubt that the mounded ceremonial *rehuekuel* still in use today is the ancient *regue* places described by the chroniclers in Purén, that the *llangi llangi* altar today is the same as the *llongi llongi* pole of the past, that the *nguillatun* is the ancient *guicha-boqui* ceremony, and that the *machi* is similar to or was the *boquibuye* administering these ceremonies.

Today, informants report that when a *kuel* was built on a *ñichi* for burial of a famous war leader in the past and when the *kuel* gained fame as an oracle that could predict events and assist people through rituals administered by *machi*, people then began to make offerings and prayers to it. It also was at this point that ceremonies like the *nguillatun* began in the open spaces around *kuel*. Through *kuel* oracles and through their relations with *machi* in ceremonies, the deities and ancestors regulated the social affairs of people in the past for the sake of continuity in the future.

Continuities return us to a consideration of the origin of Araucanian religion and to the design, symbolism, and meaning of ceremonial space. I believe that Araucanian ceremonial space is a historically replicable Andean design that represents an ancient religious and political order, which differs primarily through its location, its chronology, its incorporation of local beliefs and images (e.g., carnivores and other natural elements), and its interpretation of these beliefs and images. Ceremonial activities in *nguillatun* fields are located and emplaced in the same representational order or standard for repetition and cross-lineage participation across time and space (see Chapter 6), which suggest a deeper historical format that connects to wider Andean and possibly Amazonian processes.

Andean Continuity in Ceremonial Space as Embedded in the Trophic Socio-spatial Order

Archaeological research indicates that the Araucanian ceremonial fields and associated settlements have their beginnings at least in the thirteenth century A.D. I have located and dated late pre-Hispanic U-shaped *nguillatun* and *rehuekuel* fields and through excavations have documented a spatial layout similar to that observed today in actively used *nguillatun* fields (as evidenced by postholes, hearths, trash debris, etc.; see Chapters 4 and 6). Given this correspondence, it can be inferred that similar internal activities were performed in these fields over the past few centuries. The similarity in events and spatial designs of ceremonies described by chroniclers writing from the late 1500s to the 1800s also suggests continuity in the general form, function and meaning of ceremonies (cf. Chapter 3).

In previous works (Dillehay 1978, 1980, 1981, 1985a, 1998), I have discussed similarities in the U-shaped ceremonial structures and in the iconographic designs of Formative cultures in the Central Andes and of pre-Hispanic and contemporary Araucanian culture. Although these cultures are far removed from one another in time and space, I believe that they both reflect similar sociocultural patterns in the layout and use of ceremonial space and iconography. I am not implying that these cultures are directly related historically. Rather, I view them as Formative developments of a continuous theme that repeated itself in Andean time and space. Central to revealing one aspect of this theme is an exemplary comparison between the iconography of the Tello Obelisk at the Chavin de Huantar site in Peru (Fig. 43; Lumbreras 1974:80, 1985; Rowe 1967:99), which dates

43. The Chavin Tello Obelisk modified from Rowe (1967: also see Dillehay). Note the stepped-diamond motif in the center.

approximately 1,500 to 1,800 years ago, and the metaphorical lineage nomenclature and layout of the *nguillatun* field.

As described above, a dualistic theme exists in the symmetrical trophic order of familial nomenclature along the two wings of *nguillatun* fields. Participants seated in the central base of the U-form are collapsed into the central open area of the plaza during dance and ceremony. Lineage families seated around the wings also maintain a formal dance and congregational position in this area. Another distinguishing characteristic is the linear formation of the *nguillatufe* or *lonko* (represented by the stepped-diamond motif in the upper center of the field), the *machi* (represented by the cross icon), and the *llangi llangi* altar and *rehue* pole in the lower center area. The *nguillatufe* and the *machi* are flanked on the left and right by four apprentices, two *dunguguillatufeu* and two *dungumachifu*, respectively (Fig. 41).

The Obelisk, which is located in the central U-shaped plaza of the Chavin de Huantar site, is also characterized by a symmetrical arrangement in the faunal and floral trophic order of its binary iconographic rows (Fig. 43). Although the lower case herbivorous characters are not represented in the iconic configuration, plants do occur. The harpy eagle, jaguar, serpent, and cayman comprise the carnivorous animals. Icons with a dual carnivore representation, such as the serpent with the fangs of a jaguar and the snake with the claws of a harpy eagle, also occur. Also notable is a vertical line of individual noncarnivorous motifs in the center of the Obelisk. In the upper portion of the Obelisk is a stepped-diamond icon flanked on the left and right by smaller replicas. A plant, stemming from a human head with fangs, dominates the lower area. Flanked to the left and right of this figure are two smaller human heads. In brief, this central line of characters is somewhat reminiscent of the linear position of the *nguillatufe* and his two *dungunguillatufe*, the *machi* and her two *dungumachifu*, and the *llangi llangi* altar in the *nguillatun* field.

The general layout of the U-shaped ceremonial field and the composition and order of the Chavin iconography on the Obelisk and the *nguillatun* metaphorical nomenclature may reflect parallel spatial designs and trophic themes and possibly a similarity in social and cosmological meaning. Of particular interest is the dominance of carnivorous elements in both the iconography and the nomenclature, the similar position and stylistic expression of the stepped-diamond motif (which is a common iconographic motif throughout the Andes), and the binary symmetry of metaphorical characters separated by a center line of different features in both U-forms. Another parallel is the use of matching carnivore icons and nomenclature – for example, the jaguar-serpent, jaguar-harpy eagle, jaguar-cayman motifs on the Obelisk and the jaguar-arrow and jaguar-flint nomenclature in the *nguillatun* field. Both the Obelisk and the *nguillatun* nomenclature exhibit natural elements, albeit few, that are singularly complete in bodily form. When such elements are present, they are usually characterized in terms of contextual action. For instance, the Obelisk contains an independently positioned flying bird in the upper right hand corner. In the *nguillatun*, there are names such as the male condor (*alquiman*), the seated jaguar (*pilkinao*), and so forth that do not have their counterparts along the wings and that are whole metaphor elements reflecting action.

In particular, the jaguar theme can possibly be seen as symbolizing populated space and people's effort to achieve an ordered settled community and lifeway (Dillehay and Kaulicke 1985). The feline motif, particularly the jaguar, is not only one of the dominant animal elements in the Chavin culture, but most Andean and Amazonian cultures as well (see González 1998; Lathrap 1985). It is an icon that transcended time and space in the Andes, suggesting that the symbolic aspects of this animal always held an important communicative and mediator role in ideological syntheses. Again, I am not suggesting that there is a direct developmental connection between elements of the early Formative cultures of the Andes and the more recent Araucanian culture. However, there are parallels that suggest both cultures evolved from a repetitively occurring Andean and possibly Amazonian ideological pattern. Like the Araucanian *nguillatun* fields and their association in some areas with feline- or *nahualtue*-designated ceremonial fields, the Chavin Obelisk and similar Andean visual forms might entail the metaphorical expression of social and cosmological meanings similar to those depicted in *nguillatun* ceremonies. Taken together, these forms may represent a socio-spatially contracted cosmology of the diachronic relationship between animals and other elements, the ancestors and the living, and the persistent integrity of this relationship as manifested in the binary spatial organization of the ethereal world and the community pattern of the living as mediated through public ceremony administered by shamans and/or ritual priests.

Over the past twenty-five years, I have intermittently shown copies of the major art and iconography of several preindustrial complex societies to *machi* informants in the Purén and Lumaco Valley. Egyptian, Olmec, Chinese, Persian, and Andean art forms were depicted without any wording or identification of their sources. All of these forms shared carnivorous animals (mainly felines, lizards, crocodiles, snakes, and raptorial birds), plants, and geometric designs. Two *machi* said that the art meant nothing to them, although they recognized specific human, feline, snake, and other animal and plant elements. Three *machi* responded only to the Obelisk iconography. They said it was old, complicated, and related to the *Tren Tren* and *Kai Kai* origin tales of their ancestors and that the iconography and layout of the Obelisk represented an ancient *nguillatun* ceremony, with the stepped-diamond motif in the middle representing the symbol of authority of the *lonko*. They also remarked that the composite of the Obelisk design was too compacted and should be spread apart, which gave me the idea to draw the split design in Figure 43. We asked what the difference was between the Obelisk and the non-Andean artistic schemes they did not understand. They said it was the arrangement and combination of the elements of the Obelisk that made sense to them.

The *machi* associated *Tren Tren* and the origin story of the Araucanians with the cluster of snakes in the upper part of the Obelisk, with feline elements in it, and with the use of this iconography by *machi* (see Zapater [1978] who associates the *machi* with felines). They also said that the serpents in the Obelisk iconography were family members of the benevolent *Tren Tren* in the tale. In order to defeat the evil world of *Kai Kai*, *Tren Tren* had to increase its presence across the land, the shamans remarked, which accounted for the numerous snakes in the iconography (and numerous *Tren Tren* hills in all Mapuche communities today). They also said that the snakes were related to the Araucanian moon goddess *kuche*. Also identified in the Obelisk was the eagle or *kokorrin*, which was related to the appearance of tumultuous water (flooding). *Kokorrin* was described as a dangerous animal that kills livestock. Also identified was the *panqui*, puma, or feline, which they said was easy to manipulate. (They did not explain why it could be manipulated.) The *machi* also saw three different types of pottery vessels in the Obelisk: the *ketru-metawe*, that is used by women during ceremony to drink *mudai* (*chicha*), or when special people visit the *ruka* (home) of a relative or friend. Another is the *trewa-metawe*, which is used by important people, mainly *lonkos*, in special occasions. The last is *kawell-metawe* in the shape of a horse and is used by common people. Most significant to the three *machi* was that the entire Obelisk design represented a graphic story of the great flood and the origin tale of the epic battle between the two snakes, *Tren Tren* and *Kai Kai*, and that the moon served as a scheduling calendar for planting and harvesting crops and for ceremonies. Finally, they thought that the small central human figures in the Obelisk were *machi*.

In addition to the Obelisk, the *machi* responded to a well-made stone artifact that depicts a snake and another reptile (a cayman or lizard?) in raised relief (Fig. 44). The *machi* identified the snake as *Kai Kai* and the other figure as *Tren Tren*, saying that the artifact shows them in battle. The stone was recovered from an archaeological site in the Araucanian region but has no secure provenience. Snakes still are mentioned in ritual narratives today, as revealed in Appendix 1 (Hualonkokuel XIX: 4), when the *machi* says she is walking among snakes when speaking with the *kuel*.

In sum, several important elements are involved in the *machi's* interpretation of the Obelisk, including the ritual administers, common people, agriculture, the moon, feasting and the use of vessels to consume *mudai*, and the powerful carnivorous animals. Did the Obelisk iconography once relate an origin story similar to the *Tren Tren* and *Kai Kai* tale for the Araucanians? How much of Araucanian prehistory and history can be related to Andean and Amazonian histories? The fact that the Araucanians are most strongly related linguistically and genetically to eastern tropical lowland groups indicates that some of the

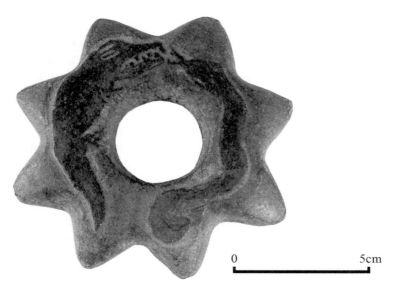

44. Stone implement with raised-relief of a reptile (cayman?) and snake. (photo courtesy of the Museo Chileno de Arte Precolombino).

symbolic and cultural patterns discussed above may have an Amazonian origin, even if they have been syncretized with Andean and local patterns (see Chapter 3). How much cultural hybridization, syncretism, and archaism has taken place in the Araucanian society over the past several hundred years? What do these patterns imply about wider social transformations in the Andes and in Amazonia?

COSMUNITIES AND CONCLUSIONS

While it would be a mistake to take Araucanian religion only as an expression of a pan-Andean religion, one may take it as representative of broader Andean and Amazonian cultural premises and tendencies. The sharing of underlying concepts makes possible historical comparison with societies beyond the geographic limits of the Araucanian region, both as observed in past times by chroniclers and indirectly by archaeologists and as experienced by modern ethnographers. The durability of this religion and its specific belief system, cosmology, and material expression reflect the Araucanian's tenacity to resist outside influence and to remain attached to their land, to their culture, and to their history.

Araucanian reference to deities and ancestors in tales, narration, and belief signify much more than a religious reverence for an anthropologically conceived "supernatural" milieu of figures who attempt to control such external forces as floods, earthquakes, climate, and crop productivity and who obligate the living populace to fulfill traditional norms of behavior. These figures are also metaphorical representations of good and false knowledge about traditional behavior, people and their environment, identity, and history. Inquiry into the temporal-spatial and structural-functional context and meaning of ancestral knowledge sources and into the social fluidity of their memory and use in the live world are important considerations for understanding the integrity and continuity of Araucanian society and especially for understanding the location, function, organization, and meaning of *kuel* and *rehuekuel* as components of an Araucanian *cosmunity*. To the Araucanians, space is a culturally derived topography of ethereal images that bounds the extent of knowledge providers and users in ethereal and living space. What they perceive in the living *Nag Mapu* world is not real space but only utopic ideas of space that are symbolically coded versions of the ancestral events that preceded them. As discussed earlier, the successive order of these events is important, since it reflects patterns of public thought and decision-making processes. That is, these ordered events are vehicles through which the living are informed about how things were done in the past and perhaps about how things should be done in the future. They also see the socio-spatial organization of lineages and families dictating the directional lines of order in the *nguillatun* and *rehuekuel* fields, all of which form the valley-long cosmunity of social history between the living and their ancestors. But it is social organization that actually follows the previous ordered ancestral lines, all of which is organized aesthetically, temporally, and spatially in the fields to create effective utopic spaces imbued with meaningful relationships and obligations between individuals, families, and different lineages.

I have studied the symbolic relationships between families and lineages and the layout of the *nguillatun* fields within which they operate ritually, seeing the latter as reflecting a microcosmic map of the larger community settlement pattern. The placement of social soil on and around the *kuel* also follows the community pattern of families and lineages in domestic space. That is, the aesthetic arrangement of ritual often reproduces the map of the spatial order of the real social world. This modeling of kinship structure is understandable in that it would seem desirable for any large-scale political apparatus (i.e., *ayllarehue* and *butanmapu*) to gain an ideological foothold in local knowledge and symbols to guarantee intelligibility, to facilitate the assimilation of its order by newly recruited lineage compatriots, and to argue for its enduring legitimacy. But it is also the reverse among the Araucanians whereby the *nguillatun* field follows the order of the domestic world and reflects a map of family and lineage settlement patterns outwardly in space. In this regard, the reverse reflection is to project the domestic lineage into public ritual to facilitate community organization and the assimilation of multiple lineages. It is this reversed representation of contracted domestic space in ritual ceremony and of contracted cosmological (and ancestral) space in domestic sites that intersect to form the *cosmunity*, which is an aesthetic utopic construct that is designed to employ effective political results and notions of appropriate social practices.

The *nguillatun* ceremony also is a diagrammatic intersection of introspection on metaphorical excerptions from past ancestral learning experiences. Other ceremonies (e.g., *kueltun*, *awn*, and *kueltun*) are similar but on a more local scale. The Mapuche become cognizant of these experiences and use them to their fullest extent only by publicly spatializing time in ritual ceremony. Thus, ceremony is a spatial *Nag Mapu* moment when the diachronic ancestral world is turned into a synchronic one. Moreover, temporally successive events are excerpted and seen in a contracted spatial side-by-side metaphorical nomenclature of lineages and families in *nguillatun* and *kueltun* ceremonies. These ceremonies provide occasions for *lonko* leaders, *machi* shamans, *nguillatufe*, *weupin*, and individual families and lineages to employ their different knowledges to negotiate trade and marriage relations and to position themselves closer to *admapu* traditional ways.

Metaphorical nomenclature and iconography also play an important role symbolizing further the diagrammatic intersection of past successive events in the ancestral ethereal world and of the ongoing live world. The aesthetic visual effects of seeing this contracted intersection in ceremony is an analog of actual behavior. However, at any moment the Araucanians can be aware of only a part of the successive events. Their selection from the collection of possible attentions to an ancestral event depends upon their knowledge of it. Thus, their knowledge at any given public moment (or ritual congregation in space) is a function of the type and level of contact the ritual intercessors (*machi*, *lonko*, *nguillatufe*, and *weupin*) have with the ancestors and deities and of their ability to act as lineage agents in the larger vertically stacked cosmological world.

All ceremonial behavior is characterized by a constant confrontation with spatial thresholds of the upper and lower cosmological world. The individual vertical planes of this world and the horizontal layout of the *nguillatun* and *kueltun* ceremonies are synchronic profiles of all ancestral behavior. Social behavior in the *Nag Mapu* world is analogically used to describe ancestral behavior in the upper space. As stated earlier, space is a temporal form of introspecting upon a live synchronic moment. Thus, there is a spatial conciliation in ritual ceremony, doing in ceremonial space what ritual narratization does in mind-space or spatialized time (see the ritual narratives in Chapter 5). Space thus brings together knowledge sources just as origin tales and ritual narratives bring together a succession of events.

There also is a hierarchical arrangement that follows the ecological trophic order of the cosmological world and the familial nomenclature. It would seem that a hierarchical strategy optimized the ethereal threshold routes between the ancestral planes of the *Wenumapu* world and the individual sets of multilineage communities which made up the living *Nag Mapu* population. The threshold route to ancestral experiences was and still is defined by a progressive agglomerative ritual contraction, beginning with the *Nag Mapu* living and the *Wenumapu* ancestors and ending with a temporal-spatial intersection of the two populations at the *nguillatun* field. The *awn* funeral rite, on the other hand, works in an opposite direction by expanding the social and spatial participation of the living, the deceased and the ancestors of different ethereal planes over a successive number of years and, in the case of the *kuel*, through a successive number of vertically stacked social soil layers that reach or expand through time and space.

This hierarchical contraction–expansion or unfolding and refolding strategy of time and space must necessarily optimize some joint meaning between the living and the dead and their fusion and fission in ceremony. As a result, the live communities through which the contraction or expansion process is initiated are not themselves necessarily optimal; the best route is obtained at the expense of the homogeneity of local and regional ritual belief, thought, and practice. I believe it is the socio-spatial fluidity and continuity of the *Wenumapu* and *Nag Mapu* contraction–expansion strategy, which has made ancestral knowledge (and its updating) accessible through public ceremony, that is the binding element that has primarily maintained persistence in and integrity of the Araucanian lifeway over the past several hundred years. Faron recognized this bond more than four decades ago:

> There has been a processual consistency with respect to traditional beliefs and action. This temporal continuity of structure is, of course, what has served to distinguish Mapuche from Chilean society. It is most apparent, because most dramatic, in the area of ritual, but it ramifies throughout the total ideological and social structure. Until the ideological orientation of the Mapuche undergoes radical change, we might expect that Mapuche society will remain relatively stable. (Faron 1964:206)

To Faron, the social behavior of the individual members of Araucanian society is dictated by religious beliefs, moral rules, and cultural values, which in turn are centered on "ancestral propitiation." He believes that "a function of ritual belief is the establishment of limits to possible variation in social action" (Faron 1964:205). To transcribe this thinking to the past, I see these limits as ways to code proper conduct by members within the society and to entrain new compatriots joining larger politico-religious organizational units such as the *rehuekuel*, *ayllarehue*, and *butanmapu*,

To conclude, most scholars of Araucanian religion agree that within local belief systems deities and ancestors can be considered as points in a system of complementary oppositions that ramify downward from the most cosmic or pan-Araucanian level through regional gods (volcanoes) to local origin shrines representing self-defined collectivities at descending levels of inclusiveness (cf. Alonqueo 1979; Bacigalupo 2004a–2004d; Cooper 1946; Dillehay 1990c; Faron 1964; Foerster 1993). Ancestral *kuel* mounds manifest the lower, more local branches of the oppositional tree, corresponding to localized kindred. That is, *kuel* mediate between people and earth; they are the agents of the upper world of the deities;

they are the progeny of earth and reside in the openings of the earth, but they are also progenitors of living people and apical members of local society. Through their mediation sacrifices go to earth, and well-being and victory come out of the *Wenumapu* world. When *nguillatun, dahatun, kueltun* and other ceremonies take place around *kuel* located on a topographically dominant *ñichi*, the combined space becomes a *rehuekuel*. The *rehuekuel* then represents a more temporally and spatially intricate history and politico–religious order that holds deeper social and cosmological meaning. In turn, when *rehuekuel* (and other sacred landscapes) are combined with cemeteries and domestic settlements, which are reflected by and are reflections of *rehuekuel*, enduring cosmological communities are formed.

FIVE:

THE ETHNOGRAPHIES OF *KUEL*, NARRATIVES, AND COMMUNITIES

With José Saavedra

In the last chapter, I presented information on the Araucanian's religion, ideology, and sources and uses of indigenous knowledge and how they relate to *kuel* and other cultural landscapes and to social history. This chapter presents an interpretative description of the ethnographic knowledge specifically related to the function, meaning, and effectiveness of *kuel* and *rehuekuel*. It remains clear from the culture memory and fading use of mounds by communities in the Purén and Lumaco area that the primary sources of knowledge about them are the *machi* and that *kuel* and *rehuekuel* are linked primarily to public congregation and political discourse, to fertility and healing rites, and to kinship linkages between the living, ancestors, and deities. As presented below, various informants provide rich data on the material, spatial, and temporal dimensions of mound building and mound use and on the names and meanings of individual *kuel* and *rehuekuel*. Especially significant are two long ethnographic ritual dialogues that I recorded in the field between shamans and *kuel*, which reveal specific historical functions and meanings of mounds that often refer to the suffering brought by increased deaths and illnesses derived from prolonged contact with the Spanish and Chileans. The following data have been collected over a thirty-year period from more than two hundred informants from many different communities scattered throught the Araucanian region. Although primarily synchronic in nature, these data provide a comparative support base for analysis of the ethnohistorical and archeological records.

Ethnographic Teachings

In 1978, when I first sought information on the mounds from local Mapuche in Lumaco, I was told that they were "*morros*" in Spanish and *winkul* (natural hills) in Mapudungun. I was also informed that the mounds were old, or *kuilfil*, and were constructed by the ancestors. According to oral tradition, important *lonko* (chiefs) and *toqui* (war leaders) were buried in them. Younger Araucanians less connected to the past said the *morros* were used today as lookouts over the valley below: some elders told us that they were towers to scout for animals and, in the past, served as places to send smoke signals in times of war and as sacred ladders to reach the deities and ancestors in heaven. Given the location of some mounds in low wet places hidden by surrounding hills, they could not have served as lookouts or signal places. Also, mound clusters that often form circles and rectangles could not have been used to send signals. Although these responses informed us how a few acculturated Mapuche perceived the use of *kuel* today, they told us little about how mounds were used in the past, why they were built, why they were placed on hilltop or hillcrest *ñichi* (*terra pleins*) and clustered in some areas, how and why they were used in ritual to sustain the relationship between the living and the dead, and why *machi* and not *lonko* were primarily associated with them, although the latter are buried in them. Five *machi* and several local elders, including *lonko* and *weupin*, were our primary informants. The *machi* were Lucinda and Juanita, and the late Cármen and Fabiana, all from the Lumaco and Remihueico areas.

NAMING AND KNOWING *KUEL*

Figure 49 in Chapter 6 shows the location of the principal *kuel* and *rehuekuel* in the Purén and Lumaco Valley, together with their names. Most named *kuel* are located in the Rucalleco, Isla de Katrileo, and Butarincón (*Fuchapichon*) communities, which border the west side of the Lumaco River and the conjunction of the Purén and Lumaco rivers. This area has the largest concentration of *kuel* and *rehuekuel*, and shamans still using them. For reasons not well understood, several *kuel* have multiple names given by different *machi* and by different individuals from different communities. However, most *kuel* have only one name, such as *Hualonkokuel* (Fig. 45) and *TrenTrenkuel* (Figs. 28, 46), or a principal name. Informants also interpret many names differently, although there often is agreement on a single or principal meaning. Further, because many names are ancient Mapudungun terms that are little used today, their exact meanings are not always known (see Faron [1964:98, 109] for discussion of the esoteric ritual terms employed by *machi*). Several possible meanings are implied for most *kuel*, which are listed below. We have worked with Maria Catrileo (1998), a Mapuche linguist at the Universidad Austral de Chile, and with several colleagues, including Gaston Sepulveda, Arturo Rojas, Raul Ortiz, and the late Américo Gordon, to derive the meanings of mound names. These meanings were verified by *machi* and other informants.

All informants claim that the largest and most powerful mound in the valley is *TrenTrenkuel*, which is centrally located on the highest crest of the chain of low

45. General view of the *Hualonkokuel* mound (arrow to right) and the *nguillatun* field in its plaza (arrow to left). Note the *rehue* pole in the plaza and the trash left behind after a recent ceremony. Compare Figure 9, which was taken from the opposite direction during a period of disuse of the field.

hills in Butarincón (Fig. 46). This *kuel* takes its name from the benevolent snake in the origin tale about the great flood (see Chapter 4). They also say that until the 1970s, *Tren Trenkuel* was a *cahuin*, or meeting place, where *lonko* met to make important decisions, *weupin* spoke, and *nguillatun* were held. Informants claim that the power of *Tren Trenkuel* is derived from its height, which is said to reach into the upper *Wenumapu* world where the deities reside, and from its history as a refuge for ancestors threatened by the great flood long ago. They also claim that the mound covers the bad snake, *Kai Kai*, that lives in the underworld of *miñchemapu*, and that the mound changes its identity to *Tren Tren* to combat the evil *Kai Kai* should it appear again. Others say that the mound's power also comes from its central and dominant view over the valley and over all other *kuel*, who are its sons and daughters. Although the top of the *Tren Trenkuel* mound has been deliberately flattened and eroded over time (see the origin tale in Chapter 4 and later discussion), it is currently about 9 m in height and 42 m in diameter; it sits on a *ñichi* platform that is 100 by 150 m. The most aesthetically appealing mound also is located in Butarincón and within the viewshed of *Tren Trenkuel*. It sits on a majestic *ñichi* that overlooks the Isla de Katrileo wetlands that are located at the conjunction of the Purén and Lumaco rivers. This mound has two names for reasons that we presently do not understand: *Rehueñichikuel*, the mound with a *rehue* pole on top which is located on a *ñichi*, and *Foyegñachekuel* (see

46. General view of *TrenTrenkuel* (center arrow) and its *ñichi* platform (marked by left and right arrows).

Fig. 10), meaning the cinnamon tree mound where sacrificial blood is offered to and consumed by the *kuel*. Informants also report that all mounds located on top of *ñichi* are associated with old *nguillatun* fields (*kuifilnguillatuhue*) where famous dynastic patrilineages once held *cahuin* and other large gatherings.

A composite picture formed by information gathered from informants living in the Butarincón, Isla Katrileo, and Rucalleco communities gives a general idea of the approximate relative chronology of mounds situated along the Purén and Lumaco River. Two mounds, *Pichikuel* and *Ñachekuel*, were built in the last ten years and are still used in *nguillatun* fields. An unnamed and unused mound in the vicinity of Rucalleco is said to have been constructed 50 to 60 years ago. The remaining mounds in the Lumaco area are believed to be even older, dating at least 100 to 300 years ago, an age also suggested by the presence of late pre-Hispanic and Hispanic sherds eroding from the slopes of mounds and by radiocarbon dates measured between A.D. 1280 and 1900 and derived from excavations in several mounds listed below (see Appendix 2 and Chapter 6). In addition to ceramics, radiocarbon dates, and oral tradition, a source of relative chronology is the indigenous names given to some mounds. Those mounds with *kuifil* (meaning ancient) as a prefix in the name are presumably older than others. All *kuel* with this prefix are located in the Butarincón cluster, suggesting that mounds situated closer to the confluence of the Purén and Lumaco Rivers are older than those located on the crest or ridge extending to the south toward Rucalleco (Fig. 47).

Listed below are the primary names and their meanings for the major *kuel* in Purén and Lumaco. Names are not remembered by informants for all mounds, especially for older and usually smaller mounds. Figure 47 shows the location of the major *kuel* in the *lov* communities of Butarincón, Isla Katrileo, San Genaro, and Rucalleco. Others are scattered throughout the valley and not depicted on the map.

> *Poremchedakuel*: A place where ritual medicine is found in human excrement and where people climb to the top of the mound to carry out sanctifying ceremonies.
>
> *Kuifilrehueñichikuel*: A mound with an old *rehue* on top located on a platform or *ñichi*. This was the personal *kuel* of the late *machi* Fabiana. It housed her *rehue* and her *fileu pullu* spirit. This mound forms part of a *rehuekuel* where large-scale ceremonies were carried out until her death a few years ago.
>
> *Piuquechekuel*: A mound built for people who are related consanguinally within the same *lov, lof, rehue*, or patrilineage.
>
> *Kuifilrochuntowekuel*: An ancient mound made up of multiple layers of old earth (*reñinmapu*) vertically placed on top of each other.
>
> *Painenikuel*: A mound of the Paine family or of dedication to the blue divinity.
>
> *Cahuelmawidakuel*: A mound that has been disturbed or trampled, or a mound that represents people from other mountains.
>
> *Kuifilingchemawidakuel*: An ancient mound considered possessive of an old community and belonging to the old mountain.
>
> *Tremewguenkuel*: A group of people belonging to the same objective, belief system, or genealogy.
>
> *Ñgaduhuinkulkuel*: A mound that is the sister of a husband or the wife of a woman's husband, or a mound composed of highly organic soil.
>
> *Nechekuel*: A mound that is observant or vigilant; it has a human eye.
>
> *Rañikuel*: An intermediate level mound, or one located between two mounds, or a mound that is thin and tall like the *colihue* tree.
>
> *Butakuel*: The great mound.
>
> *Ñachekuel*: A mound where blood is sacrificed.
>
> *Pichikuel*: A boy or young mound.
>
> *Tren Trenkuel*: The mound where the good snake of the origin tale resides.
>
> *KaiKaikuel*: The mound where the evil snake *Kai Kai* of the origin tale lives.
>
> *Pinuñichikuel*: The mound with a pine tree on top that is placed on top of a *ñichi* platform.

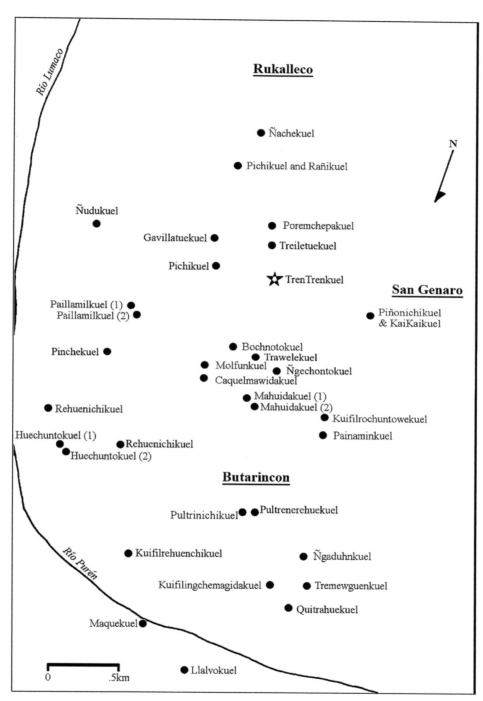

Rukalleco

N

● Ñachekuel

● Pichikuel and Rañikuel

Ñudukuel
●

● Poremchepakuel

Gavillatuekuel ●
● Treiletuekuel

Pichikuel ●

☆ TrenTrenkuel

San Genaro

Paillamilkuel (1) ●
Paillamilkuel (2) ●

● Piñonichikuel
& KaiKaikuel

Pinchekuel ●

● Bochnotokuel
● Trawelekuel
● Molfunkuel ● Ñgechontokuel
● Caquelmawidakuel

● Mahuidakuel (1)
● Mahuidakuel (2)
● Kuifilrochuntowekuel

Rehuenichikuel ●

● Painaminkuel

Huechuntokuel (1)
● ● Rehuenichikuel
● Huechuntokuel (2)

Butarincon

Pultrinichikuel ● ● Pultrenerehuekuel

Río Parén

● Kuifilrehuenchikuel

● Ñgaduhnkuel

Kuifilingchemagidakuel ●

● Tremewguenkuel

● Quitrahuekuel

Maquekuel ●

0   .5km

● Llalvokuel

47. Map of the location of *kuel* named in the chapter and located in the Butarincón, Isla de Katrileo, San Genero, and Rucalleco *lov* areas. Note the central location of *TrenTrenkuel*. All other mounds flanking *TrenTrenkuel* are the son and daughter mounds mentioned by *machi* Lucinda in her ritual narrative (see Chapter 5).

Trapunkuel: A uniting *kuel*.

Pultriñichikuel: The mound that hangs from a steep *ñichi* for a deity.

Pikulhuekuel: The mound that looks to the north and faces the north wind.

Rehueñichikuel: The *rehue* that is on top of a *kuel* which is placed on top of a *ñichi* platform.

Putrenerehuekuel: The mound where the foxes were hanging.

Tripahuekuel: The mound where the sun comes up.

Tremefquenkuel: The mound that slowly moves it head up and down.

Checodkuel: The mound that crouches to hide.

Huitranlehue: The mound that is a great meeting place.

Tralhuekeul: The mound where they celebrate meetings or where there is a group of mounds.

Quitrahuekuel: The mound where there are pipes or where there is a *tiaca* tree.

Molfunkuel: The mound covered with dew or with the blood of the mound.

Gavillatuekuel: The mound where there is blue earth.

Treilatuekuel: The mound with disturbed earth.

Maquekuel: The mound where there is the tree that produces the *maque* (*maki*) fruit.

Yalgomaquekuel: The mound where there is black *maque* tree.

Palquilkuel: The mound where there is a *palki* tree. (This is a medicinal plant used for curing illnesses resulting from heat.)

Puréntripaykuel: The mound that produces materials for dyeing.

Portahuekuel: The mound that you can climb.

Millatrentrenkuel: The mound that is a beneficial and golden hill.

Dochuntukuel: The mound where there is a *dücho* or *dochu* plant.

Paillamilkuel: The mound that is sacred and golden.

Bochontokuel: The mound that has humid vegetation.

Tripaykuel: The exit of the mound.

Rayentripaykuel: The exit of the mound where there are flowers.

Michikuel: The mound that flees or escapes.

Ngenmapunkuel: The mound where there is an owner of the land.

Wenucolla: The mound that has an oak stairway that leads to the sacred world above.

Melencahuin: The mound of a meeting place.

Retruboyekuel: The mound where there is a standing branch of the cinnamon tree or where there are goldsmiths.

Tiechekuel: The mound of people who are most distant.

Deumankuel: The mound that was constructed.

Pillanpalihuekuel: The mound that is the *palin* field of the deity *Pillan*.

Hueichahuekuel: The mound where they carried out war.

Peltrenirehuekuel: The mound where they hang weaving looms.

Kakulmahuida: The inclined mountain.

Chawivivol: Boldo (a medicinal plant) that is shaped like earrings.

Chekonakuel: The mound that is permanently positioned like knives.

Curanilahue: A ford with many stones.

Hualonkokuel: A sacred mound associated with corn and with a *lonko* leader, and possibly a mound that has water around it or has a group of people forming a ceremonial circle.

Chemamüllkuel: The mound with the ancestor's wooden statues standing on it.

Huintranlebukuel: A mound associated with a cold river or with a river in the upper world of the ancestors.

Maicoyakuel: A mound with ten oaks.

Rapahuekuel: A mound where there is black clay.

Lolonkokuel: A mound where there are holes filled with water.

Boyonkokuel: A mound where there is hot water or where bubbling water comes out.

It can be seen from this list that many *kuel* personify kinship relationships and express metaphoric connections between ecological elements and human activity. Most mound names in the valley also are related to a variety of themes that include ritual performance, sacrifice, kin relations, specific landscapes, and important spirits, deities, animals, shamans, and other figures. Reference is made to different plants, sediments, water sources, and animals that relate to the local trophic order discussed in Chapter 4. Also of interest are names associated with war, meeting places, sacred landscapes, deities, the ritual war game *palin*, sacrificial blood, and *ñichi* platforms. Perhaps the most common theme is the relationship between a *kuel* and a family or group of persons, which suggest continuity in the genealogical relations between mounds and people. In other words, mounds form kinship groups and have a domestic settlement pattern similar to human kinship and settlement patterns (see Chapter 4 and Dillehay 1995). These patterns are collaborated by informant claims that major *kuel*, such as *TrenTrenkuel, Maicoyakuel,* and *Lolonkokuel*, are the founding heads of the patrilineages residing around them in the valley. Information is not detailed enough to reliably establish kinship ties between all mounds and the patrilineages living in the valley today. However, by referential extension to patrilocal and patrilineal kinship patterns in the valley, all *kuel* are considered to be consanguinally related. Further, the residents of Butarincón and Isla de Katrileo claim that Nahual, a famous local chief whose surname means the spotted feline or jaguar, was buried in *TrenTrenkuel* and was the founding leader of the lineage carrying his name. As noted earlier, *TrenTrenkuel* is believed to be the mound that directs and fathers all others, which collectively form a valley-long network of brothers and sisters (see later discussion). Other lineages such as Colípi, Alquiman, Huircaleo, and Katrileo claim kin relations with various mounds on their lands.

Four communities in the study area still actively use mounds in *nguillatun* and other ceremonies: *Hualonkokuel, Ñachekuel, Trentrenkuel,* and *Lolonkokuel.* These *kuel* have several features in common: (1) they rest on built *ñichi* platforms of earth used by dancers who circle the mound during ceremony; (2) two narrow, deep holes dug into their east slopes, which are used during ceremony to pour sacrificial blood into the mound; (3) four- to six-foot trails passing over them from different directions, which link different patrilineal communities; and (4) ramp-like foot trails that spiral upward around the sides to the top of the mound where different rituals are performed by *machi* and their aids. When I participated in ceremony at the *Ñachekuel* mound in 1983, two wooden stakes were located on top where two animals were sacrificed (see Fig. 32). Similar features (e.g., trodden ramp ways and postholes) have been excavated archeologically at two other *kuel* in the valley (see Chapter 6).

KUEL FUNCTIONS

Several functions for *kuel* have been identified from ethnographic interviews, mound names, ethnohistorical accounts, and archaeological research: (1) to serve as burial plots for important leaders; (2) to house the *fileu pullu* spirits of *machi*; (3) to renourish the relationship between the living and their ancestors by spatially linking the historic time of ancestors and the actual time of the living; (4) to transport the spirit of the interred corpse of famous leaders to the *Wenumapu* world of the deities and ancestors by physically elevating it into this world through communal ritual (see Chapter 4); (5) to serve as "maps" or spatial nodes of historical identity for families and lineages in local communities and kin networks; (6) to serve as the central staging area for *machi* prayer and dance in *nguillatun* and other public gatherings held at *rehuekuel;* and (7) to guide people's behavior to follow *admapu* or traditional ways (see Chapter 4).

We have observed that almost all foot trails leading from different clusters of *ruka* (houses) passes over or near *kuel* in areas where mound clusters are located. Even the modern-day dirt roads for horses, ox carts, or occasionally vehicles in the Rucalleco and Butarincón areas follow the north–south line of *kuel* described earlier. Informants believe that there is a strong "pull" or sense of obligation and desire to walk by or over *kuel*, to acknowledge their presence, and to gaze at them. It is said that gazing at *kuel* provides a sense of comfort and relief and an identity to the history of the area. Also, in referring to *kuel* as "maps" or "boundaries," the mounds are perceived as physical nodes of reference to the outlying settlement pattern of related kinsmen. In other words, the Mapuche of Lumaco have a cognitive map or mental picture of the *kuel* in their physical environment and in their kinship settlement pattern that is used by the mind's eye as an orienting schema to provide structure to social and physical space (see Chapter 4). Sighting the mounds from key elevated points across the landscape gives orientation, according to several informants. People receive greater comfort and solace from places, such as *Tren Trenkuel*, where there is a wide viewshed to multiple mounds, and living communities.

As revealed in the ritual narratives discussed later and presented in detail in Appendix 2, *kuel* are renourished by the orations and prayers of *machi* during ceremony, which are designed to appease the gods *Ngenechen* (*Ngnechen*) and *Pillan* and the *machi* spirit residing in them, and by pouring sacrificial blood (*katruwen-molfun*) and *chicha* in artificial tunnels that reach deep into the mounds. Prior to ritual at *kuel* in Lumaco, families of local lineages sacrifice a small animal (usually a hen) at their houses, mix the blood of the hen with water and chili peppers to prevent coagulation, and carry the mixture in a vessel (*metawe*) to the *kuel*. Each family member takes a sip of the mixture and then gives it to the *machi* who pours it into a larger double-spout vessel (*ketrumetawe*), then mixes it with the blood of sacrificial animals and looks to the west, or left side, of the ceremonial field where her natal family is seated, and then drinks from the left spout of the vessel. She repeats the pattern by gazing and sipping to the east, or right side, where her husband's family is located. During these ceremonies, *machi* act as mediators for the living and use the *kuel* as a platform for communicating with deities and ancestral spirits in the *Wenumapu* world. It is from the top of the *kuel* and off of the mound near the *llangi-llangi* altar in the central plaza of the *nguillatun* field that the ancestors are invited and descend into the *Nag Mapu* world of the living.

As mentioned above, two functions of kuel are burial mounds of important leaders and residences of the kindred spirits of *machi*. The relationship between a ruler's burial and the residency of a *machi's* spirit in the same mound reflects two concepts. One is the role played by the *machi* in legitimizing political discourse of leaders in secular and sacred gatherings (Dillehay 1985b). This association continues after death. *Machi* oversee the funerary rites of dead leaders and aid their spirits to ascend to the *Wenumapu* world. The other relates to the *machi's* spirit taking residency in the mound once the dead leader's spirit has ascended and he has become an authentic ancestor. When the *machi's* spirit takes residency, the *kuel* becomes a living mound and kin member that is nurtured by the shaman and by the local community in *kueltun* rituals. During ceremonies at *kuel*, I have never heard a *machi* name or recognize the dead leader buried inside. In other words, the use and meaning of the *kuel* changes over time from a leader's tomb to a ritual platform housing a shaman's spirit, from a cemetery to a ceremonial center, and, if not abandoned and used in ceremony, from a center to a memorial monument.

Conversations with a *weupin* from Chol-Chol, Candelario Nancovilo, revealed that *rehuekuel* were old *palin* and *nguillatun* fields where the most powerful *weupin*, *machi*, and *toqui* gathered during public ceremonies in the past. He also related that the *kuel* in *rehuekuel* spaces are not just the burial places of important leaders but served as platforms where *cahuin* and political discourse took place between powerful rulers and where *machi* staged ceremonies independent of secular *lonko* leaders. He said that the *lonko* worked on the mounds during the sunlight and the *machi* prayed and performed on them during the moonlight. (The different daytime and nighttime functions of secular *lonko* and sacred *machi*, respectively, were repeated by several informants.) Nancovilo also told us that a hierarchical ranking existed between *machi* working at *kuel* and *rehuekuel* sites, with the highest ranking associated with the largest and oldest fields and with *rehue* poles with the largest number of steps.

Other informants report that when a principal *machi* dies, the *kuel* housing her *fileu pullu* is abandoned. Another *kuel* in the same *rehuekuel* complex is inhabited by the spirit of the *machi* who replaces her. The reason given for abandonment and rebuilding of mounds is that each *kuel* is associated with a single *machi* spirit. Upon the death of a *machi*, her *kuel* (which once belonged to the spirit of a dead *toqui* or *lonko* leader buried inside) can no longer be used by another *machi*, although the *nguillatun* field or *rehuekuel* space where it is located can still be employed for ceremony and for the construction of other *kuel* for burial of other lineage leaders. The cycle repeats itself with mounds first belonging to the dead leaders and then to active *machi* and lastly to the *fileu* spirit of the dead *machi*. The *kuel* then becomes a memorial referenced but not always ritually used in ceremony, although the surrounding off-mound space and any newly built mounds in the occupied *rehuekuel* area may continue to be used. Informants also said that a burial *kuel* was built first on a *ñichi* hilltop and then it was used as a *nguillatun* field. Patrilineal communities such as Butarincón and Lolonko that had a succession of influential leaders and that retained their land over a long period of time were associated with the greatest number of *kuel* and *rehuekuel* (see Dillehay 1995). Nancopil also stated that not all *nguillatun* fields are associated with mounds, for reasons he and other informants did not know; that only *machi*, *weupin*, *nguillatufe*, and *lonko* were allowed to sacrifice animals and to speak on top of the mounds; and that these authorities conducted ceremonies to offer *mudai*, *ñache*, burned textiles, and other dedicatory items to *kuel* and to the spirits residing in them. (Nancovilo told us that the burned textiles were usually the ponchos of *lonko* and *toqui*.) *Machi* also reported that layers of soil are placed on the mound every few years during a *kueltun* ceremony, a practice I also had learned from informants in Isla de Katrileo (Dillehay 1985a). This act gives strength, vitality, and size to the *kuel*, they claimed. It is clear from Nancovilo's testimony and from those of other informants (see later discussion) that *kuel* are initially associated with the tomb and *awn* burial rituals of important rulers and later appropriated by the kindred spirit of a *machi* shaman who performed ceremony at the mound to unite the living, the ancestors, and the deities in *Wenumapu*.

Informants also say that when the spirit of a deceased leader is still ritually nourished by the living at the tomb site, it is in historic, remembered, or authentic time. Once the dead ruler's spirit reaches the *Wenumapu* world, *kuel* are no longer maintained by the living and the spirit passes into mythical ancestor time. As more time passes, *kuel* are eventually abandoned and the name of temporally and genealogically distant ancestors are forgotten by families unless the buried persons are important *lonko* or *toqui* leaders such as Colo-Colo, Anganamón, and Lientur. Some elders claim that they know the mounds where these important rulers are buried in the valley.

Information on the number and size of individual soil layers making up a mound is derived from information on the *awn* rite in the construction of *kuel*, from the interment of the body, and from the *kueltun* or the subsequent maintenance and soil capping of the *kuel* by relatives and friends of the deceased (see Chapter 4). Two informants say that at the time of interment only one large pile of earth (*reñinmapu*) is placed on the tomb by relatives and friends. One year later another soil capping takes place and periodically thereafter (Dillehay 1985a). *Machi* and elders told us that mounds had to be capped and elevated by the living relatives in order to raise the spirit of the *kuifiche* or deceased closer to the good *Wenumapu* world above where the key deities, celestial figures, and ancestors reside and farther away from the evil forces residing in the under *miñchemapu* world.

Informants did not know of the conditions that determined the exact volumes of *kuel*, and how many capping episodes occurred before *kuel* were abandoned permanently. They did say that the terminal size of *kuel* is conditioned by the number of relatives and friends, each of whom places a pile of earth on the tomb and by the number of capping episodes necessary to fulfill whatever social obligation is required of the living. The number of relatives and friends depositing earth on *kuel* is defined by the size of the extended family and patrilineage of the deceased and by the number of friends achieved through social power and prestige (Dillehay 1995). Lineage leaders with multiple wives have extraordinarily large extended families (see Guevara 1913) and thus larger *kuel* produced by larger and more numerous capping episodes. As presented in Chapter 4, the organization of corporate-lineage labor in the periodic construction of *kuel* is similar to the seating pattern of lineages and families in *nguillatun* fields. Lineages living to the east of a mound gather and pack dirt on the east side, those to the west place earth on the west side, and so on. Local lineages pack soil in the center (*reñin*) and on all sides. Seen in this perspective, the extra layers of soil overlying a corpse serve no useful architectural purpose. Rather, these layers represent the perdurable relationships between consanguineously related lineages; they are a nucleation of "social soil" (Dillehay 1995).

The placement of lineage-specific grave offerings around a corpse and in the soil layers overlying a tomb are organized in a similar fashion, with kinsmen living to the east of the tomb placing objects on the east side of the corpse and so on. The importance of this spatial patterning of kinsmen and material goods around the tomb, which is also seen in the location of family *ruka* (houses) around the *nguillatun* field, is that the activity structure of public ceremony is organized in terms of the structure of domestic exchange relations between families and lineages in the real world. It is the mirror-like reflection of this structure in ceremony that makes it maternally and spatially easier to detect and measure the wider design and organization of production and exchange relations between discrete social units (i.e., families, lineages communities) in nucleated ceremonial sites than in dispersed residential sites.

In sum, mounds have four successive building and use phases. First, the grave and first layer of soil seals and covers the corpse. This portion of the mound corresponds to the *awn* rite, which commemorates the achievements of the entered dead leader and sends his spirit to the upper ancestral world (*Wenumapu*). Second, the periodic placement of additional layers or caps is associated with the *kueltun* rite. Participation in these recapping episodes serves to maintain the social relationships between consanguineously related lineages and, at the same time, to further elevate the mound physically in order to lift the spirit of the deceased higher into the upper world. Third, in the true sense of the term, these mounds serve as public monuments and historic places, as boundary markers between lineage and sublineage lands, and as gateway stations where footpaths from different directions meet and depart. When the first and second use-phases (which may last for several years or generations) have terminated and when the spirit of the deceased ruler has climbed into the upper world, the mound becomes a place in history and a place of residency for a living *machi's* spirit. It is ritually curated and nourished as a single monument on the landscape and as part of a nucleated family or descent group of active (first and second phases) and inactive (third phase) mounds, connected by footpaths and sacred spaces and by precedent-setting historical and spatial linkages, exchange relationships, and obligations among the persons, groups, and lineages who built and used it. In essence, a mound becomes an architectural sibling of a lineage, characterized by its own genealogical record, identity, and life history of construction, use, and rank. During phase three, it is ritually administered by *machi*, as presented later in the following ritual narratives. Upon the death of *machi*, the mounds become memorials. And fourth, in areas where mound-building lineages have been dispersed and separated from their homeland by warfare and population displacement, old (*kuifil*) mounds have become a collection of sacred architectural memorabilia lost in time and memory and detached in space and function from the people who built and worshipped them.

I think it is accurate to characterize all uses of *kuel* as an integrated set of functions and meanings that sustains the interlineage relationships between ancestors and their living kinsmen and the ceremonial participation of and the interpersonal relationships between lineage groups participating in ceremony. As both Faron (1964) and I (Dillehay 1990c, 1995) have discussed before, these relationships are important for providing a set of social and spatial nexus of several lineages united in a ceremonial nucleus and in the symmetrical exchange of goods and information, all of which sustain the total identity, memory, social, and ideological organization of communities. These are some of the more important fibers of persistence and change in Araucanian society, in both the past and present. When viewed from both a local and a regional perspective, the number and composition of multilineage membership and affinal ties manifested in *awn, kueltun, nguillatun,* and other ceremonies depend upon the importance of the deceased person (who is becoming an authentic ancestor) and the spatial and social extension of his/her kinship and friendship network. In this respect the living assemblage at successive *awn* as well as *kuel* events is not consistent in family and lineage size and content year after year. Throughout the region different numbers from different lineages participate in numerous funerals (of nonleaders who also are becoming authentic ancestors) and other rites that connect them to many different spatial and social ties in many kinship networks. There is, therefore, a common fabric in rites having regional cohesion that sustain participation in ritual ceremony, the relationship between the living and the dead, and cultural survival and political organization to resist outsiders (see Stuchlik 1976). Also recognizable in these relations are opportunities for *machi, kuel,* individuals, lineages, and communities in negotiating social and spatial relationships and in placing the communities in a best or worse position in receiving favors and goodwill from the deities and ancestors in *Wenumapu* and from the *kuel* and other figures representing them in *Nag Mapu* or living space.

THE PRIESTLY SHAMAN OR *MACHI* AND THE *KUEL*: EXCHANGING IDENTITIES AND TRANSPOSING HISTORIES

To more completely understand the meaning of the patterns and relations studied above and of the suffering, illness, malevolence and healing in society, I will now relate portions of a long discourse between a sick mound (*Hualonkokuel*) and Juanita, a *machi* from Rucalleco near Lumaco, that I documented during a two-day *llaimatun* ceremony performed at the *nguillatun* field in the Hualonko community in 1996 (see Figs. 9, 45 and 65). The ceremony was designed to heal the ill-functioning *Hualonkokuel* that threatened to bring bad times to the local community, because people in the community had not carried out proper rituals at the site and had not given the *kuel* the required offerings (i.e., *mudai* or *chicha* beer, *ñache*, food, and prayer) to renourish it and to appease its sense of duty to them. The oration also documents the *machi's* representation of the community before the *kuel* and its representation of major deities and ancestors before the community. In this regard, the narrative unfolds historical concerns, memories, social relationships, sorcery, good and evil, and a ceremonial landscape alive with the living and the dead from all levels of the cosmological world. It recalls past feats, kinship relations, social structure, and present-day malevolence. It is obvious from the text that the *machi* refers to past times when *palin* war games and ritual battles were important events and when *kuel* held more power across the landscape. It is difficult to determine how far back in time this narrative has its roots. Maria Catrileo, a native Mapuche, who translated the text from Mapundungun to Spanish states that it is a complex composite of ancient memories and that the dialect is old. After recording and translating the text, we returned on several occasions to ask the shaman about specific meanings of her discourse. Many statements she could not recall. Others were teachings she had learned from her shaman mentors. And others had meanings, which she attempted to explain to us.

A second ceremonial narrative relates to another *machi* and local community appealing to *Tren Trenkuel*, the most powerful mound in the valley, to grant us permission to excavate a trench in it and to prevent the mound and the powers in the upper world from becoming upset with the community for participating in the excavation. The ceremony took place during two days, with *machi* Lucinda of Butarincón performing a preventive ritual, *dahatun*, primarily during the nighttime. This was not a healing ceremony like that at *Hualonkokuel* but a discourse or preventive ceremony designed to ensure continued good relations between the community and to ask the mound for permission to excavate a portion of it. This dialogue also reveals historical social relations and memories, as well as the mobility of the *machi* to move between the different cosmological planes of the upper *Wenumapu* and the live *Nag Mapu* worlds. Also presented in this narrative is the role of the archeological excavation team, which was comprised of six non-Mapuche, including the author, and thirty local Mapuche workers.

It needs to be understood that the local communities encouraged our archaeological and ethnographic research in the area, because they were eager to learn more about their own history and to "look" inside the powerful *Tren Trenkuel* through the eyes of *machi*. Curiously, our excavation into the center of the mound (*reñin*) was conceptually understood by the *machi* and by the community because, as seen later in the narrative, shamans metaphysically enter mounds during ritual and take the participatory public audience with them, as was the case in this ceremony. I also should note that no ill-feelings were caused during or after our excavations. In fact, the *machi* administering the ritual gained prestige from the ceremony, because she demonstrated to the local community her ability to perform in multiple and esoteric contexts and to metaphysically enter into the interior of the mound. The *dahatun* ceremony performed at *Tren Trenkuel* had never before been witnessed or recorded by outsiders.

The *machi's* narratives are long and cryptic, with most segments referring to changing hierarchies and mutual dependencies between them, the living communities they represent, their ancestors, the *kuel*, and the creator of all, *Ngenechen*. The common focus among all involved is to direct and provide for the sharing and transfer of social energy from one cosmological level to another but primarily on the *Nag Mapu* level where the concerned living are located and to sustain the well-being of the involved communities. To achieve this, people must make offerings to *Ngenechen* through his sons, the sick and deprived *Hualonkokuel* and the excavated *Tren Trenkuel*, who control the health, fate, and vitality of the living. As mentioned in the introduction to this chapter, lineage-mates owe their existence to their common ancestor's procreative energy, which they store and transfer to the next living generation. This transfer is done through sons and daughters and through the community's or local *machi's kuel*. Thus, the basic function of the rituals at these two *kuel* is to maintain the connection between the ancestors, the *kuel* and the living, between the *machi* and the ancestors, and between the past, the present, and the future, all of which is necessary to the existence and perpetuation of the involved communities. In the traditional *machi's* language and relational structure of explanation, it makes sense to use the familial concept of ancestors to speak of the ways in which the living are embodiments of the dead at the same time that they are also representatives of future descendants. It is difficult to say whether the narratives have a beginning and ending point and whether there is a chronology or logical series of episodes. The *machi* move their discourses back and forth from the *kuel* to the deities, to themselves, to distant times and places, and to the public at large.

In the *Hualonkokuel* ritual, the *machi* addresses the presence of two *kuel* in the *nguillatun* field: the larger more important one is called *Hualonkokuel* (the *kuel* of corn or of a *lonko* ruler) and the second smaller one is named *Chemamüllkuel* (the mound with the ancestor's wooden statues). The smaller one was located about 100 m north of the large mound at the opposite end of the field (see Fig. 65 in Chapter 6). The unity of the narrative is achieved by the *machi's* attempt to justify her presence in the ceremony and to reveal her sources of medicinal and spiritual power. A struggle of identity and power can be seen in the text whereby the *machi* constantly explains her positions in the local society and her broader relations with celestial powers and gods, particularly *Pillan* and *Ngenechen*. (In both narratives, the two *machi* employ *Chaw* (*Chau*) to refer to *Ngenechen*, which is common practice today.)

Both narratives are rich in symbolic knowledge, history, and spatialities of shifting identities. In the narratives, the *machi* cross many time frames and identities, remember many histories, shift spatial locations, resituate themselves in appropriate temporal spaces, and at times, transform themselves into the *kuel*. At other times, the *kuel* transform themselves into *machi*. An understanding of the hermeneutical sequence of spatial-temporal extensions and shifts in the frames of their identities is useful for seeing that interspatial and intertemporal shifts need not necessarily be conceived of as involving real geographical and time displacement. The spatio-temporal relations of specific local lineage histories also enter into the single structure of each *kuel* narrative. The fact that spatial and temporal shifts can occur without physically displacing the shaman's body from the specific location of the *kuel*, as occurs under meditation and divining states, forcefully highlights the many possible ways in which transpatial communication and contact occur between physical, mental, and pneumatic states. From the standpoint of physical body-space reality around the *kuel*, former impenetrable barriers and chasms between the physical world or body-space, the mental world or ideational-space, and the pneumatic world or spirit-space assume a different quality when conceptualized on a framework of the permeable nature of the *kuel*. This is particularly revealed in the *Tren Trenkuel* ceremony when the *machi* and the ritual audience metaphysically enter the *kuel*. There also is a sense of historical displacement whereby the *machi* transposes circumstance of the colonial past to the present day and vice versa and whereby narratives of the past about conflicts between outsiders and Araucanians also serve to focus on today's problems.

Further, both narratives are different, but they share certain organizational and thematic elements. There are variations in the way the shaman's origin stories are given and the way that the details and events of the narratives change from shaman to shaman, but these differences stem from their individual understandings of events from the different purposes of each ceremony and from local histories and events. Nonetheless, the implications and meanings are the same to all members of the society and reflect on the broader principles of social organization and concerns with violation of proper rituals and relations between proper ritual and natural well-bring. The formal structure and content of the narratives owe everything to traditional Araucanian patterns and relations. There is no resemblance to Biblical stories and characters. *Machi* Juanita and Lucinda live in Rucalleco and Butarincón, respectively, areas only recently infiltrated by western religion. In this regard, no Biblical or Catholic references are detectable in their narrative.

The narratives also have a fragmentary quality, however. And I have turned their narratives into selected fragments again, in order to insert information relevant to my analysis in this chapter. I have organized portions of each text below in the same sequenced narrative the *machi* presented them. There seem to be, however, natural breaks where they repeat "we will conquer ten times." Further, the texts are full of redundancies, overlaps, cross-references, and allusions. For these reasons, to appreciate the coherence of the *kuel* theme here, I have pulled together partial accounts from disparate sections and interspersed them with my commentaries and interpretations to immediately clarify points, although a longer section is given to this later in the chapter. I also realize that the texts can be interpreted in many ways. Thus, I apply a strict descriptive and contextualized interpretative approach here. The full texts and order of their narratives about the *kuel* are provided in English and Mapudungun in Appendix 1. Each section below is marked in Roman numerals for reference to its place in the unabridged narrative in Appendix 1. The texts are unedited and translated directly from the tape recordings I made in the field during the ritual ceremonies. The transcriptions from Mapudungun to Spanish were by Catrileo who reports that many passages reflect old Mapudungun and old religious terms. Being somewhat competent in Araucanian ritual language, colleagues and I also transcribed some sections and verified them with the *machi*. Patricia Netherly translated most of the texts from Spanish to English. In reading the full text, the reader should keep in mind that *kuel* are artificial hills related through the origin story of the bad snake *Kai Kai* and to the benevolent snake *Tren Tren* in their epic battle to destroy people or save them, respectively (see Chapter 4). Also revealed in the texts is the "mound literacy" of ritual participants, which I will comment on later. For now, my intent is solely to employ parts of the narratives to demonstrate certain relations between shamanism, mound use and mound literacy, and public ceremony. The way the flow of the narratives is fragmented is itself an image of the way different events are remembered, isolated, and fused by the shamans and the manner in which each conducts and presents ritual discourse. Therefore, the detailed segmented fashion (i.e., stanzas, lines) in which Catrileo has transcribed the text reflects verbal features, such as emphasis, pause, and minor and major divisions by the shamans themselves. Further, although some words mean the same thing, *Nag Mapu* and *mapu*, or the earth's surface, for example, they are deliberately stated or spelled slightly differently by Catrileo in her transcription, because they reflect local dialect differences between the two *machi*. These linguistic divisions and fusions make the narrative logical and legible to the ritual participants who speak Mapundungun. Curiously, when later *machi* Lucinda entered the *Tren Trenkuel* mound when we were excavating it, she remarked that the stratigraphy and especially the prepared floors visible in the wall profiles of the trench represent different rituals performed in *kuifil* (ancient) times by other shamans in other "places," meaning the ancient shaman's connections to various planes of the *Wenumapu* world. I later spoke with her about the deeper and older prepared floors with burned offerings in the base of the mound and the younger ones above, but she was less interested in their location. To her the different colors of floor stains and ashy areas and the length and thickness of floors had meaning only with regard to different cosmological linkages rather than to time and its spatiality. The meaning that she assigned to the stratigraphy and the connectedness of soil layers was different from my archeological perspective, which she points out in the ritual narrative by noting our different views of what the layers mean. Figures 45 and 46 show the sacred spaces at *Hualonkokuel* and *TrenTrenkuel* where the ritual ceremonies were carried out. Figure 48 exhibits some of the burned floors exposed in the excavated wall profile of *TrenTrenkuel*, which *machi* Lucinda was observing.

Lastly, I do not want to lose the idea of *kuel* as special places in this chapter, and how they provide identity, security, understanding, and therapeutic healing for people. Health, suffering, and disease have spaces in Araucanian mounds and in *nguillatun* fields, along with ritual objects and gestures. Also important is the performance of ritual on and around the *kuel* mounds, which includes digging pits representing life and death and tunnels joining them, burying the dead in a grave, recapping the mound annually, dancing around the mound, and walking over and around it as a pathway to and from other areas in the valley. Each act follows a planned spatial and temporal design, each part of which carries both local and pan-Araucanian symbolic and historical meaning. These places and relations are also revealed in the narratives. Only the English translations of the narratives are provided below. Appendix 1 presents both the Mapundungun and English versions. Because the rituals were conducted at night, no flashing lights and photographs were permitted. Photographs were allowed the next morning when the sun appeared.

The Hualonkokuel Llaimatun *and* Lonkotun *Rituals*

Machi Juanita performed the *llaimatun* and *lonkotun* ceremonies at Hualonko that began around 9:30 in the evening when only a faint light was still visible on the horizon and a dim quarter moon appeared in the sky. Venus was located in the sky just below a crescent moon. The ceremonies lasted two days. Mapuche from all communities in the valley and several from Temuco, Ercilla, and the nearby coast attended the events.

The two rituals demonstrate power sharing during public ceremony, with the *machi* opening and directing the event late in the evening on the first day and then introducing *lonko* leaders and handing power to them the next morning at sunset (*lonkotun*). The separation of sacred nighttime and secular daytime power was clearly demarcated in these ceremonies, with reversed roles played by the *machi* and the *lonko*. The *machi* was accompanied by four shamans from various areas in the valley and her *dungunmachifu* helpers. She began her oration by singing, dancing, and playing the drum (*kultrun*) in front of the *rehue*, which faced the east. The *machi* and all elderly women were dressed in full ritual regalia with silver chest ornaments (*trawelfucha*), ostrich feathers, and headbands (*trarilonko*). The *lonko* wore the traditional red and white ponchos (*makuñ*) that depict the stepped-diamond symbol of authority (see Chapter 4). Also present was an official orator (*weupin*) from the nearby community of Ipinco and a ritual leader (*nguillatufe*) from Tranaman. When the ceremony began, participants gathered in a large

48. Profile of the north excavated wall of *Tren Trenkuel* showing the burned ritual floors (arrows) and the lower blue clay floor (light colored lower floor) capping the burial chamber. Gouges in the wall are places where archaeological soil samples were taken.

semicircle around the *rehue* to hear the *machi's* opening words. After terminating her initiation session, the *machi* disappeared into the nearby woods with her entourage of *dungumachifu* and *machi*. After an hour, she returned in a trance and climbed the *rehue* pole to begin her long nighttime ceremony. (I later discovered from her that she had taken a "remedy," perhaps a plant stimulant called *latue*, to induce the trance.) Her performance on the *rehue* included dances, songs, and a long discourse with the ancestors, the *kuel* in the field, ancient *machi* spirits (*fileu pulli*), the ancestors of powerful chiefs, *Ngenechen* (the supreme god), and *Pillan* (the spirit of the ancestors). The *rehue* pole was located about 40 m north of the *Hualonlokuel* and roughly midway between it and the second, smaller *kuel* located on the far north end of the field (see Fig. 65), toward which she occasionally turned to address it directly. The performance was impressive, given that she stood on the top of the *rehue* for more than three hours, often violently shaking the sacred cinnamon (*foye*) branches to awaken the deities and ancestral spirits and to invite them into the ceremonial field. On occasion, she rested by leaning against the upward protruding branches. During these moments, the *weupin* and *nguillatufe* reaffirmed the *machi's* words and spoke about lineage histories and the ancestors. During the entire nighttime ceremony, the *lonko* stood close to the *rehue* but remained quiet only occasionally singing loudly along with the *machi* or chanting to confirm her word. After finishing her performance, she climbed down and retired to a designated seating area where she rested, came out of her trance, and consumed *mudai* and food. During the remainder of the evening, people rested, dispersed, mingled, and conversed.

Between five thirty and six o'clock in the morning when the moon was disappearing and streaks of sunlight were visible on the horizon, the *machi* terminated the *llaimatun* and began the *lonkotun*. The transition from sacred to secular power was administered by the *machi* who calmly introduced each *lonko* by naming them and speaking briefly to their accomplishments and legitimizing their powers. Once they took the word, she was seated behind them, softly tapping her *kultrun*. One *lonko* remarked that the *machi's* primary duties were nearly over and that she would now pass the voice of authority to the *lonko* when daylight appeared. Later, the *lonko* killed a sheep and placed its skin on top of the *rehue* with its head looking to the east. The *lonko* told us that in the past a puma skin was draped over the *rehue* to represent the son of the Sun (*Mareupuante*) at the ceremony. At this point the *lonkotun* and a lengthy political discourse followed. Each *lonko* spoke of the accomplishments of their lineage, the battles fought and won with the Spanish and Chilean armies, the atrocities committed by the armies, and the present-day problems with lumber companies and government authorities. After this discourse, *palin* was played by competing local and nonlocal lineages and then a more relaxing mood took place, which involved the consumption of *mudai*, wine, and food and the exchange of gifts. (I should note that in comparison to many other areas where I have worked with the Mapuche, the local elders and leaders in the Purén and Lumaco Valley sustain a remarkably detailed memory of battles, war chiefs, toponyms and other events that coincided with details in many Spanish chroniclers. None of these individuals have ever read and only one knows of the published accounts. This memory is sustained by oral tradition and tales recounted at ceremonies and other events.)

Presented below are several important themes extracted from the *Hualonkokuel* narrative, with my occasional comments and interpretations. References to sections are in Roman numerals and to verses in Arabic numbers. These are cross-listed to the complete narrative in Appendix 1. The reader is strongly encouraged to read the full text in the appendix in order to gain a more detailed idea of the incredibly rich interplay between kinship relations, and shamans and subjects and how mounds and rituals performed at them are spatialized and materialized.

At the outset of the narrative the *machi* tells why she has been commissioned by the local community to the Hualonko *nguillatuhue* and how the *Hualonkokuel* had threatened bad deeds against the community. The unifying premise of the text is the *machi* who attempts to use her powers to cure the largest and southernmost *kuel* in the Hualonko field, which has become incapacitated and has been acting badly, because the local community no longer prayed and gave offerings to it. We learn during the opening part that only the *machi* can establish the discourse with the *kuel* and cure its illness. She also considers the two *kuel* in the *ngullatuhue* field to be sons of *Pillan* and to represent or to become her at times. The *machi* says that the *kuel* spoke to her and goes where she goes (I: 2–3). She states that he has been treated badly by the local community, he has no affection for them, and thus he has been treating them badly in return. It is for this reason that she has been summoned by the community to conduct a *llaimatun* and to make offerings to *Ngenechen* (or *Chaw*) in order to cure the bad *kuel*. She then relates her visions (*perimonton*) to the audience.

The following verses near the end of the narrative reveal the disposed historical context of the narrative in past times of Araucanian successes in war, battles with *huinka* (huinca, winkga, outsiders), oration of the *machi* in the context of a *palin* ceremony to prepare for war, and gaze of the *kuel* toward his kinsmen the living, other *kuel*, and the *rehuekuel* of *Hualonkuel* where he, the sick *kuel*, is located.

> LV: 29–41: in all areas, they [Araucanians] cornered the *wingka* [Spanish and Chilean armies]
> today people don't remember these successes, friends. . . .
> the new generations no longer do these things. . . .
> they no longer do this with the poor son [*kuel*]
> I have said this for all of you in the *palin* of war
> I have said it for you, beloved *Chaw* [*Ngenechen*]. . . .
> You want to defend your bloodline, well, *kuel*.
> But you returned your gaze towards your kinsmen [living communities and other *kuel*] and your *rehuekuel*, well
> In other types of matters in order to do something different.

Later passages reveal that the *kuel* is *kunifal* or needy for having been envious and having done bad deeds. He has become before the *machi* from the world above (*Wenumapu*) where he was a servant to and a son of the supreme spirit *Pillan*. We also learn that the *kuel* was abandoned (by the community or by the deities above?) and that the *machi* has done him a favor by calming and settling him into the Hualonko field. She tells the *kuel* that she also has power and has been in the upper world of the supreme gods, *Ngenechen* and *Pillan*. At the end of this stanza, she describes more of the visions (*perimontun*) that she has had in the *nguillatun* field. The visions have come to her when she stood on the golden *rehue* (see XIII). Dances around the needy *kuel* also are mentioned, a pattern that still takes place today around "needy" and sick *kuel*, such as *Ñachekuel* in Rucalleco and *TrenTrenkuel* in Butarincón. The dance and vision are employed to search for medicine to cure the *Hualonkokuel* who has *kalkuluwma* — a disease that bewitches the earth (see XV: 23). This disease is caused by the *miñchemapu*, or evil, world

237

that lies below the earth's surface (see VXII: 4). She also informs the sick *kuel* that her motive is to fight evil (see XVII: 26), to help him, and to return him to his beloved land, which must be the upper world (see XIV: 34).

In the following verses (LVI: 1–7), the shaman addresses the living ceremonial group at large and refers to the union of local communities with the two mounds in the *nguillatuhue* field. (The term *nguillatuhue*, meaning the place of the *nguillatun*, is employed below because it is used by the *machi* in her narrative.)

> Well, well, well, this is the way things are.
> Now, only now, you [ritual audience] have worked hard
> here . . . you have come to work on the needy [*kuel*]
> Two, three, you people are Mapuche for certain,
> a pair, in a pair of *kuel* [in the *Hualonkokuel* field].
> In a pair of *kuel* you have come together.
> At midnight, at midnight, well.

In these and other verses, the *machi* mentions two other needy *kuel* that are present in the same area and that also walk on the earth's surface (*Nag Mapu* or *mapu*). (This reference may be to two ancient *machi*, or *fileu*, who have transformed themselves into the two *kuel* in the Hualonko field in order to compete or consult with *machi* Juanita in the *mapu* world of the *nguillatun* field.) Or it may refer to two *kuel* situated about 1 km to the north of Hualonko in another *rehuekuel*, which can be visually sighted from the Hualonko mounds. I suspect that two ancient *machi* have transformed themselves into the two Hualonko mounds, because *machi* Juanita references old *machi* several times during her discourse, as if they were present among us. (The references to visible and invisible *kuel* and to the two ancient *machi* also indicate the interchanging identities and roles of the host *Hualonkokuel* and *machi* in the field and of the ethereal *kuel* and *machi* from *Wenumapu* spaces.) *Machi* Juanita also refers to herself and to her two *dungunmachifu*, or assistants, as servants to the two *kuel*, or mounds, at Hualonko (see VIII: 10–14). She claims that the two *kuel* should no longer be disgraced and should be reanimated to help the living community. (Perhaps she is more tolerant of the bad *kuel* at this point in the ceremony, because she is curing him of his sickness and bad ways and now believes that he is calmed and thus can be reincorporated into the local community.) During the ritual, when she climbs the golden *rehue* to *Wenumapu* in order to consult with the supreme deities and spirits (see XI), she says that she is the owner of the powerful medicine to remedy the sickness of the *kuel*. She also asks why no one else helps her with the curing ritual. She makes it clear that her power to cure is derived from her contacts with the supreme being in the upper world – *Ngenechen* – which only she can contact only by climbing the golden *rehue*. In section XI, she also refers to the help that *Ngenechen* gives her to transport more power from the upper world to her immediate task of curing the sick *kuel* below in the *mapu* world.

In sum, four pervading themes seem to order the narrative at this point. One is that the shaman has been commissioned by the people to heal the sick *Hualonkokuel*. Not yet fully revealed in the early parts of the narrative is why the *kuel* has turned bad, although hints are that people have neglected their religious duties and offerings to it; that is, they have not been staging ceremonies with him, not offering him *chicha*, and not recognizing his powers and his kin relations to them and to the ancestral world above. The second is that the *machi* is the only one who has the earthly or *Nag Mapu* power to cure the *kuel* and who can unite all elements to overcome evil (cf. Faron 1964). The third is that the *kuel* is not just an isolated landscape feature, but he is associated with the sacred spaces where the rituals take place – the *palihue* and *nguillatuhue* – and with other landscapes in the community as well as the living and the dead. Fourth, the *kuel* is perceived as a living force and a kinsman – it prays, it contests, it fears, and it feels, and it is feared like humans. But unlike humans, it communicates and transposes itself from one world to another like the *machi*. It also has multiple histories and multiple identities – it can transform itself into a *machi*, and she can transform herself into a *kuel*. The interchangeable identities between the *machi* shaman, her kindred spirit (*fileu pullu*), and the *kuel* are obvious throughout the narratives. While the *machi* prays for the *kuel* and the local people, the two ancient *machi* or *fileu*, in the field also are praying for the sick *kuel* (XXX: 1).

Considerable spatial dislocation and identity change can be seen in the narrative at this point. There are struggles between the *machi*, the *kuel*, and other figures over sacred spaces that seemingly relate to population disruption and other events in the past and present, to the deaths of important *lonko* and *machi* (including those whose spirits once resided in the *kuel*), and to the neglect of the *kuel* by the local community. *Machi* Juanita speaks about the power of her medicine (which draws on a *rehue* made of cinnamon and gold and on her relation to snakes and other creatures) and about the possessor of medicine owning the earth (see XIV). In section XXXVI, the *machi* also tells people attending the ceremony that "they must maintain good relations with someone [like her?] who has the medicine or power from above [*Wenumapu*] . . . and that she is the only one who has the knowledge and power to use the medicine (see also XXIV)." In these same stanzas, she reveals her personal struggle with the sick *kuel* and recognizes him as the son of *Ngenechen*. She also comments on the *kuel's* lack of respect for her, by saying that "for a longtime, it [*kuel*] has laughed at me, he who possesses objects of laughter, this poor son" (VIV: 26–27).

In other verses, the shaman further reveals her competitive nature and her venues of power: "[the *kuel*] makes a competition with her who has the medicines" (VIV: 67) and "you will win against her who possesses the medicine" (VIV: 68). Another theme is the *machi's* inability to achieve her objective without help from the people she serves and from the deities above, both of whom are the sources of her medicinal power and knowledge (see XXVI: 13). Other passages reveal power struggles between various *machi*, between the *machi* Juanita and the *kuel*, and between various deities and ancestors. It is clear that the *machi* also receives power from her *rehue* and from its central place in the *nguillatuhue* field, which she considers to be her personal sacred space: "all are present in her space" (XXI: 1), she says. The *rehue* also is powerful, because it is the instrument and pathway to *Wenumapu*. She also remarks on the *kuel's* inability to return to *Wenumapu* space, because he has no *rehue* to climb. She states that: "People have come to buy the *kuel* a *rehue* [of his own] in order for him to return to the earth above" (XXI: 5). The *kuel* and its space also are referred to as places where the recent dead were removed (see XXVI–4). Moreover, the *kuel* does not have his own space or a *palihue* made of gold like that of the *machi* (see XXVII: 2–3). In stanza XXVIII, the *machi* ask how she can pray for the poor *kuel* who has no space of his own. (After the ceremony, Juanita told us that in order to return to *Wenumapu*, the *kuel* must have his own *rehue*, space or portal, to pass to and from the upper ancestral world.)

The following passages further relate several themes mentioned above and the spatiality of relations between and interchangeable identities of the *kuel, Ngenechen*, shamans, and an unknown dead *machi* [*nana*] who is associated with another *kuel* located in another place or on a distant pathway in the valley. *Machi* Juanita asks why a foreign *machi* has intruded into her space and recognizes that *Wenumapu's* powers also are present in the *nguillatuhue* field, presumably because the other *machi* has come into her personal ritual space and a mediating force from above is needed.

> XXXXIV: 3–9: Why do you [another *machi*] give advice in this land?
> I have seen that he [the *kuel*] is on another path,
> the *nana* [*machi*] of the other *kuel* has dried up [died].
> How did she arrive here?
> In the space of my own *mapu*
> She brings something too.
> The *Wenumapu* is working.

The solitary or independent nature of the *machi's* work in the *mapu* world is described below, as well as her dependency on the collective powers of the *Wenumapu* world. The sick *kuel* also possesses spiritual and shamanic powers derived from his ability to transform himself into a *machi* and from his kindred affiliation with *Pillan* and *Ngenechen*. Identity and occupational competition between the *machi* and *kuel* are shown below when the weakened *kuel* asks the *machi* not to be competitive with him and not to perform ceremony on top of him. The *machi* states in section XXXXI: 1–10 that:

> You [*kuel*] believe that you can govern the *machi*,
> but *Wenumapu* does not believe this.
> The *machi* does not govern alone. Friends [ritual audience]

a different person [*machi*] takes a different path.

A different *machi* who follows the paths of others can be harmed.

For this reason each *machi* has to go a long way; friends

for this, for certain, one must consult with the owner [*Ngenechen*] of the medicine [in *Wenumapu*]

so that one from the same *mapu* [place on earth] does not have so many problems; friends

these two [*kuel*] are asking that we not be competitive with them . . .

[the *kuel*] that I don't initiate my prayer ceremony on top of them.

The visionary and spiritual powers of the *kuel*, *machi*, and gold (*milla*) are shown below. This is significant because it ties the narrative to certain Andean themes, especially the relation between power and gold. (*Milla* is the gold offering given to renovate the spirit of the *kuel*.) As yet, there is no conclusive archeological and ethnohistorical evidence to indicate that the pre-Hispanic Araucanians possessed gold or revered it as an object of metaphysical power and social status (see Chapter 3). The association of power and gold likely stems from late pre-Hispanic Andean or Inka influence on the Araucanians, which they incorporated into their beliefs and stories. Once again, the following verses make clear the interchanging roles between *machi* and *kuel*.

She relates in sections XXXXII: 1–13, XXVI: 63, and XXVII: 7 that:

And the others [other ritual audiences in other rehuekuel] are still, still alert in another *rehuekuel* [in the valley].

Hay, other work awaits me there [in another *nguillatun* field]

I have the medicine

There is a *nana* [another *machi*] who has died and been buried there [in the Hualonko field] before.

She too [the other *machi*]: she too is in another *kuel* and this too is a poor *kuel*;

there also are visions coming from this *kuel*, Hay,

I believe that I have to continue working with them [the *kuel*], well

hay, I passed over that woman [the other *machi*?], says the *kuel*.

In my presence I have gold, well your past orin [sic] of gold.

And from the golden cinnamon tree I take favors. . . .

. . . someone [*Ngenechen*] who has gold on this stairway [*rehue*].

In a golden space located on another hill [*kuel*].

At the outset of these verses, the shaman mentions another ceremony in another *rehuekuel* in the valley. In section XXVI: 59, the *kuel* asked people in the local community to loan him the hill where the *nguillatun* and *palin* fields are located in Hualonko in order to conduct his affairs and to return to *Wenumapu*.

Later, he says that he will bewitch or cast an evil spell on neighboring communities if his requests are not met. We also learn from these stanzas that other "hills" and "fields" have powers. The *machi* later told us that "this hill," meaning Hualonko, and other "hills and fields" refer to other *kuel*, *rehuekuel*, and *nguillatun* sites in the valley. The competitiveness between *kuel*, *machi*, and sacred places is described, as well as other kinds of power. In later interviews, the *machi* said she did not know what she meant by other types of power, although she thought that they were other powerful *kuel* or *machi* present in the ceremony. She noted that a *machi's* power is diminished when she performs ceremony on top of a *kuel* that she has never visited before or does not know whose shamanic spirit resides inside, which was the case at Hualonko. *Machi* Juanita's personal *kuel* where she receives her maximum power and where her spirits resides is located about 20 km to the east in Rucalleco. Visitation from other *machi*, both living and dead, also occurs through the sighting of other *kuel* and *rehuekuel* during ceremony. During other ceremonies that I have attended, *machi* often pointed to other *kuel*, *visible* in the distance (ca. 0.5 to 2 km away), and stated that the *machi* spirits residing in them were coming to visit us and were participating in her ceremony, because they could see from these distant *kuel* to her *kuel*. The *machi* claim that all *kuel* have *wedange* (eyes and evil eyes) that allow them to visually travel. In order for the living to be aware of the eyes and the movements of *kuel* across the valley during ceremony, people had to cut the forest to open and maintain lines of sight between related *kuel* and *rehuekuel* (see Chapters 4 and 6).

In section XXVI: 59–62, she says

> I am going to borrow this hill [*kuel*].
> What would be the effect of the *machi's* kneeling down
> on this hill [*kuel*]
> in front of someone [*Ngenechen*] who has another type of power?

Sections LVI to LXVI end the shaman's oration by addressing the ancestral dead and the living and by stressing that the local communities attending the ceremony must conduct themselves properly in life. In the passages presented below, she also talks about other *kuel* as sons of *Ngenechen*, and asks how many *kuel* are really present in "the other *mapu*," implying the remainder of the valley. She also asks how many *kuel* are present in the ceremonial field, what strengths they possess, where they plan to travel, and why they are communicating with her. She and her *dungunmachifu* later told me that *kuel* may appear in the form of ancestral *machi* or *kuel* and that during ceremonies she must always ask whether other dead *machi* are present in the form of *kuel* in the ceremonial field where she is performing her rituals. If other *machi* are unknowingly present, they can inflict sorcery on her and the community or oppose the strength of her medicine. During these interviews, she also stated that other *kuel* and *machi* can be present in ceremony by hiding on other planes in *Wenumapu* and *miñchemapu* worlds and that she constantly has to travel between them to solicit their aid in combating evil and in achieving her goals. This again brings up the idea that under certain circumstances *machi* and *kuel* transform themselves into each other and that they possess visible and invisible forms in sacred spaces.

She also remarked that it is important to leave wide open spaces between *kuel* in ceremonial fields for other *machi* and *kuel* to visit the ceremony (which accounts for the open spaces between mounds) and for her to see where these visitors are located. I asked her about the large *ñichi* platforms where the *kuel* are built, why they are built so high, and flat and why they have open spaces cleared of vegetation. She said that many people attended the ceremonies and needed space to see, sit, cook, dance, and pray and that the people are always ordered and seated where the *lonko* tells them to locate. Colípi also stated that people usually remain in their designated spaces during ceremony and that only important officials occupy the central spaces of the ceremonial plaza (a pattern that I have seen in all *nguillatun* and other ceremonies I have known over the past thirty years.)

> LIX: 27–38: Here I have my poor horse, friends.
> It will remain tied up in this space of the *kuel* of the past.
> Then, also, there are other successes, for certain,
> I admire one son [*kuel*] that is on top of the [Hualonko] *ñichi*.
> This son [*kuel*] that is one. Where are you?
> This *kuel* of the past that is in the other *mapu*, I ask you.
> He who comes a long way, he who comes a long way.
> Also present is the other [second *kuel* in the Hualonko field]. What is
>   your name?
> This is, this is. Where are the sons [other *kuel*] from the past?
> Where have you gone? We are asking.
> Where are you, Chaw [*Ngenechen*]?

> LXIII: 2–10: Is there another one [*kuel*] in this mapu?
> Here where one climbs [into the upper world], here, well, I will do
>   you [*kuel*] a favor,
> I am telling you, well. . . . [pause]
> What gives you strength, you, poor you [*kuel*]?
> It's nothing bad that you have fallen here [from *Wenumapu*].
> This is the matter?
> Let us hear from you two [*kuel*], brothers.
> Are there three or four of you [*kuel*]
> says the parent of the earth [the deity *Pillan*].

After curing the *kuel* of his illness, she ends the ceremony by telling the two mounds in the field to travel safely upon their return to the upper world and that they have not conducted themselves so badly in the *mapu* space of the living (see LXIV). She also makes it clear that she has descended (with others?) from *Wenumapu* to *mapu* space to terminate the ceremony and that she brought *mudai* to cure the sick *kuel* (see XXXV: 3–6): "When the ceremony begins, we will come down [from *Wenumapu*] and carry *muday* [*mudai*] for the *kuel* and scatter the *muday* and the earth of the *kuel*" (XXXI). She says that she experimented with sicknesses while she was in the *Wenumapu*, that she is a "golden crest" when she is up there, and that she continues to have a *lonko* mentor in *Wenumapu*. In other passages, she mentions how difficult it was to cure the *kuel*. She also speaks with *Ngenechen*, makes reference to the past and to lost spaces (see XXXI), and laments that people today don't remember their history (see XXXII: 1–10). In passage XXXIV, she mentions that her work to cure the *kuel* was "the product of an enormous amount of energy."

Tren Trenkuel *Narrative*

To set the context, *TrenTrenkuel* is surrounded by more than thirty other mounds within a 1 km radius. Its location is referenced with regard to all other *kuel* and to other sacred places in the valley. The ceremony at this site began at a *rehue* pole in a *nguillatun* field located 0.5 km to the north. All participating lineages and project members first gathered in the field at midnight and then around 5:00 A.M. proceeded to *TrenTrenkuel* to conduct the preventive *dahatun* ritual to ask the mound for permission to excavate. We wanted to excavate *TrenTrenkuel*, because it is one of the largest and most centrally located mounds in the valley, because it is the only mound named after the benevolent snake, *Tren Tren*, and because the local Mapuche in Butarincón were interested to know what was inside the mound. Multiple speakers are recorded in this narrative, which are listed as the *machi* and her *dungunmachifu* or helpers.

For reasons discussed earlier, the narrative is presented in paragraphs rather than the individual verses of the *Hualonlokuel* text. I present a summary of the main points in selected paragraphs, starting at the beginning of the ceremony. Selected passages also are directly quoted to provide specificity for commentary. Both the paragraphs and verses are numbered in Roman numerals and referenced to the full text in Appendix 1. In this narrative, the living world is called both *Nag Mapu* and *mapu*. Again, only the English version is given below.

I. In the opening passages of section I, *machi* Lucinda establishes her place in the *rehuekuel* of *Hualonkokuel* and in the *Wenumapu* world by referencing her movements from one plane to another, instructing us where her sources of knowledge and power are located, and revealing that the supreme deity *Ngenechen* is responsible for commissioning the ceremony and for assigning her the sacred administrative role. She asks for his help in carrying out the ceremony and informs him that people have come to this event with good intention and proper conduct. She also recognizes that *Ngnechen* and the upper world are the "owners" (meaning father and supreme stewards) of all mounds, including *Tren Trenkuel*. The *machi* also credit's the importance of people's dreams for instructing their conduct and guiding their future.

> *Machi*: Here I am standing in this *rehuekuel* of supplication [*nguillatun*]. Here in this place of supplication they gave me strength, *Ngünechen* [the Father Guide: *Ngenechen*] gave it to me. And today in the midst of these mounds I am beseeching, kneeling, praying. . . . And this is happening because *Ngünechen* makes it possible. And I beg of you, that we enter into the place of ceremony [*Tren-Trenkul*] with respect and good order. Father Guide, and all you up there, aid me in this ceremony in which we are praying on our knees, only with the good thought we have at this moment. We wish to begin everything in good form, for this reason, grant me the necessary strength Father of *Rangiñ Wenu* [the Middle World Above], oh thou *Ngünechen*, aid me and help me to stand and raise me up in this special matter of this moment. Also all [of] you behold my brothers and sisters [ritual audience] here in *Nag Mapu* [the World Below of the Living], we are all attentive in this ceremony taking place in this place. But, indeed, please hear them.

II. As revealed below, *kuel* are sacred places that are traversed daily by people. The *machi* mentions that the community is sponsoring the ceremony, because there was a vision (*perimontun*) calling for prayer at and offerings to the *kuel* and because this is what *Ngünemapun* (*Ngenechen*) wanted.

> *Machi*: Oooooooh . . .! Oh . . .! What a beautiful meeting we have! Here lie our forefathers. On this hill many people walk across or around this mound. But we are here because of a *perimontun* [dream] and because the *Ngünemapun* [he who rules this space] desires it so. Good day to all the sons and daughters!

III. The *machi* locates the *kuel* in *mapu* or *Nag Mapu*, the earth's surface below the *Wenumapu* world where the *nguillatun* field and the living are located. She specifies that the ceremony is necessary because someone (the archeologists) will be performing an activity (excavation) at *Tren Trenkuel*. Later, in this section, she refers to the audience as "*kona*," which means warriors in times of past conflicts. At the end of this passage, she again mentions the power of her vision and how it has produced a *millariku* or wealthy person, which is in reference to the author and his archeological crew.

> *Machi*: Thus this is how my song and my gaze are in this *Nag Mapu* [World Below *Wenumapu*]. *Ngünechen* gazes upon us here where we are in this place below. There is a *kuel* here in this place below. Here they left thee a space to kneel, to make supplications. And thus supplication is made, a golden *Ngillatun* is made which raises dust. Then each one will come into this place of supplication. This *Ngillatun* shall be held because someone [people of the community] call [on me] and intend to carry out a [ceremonial] act in this place, here in the World Below [*Nag Mapu*]. There they go, standing. There go the *longko* [*lonko*: chiefs], those who truly think with their hearts, they are going to kneel in this place of supplication.

IV. Important here is the *machi's* description of the floor or surface of the *kuel* that we are standing on during ritual. Throughout the ceremony and typical of other rituals is recognition of the *Nag Mapu* surface upon which live ritual is performed, danced and offerings are made, ashes of the *foye* (cinnamon) and other sacred plants are scattered, *chicha* is poured over the mound, and pottery vessels are smashed over it. (The *machi* considers the floor to be a cultural surface prepared and blessed by the ritual gathering. When she later entered a trench excavated from the base to the center of the mound and looked at the prepared floors and burned areas, she stated that those were the places where *fileu pullu* (ancient spirit shamans) had conducted ceremonies and made offerings long ago.) Use of the term *kunifal* (orphans or needy people) also is significant, because it refers to displaced people in the ceremony who have no home or history. She later told us that she was referring to the past when people had to move to the lands of other Mapuche due to intense warfare in their homelands.

> *Machi*: Yes, [this] is the ground we walk on. This is never lost. The place below [*mapu* space], a place of ceremony, a place of gathering is never lost. But, I say, this is a place of speeches. Here I am standing, thinking on my knees on this ground below. Here is the *Ilo Nag Mapu* where the *Wenumapu* [the World Above] inclined [unto us] according to the *perimontun* [vision] which we have had, [we] the *kuñifall* [orphans in this place].

V. This section of the narrative is especially illuminating, because it describes the need for obedience and attentiveness of the ritual audience and for the audience to observe and learn from ceremonial experiences at *kuel*. She stresses that we should not be disruptive and disorderly during the ceremony; she assures the *kuel* and other powers that our conduct will be correct. The *machi* also states that the archaeologists (*wingka*) had other ideas about the *kuel* that were different from the Mapuche's thinking about them. Here she refers to a conversation we had with the community in order to obtain their permission to excavate. We told them that our archaeological experience led us to believe that the *kuel* might be very old and that it and other *kuel* were probably constructed at different times. The *machi* differed in her opinion and believed that *Tren Trenkuel* and other *kuel* were all built at the same time. This was the only major discrepancy that we had between our interpretation and her vision of the mounds. She also recognizes that we *wingka* know much about Mapuche culture and history and that we are acquainted with other *machi* who perform rituals at *kuel*. (*Machi* Lucinda knew that I had worked with other shamans in the valley.) In the following passages, her ritual helper speaks.

> *Dungumachife*: It is true that there are non-Mapuche people here, but in like fashion they also want to hear the discourse. Yes, it is true that these *wingka* [archaeologists] come from another place. But they are silent and respectful in this place. They want to see and learn what is happening in this place of prayer. There is no disorder or actions which can disrupt the ceremony. They [the *wingka*] thought that this place of discourse and decision-making [*nguillatun* field and *kuel*] had other histories; this is why they wish to witness all this. Moreover, they are familiar with this land and know that in another place there was a person of power [ancestral *machi*] who could come to this place of discourse. And in that they worked together. This also is why [the ritual audience] are here as well. [Translator not sure of this latter interpretation, since the *dungamachife's* speech was barely understood.]

VII. In this narrative use of the term *llonagwingkulmalonmapu* means the layered soils of the *kuel* which overlie *Kai Kai*, the evil snake in the origin story that brought flood waters to devour people (see Chapter 4). In this regard, the evil snake living below *Tren Trenkuel* is capable of transposing living people from the *mapu* world and placing them in the evil underworld. (The *machi* also told us that the soil used to build the evil mounds of *Kai Kai* is different from the soil placed in the good mounds of *Tren Tren*. She did not know why different soils were used to build the good and bad mounds.) Later, she states that we will excavate the "waters" of the *kuel* located in these hills. Here, she metaphorically references the flood waters absorbed by *Tren Trenkuel* when the people were threatened by rising waters (see origin story in Chapter 4). The last part of this oration mentions the power derived from the world above and from her *rehue* made of gold, which is the altar where she conducted previous ceremonies and often had painful experiences. She ends this section by describing here powers again and by offering *chicha* to the mound.

Machi: Here is a discourse [ceremony] which we are all holding today including the totality of our brothers and sisters, the *wingka* as well. We are all gathered here in this *Ilo Nag Wingkul Malon Mapu* [land of the mound that draws people down below the earth's surface and encircled by people [the participants].] [Translator not sure of the meaning.] And I am standing here in this place. So it is, sons and daughters, brothers and sisters, say I. . . . But I am moved by what all of you are going to hear. . . . They [archaeologists] go and come to excavate the water of the mound in this range of hills. . . . Until today when it has become a height on the mountain, a mound, a height on the mountain in the land of these hills [mounds]. But this mound does not exist by chance. There is a spirit of the land there. Oh brothers and sisters for always!! They [archaeologists] have been spoken to through a *machi*. They have been brought to the place of supplication. In a discourse similar to that of a *machi*, they have been encouraged and directed in the matter present here, in a ceremony of prayer and according to the order of the ancestors. I have my own ceremony of prayer. We have someone with power here with us, although you [*Newenngleu* or *Ngenechen*, the supreme deity who gives power] do not have it here in your land. But in this moment you have someone from another place. Now we can say, "Here is our *koyag* [discourse]," we can say now. This is what we can say now. Someone [*Newenngelu*] of power has come down to replace [the mound, his son] among our sons and daughters, he is here, he is speaking. Just as she who posseses the power, we are also going to enter [the *kuel*]. But the *Newenngelu* [the power that has the resolution] has come down to this place among his sons and daughters and is standing here, speaking. . . . In like fashion we are going to enter together with the one who holds the power [the *machi*], but I swear that I shall not use this place of prayer and meeting wrongly. I shall not profane the *millarewe* [the golden *rehue*] where I have suffered, where I have undergone much affliction for many things, where I have ordered others who also possess the power. We are praying and we are holding this discourse for all these reasons.

XII. Revealed below is the *machi* instructing people how to perform the ceremony and that they should listen to her because she has the powers to conduct the ritual and to guide people to the *kuel*. Up to this point, the ceremony had been performed at the *rehue* in the *nguillatun* field located about 500 m north of the mound. She now leads the ritual procession to *Tren Trenkuel* and instructs us to stand on its east side to face the rising sun. She tells the mound that we come to pray and to converse with it. If she is successful in praying to and in appeasing the mound, then we can later make offerings of gold to it and asks its permission to excavate. Offerings of gold are listed as *chicha*, ashes of burned sacred plants, food, and sacrificial animals (a black and a white sheep). In this and other ceremonies that I have attended with *machi*, they always caution the ritual audience of the uncertainty of ceremony and that she may not always be successful in achieving her stated purpose. Most *machi* fear the opposition and sorcery from bad *machi* who might enter the ceremonial field to manipulate *kalku* and to negate the force of their power and knowledge. This uncertainty and insecurity are prevalent throughout this ceremony as well as the one performed by *machi* Juanita at *Hualonkokuel*.

> *Machi:* That's right, sons and daughters. Everything is ready among you. This is what you have. But first you must pray here, you have to listen to the person with the power [*machi*] who will make the prayer and then you can walk and go to the mound. Thus you will be able to continue the prayer and reach the place of prayer and supplication. Before standing on the right of the *Treng Treng kuel*, the person with the power must pray and say what must be said in her prayer. If she is successful and something positive results, once she has finished and has good results, you shall also enter carrying something like gold [Translator does not fully understand this expression], which you shall place just there.

XIII. After describing the prayer we will offer the *kuel* and the excavation that we will perform there, the *machi* informs us that the mound is not alone and that there is a horse buried inside it (the bones of which we later excavated in the mound). The *machi* also describes a golden cave of the ancestors that lies inside the mound and inside the flat *ñichi* hill it stands on. Here she refers to the place of the kindred spirits inside the mound and the different places in the valley where the ashes of burned sacrificial plants have been ritually deposited during other ceremonies in other sacred places. Also important is her description of *Tren Trenkuel* and other mounds in the chain of *kuel* located in the hills stretching from Butarincón to Rukalleco. These are the named mounds shown in

Figure 47, many of which are those listed previously. After referencing all of the mounds within view of *Tren Trenkuel*, she identities them as extensions and subjects of *Tren Trenkuel*. They are the sons and daughters of *Tren Trenkuel*.

> *Machi*: That is, according to my understanding, what he [*Ngünechen*] who holds the power says and has. He knows all this and because of that has agreed to participate in this matter. And this is why we are here. And thus, supplication will be made to the *Trengtreng kuel*. I see that they are carrying out their work and excavating earth in the *Trengtreng kuel*, indeed. But I tell them that the *Wingkulmapu* [mound] is not thus alone. The *Trengtreng kuel* is not alone. He has his power there, he has his saddled horse. . . . And here we are sons and daughters, brothers and sisters. . . . Thus he also has his *millarenü* [the golden cave [tomb] of the forefathers] in the mound and mountain. It has its *fumarole* and its power. The earth on all the mountain mounds seems like ashes. There his heart is, there his thought is wont to be. . . . Then the mounds come together in rows [meaning pathways in the valley; see Chapter 6], and thus there surely is *Trengtreng kuel* in all the mounds. There are the *llellipun* [supplication], the *kimün* [wisdom], the *witranewen* [the power or force that attracts]. Everything appears as a place of ashes here in all the mounds and on the mountains. His heart has entered these places and settled [there]. So he is to be found bound thus to all these mounds of *Trengtreng kuel*. In this way we come to recognize our being. All you are going to participate in this supplication as masters of the ceremony. And thus, you will have to make the supplications. You will have to prepare yourselves with the *millamuday* [the golden drink, *chicha*], the bread and some marks of color, my dear sons and daughters. Once she [*machi*] who holds the power has prayed, then you shall go to make a supplication to the mound, leaving there your *millaseña* [golden sign], in a very orderly and respectful way, my dear sons and daughters. Thus it is . . . let him go who has the *millabandera* [the golden banner]. There has never been a *kuelbandera* [banner of the *kuel*] in this place. Is there a horse? . . . He who has the *kuel* banner. Then, listen, there should be a banner. How many *kuel* banners are there, brother?

Near the end of this long passage, she mentions the various kinds of ceremonies and powers possessed by places where "ashes are deposited." She also states that *Ngenechen*, the supreme deity who possesses the great power, has located his "heart" in all *Tren Tren* mounds. She also informs the audience that they will know these things by participating in ceremony and that they will have to pray to the mound and to the deities. This section ends by describing the gold offerings made to the mound and the placement of golden flags and emblems of each lineage around the *rehue* and the *kuel* (see also Section XIV).

XVIII. Additional description is provided of the sacrificial offerings made to the *kuel* and to *angkatraru*, the latter being the fragments of pottery vessels intentionally broken by the ritual audience on the exterior surface or floor of the mound. The *machi* then remarks that after we had poured the "golden *chicha*" into the tunnels of the mound and onto the surface, the *chicha* vessels were smashed *in situ* and mixed with the ashes of sacred plants. The result was a burned area with ashes and burned plant remains, *chicha* stains, and broken drinking vessels. These ritual acts are remarkably similar to those described by the early chroniclers and in the origin myth (see Chapters 3 and 4) and inferred from burned areas and broken vessels later retrieved from excavated floors inside the mounds. In Rosales' version of the origin story, studied in Chapter 4, pottery vessels smashed and broken on *"Ten Ten"* (*Tren Tren*) hills were used to cover the people to protect them from the burning sun above. The *machi* insisted that the *chicha* vessels we were using in the ceremony had to be broken and that the sherds be properly distributed among all participants in ceremony. After the ceremony, we had to leave the sherds on the used surface of the *kuel*, so they would protect the mound from evil forces. As seen below, she later scolded the ritual audience for not placing the sherds in their correct location around the base and on top of the mound, which is in reference to proper spaces of participates and ritual objects and to designated space areas determined by social and settlement placement in the local community (see Chapters 3 and 4 for designated ceremonial spaces mentioned by early chroniclers).

> *Machi*: Now, bring the *millawangku* [the golden seat] and the *kuel muday* [the *kuel* drink *chicha*] and the *angkacharu* [the ceremonial pottery vessel]. We are in this ceremony and we are carrying it out thus. Now! You have to pay attention, the volcano [or the deity *Pillan*] is coming. The volcano rises upward and we are going to enter [it] only with words. The grandfather and the youth, they are two in the place of discourse. They look very well. Now, you *kuel*. You could not remain outside the ceremonial sherds. All should be alive within the golden vessel [containing the *chicha*]. That should be considered. And you will have to pray thus. So also you will have to cut the animal [to be] sacrificed and do it in the same way. There you will have to cut and make the sacrifice.... I am already praying

with the golden *muday*, with the *kuel* hominy, and the *kuel* blood. Now . . . you must take the blood of the *kuel* and you have to beseech him for all that is needed. The *küme wenu* [good world above], my son, is very beautiful, my brother [*kuel*]. Take care, for the *küme wenu* can be angered, sons and daughters [the ritual audience]. But it can feel sorrow, since it gazes upon you from above. Sometimes you [*kuel*] do not walk rightly, you are stubborn like a bad son. There is the *küme wenu* in its majesty and beauty, my son. But all the forms of life depend on the kindness from above.

She also tells the audience to pay close attention to the arrival of the volcano, which is the deity *Pillan* who resides in the visible Andean volcanoes to the east (Tolhuaca, Llaima Llaima). She instructs us that we will soon enter inside the mound and that we should be alert. For reasons not understood, she mentions that the *kuel* should remain outside of the sacred ceramic pieces. (I think she implies that the vessel fragments are intended for our use only during ceremony.) She also asks us to continue offering special food and drink to the mound. She then speaks of the good world immediately above us (*kumewenu*) and to the *kuel* as her son. She informs him that the world above is watching the ceremony and that it could become upset with her, the *kuel*, and the ritual audience. The *machi* also states that the *kuel* does not always conduct himself well and that he has been a bad son (to both her and to the upper world). In later interviews, she said that all *kuel* act badly from time to time and must be kept in line by praying to them and by offering food and drink to them (see Appendix 1).

XVII. The *machi* mentions the beauty of the upper world and that all of us will soon climb on top of *TrenTrenkuel* to celebrate and pray to it. (At present, most of the ritual congregation is still standing at the base of the mound.) She again informs us that we will soon enter inside the mound, that we should not fear being there, and that she will pray to the mound for our protection and good will. When she says that she has "breadth," she refers to her spiritual powers. She also refers to the *kuel* as a kin member in the following passages. She pleads to the *kuel* not to be upset with the ritual chants and noises that the audience is making. The *machi* then addresses the "*kuel* of history" and the supreme deity of all *kuel* – *payllangenwingkul* – to ask if they are still present in the ritual space and if they had thought about the sacred ceramic pieces. These verses reflect the *machi's* insecurity about the different figures and forces present at the ceremony, which also is a pattern repeated often by the *machi* in the *Hualonkokuel* ritual. This again reveals the kinds of invisible and inaccessible forces that intrude into ceremonial space and that are seen only by the *machi*. She again informs us that we had not broken the pottery vessels in proper order (which meant hierarchical kinship and spatial lines across and between lineages) and that we should be more attentive and careful. She said that the broken vessels had to be placed closer to the center (*reñi*) of the *kuel*. (The excavations later revealed a higher concentration of broken sherds and ashy burned areas near the center of the mound.) The *machi's* concern with the broken sherds and their proper placement on and around the mound is remarkably similar to Nuñez de Pineda's description of designated places for pottery vessels smashed during ceremony and to broken sherds in the origin story the (see Chapter 3). She tells us that we need to kneel, pray, and make offerings to the mound and to do all of this with our own breath or spirits.

> *Machi*: Yes, the *küme wenu* exists . . . it is very beautiful. Now you are going to reach that immense mound where the prayers are offered. You are going to arrive where the *Trengtreng kuel* is, surely. . . . We are going inside the *Trengtreng kuel*, but do not feel badly. I am going to pray to him. I am like the wind. I have the capacity to behave like the wind in this place, kinsman *kuel*. Grant us this favor, decide with compassion in this matter. . . . Do not be angry, *Trengtreng kuel*. Thou hast the *newen* [power], do not be angry because we are making noise. Yes, we are going to go as guests but we are only going to leave standing a *millaseña* [a golden marker]. But, please, grant us the favor *Trengtreng kuel*, give us an affirmative answer. *Kuel* of spoken history, *payllangen wingkul* [sacred guardians of the mounds], you [all] are here. Now you have already reflected with the *angkacharu* [sacred vessel]. Brothers and sisters, the *angkacharu* is not correctly placed. You [ritual audience] are not paying attention to this. Alas! That [the sacred sherds] has to be placed near the center to offer the supplication so that it reaches its goal. This is our ceremony. Indeed, all have to kneel. The outsiders as well who have been permitted to be here. The *millawingka* [the non-Mapuche in the sacred place] have to kneel and thus, in their own breath . . . and they must follow their own breath. We are standing and very involved in this task.

XVIII–XI. These verses again document the instructions that the *machi* gives the congregation to pray to the mound, to recognize the different ethereal planes where the deities and ancestors are located and where she ascends and descends, to continue making offerings of *chicha* and other items to the *kuel*. She also asks the *kuel* and, by extension, the celestial figures not to be upset with us for performing the ceremony.

XXII. The shaman speaks to the congregation, the *kuel*, and the deities, and refers to the different types of ceremonies she is performing: speaking with the powers above (*dungutun*), praying to the powers above (*llelipun*), and conversing with the congregation (*nütramtun*).

> *Machi:* Now then, brothers and sisters! Now then, sons and daughters! Let us warm the place above a little, sons and daughters. Ay, sons and daughters! Our good land above has always been beautiful, my brothers and sisters. It is within you, because its goodness is so great. This is our word, here. But everyone should have an attitude of respect. No one should joke or laugh. All thoughts should be concentrated on our present endeavor so that we may have the desired results. Any contrary thought can go against you. You are sharing the word. And here we are standing on this space below offering our prayer.... Eeww!... Now, brothers and sisters, this person with power has not brought her *llellipuwe* [what is used in the supplication]. Perhaps she forgot it. This person [*machi*] who has the power seems to have become drunk [in a trance] in the course of our ceremony. Bring the *kuel muday* [gloss], right away, friends. Right now! Stand up and then all will have to kneel and pray. Thus is *Ngen Wenu Chaw Ngünechen* [Father Guide, master of the world above]. If there is a sister in black, may she blow out her breath and make it circulate ... yes, a sister. Well now, friends, everyone has to kneel.

XXIII-IV. She tells the congregation that it must respect the *kuel* and the ceremony being performed and conduct it properly. In these passages, the shaman associates the *kuel* with volcanoes and the ritual she conducts as a healing performance.

XXV. The *machi* seeks respect for the owners (deities and ancestors) of the medicine [her shamanic powers] who are attending the ceremony. She asked the *kuel* again not to be upset with the audience.

> *Machi:* Now, then, we who have made an effort and suffered, my dear brother [*kuel*]. We the defenseless [*machi* and ritual audience], here we are. Well, we [*machi* alone] who have had these visions! But for now, they no longer reprove us [*machi* and her assistants], they are not angry with us any more.

Between Sections XXVI and XXIX, she repeats the idea that the ritual audience must be obedient and respectful and listen to the advice of the *kuel* and the deities.

XXXI. She tells the congregation that if they are not obedient, then the powers above will "castigate" them and evil forces (in the *miñchemapu* underworld) will speak with them (meaning enter into their lives). She further remarks that they will suffer if they do not believe in her vision, follow the advice given to them to resolve their problems, be more cautious in listening to beggars (*lukutun*), and agree more among themselves (regarding community affairs). If they continue in their present ways by not following these instructions and acting improperly and disrespectfully, then the snake (*Kai Kai*) who lives in the underworld will inhabit the *kuel* (and the land) again. She discusses the good powers of the upper world (*Ngünemmapu*, *Wenumapu*) and the sacrifices it has made on behalf of people.

> *Machi*: Thus, I understand . . . some people do not pay a lot of attention to the person who holds the power. And thus she is not taken into consideration when an event occurs. But yes, . . . now the *perimontun* [vision] comes. From above one can see how the punishment comes in first place. Up there the vision and the punishment are together. When this measure comes about, then there the world below [*Nag Mapu*, the surface of the earth] will speak. And there is the reason for which *Chaw Ngünechen* [the Great Father or Father Guide]. And you all [ritual congregation] will say this. Until then, when you all will have reflected, then, thus you all will know each other better. For those [in the ritual congregation] who do not believe in visions, who do not follow the steps they should to solve a problem, who do not believe in prayer, and who do not agree, there is no agreement among all [of them]. There is no union around a single problem; there is no *lukutun* [ceremony of prayer], no looking upward, toward the one who has the power [*Chaw Ngünechen*]. They say they would rather remain as they are. They think that they can continue weeping alone. But yes, but yes, if they remain thus, they shall see the vision come nearer and this [the vision] thus will be seen in *Nag Mapu* and thus will remain a vision. A serpent shall come in which shall enter the dwellings. The whole vision shall enter there. It shall also enter the field of prayer and around the *Ngenmapu* [the steward of the land]. But *Chaw Ngünechen* shall seek the earth that rises up when his gaze is turned here. And thus, also,

other spaces are grouped together. And in this mountain [*kuel*] of yours [*Chaw Ngünechen*], the *Ngünenmapu* [the Great Father who controls the space] makes sacrifices on this beloved earth. Until this time, in reality, this is the power which the *Ngenmapu* has. Then, he has all these spaces together until now, it will be he [*Chaw Ngünechen*] who gives power.

XXXII-III. She ends the ceremony by referencing the powers of the upper world where she has been traveling during the ceremony and the importance of her visions. The ceremony terminates when the audience chants and dances around the *rehue* placed at the base of the east side of the mound. We then return to the *nguillatun* field where we had started the ritual and sang, danced, and feasted during the remainder of the day and into the next night. In many ways, this narrative is similar to the *Hualonkokuel* one except that we *wingka*, or archeologists, were major actors in the ritual congregation. The acts by which both narratives focus so exclusively on the *kuel* reveals how these structures bring other mounds, deities, lineage groups, individuals, and landscapes into being. Even in large-scale *nguillatun* and other ceremonies that are administered in other sacred localities where there no *kuel* are present or can be seen in the distance, the shamans constantly reference them as if they have intruded into ceremonial space and thus are always present (albeit only *machi* may "see" them in the same manner that she saw the ancient *fileu pulli* during the *Tren Trenkuel* ritual). Unfortunately, we were unable to record one of the more important moments of the ritual when we entered inside the *kuel* with the *machi*. (The tape recorder malfunctioned at this moment.) When we "entered" the mound with the shaman, which was about 5:30 a.m. and still dark outside, the congregation was very quite and serene. The *machi* briefly described to us what "we were viewing" inside the mound: ancient *machi* were playing flutes and drums in tunnels and galleries in the base of the mound, people were gathered around the golden tomb inside, and other people were consuming *chicha* and food. She also emphasized how respectful and obedient we had to be to the *kuel* and to the spirits inside it. It can be seen in both narratives that the shamans have a mesmerizing dictatorial power over the ritual congregation and over several processes by which the society publicly conducts itself, including important decisions about people's rights and duties in interacting with the deities and the mounds. Further, it is clear that *kuel* are perceived as living beings and kinsmen, members of local lineages. In Lumaco, traditional Mapuche view them as real persons, material in form and mobile like humans but animated by spirits.

POSTCEREMONY CONVERSATIONS WITH *MACHI* JUANITA AND LUCINDA

José Saavedra and I visited *machi* Juanita and her *dungunmachifu* several times after the *llaimatun* ceremony in Hualonko and asked her about the meaning of her discourse with the *kuel* and about specific events and relations she expressed. In general, she was distant with us and said that she had little knowledge of the specific meanings of her narrative, saying it was a *fileu pulli*, an old powerful *machi* spirit, who was speaking through her during the ceremony. This statement suggests that she might have been in a trance during the night of her *llaimatun* and that she was possessed by a mentor *fileu* spirit. She also believed that she was the sick *kuel* at times and an old ancestral *machi* at other times. She told us that the *Hualonkokuel* was not her personal *kuel*, that he was sick and had turned bad, and that he was in need of her curing. She solicited help from *Wenumapu* in curing the *kuel* because her powers were diminished by having to work with an unfamiliar *kuel* outside of her territory. She also said that the *kuel* turned bad because the local community had not been praying enough to *Chaw* or *Ngenechen*, and that the *kuel* had absorbed the bad ways of the people. (The "bad ways" also referred to growing evangelical influence in the region and to the demise of the traditional lifestyle.) As a result, crops were failing and several families had fallen on bad times. Thus, she was commissioned to cure or heal the mound, although it had belonged to another *machi* who died long ago. She stated that old *kuel* fall to illnesses and become weaker after their *machi* dies. However, old, powerful *kuel* could be revitalized by being incorporated into an active *nguillatun* field like Hualonko and by feeding it *mudai* and food, by praying to it, and by helping it to return to the *Wenumapu* world.

We asked her about other old *kuel* and *nguillatun* fields in the valley. She said that many were inactive and spiritually living in and adopted by other *mapu* worlds, meaning other *rehuekuel* complexes in the valley. This again implies a kinship relation between *kuel* and kindred spirits and possibly the metaphysical incorporation of weaker or inactive mounds into stronger active ones. (To her, active meant a *kuel* "in use" or "attended to" by a *machi* and *nguillatun* community.) This pattern is similar to the real world relations between lineages in historic times when fragmented groups were adopted by stable groups (see Chapters 3 and 7). She also noted that all *kuel* were related historically and were the sons and daughters of *Pillan* and *Ngenechen*. She verified that the *kuel* are kin related to each other and to people in the same manner that humans are. We asked about the gender of *kuel* and why some are sons and daughters. She said that she knew little about these matters and had heard of only two daughter *kuel*. Most *kuel* are males. All of this information confirms not only a kinship pattern among the *kuel* but a system of rejuvenation of kin ties based on local histories and linkages between them, active *nguillatun* fields, and local communities. She also said that the land is spiritually motivated and active by these types of kin relationships.

Juanita and her *dungunmachifu* also reported that many *kuel* are active in ways other than participation in public ceremony, such as housing evil spirits, or *kalku*, and being inhabited by bad snakes or *filu* (which is in reference to the origin story and the struggle between *Kai Kai* and *Tren Tren*. See Chapter 4). Bad *kuel* are unattended by and unaffiliated with living communities. Although bad *kuel* can make you ill, they can be cured and converted to good *kuel* by praying for them and by giving them offerings, as she has done for the sick *Hualonkokuel*. The living and the *machi* give *mudai* to the *kuel* to cleanse it of evil forces and to nourish it into the upper world, she emphasized. The *mudai* runs through the soils of the mound like water in a stream and in the human body, washing away bad thoughts and evil spirits (see Chapter 4).

She also noted that the *Tren Trenkuel* in Butarincón had been abandoned by its *machi* and thus thought to be an evil place inhabited by snakes (i.e., *Kai Kai*). She related a story of two Chileans, or *huinca*, who once looted a portion of *Tren Trenkuel*. After digging the mound, she later heard that the two had severe economic problems, which the local community blamed on their intrusion into the mound and on not having performed a *dahatun* ceremony at the mound beforehand. She also said that people and *kuel* cry during ceremonies, because they needed water and *mudai* and that *kuel* do not bless people and help them the way they once did in the past. In the past, she told us that most *kuel* defended people and brought them together to defend themselves against outsiders rather than turning against people. She also said that *kuel* teach people all of these ways.

Juanita also reported that *Nahualbuta (Nahualfuta)*, the large mountain range to the west, means the great spirit of *nahual*, or the jaguar, the large spotted cat from the other side of the Andes (Argentina), and that *ñichi* refers to each *machi's* personal *kuel* that is positioned on an artificial hill. (Her interpretation of *nahual* partially coincides with that of the late *machi* Lucinda in Butarincón who told us that *nahual* is a feline and a jaguar-person, that Nahualbuta means the great spirit, and that *kuel* are extremely powerful and if destroyed, they could harm people.) Juanita referred to *Pillanwenu* as the spirits of dead *machi* or *fileu* that reside in all *kuel* and as the spirits of the two dead *machi* who were conversing with her during the *llaimatun* in Hualonko. Each *machi* has a *fileu* and a dead *machi's pillanwenu*, according to her. Her *Pillanwenu* comes to her when she solicits it. *Dene* or *dengue* is the great spirit in *Wenumapu* who names the *kuel* for shamans.

Juanita also related that all *machi* in the Lumaco area have their own personal *kuel*, and that *machi* in most other areas understand the meaning of *kuel*, but never had them because they were not traditional in those places. She also stated that *kuel* house spirits in order to become *machi*, that some *kuel* do not house the spirits of *machi*, and that some *kuel* are male (son) and others are female (daughter). She also told us that not all *kuel* are associated with *palihue* and *nguillatuhue* fields, that some stand alone as memories of the past, and that all *kuel* also are the sons and daughters of *Ngenechen* and *Pillan* who originally placed all mounds across the landscape and then told them they were the sons and daughters of *Tren Trenkuel*. According to her, *Tren Trenkuel* is the oldest and most powerful *kuel* in all of the land. We also asked her why she spoke of gold as an important offering to *kuel*. She did not know why it was so important; she said that the Mapuche never used gold, but that they know of its power. The *kuel* today do not have benediction, she said.

Machi Juanita was informative about other matters too. For instance, the largest and best-preserved mound in Butarincón, *Kuifilrehueñichicuel*, is the spirit of a powerful *machi*, the late Fabiana, who died a few years ago. Juanita also informed us that she occasionally takes something (*latue?*) before she conducts a *kueltun*. *Pelonquimumtun* is a person who looks into the *kuel* and into the earth to see events and to predict the future. These persons no longer exist she said, although old, wise *machi* and *weupin* come close to performing these services today.

We also asked her about dual secular leaders in ceremony. She said that one *lonko* was for praying (*nguillatufe*) and the other was for secular organization of people (*lonko*). Both leaders are capable of performing both roles, and they rotate them from year to year among the three *trokinche* communities sponsoring a *nguillatun*. Thus, each year two *lonko* are active and one is administratively inactive but every third year rotates back into an active role for a period of two years service (see discussion of *nguillatun* rituals in Chapter 4). In a sense, this is a dual but also tripartite division.

Lastly, she says that the intimate historical and spiritual relationships between a *machi* and a *kuel* is called *nauchi*. (Other informants also spoke of *nauchi*, but she was the only *machi* who knew what it means.) I interpret these relationships as the ability to speak with the *kuel*, to know its feelings, to predict the future through the *kuel*, to relate it to one's spirit, to become a *kuel*, and to teach the living how to respect and live with *kuel*. She said that very few *machi* and Mapuche understand these relationships today. Only a few *machi*, *lonko*, *weupin*, *nguillatufe* and *ülmen* who live in areas where *kuel* are still used or stay in the cultural memory of the community know the meaning of mounds and how to live with them and learn from them. She lamented that in the past everyone comprehended the importance of *kuel* to the community and knew how to interact with them and to interpret their feelings and visions. This comprehension and interaction, which she (and other *machi*) names *nauchi*, is what I call "*mound literacy*"; that is, people need to know how to read and live with the *kuel* and how to correctly use its knowledge and place in history and society.

In regard to *machi* Lucinda and the ritual held at *Tren Trenkuel*, she said that the old people built the *kuel* and maintained it during *kueltun* rituals. Three local *lonkos* would perform *trawün* (*cahuin*-like meetings) and *nütramcahuin* (decision-making meetings) at this *kuel*. She also described the four arms and legs of *Tren Trenkuel* and stated that the mound had a *nien*, or owner (meaning spirit), inside it, which served as a guiding light that radiated to all other *kuel* in the valley who are its sons and daughters. The most important part of the mound, she claimed, is the east side – the *Tripahueantu* – or side facing the sunrise. For reasons that she could not explain, she said that old people could read the condition or conduct of the mound by examining the way the sunlight struck its east side early in the morning. Further, the *Tren Trenkuel* has a heart (*piuke*) and it commands all other *kuel*. Public ceremony at *kuel* always takes place during the nighttime when the moon is visible and powerful. The moon is a woman that brings clarity (*Tripapale*) and motherhood to the *kuel*, she says. She said that it is important in all ceremonies for the *machi* to burn medicinal plants (e.g., *foye* or cinnamon, *boldo*, and *maqui*) and tobacco and to spread the smoke over the ritual ground in order for *Pillan* to use his powers to control evil forces and to send warriors into battle and *lonkos* to negotiate political issues. This latter comment reminds us of Rosales description of the use of ritual smoke during ceremony in the early 1600s.

> Esparcieron por el campo yerbas, que los Echizeros [*hechiceros*] les dieron, y zahumaron el lugar, donde auía de ser la batalla, con tabaco, lamando en su fabor al Pillan, y echando el humo azia la parte de los Españoles, para que los dehiziesse como el humo. (Rosales [1674] 1989:445)

> They sprinkled herbs which the witchdoctors [*hechiceros*] gave them over the field, and spread tobacco smoke as incense calling on *Pillan* for his favor and throwing the smoke toward where the Spanish were so that they might disperse like the smoke. (Rosales [1674] 1989:445)

Both *machi* Juanita and Lucinda reported that the location of mounds often impedes the construction of other mounds. I asked what they meant by this and they said that people had to seek the permission from existing or old mounds to construct a new or "kin" mound on local lineage land and that permission was not always granted. They said that it was often easier to build a new mound in a distant but visually connected location in order to prevent social conflict between the local community and the existing *kuel*. These comments seemingly refer to interlineage conflicts in the past and to the use of mound building to establish new lineage settlements in neighboring lands to prevent further disorder.

Lastly, *machi* Lucinda said that public ceremonies performed in the dark at night or under a pale moonlight are more sacred than daytime rituals, because the former are conducted under the *"melange"* (gaze) of the moon. I have observed that nighttime rituals also use torch light, which is used by shamans and their helpers to focus the full attention of the ritual audience on the *rehue*, the shaman, and her activities around and on the mound. Set in this context, shamans can manipulate the sources of light and thus what is being seen by the public audience. During daytime ceremonies, peloe tend to wander away and to gaze at distant horizons and other vistas (cf. Moore 1995 for a discussion of public viewsheds in the pre-Hispanic ceremonial architecture of Peru).

ETHNOGRAPHIC DESCRIPTIONS
BY OTHER INFORMANTS

Other *machi*, *lonko*, *weupin*, and elder informants present at the *Hualonkokuel* and *TrenTrenkuel* ceremonies confirmed most of the information given to us by *machi* Juanita and Lucinda, providing similar stories about the past, sacred landscapes, and the meaning of *kuel*. They generally were unable to give detailed commentary on the dialogues between the *machi* and the *kuel*, saying that only the shamans could interpret their own narratives. However, these informants and others from areas outside of Purén and Lumaco provided valuable information about other aspects of local history and *kuel* that are useful to this analysis. Presented below is some of this information. I also draw on the theses and technical reports written by several ethnographers working with the project in the Purén and Lumaco area (e.g., Ortiz 2005b, 2006; Poblete 2002; Rojas 2005, 2006; San Martín 2002). Some of this information is repetitive, but I include it to affirm the accounts given above by the two shamans and by other informants about other matters.

Elders of the Butarincón community stated that their great-grandfathers had told them that *kuel* were present when they were born, placing the minimal age of the mounds before 1850. In particular, Jacinta Katrileo Cheuque mentioned that *machi* who worshipped at *kuel* are both good and bad (*kalku*) shamans and that conflicts often arose between *machi* about rights to perform ceremonies in certain communities, to access sacred power sources, and to use the ritual paraphernalia of dead *machi*. To give an example of one conflict, she related that when *machi*

Fabiana died, *machi* Cármen wanted the twelve quartz stones of *lican* power that were inside Fabiana's *kultrun* (drum), but the dead *machi's* daughter did not give them to her. This resulted in an argument between *machi* Cármen and the daughter of the dead *machi*. The stones were powerful and had been used by *machi* Fabiana to predict the future during *machitun* (initiation rites) at her *kuel*. We were told that the conflict resolved itself two days after the death of Fabiana when the stones suddenly disappeared on their own accord.

The daughter also told us that her mother, Cármen, had said that *kuel* were powerful and that they could bring good luck if they were pacified and treated well by the living. She said that when *machi* seek medicine to cure the sick, the community worships at a local *nguillatuhue* and *kuel* to help the *machi* procure powerful medicines from the *Wenumapu* world (a scenario similar to the *Hualonkokuel* and *Tren Trenkuel* ceremomies). She also reported that *kuel* had *rehue* placed on top of them in the past, which served as *machi's* golden stairways to *Wenumapu*, and that spirits of *machi* reside inside mounds. (We have inferred the presence of *rehue*-like poles on top of mounds from our excavation of large post holes ca. 45–50 cm in diameter in *kuel*.) *Machi* Cármen also informed her daughter that *machi* regularly visited their personal *kuel* to receive power and to empower their medicine from the *Wenumapu* world. She said that *kuel* serve as spirit companions to *machi*.

Located north of Purén is *Wenucolla*, which is an old volcano and the largest and most physically distinct mountain in the valley. *Ngenechen* protected *Wenucolla* and all *kuel* and gave all *machi* their power and their *fileu pulli*, which reside inside *kuel*. Local Mapuche believe that *Wenucolla* is a long "stairway," or *rehue*, that reaches from the *Nag Mapu* to the *Wenumapu* worlds. Oral tradition, as told by Jacinta Katrileo Cheuque, has it that a lock of gold hangs from the doorway to *Wenumapu* at the top of the mountain. When the sea is frustrated (by whatever cause), it bumps against the lock making a *trueno* sound. She also told us that *Tren Trenkuel* was the most powerful *kuel* in all the land and that *hualfilu* (the evil snake in the origin story of *Kai Kai* and *Tren Tren*) lives in it. She said that in order to pacify the snake and to calm the evil inside the mound, the Mapuche periodically give it *mudai*. Gabriel Chicahual (husband of the daughter of *machi* Cármen) said that people from the valley always asks *Tren Trenkuel* in Lumaco for rain, because it is the most powerful *kuel*. He said that a great *lonko* named *Nahual*, meaning "tigre" or jaguar, is buried in *Tren Trenkuel* (see Chapter 4 and Dillehay [1999] for discussion of the feline in Araucanian culture). *Nahual* was the founding leader of the *Nahual* lineage, he claimed. Santiago Cheuque reported that his father told him that there once was an underground doorway or gallery located in the base of *Tren Trenkuel* and that when he entered it, he saw evil creatures and witches playing musical instruments and having a feast inside the mound. (This account is similar to *machi* Lucinda's description of people playing flutes inside the *Tren Trenkuel* mound during ceremony.) He also said that some *kuel* house evil snakes that reside underground, a notion that bodes well with the evil *miñchemapu*, the *Kai Kai* snake living underground in the origin story, and *machi* Lucinda's description of the snake living below the mound.

These and other informants also said that *Tren Trenkuel* has four legs, which can be seen from the top of the mound, and that *Tren Tren* came from the sky or the *Wenumapu* world where it was a *nahual*, or feline (i.e., jaguar), which transformed itself into a snake when it reached *Nag Mapu*. They also report that this four-legged "feline mound" walks throughout the valley at night to visit its son and daughter *kuel*. They also informed us that other *kuel* also have legs so they can travel and move into the upper world. Not known is why some *kuel* have legs and others do not. One informant claims that *Tren Trenkuel* also has a head that shrinks into the interior of the mound like a turtle's head. Juana Painenao and others relate that during floods *Tren Trenkuel* grows higher so people and animals can climb on it to save themselves from rising flood waters, a reference to the origin story and to the good deeds of this mound (see Chapter 4). She also remarked that *Tren Trenkuel* can consume the earth of the smaller son and daughter mounds so that it can grow larger and that this often results in the disappearance of some *kuel* from the land (see Chapter 6 and the comments above by other informants). Collectively, these reports reveal the anthropomorphic quality of some *kuel*, their mobility across the *Nag Mapu* landscape and into the upper world, the kinship relations between mounds, and the dominant fatherly role of *Tren Trenkuel*.

Alonso Painao, the head of the Lolonko community where several large *kuel* are located, told us that important leaders who died in battle were buried in mounds located on the hillcrests above Boyeco, near the town of Purén. In Lolonko, Manuel Katrileo stated that *lonko* climbed on top of mounds to converse across the open areas or plaza between them during important political and religious meetings (*cahuin*; see Figs. 62 and 63). He said that many *lonkos* from different valleys came to meetings held at Lolonko.

Interviews with Francisco Millao, Manuel Catrileo, Juan Chicahual, and José Luis Nahuelpan of Tranaman, all of whom are *lonko*, *ülmen*, or *weupin*, relate the following. Most *kuel* were built before the arrival of the Spanish and were made larger after the Spanish entered their land. There are two types of *kuel*, each with different kinds of power. One type is old, or *kuilfilkuel*, which are larger and more powerful than other mounds and are associated with the source and flow of water and with producing healthy animals and crops. They said that some older *kuel* can turn bad, like *Hualonkokuel*, and house large *Kai Kai* snakes that are destructive and evil. Young *kuel* were built after the arrival of the Spanish and are associated with large public ceremonies between many groups. *Nguillatun* are performed at both old and young *kuel*. They also said that the mounds in *Lolonko* are very powerful and associated with political and military might and that *toqui* war leaders at *Lolonko* would stand on opposing *kuel* and converse across the open plaza between them.

Luis Ancamilla, *lonko* of Ancamilla, also informed us that *kuel* were places of *cahuín* where people gathered to listen to the speeches of powerful *ülmen* and *toqui*. He said that *kuel* are always located on high points above agricultural fields and habitational settlements and that large *kuel* and *ngullatun* fields indicate a large population and a powerful *lonko*. He stated that before the arrival of the Spanish, the *kuel* were built to bury important people. After Lautaro, a famous war leader, defeated Pedro de Valdivia (in mid-1500s), *kuel* were constructed for *cahuin* and *nguillatun*. When asked about *rehuekuel* sites with multiple *kuel*, he said that some powerful *toqui* rulers, such as Colo-Colo, oversaw several secondary leaders and that during *cahuin* in *rehuekuel* each leader had his own *kuel* to stand on in order to see out over the people and to address them during ceremony. According to him, the location and orientation of secondary mounds around a central *kuel*, like those found in many *rehuekuel*, correspond with the cardinal direction of the secondary ruler's outlying homelands, which is the same type of designated spatial patterning associated with the seating patterns of families and lineages in *nguillatun* ceremonies (see Chapter 4). In other words, the spatial layout of the individual mounds in a *rehuekuel* is a microcosmic reflection of the ruler's settlement pattern in real domestic space.

Nicolás Millao of Tranaman said that *kuel* and *rehuekuel* were places where the *machi* would predict important matters. Another informant, Jaime Alquiman, near Temuco said that *kuel* were places where *machi* were initiated into shamanhood and given their *fileu pullu* spirits by *Wenumapu*. Faustino Tramulao, a local *weupin* from Chequemilla, said that all communities have their *kuel* and that they are located on high, flat hilltops, or *ñichi*, overlooking wetlands and that they are associated with old *kuifilpalihue* and *nguillatuhue* fields.

Candelario Nancopil, *weupin* of Chol-Chol, said that *machi* and *kuel* possess interchangeable identities and represent the same spirit force. He stated that there are always two *kuel* in each *nguillatun*, although they are not always seen, because some mounds have been destroyed, and others are low and difficult to see (which is similar to *machi* Lucinda's experience in the *Tren Trenkuel* ritual). He also used the term *winkulkuelchetue* to refer to the ritual act to build a mound in a specific place, usually on a high crest that overlooks a river and adjacent lineage land.

Katrileo Cheuque also noted that specific events and meanings are associated with other mounds in the area. For instance, *Paltrenechekuel* was formed by a rising sea, implying it too is associated with the *Tren Tren* and *Kai Kai* origin tale. He said that all mounds are associated with old *nguillatun* fields, and that all *machi* are buried with their ritual instruments except for the sacred stones inside their *kultrun*, and these are usually given to their disciples. When used upright, the top part of the *kultrun* symbolizes the *Wenumapu* world and the bottom part the *miñchemapu* world.

In Rukalleco, Francisco Huichaleo said that *machi* and other people danced around the base of a *kuel*, and made offerings to it by placing pottery vessels filled with food around its base and on its top surface. They pray to the *kuel* to ask the ancestors and deities for good crops and for more land. He also said that mounds serve as lineage markers to connect and locate people on the land and within the local kinship network. Andre Katrileo, also of Rukalleco, said that the alignment and layout of the *kuel* relate to kinship genealogy and to the patrilineage and patriterritorial divisions of local *lonko* (see Dillehay 1990b).

These same informants report that old *nguillatun* fields are abandoned for various reasons, including religious changes, the death of a local leader whose land they inhabit, to the loss of lineage lands resulting from warfare in the past and from changing land tenure laws today. These informants imply that the length of use of a *kuel* depended on leadership ability and on the succession of dynastic lineages (see Dillehay 1995). In this regard, *nguillatun* fields may shift location as leadership changes from one lineage to another in a *trokinche* community. In Quitrahue near Lumaco, a local *machi* showed us four old fields used in the late nineteenth and early twentieth centuries that had been abandoned because powerful rulers had died and were replaced by weak ones who were incapable of holding alliances together and maintaining the dynastic rule of their lineage. She said that each field ranged in use between twenty and forty years.

Also significant are reports that ceremonies at old *nguillatun* and *rehuekuel* localities were attended by many more people in the past and that people would participate in ten to fifteen ceremonies every year (see Chapters 3 and 4). Several elderly informants from Butarincón, Huitrenlehue, and Tranaman told us that there were designated places and times of the year where the ceremonies were held, that they always followed a pattern, and that the leadership at each would alternate between local lineages. They also claimed that the ceremonies moved back and forth across the river and would start in the Purén side of the valley to the west and then move toward the conjunction of the two rivers near Butarincón. No one described the ceremonial schedule as a zigzag-like movement, but it seemed clear that a relatively fixed and cyclical pattern once existed, that the valley-long ceremonial calendar was more regular and predictable, and that the valley was once more united than it is today (see discussion of these patterns in Chapters 7 and 8).

Mound complexes at *TrenTrenkuel*, *Huitrenlehuekuel*, *Huitrenlebuekuel*, *Maicoyakuel*, *Rapahuekuel*, *Hualonkokuel*, and *Lolonkokuel* were said to have been very active ritual and political localities at one time. They were places where famous leaders such as Anganamón, Lientur, Colo Colo, Colípi, Butapichón, Caupolicán,

Lautaro, and others lived, celebrated, and ruled. All of these leaders are remembered today by nearly all elders and especially by *machi* and *lonkos*; all of these rulers are repeatedly mentioned by the chroniclers (see Chapters 3 and 7). Anganamón, Lautaro, Lientur, Pelantaro, and Butapichón date back to the sixteenth and seventeenth centuries (see Chapters 3 and 7). Colípi was active in the nineteenth century.

Several informants also reported a strong linkage between water, fertility rites, and *kuel*. In particular, Santo Millao of Tranaman mentioned the topographic linkages between water, hills, ridge crests, and *kuel*. He said that they work together to direct the flow and course of water, although each also functions independently in its own way to move water and energy in certain directions. He also stated that the communities of Tranaman and Centinela are related to the large *kuel* or mountain of *Wenucolla*, which extends from the *Nag Mapu* world to the *Wenumapu* world.

Several informants report the following: *wampu* is the place where food remains are burned in front of the *llangi llangi* altar in *nguillatun*; offerings to the god *Pillan* in the *nguillatun* field are located near the *llangi llangi* at the *pillankutral*; *curacahuin* is the sacred name of the *machi's* drum or *kultrun*; and some *machi* still use a sacred plant (*latue* or *miyaya*; see Chapter 4) to induce a trance before they perform on top of *kuel*. *Machi* who cure the sick often engage in sorcery or *kalku*. The evil spirit directing a *machi* is *wekufe* or *pelonneupin*. *Kalku* often bring excessive flooding and destruction of crops; *machi* bring rain during droughts. In the past, informants also say that people never approached a *kuel* at night. Evil forces (*weukufe* or *kalku*) may be inflicted on anyone who passed beside these places in the dark or who neglected the necessary rituals and offerings to them. As seen in the above narratives, *kuel* are placated by ritual payments or offerings (i.e., *chicha*, blood and flour, imagined gold objects) to ensure personal safety and the fertility of one's animals and crops and family and, if angered, *kuel* can cause personal or collective damage to the community. In order to pacify *kuel*, sacred tributes are often made to them by individual families several times a year at household rituals and by the community at large during public *nguillatun*.

There also are accounts that several *kuel* once had large stone monoliths standing on them, but they were later removed by the Chilean army that defeated the Araucanians in the late 1800s. Today, in the Lumaco area there are many worked monoliths scattered along hill crests and usually located near old *nguillatun* ceremonial fields, which are said to be old boundary markers located between lineage lands. All informants claim that *kuel* also serve as lineage markers (Dillehay 1990b). Informants report that there is a strong "pull" or sense of obligation and desire to pass over and by the *kuel*. Not only do the *kuel* impart a sense of solace and comfort, but they function as boundaries and nodes of reference to outlying communities as well. That is, in a sense, *kuel* sustain kinship patterns in times of stress and growing social cohesion by spatially reminding people of interlineage boundary markers and of their obligations to intercommunity relations.

Lastly, informants told us that *kuel* were made by thousands of earth loads carried by individuals from local and nonlocal communities during *winkulkueltun*-building ceremonies. People carried soil in baskets, ponchos, and large gourd vessels. Different colored clays and soils were dug from different places in the valley. When we visited our excavations in the mounds, several informants told us that they knew the source locations of the different clays and sediments that make up the mound sediments and that these localities were the properties of specific lineages.

ANALYTICAL MEANING AND PERSPECTIVE

The two ritual narratives give prima facie context and structure to mound use and mound worship never before recorded in ethnoarchaeology and anthropology. It is evident in the *Hualonkokuel* and *Trentrenkuel* narratives and in the information provided by other informants that there is remarkable continuity in many ritual forms and meanings between the ethnographic present and the ethnohistoric past. What social and religious patterns do the narratives and the insights from other informants represent? The meaning of some linguistic indices such as the use of *ülmen* for powerful leaders and *fileu* for ancestral shamans are not clear but suggests some association with the use of similar terms in the sixteenth- and eighteenth-century documents (see Chapters 3 and 4). Traces of these and other old terms indicate teachings influenced by patterns and concepts whose ancient forms persist as residual features in the Purén–Lumaco area just as the continued use of the *rehuekuel* and *kuel* do. All of this evidence points to the narrative as an artifact of old Araucanian religious traditions and historical experiences, which is what the *machi* and elders also report.

The *machi's* complementarity of form, function, and, at times, interchangeable identity with the *kuel* at Hualonko and TrenTren suggests that rituals construe a memory of armed conflict, stress and healing, *palin* and *nguillatun* ceremony, and ancestral dialogues as an ideology of affinal interdependence. Clearly, *kuel* and *machi* are interchangeable in many schemes. Their interchanging identity is done through the spiritual media of the *machi* shaman whereby *kuel* are the spirit companions of *machi*. The relations between the *kuel* and the stress in the local community are another theme repeated many times in the narratives. Both *kuel* carry within themselves a past power and a present agency that the contemporary population cannot see but fears. Only the *machi* know of them and of other good and bad *kuel* located across the landscape where the spirits of powerful dead *machi* reside.

Several passages in the narratives detail the shamanism, oracles, offerings, ancestral relations, and deities that ritually organized and interrelated communities with *kuel* and history. Although the relationships between the deities and the living are complex and often far from obvious, one unifying feature is clear: the affinity between the *machi* and the *kuel* is ideolized in terms of affinal ties between the *kuel* and the highest deities and between the *machi*, the *machi's* spirits, dead *machi*, and other *kuel*. In this scheme, the female shamans play an important role with the male *kuel* who are the sons of the great *Ngenechen* (*Chaw*) and *Pillan* that reside in the upper *Wenumapu* world. Yet, in *Nag Mapu* space, the *machi* act as mothers to the *kuel*. Whereas the affinal relations of the *kuel* are stories of social relations, they express not only an ideal of productive and reproductive union but also an image of the many tensions involved in sustaining relations between the living and the dead. The *machi* inform us that the affinal ties between and distribution of all *kuel* in the Purén and Lumaco Valley emulate the kinship and spatial organization of the living lineages in the valley, a pattern repeated by several informants.

In establishing a parental relation between female shaman and male *kuel* and between male deities and female shamans, the rituals may have followed earlier prototypes set in the historic period. Within the dominant synthesis, ritual order embodies the idea of the shaman as healer coming to the rescue of the *kuel* and of the population at large. The abundance of details in the narratives also reflects the function of the discourse as a memory bank of information about the shaman's claims to power and their access to the powerful *Wenumapu* world. The *machi* constantly detail the sources of their power and that only they can bring remedy and medicine to the situation. Although some of the rituals also have to do with the possible demise of power, there is a clear hierarchy here of gods, ancestors and shamans, and oracles in the form of *kuel*. There also is a sense of urgency, rescue, and dependency between them. The treatment of the discourse tends to express ideas of rescue and proper dedication rituals much like those in the origin tale presented in Chapter 4 – the struggle between good and evil forces, the benevolent snake that rescued people from the floodwaters, and the *toqui* war leaders who saved the Araucanians from the Spanish conquistadors. Further, there is a theme of indebtedness with the people, the deities, and the *kuel*; they become indebted to the *machi* for administering the rituals and for seeking the medicine or power to overcome their disobedience and unattentiveness, sickness and evil ways, and healing practices, respectively.

The narratives and informants also make it clear that *kuel* are living social bodies that are animated by *machi* spirits. The mounds have individual functions, affinities, and local histories, as suggested by the narratives and by the individual names for them. *Kuel* also manifest the primary deities, *Ngenechen* and *Pillan*, and the shamans; thus *kuel* become temporal and spatial intersections of the *Wenumapu* and *Nag Mapu* worlds, as explained in Chapter 4. Thus, in a sense, *kuel* are both the mythical and authentic ancestors of people who represent a genealogical continuity between the living and their ancestors and between the materialized form of deities in *Nag Mapu* space and their places in *Wenumapu* space. The ancestors survive in the form of mounds and *chemamüll*, the anthropomorphic statues made of wood, that are humanized shrines standing in *nguillatun* fields and on top of *kuel*.

There is no fixed size or spatial extent of *kuel*, although it's apparent in their form and in their capping episodes that there are hierarchies between them and divisions in time and space. *Tren Trenkuel* is said to be the oldest and largest mound in the valley; it dominates all others and is the center of mound unification. The *machi* claim that active *kuel* spiritually incorporate inactive ones, which is a form of consumptive performance in kin relationships between *Tren Trenkuel*, the father mound, and its younger and smaller son and daughter mounds. People also act as kinsmen of *kuel* and consume them. Several informants report that small inactive mounds no longer remembered and related to a particular lineage were ritually dismantled in the past, with the soil that once comprised them transported to and used in the construction of other *kuel*. In referring to this transfer of soil, they said that powerful *kuel*, such *Tren Trenkuel*, would "eat" the less powerful ones. Also reported is the transport of soil from old lineage habitation sites to newly built mounds in order to include the *pullu*, or spirit, of the ancestors. (See the ritual narrative by *machi* Juanita in Appendix 1 [XXXVI:6], where she refers to soil taken from a *kuel* and then scattered in another place.) These consumptive relations between *kuel* and between *kuel* and ancestral sites parallel those of past and present human groups whereby large stable lineages incorporated smaller less stable, displaced ones and altered their identities (see Chapters 7 and 8). The transfer and consumption of soils from one place to another is a form of identity-breaking and identity-making of *kuel* as they become affiliated with newly formed or expanding lineages and unaffiliated with fragmented and migratory lineages.

In comparison to the deities and shamans, the narratives have little to say about the power of non-shamans such as *ülmen* and *lonkos*. However, the kindred spirits of the dead rulers buried inside mounds that reside in the *Wenumapu* world are believed to look after the well being of the living. Curiously, religious ideas also are not detailed in the narratives. Despite the reference to the sun and moon, these elements appear only as objects. Neither is personified in the tales except for reference to the moon in two passages. Araucanian religion can be partly understood from these dialogues, but not because they explicitly describe it. Most important is to understand the broader meaning of the social discourse of the *llaimatun, lonkotun, dahatun*, and other rites conducted by the *machi*, which speak to suffering, contact with outsiders, disease, death, healing, spiritualism, shamanism, and survival.

In sum, these ritual narratives relate to real-life mounded landscapes in the Purén and Lumaco Valley and to the historic conjunctures that generated them. Many elements of the narratives can be read as combined ideological and political characters for the accepted ways that communities and agents should treat each other to establish and maintain order. Every aspect of the narratives reflects the pressure of social stress and the need for agency, leadership, identity and memory, and mutual understanding between the community, the deities and their representatives (the *kuel* in this case), and the shamans. All of this is focused on the sustainability of social unification and on the independent and, at times, interdependent agency of these actors in negotiating community relations.

KUEL, MACHI, AND THE SPIRIT WORLD

As mentioned in Chapter 4, the Araucanian cosmos consists of a fundamental distinction between the visible world of human form and the invisible world of animating spirits. The relationships between these elements constitute different levels of existence that are based on the amount of spirit-matter within human and animal bodies and across the landscape. Inanimate objects such as rocks are predominantly visible and static, and have little or no spirit-matter; small birds and insects have more, while humans and animals have spirits which are semi-detached and transformable out of their bodies to the different planes of the ethereal world. Live creatures cannot travel between adjacent planes, because that is the prerogative of the invisible spirit world; however, humans in states of awareness arising from dreams and visions can make contact with spirits (see Faron 1964:4, 60–65). *Machi* spirits are especially transportable between all surfaces but reside permanently in *kuel* on the *Nag Mapu* surface. Shamanic knowledge and power is about temporarily transposing and recollecting these separated surfaces in order to gain access to powers which can cure and restore order. This process is enacted and located in the visible and invisible spaces of ceremony and in the *Nag Mapu* and *Wenumapu* worlds and of the living and the spiritual world of the dead.

Faron recognized the symbiotic dependencies between the living and ancestral spirits.

The most dramatic aspects of social action involved in the central concept of Mapuche religious morality revolves around sacred and influential spirits whose existence regulates and depends upon human moral conduct. Among the several visible forms assumed by ancestors are "hawks of the sun" (*antüpainamko*), a designation used by the Mapuche and employed here to symbolize all ancestral spirits. Hawks of the sun, then, are beneficent ancestor spirits who intervene in the affairs of the living, who are responsible to the living, and, at the same time, who govern human conduct. Mapuche die and become hawks of the sun. In this simple belief is expressed the notion of continuity between the living and the dead on which hinge concepts and practices of a ritual nature that order and sanction human relationships. (Faron 1964:4)

In general, ancestral spirits are felt to live with kindred souls in the afterworld. . . . It seems of significance that ancestral chiefs look after the well-being of the living, not the dead. In turn the responsibility for the eternal ease or beatitude of the dead lies with the living. The social structure of the ancestral world is, therefore, clearly meshed with that of contemporary Mapuche society and is not an entity completely apart. These pneumatic ancestral spirits, after all, comprise direct links between mortals and the major and minor deities. (Faron 1964:60)

The invisible spirit world of the Mapuche consists of unfettered spirit-matter, which takes on the ephemeral form of the visible *Nag Mapu* world. In this way, it is possible to see that animals (particularly raptorial birds such as hawks) are cosmologically closer to humans than inanimate objects. Spirit-matter connects all life because the same invisible characteristics animate everything; at the same time, it takes different forms according to certain criteria. *Puam, kuifiche*, and *peuma* (dream spirits) take different forms. (The term *puam* usually refers to the image which spirit-matter takes and manifest as the form of a visible body.) Spirits are invisible to waking vision and consequently outside of time and space. Mapuche can see them only in dreams (*peuma*) and by interpreting the forms that are imposed on the spirits from the visible world. Spirits react to events in the visible world. The dangers in the spirit world come from uncontrolled spirit-matter, which takes the form primarily of concentrated harmful spirits (*kalku*), which shamanic techniques and ritual try to tame. By being beyond living space and time in *Nag Mapu*, ancestral spirits are more knowledgeable than humans and understand the potential inherent in the *Wenumapu* universe. Thus, only *machi*, who have the powers to move about in both the visible and invisible worlds and whose spirits reside in *kuel*, work with the deities (*Pillan, Ngenechen*), important dead leaders who were the heads and founders of patrilineages (*karuhua*), and other ancestral figures (*antüpainamko*) to counteract evil forces. Set in this context, *kuel* become powerful mediators who can transform themselves into *machi* who live and work in the living *Nag Mapu* world and who travel between all planes of the cosmological world to unite the past and the present. According to shamans, certain *kuel* spirits have developed a reputation for their power in resolving disputes, settling warfare, ameliorating misfortunes due to sorcery, advising on important undertakings, and predicting future events. *TrenTrenkuel, Lolonkokuel,* and *Ñachekuel* are three *kuel* complexes said to have these kinds of powers and especially visionary powers to see the future.

KNOWLEDGE, *KUEL*, AND MOUND LITERACY OR *NAUCHI*

Despite colonialism and warfare in the sixteenth to nineteenth centuries and settlement shifts brought about by conflict and alliance-building, some Mapuche communities have continued to develop their religious and spatial organization around traditional political and demographic orders. Use of the terms *rehuekuel* and *ayllarehue* still implies the local *kuel's* spatial domain, its adjoined domestic settlements, and cemetery space of the ancestors. Taken together, these sites represent social history — a history that is a mental template of lineages and fragmented groups materialized in *kuel*. Thus, *kuel* implies historically constructed social relationships as well as landscapes and religious features.

Shamanic knowledge of and communication with the *Wenumapu* world is locally based and bounded. It is focused primarily on *kuel* and on deities and *fileu pullu*, who are the primary sources of shamanic power and of fertility, who embody the remote ancestors, and who are the guardians of local communities. *Machi* are a class of people identified as those who know how to read and interact with the *kuel* through ceremony and prayer at the *rehue*, who can enter into communication with the upper world of the deities and ancestors. The term *machi* is used for those who have participated in *kueltun* and other ceremonies and used esoteric knowledge, often developed by learning from an already established *machi* (see Chapter 4). This knowledge derives from two particular skills: the art of divination by reading the *kuel*, and the strength to speak to and interact with the *kuel* and the ancestors. These specialists of esoteric knowledge are healers as well as priests and diviners. And they are central to the performance of any ritual that involves the mountains, *Nag Mapu*, the *kuel*, deities, and ancestors. Traditional knowledge in this context is not only a question of knowing the stories of ancestors but even more one of knowing how to relate to them through the *kuel*, and both of these aspects of knowledge are handed down from one generation to the next though daily routines and through ceremonies. The good narrator's knowledge is authenticated by having been learned and inherited from a previous generation of ceremonial participants. The central value accorded to the land and to particular *kuel* in articulating the present with the past of this world is exemplified by the importance attached to living with, reading, and understanding *kuel*, which traditional *machi* today call *nauchi* and I refer to as *mound literacy*. Although most shamans today are healers and diviners, some in areas such as Lumaco manifest a wider knowledge base and political and religious role in society. Thus, I refer to them as priestly shamans. Given the idea that the Purén and Lumaco Valley was more politically united in the past, perhaps these and other ritual specialists were more institutionalized in status than are present-day shaman.

The ways in which the representation and interpretation of knowledge and literacy about *kuel* are culturally and ideologically linked to the legitimated forms of Araucanian polity development require further discussion. A guiding principle of this book is the manner in which *kuel* were and are used is not simply political, economic, and religious enactment, but that it is also a cultural performance in public ceremony at mounds and other sacred spaces. The poetics of such cultural performances may be enigmatic to archaeologists who envision them largely as objects produced in the past by politically controlled public labor, rather than as participatory agents also experiencing society and history. Such cultural performances have an intended *audience* as seen in the ceremonies presented in the above narratives. Audiences experience and interact with *kuel* and vice versa, requiring both audience and *kuel* to become mutually literate in reading and understanding each other. This again suggests that a more developed understanding of mound literacy and its role in the social and cultural relationships between individuals and communities is necessary. Simply put once more, the logic and meaning of *kuel* cannot be understood without reference to these wider cultural values and practices. These practices have meaning in regard to the traditional and proper ways to act as members or compatriots of the newly constructed society in order to insure order and cultural continuity.

To conclude, the kinds of *kuel*-related rituals and discourses studied here are fraught with different experiences and meanings. They have resulted, I believe, in a distinct and new view of mounds and mound complexes as not only burial and ritual locales but also kinship, shamanic, deity, and community agents; moreover, in studying the statements by informants, it becomes apparent that the "reality" of mounds as conceived within an empiricist and rationalized tradition of archaeological thought is quite different from the "reality" for those who live around and with them and their consequences. This is why the study of these kinds of monuments must be approached as a form of discourse between the mounds as sacred geographies and the people whose practice is simultaneously and in varying degrees verbal, emotional, psychological, metaphorical, spiritual, sociological, and cultural – in other words *real* and *living*. *Kuel*, therefore, are not just a matter of archaeological material evidence but pneumatic reality. The ritual narratives studied in this chapter reveal how the Araucanians envision history as an interaction between people and their patron *kuel* – the deified features of the landscape that connect to forces of the cosmos itself.

SIX:

AN ARCHAEOLOGICAL VIEW OF *KUEL*

AND *REHUEKUEL*

This chapter provides a synopsis of the architectural archaeology of mound cultures in the Purén and Lumaco Valley, relates the chronological and spatial patterning of this record to the ethnography and ethnohistory reported earlier, and presents a broader, more scholarly analytical perspective of the sacred geographies of *kuel* and *rehuekuel* as a form of Araucanian monumentalism. More archival, chronological, and functional research is required to better understand these cultures and their formation processes, to relate *kuel* and *rehuekuel* to specific lineages and leaders named in the texts, and to infer lineage and polity development in the south Andes. Since this chapter is a preliminary report on the archaeology and its broader social and landscape meaning, the methodology is only briefly discussed.

Prior research in south-central Chile suggests a singular picture of late pre-Hispanic and early Hispanic Araucanian culture, which consisted of decentralized settlement of dispersed households occupied by kin-based group of chiefs and commoners (Dillehay 1976, 1990a, 1990b; Aldunate 1989; see Chapter 3). Settlements were supported by various combinations of cultigens, hunting, gathering, and fishing. The idea of a singular Araucanian pattern gives way on closer inspection to a regionally varied group of dispersed and nucleated settlements incorporated through local historical contexts and linked through shared cultural tendencies and widely held belief systems. Some areas developed nucleated settlements associated with isolated mound building, incipient agriculture, public rituals, and partly centralized leadership in rich and geographically circumscribed valleys (i.e., Purén, Lumaco, Liucura, Tucapel, Arauco, Villarrica). Other areas were characterized by advanced hunters–gatherers and probably incipient horticulturalists (Dillehay 1976, 1981, 1990a, 1990b; Aldunate 1989). Both ethnohistorical and archaeological studies indicate that social complexity partly developed through contacts with Andean cultures to the north and on the eastern flanks of the Andes in Argentina (see Chapter 3).

Much of the late Purén and Lumaco archeological culture was influenced by the El Vergel (a Formative development dating between approximately 1200 and 1500) and probably the Inka cultures (see Chapter 3). As discussed in

Chapter 3, while the notion of Andean diffusion south of the Bio Bio River has its advantages and explains early historic social complexity and resistance for scholars who believe the Araucanians never developed much beyond a hunter–gather society, it fails to explain many of the significant elements of their culture. Emerging analyses of the Pitrén (ca. 500–1000?) and El Vergel cultures indicate that there are developmental differences between Araucanians living in central Chile and those living south of the Bio Bio River. The southern groups had higher population densities, more widespread mound building, and more centralized political organization.

The Purén-Lumaco culture also represents the elaboration of social trajectories that had been underway in the south Andes for centuries (Dillehay 2003). Between 1300 and 1600, the population increased, interregional exchange intensified, mortuary customs became increasingly elaborate, reliance on horticulture increased, and social organization and intergroup relationships became more complex. Some of these trajectories, however, changed more than others and in unique ways, and it was the expression of some cultural elements (e.g., mounds, fortresses, large domestic villages, raised agricultural fields) that gives highly visible distinction to Purén-Lumaco in the archaeological record, setting it apart not only from indigenous cultures in central Chile but even from other mound cultures in the Araucanian region.

This chapter is divided into three parts. The first part presents a summary of the general archaeological methods and findings to date. The chronology, location, size, and internal characteristics of major *kuel* and *rehuekuel* localities, domestic sites, fortresses, and agricultural terraces and canals are discussed. The second part provides a brief summary of the settlement patterns and cultural developments in the valley over the past millennia. The last part is a conceptual analysis of Araucanian monumentalism, which builds on the spatial and physical record of the archaeology.

GENERAL ARCHAEOLOGICAL OBJECTIVES, METHODS, AND FINDINGS TO DATE

While the ethnohistorical and ethnographic data have enabled us to suggest principles of late pre-Hispanic settlement and social organization, the most important first step in the archaeological analysis was the building of a detailed inter-site chronology, the complete survey of the Purén and Lumaco Valley, and the excavation of selected sites. For this, 100 percent survey coverage and well-oriented excavation were essential in order to understand site stratigraphies and changing site functions and meanings. The survey has recorded 380 pre-Hispanic and Hispanic localities to date, including residential, agricultural, defensive, cemetery, and mound sites of different types and scales. Research on the late pre-Hispanic period focused on incipient complexity, which was related to the adoption of cultigens, settlement nucleation, and social ranking in the rich, circumscribed setting of the valley. This research recorded a shift from small, isolated burial mounds associated with dispersed household communities and dating between approximately 1200 and 1500 to clusters of small and large multifunctional mounds (i.e., ceremonial, administrative, and burial) related with nucleated household villages and appearing between 1500 and 1800 (Dillehay 1985a, 1999, 2003, 2004). Not presently well understood are the late pre-Hispanic political shifts that occurred from the inaugural burial mounds to the later large mound complexes, although it is suspected that leadership began changing from individual lineage heads to centralized multilineage rulers (see Chapters 7 and 8).

The results obtained from the survey and from the written records provided the rationale for site selection for excavations in various types of sites. Based on diagnostic sherds and radiocarbon assays, excavated sites have been correlated with major periods of occupation at mound complexes, domestic settlements, and fortresses (Dillehay 2004, 2005). This suite of sites represents different settlement sizes and functions, geographic locations, and temporal periods derived from the written records but also from temporal and settlement relations suggested by archaeological patterning. The objectives of the excavations were sharply focused on (1) exposing site stratigraphy to document use, expansion, and abandonment processes; (2) obtaining precise data on site chronology, cultural affinity, and site function; and (3) and relating them to events and places specified in written documents.

Based on this work, we have partly completed one of the fundamental objectives of the archaeological work, that is, the establishment of a radiocarbon (C^{14}) and thermoluminesence dated ceramic typology and a site typology based on size, function, presence and absence of domestic zones, stratigraphy, and proximity to natural resources (Dillehay 2004). This typology permits a general ordering of sites on the basis of rank-size, internal site structure, chronology, and general characteristics of the settlement history. Given the diagnostics of late pre-Hispanic Araucanian and central Chilean-influenced (i.e., Molle, Llolleo), Inka, early and late Spanish, and other European artifact styles and the dated events and named places in the historic texts, we can place many sites within specific 50- to 100- year time spans (see Chapters 3 and 7). Further, the connection of some archaeological sites to specific events and places mentioned in the texts and by ethnographic informants provides continuity from the past to the present and insights into various social processes such as the recruitment and adoption of fragmented groups by stable lineages.

Recruitment is suggested to involve the incorporation of fragmented groups and their assimilation into the local kin system through public ceremony and the construction of public works (see Chapters 3, 6, and 7). Annexation or segmentation probably involved the reverse whereby people from the intact or recruiter's territory were sent to live in segmented lands. We have learned that these two different processes generally have different archaeological implications (Dillehay 2004). That is, intact domestic lineage lands engaged in recruiting defeated groups to their homelands are characterized by a higher variability of ceramic decorative and manufacturing styles. In these areas, exotic sherds are usually isolated within sites. Annexed lands reflect noticeably less variability and an admixture of local and exotic styles, which are not spatially separated. These findings have been useful in relating specific places and events in the written and sometimes oral records to specific artifact and spatial observations made in the archaeological record. This in turn has permitted greater confidence in inferring settlement patterns, social processes, and developmental trajectories.

The ways in which processes of recruitment and segmentation, including degrees of intracommunity cohesion, may be reflected in the archaeological record, particularly ceramic and settlement patterning, also have been examined through the application of models of artifact formal variation, particularly those that focus on seriation and chronological markers of change, artifact style and technological choice, and intracommunity spatial patterning. Our excavations at several sites in the Purén and Lumaco Valley indicate multiple, ephemeral occupations and/or periodic cycles of use and abandonment over relatively brief time intervals. In some areas, complete abandonment in the sixteenth century at or immediately after Spanish arrival is indicated by the presence of diagnostic Spanish goods and late Araucanian ceramics with Spanish inclusions (e.g., glazed ceramics used as temper, glass beads). My previous research in the study area has excavated several small and large domestic sites and radiocarbon dated them between 1280 and 1780. Nearby domestic sites with continuous and relatively deep midden deposits (40–90 cm) containing a long sequence of proto-Araucanian (1200–1500), Valdivia polychrome (an Inka influenced style dating to the 1500–1600?), ethnic Spanish (1550–1750), and ethnic Chilean (> 1750) ceramics are present in the majority of sites. We also have documented a great variety of local and nonlocal ceramic wares in some large domestic sites, as determined by surface treatment, temper, decoration, vessel form and stylistic heterogeneity, which suggests the co-residence of different population sectors.

Although a secondary concern, fieldwork also has generated valuable interdisciplinary data to understand the environmental features and past climates in the valley. As noted earlier, the valley was mentioned by chroniclers as one of the richest agricultural sectors in the south (see Chapter 3). It was and still is characterized by deep, rich, dark soils formed by boggy terrain partly drained by the Araucanians and Spanish over the past few centuries. During archaeological excavations at cultural sites, Mario Pino, the project geologist from the Universidad Austral de Chile recorded and analyzed all stratigraphic profiles for evidence of major environmental events and site histories (Pino and Sequel 2004). His current paleoenvironmental research continues three related sets of activities:

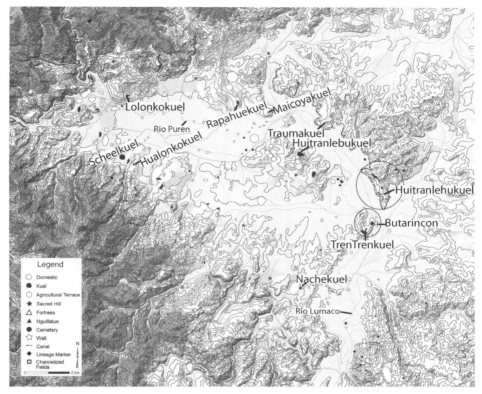

49. General location map of *kuel*, *rehuekuel*, cemeteries, domestic sites, fortresses, and canals in the Purén and Lumaco Valley.

(1) geomorphological and landscape analysis of targeted agricultural features and mound features, (2) river terraces, alluvial fans, wetlands, and adjacent areas to more precisely map diagnostic signatures of major sedimentation and geomorphological events, and (3) settlement location as a function of paleogeomorphology and paleoenvironmental conditions.

Figure 49 gives the distribution of the different types of archaeological sites within the study area. Circles have been drawn around the named *rehuekuel* centers. In several areas, there are single mound sites that are just outside the boundary of these centers, but which are packed too closely between adjacent zones to allow for the construction of intermediate circles. These have, therefore, been identified by the construction of smaller circles. Fortresses, canals, terraces, cemeteries, and other sites also are marked.

Kuel *and* Rehuekuel

More than 300 individual *kuel* have been recorded in the Purén and Lumaco Valley, 78 of which are grouped into nine and possibly twelve *rehuekuel* complexes

279

(Dillehay 2001). We have documented a shift from small, isolated burial and ritual mounds dated at least to the twelfth to fourteenth centuries to *rehuekuel* dated in the fifteenth to seventeenth centuries (The deeper levels of some small isolated mounds date between 200 B.C. to 500 by radiocarbon means [see Appendix 2], but more archaeological research is required before earlier mound-building cultures can be confirmed.) The earlier small, isolated *kuel* are associated with incipient agriculture, dispersed communities, and emergent social complexity. The later *rehuekuel* complexes are defined by specific locations, restricted and equidistant distributions in the valley, relatively standardized sizes, ceremonial landscapes, and polity development. The development of these complexes is a strong archaeological indicator of a centralized political system in operation by at least the fifteenth to sixteenth century These complexes either do not occur in other valleys or are present in dispersed and low densities in places such as Rucaray on the Pacific coastline west of Purén, Boyeco, and Chol-Chol near Temuco, and Pucón near the Argentina border, suggesting dispersed to small nucleated communities with less cultural development and political centralization (Dillehay 1985a, 1995, 1999).

Based on archaeological, ethnohistoric, and ethnographic records, we know that *kuel* were multifunctional with differing combinations of burial, administrative, religious, and ceremonial roles (Dillehay 1985a, 1990a, 1990b, 1999; see Chapter 3). *Kuel* are normally conical in shape, but a few are oval or rectangular in form. Numerous small stone and earth conical mounds were built, especially in upland locations in the Boyeco and Huitranlehue areas in the Purén and Lumaco Valley. Many of these were burial mounds, but not all were, and as a group the smaller, isolated mounds are not well understood. Better known are the large mounds of the *rehuekuel* complexes that are equally distributed throughout the valley, with the largest concentration located in Butarincón.

The ritual mortuary function of most mounds has been reconstructed from the combination of archaeology, ethnohistory, and ethnography (see Chapter 3 and Dillehay 1985a). Our mound excavations have located several burial contexts associated with late ceramic wares. In the early 1980s, I carried out salvage archaeology at two small, cistern burial chambers in two pre-Hispanic mounds that had been cut by road construction near Lumaco (Dillehay 2004). Gordon (1978, 1984) also excavated cistern burials in a mound at Trapa Trapa near Lago Budi and in a mound near Galvarino (A. Gordon, personal communication, 1989). He reported that during the excavation of the latter site, three elderly Mapuche women visited him and asked him why he was excavating their grandfather. He immediately terminated the excavation upon their request. I report this story, because I also have been asked by Mapuche communities not to expose the human remains of ancestors. The Purén-Lumaco Project that I direct in the study area also has respectfully honored this request. Mapuche communities have granted us permission to expose only the top layer of burial chambers just to record their depth and size. It is for these reasons that no burials are discussed below.

In simplest outline, the initial building of burial mounds consisted of four steps, as defined by ethnographic, ethnohistoric, and archaeological research: (1) a special surface or floor was prepared according to the prevailing ritual; (2) a tomb was dug; (3) the deceased person(s) to be interred beneath the mound was ritually prepared; and (4) then he was placed in the grave (Dillehay 1985a; see Chapter 3). Every few years a new soil cap was placed on the mound. (To remind the reader, mound building is a ritual called *winkulkueltun*. Later capping episodes are *kueltun* rituals. Ancient cemeteries are named *kuifeltun*; old habitation sites are called *kuifumelewe*.)

Two mound-building models have been documented. One consists of a larger cone-shaped mound built over the primary mound as exemplified by capping episodes and mound fill of the secondary mound as it took shape (see Chapters 3 and 4). At some future time, additional burials or mounds and soil layers were added above the primary mound, after which only a single, larger mound existed, as exemplified at *TrenTrenkuel*. This is vertical accretion of a single mound or *kuel*. Another model consists of building one or more successively built mounds adjacent to each other, as seen at most mound complexes or *rehuekuel*. This is horizontal accretion. Whatever the history of a single mound or multimound complex, it is clear that the mortuary ritual called for conical or near-conical monuments to mark the graves of deceased leaders, who were determined worthy of burial and commemoration in this fashion. Not yet well understood is the transformational shift from earlier small isolated mounds to later multimound *rehuekuel* complexes.

As mentioned in previous chapters, most *kuel* are built on *ñichi* promontories flanking the marshes or *ciénegas* in the valley floor (Fig. 49). The mounds range in size between 8 and 50 m in diameter and 1 and 15 m in height. *Rehuekuel* are often oriented with their long axes parallel or perpendicular to a body of water, usually a river or wetland. Because the streams in the valley flow in an east–west direction, most mound axes face east and west. The greatest cluster is situated on the crest of a continuous north to south chain of low hills overlooking the Purén River to the north and the Lumaco River to the east. The largest concentration of *rehuekuel* within this cluster is on a series of low hillcrests that form a rough U-shaped peninsula positioned between the juncture of the two rivers at Butarincón (Fig. 49). These two arms, which contain the highest density and largest *kuel* in the valley, are called *Chawivivol* for the east arm and *Kawulmawida* for the west arm (Ortiz 2005b, 2006; also see Chapter 4). The remaining *kuel* in this concentration are scattered southwardly along the crest of an 8 km long, north–south oriented chain of low hills that parallel the Lumaco River. All others are isolated features on the valley landscape (Fig. 50).

50. Butarincón area where the majority of the large mound complexes are located and named arrows. Far left arrow points to *Chawivivol*; Far right arrow points to *Kawulmawida*.

Each *rehuekuel* occupies between 1 and 10 ha, with adjacent village and cemetery zones often spread over an additional 10 to 25 ha. The average number of mounds per *rehuekuel* is four and the median number is three. Butarincón is the largest complex with thirty-three mounds occupying about 110 ha. (The closest site of comparable size is 220 km away in Pucón where thirty-two mounds comprise a single *rehuekuel*.) Judging from associated El Vergel ceramic diagnostics and from radiocarbon dates obtained from excavations in several mounds, most *rehuekuel* in the Purén and Lumaco Valley were built from the late pre-Hispanic to early Hispanic period (see Appendix 2).

The immediate peripheral area surrounding *rehuekuel* is one within which there is a spatially compact nesting of hierarchically ordered places ranging from the *rehuekuel* on an elevated *ñichi* downslope to a domestic site and further downslope to a cemetery. *Rehuekuel* are thus defined by (1) location on bounded promontories or low hills overlooking the valley floor that have been culturally modified into *ñichi*, upon which three to eleven mounds flank a large ceremonial plaza (Fig. 51); (2) restricted and relatively equidistant distribution in

51. Aerial view of the *Maicoyakuel* complex, the central mound (A), accompanying mounds (B–C), plaza (dotted lines), and nearby old habitation sites (see Figs. 8 and 61).

the valley; (3) relatively standardized mound sizes and shapes (mainly subconical but a few stepped platforms); (4) ceremonial complexes (i.e., plazas, excavated subsurface rows of hearths, broken vessels, and other ritual evidence); (5) association with dense domestic debris, cemeteries, and agricultural terraces that are located below at the foot of the *ñichi* or on the nearby valley floor; and (6) occasionally one or more dry ditches, or defensive moats, cutting across relatively gentle access slopes or ridges below the sites.

The fact that the same suite of mound, domestic, cemetery, and occasionally defensive sites is found in and around each *rehuekuel* complex suggests that the socio-environmental stimuli and factors affecting the system – including warfare and the establishment of irrigation agriculture – were essentially the same everywhere in the valley. Indeed, the internal nature of the nine to ten *rehuekuel* characterizing the subsistence-settlement pattern suggests not only a remarkable degree of area-to-area similarity in the valley sectors, but the probability that each *rehuekuel* operated both independently of and complementarily with others (this also is suggested by informants; see Chapters 4 and 7). All three of the smaller *rehuekuel* (*Traumakuel*, *Scheelkuel*, *Huitranlebukuel*) contain the same three components – individual *kuel* and *ñichi* platform, cemetery, and one or more habitation sites. One *rehuekuel*, *Rapahuekuel*, is associated with an extensive moated or palisaded defensive system. The distribution of *rehuekuel*, on the other hand, is somewhat more complex. Here, there is a system characterized by what appears to be strategic placement of outlying habitation sites and agricultural terraces near mounds, and strategic location of a few *rehuekuel* sites at wider intervals in the valley and at key passes, such as Centenario, Purén, Butarincón, Guadaba, and Lumaco (see Fig. 49).

Seven complexes (*TrenTrenkuel*, *Maicoyakuel*, *Rapahuekuel*, *Gundermannkuel*, *Huitranlebukuel*, *Scheelkuel*, and *Traumakuel*) have been partially excavated. Collectively, their lower and upper layers are C[14] dated between 1310 and 1900 (see Appendix 2), suggesting short periods of use over four centuries and sequential and/or overlapping construction, use, and abandonment phases. These phases may represent lineage rotation associated with ritual activities at these complexes. As discussed in Chapters 3 and 4, early texts describe "*regua*," or *rehuekuel*, as places where feasts and *cahuin*, or political meetings, were held (e.g., Butapichón, Ipinco). The Butarincón or Butapichón complex at the confluence of the Purén and Lumaco Rivers is particularly notable, because it is referenced by the early chroniclers as a place where a large indigenous population was located and where numerous battles were fought with the Spanish (see Chapter 1). (Oral accounts today in the valley relate similar functions and the same toponyms mentioned by the texts. See Chapters 3 and 5.) Ethnographic interviews and ethnohistorical texts suggests that *rehuekuel* are ceremonial centers that belonged to single dynastic patrilineages, or *rehue*, which ruled lineages of lesser rank (Dillehay 1990a, 1995). We do not yet know if each *rehuekuel* in the historic past represented (1) a single, independent, lineage polity that emerged and fell from power and was followed by another lineage polity and its *rehuekuel* complex; (2) a member of an allied subgroup of 2 to 3 lineages and their respective *rehuekuel* organized at higher politico–religious units in the valley (i.e., *ayllarehue*; see Chapters 3, 7, 8); or (3) both or other models operating in different places at different times in the valley. Whether individual *rehuekuel* are members of clusters of contemporaneous collectively allied centers or sequential independent centers, they still reflect continuous mound construction, domestic settlement, and political power in Purén-Lumaco. The appearance of sequentially and/or contemporaneously used *rehuekuel* also suggests a rotating centralized politico–religious system that emerged at least between 1500 and 1600 and was fully operational by 1600 to 1700. As noted earlier, four *rehuekuel* complexes (*Lolonkokuel*, *TrenTrenkuel*, *Hualonkokuel*, *Ñachekuel*) are still used today by the Mapuche in rotating public ceremonies and *cahuins* in the valley, which I believe to depict ancient patterns of interaction as well (Dillehay 1985a, 1990a, 1999, 2003).

52. Aerial view of *Ñachekuel* and *nguillatun* field. Note the *rehue* pole in the center of the plaza and the archaeological habitation site nearby (see Fig. 28). The *palin* field is where a ritual war game is played between competing lineages.

PRIMARY *REHUEKUEL*: Since *rehuekuel* are one of the primary features of this study, I briefly describe twelve *rehuekuel* in the study area in terms of their location, size, number of mounds and associated sites, and their chronology. When applicable, I also present written texts that relate the *rehuekuel* to specific historical events.

> *Ñachekuel* (LU-23): This *rehuekuel* is located on a high crest of a hill near the south end of the Rucalleco and Butarincón hills in the present-day community of Rucalleco. The mound is called *Ñachekuel* (bloodletting mound) and is positioned on top of a low prepared earth platform in an active *nguillatun* field built on top of a *ñichi* measuring about 150 by 200 m in length (Figs. 52–53). The mound is located at the south end of the field and is used by shamans to pray, to access the *Wenumapu* world above, to sacrifice animals, and to dance. A *palin* and *nguillatun* field of 130 m extends from the base of the mound to a circular, slightly sunken pit (ca. 11 m in diameter) located at the far north end of the field. During the *nguillatun* ceremony, the field

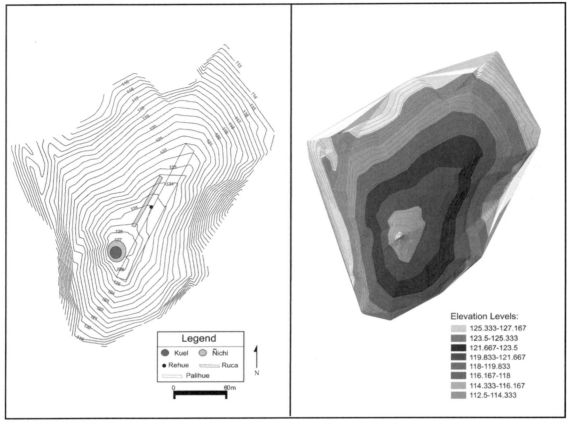

Legend

● Kuel   ○ Ñichi
● Rehue   ⌐⌐⌐ Ruca
— Palihue

N

0   60m

Elevation Levels:
- 125.333-127.167
- 123.5-125.333
- 121.667-123.5
- 119.833-121.667
- 118-119.833
- 116.167-118
- 114.333-116.167
- 112.5-114.333

53. Topographical and three-dimensional view of *Ñachekuel*, its *ñichi* platform, its *ruca* dwelling, and its *nguillatun* field.

is flanked by the two arms of family *ruka*, which serve as the inner plaza of the elongated U-shaped space where public dance, prayer, and *palin* are performed. This complex of features is particularly important because it is one of the four actively used *rehuekuel* that visually and ritually reveal the union of the *nguillatun*, *awn*, *palin*, and *kueltun* rites and of their corresponding architectural components. (To consider the importance of this integration in archaeological terms, the site forms a ceremonial center defined by an elite burial platform mound, a ritual area, and space demarcated for the *palin* war game; see Fig. 52.) Test excavations and surface collections have yielded diagnostic ceramics dating from the terminal late pre-Hispanic period to the present day, with the highest frequency belonging to the eighteenth and nineteenth centuries. No radiocarbon dates have been attained from this site. The site is flanked by several moderate to large-sized domestic settlements located at the base of the hills just above the valley floor.

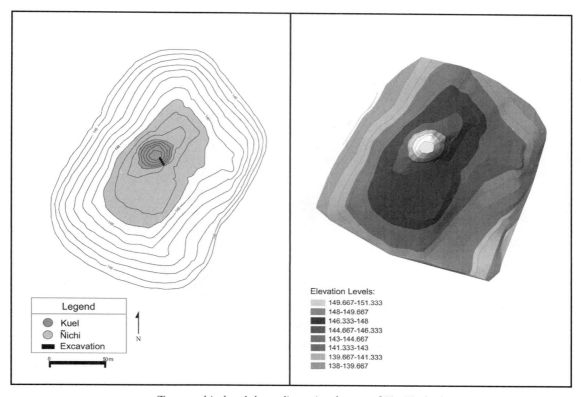

54. Topographical and three-dimensional maps of *Tren Trenkuel*.

I have participated in *nguillatun* ceremonies at this site and directly observed many of the ritual stages discussed in previous chapters. Of particular interest is the presence of tunnels dug into the mound for the purpose of feeding it *chicha*, food, and the sacrificial blood of animals during ceremony (see Chapter 4 for informant comments on these features).

Tren Trenkuel (PU-69): This *rehuekuel* has been discussed in many places in this volume, especially in regard to the long ritual narrative gathered there during a live ceremony (see Chapter 5 and Appendix 1), and will be described here only briefly. It is built on the highest crest point of the chain of hills in Butarincón that runs from north to south along the Lumaco River (see Figs. 2, 28, and 54). The mound is approximately 9 m high today, although considerable erosion from use can be seen on top. The base is about 42 m wide. The *ñichi* platform upon which it is built has been modified greatly not only with sediment deliberately having been removed and deposited downslope on the north and south side of the crest but different sediments have been imported from the valley floor to cap the crest and to smooth the flattened *ñichi*

55. Ritual sight lines from *Wenucolla* to Andean volcanoes where the deity *Pillan* resides (1, 3, 5), to *Kai Kai* (4), to *Miradorkuel*, and to *Tren Trenkuel* (2).

surface (Pino and Sequel 2004). This is the most stratigraphically and architecturally complex *ñichi* that we have excavated in south-central Chile. The entire *rehuekuel* complex is constructed of different colored and textured sediments brought not only from the valley floor but probably from other valleys as well (Pino and Sequel 2004). Flanking the base of the *ñichi* are five small mounds said by local informants to be the most recent sons and daughters of *Tren Trenkuel*.

    This is the most dominant *kuel* in the whole valley and takes the name of the benevolent snake in the creation story (see Chapter 4); it is the father *kuel* to all others. It can be seen by and can see all other *kuel* and important sacred mountains and hills in the valley.

Miradorkuel (LU-45): This is a single mound built on a high hilltop in the mountain range east of the Lumaco Valley. The mound is 2.5 m high and 12 m wide and sits on a *ñichi* that measures 40 by 50 m. Antonio Raiman of Hueico says that this *kuel* is known for its line of sighting across the valley from *Miradorkuel* to *Tren Trenkuel* to *Wenucolla* to form a *kuifirupu* or old (visual?) road across the valley (see Fig. 55, line 2). *Rupu* means road or stone boundary marker that divides spaces (see Tellez 2004).

56. General view from *Huitranlehuekuel* and the sacred lagoon to *Tren Trenkuel*.

Huitranlehuekuel (PU-172): This complex of mounds, agricultural terraces, and other spaces constitutes the second largest *rehuekuel* in the valley. It is located due north of Butarincón on the north side of the river. Thirty mounds ranging in size from 1 to 5 m high and from 5 to 20 m wide are scattered over an area about 1 km². The two largest mounds are associated with a natural U-shaped hill facing south to Butarincón and overlooking a small artificial lagoon (Fig. 56) that was built around a natural spring seeping from the hillside. The mounds were built on the southern edges of two long, flat natural knolls forming the U-shape. The lagoon measures about 40 by 45 m and was constructed in ancient times, according to informants and to Pino's analysis of its stratigraphy and the sediments (M. Pino, personal communication, 2004). The south wall of the lagoon is a 3-m high dike, which according to locals, was used during ritual ceremonies in the past to drain water onto three stepped artificial benches constructed just below the lagoon. Locals refer to the spring and lagoon as the "*wedange*" or evil eye, saying that both good and harm come from it and that in the past their grandfathers offered it *chicha* and food to calm it. This complex directly faces and can be observed from *Tren Trenkuel*.

Huitranlebukuel (Pu-56): Three *kuel* measuring about 1.5 m, 1.8, and 1.9 m high and 11 m, 15 m, and 20 m wide are located on a long flat *ñichi*

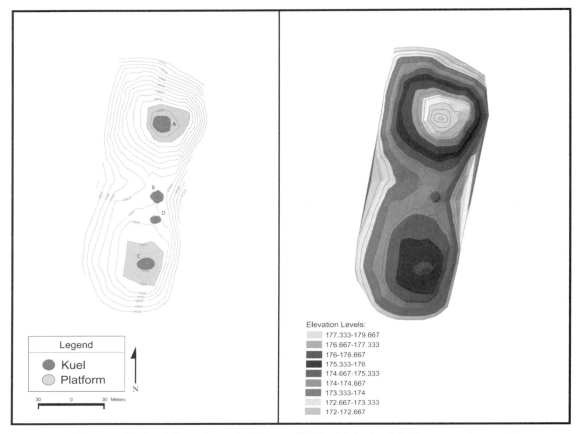

Legend

● Kuel
○ Platform

30   0   30 Meters

N

Elevation Levels:
177.333-179.667
176.667-177.333
176-176.667
175.333-176
174.667-175.333
174-174.667
173.333-174
172.667-173.333
172-172.667

57. Topographical and three-dimensional maps of *Huitranlebukuel* and the four mounds comprising it.

platform high above the valley floor in a chain of hills on the south-side of the Purén River about 2.5 km southeast of *Maicoyakuel* and directly across valley from *Traumakuel* (Fig. 57). Informants report that a fourth and smaller mound once existed in line with the other three, but was destroyed several years ago. Remnants of it are still visible. Informants also state that *nguillatun* were performed at the site in the early 20th century and that local *machi* once used it to communicate with *Wenucolla* to the west and *Tren Trenkuel* to the east. Nearly all *kuel* and other sacred places in the valley can be seen from *Huitranlebukuel*. Approximately 25 small to large domestic sites, agricultural terraces, cemeteries, and channelized fields are located within 1.5 km of this *rehuekuel*. Diagnostic ceramics suggest that the site dates from the late pre-Hispanic to modern period.

Local informants give the name of the largest *kuel* as *Huachikuel*. The two smaller ones are called *Ankakuel*, which means second in

58. General view of *Rapahuekuel*, Mound A. Note the trees planted around its base.

order. Located below the *ñichi* and the *kuel* are three smaller *kuel* (80 cm high and 5 m in diameter). These are said to be the feet of the *rehuekuel* that it uses at night to rise from the earth and to walk across the land. These smaller *kuel* are named *Natalkuel*, which means that they are not only lower in elevation but also lower ranking to the other *kuel*.

Traumakuel (PU-88): This *rehuekuel* has two small mounds associated with a central plaza and a fortified or palisaded homestead (Fig. 49). The mounds measure about 1.2 m and 1.8 m high and 8 m and 16 m wide. The fortified structure measures about 80 by 80 m in size and is defined by a square moated trench alignment. A similar structure exists in Butarincón and is believed by local informants to have been the home of a famous war leader, Colípi, who ruled the valley in the middle 1880s and still has descendents living in the area today. The form and artifactual debris from both structures are similar, suggesting a chronology for the *Traumakuel* structure in the nineteenth century. Ceramics associated with the *kuel* indicate an earlier chronology in the sixteenth and seventeenth centuries. The *ñichi* has been leveled considerably, with approximately 1.2 m of top sediment removed from the hill crest. Several domestic sites are positioned below this site near the valley floor.

Rapahuekuel (LU-34): This complex of four *kuel* and a heavily modified and very extensive *ñichi* (Figs. 58–59) are located on the north side of the middle valley about 2 km west of *Maicoyakuel*. The *ñichi* measures

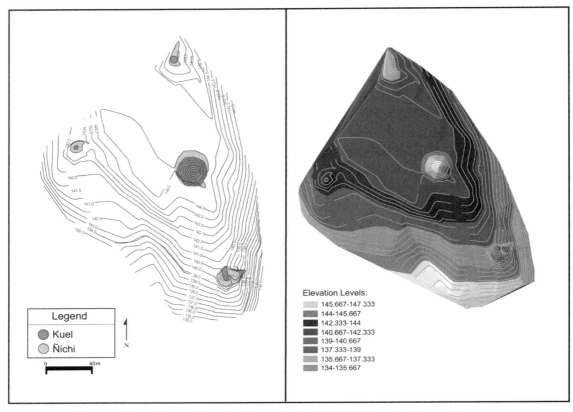

Legend

- ● Kuel
- ● Ñichi

0   40m

Elevation Levels:
- 145.667-147.333
- 144-145.667
- 142.333-144
- 140.667-142.333
- 139-140.667
- 137.333-139
- 135.667-137.333
- 134-135.667

59. Topographic and three-dimensional maps of *Rapahuelkuel*. Mound A is located in the center.

about 300 by 350 m. Mound A is the largest structure and measures about 8 m high and 22 m wide. Positioned equidistance around the base of the mound are ten large oak trees, which were planted by the Araucanians at least two centuries ago, according to informants and to a count of the tree rings in one cored tree. Mound B is located 150 m south of Mound A and has been cut by a logging road. It measures 1.6 m high and 17 m wide. Mounds D and C are small and measure about 1.2 m high and 9 m wide. They are placed about 100 m northwest of Mound A. Excavations in Mounds B and C revealed intermittent layered floors with burned areas and broken sherds and culturally sterile fills similar to those observed in other excavated mounds. A radiocarbon date of 1310 to 1370 was produced from charcoal recovered from a burned feature in a middle level of Mound C (see Appendix 2). Located immediately east of Mounds A and D are several elongated and flattened earthworks that suggest no apparent function. A large domestic site associated with a deep moat is located 500 m downslope on the southeast side of the hill near a rich wetland. Other

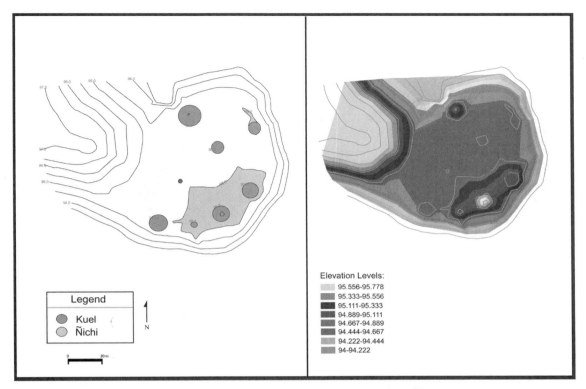

Elevation Levels:
- 95.556-95.778
- 95.333-95.556
- 95.111-95.333
- 94.889-95.111
- 94.667-94.889
- 94.444-94.667
- 94.222-94.444
- 94-94.222

Legend

● Kuel
● Ñichi

N

0   20 m

60. Topographic and three-dimensional maps of *Kuifilkue*.

large domestic sites and two cemeteries are located west of this complex. Pino has trenched the modified surface and hillsides of the *ñichi* at *Rapahuekuel* and shown that approximately 1 m of top sediment was removed to create its flattened surface.

Kuifikuel (PU-166): This site is located 1 km north of the Lumaco River and 1 km east of *Huitranlehue*. *Kuifikuel* is on a low hill spur that overlooks a wetland about 2 km north of *TrenTrenkuel* (Fig. 60). The site is comprised of eight small mounds, measuring between 0.7 to 1.4 m high and 8 m wide. Three mounds are positioned together on a 0.6 m high *ñichi* platform. Excavations in the largest mound yielded a burial chamber and several burned floors and offerings. Ceramics and radiocarbon dates (see Appendix 2) suggest that it dates to the late pre-Hispanic to Hispanic period. Informants report that this mound complex was associated with ritual activities that once took place at the *nguillatun* field and artificial lagoon located in the *Huitranlehuekuel* about 0.8 km uphill to the northwest.

Maicoyakuel (LU-19): This is another large complex defined by a plaza, five *kuel*, and several large domestic sites (Figs. 51, and 61). The central Mound A is 10 m high and 22 m wide. Four small mounds (B–E)

293

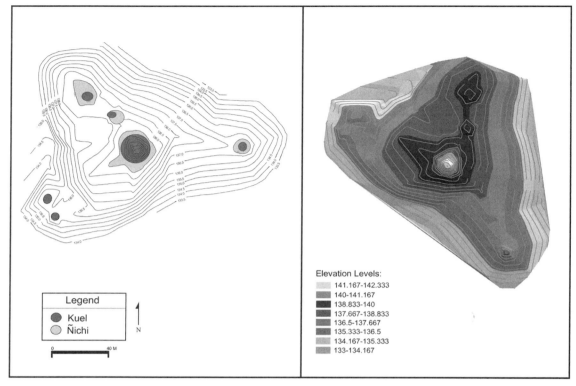

Legend
● Kuel
○ Ñichi

N

0   40 M

Elevation Levels:
░ 141.167-142.333
▓ 140-141.167
■ 138.833-140
■ 137.667-138.833
■ 136.5-137.667
▓ 135.333-136.5
▒ 134.167-135.333
░ 133-134.167

61. Topographical and three-dimensional maps of *Maicoyakuel* (see Fig. 51).

measure between 0.5 to 1 m high and between 4 to 6 m wide. *Maicoy-akuel* overlooks the ecologically richest wetland in the valley where Ipinco, Purén, and Guadaba creeks and two chains of hills converge to form a bottleneck basin between the east and west sides of the valley. These areas are mentioned frequently by the chroniclers as important defensive localities and places where "*sementeras*" or agricultural fields were located (e.g., see Rosales [1674] 1989:583; see Chapter 3). Several agricultural terraces are located about 1 km north of *Maicoyakuel* and *Rapahuekuel* in the headwaters of Guadaba Creek and near *Huitranle-bukuel* (Fig. 49). Extensive excavations were carried out in Mound A and the plaza. Several TL and C[14] dates obtained from burned floors in the base and on the top of the mound were processed between 535 and 1770, respectively (see Appendix 2). Around the base of *Maicoya* hill and on flat knolls to the west are several domestic sites which contain late pre–Hispanic and late Hispanic materials. Local informants report that *Maicoyakuel* was an important *cahuin* locality where leaders from different lineages gathered for political discourse and ceremony. Each leader spoke to the ritual audience from his own designated mound,

62. View of mound B at *Lolonkokuel*. Second mound is located behind trees to the right.

which was located in an area of the *rehuekuel* complex that corresponded to the cardinal direction of the lands he ruled in the valley.
In other words, leaders and groups participating in events at the site
had designated activity areas. If a leader lived in the northeast end of
the valley, he spoke from Mound E, a leader from the south side of
the valley orated from Mound D, and so on.

Lolonkokuel (PU-12): This complex is located about 1 km northeast of the
town of Purén in the west end of the valley and at the headwaters
of the Purén River where it descends from the Elicura Valley to the
town of Purén (Figs. 62–63). The site is comprised of two large *kuel*
that are elongated in form and situated on a high hill overlooking the
valley floor. The sacred mountain of *Wenucolla* is located due north
of and directly above *Lolonkokuel*. The two mounds and a *nguillatun*
field, located immediately north of the mounds on a flat bench, cover
approximately 5 ha. The largest *kuel* is Mound A and measures about
50 m long and 12 m high. It is a natural hill that has been modified
extensively to form a leveled *ñichi* platform on top. Test excavations
and coring indicate that about 70–80 cm of sediment was removed
from the hilltop to shape a flat ritual surface. The modified hilltop is
characterized by a high density of grinding stone fragments and chunks
of white quartz rocks, the latter brought from downslope outcrops.

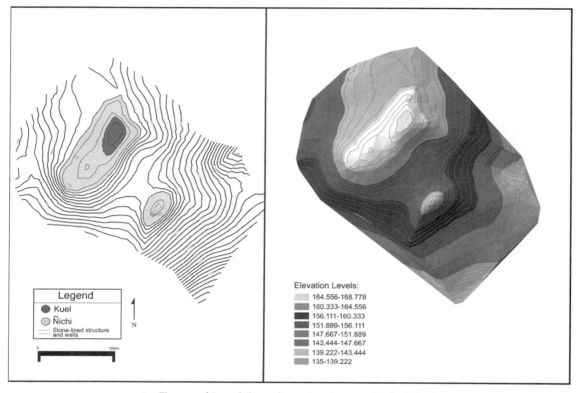

Legend

● Kuel
○ Ñichi
⋯⋯ Stone-lined structure
   and walls

0   100m

N

Elevation Levels:
☐ 164.556-168.778
■ 160.333-164.556
■ 156.111-160.333
■ 151.889-156.111
■ 147.667-151.889
■ 143.444-147.667
☐ 139.222-143.444
■ 135-139.222

63. Topographic and three-dimensional maps of *Lolonkokuel*.

Located about 50 m east of Mound A is Mound B, which also is a low natural hill that has been modified into an elongated mound. It measures about 40 m in length and 10 m in height. The four corners of the mound have been lined with imported stone blocks to form a rectangular-like base around the structure. Two stone-lined entryways were built at the base of the south end of the mound. The slope above the entryways has been built into four stone-lined platform terraces that serve as a stepped stairway to the top where another rectangular stone-lined structure has been built. Situated about 250 m downslope from the mounds on the southside of the hill is an ancient cemetery. Farther downslope at the base of the hill is an ancient domestic site and the present-day indigenous community of Lolonko. Diagnostic artifacts recovered from the surface of the entire complex date from the late pre-Hispanic to modern period.

Informants living in Lolonko recognize the site as an ancient *rehuekuel* and say that their grandfathers told them that it was an

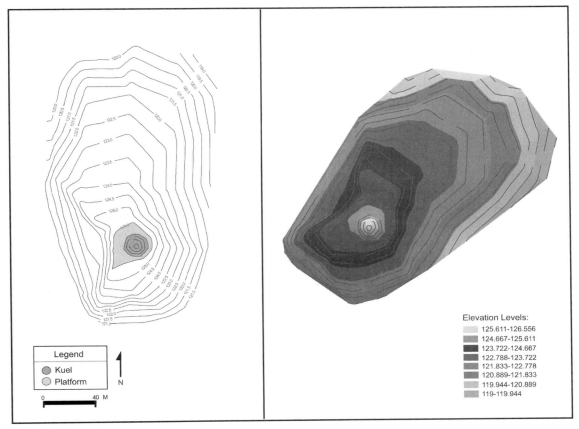

Elevation Levels:
125.611-126.556
124.667-125.611
123.722-124.667
122.788-123.722
121.833-122.778
120.889-121.833
119.944-120.889
119-119.944

Legend
Kuel
Platform

0   40 M

64. Topographical and three-dimensional maps of *Scheelkuel*.

important place where large *cahuin* and *nguillatun* were attended by thousands of people from all over the valley and from other places. They were informed that two *lonko* administered gatherings at the site and that each stood on top of a mound and conversed across the open space between them. This use pattern is similar to ones described by other informants for *Maicoyakuel*, *Tren Trenkuel*, and *Ñachekuel*.

Scheelkuel (PU-44): This is a single mound that is 2.5 m high and 18 m wide. It is located on one of the smallest *ñichi* (Fig. 64) in the west end of the valley about 2 km east of the town of Purén and 2.5 km due south of *Lolonkokuel*. The mound sits on a high bench above the valley floor and is surrounded by one of the largest and densest domestic sites in the valley, PU-41. Possibly affiliated with *Scheelkuel* is an isolated hill located about 400 m to the north. The hill has been modified considerably and has a deep moat around its base. Both indigenous and Spanish artifacts were recovered on and around the hill. Local informants report that it was the fortress of the Spanish governor Oñez de Loyola when he occupied the valley in the early 1600s. They also state that *nguillatun* were once held at the *Scheelkuel* complex.

Hualonkokuel (PU-41): This complex is an actively used *nguillatun* and *palin* field where two *kuel* are located and where the ritual narrative about the sick *kuel* was collected and analyzed in the last chapter (Fig. 65; see also Figs. 9 and 45). It is located on a high promontory overlooking wetlands on the southside of the Purén Valley about 3 km east of the town of Purén. The field is approximately 300 m long and 60 m wide, with the larger Hualonko mound, the sick one in the narrative, situated on the far south end and the smaller one located on the far north side. The large mound (A) measures about 4 m high and 12 m in diameter; the small one is 1 m high and 8 m in diameter. Lying between the two mounds is the *nguillatun* and *palin* space, which today is characterized by a *rehue* pole and several *ruca* structures where families are seated during ceremony (see Fig. 45 in Chapter 5). Both pre-Hispanic and modern ceramic wares have been recovered from the surface of the site. Located within 1.5 km of the site are several small to moderate sized domestic sites.

Other mound non-*rehuekuel* complexes and isolated mounds exist throughout the valley but will not be presented until the ongoing archeological research is completed. Figure 49 shows the location of the complexes and their spatial relation to other complexes and site types.

In sum, from a strictly archeological perspective, the practice of building mounds reflects important changes that were occurring in the way of life of local people, especially in the religious and political realm. Although mounds are typically thought of as burial monuments, clearly not all were built for that purpose by the Araucanians. Excavations reveal that some mounds cover the remains of previous structures or prepared surfaces and contain few graves, and others seem to be independent of any preexisting activity (Dillehay 2004, 2005). Small isolated burial mounds, however, were repositories for dead leaders, and they were also memorials to the dead whose bodies they covered and enveloped and later were public meeting places and ceremonial centers (see Chapter 5). The fact that the burial mounds required a special effort to construct them indicates that the deceased were sufficiently respected by their group to warrant the investment of time and labor required to erect the memorial – one that became the resting places of *machi* spirits and the staging grounds for large-scale public ceremonies. Above all, the burial mounds also served the living, for they provided a visible and permanent statement of a group's commitment to its own lineage, to any other

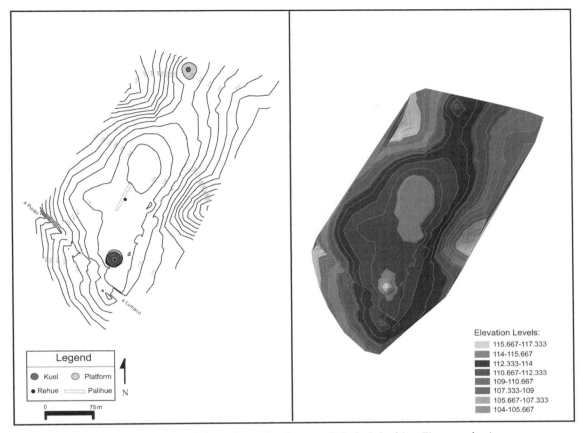

Legend

● Kuel   ● Platform
● Rehue   ▭ Palihue

0   75m

N

Elevation Levels:
115.667-117.333
114-115.667
112.333-114
110.667-112.333
109-110.667
107.333-109
105.667-107.333
104-105.667

65. Topographical and three-dimensional maps of *Hualonkokuel* (see Figs. 9 and 45).

social entity of which it was a part, to its ancestral claim to its territory, and to a gradual unfolding ritual process across the landscape that continuously connected and transformed mounds with mounds, people with people, and people with mounds. Beyond the self-interest of the group, mounds, whether built for burial, ceremonial, or other purposes, also functioned as territorial and diplomatic markers – statements of the vested interests of one lineage, or closely allied lineages, in a given territory or to each lineage, or closely allied *ayllarehue* lineages, in a given territory or to each other (Dillehay 1990b, 1990c, 2003). From an archaeological perspective, the appearance and elaboration of mound construction among the Araucanians, therefore, reflects the intensification of population nucleation, agricultural production, the tendency toward greater aggregation and home range affinity, and the probably need to more securely and clearly demarcate and defend territories and declare and affirm alliances and reciprocal responsibilities within and among groups – all sufficiently important reasons to invest corporate resources in mound construction.

Domestic Sites

Small to large domestic sites of all ceramic periods are distributed more or less evenly on the lower hill slopes and occasionally on low ridge spurs just above the valley floor, especially near wetlands, and below *rehuekuel*. Several C[14] and TL dates place the domestic contexts of sites between roughly 5150 B.C. and 1850 (i.e., LU-11, PU-165, LU-36, LU-13, LU-41, PU-41, see Appendix 2). Undifferentiated habitation sites of the late El Vergel (ca. 1200–1500), particularly of the early historic period, range in size between 25 and 50 ha and contain deposits averaging between 20 and 50 cm in thickness. Their average size is about three times greater than that of the earlier Pitrén period (ca. 500–1000) sites (see Chapter 3). Between 1500 and 1750, sites generally range in size between 3 and 15 ha, contain deposits extending in thickness between 30 and 80 cm, and reflect population nucleation and stability. In some areas outside of Purén-Lumaco, sites dating between 1700 and 1850 generally cover less area, are characterized by periodically refurbished structures, and exhibit less midden deposits. This latter pattern suggests the reverse – less population density and stability in some valleys. Late nineteenth to early 20th century sites throughout the entire Araucanian region, including Purén-Lumaco, are usually less substantial; the middens take the form of thin sheet deposits, suggesting relatively ephemeral occupations that are probably related to intense conflict, population displacement, and political instability in some areas. These site and settlement patterns likely represent shifts in political and economic relations, including lineage fragmentation and displacement, waxing and waning involvement in warfare, differential reliance on agriculture and other subsistence means, and cyclical changes in leader's authority (see Chapters 3, 6, and 7 for discussion of corroborative historical accounts and oral histories of these patterns.)

Although we have surveyed more than 250 domestic sites and excavated portions of several domestic sites, the plan and organization of residential communities are poorly understood at this time. Few site plans have been fully exposed and our knowledge is limited to test and block excavations in stratified sites. There does not seem to be evidence for any obvious community plans at non-mound sites, although postholes and open areas suggest houses (*rucas*) dispersed across areas located just above wetlands in the valley floor (Dillehay 2004, 2005). Excavated habitation features consist principally of hearths, ceramic concentrations, and fire pits and ovens (Fig. 66). Few houses or other construction features have been excavated at any of these communities.

When coupled with the ethnohistorical data, this evidence offers promise for understanding several social processes, including settlement nucleation, fragmentation, and recruitment. While local patrilineage life was penetrated by developing networks of fragmented groups, local communities in the valley increasingly opened up their lives and their lands to public participation in multiple

66. Excavated ovens outside of a *ruca* house in a domestic site that are radiocarbon dated between 1450 and 1660.

ceremonies across and outside the valley (see Chapters 3, 6, 7). Written texts and oral accounts name outside groups coming into the valley to reside with local lineages and often specify the northeast or other sectors in communities where these newcomers lived. This kind of information is archaeologically testable, with preliminary findings suggesting exotic ceramic wares generally isolated in the northeast sectors of domestic sites (Cecil and Glasscock 2005; Dillehay 2004, 2005).

Some domestic sites also contain a wide variety of local and nonlocal indigenous types of ceramics, as determined by surface treatment, temper, decoration, vessel form, trace element analysis, and so forth. This pattern may suggest co-residence of local and nonlocal groups, which may reflect recruitment of fragmented and/or annexed groups. Not well documented to date is the settlement/community pattern of recruited and annexed areas, although clues to the location and structure of these patterns are available from prior ethnohistorical and archeological studies. For example, research at Boyonco-Ipinco in the Purén area has recovered nonlocal ceramics in sectors of domestic sites that correspond with those found at domestic sites located 15 to 30 km to the south in Repocura and Chol Chol (Cecil and Glasscock 2005). The ceramics in these areas are red slipped jars and incised plates with compositional percentages of grog, sand, and mica that are significantly different from those in domestic sites in Purén (Dillehay 2002), suggesting co-residency of Purén and Chol Chol groups, possibly the adoption of the latter by the former, and/or women from the latter marrying and moving to the former.

AGRICULTURAL CANALS AND RAISED FIELDS

Also in association with *rehuekuel* and domestic sites are agricultural terraces, canals, and raised fields, which have never before been recorded in this part of South America. Ancient canals, channelized field systems, and canals were found along the valley margin on both sides of the Purén and Lumaco River. Aside from their fragmentary nature and the silt that partially filled them, there are three criteria that aid in assessing these systems as late pre-Hispanic to early Hispanic in date. First, in areas where modern canals presently run, the ancient irrigation ditches are invariably located several m higher in elevation. For example, the modern canals run at or slightly below the 180-m contour level, downslope to the west of the two probable ancient canals located here. Whether or not this indicates that earlier canals generally were longer than more recent ones, it is clear from our research that the area drained and/or irrigated by traditional contour canals is located near the higher *rehuekuel* sites and their large domestic sites. Second, in almost all areas of the valley numerous late pre-Hispanic or early Hispanic fortresses and other sites were found in close association with the canals shown on the maps (e.g., Figs. 49, 67). Third, in at least two areas of the valley, the remains of raised and channelized field systems were found adjacent to the fragmentary remains of the main ditches and raised fields in the valley floor (e.g., see Fig. 67). Both systems are located in wetland areas where irrigation agriculture does not appear to have been practiced since the early to late Hispanic period, judging both from the deteriorated state of the systems in some places and from the absence of any settlements of more recent times.

In the latter part of the late pre-Hispanic to early Hispanic period the most impressive feature was agricultural ridged fields located in limited parts of the valley and in backwater estuaries situated along the Imperial and Budi coastline to the southwest. In the valley, they occupy small areas between 5 to 10 ha that are characterized by low, 1 m high and 10 to 20 m long, usually sinuous ridges that follow the natural terrain of semiparallel and amorphous-shaped natural contours of the levees. Channels have been cut between levees to facilitate and manage the flow of water for cultivation of the flat levee surfaces. These channelized fields are similar to those reported for the Palenque region in Mexico (see Liendo 2002:178–84). Along the Lago Budi coast south of the Rio Imperial (see Fig. 7), these are parallel side-by-side arrangements of massive raised fields located in backwater estuaries protected by sand dunes and a sea wall. The individual ridges in the valley are 1 m or more high, 5 to 6 m wide, and, in some instances, more than 20 m long. Those on the coast are much larger, often measuring more than 300 m

67. View of a late pre-Hispanic to early Hispanic canal near Butarincón.

long, 2 to 3 m high, and 20 to 22 m wide (Figs. 68–70). It is presently uncertain what kinds of crops were grown in these plots. A single radiocarbon date places a segment of the Budi coastal system at 1280 ± 40 (see Appendix 2). The coastal system is called *deume* by the local informants, meaning large constructions in Mapundungun. This evidence implies expansive water management systems built and used in late pre-Hispanic and Hispanic times.

Fortresses

A special category of upland earthworks is the hilltop enclosure (Fig. 71). These enclosures are formed of rectangular embankments, typically located on top of, and extended around, all or part of the perimeter of isolated or semi–isolated high points. Several of these enclosures occupy isolated mesa-like outliers at the edge of the valley floor or on promontories extending into the valley, and are thought to be fortified settlements. Most *rehuekuel*, both large and small, were located near fortifications in the form of embankments, ditches, moats, or wooden palisades, especially at *Rapahuekuel* and *Lolonkokuel* (Fig. 71). Some hilltop enclosures have produced evidence of having been built in multiple stages, and it is reasonable to suspect that most if not all had similar histories. Several fortresses may date to the late pre-Hispanic period, although I suspect that most are of early Hispanic origin (see León 1986 for a discussion of Araucanian forts).

68. a. Channelized field showing amorphously shaped agricultural growing platforms (white areas, arrow points to a canal). b. A regularly shaped raised platform in a field near Butarincón.

Population Estimates

Based on ethnoarchaeological and archaeological evidence, I have estimated that 1/2 ha of settlement contains one house lot (Dillehay 2004). If each house lot (*ruca*) contains approximately seven persons, as it does today, it follows that a family would include homesteads of 1/2 ha or less. Small communities would consist of settlements that have an area between 4 and 17 ha and moderately sized villages would have an area between 18 and 35 ha. Large *rehuekuel* complexes accommodate between 2 and 80 ha, providing that they also have the associated domestic sites. Based on these figures, I would estimate that small to large domestic sites may have been occupied by as few as 25 to 40 persons and by as many as 2,000 to 3,000 persons, respectively. However, this figure can be misleading, because each site is defined as a self-contained spatial unit. Some *rehuekuel*, such

69. Raised fields along the Pacific coast southwest of the Purén Valley. The arrow to the right points to a remnant canal complex. The raised platforms are between 100 and 400 m in length, 2–3 m in height, and 20–25 m in width. Arrow to the left points to a raised field.

as *Rapahuekuel, Tren Trenkuel,* and *Maicoyakuel,* are flanked by three to four large domestic sites around the hilltops they occupy, thus implying a larger affiliated population. Based on the presence of more than 80 contemporaneous domestic sites for each cultural time period (i.e., late pre-Hispanic El Vergel, Contact, and post-Contact), I would estimate that roughly 4,000 to 8,000 people were living in the valley at any one time from 1200 to 1800.

Additional population estimates can be derived from the number of *lanzas,* or warriors, described by the sixteenth and early seventeenth century Spanish for specific areas in the valley at the time of early contact (Inostroza 1991). Inostroza has estimated the overall number of warriors for this period at 5,960, with 3,855 in Purén, 1940 in Guadaba, and 150 in Lumaco. Each *lanza* must have belonged to a family, implying an estimated total population of several thousand individuals. (We do not know how the early Spanish divided the valley into these sectors and how these figures were derived. I suspect that they were following the layout of streams in the valley, which would explain why Lumaco has such a low population estimate. The Lumaco River and especially the Butarincón area, where the highest density of archeological sites are located, must have been included in the Purén estimate.) Although this is not the place to provide a detailed comparison of the written and archeological records, the two generally agree on a minimal

70. Closeup of the raised fields in backwater estuaries. Arrows in the upper area of photo point to a dike to define the limits of the field system and to protect it from intruding sand dunes.

population range between 6,000 and 10,000 people for the valley during the period 1500 to 1700 (see Chapters 3 and 7 for discussion of the number of warriors in some battles in Purén).

Settlement and Other Patterns

I consider three aspects of the valley settlement pattern in this section: settlement location and spacing relative to local topography and settlement organization; relations between mounds and other site types; and the placement of mounds with respect to open or plaza areas.

The emerging archaeological picture suggests that mounds were increasingly becoming the focus of interest within the valley over time. The current evidence suggests that their size and complexity increased and their function changed from mortuary ritual at isolated mounds from ca. 1300 to 1500 to increased public ritual at *rehuekuel* to accommodating more expanded segments of society by the late 1500s. In the early Hispanic period (1550–1650), we begin to see a clearer picture, in part because the archaeological and ethnohistorical data are richer and complement each other. Mound communities are increasingly bounded and differentiated from surrounding contemporary populations, as revealed at the

71. Deep moat associated with a hillside fortress near *Rapahuekuel* (see Figs. 58 and 59).

rehuekuel complexes. At this time, community patterns show a shift toward the adoption of the *rehuekuel* mound-and-plaza arrangements and the emergence of larger domestic sites. Mound construction and the notion of a mound-and-plaza arrangement of community planning appeared to reach its peak in the late seventeenth and early eighteenth century. During this time, we see the emergence of people living near the *ñichi* platforms of large *rehuekeul* complexes, and there is increasing evidence that larger populations are living within a 1 to 2 km radius too. Beyond the *rehuekuel* complexes, the settlement evidence indicates that a substantial population was scattered across the landscape and that its subsistence base was agricultural, supplemented by hunting, fishing, and gathering. During the later Hispanic period (ca. 1600–1700), mound groups and domestic sites continued to expand in size and in their restricted access. At sites such as *Rapahuekuel*, *Maicoyakuel*, and *Lolonkokuel*, mounds and their elevated position on top of the *ñichi* platforms effectively enclosed a central plaza, thus symbolically shutting out and elevating access to special places.

The arrangement of mounds at *rehuekuel* often indicates the presence of plazas and public spaces, suggesting a deliberate plan of the builders. This formality results from the alignment of some *rehuekuel* facing each other (e.g., Fig. 49). Four sites contained aligned mounds. Eight sites had both aligned and nonaligned mounds. The mounds at Butarincón are clearly aligned with each other, as evidenced by equidistance and regular placement along the U-shaped ridge crest discussed earlier. This formal arrangement may reflect a strong central authority at Butarincón, an inference supported by ethnohistorical data in the area (see Ovalle [1646] 1888; Tesillo [1647] 1911: 22–26; cf. Bengoa 2003:390–500). At *Maicoyakuel* the site history demonstrates a pattern of spatial exclusion and restriction of access to the interior plaza spaces. At this site and other large mound complexes, the largest central mounds occupy strategic positions opposite one another, with flanking structures being lower in height, smaller in scale, and less complex in their architectural features. Sites with aligned mounds appear to be larger (in number of mounds) than sites with nonaligned mounds. The internal arrangement of individual *kuel* in the *rehuekuel* also varies, but two common patterns can be discerned. The principal mound stands at the edge of the mound precinct at five localities: *Hualonkokuel, Ñachekuel, Huitranlebukuel, Kuifikuel,* and *Huitranlehuekuel.* The main mound stands roughly at the center of the precinct at five places: *TrenTrenkuel, Lolonkokuel, Rapahuekuel, Scheelkuel,* and *Traumakuel.* As we learned from the ethnography, central location may result from the addition of smaller mounds for secondary leaders to speak (see Chapter 5). This pattern suggests that formal arrangements may result not from a plan laid out at the beginning of a site's history but from the presence of a continuing politico–religious activity (i.e., alliances and public ceremony) that dictated or influenced the relationships of mounds to each other in special designated places. Of course, the mounds and other earthworks that existed at the time that a site was abandoned – or, at least, at the time that construction was halted – represent the stage of development of the complex upon abandonment, not necessarily the completion of a grand plan that had been envisioned when the site was initially occupied by the original occupiers decades or centuries earlier.

Whatever the reasons underlying the decision about where to place mounds and how they were arranged, topographic prominence, lines of sighting from one *rehuekuel* to another, defense and close social distance seem to have been important objectives. While it is impossible to fully determine today what the visual opportunities for any given site might have been at the time that it was selected, because we do not know the precise status of vegetation or land use by peoples at the time, it appears to have been important that *rehuekuel* could be seen easily from settlements and from other mound complexes. Today, local shamans report that visual sighting was and still is important to distant participation in, or "visual pilgrimages," to ceremonial events held at *rehuekuel* (see Chapters 3 and 4 and later comments in this chapter). Consequently, mounds in upland locations were typically placed on ridge crests, hilltop bluff lines, and the tops of promontories such that they could be seen easily and silhouetted against the sky. Mounds in lowland locations were usually placed on higher terraces of flood plains, sites that would allow them to be visible from the waterways or the adjacent uplands, yet secure from all but the largest floods. The fact that clusters of mounds often developed in these upland situations further suggests that intergroup identity, distant ritual communication, and symbolism were important dimensions of the development of the local monumental landscape.

The domestic settlement pattern of the late pre-Hispanic period appears to be made up of two elements: small dispersed communities and family dwellings, and larger often single-mound communities of greater size than other contemporary settlements. In the Purén area, the Pitrén settlements are small and spatially homogeneous. The basic community plan is manifested archaeologically in scattered middens, sometimes found in discrete clusters near a stream confluence or wetland. Comprehensive controlled surface collections of and limited excavations at these small sites indicate clusters of spatially confined activity areas probably associated with individual extended families (Dillehay 2004, 2005). A generalized economy dominated by hunting and gathering and some gardening characterized this period. No mounds are securely associated with the Pitrén period.

The late pre-Hispanic El Vergel period appears to mark a series of transformations in the cultures of the region. This period represents a time of notable shifts in local and regional behaviors on a number of different levels. Mound building begins in this period. The subsistence base is poorly understood but seems to have consisted of a broad-spectrum hunter–collector–horticultural pattern (Aldunate 1989; Dillehay 1990a, 1990c). Several domesticates, including potatoes (*Solanum tuberosum*), beans (*Phaseolus vulgaris*), corn (*Zea*), quínoa (*Chenopodium quinoa*), zapallo (Curcubita sp.), madi (*Madia sativa*), mango (*Bromus mango*), lanco (*Bromus stamineus*), teca or tuca (*Bromus berterianus*), and wild-plant species (*Fragaria chiloensis*, wild fruit; *Cryptocarya alba*, peumo; *Typha angustifolia*, totora; *Muehlenbeckia hastulata*, quilo) were consumed throughout this period and the following early Hispanic era, as evidenced at excavated domestic sites in the Purén and and Lumaco (Silva 2006). In some areas, small singular mounds were constructed for the interment of the dead. Changing burial practices seem to indicate a greater emphasis on individuals and their achievements or accomplishments, and evidence for communal mortuary ritual increases. Settlement patterns represent a dichotomy between single mound sites and what are presumed to be single-family or possibly extended-family settlements ranging between 0.5 and 5 ha in size. Some non-mound communities appear to become larger and may represent the development of small community groups. No defensive sites and agricultural canals have been securely recorded for this period, although raised fields and terraces appear in the thirteenth century The terminal pre-Hispanic culture also can be identified as possible Inka influenced for reasons discussed in Chapter 3. This influence probably concerned architectural patterns, settlement organizations, ceramic decorative techniques and styles, subsistence practices, and political and religious ideas.

The Spanish Contact period marks a change in settlement and subsistence pattern of the Purén and Lumaco Valley. The early Hispanic pattern appears to be an evolved form of that witnessed in earlier times. Smaller population and mound centers of the kind first noted as early as 1300 to 1500 appear to increase in number and also in size. The standard late small-mound site plan is often enlarged to include up to three to five more mounds. Non-mound communities are not well explored but are present in some numbers. These communities are frequently of moderate to large in size, suggesting something on the order of small to large communities as opposed to a pattern of scattered dwellings. Population seems to increase or nucleate dramatically in some places, and there is strong evidence of a growing cultural and political complexity. As a result of excavations at several domestic sites in the study area, we now have a reasonably good picture of this period's subsistence practices in the valley (Dillehay 2004, 2005). The typical site plan, consisting of dense ceramic and grinding stone scatters arranged around a base of a *rehuekuel* complex, begins at least by 1500 to 1600. Similar plans seem to emerge across much of the valley at this time, indicating perhaps the development of incipient dynastic patrilineages. By about 1700, there are more moderately large non-mound communities scattered throughout the valley.

The corporate life of people living in the Purén and Lumaco Valley during the early Spanish Contact period also was different from any predecessor in the valley and represents the most extreme development of institutionalized architecture and associated corporate ceremonialism ever realized in the area. Certainly, ancestor worship and funerary practices seem to have been anchored at many sites around which monumental mound and earthwork complexes developed. But whether it was mortuary practices or other important ceremonial functions that identified places as special, some and perhaps all of the sites that developed earthwork complexes fulfilled multiple corporate functions and probably, with time and the development of tradition, assumed expanded symbolic importance. Also notable during this period is an increase in the construction of agricultural raised fields and terraces and fortresses, which probably relate to greater population nucleation in the valley for defense purposes.

With regard to the nature of local intersite relations, perhaps the most important interpretation to be drawn from the relative number and distribution of different site types is the improbability that the valley was characterized by autonomous, mutually bellicose settlements in the contact period. First, if we assume that the widespread distribution of fortresses is an ample indication that warfare was a critical stress affecting the entire valley, the relatively small number of fortresses in the study area, as well as their strategic location, both suggest that groups of several surrounding habitation sites were focused on the same *rehuekuel* for defense. Second, the presence of nine to ten centrally located *rehuekuel* suggests that public and/or religious activities were also carried out on a supracommunity basis, perhaps having to do with aspects of the ritual and agricultural cycles and warfare. This does not imply that sporadic domestic disputes did not occur between some local groups, but it is unlikely that prolonged conflict happened between them.

Another primary objective of the archaeological study is to define religio-political boundaries. For that purpose, I am not primarily concerned with *rehuekuel* as central places per se but rather with what they can tell us about the way in which places were distributed among and produced by political alliances such as *ayllarehue* and *butanmapu*. Thus, I am focusing upon the multiple *rehuekuel* in the study area as the individual centers of small semiautonomous patrilineal chiefdoms in the 1300s to 1500s and collectively as a single large polity in the 1600s and 1700s. Further, the relationship between an individual *rehuekuel* and its complementary area appears to be one of mutual dependence. The *rehuekuel* probably supplied specialized services to the complementary region, the inhabitants of which in turn contributed labor and commodities needed to support the population of the *rehuekuel*. In accordance with my *rehuekuel* model of complementary religio-political areas, we can estimate that a chiefly patrilineage territory in late pre-Hispanic times was approximately 25 sq km (see Fig. 49) and associated with an estimated population of 1,500 to 3,000 people. During the period from 1600 to 1800, the larger patrilineage polity in the valley covered about 150 sq km and probably comprised of about 6,000 to 10,000 people.

A corollary of the above is that nearby populations that fell outside the complementary areas were not, strictly speaking, members of a *rehuekuel*. They may, however, have fallen within the sphere of political and/or religious influence of a single patrilineage chiefdom and later the larger polity and may, therefore, have been politically and economically subordinate. In such cases, they may usefully be regarded as dependent annexed neighboring territories of a chiefdom or the polity. The distinction between late pre-Hispanic chiefdoms and the later polity per se and their respective dependent territories is a critical one for purposes of estimating population size and analyzing recruitment and segmentation networks. The distinction is also critical to our understanding of imbricated or overlapping politico-religious boundaries. So far our knowledge of the frontier between the Purén and Lumaco polity and others (e.g., Tucapel, Arauco, Catiray) is limited to knowing the place where the their complementary regions may have intersected. Conceivably, however, independent territory administered by each of the respective patrilineages (and probably their associated *rehuekuel*) extended out in space beyond the immediate intersecting points of any of them. Less is known about the organization of these patrilineages within *ayllarehue* and *butanmapu* networks and the overall polity structure of the Araucanians in the seventeenth to nineteenth centuries. Additional ethnohistorical and archaeological information is needed, if we wish understand these relations.

Summary and Discussion

The purpose of this part of the chapter has been to present a synopsis of the preliminary archaeological findings in the study area. It can be determined independently from the archaeological record and from the ethnohistorical and ethnographical evidence that there is cultural continuity from at least 1300 to 1900 in the practice of building earth mounds in the study area. Given the few ethnographic accounts and the presently limited number of archaeologically known *kuel* and *rehuekuel*, it is safe to assume that this type of constructive burial practice was most likely reserved for selective patrilineage leaders and powerful multilineage alliances, respectively, like those in Purén, Lumaco, Tucapel, Arauco, and other places scattered throughout the Araucania. The *kuel* and *rehuekuel* complexes described here fit the expected pattern of religious and burial architecture for the interregional polity level of sociocultural development attained by the terminal pre-Hispanic and early Hispanic southern Araucanians. Although this study has focused on the Purén and Lumaco Valley, it was not alone in experiencing these developments as shown in Figure 7. We can hypothesize that the absence of archaeological *kuel* in some areas suggests that local societies never activated a necessary and sufficient level of social stratification and complexity to develop mound building, although they may have been participates in the polity-wide developments occurring south of the Bio Bio River after 1550. As an extension of this discussion, Chapters 7 and 8 present a more detailed historical trajectory of the political, social, and religious transformations underlying the creation and use of mounds.

Several functions of *kuel* also have been discussed, and some of the social, ideological, and ritual factors that condition their location, number, size, height, and postinternment maintenance have been identified. These functions differ according to different temporal and social contexts. For instance, the initial functions of the mound were twofold: to bury the corpse and to provide a social and ritual staging area (i.e., *awn* burial rites) to sustain the interpersonal relationships between ancestors, the deceased, and the affinal living, particularly as the latter assist the dead person's spirit in passing to the good *Wenumapu* world above. During the postinternment context this relationship persisted in the form of capping mounds with more "social soil" that served to further assist the spirit of the corpse by lifting it physically closer to the upper world of the ancestors (see Chapters 3–5). The postinternment period also entailed the use of the mound as a node of social, religious, and spatial reference in local community patterns. There is a clear historical association between *kuel, rehuekuel,* and *nguillatun* ceremonies in the area. Several presently used *nguillatun* and *rehuekuel* fields exhibit *kuel* inside their open plazas (e.g, *Hualonkokuel, Ñachekuel*) where *machi* still perform ritual services and the public congregation dances during ceremony.

Not understood well are the forces influencing the abandonment or the vertical and horizontal accretion of mound building. Some mounds were continuously reused and recapped for several decades or intermittently for several centuries, thus resulting in vertical accretion. They were eventually abandoned. Other mounds were abandoned much more rapidly, perhaps after 30 to 50 years use, and new ones were built next to them, thus forming a cluster or horizontal accretion of *kuel*. Although the data are presently incomplete, there is some evidence to suggest that the dynamics of vertical and horizontal accretion were determined by the rise and fall of dynastic lineages and by the influence of priestly shamans whose death also led to the abandonment of mound complexes (Dillehay 1990a, 1990b, 1995; also see Chapter 5).

At this point, it may be helpful to turn to a few questions and findings published from my previous anthropological research in the study area and their implications for understanding some of the issues raised above (see Dillehay 1985a, 1990b, 1990c, 1995, 1999, 2003). I present a slightly modified version of these implications for the purpose of this discussion.

1. How do we explain the historical association and spatio-temporal alignment of *kuel* and *rehuekuel* and the emergence of more complex *nguillatun* fields in Purén and Lumaco during the fifteenth to seventeenth centuries? Previous ethnographic reconstructions of kinship settlement patterns, historical records, and archaeological data suggested that the temporally and spatially successive construction of *kuel* and *rehuekuel* across the landscape corresponded to the firm and enduring establishment of a corporate, localized kinship network – the three consanguinally-related lineages (*trokinche*) hosting periodic ceremony and participating in rotating neighboring ceremonies in the valley over the past few centuries (see Chapter 4 and Dillehay 1995). Although the late pre-Hispanic and Hispanic people in the area experienced armed conflict, economic setbacks, lineage displacement, and settlement shifts, they seem not to have been disrupted as much as populations in other areas (Dillehay 2004, 2005). The stability of residentially fixed and consanguinally allied lineage groups over a period of several generations (as long as 100 to 200 years), which I previously called lineage "*sedentariness*," coupled with economic gains made by agricultural intensification, by strategically placed marriages in distant lands, and by exchange relations brought into being a more enduring social and economic development, integration, and expansion of local population and the emergent polity.

I also suggested that the development of a lineage sedentariness in the study area was commemorated (1) architecturally and symbolically by the construction of mounds over the tombs of dynastic lineage rulers and other probably important persons (i.e., shamans and wealthy elders); and (2) socially by participation of kinsmen in *kueltun* rites (i.e., soil-capping episodes) of spirit passage of important persons into the ancestral world. On one level, the successive burial of leaders and the construction of mounds across the landscape between approximately 1400 and 1700 signified a process of patrilineal gentrification of the land, a mode of asserting permanent claim to use rights and locking local agnatically and cognatically related kinsmen into perdurable relationships of ceremony and marriage exchange, all of which served to foster the growth and domination of local lineages and their allied *ayllarehue*. In this case, mounds and ceremonial sites, as architectural motifs of lineage assertion and linkage, served as perpetual sites for the organization of social and political authority and for interlineage negotiations over marriage exchange and other relations.

Prior research also revealed that kinship sedentariness provided the basis for jural order and continuity, and for the persistence of corporate lineage groups. I suggested that large-scale ceremonial congregation and *rehuekuel* mound building emerged when social units like the *trokinche*, as local expressions of corporate grouping and continuity, developed into conterminous and overlapping administrative and localized kinship units interacting with similar contiguous units. This is not a development that occurred rapidly, or one that probably emerged under the rule of a founding lineage leader, but one that evolved over successive generations of lineage rulers that began to form the multiple lineage *rehuekuel* and *ayllarehue* units between approximately 1550 and 1750. It probably occurred when a lineage (or a set of lineages interacting within a *trokinche* unit) was in a state of transition from a loosely structured, and possibly displaced or semisedentary kinship unit to a corporate, territorially based multilineage polity. I also suggested that this transition took place when individual ties of kinship, rules of residence generated by marriage alliances between contiguous communities, ceremonial congregation, and inheritance of land-use rights constituted a permanent social and jural precinct of interlineage cooperation regulated under the stewardship of localized dynastic lines of rulers whose placement in burial mounds at the time of death marks lineage rights to the land. Given the absence or light scatter of mounds in many areas in the Araucania, it seems that this transition and development did not occur often in terminal pre-Hispanic and early Hispanic Araucanian populations. This suggests that most patrilineages were probably short-lived (perhaps lasting only a few decades), and that localized dynastic polities in areas like Lumaco and Purén, where a dynasty might have endured for 100 to 200 years, emerged infrequently. In building on this prior work in recent years, I now see that lineages also expand as a result of the recruitment and adoption of fragmented groups and of the annexation of weaker neighbors (see Chapter 3 and 7).

2. What determined the number of mounds built in a particular area and who was buried in them (Dillehay 1992a–1992c, 1995)? Initially, I thought that mounds were built just for the interment of the founding rulers of lineages. However, that does not always seem to have been the case. Although the data are sketchy, some informants claim that second-, third-, and fourth-generation leaders of dynastic lineages also were buried in them. This information makes sense, because if all founding rulers were placed in mounds, we would find mounds in all lineage lands. Instead, we find only isolated occurrences and clusters of mounds in certain fertile lands in the Araucania where corporate, localized descent groups resided permanently. Informants and written records do not explain why leaders of later dynastic generations were placed in mounds. Although several conditions could explain this phenomenon, including social and economic factors not discussed here, it was my guess that it relates to principles of genealogical continuity, lineage sedentariness, and residential continuity as bases of common social and ritual action. Recently collected ethnographic and ethnohistorical data

(see Chapters 3, 7, 8) indicate that successful *toqui* war leaders and great orators who negotiated alliances between lineages were the individuals most often buried in mounds. Some of these individuals were both founding leaders of splintered lineages and later generation leaders.

3. What was the temporal relationship between permanent mounds, cemeteries, and habitation sites? I know from ethnographic and archaeological research that mounds and fields with their special activities were and still are in more continuous use than domestic sites, though because they are ritually cleaned from time to time, they tend to accumulate less debris. (Some trash and broken objects are discarded around mounds and fields but rarely inside them.) I stated previously that mounds were in use for several centuries, whereas the domestic sites generally are occupied for only a few generations (Dillehay 1995).

Based on archaeological data retrieved in recent years, I now know that this statement is not necessarily true. The *rehuekuel* complexes are flanked by cemetery and habitation sites that integrated sacred and secular domains. Radiocarbon dates obtained from the upper and lower strata of several sites suggest intermittent use for only a few decades or for only a century or more. As discussed above, several habitation sites were occupied for lengthy periods of time as far back as 6,500 years ago (Dillehay 2005; see Appendix 2). Others reveal rapid abandonment and reuse episodes suggesting occupational instability. And others indicate long-term stability, as suggested by thick and extensive deposits, features, and house remains. Stability and instability seem to be related in late pre-Hispanic and early Hispanic times to settlement location in the valley near stable social groups and adjacent to rich agricultural lands.

4. Does the labor invested in the periodic reconstruction of the *nguillatun* ceremonial field and recapping of a *kuel* mound reflect more about the corporate roles of related kinship units than about those of individual leaders? The organization and administration of *nguillatun* ceremonies are periodically dispersed and rotated among the three leaders of a *trokinche* (three patrilineages sponsoring a ceremony) unit (see Chapter 3). What accounts for this arrangement is not well understood; however, I suspect that it relates to the way political power emerged through the need for recurrent alternatives to, and competitive succession of leadership, which eventually resulted in the accession and centralization of one ruler's power, as manifested in the case of the Purén and Lumaco *nguillatun* and *rehuekuel* platform mounds.

I also stated that standardized *nguillatun* ceremonial fields expanded by rotational spinning of sublineating groups, which established new settlements and fields in newly occupied and/or annexed areas (Dillehay 1992a–1992c, 1995). There is a resultant pattern of kin-related ceremonial fields with spatial patterns (e.g., designated family and lineage patterns and location of *rehuekuel*) similar to their home field but eventually with their own social and demographic history of descent, a pattern similar to the kinship relations inferred between *kuel* (see Chapter 5). While there is no formal political hierarchy among these fields, there is a social and religious one among the hierarchically ranked *machi* conducting ceremony in them. Most interesting, the spatial layout of both ceremonial fields and mounds across the landscape denotes the historic and demographic development and affiliation of local lineages and later of their place within the larger *ayllarehue* units.

5. Standardization of ceremonial fields and ritual ceremonies involves the creation and duplication of a set of exclusive residential rights and religious and social rules (i.e., *admapu*) that budding, sublineating, and annexed members follow. Standardization and compliance in the seating pattern of families and lineages in ceremonial fields and in the usage of pan-Araucanian beliefs and symbols are necessary for regional social and religious integration in the absence of a highly formalized centralized political authority. Standardization also ensures consistent recognition of established family and lineage identities (see Chapter 9).

Based on evidence gathered in Purén and Lumaco, is it plausible to suggest that the size of a mound is one method for measuring the rank of a deceased lineage ruler and, in turn, of his lineage? The size and number of mounds associated in a cluster seem to indicate the demographic continuity and historical integrity of a patrilineal kinship network in a particular area. I believe that lineage history and thus status differentiation are reflected in the number and size of the mounds – not so much resulting from the prestige and wealth of rulers but from the size of the kinship groups related to the dead leader buried inside (Dillehay 1995). That is, the size of the mound is a direct expression of the number of kinsmen and allies placing earth on it during the initial burial ceremony and subsequent soil-capping episodes. Thus, a powerful leader with fifteen wives, for instance, may have an extended family of several hundred individuals capping and recapping his mounded tomb over time. A stable dynastic patrilineage with successive rulers buried in mounds results in the creation and use of a *rehuekuel* ceremonial complex comprised of several mounds like those described earlier in the chapter.

Lastly, although this is not the place for a detailed discussion of the spacing principles of *kuel* mounds and *rehuekuel* plazas and how they compare with other mound-building cultures in the Americas, a brief commentary is necessary to relate them to other areas. Unfortunately, the neighboring mound-building cultures in central Chile and western Argentina have not been studied enough to compare their community and spatial structure with the Araucanian mounds. However, it appears that the Araucanian communities that emerged in the fourteenth to sixteenth centuries most resemble those of the Formative period in Mesoamerica and the Woodland period in the eastern United States whereby large households and public architecture were integrated. In Formative Mesoamerica, at the early sites of San José Mogote, Paso de la Amada, Cuello, and La Blanca, public architecture appears in the form of public spaces and mounds (e.g., Blake 1991; Hammond 1991). Although they are much like the Araucanian sites, they are not always arranged in a way which suggests formal structuring of space and the households do not always present clear evidence of social differentiation. The late pre-Hispanic Araucanian case is perhaps most similar to the Hopewellian and early Mississippian cases whereby there were few to no large nucleated villages but rather single household farmsteads consisting of one two houses with their associated features (e.g., Milner 2004). Unlike Hopewell the Araucanians did not accumulate moderate portions of wealthy material objects through long-distance trade, although they did later through marauding and raiding. In the sixteenth century, the Araucanian mounds become more integrated into more nucleated settlements whereby the mortuary, domestic, and ceremonial functions are spatially close and more planned.

Hundreds of early Mississippian and Fort Ancient mound sites are known throughout the eastern United States. Some are large complexes, often built around plazas, and associated with features like palisades and ditches. They were related by exchange and communication networks and also held similar beliefs and ritual practices that are expressed architecturally in a complex of traits called the Southeast Ceremonial Complex (e.g., King and Freer 1994). Further, variation in the scale of Mississippi mound building is an important criterion for determining social hierarchy and political order. Most archaeologists view mound volume related to the duration of use or size of the labor force. As discussed previously (Dillehay 1995 and above), the duration of use and the size of Araucanian mounds primarily depend on the longevity and stability of dynastic patrilineages and their association with a specific *rehuekuel* location and on the number of wives and extended family members of a deceased leader placing earth on his burial mound.

In other ways, the settlement patterns described for the Mississippi culture fit more closely with the Araucanian model. In most Mississippi polities, a settlement hierarchy can be seen. At the bottom are the farmsteads of one or two households. Many of these are clustered to form hamlets, although they remain dispersed rather than nucleated. Next are the central settlements, with one to two mounds, which are interpreted as the residential and ritual centers of the elite and local leaders. Lastly, there is the one large site with multiple mounds which are seen as the paramount chiefs for the region. Over time these developed and declined, each with a different chronology and pattern despite the common traits. Like the Araucanians settlement pattern numerous dispersed settlements of one to three households sometimes clustered in small hamlets and concentrated in the vicinity of large ceremonial centers (cf. Smith 1990).

In looking at local Araucanian community patterns, the basic layout of domestic sites consist of differently elevated and landscaped irregularly shaped rings of mortuary, habitation, and refuse disposal areas surrounding a *rehuekuel*. Isolated low earthen mounds and palisaded outer parameters are associated with some habitation sites, especially those in the vicinity of the *Huitranlebukuel*, *Maicoyakuel*, and *TrenTrenkuel* complexes. Variation in the internal organization of these complexes is related to several factors, including topographic setting, cultural preferences, and/or a complex's particular occupational history. The shift from households as the fundamental loci of activity and competition to the public ceremonial space occurred during the sixteenth century. Isolated *kuel* mounds once serving smaller kinship based groups were transformed to multiple lineage *rehuekuel* landscapes, which served as places to unite larger corporate groups, to establish and practice compatriotism, ethnicity, and nationalism, and to politically rally allied communities to resist the Spanish and other outsiders.

These relative limited comments will be extended with the developments traced in the following chapters.

ANALYTICAL PERSPECTIVES ON ARAUCANIAN MONUMENTALISM

Kuel, rehuekuel, and *nguillatun* fields have shaped the sacred landscape of the Araucanians, so it is appropriate to ask how they relate to history and identity. What do these mounds mean across the physical landscape? Where are they located? How are they spatially positioned to each other? How do they interrelate with special topographic and aesthetic features? How are they perceived as organic bodies that are affinally related like human society? How do local traditions of Araucanian monumentality fit into processes of social landscape development and into the utopic spatiality of Araucanian cosmology? How can we read them archaeologically?

I view the sacred geography of the Araucanians as a form of monumentalism, which I defined earlier as a symbolically interactive, topographically bounded, aesthetically effective, and meaningfully holistic landscape (Dillehay 1999). *Kuel* and *rehuekuel* are monuments defined by specific location, restricted distribution, relatively standardized sizes and forms, and a landscaped architectural complex. Along with sacred natural features (e.g., volcanoes, mountains, bodies of water) and with other historical localities, these monuments collectively form topographic pathways, which serve as the traditional routes used by people to move from one public ceremony to another in the valley. By definition, a topographic pathway specifies the differential nodality and directionality of historical social and ritual relations in the Purén and Lumaco Valley – the zigzag pattern of rotating *nguillatun* ceremonies held at *rehuekuel*. The term nodality refers to places on the landscape where social linkages occur between different patrilineages. Examples are the *rehuekuel* mound groups and the isolated *nguillatun* ceremonial fields, which merge two or more lineages into a single unified pathway and activity. These pathways and nodalities are illustrated in the distribution of mound groups, ceremonial fields, and connecting trails shown in Figure 72, which in the past

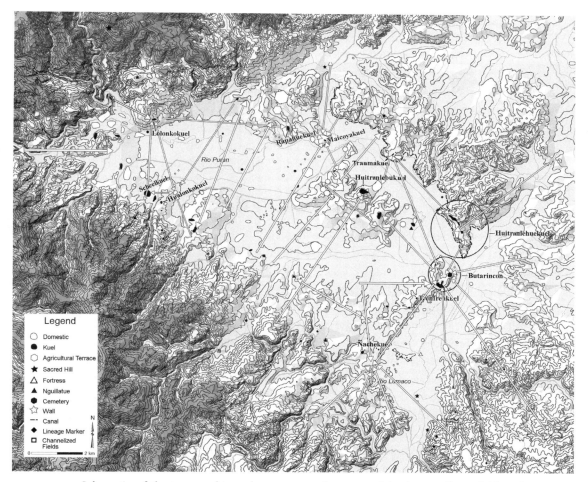

72. Schematic of the topographic pathways connecting co-participating *nguillatun* fields and *rehuekuel* and lineages across the valley today. Circles shown the places where the heaviest concentration of mounds are located.

and present organize networks of local and invited lineages in intracommunity and intercommunity contexts.

These nodalities also have special meaning. They represent points along the topographic pathways such as Butarincón to Huitranlebu and Lolonko to Rapahue that were used as lines of sighting and to sequence public ceremonies, congregate warriors to pray for victory in battle, establish sacred refuge areas for civilians in times of conflict, and defend certain strategic areas. These pathways were transformed symbolically through a system of interlocking public ceremonies, memorials, and historical events at these sacred places, which were operationally manageable only in small, circumscribed settings like Butarincón, Lolonko, Boyeco, Ipinco, and others. Most importantly, these pathways organized

Araucanian religious concepts and allied lineages with respect to one another. Pathways constituted (and in a few areas still constitute today) fluid frameworks or "landscapes in motion" (Sahlins 1985) that were continually created and enlarged by human events and components. Pathways and nodalities thus provide a spatial framework for social interaction and community organization in the valley. Particularly important is how this framework organizes, regulates, enhances, or delimits contact between lineage communities. This framework also represented a more restricted religio-political network for sharing economic production and military defense of the valley in the sixteenth to nineteenth centuries.

History, Landscape, and Meaning

To reiterate briefly several points developed in Chapter 4, we saw that within the Araucanian belief system deities and other important figures are points in a system of complementary oppositions that ramify downward from the most cosmic or pan-Araucanian level through regional gods and mythic ancestors to *kuel* and *rehuekuel* representing self-formed religious and political collectivities at descending levels of inclusiveness on the living *Nag Mapu* landscape. Ancestor mounds manifest the lower, more local branches of the oppositional tree, corresponding to localized patrilineages and alliances. Mounds mediate between people and the upper *Wenumapu* world; they are the progeny of the great deities *Ngenechen* and *Pillan* and reside in the openings of the earth, but they are also progenitors of important ancestors, *machi*, and apical members of local society. Through ritual mediation sacrifices to deities and earth, health and victory come out of the upper world. Increasingly elaborate public ritual was and is a major way in which dynastic patrilineages with gentrified pretensions appropriated symbols of hegemony to constitute their own social value to make themselves living *antumallen* (authentic) ancestors in their own domain. Worship at the burial mounds of leaders of these patrilineages ensured their ancestry and their valued place in history. Set in this context, *kuel* and *rehuekuel* were and are monumental objects standing on the landscape as remembered symbols of powerful ancestral traditions, dynastic lineage authority, priestly shamanistic knowledge, and one of the most successful and prolonged indigenous resistances to European invasion.

We also have learned that similar forms and spatial configurations of mounds and ceremonial fields in Purén-Lumaco and other valleys (e.g., Liucura, Boyeco) suggest a certain degree of social continuity, at least in regard to mound-building and politico-religious activity. Oral accounts from elderly informants, whose fathers and grandfathers fought in the Araucanian wars of the late nineteenth century and worshipped at mound oracles and other sacred places in these valleys, report a spatial and temporal pattern of circulatory or rotational participation at *rehuekuel* sites located along ceremonial topographic pathways specific to each valley (see Chapters 4, 5, and 8). Participation was first required at special ceremonies administered by high-ranking shamans and rulers. Lower-ranking events in individual communities along pathways were attended later. These are not pilgrimages designed to worship deities and other figures but commensal feasts (*sensu* Dietler 1996) and reunions focused on local and regional interlocking sets of lineages and social landscapes in motion.

As stated in Chapter 3, the general conditions accounting for the formation and distribution of mounds, fields, and pathways are related to changing social relations between different lineage groups and to a set of historically contingent factors – that is, long-term kinship sedimentation or permanency in a patrilineage homeland, residential contiguity of related lineages, protection of land use rights, profitable marriage alliance-making and trade-exchange affairs, and adoption of other groups. Increased social and political complexity was occasionally achieved by local leaders when they regulated the annual itinerary of multiple public events at special ceremonial sites (Dillehay 1990c). The corresponding spatial and architectural expression of these relations was locally interlocking sets of *nguillatun* ceremonies, occasionally *kueltun* mound-related rituals, and obligated pathways of ceremonial participation at all *nguillatun* fields, with the former related primarily to agricultural and marriage festivals and the latter two to funerary rights and interlineage solidarity, especially in times of war (see Chapter 4).

The monumentality of the Araucanian sacred landscape is thus more than a single large mound or group of structures. It is a concept and an activity that unites mounds and other features into a socially dynamic system of religious and political interaction. From this perspective, Araucanian monuments become memorials and historical places that are designed and intended to communicate lasting meaning. They also are endowed with the spirits of important ancestors that are of special consequences and meanings to past, present, and future generations. As such, monuments are therapeutic spaces that alleviate anxiety, suffering, disease, and fear, and they impart aesthetic value, home place, and ancestry to the cultural landscape (Dillehay 1990c, 1999), from which the Araucanians have derived inspiration. Analogously, they understand a group of monuments as a vertically and horizontally layered network of historical social relations between the living and their ancestors. This network is defined metaphorically by a proliferating kinship network of new son:daughter and brother:sister mounds through which history is made, recorded, and perpetuated across the countryside (Dillehay 1990c, 1992a–1992c, 1995; see Chapter 5).

Volcanoes, Mountains, Mounds, Nodalities, and Topographic Pathways

Mountain peaks and other high places are regarded as sacred sites since ancient times. The Araucanians view the *kuel* as minature mountains (*winkul*) and as volcanoes where the spirits of lineage ancestors reside. (The word *kuel* is derived

73. View of volcanoes in the Andean mountains to the east, from which *kuel* are said to take their form. Arrows show the volcano platform similar to the *ñichi* platform where *kuel* mounds are built. In Mapundungun, the volcano's mountain or platform is called *ñichi*.

from *kul*.) *Kuel* and their beveled *ñichi* platform are said to take their shape from the volcanoes of the Andean mountain chain to the east, which can be seen from the largest mounds in the valley (Fig. 73). Moreover, some mountain tops in the valley have been converted to earth shrines where important deities live and where some high-ranking shamans still perform annual rituals dedicated to important ancestors. (As discussed earlier, one such place is *Wenucolla* [the stairway to heaven], located just north of Purén [see Chapter 5].) Thus, volcanoes, mountains, and *kuel* are conceptual and structural equivalents in Araucanian society in that they serve as dwelling places for the ancestral gods (e.g., *Pillan*), their spirits, and the spirits of *machi*, and as symbols of significant political and religious gatherings. By duplicating or mimicking the volcanoes where the great ancestor spirit *Pillan* resides, the Araucanians are symbolically linking the qualities and powers of ancestors and *Pillan* and transferring them to the *kuel* and local communities. This is reinforced constantly by ceremony given to their belief systems and the creation story.

As described earlier, most mounds are situated along second-order streams where two or more first-order streams come together to form a drainage basin at the base of a low hill range. The mounds are built on spurs, crests, or promontories, usually at their highest point or at a unique angle that visually sets them apart and visibly contrasts them on the horizon in multiple directions in the same manner that mountains and volcanoes are against the horizon. Mounds also are cleared of vegetation so they can be seen from various angles and distances. The promontories are not always well defined but are often located between or near mountain passes or large isolated, sacred hills. Other mound groups are defined variously by streams, slopes, or other noticeable topographic features. In fact, the natural contour and location of certain hilly topographies in the valley attract mound-building and "place-worship," by providing historically significant or special settings, which influence the form, function, meaning, and placement of these aesthetically solacing sacred places (*sensu* Bradley 1998, 2000; Scarre 2002a, 2002b). This succession of spaces – mounds, crests, ridges, passes – imparts an alignment in plan that is a general feature throughout the Purén and Lumaco Valley. Formal rigidity, however, is secondary, as many examples indicate – in particular those mounds on *ñichi* platforms that are flanked by smaller mounds. No two *kuel* or *rehuekuel* complexes are the same and yet all evidence suggests a level of identity arrived at through subtleties that transcend the scope of mere formal repetition, and imply a strong sense of interpretative standardness, flexibility, and deliberate boundedness.

The creation of boundaries as physical features is mainly associated with needs of defense, territory, shelter, containment, and relational identity with and memory of *Pillan* and the volcanoes. Entrances and physical barriers, such as walls, crests, steep slopes, and other earthworks, mark differences in domains and thus restrict and control access between them. By physically dividing up and demarcating space, the Araucanians classify and control places and relationships more readily. That is, the landscape is ordered by highlighted topographic features and by paths that represent history, memory, and destiny.

The intermittent location of mounds and fields in the valley also suggests that boundaries were concerned with the practicalities of lineage territories, with demarcating ritual territories, and with sanctifying political alliances. In producing boundaries, the concern of the Araucanians has been to confirm the definition of small enclosed areas, the boundaries of which were already at least partly visible in the contours of the land, the courses of the streams, and other features. Enclosed or bounded areas not only were important for easement of coordination but served as models for organizing lineage territories. The location of existing lineages and the topography and routes of communication shared by them have determined the location of additional sacred hills and other features.

Abstract or visual boundaries, pathways, and radiating lines between special places also exist. These boundaries are imposed by visual sightings (see Rappoport 1985 for a similar case among the Cumbales of Colombia; see also Rappoport 1998). That is, the Araucanians conceptualize the boundaries of their lineage lands and sacred ancestral places by sight. Elder informants report that paths and large sections of forests were cut in the past to visually connect mountain top shrines and mounds in *rehuekuel* localities (see Chapters 3 and 4). When the Araucanians look at a distant mound, a pathway cut through the forest, or a line or territorial boundary, they establish a field of vision that defines the boundary of their territory and those of neighboring lineages and thus the places where they participate in rotating multilineage ceremonies. *Machi* claim that by standing on a mound and looking to other mounds up, down, and across the valley, a historic bondage and trust are established between particular places and between multilineage histories. Conspicuous *rehuekuel* with imposing views are essential to enunciating the importance of these feelings and connections and to be seen by and to gaze at other places. Mounds also show some axial alignments as well. Local shamans inform us that these alignments represent astronomical sight lines, kinship lines, and ritual lines (see Chapters 5 and 7). They say that one reason mounds are placed on crests and high points and cleared of vegetation is so they can be seen from various angles and distances. That is, physical positioning and visual sighting connect all horizon points back and forth across the valley to involve total intercommunity participation in ceremony. When lineages both physically and visually participate in ceremonies at different *nguillatun* fields today, they zigzag back and forth across the valley. This dual type of participation establishes solidarity and regularized rhythms of pilgrimages between communities (see Chapters 5, 7, 8).

Although little is presently known of the way the past Araucanians used celestial bodies and astronomical features in their cosmological system to align mounds and ceremonies, we know from texts and ethnographies that these phenomena played a role in the design, placement, scheduling, and visual sighting of places located along the horizons in the valley. For instance, *machi* informants report that the sacred mountain top of *Wenucolla* and its terraced structures are connected to the sun's rays and to the stars and moon. (This is the place where the "*usnan*" stone structure is centered on the hilltop and flanked by numerous ritual terraces and other small edifices. In Mapundungun, *usdnan*, *udan*, or *unan* mean to divide or to give primacy to something. These terms and their conceptual meanings are reminiscent of the Inka word *ushnu*, which was a shrine used in town plazas to serve as an *axis mundi* to intersect lines and as an authority between the Inka and the sun. *Ushnu* also connected the upper and lower worlds of Inka cosmology. See Chapter 3.) Mapuche informants claim that their harvest cycles are determined by changing sun and moon cycles and by what we call the zenith and anti-zenith of the sun. These patterns may be further evidence of Andean and Inka influence in Araucanian society. To elaborate briefly, Zuidema (1977; cf. Urton 1981, 1990) has established the importance of the zenith and anti-zenith of the sun in the ritual and agricultural practices of the Inka. These and other celestial features were mapped onto physical spaces (i.e., horizons, sacred landscapes, huacas) and into the state ritual calendar. The sight lines between celestial points and places on earth also were used by the Inka to structure time and space. As discussed in previous chapters and above, informants in Purén and Lumaco state that ritual sight lines or pathways (i.e, *kuifirupu*) across the valley are important for connecting special places along topographic and visual pathways and for recording lineage histories in space.

Although the sequence of monument building and all nodes of the valley-long pathway shown in Figure 72 are not fully known and understood, the large mound groups of the valley were built first at critical topographical points then the rest of the valley was filled in later, as suggested by diagnostic ceramics and radiocarbon dating of sites (Dillehay 2004, 2005, and forthcoming). These critical places are the entry points into the valley from the west near present-day Purén and at Lumaco from the north and south and near rich wetlands where agricultural lands occur. A linearly expansive network of high hills and low promontories scattered along the valley floor and the valley walls is the organizing principle of each pathway. Complementary opposition also is an essential feature as evidenced by several paired mound groups located across the valley from each other at *Hualonkokuel* and *Lolonkokuel*, *Rehueñichikuel* and *Huitranlehuekuel*, *Ñachekuel* and *Hueicokuel*, and *Maicoyakuel* and *Huitranlebukuel*. Physical prototypes for these opposing *rehuekuel* include riverbanks, especially where two hillsides or promontories closely face each other, and natural embodiments or opposing hills in narrow ravines and passes.

Opposition is also expressed in the *nguillatun* and other ceremonies. (As discussed in Chapter 4, the *nguillatun* field is defined by two opposing wings.) The *nguillatun* also is administered by two lineage leaders, with a third lineage hosting the event the next year with one of the two previous lineages. Complementary opposition between the wings of the field and the two leaders presupposes the perpetuity of the ceremony as a balanced whole. At another level, *nguillatun* fields and their connecting paths are combined to express the complementary relationship between local lineages in a rotating ceremonial network of interlocking communities, which in the historic past was administered by *toqui* war leaders defending their territories. Today in ceremony, the oppositional tension set up between a built mound on a *ñichi* and a mental map derived from participation in real physical or distant visual ritual is the key to the homogenization of the setting, by asserting a continuum of spatiality that transgresses the distinction between architectural space, historical imaginary, and the cosmological planes of the Araucanian world. The imaginary never relinquishes its connection with the openness and boundedness of the ceremonial space. In this sense, the settings of *rehuekuel* are never merely isolated physical (or archaeological) sites; rather, they are settings of immense aesthetic richness, fueling feelings of deep history and spirituality, memory, and substantiating a participant's situatedness in the larger scheme of things, and thus in the political and, above all, cosmic order of deities, ancestors, and the living.

Bounded and Holistic Monumentalism

The initial step of mound building probably was the transformation of natural hills (*winkul*) as natural "objective" phenomena into *kuel* as sociocultural "subjective" phenomena, which were then viewed from the perspective of the cultural definition – that is, sacred places (see Trigger 1990) as an aspect of a public culture. Hills and promontories located at strategic nodes of communication and special places (such as historic battlegrounds, large rock outcrops) produced the topographical pattern of sacred places. Located at these sacred places are the *rehuekuel* ceremonial fields and *kuel* burial mounds. Taken together, these places in the natural environment are symbols that connect the Araucanians to their creation, to their ancestors (and thus history), and to the future. As such, the enclosed form and valley-long spatial configuration of mountain shrines, mounds, ceremonial fields, lineage boundaries, and historical places and the connecting trails between them constitute the local pathways for lineage religious and social organization. I characterize this entire system as *bounded monumentalism*.

In essence, this system reifies the socially transformed natural environment of the valley. Geertz (1983:58) calls these reified elements "experience-near concepts," by which he means "that ideas and the realities they inform are naturally and indissolubly bound up together." Viewed from this perspective, the Araucanian monuments represent experience and knowledge; that is, they are locational epistomologies about local history and the world in general. These epistomologies are juxtaposed by the participation of each lineage in multiple *nguillatun*, *kueltun*, and other ceremonies that are held throughout the year at various localities along the topographic pathways in the valley (see Chapter 4). These epistemologies give meaning, reference, order, and security to life.

Mounds and fields also are given a life of their own by these ceremonies. That is, these monuments become both physical beings and kinsmen, affiliated with but also bounded and set off from the human population and from the natural environment by the pathway of special places to which they belong and by a contained subset of local elements (i.e, ancestral history, beliefs). Each mound in a *rehuekuel* projects an in-out orientation onto other mounds, onto other physical objects, such as hills and promontories, and onto living human communities that are bounded by the valley topography. Thus, mounds are viewed as containers with opposing inside and outside dimensions. The bounded natural world imposes this orientation on the Araucanians, and they in turn impose it on the mounds. The mounds also impose a boundary – marking off a lineage territory and a vertical territory consisting of the mounds and sacred topographic features (e.g., mountains, streams). In short, whether they exist naturally or socially, boundaries appear everywhere, so that they have an inside and an outer bounding surface – whether a clearing in the forest, a modified hilltop, a mound, a wall, or an abstract line or plane formed by sightings to and across these places. But, on the other hand, these boundaries are highly permutable, allowing cross-valley participation in ceremonies and fluidity in kin relations.

It is important to know that individual lineages in the valley do not have to understand the specific interconnections between all parts of this bounded network in order to have a complete and comprehensive understanding. Rather, they practice *holistic monumentalism*: whereby the patrilineal *rehuekuel* locations (i.e, *Huitranlehuekuel, Maicoyakuel*), for instance, which have played an important role in the history of a dominant lineage, is equivalent and historically related to all mound groups or networks in the valley. Thus, participation in one or more ceremonies at these groups provides a valley-long experience (see Chapter 5 for informants' discussions of intervalley ceremonies). This type of network functions best in an enclosed geographic setting, where ease of communication and travel exists and where boundaries are created and reinforced by regular use, ritual confirmation, and visual sighting. Essential to the operation of this system is intersite visibility, aesthetic effectiveness, social connectivity, and standardization of form and function among *nguillatun* and other sacred places.

Analytical Classification of Araucanian Monuments

Brief consideration of the monuments by functional types enables additional locational and organizational characteristics to be recognized, after which the interrelationships between the various mounds are considered. Based on interviews with *machi* and other informants, on the ethnohistorical record, and on variation in the archaeological content and structure of mounds, I define three types of *kuel*: *generational, orientational*, and *relational* or *ontological*. None of these types is mutually exclusive but represent primary single functions.

Kuifikuel, or ancient mounds, are generational mounds: they are related to temporality and history. There are three modes of temporality: past, present, and future. These are mounds in which the relationship between space and local lineages is oriented exclusively toward the past, toward history. After their construction and use, these mounds are abandoned and unused, and contain the burial remains of important leaders. Since these mounds belong to past experiences, they exist only as memorials or *kuifilkuel*, as archaeological or historic sites scattered across the landscape and suspended in memory (Dillehay 1990c). Other mounds, many of which were built in the last one hundred years and are still used today, are different. They have "the being" of present experiences. The being of these *kuel* is something that is experienced by the local population if certain local conditions are met. These conditions are physical maintenance of the mound and periodic ritual (*kueltun* and *llaimatun*, such as occurred at *Hualonkokuel*; see Chapter 5) at the mound by a shaman whose spirit resides there. Stories are usually told about these mounds, such as the feats of famous *toqui* warlords buried in them. (Today, informants point out the burial mounds of warlords such as Colo Colo, Colípi, Lientur, Pelentaro, and Anganamón [see Chapter 7]). Finally, there are mounds that bring some future reference into relation with a local lineage. As such, these mounds always point to the future. Ceremony at these mounds seeks good weather, successful crops, victory in warfare, or today political dealings and rewarding marriage alliances. Recently built mounds such as Ñachekuel and *Pichikuel* fall into this category. Although they are of historical or contemporary origin, their permanent institutionalization is not yet ensured. This last type is usually associated with currently used *nguillatun* fields. Thus, although all mounds are monuments, each has a temporal or generational context in the past, present, or future. Even though old mounds are abandoned, they are still formally visited by shamans (like the case of *Hualonkokuel*) and, along with recent mounds, constitute parts of the culturally coded pathway of social relations, historical events, and geographical places in the valley. Ancient paths connecting different lineage lands in the valley pass over or near almost all mounds, which ensures that all mounds, old and new, are seen and remembered by all members of the living community.

There also are *orientational* mounds that provide spatial orientation and clear discretion and enclosure. This way of viewing physical phenomena is employed by the Araucanians to satisfy certain purposes: locating mountains, meeting at stream confluences, and organizing the valley-long ceremonial pathways or networks. As discussed above, the Araucanians impose artificial boundaries that make mounds, ceremonial fields, and sacred places and their physical settings discrete just as their lineages are: entities bounded by a place, by a kinship system, by radiating lines that connect spatially separated places, and by history or experience. Each mound also has its own life history on the landscape, as we have seen in the case of *Hualonkokuel*. When *kuel* and *nguillatun* fields "die" (meaning the *machi* died who had her *fileu pullu* in the mound and/or the patrilineage that performed ritual at the field moved or lost its land, respectively), they are abandoned and mark the landscape as a memorial or historic trust site that continues to give orientation to special geographic places, to connective radiating lines of sight, and to define boundaries. All mounds located in *rehuekuel* are orientational *kuel*, as well as those that are conspicuously situated on the crest of highly visible ridges that are constantly seen or traversed by locals.

Just as the basic experiences of Araucanian spatial orientation have given rise to orientational monuments, so their experiences with each other and with topographic features have provided the basis for a wide variety of *ontological* or *relational* mounds; that is, *kuel*, fields, and pathways that record the particular events, activities, and ideas of past shamans and rulers. They are relational mounds in the sense that can be connected visually, ritually, socially, and historically with other *kuel*, domestic sites, cemeteries, structures, or natural features. Stories and myths are told by *weupin* and *machi* about certain mounds and their relation to mountain deities, important ancestors, and historical events. *TrenTrenkuel* best fits this category. Expert knowledge of ancient mounds, fields, and pathways is an essential part of the responsibility of the shaman, *weupin*, and leader. Great power can be harnessed by a wise *machi* who, upon learning, can narrate a story accounting for some earlier mound, for instance, which has established itself as a node along a boundary or pathway. Another example is *kuel* affiliated with the creative tales of the Araucanians. While each mound emphasizes particular aspects of the creation story, together they incorporate the principal features of the act of creation, as was the case with *Tren Trenkuel* and *Kai Kaikuel* in the creation story presented in Chapter 4. The ontological mounds are *Hualonkokuel, Tren Trenkuel, Lolonkokuel, Rehueñichikuel, Ñachekuel, Pichikuel,* and many others. These are all actively used mounds or places where stories are continuously told about them.

As noted above, these three types of monuments are not mutually exclusive. For instance, an old mound may be a historical marker, serve as an orientational feature, and have special symbolic meaning. Other mounds and features may be old or new and have little social significance. Most significantly, these analytical types of monuments represent a coherent structuring of the historical experiences of local Araucanian communities. Although the types are points along a historical continuum, they also form together in a coherent fashion to link, people, places, and histories.

Finally, what was the integrative effectiveness and success of this bounded, holistic system in the Purén and Lumaco Valley? We know from historical records that this valley successfully integrated because this was the center of strongest resistance to the Spanish from the early sixteenth century through the late nineteenth century. The leaders of the valley accomplished order and maturity out of a volatile historical period. There are several reasons why the success of integration was greater in this area. In the first place, the economic base of the valley with rich agricultural lands likely resulted in stronger and tighter interdependence of lineage sectors. Second, land was occupied continuously and the genealogical power was less challenged. Scattered communities were connected by overlapping ties of alliance and hostility. The valley population became a total polity in the early seventeenth century only when these linkages were organized by the unifying forces of public ceremony and the valley-long topographic pathway of public monuments and ceremonies. It also seems that the complementarity of the nature of public ceremonial life and the boundedness of the valley-long religious and political network worked at higher levels of integration to fend off the Spanish and to build successful military alliances with neighboring groups, especially those to the north in Arauco and to the south in the Imperial and Cautín valleys (Inostraza 1991). Yet, all of this points once again to the tactical and strategic organization of the Purén and Lumaco patrilineages *vis-à-vis* their religious and political structure.

DISCUSSION

At a specific level of historical generality, Araucanian monumentalism involved (1) instances in which the nature of the local land forms themselves attracted *kuel* and *rehuekuel* monuments by providing meaningful or dramatic locations and a series of ideas that played some part in influencing the form of those monuments – that is, the monumental form of *ñichi* platforms and of *kuel* suggested itself through the natural appearance of distant volcanoes on the horizon and the symbolic meaning of these natural features to the Araucanians; (2) the total social and natural system of enclosed areas – small administratively manageable valleys (or pockets and tightly constricted river confluences in valleys) and how the valleys acted as bounded socio-politico-religious systems, which, for our purposes, were most significantly characterized by tight mound clustering at *rehuekuel*; (3) the interplay of a variety of spatial forms structured in terms of discrete geographical pathways and nodal places connected by circulatory participation in ceremony and by participatory visual sightings; and (4) the periodic channeling of social, political, and ritual activity through these pathways and places. The social landscape of the Araucanians was articulated to engage monuments and pathways in channeling social activity and in directing the course of politico-religious change in the face of exogenous factors such as warfare and sudden demographic shifts in the population. To me, all of this implies monumentalism as a form of *bounded holism* and *symbolic interactionalism* and as a graded series of constricted social relations and physical settings. Boundaries were physical, social, historical, aesthetic, and cultural, and they played out in visual, aesthetic, auditory, and mental terms. The sacred landscape was a kaleidoscope of intentions, claims, and structurations for a utopic future.

The physical definition of Araucanian monuments has survived for a considerable period. As seen in the Purén-Lumaco area, the presence of mounds, ceremonial fields, and pathways has maintained the spirit, if not the character, of these places in the historic and present-day cultural landscape. Although the use of mounds and fields for the definition of sacred areas in the landscape would appear only to have been temporary compared with the permanency of mountain deities, for instance, in the case of those bounded areas where substantial mound groups can be found, it is a lasting value. These groups code historical information, political transformation, and lineage integrity. Monuments also served as historical signs of stages of institutionalized development. The fact that boundaries and pathways have formed overlying *rehuekuel* complexes, each complex mirroring and thereby reinforcing other complexes, might lead to the conclusion that this network is essentially static. But monuments have coded the valley-long social process in terms of episodic kinship sedimentation, whereby lineages established residential permanency in a specific terrain, which resulted in greater social, economic, and religious organization (Dillehay 1990c). This process has been suggested for both the *rehuekuel* complexes and the *nguillatun* ceremonial fields. Each is seen as a religious and political unit in space, and each is duplicated in space (Dillehay 1990a). The reduplication or redundancy of sets of mounds within mound complexes also serves as a sign of historical depth, the absence of population displacement in the valley, and layered reinforcement and cultural development. All of this points to a socially engineered utopic landscape that was effectively designed to remember and retrieve powerful ancestral knowledge and thereby to influence the future.

In turning to a different matter, it is apparent by now that it may be misleading to artificially isolate a single large mound or a group of mounds for the purpose of orderly archaeological site definition and analysis. (It is for this reason that I ended this chapter on archeological data with an analytical discussion of their social and symbolic landscape meaning.) As long as abstract awareness of the structure and holistic connectedness of the monuments in the Purén and Lumaco Valley is realized (and archaeological and historical contemporaneity can be established), the nodalities and pathways could be treated independently, but when social processes are under consideration, complex historical relations and effects become the rule rather than the exceptions. These relations produce and unite the ceremonial sites that comprise the entire topographic pathway in the bounded setting. What makes this system work is annual participation by local lineages in multiple political and religious events throughout the valley. Once again, such participation is possible only in a manageable enclosed area where communication and travel are facilitated and where effective aesthetic vision unites and solaces dispersed communities.

PART TWO
ANALYSIS AND INTERPRETATION

SEVEN:

CONTACT, FRAGMENTATION, AND

RECRUITMENT AND THE *REHUEKUEL*

Contact with the Spanish in the middle 1500s produced a domino effect along the Bio Bio frontier that altered social formations in several ways, creating bounded areas, shifting exchange patterns, formalizing informal and contested indigenous hierarchies, promoting local leaders to paramount warlords, and forming a regional polity of different types of rulers. In this chapter, I am interested in how Araucanian society responded to contact, how it was organized politically, and how it was represented spatially and materially by the mounded landscapes in the Purén and Lumaco Valley, an early center of contact with and resistance to the Spanish.

I stated in Chapters 1 and 3 that the Araucanian case represents an emergent confederated regional polity in which central authority, often of a military nature, was paired with a religious power structure that was diffused, segmentary, hierarchical, and heterarchical (this latter term is nothing more than many various kinds of hierarchies), as well as groups in which considerable complexity was achieved through horizontal differentiation, consensus building, and incorporation of fragmented groups. The distribution of power among several corporate entities (i.e., patrilineages, ceremonial groups, military alliances) was a tactical strategy that successfully resisted the invasion by the Spanish, the Chileans, and, perhaps earlier, the Inka for more than 350 years. This case also provides clear historically documented examples of secular and sacred agents practicing negotiations between different groups in times of intermittent warfare and peace to intentionally restructure the society and to gain individual power.

More to the point, the outbreak of prolonged and low-intensity warfare with the Spanish created frontier places of heightened possibilities produced by population dislocations and disjunctures in many areas and by increased social complexity in others. Certain Araucanian leaders, acting as lineage agents in response to the imperatives of increased conflict, imposed a new strategic or tactical organization that led to a competitive leadership, a drawing of boundaries of inclusion and opposition among lineage communities, upon the nuances and adjustments of social life in times of duress. Written records from the sixteenth to eighteenth centuries suggest that some powerful rulers built alliances and organized a culture of recruitment of defeated and fragmented lineages through ceremonial feasting and through annexation of neighboring lineage lands that became the instruments and consequences of this situation and that produced the formal landscaped monumentality under study here. It was alliance-building and especially the recruitment of distressed lineages that created new spaces for the exercise of agency and actions by various types of leaders and by common lineage members, which was politically negotiated and ritually enacted in places like *rehuekuel* to bring about greater social cohesion. I suggest that it also was the context within which new and different demands were placed on members of individual lineages and of the wider society to act as new compatriots of a restructured movement focused on polity-building, appropriation of selected symbols and organizations (some of which were Inka and Spanish) to enhance the tactical organization of the polity and to define the parameters of participatory compatriotism through public ritual and peer-pressure to conform to traditional *admapu* (ancestral) ways in order to become a contributing member of the new order. New forms created a more complex framework of political authority that significantly restructured the institutionalized social, economic, religious, and demographic organizations of the Araucanians. There also were important variations in Araucanian aggressiveness among lineages, with some lineages more assertive and "nationalistic" than others. Others were weak and submissive to the Spanish or to more powerful indigenous leaders, such as Pelantaro, Anganamón, Liempichu, Lientur, and Butapichón in the study area (see Bengoa 2003; Guevara 1925; Villalobos et al. 1989; Zapater 1973, 1974, 1978, 1992). These variations were in many instances a function of differences in the political culture of local lineages and multilineage organizations (i.e., *ayllarehue*) during the late pre-Hispanic and early Contact periods.

During these periods, the traditional political organization of the Araucanians was the replication of local-level, lineage-based politics at ever-higher levels of political (i.e., *ayllarehue* and *butanmapu*) and religious (i.e., *rehuekuel, nguillatun*) incorporation. The local *lov* community of several extended patrilineal families and the supralocal *rehue* (*regua*) unit of multiple *lov* were at the core of the economy, politics, and religion. Differences between experience and power within these lineages enabled certain men to claim wartime leadership roles (*toqui, ülmen*); they regulated conflict within the group and organized it for defense or aggression against enemies. Growth of larger units such as *ayllarehue* in the late sixteenth century was an attempt by ambitious leaders taking advantage of the changed circumstances to combine ever-greater numbers of groups under their control and to defend their territory. This process eventually resulted in the creation of a broader territorial system in the early seventeenth century – the *butanmapu* territories – but the power of *toqui* and *ülmen* war leaders was largely personal and based on their personal networks and on their ability to gain it by persuasion from the collective and especially to favorably negotiate the organizational and locational settings (*sensu* Wolf 1999) of public ceremonial places such as *rehuekuel*. Set in this context, ritual specialists (e.g., *machi, boquivoye, hechicero*) also became powerful figures with both independent and dependent powers (see later discussion). In effect, the assumption of the *ayllarehue* and *butanmapu* and their leaders was that they acted as the agents of an ethnic- and nation-building diffused authoritarian rule, which was the root of the tactical and strategical modes of organization of Araucanian power and resistance.

In addition to regulating traditional institutions to legitimize their authority, leaders reorganized a supra-local military system to defend their territories. As discussed in Chapters 3 and 6, I believe that this system was closely associated with the ritualized topographic pathways between *rehuekuel* complexes in select enclosed valleys like Purén–Lumaco where close and regular contact occurred between lineage communities, where lineage territories were sustained by regular ritual feasts, and where the local terrain facilitated defense of the homeland. Although the populations occupying these valleys were never highly centralized politically and economically, they did achieve a supra-local level of military solidarity and religious organization during the sixteenth and seventeenth centuries that constituted the polity-like structure mentioned as an "*estado*" by Ercilla ([1569] 1982) and others. This newly formed structure does not neatly fit popular definitions of chiefs and states that tend to be space centered with near absolute sovereignty and spatial overlap between their political, social, economic, and religious domains (see Chapters 1 and 3). Rather, they were multicentered, fragmented, segmentary, and unevenly developed, although all of them had similar utopic notions of a pan-Araucanian organization and purpose designed for survivability and future advances.

To understand the intricacies of these relations and organizations and how they relate to sculpted places like *kuel* and *rehuekuel*, it is necessary to review the indigenous political structure and power of the Araucanian prior to the Spanish Contact period and how this structure changed from 1500 to 1700. Based on this discussion, I will turn to the relationship between leadership roles and other institutional organizations and then to the spatiality of these organizations.

INDIGENOUS POLITICAL AND RELIGIOUS STRUCTURES: LEADERS AND VENUES

Although the early written records are scarce, we can surmise from the early chroniclers that the fundamental social structure of the proto-Hispanic and early Hispanic Araucanians was based on large and mostly patrilineal groups with patrilocal residence (cf. Melville 1976). Patrilineages comprising several extended families were the main socioeconomic and ritual units. Multiple lineage organizations were *ayllarehue*. Land was held communally by the lineage.

Depending upon place and circumstance, the Araucanians had a diffused, heter-archical, hierarchical, and horizontally differentiated corporate power structure shared by different but complementary leaders (Dillehay 1990a–1990c, 1995; see subsequent section for definition and discussion of power). The political struc-ture within lineages was hierarchical and within multiple lineage entities (e.g., *ayllarehue*) was heterarchical with principal leaders situationally drawn (e.g., for administration of *cahuin* political meetings, large feasts, warfare) from different lineages.

Generally speaking, early secular leaders were called *reche, ülmen,* and *gentyoke* (see Chapter 3; Boccara 1999); early ritual leaders were known as *hechicero* (an adopted Spanish word), *boquivoye,* and *machi.* In later periods, the secular leaders came to be recognized as *toqui, ülmen, weupin,* and *lonko* and the ritual ones as *machi* and occasionally *nguillatufe,* respectively, as described for some titles below by the social historian Boccara (1999:449; see Chapters 3 and 4).

> El "gran hombre" reche que se distinguía por sus cualidades guer-reras y su habilidad oratoria es progresivamente remplazado por un ülmen que se lanza en una nueva competición económica y en hábiles negociaciones políticas. El cacique mapuche sigue sin ejercer un poder coercitivo, pero concentra desde ahora todas las funciones de organi-zación de la sociedad que antes competían a personas distintas (genvoye, gentoyui, boquivoye). (Boccara 1999:449)

> The *reche* "big man" who was distinguished as a warrior and for his skill in oratory was gradually replaced by the *ülmen,* who threw himself into a new economic competition and skilled political negotiation. The Mapuche cacique continued without coercive powers, but from this time he concentrated in himself all the organizational functions of the society which formerly were exercised by different individuals (*genvoye, gentoyui, boquivoye*). (Boccara 1999:449)

Toqui, ülmen, and *lonko* were renowned for their military prowess, for their power of persuasion, and for their ability to inspire a following. The *weupin* were also individuals of authority; their power was based on their oratory skills and on their narration of history and customs as revealed through genealogical accounts of past achievers and heroes at public ceremonial events. The *boquivoye, hechicero,* and *machi* (and later the *nguillatufe*) also held important positions because of their ceremonial and medicinal services and their special relationships with ancestors and deities in public ritual. The similarities and differences between these ritual specialists are not well understood, but it is likely that they both had different and overlapping roles with different names (see Chapters 3 and 4). Social prestige was allotted to these different authorities for different reasons: to the *genvoye, reche, ülmen, toqui,* and *lonko* for their leadership qualities; to *weupin* for their knowledge of history; and to *hechicero, boquivoye,* and *machi* for their ethereal contacts, esoteric knowledge, and healing powers. Although distinct in practice and purpose, these categories also shared power and legitimized and complemented each other's authority during public gatherings. Diffused but complementary corporate leadership thus was the most efficient and advantageous model of political organization. All of these categories of authority still function in Mapuche society today, although the terms *toqui, reche, boquivoye,* and *hechicero* are no longer used. *Ülmen* have become elderly authorities that accumulate wealth in animals and land. *Weupin* still serve as orators and historians. *Machi* and occasionally *nguillatufe* are the sacred leaders.

Each of these different categories of authority was associated with different domains of influence and often with distinct but overlapping spaces where their powers were exercised. For instance, *toqui* and *ülmen* ruled in matters of warfare and political decision-making at *parlamentos, cahuin,* and public feasts. *Hechicero, boquivoye,* and *machi* oversaw healing and other rituals in ceremonial fields. I suspect that their past domains and spaces operated in ways similar to those today. A present-day example of the configuration of these spaces is shown in Stuchlik's map of heterarchical intercommunity *nguillatun* ceremonies in which three kin-related lineages (*trokinche*) host the ceremonial event and invite others to participate. (See the rotational shifts in interlineage participation in *nguillatun* ceremonies in Figure 74; see Stuchlik 1976:150–156.) Today, each lineage is headed by a *lonko* (a term that eventually replaced *ülmen* to represent community leaders) and invites different *machi* to administer the event in their community, with the result being different admixtures of secular and sacred leaders rotating and sharing places of authority as different sets of communities interact as hosts and guests. The ranked or unranked position of each community as a host or an invited participant, respectively, changes in a number of different ways during different ceremonial cycles, with each host and guest lineage constantly realigning its ritual and other alliances with different sets of local and nonlocal communities (see Chapter 4 for discussion of host and guest lineages in ceremony). Revealed in the rotational arrows in Figure 74 is an amoeba-like spread of these different but overlapping concentric spaces comprised of differentially ranked host and guest ceremonial groupings, which represent different communities whose members participate in different ceremonies and whose secular and sacred leaders serve in different authority categories that annually interact as heterarchically ranked units depending on the location and multilineage grouping of each ceremony. Over a period of several years all participate communities act as equals as they invariably occupy and reoccupy ranked host and unranked guest roles. There also may be sequential or overlapping activities that situationally correspond with different secular and sacred authorities in each concentric space (e.g., *machi, lonko, weupin*), although only one authority rules at any one time in any one space. For instance, a

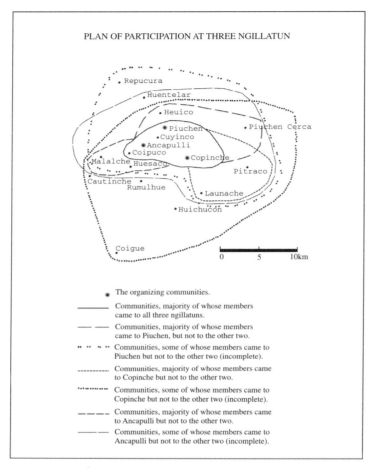

PLAN OF PARTICIPATION AT THREE NGILLATUN

- Repucura
- Huentelar
- Heuico
- Piuchen · Piuchen Cerca
- Cuyinco
- Ancapulli
- Coipuco
- Copinche
- Malalche Huesaco
- Pitraco
- Cautinche
- Rumulhue
- Launache
- Huichucón
- Coigue

0   5   10km

- The organizing communities.

————— Communities, majority of whose members
came to all three ngillatuns.

— — — Communities, majority of whose members
came to Piuchen, but not to the other two.

·· ·· ~ ·· Communities, some of whose members came to
Piuchen but not to the other two (incomplete).

·········· Communities, majority of whose members came
to Copinche but not to the other two.

···●··●··· Communities, some of whose members came to
Copinche but not to the other two (incomplete).

— — — — Communities, majority of whose members came
to Ancapulli but not to the other two.

——— — Communities, some of whose members came to
Ancapulli but not to the other two (incomplete).

74. Plan of participation at three *nguillatun* fields near Temuco (after Stuchlik 1976:160). Note the distinct and overlapping spaces of different community activities. Piuchen, Copinche, and Ancapulli represent multilineage *trokinche* units.

lonko from Copinche administering the *nguillatun* may co-host the event with *lonko* leaders from Anacapulli and Piuchen and the *machi* may be from an outside area such as Coigue. When the event shifts the next year to Repucura, for example, the set of leaders changes entirely according to new co-hosts and participants, but the same *machi* may be invited to administer the ritual aspects of ceremony and the prior ranked *lonko* may be a guest leader. In short, each *nguillatun* ceremony annually rotates through different sets of host and guest lineages and with each lineage cyclically occupying different roles with different lineages each time. This rotational spin of hosts and guests leaders and communities is greatly facilitated by standardized ritual codes and beliefs, material and spatial symbols, and seating spaces of families and lineages in *nguillatun* fields (see Chapter 4) and, above all, by the spatial uniformity and design of the U-shaped fields in different localities.

Schematic Representation of Reservations in a Ritual Congress

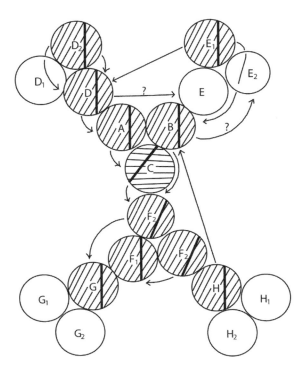

Blank areas indicate absence of reservations. Ritual
and marriage ties of peripheral units jump such areas.

75. Schematic representation of intermarrying lineages and ritual congregations in the 1950s (after Faron 1964:110).

Faron also has examined the pattern of cyclical rotation among lineage communities in what he calls a "Ritual Congress," which reveals intergroup connections and the spatial flow of ceremonial participation, according to the local settlement pattern and the way it is distributed topographically across the landscape (Fig. 75; after Faron 1964). This type of patterning produces solidarity among groups and also requires uniformity in the design and meaning of *nguillatun* fields. In linear river valleys like Purén and Lumaco, past patterns of rotational spin moved in a zigzag clockwise direction from Butarincón to Hueico to San Genaro to Huitranlehue to Trauma and back to Butarincón (see Fig. 72 in Chapter 6). As described above, also moving from ceremony to ceremony among these communities is the authority of each set of *lonko* and *machi* leaders whose secular and sacred powers, respectively, shift heterarchically from ranked to unranked ones as their status changes from organizing hosts to invited guests (see comments of informants in Chapter 5).

This is not to say that more permanent hierarchies did not exist among authorities in the sixteenth and seventeenth centuries, because paramount *toqui* and *ülmen* held considerable enduring power over other secular leaders and probably over *hechicero, boquiboye,* and *machi* as well. As revealed in passages discussed in the next section referring to the power of several Purén leaders (i.e., Pelantaro, Anganamón, Liempichu), centralized control by paramount leaders was both periodically and permanently exercised over other authorities in moments of intense conflicts. Political organization was thus hierarchical but in the service of a situationally ranked or heterarchical political, social, and religious system that was more segregated than integrated even when different leaders shared the ceremonial and political space.

Araucanian power thus refers to different kinds of influences and to different places and settings of power – for example, the power of a *machi* in the *rehuekuel* field, the power of the *toqui* war leader on the battlefield, the power of the *ülmen* and *lonko* in the local residential community, and the power of the *kuel* activated by ritual to cause damage or bring good luck and fortune. However, *toqui* were not merely persons who could enforce their will on their people. They also were the axis of defense against outsiders, the symbol of intergroup unity and exclusiveness, and the embodiment of essential Araucanian values. To the extent that central war leaders were recognized, it was likely that they had much military authority in times of war and less political and ritual power in times of peace, since power also was effectively distributed among the heads of the founding lineages in each community and among local ritual leaders as well. That is, power was seated in the belief that survival on the land depended not only on strong *toqui* war leaders but also on the maintenance of a lasting accord between local ancestors and living kin groups. While *toqui* warlords could occasionally control resources and military labor, the vast proportion of their political territory often remained under the autonomous control of local patrilineal kin groups and their leaders, and the basic relationship between regional alliances administered by *toqui* and local patrilineages probably remained that of ritual suzerainty, which was permanently regulated by sacred leaders (e.g., *hechicero* and probably *machi*), rather than political sovereignty. It also is probable that the most established founding patrilineages in allied communities of multiple patrilineages, by virtue of the pact they had originally made with the divinities and their ancestors, claimed a privileged rank with ancestors and with the cosmological world. Again, power was not unified in any one person, lineage, or religious or political institution but heterarchically structured in different local and regional situational settings whereby one or more categorical leaders dominated over others whether it be in a ritual, battle, or political setting. Additional power was achieved by some leaders who tactically structured these settings in such as way to gain extra prestige and status. Set in this segmented and situational context, Balandier's comments on traditional African political structures seem appropriate to the Araucanian society: "In 'segmentary' societies, the diffused political life is revealed more by *situations* than by political institutions" (Balandier 1970:64). Although the traditional religious and political institutions of Araucanian society were (and still are) powerful social forces that sustained cultural continuity and fostered prolonged resistance to outsiders, I believe that it was the diffusion and manipulation of political power in different tactical settings by different secular and sacred leaders that also played an important role in positioning the society to survive.

While a permanent, formal centralized hierarchy as defined by Johnson (1973; involving permanent, ranked, decision-making structures, and leadership positions) did not emerge in the Araucania, local lineage-level sequential hierarchies were transcended, without undermining structural continuity in most cases, by the emergence of specialized decision-making within the regionally organized horizontal subgroups of *ayllarehue* and within the larger scale of the *butanmapu* organization in the late 1500s and throughout the 1600s. (*Butanmapu* is not specifically mentioned at the end of the sixteenth century but there is reference to a *butanmapu*-like political organization by L. de Valdivia in his text of 1612 which is published by J. Medina ([1852] 1952, Volume 11) and to "*cuatro cabezas generales,*" with Purén as it principal head, by Tesillo ([1647] 1911); cf. Rosales [1674] 1989:1026–1027. Núñez de Pineda [1673] 2003:292] also mentions "*utanmapues*" in the middle seventeenth century. Also see Padden 1993:78.) The relative rank and geographic position of the *butanmapu* territories were to defend the territory against outside invaders, but this seems not to have always been the case and alliances were constructed in all directions, with some *ayllarehue* dominating over others in particular situations, which further suggests the malleability and heterarchical nature of the political structure above the patrilineage level (see Bengoa 1985 and 2003 for examples). In essence, I suggest that this structure was an effort to remap the domestic, pan-Araucanian cosmos and ancestral worlds together in the same locality (e.g., *rehuekuel* and *nguillatun*) to form locally and regionally unified cosmunities and their religio-political singular sovereignty. It also was localized and controlled by local rulers. This meant it was an occasion both for periodically synchronized *ayllarehue* celebrations at *rehuekuel* and for multiple and highly individualized temporal rhythms of local groups and harvesting and other cycles. The aim was to create a landscape that reflected the organization of hierarchically and heterarchically ranked lineages all bound to the Araucanian cause, enabling a history of patrilineage loyalty and dependents to be read through the material traces of ancestor cults and such aesthetically visual and physical effects as *kuel* and *rehuekuel*. This permitted considerable increase in and flexibility of the social complexity without recourse to formally integrated and permanent vertical structures. Nearly all early documents record numerous cases of local and regional alliances that continually fragmented and then reorganized themselves, always maintaining the same basic political structure and objective and the same core group of ruling patrilineal leaders (Zavala 2006).

Of particular interest from this perspective is a process in which larger, more complex *ayllarehue* at centers like Purén, Tucapel, Catiray, and Angol gave rise, through the fission and dispersal made possible by sublineage budding, fragmentation, recruitment, and annexation, to smaller groupings in outlying areas. Many other populations apparently were not centrally united at all and consequently formed a large cloud of dispersed, usually short-lived, small satellite communities (with their respective *kuel* and *rehuekuel*), often allied with political centers like those in Purén and Lumaco. This pattern illustrates the fundamental characteristics of a diffused, segmentary, and *confederated regional polity*. That is, the Araucanian polity was comprised of regional groupings of short-lived and long-lived patrilineages – some acting alone and others allied into larger entities – all given to the single cause of defending the homeland and of striving to form and sustain a larger unified political organization. The end result was a confederation of increasingly larger geopolitical organizations that were first organized on the local multipatrilineage level at *rehuekuel*, then on an intervalley and, at times regional, multi-*rehue* or regional *ayllarehue* level, and eventually at the interregional *butanmapu* level.

I have two more points to make before leaving this section. First, although differentiation in power and authority were clearly marked in titles in early Araucanian society, there were and still are relatively little material differences between different rulers. Prior to the Araucanian expansion into Argentina in the middle 1700s, role differentiation and political specialization were more prominent than economic specialization and the display of power in elaborate wealth goods and symbols. There was a highly developed appreciation of and competition for prestige and respect and for more control over people than land and material wealth. That is, in my opinion, most rulers' wealth lay in people and in the organizational tactics of war, ceremony, and public projects rather than in land, and most rulers' powers were nearly always balanced by those vested in other persons or interest groups. Power also accrued to leaders who had multiple wives derived from alliances with other lineages and who allocated lands to migrants and fragmented populations. In this regard, maximizing fertility and labor in times of warfare through polygyny made wife exchange, alliance building, and recruitment of defeated populations a more important historical dynamic than the accumulation and display of wealth goods. In this sense, a ruler's purview and responsibility was to orchestrate and manage resources – human, material, and events – with the kind of segmentary and heterarchical complementarity discussed above being the most efficient and advantageous model of political development. Hence, the distribution of different kinds of power (economic, military, and ideological *sensu* Earle [1991]) among several corporate entities was a strategy that successfully resisted a formal, more permanent hierarchical centralization of power by any individual or set of individuals.

There are many passages in the chroniclers that demonstrate how leaders from Purén and other areas articulated their prominence and power in terms of unique ritual connections, titles, and prestige items (see Chapters 3 and 8). Oral tradition in the valley today relates that status in the past also was achieved through *admapu* contracts that leaders struck with *machi* and ancestor spirits to reproduce social unity among the descendants of their lineage. Prominence also was defined by a set of group symbols broadly identified as Araucanian, anything from decorated ponchos, ceramics, jewelry, and ceremonial fields, to common descent to a set of shared cultural practices, objects, and beliefs. Leaders often revealed their prominence by flaunting the trophy heads of decapitated Araucanian enemies and Spanish soldiers and by giving gifts to visitors during public feasts (see Núñez de Pineda [1673] 2003:520–80), the latter practice still widely performed today. Political symbols and signs of dead ancestors were particularly effective in maintaining intergroup corporateness and in organizing consanguinally related lineages, especially the wooden *chemamüll* (see Chapter 4) that served as memorial statues of famous ancestors to foster a sense of political obligation among the living. These signs were political weapons or agents in the hands of some leaders, because they symbolized life crises that moved people to action and to allegiance to those leaders. The permanency of the *chemamüll* and other ancestral symbols placed in visible localities across the landscape and referenced repetitively by leaders and shamans in ritual ceremonies were important acts to raise the political consciousness of the group (see Chapters 3 and 4).

Second, it should be noted that this case undermines the generally held notion that political control by those at the social apex and coterminous accumulation of material wealth and ritual power are universal hallmarks of complex societies (cf. Earle 1991; Feinman 2000; Smith 2003; see Chapter 2). Economic status derived from material wealth did not fully emerge until the late eighteenth and early nineteenth centuries as a result of increased raiding and marauding of Spanish and later Chilean and Argentine lands, which was linked to the development of capitalism in the southern cone of South America (see Jones 1999). During this period, the increasingly more powerful *toqui* leaders successfully extended their tactical influence throughout south-central Chile, providing effective leadership and organizational strategies to previously scattered local groups, and trading with and attacking Spanish settlements in central Argentina that was staged from various Andean mountain passes.

POWER VENUES AND LEADERSHIP ACTION

I argued above that power in the early historic Araucanian society was situationally centralized with individual leaders and patrilineages lineages employing social, tactical, religious, and military strategies to maintain and expand their influence.

Rather than assuming hierarchy and centralization as givens and then concentrating on how leaders maintained power and control through political and tactical leverage or coercion, it is more useful to examine how power was achieved and how social and economic resources were mobilized and collective action made possible in the absence of significant economic development and control during the sixteenth and seventeenth centuries. Before turning to these matters, I briefly define power (see discussion in Chapter 2 also).

Power is the ability to coerce physically and to enforce political decisions (*sensu* Adam 1991; Barnes 1988; Wolf 1999; Foucault 1984). Given my interest in the role of ideology and religion in the rise of the Araucanian polity, I see ideological power as analytically separate, with ideology in a dialectical relationship reflecting and legitimating authority and other sources of power. Ideological power thus consists of control over the symbols of power that define and interrelate institutions in other realms of power. As I stated in Chapter 1, I consider ideology an epistemology or concept of the way people know their world. I view cosmology as the way people ideologically and metaphysically construct their world, ritually teach it to the society at large, and practice it on a daily basis. Power and agency are derived from knowing and negotiating the epistemology and the constructed world.

In studying the concepts of leadership, some recent studies in archaeology have focused on individual aggrandizement, agency, exclusionary strategies of centralized authority and social power gained through connections or "networks" among leaders of different communities (Blanton et al. 1996; Hayden 1995). In contrast, collective or "corporate" strategies (cf. Blanton et al. 1996; Feinman 2000:453) view leadership as less personalized, with reduced individual aggrandizement and ostentatious display. In corporate strategies, leaders draw power from the collective, and therefore, are less dependent on individual prestige created through network relationships with nonlocal leaders from other communities. Instead, communal ritual, public construction, large cooperative labor tasks, shared power, and social segments that are woven together through broad integrative ritual and ideological means, and suppressed economic differentiation are emphasized.

The Araucanian case does not fit neatly into the network or corporate strategies of political leadership; rather, it combines the two and also engages in other strategies. Leadership was invariably achieved, ascribed, or hereditary (cf. Dillehay 1976). Leaders opportunistically employed both network and corporate strategies to achieve some goals, depending on the situation and scale of activity. In a way, individual *toqui* and *lonko* acted as lineage agents to build patrilineal kin networks and political alliances through marriage exchange, public ceremonies, communal labor projects, and polygyny in times of sporadic low-intensity warfare. Each leader had his personal networks, outside contacts, specialized status-related wealth objects, and burial patterns, all of which differed at different times.

Individual leadership networks also were constructed within the contexts of feasting and interlineage projects. In another way, leadership was partially representative of a corporate structure, whereby power was shared situationally by several different but complementary leaders (as discussed earlier). This structure was characterized by large-scale public projects, intensified food production, and different associations linked through ritual and ideological media. Leaders drew corporate power from public events, such as ceremonial feasts, labor projects and warfare, and from an ideology centered upon ancestral worship, mound ceremony, and marriage alliances (Dillehay 1995). Thus, in a sense, "corporate networks" defined both by personalized agency, ceremonial display, performance, and aggrandizement and by power sharing, communal cooperation, and action characterized early Araucanian leadership (see Chapter 2). As noted above, leadership also tended to be over people rather than land, and goods were redistributed more readily than accumulated, through feasting and through bridewealth payments for as many wives as one could afford. Thus, in effect, the head ruler of a lineage and multilineage grouping was not a centralizing agent or a distributor of material wealth. If he was not a *toqui* war leader, his principal duty was to establish and sustain political alliances with other powerful agencies, which would secure a stable milieu for his group. (Many lineages had a dual political structure with one leader for peace [*ülmen*] and one for war [*toqui*].) To this end, an elaborate system of ceremonial exchange developed during the sixteenth and seventeenth centuries within communities. Leaders, endowed with ancestral knowledge of genealogies and political controls and with support from shamans and other ritual leaders, sought to uphold a balance of power among lineages residing in the valley while maintaining workable and generally harmonious interaction with allied outsiders.

Rulers' control over the labor of kinsmen, nonkinsmen, transients, and captive slaves and their relations with shamans to appease the gods and ancestors and to mobilize sorcery against enemies also constituted power over the settings where this labor was enacted (e.g, Arnold 1996; Saitta 1994). Leaders regularly involved followers in ritual events, alliance formation negotiations, political rallies for the purpose of spreading rhetoric, and similar activities that may appear completely benign with respect to direct physical labor. Even generalized contacts between leaders and constituents were interwoven with requirements for followers to contribute to leader-sponsored labor projects such as ceremonial feasts and cooperative *minka* or *mingaco* harvests (a concept derived from the Quechua term *minga*), which is the case today (e.g., Stuchlik 1976). In these multiple ways, followers expressed their allegiance to leaders or expressed their resistance through noncooperation. Power, in this sense, was the leader's ability to engage others – people not material resources – in various actions and to tactically control the settings within which social relations were negotiated. In this regard, a leader's agency was relational and tactical – reflecting connections among various factions and between people of those factions and public display in feasts and political events – and it was, most fundamentally, the capacity to bring about action in the political and religious settings they controlled. Thus, the definition of a successful leader is one who succeeded in persuading followers, first, to believe in an agenda of action, second, to schedule and organize it in preferred settings, and third, to make themselves available to execute it, and, to win battles against enemy outsiders. Similarly, a loss of leadership was defined by the defection of followers (and their labor) to competitors (*sensu* Arnold 1996:15) and particularly by inaction.

To give examples of several of the circumstances developed above, observing in the middle 1500s, Bibar specifies the relationship between a *lov* social unit, a designated feasting area where celebrations and political decisions were performed, and paramount leaders who scheduled and controlled these events and their settings (see other examples in Chapters 3 and 5).

> Tienen esta órden entre ellos que cada lebo, que es una parcialidad, tiene un señor, y estos principales obedecen aquella cabeza. Tendrá un lebo de estos MD y 2.000 indios y otros más, y todos se ajuntan en ciertos tiempos del año en una parte señalada que tienen para aquel efecto. Ajuntados allí, comen y beben y averiguan daños y hacen justicia al que lo merece, a allí conciertan y ordenan y Mandan, y esto es guardado. (Bibar [1558] 1966:155)

> They have this organization among them such that each *lebo*, which is a parcialidad [patrilineage], has a lord, and these leaders obey the paramount chief. One of these *lebo* has 1,500 and 2,000 indian men and some have more, and all come together at certain times of the year in a place they have designated for this purpose. Gathered there, they eat and drink and judge injuries, and they award justice to those who deserve it, and there they make agreements, and issue orders and commands and these are obeyed. (Bibar [1558] 1966:155)

Observing and writing in the late 1800s, Guevara comments on the relation between leader's prestige and the ability to retain followers.

> En épocas de guerra i particularmente cuando un grupo patriarcal tomaba grandes proporciones, algunos miembros de él se ausentaban extraordinariamente para ir a establecerse a otro lugar. EI cacique hacía lo posible por impedir estas segregaciones, que a veces asumían el carácter de deserciones porque el mayor o en menor número de parientes y allegados regulaba su prestigio . . . Cacique ha perdido, pues, su prestigio de jefe, cuando no lo tiene personal. (Guevara 1925:289–291, 297–98)

During times of war and particularly when a patrilineal group became large, some of its members left extraordinarily and went to live in a different place. The chief did everything possible to prevent these separations, which at times became desertions because his prestige was tied to the greater or smaller number of his lineage-members and clients. . . . Thus, a chief lost his prestige as a leader when he did not have followers. (Guevara 1925:289–291, 297–98)

These and other passages (see Chapter 3) suggest that the power of individual leaders was largely personal and associated with success in warfare, in aggregating labor for public projects, in retaining followers, and in sponsoring large feasts. Power and prestige also stemmed from skillful manipulation of force, feasting schedules, and excess food and other materials within an elaborate network of ritually linked communities at designated places like *rehuekuel* and *nguillatun* fields. Such rulers were usurpers of power, and at their death their personal empires often dissolved back into their component lineage parts unless their successors were competent leaders who maintained the lineage dynasty. Some leaders also were the popular choices of political movements. Choice was a complement to coercion, because rising leaders attracted voluntary followers by their success in war and raiding and in recruiting fragmented groups. Upon their deaths, the movement often dissolved. In this regard, some *ayllarehue* organizations headed by a paramount *toqui* or other leader were inherently ephemeral and cyclical, with the organization often disappearing upon the death of its founder. Patrilineage polities, therefore, usually only temporarily dominated a local political organization. But there were exceptions with some areas sustaining political power for several decades or even centuries such as the case of the Purén and Lumaco Valley.

There are several cases of high-level or paramount rulers and patrilineal dynasties of one or more centuries in the Purén and Lumaco Valley, especially during the late 1500s and early to middle 1600s when the area developed as the center of resistance. During this period, some of the great Purén *toqui* leaders were Anganamón, Pelantaro, Pellagen, Butapichón, and Lincopichón (see Bengoa 2003:422–500; Ovalle [1646] 1988: Rosales [1674] 1989). Anganamón was famous and powerful by ascending the hierarchy from an *ülmen-cona* (warrior leader) to *toqui* to *gentoqui* between the later 1500s to the early 1600s (see Núñez de Pineda [1673] 2003:90–95). Even in the valley today, oral tradition still refers to him much in the same fashion as Lincoln, Roosevelt, Kennedy, and Churchill are remembered in the United States. The early Araucanian leaders articulated their prominence in terms of unique alliances, ritual connections, titles, and prestige items, which set them off from the commoners and other leaders. Several of these leaders probably started as wealthy and respected lineage headmen and gradually secured their reputations by skillful mediation of conflicts.

In some cases, they eventually established themselves as leaders over many lineages, with resulting synchronization in multilineage and ceremonial formations within this area.

The political power and geographic prowess of some leaders in recruiting distant groups and in forcing allies to remain loyal to them is revealed below, especially in the case of Tucapel, an allied leader who wavered in his commitment to those from Purén.

> Por ser la gente de Purén la más belicosa, y la que tras sí se avía de arrastrar a todos los demás principalmente Anganamón, que era tenido por Señor de toda la tierra y entre el y Pelantaro avía sus competencias, que cada uno dezía; que el era el Rey. (Rosales [1674] 1989:903)

> Since the people of Purén were the most warlike, and the ones who had to drag the rest after them, especially Anganamón, who was held to be the ruler of all the land and between him and Pelantaro there was competition and each said that he was the King. (Rosales [1674] 1989:903)

> Hasta que Anganamón fuesse a la Imperial, Valdiuia y Osorno y las demás partes reueladas, para unir a todos los Indios en un parezer, como persona, que tanto poder y mando tenía en toda la tierra.... (Rosales [1674] 1989:906)

> Until Anganamón went to Imperial, Valdivia, and Osorno [the latter more than 400 km away] and the other rebellious areas to unite all the indians in one purpose as a person who held so much power and authority in all the land.... (Rosales [1674] 1989:906)

> Los Indios de Purén, viendo que Tucapel blandeaba, y que los confederados se les avían de entrar por las puertas como enemigos nuevos, amenazaron a los Caciques y soldados de la costa con guerras ciuiles. Los quales por no venir a las passadas, de común acuerdo formaron campo de mil ochocientos Indios de a pie, y de a caballo, para pelear con el Coronel y sustentar la Guerra. (Rosales [1674] 1989:826)

> The indians of Purén, seeing that Tucapel was wavering, and that the allies were going to come in the doors like new enemies, threatened the *caciques* and warriors from the coast [those from Tucapel] with civil war. These, in order not to be outdone, by common agreement formed a host of one thousand eight hundred indians on foot and on horseback to fight the Colonel and wage the war. (Rosales [1674] 1989:826)

The pervasive geopolitical power of Purén leaders like Anganamón, Aipuavilo, and Pelantaro is expressed by most early chroniclers. For instance, writing the period between 1605 and 1612, Luis de Valdivia describes long-distance alliances between Purén, Villarrica, and Osorno, the latter two located approximately 250 and 400 km, respectively, from Purén (Luis de Valdivia [1612] 1887:318–319; Zavala 2006). Yet, the actions of these leaders were not always theirs alone: even if they devised and controlled everything they performed, it is still important to remember that their actions were produced within a variety of lineage-based discursive practices and traditions. Their leadership styles were assembled from the thoughts and acts of many different aspects of traditional knowledge, and their visual images of power were drawn from the conventions of *machi* and ancestral representations that circulated in ritual ceremony, in oral tradition, in the wooden *chemamüll* sculptures, in the architecture of the *kuel*, and in other material media. Indeed, in order to be as effective as they were, leaders also had to speak intelligibly to the cultural experiences and perceptions of their audiences. Their voices were credible precisely because they engaged so provocatively with ongoing cultural conversations about warfare, change, power, ritual, and lineage ancestry. But their power as lineage agents also was fragile and fleeting, especially if they made critical errors in judgment that cost the lives of their kinsmen.

An aspect of the responsibility and despair of leadership is shown in the following passage whereby women from communities in Purén and Lumaco asked for compensation from *toqui* war leaders for the loss of their husbands who were tricked by the Spanish into attending a political meeting to discuss peace but instead were captured and executed. The women blamed the surviving *toqui* for irresponsibly sending their husbands to their death, as related in a passage by Rosales in the middle 1600s, who mentions the responsibility of *toqui* to their followers. In another passage, he also shows the power of ritual leaders, in this case a *hechichero*, to make secular leaders accountable for their mistakes in times of war and to compensate the loses of people.

Mucho sintieron los generales de Purén, y Lumaco la prisión y muerte de estos treinta Caciques, y el llanto de sus mugeres, hijos y parientes, fue inconsolable, y quexándose de los que avían dado tan mal arbitrio, y poniendo pleito en forma ante sus Toquis generales, pidieron, que les hiziessen pagar las muertes a su usanza, y aunque ubo sobre esto varios pareceres, resistiendo los reos, y alegando, que la guerra trahía eso, y que muertes en la guerra, no se debían pagar, pues todos estaban obligados a poner las vidas en la defensa de la patria, y de la libertad. Con todo eso preualeció la parte de los demandantes, por dezir que no avían muerto peleando; que si assí ubiessen rnuerto, ubiera sido una muerte gloriosa, y estubieran sobre las nubes conuertidos en truenos y relámpagos, como los demás que mueren en la guerra; que avían muerto por mala disposición, y por un ardid rnal trazado, y assí se mandó, que les pagassen las muertes, y se execute la sentencia: que no es mal gobierno este. Porque como es bien que se premie un acierto, es bien que se pague un yerro, y como se remunera una buena traza y una victoria, se debe castigar una mala, y una pérdida. (Rosales [1674] 1989:827)

The generals from Purén and Lumaco were greatly affected by the capture and death of these thirty *Caciques* and the tears of their wives, children, and relations were inconsolable and they complained of those who had rendered such a bad decision, and they brought the case before their *toquis generales* [high war chiefs]. They asked that they [those responsible] be made to pay for the deaths according to their custom and, although there were several opinions about this, with the prisoners opposed saying that these things happen in war, and that deaths in war should not be compensated since all were obliged to risk their lives to defend the homeland and freedom. Despite this [argument] the cause of the plaintiffs prevailed, because they said they had not died fighting; that if they had died in that fashion, it would have been a glorious death and they would have been above the clouds transformed into thunder and lightning like the rest of those who died in war; but they had died because of a bad decision, and because of a badly laid scheme, and thus they ordered that the deaths be compensated and that the sentence be carried out; which is not bad government. Because just as it is good to reward a success, it is good that an error be paid for, and as a good plan and a victory are compensated, so a bad plan and a loss should be punished. . . . (Rosales [1674] 1989:827)

Mientras andan los soldados en la Guerra, estan los Hechizeros consultando al demonio sobre el successo de los suyos, incensando con tabaco a las tierras de el enemigo, i haziendo sus invocaciones. . . . En aviendo algun mal successo, le echan la culpa al Toqui general, que convocó los soldados, para la guerra, y ha de pagar las muertes con chicha, i ouexas de la tierra, y con hazer otra suerte buena. . . . (Rosales [1674] 1989:135)

While the soldiers are at War, the sorcerers consult the devil about the success of their [warriors] blowing tobacco [smoke] toward the lands of the enemy and making their invocations. When there is a bad outcome, they blame the highest-ranking *Toqui* who called up the soldiers for the war and who must pay for the deaths with *chicha* and sheep of the land [llamas] and make another good fortune. . . . (Rosales [1674] 1989:135)

Given the prior indepth treatment of *machi*, *hechicero*, and *boquibuye* and other ritual leaders in Chapters 4 and 5, I briefly address their political status here. Bacigalupo (1996, 1998, 2004a, 2004b, 2004c, 2004e, 2005, 2004a, 2004b, 2005) has studied the various relational personhoods of *machi* and their changing identities in ritual and political contexts (see also Dillehay 1988). Her work is particularly valuable for illuminating the historical and contemporary shamanization of identity politics and resistance among *machi*. She has shown that contemporary *machi* still exercise considerable power over ritual and political gatherings and address past and present nuances that have bearing on Mapuche land tenure, cultural patrimony, history, and social placement in the Chilean society.

As for the past roles and identities of ritual leaders, the chroniclers provide little insight. There is continuity between the past and present, because *machi's* roles today are similar to those described in the texts. As examined previously, leaders are described as healers, devil worshippers, and persons with great powers. *Machi* bring together people and gods, animated and inanimated things, and the living and the dead members of lineages in ceremony. They are primarily responsible for communication between these different categories, which itself is a venue of power and agency. *Machi* also understand the naturally and socially construed places of numinical power and the means by which this power can be obtained by spatial proximity and alignment with *kuel* and other sacred places and by understanding and "reading" these features. Only *machi* move across the different levels of the ethereal world with the help of ancestors and by means of ritual and paraphernalia (see Chapters 4 and 5). Through travel shamans bring power, wisdom, and knowledge, which often invest secular leaders with the authority to speak, to lead, and to command. Shamans also are solicited by leaders. In the past, *machi* and other ritual leaders probably enabled secular rulers to gain critical assess to divine and ancestral wisdom, which was a basis of their political authority.

In the early development of the Araucanian polity, its supernatural cooptation of local knowledge and material symbols and the scaling up of existing ceremonial architecture and ideology from the local patrilineage to the *ayllarehue* and *butanmapu* levels of organization were related to expanded religious and political orders. This development must have entailed greater participation by ritual leaders in affairs broadly affecting the society, stronger complementary relations between ritual and secular leaders, and greater knowledge and manipulation of Araucanian cosmology. The traditional roles and identities of ritual personnel also must have undergone significant transformations as patrilineages expanded their alliance networks and interacted within larger public ceremonial settings, which required more knowledge of and negotiation with regional deities and ancestries. In addition to performing ritual ceremonies and consulting with deities and ancestors in the upper world, *machi*, *hechicero*, and *boquivoye* affected the relationship between leaders and followers by reprimanding them, by creatively reworking political symbols, and by administering important ritual events at sacred places (e.g., *rehuekuel, nguillatuntue*). It also may be that ritual leaders tapped into and co-opted traditional symbolic themes to fashion related but more abstract themes applicable to *ayllarehue*, and even further, to invent new material symbols (e.g., rounded stone disks to serve as portals from the natural world to the ethereal world).

In summary, Araucanian society has characteristically shown a pattern of role differentiation in which political specialization has been more prominent than economic specialization. Although differentiation in power and authority were clearly marked in titles, actions, and places, there were relatively little material differences between different rulers in the sixteenth and seventeenth centuries. Most rulers' wealth laid in people rather than in land and material goods. Wealth in land was often given up by leaders who handed over land for designated ceremonial spaces and for domestic space for recruited groups whose loyalty and labor they received in return (see later discussion). Charisma, knowledge, and oratory skills were effective political tools; self-aggrandizement and display and accumulation of wealth goods usually played minor roles. We also have learned that shamans and other ritual leaders wielded considerable power and that people learned to respect, and in some cases even to have feared, shamans. Leadership thus involved the organization and employment of social-, ritual-, and knowledge-based forms of power.

POLITICAL EFFECTS OF POPULATION FRAGMENTATION: RECRUITMENT AND ANNEXATION

Beginning in the middle sixteenth century, the social landscape across south-central Chile was in considerable upheaval. The Spanish frontier war and a rise in inter-Araucanian warfare contributed to the conditions which some local populations were defeated, fragmented, and moved (Zavala 2006). This wider context of movement, upheavals, and forced migrations is relevant for several reasons (cf. Handlin 1951; Scott 1986). Lineages were heavily fragmented in some areas and were seeking movements to peaceful or protected places, even those along the frontier where conflict was sporadic and usually low intensity. The other is that the ongoing threat of violent confrontations had an immediate bearing on the reproduction of leader–follower relations throughout the Araucania. People's propensity to move about and to be recruited emerged as perhaps one of the most noteworthy traits of the period from approximately 1550 to 1850. Political alliances or migrations were unquestionably the keys to continued survival in those areas most affected by conflict. Movement tied people to more powerful lineages that could expand in size and militarily protect themselves against the Spanish, to local feasts and social structures that reinforced traditional religious and social institutions, and to productive and predictable economies. A culture of mobility and group expansion in the form of dynastic patrilineages and *ayllarehue* was thus developed, which was based on rational decisions made in response to the inescapable need to avoid conflict and to survive. This also created different opportunities and problems of identity and leadership (see Bengoa [2003:310–316 and 510] for comments on population fragmentation, depopulation of areas and shifting power alliances and González de Nájera [1614] 1971:97] for uncertainties, risks and movements during the late sixteenth-century period).

In referring to the demographic and social consequences of these movements in the sixteenth and seventeenth centuries, Rosales wrote in the late 1600s that:

> Yassimismo halló que se avía ya venido a sus tierras el Cacique Toncogueno, Toqui general de Angolmo, y que estaba muy contento, y agradecido de verse en ellas con toda su gente. Y assimismo, se fueron poblando todas las quebradas de Lincoya, Cayucupil, Tucapel, y Moluilla, que con el furor de la guerra estaban despobladas, y desiertas, por aver echado de ellas a los habitadores, apretándolos, y obligándolos a meterse la tierra adentro, a viuir en tierras estrañas, por huir de la muerte, y de las inuaciones de los Españoles. (Rosales [1674] 1989:1141)

> And he also found that the *Cacique* Toncogueno, the highest-ranking *toqui* of Angolmo, had come into his lands and he was very pleased and grateful to find himself in them with all his people. And likewise they settled in all the valleys of Lincoya, Cayucupil, Tucapel, and Moluilla, which had been depopulated and abandoned in the fury of the war, since they [the Spanish] had driven the inhabitants out of them, forcing and obliging them to move inland, and live in unfamiliar lands, to flee death and the invasions of the Spaniards. (Rosales [1674] 1989:1141)

In a passage referring to Utaflamme, a principal leader of Purén at the turn of the sixteenth century, Luis de Valdivia ([1612] 1887) states that:

> [Utaflamme] levanto voz y nombre de su regua [*rehue*] y de la provinica de Purén . . . y dijo, lo primero, lo contento que habia recibido toda la tierra de guerra con las buenas nuevas que su senoria y yo le habiamos enviado, y aunque hubo varios paerceres de conas y capitanes mozos e inquietos en el interin que no se unieron las cuatro cabezas principales de la guerra, pero que despues se acabaron de unir y conformer, lo cual concluyo tres dias habia, que no hay ni Habra cona ni capitan

que ose tomas las armas en las abarequas [sic] que al presente estaban en Guerra, y que les sera muy facil echar de sus tierras a los retiraos y estranjeros, naturals de las provincias de paz, fugitives de Arauco, Tucapel y Catiray.... (cited in Silva 2001:11–12)

[Utuflamme] spoke and in the name of his *regua* [sic] and of the province of Purén...and said, firstly, that all the land at war had received with great content the good news that His Lord, and I had sent, and although there were various opinions [expressed by *conas* (warriors)] and restless young captains during the interval while the four principal heads of the war were not united, but afterward they ended by uniting and agreeing, which concluded the three days. There is not, nor will there be any *cona* [warrior] or captain who dares to take up arms in the *abereequas* [sic] which at present were at war, and it will be very easy for them to expel from their lands the refugees and outsiders, native to the pacified provinces, fugitives from Arauco, Tucapel, and Catiray. (cited in Silva 2001:11–12)

Other chroniclers and historians have described lineages as continually fragmenting or expanding and then generating new fugitive social units resulting from internal conflicts or population pressure on the land, which in turn often repeated the fragmentary and expansionary cycle (cf. Bengoa 1985, 2003; Cooper 1946; Guevara 1925; Jones 1999; Núñez de Pineda [1673] 2003:704–705; Zapater 1992 for discussions of chroniclers). The logic of these cycles concerned intergenerational relations of exchange and obligations, both among stable patrilineages and the people they recruited and annexed. Outsiders who were incorporated became new lineage members, either as laborers, spouses, or children. As conflict spread between the Spanish and the Araucanians, and in some cases between the Araucanians, it must have generated a political and social bifurcation between stable and unstable areas. There were various political, economic, and other repercussions that cut across these areas, as well as opportunities to erase old identities and to produce new identities and social relations. At the same time, in times when they penetrated Araucanian territory, the Spanish sporadically repositioned themselves across the landscape through dealings with allied indigenous leaders, who often had titles and tribute privileges from the Spanish crown. This wider context provided new tactical and strategical options for various allied and unallied leaders and groups, which also had local repercussions as patrilineages were constructed, reconstructed, and reproduced in rituals, exchanges, subjects of action, and changing identities vis-à-vis alliances with the Spanish or with resisting indigenous groups.

Writing in the late 1800s, Guevara comments on the internal conflicts among indigenous populations and the resultant fission of groups.

En épocas de guerra i particularmente cuando un grupo patriarcal tomaba grandes proporciones, algunos miembros de él se ausentaban extraordinariamente para ir a establecerse a otro lugar. El cacique hacia lo posible por impedir estas segregaciones, que a veces asumían el carácter de deserción, porque el mayor o en menor número de parientes y allegados regulaba su prestigio. (Guevara 1925:289–291)

In epochs of war and particularly when a patriarchal group expanded to a large size, some its members left extraordinarily to establish themselves in another place. The chief would do everything possible to prevent the separation, which at times was seen as desertion, because the greater or lesser number of relatives and clients determined his prestige. (Guevara 1925:289–291)

Bengoa also describes the situation of leaders losing followers and their desperate attempts to recruit others and to biologically expand the size of their own group by encouraging women to mate with available young men.

La sociedad indígena, a partir de esos años, se obsesionó por el problema de la despoblación y la necesidad de población. Era la condición de su libertad tener muchos hombres que pudiesen esgrimir la lanza. Las mujeres tenían libertad para buscar a los jóvenes. . . . Los caciques aconsejan tener muchas mujeres y envían a sus *conas* a buscar mujeres criollas con el fin, además, de tener más hijos. La poligamia se convierte en ese entonces en una necesidad e instrumento de sobrevivencia para la sociedad indígena. . . . (Bengoa 2003:423)

Beginning in those years, indigenous society became obsessed with the problem of depopulation and the need for [a larger] population. Having many men to take up the lance was a requirement for freedom. Women were free to seek out young men. . . . The chiefs recommended having many wives and sent their *conas* [warriors] to get creole women [*criollas*] also in order to have more children. At this time, polygamy became a necessity and a means of survival for indigenous society. . . . (Bengoa 2003:423)

Population displacement, recruitment, and adoption continued into the late twentieth century and, in different ways, to the present day (see Stuchlik 1976). In the late 1800s in the Butarincón area of Lumaco, for example, Colípi, a powerful local leader, received people displaced by warfare (Bengoa 1985:71–80; cf. Guevara 1913). The adopted recruits were allotted lineage lands and, in some cases, even formed new sublineages and new congregational ceremonies under the guidance of Colípi. But, most importantly, the recruits extended the size and holdings of his family, which gave him more political power. (For a detailed account of the changing alliances and the fusion and fission of specific leader's political power, see León's (1999) excellent treatise of the *toqui* Allapangui who ruled in the latter half of the eighteenth century in the Malleco province.)

There is no doubt that the kinds of crises described above brought distant and often related lineages closer together into coresident and interdependent entities. Local patrilineages played key roles in fragmentation, recruitment, and adoption cycles. Through patrilineality and exogamy, recruited populations usually had roots with other lineages in distant areas through the prior exchange of women and the occasional migration of family members. Once lineage roots had been established in another place by inmarried women, allied rulers, or others, those places (if stable) usually became agents for the migration or recruitment of other fragmented groups. In the long run, both the stable and the fragmented lineages needed the other in order to keep the society functioning smoothly and to resist outsiders. These ties were far stronger in the early years of the war in areas like the *estado* and along the frontier in Purén, Lumaco, Arauco, and Tucupel, which were under constant stress due to warfare and in need of a continuous influx of people whether they were migrants, distant fragmented groups, or annexed neighbors. The most visible (though certainly not the only) consequence of this influx was the overall population growth of lineages in stable areas. Population densities were usually higher in areas like Purén where defense against the Spanish was more successful and where fragmented populations were continuously recruited to maintain large warrior and support populations for defense purposes and for productive agricultural economies.

Revealed below are the large number of warriors ruled by Anganamón, Pelantaro, and other war leaders from Purén who protected the northern Araucanian frontier in the late 1500s and throughout the 1600s. (Particularly noteworthy is mention of the "Butapichón" or Butarincón area where the large concentration of *kuel* and *rehuekuel* are located today.

> Anganamón esperando, en los campos de Tabón con dos embocadas de seis mil Indios, los más valientes, y animosos de la tierra, quales eran los de Purén, y Lumaco. (Rosales [1674] 1989:729)

> Anganamón waiting in the fields of Tabon with two groups of six thousand indians, the bravest and most daring in the land, which were those from Purén and Lumaco. (Rosales [1674] 1989:729)

> Pero desde lo alto de los cerros Butapichón y los *puréninos*, guardianes fronterizos, lo [the Spanish army ander Don Luis] estaban esperando. Dicen que eran unos tres mil los que se le vinieron encima. Les

arrebataron los ganados y liberaron a todos los prisioneros y a Don Luis le costó el cargo. (Rosales [1674] 1989:406)

But on the heights of the Butapichón hills and [sic] those of Purén, guardians of the frontier, were waiting for them [the Spanish army under Don Luis]. They say there were some three thousand [warriors] who attacked him. They seized the livestock and freed all the prisoners and cost Don Luis his command. (Rosales [1674] 1989:406)

la junta quedaba tres leguas de Ilicura, y dentro de cuatro, daria en Arauco;... no era junta ordinaria ni de poca gente sino de siete mil Indios, que avía casi un año que se juntaban a costa de mucha chicha y carneros de la tierra, que avían gastado los generales de la junta Butapichón, Queupuante y Lientur. (Rosales [1674] 1989:1052)

the assembly was held three leagues from Ilicura [near Purén] and within four, it would be in Arauco . . . it was not an ordinary gathering with few people, but rather there were seven thousand Indians, it was almost a year since they had met at the cost of a lot of *chicha* and llamas, which generals Butapichón, Queupuante, and Lientur had furnished. (Rosales [1674] 1989:1052)

Warfare clearly led to a reduction in the population density of many areas and in the number of warriors to defend the frontier, which could only be offset in the short term by recruiting and adopting other groups, especially their males, to increase the population size. As a result of intense, albeit sporadic, warfare along the frontier of the *estado* and occasionally into the interior of the Araucania, migrants and fragmented groups must have determined much of the social makeup of some areas and must have become an integral part of the social change processes affecting not only local lineages but leaders as well. Leaders acting as lineage agents were manipulating recruitment to solidify their power inwardly within their own lineage and then outwardly by incorporating other lineages (Zavala 2006). In doing so, they must have employed knowledge of traditional kinship structure and ceremony to enhance their own geopolitical position. Written texts suggest that there was a constant interplay, or negotiation, between existing and new usages of their knowledge about the organization and structure of the social and religious system that they operated within, particularly with regard to ritual and interlineage relations, which allotted additional prestige to leaders (see Boccara 1999; Leiva 1977; Montecino 1980). Again, the focus was on individual accumulation of social and political prominence by leaders and not so much on their accumulation of material wealth, which resulted in mobilization of all available manpower for productive efforts and created cumulative processes resulting in, for instance, population expansion past the limits of a local rulers's own procreative capacity and power over the labor of non-kin recruits. In fact, the sixteenth century shift of the Purén-Lumaco war leaders from small-scale leaders to polity rulers, such as Pelantaro, Liempichu, and Anganamón partly rested with their ability to recruit non-kin from distant areas as the latter did in Valdivia and Osorno to the south (see earlier quote). These followers provided additional labor to construct community infrastructures that we see archaeologically in the form of fortresses, agricultural terraces, roads, and mounds in sites in the Purén and Lumaco Valley. Adopted groups from different areas also account for the increased variability identified in the ceramic assemblages recovered from domestic sites dated after 1550 in the valley (see Chapter 6).

Lastly, the institutions of recruitment and adoption also must have been related to inflationary pressures placed on agricultural production for expenditures concerning warfare and population increase and for holding onto favored lands requiring lineage members for rituals and for linking lineages with their ancestral world. The impact that adopted groups had on resources extended beyond direct degradation, often inducing local communities to change resource use arrangements as a result of population increase. Land resource rights (land tenure) must have played a primary role in how recruits intersected with local resources and communities, and the resulting environmental and resource use consequences, especially in times of warfare when the Spanish often burned crops (see Rosales [1674] 1989 and Núñez de Pineda [1673] 2003 who detailed the destruction of crops throughout their chronicles). Often the first and most important interaction between adopted groups and local communities was over access rights to resources, and most often, the land resources needed for food security. In this context, how migrants and adopted groups obtained a set of rights to land resources in destination lineage areas, the composition of the set, and how this composition intersected with other social patterns and aspirations involving land (i.e., security, inheritance, exclusion, political obligation) probably became fundamental issues to the viability of both adopted and host resource use systems and leader–follower relations.

Lasting Outcomes of Recruitment and Adoption: Compatriotism, Political Unity, and Ritual Feasting

In the late 1500s and early 1600s, I suggest that expanding warfare and adopting others subverted many prior lineage separation pressures toward a new form of organization that could transcend the narrowness and limitations of the single patrilineage organization. This new form was the community of the *faithful*, built up around the worship of ancestors, the *Tren Tren* and *Kai Kai* origin story, and overarching deities like *Ngenechen* and *Pillan*. I also suggest that it was during this period that those ancestors and gods, previously only the deities and ancestors of local kinship units, were now installed as the dominant figures of the entire collectivity of kin and non-kin members – now recodified as a unitary and wider body of Araucanian *believers and compatriots-in-the-making* rather than as members of separate, localized bodies of lineage kin. I also submit that public ceremonies held at *rehuekuel* and administered by *machi*, or other sacred leaders, increased the area of ancestral knowledge and reverence, as well as enshrining the whole religious system in ritual, giving a sense of confidence, faith, security, and place to ordinary and/or adopted folk and enabling them to glorify their *toqui* war leaders, who in turn glorified warriors in glorifying themselves (see Leiva 1977:120–130). Public ceremony also would have been effective in securing compliant behavior and resolving disputes, in healing and solacing a wounded society, and in connecting social organization with a structure of new and wider civic rights and duties. To social order and political unity, the Araucanians had to anchor the new idea of compatriotism in appeals to a historically formed common origin, culture, religion, and language as a basis for their collective being and resistance.

An extensive literature exists on religion and political authority in the Araucanian culture, with much written about the role of ritual in constructing traditional authority and how ancestor cults were implicated in the historical emergence of resistance (cf. Alonqueo 1979; Cooper 1946; Dillehay 1990; Foerster 1993). As a result, scholars have tended to subscribe to the anthropological convention that ritual played a key role in creating and conveying shared cultural meanings and social values as well as in sustaining historical references that define social groups. I propose that ritual not only elaborated bonds between local groups, local ancestors, and their owner priests, it also placed the Araucanians as subjects and compatriots in the polity (see Chapters 3 and 4). Araucanian polity-builders appear to have drawn on the power of ancestors through three complementary kinds of ritual with one centered on the burial of leaders in *kuel*, another focused on large public feasts, and another on human and animal sacrifice.

I also think that leaders' burials in places like Purén and Lumaco after the 1500s usually occurred in large multiple mounds set in *rehuekuel* contexts and public ceremony. As leaders' mortuary practices became more elaborate and consuming of time and financial resources, they came into the hands of successive rulers with the idea to capture the labor and loyalty of commoners and of shamans who controlled access to ancestors and to employ mortuary ceremony as a means to build alliances with other leaders (Dillehay 1995). From this vantage, I further believe that repatriation of ancestors through funerary ritual served to affirm social relationships at the local level and to strengthen the political autonomy and power of patrilineal descent groups in their transactions with recruited outsiders. By centralizing power and consuming resources, these cultural practices in turn were among the enhancements to rulers' attempts to control the fragmented and adopted lineages and to maintain local loyalty. Thus, a fundamental dimension of the life cycle and social identity in mortuary ritual was equally an arena of political struggle and identity.

In other areas, by contrast, rulers attempted to deploy ancestors in polity-building by involving the sacrificial prerogative. Sacrifice of outsiders (Spanish or indigenous) was part of the way rulers symbolized and created subjects. Outside victims were sacrificed to the ancestors of lineages. In this way, *kuel* where important leaders were buried and where sacrificial and other ceremonies were performed became the roots, *de facto* leaders, and conduits to ancestors (see Chapters 4 and 5 and role of ritual sacrifice). At the same time, both old and new lineages were worshipping at and giving kin affiliation to *kuel* at public ceremonies. (It is for this reason that in both ritual narratives in Chapter 5, the shamans constantly invoke the ritual congregation of both insiders and outsiders to recognize and to be obedient to the kinship ties of *kuel*.) Despite the influx of new recruits of fragmented groups into local lineages, the aim of prominent and visionary leaders was to create a new utopic social order by transforming and enhancing traditional institutions and by organizing the population into kin-related *kuel* that owed their ritual status and political rank to local ancestries. In this way, the practice of the sacrificial cult of both humans and animals in public ceremony set in motion a dynamic of self-generation and self-legitimization. (See quotes in Chapter 3 for the importance of this prerogative in constituting and displaying power in the sixteenth century.) In addition to promoting self-generation through human sacrifice, these ceremonies encompassed social value, knowledge, history, and power, which was an ideal way of integrating vulnerable, rootless, and fragmented lineages as devoted subjects and compatriots in the Araucanian cause. Through these ceremonies, newly adopted lineage subjects were suddenly transformed from fragmented and displaced "people without history" and without identity to members of local patrilineages and thus "people with history" and with identity.

Today, informants in Purén and Lumaco report that *nguillatun* and other ceremonies over the past century addressed connections between the authentic ancestors of local residents and people recently incorporated within the lineage. This served to enculturate adopted groups into local histories and to remove them from their own ancestries and histories. In other words, people displaced geographically were now displaced historically by ritual extraction from their own ancestral time and relocated within the ancestral history of the host or local patrilineage adopting them. In this configuration, rituals were continuously referenced to ancestral premises and rationales, which was and still is the role of the *weupin* orator – that is, to recount lineage genealogy and history. These orations involved recourse to origin stories, tales, and historical events to portray how the world of the local patrilineage came to be. In these ceremonies, internally to the locals and externally to the outsiders, the *machi* and other leaders incarnate the original lineage founders, and perpetuate, down through ancestor-historical time, both the privileges accorded them by the lineage founders and ancestors and the obligation to guard and execute the obligations and requirements imposed on them through the original contracts with ancestral spirits.

These venues of identity-erasing (or breaking) and identity-making were probably manipulated by secular and sacred leaders to promote their own political agendas. For instance, the subject of ritual action by *machi* and others may have turned relations from local level concerns between a single lineage, their ancestral spirits, and *kuel* to the hierarchy of deities and spirits beyond the level of local ancestors toward larger multimound *rehuekuel* and *ayllarehue* goals and wider polity concerns. That is, single mounds were ritual units with a single set of ancestor spirits representing a single lineage and lineage leader. *Rehuekuel* localities with multiple mounds represented numerous spirits and multiple allied lineages or *ayllarehue* organizations. This would have made the multiple lineage spirits of all lineage groupings, both fragmented and unfragmented, extensions of the ancestors' and deities' abilities to take care of all lineages.

I suspect that the relative size and number of *kuel* in areas like Purén and Lumaco, where the *rehuekuel* mounds are larger and more numerous, may be expressions of the notion of fragmented lineages or "people without history" (i.e., people whose history has been joined or subsumed in another lineage). Those local lineages and leaders that adopted outsiders would have gained additional kinsmen through intermarriage and through redefined descent lines. Thus, the burials of these leaders in mounds would have been attended by larger numbers of real and perhaps fictive (adopted) relatives who placed more "social soil" on the tombs, thus making them physically larger than the tombs of other leaders who perhaps lived in areas where less recruiting and annexing occurred and thus had fewer kinsmen adding volume to their mounded tombs through ritual capping episodes (see Chapters 5 and 6 for discussions of mound-building). Although there is no present way to prove this proposition, an aim of some leaders may have been to create a landscape of hierarchically ranked lineages comprised of ranked locals and outsiders all bound to local authentic ancestors, thus enabling a history of loyalty and dependents to be visibly read through the expanded material and spatial traces (i.e., *kuel* and *rehuekuel*) of local genealogy and history.

In Purén and Lumaco, this landscape may have been associated with the multiple mounds in *rehuekuel* and with more *chemamüll* (wooden ancestral statues) and other symbolic lineage markers placed in visible localities such as hillcrests, ceremonial plazas, and crossroads than other areas, suggesting the need to visibly demonstrate to both locals and outsiders the primacy of local genealogies. For example, the *Huitranlebukuel* comprises three mounds ranked by local informants according to size and to names, with the largest mound called *Huachikuel*, and the secondary mounds referred to as *Ankakuel*, meaning second order, and *Natalkuel*, meaning a lower or third level (see Chapters 5 and 6). Another example is *Maicoyakuel* where informants report that the large central mound is flanked by smaller outlying ones where secondary leaders spoke to ritual audiences positioned in the open spaces between mounds on the *ñichi* platform. Although ideological and religious canons primarily account for the location, elevation, layout, and meaning of these and other *rehuekuel*, the political and genealogical relations between locals and adopted refugees may explain the hierarchical structure between the individual mounds with smaller ones representing some adopted groups. In practice, however, some local mounds and *chemamüll* also may be historically "invisible" and less important to some adopted outsiders, because they were not built in their distant homelands. I say this because some of the local narratives that I have collected among present-day inmarried women and other outsiders often reveal local *kuel* and other sacred places as representing other histories and not their histories (Dillehay n.d.; see also Ortiz 2004). That is, inmarried women explain that they do not always feel fully incorporated into their adopted lineage and thus have not yet affiliated with local genealogies and histories. This signals that landscapes are socially in motion and are in a constant state of flux with well-entrenched insiders or locals, adopted and established outsiders, and newly incorporated outsiders who often feel estranged. It is these conditions that partially establish ranked social groups within lineages.

There is another feature about *kuel* that is relevant here. In Chapter 5, I discussed how *machi* and other informants tell stories of "living *kuel*" that move across the landscape at night and of the consumption of one mound by another. To reiterate briefly, mounds are perceived as human bodies that have arms and legs, walk across the land, and consume other mounds. Metaphorically speaking, given that mounds are kinsmen, then the movement and consumption of mounds may convey and sustain recollected knowledge of past migrations and adoptions of displaced lineages who have become the "inmarried kinsmen" of local lineages and thus the fictive kin of local mounds – mounds that newly adopted groups may have helped to build through participation in the ritual burial of local leaders.

REFLECTIONS

The collective archaeological, ethnohistorical, and ethnographic evidence for the Purén and Lumaco Valley suggests how ritual mediated statements about multiple lineage formations, with secular rulers' power being characterized by a monopoly on important public ceremonies and nonegalitarian settings by feasting systems at *rehuekuel*. Leaders' control and prominence expanded in the valley throughout the sixteenth and seventeenth centuries, with large-scale feasting becoming more unevenly distributed to localities periodically controlled by different patrilineage dynasties. In the late 1500s, I believe that there emerged a greater pressure on these lineages to assert themselves as politico–religious units through the kinds of feasts and rituals described in the chroniclers and performed today in the valley. Later in the eighteenth and nineteenth centuries, public feasting drew largely on the economies of raiding and intensified farming, although ceremonies like the *nguillatun* also continued.

I do not want to leave the impression that the Araucanians' religion and ideology remained static throughout the period under study, because the power and status of rulers grew considerably as conflict with the Spanish spread south of the Bio Bio River and they had to find new tactics to defend themselves against outsiders and as they sought more legitimacy for their actions from deities and ancestors through mediation with shamans and the public at large in public ceremonies. I have argued for a standardized ideology and sacred landscape throughout this period (see Chapter 6). This also does not necessarily imply continuity but enhancement of certain and architectural and spatial forms. That is, small isolated burial mounds on hilltops and hillcrests and scattered domestic settlements and cemeteries were the norm in the late pre-Hispanic and early Hispanic periods. Beginning in the middle to late 1500s, several important transformations occurred as evidenced by the increased presence of multiple mound complexes, the *rehuekuel*, larger and more aggregated domestic, cemetery, and defensive sites, all forming nucleated communities. By the mid-1600s, more complexes and larger and more nucleated communities are evidenced and a wider variety of material traits (e.g., ceramic styles) are documented at these sites, all presumably resulting from an increased population in the valley associated with local settlement growth and the recruitment and annexation of outsiders. In the late 1600s and throughout the 1700s and 1800s, stability is seen in the continued use of *rehuekuel* and major settlements but also more instability is documented at smaller and outlying or marginal settlements, probably resulting from intermittent periods of peace and low intensity warfare. Further, I believe that as more *kuel* and *rehuekuel* were added to the landscape, with some being abandoned for reasons discussed previously and others being ascribed new and different meanings, the overall inscribed meaning of the sacred landscape also was transformed. I envision a landscape, to apply academic terms, comprising the kinds of generational, orientational, and relational monuments I discussed in Chapter 6, which represents a constantly rearranged landscape in aesthetic motion and of inscribed and ascribed meanings. Rearrangements involved shifts in the location, size, and social composition of domestic settlements and the building, abandonment, or continued use of *kuel* and *rehuekuel*.

I also have mentioned several venues of political, economic, ideological, and tactical power. I stated that political power, in order to be fully translated into authority, required a cosmology – an understanding of the traditional or ancestral forces that effected outcomes in the world and the knowledge to influence them. The mobilization by leaders of the appropriate specialist knowledge and ritual power of *machi* and others (Dillehay 1990c, 1995, 1999), including the symbols of power of the fallen Inka empire, was a key element of the capacity for effective action in Araucanian society. Mobilizing different types of knowledge – ancestral, technological, ecological, agricultural, and ritual – made possible a successful life in the uncertain political environment of the time. Both secular and ritual leadership was the capacity to do this effectively. Ritual leadership of *buquivoye* or *machi* and other ritual leaders thus involved creativity to ensure that power was always properly socialized, legitimate, and morally warranted. An important goal of leaders thus was to create a sphere of effective ritual control, which was operated spatially by *rehuekuel* and organizationally by *ayllarehue* alliances. A fundamental purpose of alliances was thus the creation of spheres of ritual control and knowledge, which functioned through the kinds of linked *rehuekuel* networks headed by individually powerful patrilineages found in Purén and Lumaco Valley. As suggested by archaeology, ethnohistory, and ethnography, most other valleys in the Araucania did not initially have these or at least not to the same extent, which again indicates the early political response and polity formation of this valley to defend the homeland against the Spanish.

In the early Araucanian polity, power was never fully centralized but segmented and effective because the major characteristics and boundaries of the traditional political system were shaped by a wide variety of specialized roles and coalitions of different leaders and specialists (e.g., secular and sacred administrators, warriors, traders) in various settings, who had different modes of controlling and regulating power, creating systems of meaning, and articulating different ideologies derived from overarching principles of cosmological organization. I believe that the confederated polity of the Araucanians could never have been transformed into a lasting unitary state, because there was no transformation from a diffused or segmentary structure to a fully realized unitary organization in any situation. Even the ideology of domination in the superarching *butanmapu* structure was precisely the same as that of the lower units comprising it (i.e., *ayllarehue*, *rehuekuel*, and *lov*). No institution, setting, or situation ever transformed the *butanmapu* to a higher unit of centralized authority.

Along similar lines of concerns with political centrality and permanency, I turn briefly to "chiefly" cycling within the polity organization of the study area (see Chapter 2). I am convinced by the oral traditions of informants and by the standardization of mound form and location that *rehuekuel* were sequenced in close relatively spatial proximity in the valley in order to accommodate the historical cycling of dynastic lineages rather than their permanence or *longue durée*. That is, it can be inferred from the numerous written texts that many lineage leaders and thus their lineages fell from power for various reasons, including defeat in warfare, internal conflict, and so on. On the other hand, it is obvious that other leaders and lineages gained power and endured for considerable periods of time, perhaps as long as fifty to one hundred years, some of which developed into dynasties referenced in written texts and oral traditions and associated with complex archaeological records. Some of these lineages and multilineage organization like the *ayllarehue* waxed and waned between petty headmen leading single lineages to paramount polities heading several large lineages. I am not certain whether all of this is "chiefly cycling" or simply history unfolding in variable ways or other forming of cycling and rotating power.

In the past, it is probable that public gatherings at *rehuekuel* functioned much in the same way they do today. That is, they rotated from place to place depending on the social and political connections between lineages and their leaders. As studied in Chapter 4, today in the valley, local *trokinche* units composed of three lineages always sponsor gatherings in their respective *rehuekuel* or *nguillatun* fields, with two units administering it one year and then rotating the event to the next set of two combined units the next year. Lineage leaders stay in contact to schedule events and to shift local power relations, according to the political, economic, or social issues momentarily at hand. Although the spatial placement and form of ceremonies at *rehuekuel* largely remain the same, the meaning attached to them varies situationally from year to year and from sponsoring group to sponsoring group much in the same fashion cited earlier by Faron (1964) and Stuchlik (1976).

Lastly, I discussed previously that a *rehue* is a multi-*lov* patrilineal unit, and I have proposed that each *rehuekuel* in the study area is the *cosmunity* of one powerful patrilineage overseeing several local *lov* communities. As discussed in Chapter 3, the chroniclers document that the *ayllarehue* political organization comprised nine to ten *rehue*, or lineages, and that Purén and Lumaco belonged to an *ayllarehue*, which may have included areas outside of the valley or the entire valley itself. In Purén and Lumaco, there are nine major archaeological *rehuekuel* that roughly date to the same period and exhibit similar forms and artifacts (see Chapter 6). It is possible that these nine to ten *rehuekuel* formed the Purén and Lumaco *ayllarehue* that is mentioned by the chroniclers and that held power from at least the late 1500s to the early 1700s, as suggested by radiocarbon dates from the mound complexes and by the early written texts discussed through out this book. Although I am unable to assign a specific *rehuekuel* to a specific lineage leader, considering the facts that Butapichón, for example, ruled at the conjunction of the Purén and Lumaco rivers, that the written texts mentioned him in the early 1600s, that there is an indigenous community named after him, Butarincón, at the juncture of these two rivers, and that he is remembered through oral tradition by several elders in the valley, it is possible that he is buried in the large mound called *Rehueñichikuel*. This is what some informants report. We also known from oral tradition and from texts that Anganamón, Lautaro, Pelantaro, Colípi, and other leaders resided in the valley during the late 1500s and early to middle 1600s. Informants place Anganamón near Tranaman, which might associate him with *Rapahuekuel*, Pelantaro near *Hualonkokuel*, Lautaro near *Lolonkokuel*, Lientur near *Maicoyakuel* (although he was from the Imperial area farther south), and Colípi near *Ñachekuel*. We have no information to affirm these associations, but so far the oral traditions from informants generally have been fairly consistent with the ethnohistorical and archaeological findings.

EPILOGUE

Although the Araucanians indigenously and independently developed their polity, it was not without some indirect or direct outside influence from the Inka and later the Spanish. Thus, in part, although not stated explicitly, this chapter partially has been about the power venues of leaders and about secondary polity formation and what they look like organizationally and spatially. Araucanian political formation between the sixteenth and eighteenth centuries showed a range of outcomes in terms of heterarchical, hierarchical, and horizontal multilineage organizations and of settlement stability and instability that do not lend themselves easily to Andean or Inka-influenced characterization of the society. The range of simultaneous variation in political and settlement formations reflects a regional geopolitical mosaic. This mosaic is the outcome of inequalities internal to low-intensity but prolonged conflict, migration, recruitment, and annexation. In the late sixteenth century, these inequalities along the northern Araucanian frontier, primarily defended by the Purén and Lumaco Valley (and the larger *estado*) during the early half of the war with the Spanish, were different from those of the interior populations, where the articulation of local ambitions in the context of public ritual engagement at places like *rehuekuel* had different outcomes in terms of their material and spatial expressions, as evidenced by more mound building and larger villages in Purén and Lumaco. Other localities were influenced, if not incorporated, by these places or simply stayed locally autonomous lineages that were later defeated by the Spanish and/or incorporated by stable lineages.

The early polity of Araucanian lineages was constructed segmentally and unequally. Some people and groups were drawn or propelled into the central orbits of resistance; others were defeated and fragmented all together. There were winners and also losers, unequally distributed over the terrain and unequally represented in the symbolization of the polity. As patrilineages became partners in wider alliances and participants in transvalley networks of exchange, many of them reemerged with agendas on their own behalf that tested the limits of integration within the polity. These simultaneously encompassing and differentiating processes were mirrored in the organizational concepts of *ayllarehue* and *butanmapu*, all of which was a process of ideology making and ideology breaking (Wolf 1999). We must be aware of these spatial and temporal differences across the political landscape of the sixteenth and seventeenth centuries in order to avoid unduly making local religio-political formations in the Purén and Lumaco Valley and elsewhere "global" in the Araucania region and thus homogenously developed at the same sociocultural level everywhere, as some historians have done in previous studies, when they most clearly were not (see Padden 1993; Dillehay 2003; see Chapter 2).

As part of the utopic vision of the polity, the ideology making of the Araucanians probably relied heavily on rulers' skills of rhetoric and oratory. Relevant
cosmological and ideological stories probably were recited publicly by both secular and sacred leaders and members of their lineages holding appropriate rights,
thus granting the stratum of power holders a near monopoly over the messages
and channels of ideological communication in public ceremonies and political
unions. These oratorical acts likely did more than reiterate rights to privileges;
in stressing the ontogeny of these privileges, they placed the war leaders and
shamans within a cosmology of the Araucanian ancestral world as a whole and
fortified their possession of a distinctive status. Just as they do today, past *machi*
shamans and other specialists propounded cosmological propositions and ancestral
myth-histories with the aid of politically approved agendas. The speakers delivered
major orations in ceremony in which they upheld the virtuous and castigated the
evil and negligent. These moralizing discourses did not merely advertise norms
of proper conduct and compatriotism in the new political order but projected
the hegemonic values that governed a newly formed cultural and social world;
and the ancestral myth-histories were not so much narratives of actual events as
allegorical accounts of the Araucanian past that enshrined a political teleology
for polity expansion and the future. Such discourses and narratives, coupled with
ritual performances, with the symbolic emblems drawn from them, and with
the sculpted *rehuekuel* landscapes where public gatherings occurred, projected an
imagined or utopic world where power was assigned a strategic position and
a religio-political structure and where the Araucanians imaginatively controlled
both authentic and mythical time and space and thus their own destiny. Curiously,
oratory had a similar truth-defining and destiny-controlling role among the Inka.

Finally, full regional political unification never fully occurred among the
Araucanians, but only emulation and organizational recursiveness in the form of
kuel, rehuekuel, and *ayllarehue* in places like the Purén and Lumaco Valley, which
was not universal among all Araucanian populations. Thus the relevance of local
lineages – both stable and fragmented – was defined in terms of the grand narrative
of a self-determining utopic destiny that was spatially engineered and materialized
in the sacred geographies of *kuel* and *rehuekuel.* In my opinion, groups, living or
dead, are and were relevant only insofar as they shed light on the universal story
of Araucanian control of space, history, identity, and destiny.

EIGHT:

RECURSIVENESS, KINSHIP

GEOGRAPHIES, AND POLITY

This chapter is an interpretative continuation of several themes presented in the last chapter, but with emphasis given to the wider political policies and demographic settings that are materially manifested by *kuel* and *rehuelkuel*. This chapter also reflects on some of the conceptual approaches developed in Chapter 2. Specifically treated are identity, compatriotism, and memory, which are important to the transformative composition of the Araucanian polity.

I stated in Chapter 4 that the Araucanians perceive humans being embedded in a larger time–space or cosmic society whereby life cycles are circular with ancestors and the living constantly linked (see Faron 1964; Dillehay 2003) in a landscaped geography characterized by a network of mental images, visual sightings, and physical pathways that connect historical places, sacred spaces, and the *kuel* and *rehuekuel* with figures in the ethereal upper world. This network of ancient settings gave historical significance to the organization of ritually sanctified political alliances among the Araucanians in times of sporadic low-intensity warfare with the Spanish and later with the Chileans. In places like Purén and Lumaco, *kuel* were the architectural landmarks that served as the physical evidence of the movements, effects, and responses of increased contact between the Araucanians in late pre-Hispanic times and later with the Spanish in Purén and Lumaco and other areas. In this context, mounds and other sacred features represent an architectural ideology that formed the ceremonial landscape (Dillehay 1990c), which contributed to the vitality and integrity of the warring indigenous population. This ideology stemmed from beliefs about the natural and social world, from the experiences in that world, and from the employment of *kuel* and *rehuekuel* to link aspects of both worlds.

Socially, mound building and participation in ceremonies developed into a networking society that permitted cost-effective social expansion, goal-driven politics, and the creation of local religious *rehuekuel* units and controllable political organization. The network form of *rehuekuel* organization in Purén and Lumaco divided the society into participants and nonparticipants, according to the active and inactive status of rotating ceremonial fields. Culturally, the dominant ethos was warrior "prestige," in which symbols and images made up the actual experience of most lineage members (see Chapter 3; cf. Bengoa 2003; Boccara 1999; Leiva 1977; Montecino 1980; Zapater 1973). Not only was the society preoccupied with a growing "warrior class" to defend the frontier but ordinary individuals making up the remainder of the society also had changing values, roles and duties as agriculturalists, craft specialists, emissaries, ritual leaders, and so forth. Cultural expressions were recombined and rearranged within the network and burial of important leaders defined the first function of mounds. However, mounds and mound-related rituals had (and still have) a life beyond the theme of death and burial; as a second function, they were memorabilia and ceremonial places actively used and, through the death of a leader and the reconstruction of alliances by new leaders, actively restructured who participated in ceremony and who formed alliances. Thus, mound politics culturally transformed social structure as death did political structure (Dillehay 1990c, 1995). A third function relates to the role of *kuel* as places of healing and solacing and as living members of local communities who acted as intermediaries between the living, the dead, and the deities. In this capacity, *kuel* held and still hold a powerful influence over the affairs of local communities, as shown in the *Hualonkokuel* and *TrenTrenkuel* ceremonies.

As members of kinship networks in the Purén and Lumaco society, *kuel's* social positions are ambiguous. They started as burial mounds. But in a more advanced mound state, larger more numerous networks – multiple *rehuekuel* – were needed for alliance building, population nucleation, information flow, increased public congregation, and greater parliamentary power. Related and standardized *rehuekuel* complexes were designed to facilitate the increasing complexity of Araucanian society in the course of growing conflict, population movement, population nucleation in some areas, and a developing new society in general. Mound literacy or *nauchi*, knowing how to read and interact with the mounds, became a prerequisite for the conduct of their lives as literate compatriots forming in a new society. Mounds demanded a special way of interaction and socialization with local communities, which carried with it uniform ritual offerings and feastings (see Chapter 5). This interaction also communicated to people's values. *Kuel* and *rehuekuel* thus served as the control centers of the myriad links that maintained the past in the present for the future. Ceremony at these standardized centers narrowed the spectrum of learning curves and experiences for rapidly changing communities that were increasingly exposed to new and different challenges. Uniformity in the form, meaning, and topographical setting of the mound society developed to deal with different experiences and to form new partnerships between stable and adopted lineages. The significance of the formation of mound-building, viewed in this perspective, ultimately was that of providing new instruments for the moral and cultural regulation of these partnerships and for a utopically engineered social order that was materially manifested in the form of a sculpted ritual landscape. Local leaders, in drawing on the techniques and rhetoric of feasting and discourse relations, provided the opportune context in which local host lineages and recruited nonlocal lineages could be brought together to form the new society.

As discussed in the last chapter, particularly important to the articulation of this order was recursiveness in administrative and religious thoughts and practices and in the form and meaning of *kuel* and *rehuekuel*. With regional population increases and alliances, the homogenization of needs and experiences, and the need of a uniform knowledge system, a pan-Araucanian cosmology of beliefs, norms, values, deities, and ancestors eventually replaced individual patrilineage attention to local ancestors. Important to these practices were the different kinds of mounds and monuments inscribed with historical meaning across the landscape. Both *kuel* and *rehuekuel* represented generational, orientational, and relational spaces (see Chapter 6) that reflected ancestral history, traditional *admapu* ways (codes and beliefs) of doing things, and new tactics for organizing peoples and places. These different elements, which were employed in the development of the religio-political system exercised at contemporaneously occupied *rehuekuel* (which generally was similar in content and structure through the period under study; see Chapters 4 and 5), became so interdependent that they were seen in terms of an integrated ideological scheme related to problems of the individual members of the group and his or her place in society, as well as the individual lineages comprising the larger *ayllarehue* groupings. Thus, a cosmology of this kind was itself a significant element in its own right, contributing further to the development and functioning of the group. This cosmology functioned only if it was maintained and kept alive by continuous indoctrination, conditioning of moods and sentiments, and affirmation of beliefs in ceremony (cf. Bacigalupo 2002, 2004a; Dillehay 2002). This was mainly achieved by the large-scale political and religious gatherings at designated places like *rehuekuel* that were frequent and repetitive (1) to prevent duplication of efforts and individualism, (2) to facilitate cohesion by providing familiar settings, and (3) to fulfill the purpose of maintaining a new order (see Chapters 4, 6, and 7). These inseparable activities created and maintained the new organization as a utopically and aesthetically constructed religio-political entity. Each activity was not a "variable" but part of the dialectical processes of leader's power and symbolization of the structural reorganization of the society (see Chapter 7).

In sum, *kuel* and *rehuekuel* helped to create memory, unity, identity, and compatriotism in the new order. To operate effectively in times of duress, the Araucanian population had to define its growing membership and its sphere of operation by defining its identity, its compatriotism, and its inclusiveness within the increasingly larger political field in which it operated (see Jones 1999 for a general discussion of the expanding political influence of Araucanian culture in the southern cone). Groups adopted one or more of a number of similar symbolic forms to define their uniformity, creating similar stories and ritual practices, for example, which were legitimized by the moral inclusiveness and style of life of the participants. Participation in this new system was essentially dependent on a set of group symbols broadly defined as Araucanian, anything from decorated ponchos, ceramics, jewelry, *chemamüll* statues, and standardized U-shaped *nguil-latun* ceremonial fields, to common descent to a set of shared cultural practices, objects, and beliefs. As mentioned previously, several of these were Andean and Inka symbols that were transformed into political symbols through direct or indirect (i.e., *yanacona*) contact with the Araucanians prior to and during the Spanish conquest (see Chapter 3).

BECOMING ANDEAN AND INKA

I have argued throughout this book that in some ways, the late-sixteenth-century Araucanians reenacted part of the Inka empire that the Spanish had defeated half a century earlier in Peru but also went beyond it: I suggest that there was an immersion and intervention into parts of the immediate (perceived) historical record of the Inka that was profoundly transformative to the Araucanians (see Chapter 3). Collectively, the ethnographic, ethnohistorical, and archaeological records suggest that the southern Araucanian leaders (those south of the Bio Bio River) of the late-sixteenth and early-seventeenth-century *estado* reinterpreted certain aspects of Inka state identity and resistance identity as processes of various ambivalent identifications: they reopened and continued local lineage histories with accounts of entangled engagements between different lineages and between their people and the Spanish, resituated histories of resisting outsiders, incorporated indigenous outsiders, and rebuilt and rememorized their own history through homogenized and commemorated mounded landscapes. Here the purpose was not only to appropriate and reference aspects of the Inka past and ethos but to enhance an old Andean/Araucanian religious landscape and to design a new political landscape and a new conception of authority and religious order that emerged in the face of Spanish contact. It is important to realize that the Araucanians did not simply mimic certain Inka styles; they created and hybridized a new and distinctive one, defining new identities and relations that are becoming more evident in these records. What they adopted and structurally adjusted were military and administrative organization, as well as religious codes, which went through several transformations in solidifying power in south-central Chile and in expanding into Argentina in the early 1700s. This was a ritually sculpted landscape style that was socially anchored in the past via ancestor worship, ritually participated in the present via repetitive ritual at *rehuekuel*, and utopically grounded in the future via priestly shamanic vision quests and planning by secular leaders. Leaders employed the sacred past of ancestors to establish their legitimacy. I argue that these processes of polity building and sacred legitimization of rulers are suggested in the past and present mounded landscapes of the Araucania region, particularly in the Purén and Lumaco Valley.

This happened at the same time that mound construction was developed further to define new ways to relate to existing *kuel* and *rehuekuel*, to establish new identities with them, and to incorporate new social groups. The result was a new and more sacred form of architecture that spread from the *estado* to other areas in the late 1550s and early 1600s. The political construction and spread of this architecture was grounded in the conception of a formal frontier military society assigned defense of the polity. What made aspects of some changes Inka was how the Araucanians enhanced the politico-religious landscape to reflect political expansion and incorporation of outsiders. Reconstituting part of the ethos of the Inka past in the Araucanian present was, of course, an impossibility, but I believe that it was precisely the tension of impossibility that charged the critical spark on which the Araucanians partially thrived. And part of that history – the ethos of the past for the future – entailed revitalized memories of Atahualpa, Inka resistance, and Araucanian utopics. Much of this ideology insisted that the kindred spirits in *kuel*, the ancestors of the past and the deities of the present, could be kept alive and in memory by worship and could be projected onto the future by keeping the *admapu* or ancestral ways.

As stated in Chapter 3, I believe that the political, religious, and knowledge structures of the Inka and Araucanians, were, upon initial contact between them, mutually legible because both were essentially Andean societies at their core. This familiarity opened the opportunity for the Araucanians to adopt certain Inka ways. This does not always imply that exact Inka knowledges and practices were executed but that they might have been cast in new ways. These local and pan-Andean knowledges were absorbed, mixed, and banked in memory and repeated in material form in mounded landscape, in ritual, and in stories about Atahualpa such as those today, and in the *khuipu*, ceramic styles, and other objects and symbols (see Chapter 3). Not only were the Araucanians partially drawing on the past power and identity of the Inka but also reacting to a past with the Spanish they knew and could relate to. By practicing a form of archaism (*sensu* Patterson 2004) recent Andean history and symbolism, the Araucanians established their social integrity and purpose and found a source of additional identity and strength.

On the basis of the currently known ethnohistorical, archaeological, and ethnographic data, I cannot say for certain how many of these elements were pre-Hispanic Araucanian or Inka or just plain Andean or a hybridization of all three. Although the Araucanians were building mounds (a trait probably derived from earlier Andean influence) before contact with the Inka, I think that they learned from the latter that mounded landscapes and multiple mound complexes (*rehuekuel*) and not just single burial *kuel* mounds could be used to increase or decrease the differences between people, particular places, and historical contingencies. Although I lack the precise evidence to prove it at this time, I believe that given the prior mound-building experience of the Araucanians and of their legible principles of organization, they quickly learned either directly or indirectly from the Inka prior to or at the time of contact with the Spanish how these principles could govern the ordering of an expanding political space. The character of the relationships and emulations that is inferred from the data is the employment of similar tactics of subjection of conquered, recruited and adopted *rehue* and *lov* peoples, a pronounced emphasis on teaching people how to belong to a larger polity and to be productive compatriots or citizens, the organization of collective labor, how to incorporate and organize outlying or hinterland groups through public ceremony and topographic pathways and visual lines of contact, and the value of standardization in organizing large-scale productions. The Inka variant of this pattern is exemplified in the spatial layout of the *ayllus*, *ceques*, and *panacas* of Cuzco and its surrounding region and the temporal model constituted by the Inka astronomical system and ritual calendar (e.g., Zuidema 1977; Urton 1981). Thus, what made aspects of the Araucanian polity "Inka" were principles of an expansive geopolitical ceremonial landscape organization. To have achieved this emulation, I believe that the Araucanians must have had a social memory, a collective notion about the Inka past. This emulation was grounded primarily in an ideology of both the Inka and the Araucanian needing to expand and defend their territories. What were conquered ethnic enclaves to the Inka were the fragmented lineage groups adopted by the Araucanians, both indicative of the incorporation of groups but through different means and for different purposes. But the principle was the same – that of an ideology that defined rights to and obligations of membership and compatriotism (or citizenship in the Inka case?) in a newly ordered society and that created a religious and political landscape to insure this order.

Spatializing Gatherings at and between *Rehuekuel* for *Ayllarehue*

Informants reported that the names and similar locations and forms of individual mounds and the visual links between them were the frameworks for the symbolic kinship relations between living people and "living" *kuel* and thus between the people and their ancestral spirits and deities, all of whom actively revealed themselves through direct or indirect participation in various ceremonies and through narratives, tales, and myths. In Chapters 4, 5, and 6, I discussed the participatory solacing power effected by the visual sightings of *kuel* and *rehuekuel* in ceremony. One of the architectural innovations of the valley's mounded landscapes consisted of lineages participating in active ceremonial fields and looking outwardly from them to *kuel* in distant inactive fields (usually located approximately 0.5 to 2 km away), where nonlocal lineages participated in physically active public ceremony through "visual pilgrimages," thus combining the functions of direct and indirect ritual participation, of kinship and ancestry between mounds and between mounds and people, and of wider festive solidarity. During the next seasonal rotation of valley-long ceremonies, the roles were reversed whereby previously active fields became inactive ones, inactive ones became active, and visually participating pilgrims became physically active participants, and previously active ones became visual participants, and so forth. Collectively, rotation of ceremony, organizational emulation, continuity in religious ideas and practices, visual pilgrimages, and standardization in mound forms and topographic settings fostered familiarity of and participation in ceremonies. In this regard, the sixteenth- and seventeenth-century ceremonial spaces were probably unprecedented in the social effort they devoted to the organization of commensal feasting (*sensu* Dietler 1996) arranged for increasingly larger and often unrelated lineages.

The architectural media of *rehuekuel* ceremonial fields and their uniformity enabled individuals to interact with one another across spatial and social distances, although the nature of architecturally mediated visual interaction may have differed significantly from the kinds of interactions which were typical of face-to-face ceremonial situations. This form of interaction allowed ceremonies to be detached from their local contexts and transmitted via visually seen and spatially accessible ceremonial places in distant contexts. By virtue of this visual transmission, the deployment of visual ceremony integrated social interaction with separate physical locales, so that individual lineages interacted with one another even though they did not always share a common spatial-temporal setting. By linking the past and present and the living and dead, ritual interaction at *rehuekuel* combined extended availability in space with temporal simultaneity, which ultimately solidified the religio-political organization even more.

Mounds thus located local host and recruited guest audiences at the spatial pinnacle of the new order under construction in the Purén and Lumaco Valley in the late 1500s. They installed them at the threshold of greater things to come – the utopic vision of the sixteenth-century political society – to unify host and fragmented lineages, which was ultimately achieved in the form of the *ayllarehue* and later the *butanmapu*. But in their interrelations, the mounds constituted the order of things and of peoples which, reaching back into the depths of past ancestral time as well as encompassing all corners of the Araucania, rendered the world metonymically present, subordinated to *Ngenechen* and *Pillan* powers and to past ancestral achievements. All of this was reinforced by the visual tracks between the spatially accessible *rehuekuel* complexes – the visual pilgrimages from one *nguillatun* ceremony to another taking place at those complexes. The large complexes of *Huitrenlehuekuel*, *TrenTrenkuel*, *Maicoyakuel*, *Lolonkokuel* and others not only integrated distinct vision tracks from across the valley but also extended them to sacred mountains like *Wenucolla* and the sacred horizons to the east where the great snow-capped volcanoes are located (see Chapter 6). Distinctive powers were and still are obtained from directly and indirectly moving among and participating in *nguillatun* or *rehuekuel* fields in the valley today, and simultaneously seeing the maximum number of sacred places and horizons possible (see Chapter 5). The simultaneity of this also marked a transition and a passage into the ethereal *Wenumapu* world. Thus, vision to all geographically available *rehuekuel* and other sacred spots on the horizon gave these places a "vision of power," which, is appropriately expressed in the names given to several localities today: *wedange* or evil eye, *ojos de canelo* (eyes of the sacred cinnamon tree). In effect, the visual pilgrimages between *rehuekuel* constituted a mental bridge and passageway between the individual *kuel* that formed part of the valley-long network of kinship topographies. Mounds were located in the most dominating geographic positions in the valley where they acted as embodiments of power and where they showed unity and advancement for future actions, which sought to incorporate people into more public projects and into defending the area against outsiders. The pilgrimages across these complexes closed symbolic kinship spaces and real physical spaces and rendered them historically as one united religious and political space.

Paradoxically, mounds not only represented the crystallization of past and present experiences through ritual practice but also something far more immediate: a direct communication from the ancestors who first built them and from the deities who viewed them as their offspring and representatives in *Nag Mapu* space and who entrusted them to their descendants. This is the way that *kuel* (and their grouping into *rehuekuel* complexes) embodied the past directly. They constituted the regenerative powers of the ancestors. They were celebrated with offerings of *chicha*, food, and animal and human sacrifices. (Mountains and other sacred features, especially those relating to the upper *Wenumapu* world, such as *Wenucolla*, have something of the same status. They too are celebrated with offerings.) Instead of being solid archaeological objects, *kuel* became through offerings and through "walking" around the valley (see Chapter 5), a combination and recombination of people, kinsmen, and histories.

The redundant spatial and visual organization of *kuel* and *rehuekuel* may have been the ideal structure of religious and political order based on the cosmological themes of *Ngenechen*, *Pillan*, volcanoes, and ancestral spirits, but their location and replication also related to political struggle and social reorganization. Although activity within the Purén and Lumaco Valley was directed by the architectural arrangements of the *rehuekuel*, the architectural form of the individual *kuel* was a product of cosmology and political circumstance. The ceremonial activity and geography of the mounds formed parts of a symbolic organization in which each affected and reflected the other. Not only did the undertaking of different activities at particular places and along specific topographic pathways within the valley draw on this structure but also the traditional *admapu* principles of order underlaid its organization and provided an ontological status to those actions which inevitably involved both secular and shamanic agency, authority, and interlineage heterarchical relations (see Chapter 7).

Symbolic uniformity, organizational emulation, and direct and indirect participation in ceremony in core areas like Purén and Lumaco alone, however, were not enough to create a larger functioning political organization. Members of expanding *ayllarehue* and *butanmapu* groups had to exchange information, pool their separate experiences, and identify problems by which they could then develop some kind of common denominator or agreement. This was largely achieved through political *cahuin* (*parlamentos* in Spanish texts), and through other gatherings. Even though organizational uniformity and communication contributed to the emergence of more complex interregional political groupings, especially the *butanmapu* in the late 1500s and early 1600s, a more powerful vehicle was necessary to enable patrilineages to more fully integrate. The groupings must have had a procedural pattern for the regular collection and exchange of important information, for discussion, and for deciding the appropriate action. Decisions were implemented only if they were backed by some type of authority, and by the tactical exercise (*sensu* Wolf 1999) of the complementary power of paramount leaders and shamans. What was this higher order?

As discussed in Chapter 7, authority was seen through its symbolism and public ceremonies, and leadership was fulfilled as *toqui*, *ülmen*, and other leader types manipulated symbols through power given to them by the lineages themselves and through the power of flows of people, ideas, and things through special places like the *rehuekuel* centers. Thus, power was essentially symbolic and leadership was a process of mutual stimulation between the members of larger groupings. Ritual mediated statements about social formation also were important, with leader's power being characterized more often by a monopoly on important ceremonies and more egalitarian settings by much more open feasting systems. It can be seen in the written texts that as leaders' power grew in some areas, commensal feasting became more important, and there emerged a greater pressure placed on leaders to assert themselves as social units through more feasting and ritual. Cosmologies and shamans also were very important to secular leaders, because they guaranteed uniformity in thinking and policy vis-à-vis authentic and mythic ancestors and a common language that had depth and breadth. Shamans did not just legitimize the actions of secular leader's actions, they also forced leaders to use *admapu* or traditional law (Bacigalupo 2004a, 2004b; Dillehay 1985a, 1985b), and they often acted as cultural interruptors who employed their power to support certain leaders and causes. It was the *machi's* (or other ritual leaders) mentality and cosmologies that gave a similar language and influenced leaders to be less individualized and personalized. They also encouraged leaders to place their personal networking with a corporate *ayllarehue* structure and provided a check and balance system of power. These were not coercive matters, but they were instruments engaged in the organization of consent and cooperation. Nor does it imply domination and subjugation but tactical organization and coordination by both the secular and ritual leaders.

In effect, the mounded landscape became a fundamental institution of the early *estado* in the Purén and Lumaco Valley and the relations between four historical times – Andean, Araucanian, Inka, and Spanish – which resulted from an increase in the vertical depth of historical time as it was both pushed further and further back into the past and brought increasingly forward in order to compact it into intersected ceremonial spaces (e.g., *nguillatun*) that ideologically served the founding and eventual expansion of the *estado* polity. The cultivation of mounds, the reenactment of ancestral rituals, the appropriation of past symbols, and the local anchoring of origin stories all contributed to the cult of politics associated with an Araucanian polity, ethnicity, and nationalism that developed in the early seventeenth century. For sacred histories, the Araucanian origin tale of the struggle between the two reptiles – one bent on destroying humankind and the other given to saving it – was fundamental to the constitution of the *kuel* narratives studied in Chapter 5. The significance of these accounts resides in their narrative structure where the living and the dead both worked as agents yet with different roles and where key episodes or events in the origin story and the narratives reveal both divine intention and the attachment of human significance to these events. Strictly speaking, in these narratives and in other tales chronological time is replaced by sacred time, a time controlled by the ancestors, when something of significance was made manifest. As stated earlier, I am convinced that these histories were partially annexed to Inka histories of resistance and expansion as memorials of achieved and remembered Andean history but also as new Araucanian histories. Although functionally, the mounds served for burial, ceremony, and commemoration, symbolically, they were vehicles for the edification of a pan-Araucanian (if not pan-Andean) resistance and the confirmation of its utopic vision.

While the Araucanian polity may have historically achieved a wider geographic expression as a result of regional processes at the *estado* level in the sixteenth and seventeenth centuries, the organizational dynamics within the populations initiated processes of cultural change locally and independently of regional forces. As a material manifestation of these processes, *rehuekuel* were found only in places where people experienced high population density, heterogeneous lives embedded in emulated religious and political organizational structures, and "inscribed" mounded landscapes. People in conflicted frontier zones such as Purén, Lumaco, Tucupel, and Arauco created institutional roles for themselves that stood in sharp contrast to the interior hinterland and created a template for organizational behavior that made sense only in this setting (see Chapters 3 and 7). The concentration of dynastic political power in the Purén and Lumaco Valley brought about behavioral possibilities and new ways of acting out compatriotism that either were absent or denied to other areas. Although the boundaries of these places emerged through regional dynamics, valley residents perceived the density and cultural homogeneity they experienced as circumscribed by the limits of the valley space. (Even today they call the Purén Valley the "cave in the ground," implying a deep boundedness and serenity in the Mapudungun language.)

This reasoning may explain why *kuel* and *rehuekuel* do not occur everywhere in the Araucanian region (and why local-level, non-*rehuekuel*-oriented, individual burial mounds were continuously built along with the larger multi-mounded *rehuekuel* fields; see Chapter 6). As the material correlates of larger patrilineal groupings and *ayllarehue*, the *rehuekuel* complexes, while conferring a wider degree of geographic and political unity on the regional level, provided a different effect on the local social and political institutions comprising them. If these complexes gave the region a solidity and permanence, this was achieved at the price of a lack of ideological flexibility on the local level. These complexes were not well adjusted to respond to local and to short-term ideological and historical requirements, because they were more oriented toward regional and future needs. I see no evidence to suggest that local needs were always met by these complexes. However, the continued use of single, isolated burial mounds of locally important leaders, which were never built for or incorporated into *rehuekuel* complexes, probably met this need by continually injecting new and local life into patrilineages. They made the order of local affairs dynamic, mobilizing them strategically in relation to the more immediate ideological and political exigencies of the particular patrilineal moment but also connecting them to the larger regional processes through ceremonies in the multi-*lov rehuekuel*.

To conclude this section, the succession of ritual spaces – mounds and *nguillatun* fields – imparted an alignment in plan which is a general feature throughout the Purén and Lumaco Valley. Formal rigidity, however, was secondary, as many examples indicate – in particular the small mounds located on regular plots and terraces that flank larger mounds. Although no two mounds or mound complexes are the same, they collectively suggest a level of architectural uniformity and social identity with them arrived through topographic subtleties which transcended the scope of formal repetition, and imply a strong sense of interpretative flexibility and familiarity. They also are silhouetting the familiar and sacred volcanoes (where the great deity *Pillan* lives) visible along the eastern horizon by duplicating their profiles. In this sense, the mounds were "analogical" monuments that were visual analogies with other mounds or natural features (*sensu* Pearson 1994:56). The mounded landscape was ordered by topographic pathways in the valley that represented destiny and the pathways of the participants in rotating ceremonies. The creation of pathways and boundaries as physical features also was associated with needs of defense, territory, and containment. Entrances and physical barriers, such as walls, crests, steep slopes, and other earthworks, marked differences in lineage domains and thus restricted and controlled access between them. By physically dividing up and demarcating the valley, they classified and controlled places and relationships more readily. All of this transposed a series of elements or ideas into a nest of symbolic parts and into parallels with the original creation. While each emphasized particular aspects of the creation story, together they incorporated the principal features of the act of creation, that is, the primordial mound. The categories of order inherent within the mounded architecture of the valley formed part of a wider symbolic classification embracing many spheres of meaning. Such meanings could be mobilized only through repeated social and ceremonial practices. Not only did the undertaking of different activities at particular places within the valley draw on this symbolism, but also the religious principles of order that underlaid its organization provided an ontological status to those actions which inevitably involved authority and dominance.

NAUCHI: MOUND LITERACY AND THE SOCIAL WORKING OF REHUEKUEL

Archaeologists often interpret monuments as forms and places of exclusivity and confinement for elite activity and burial (see Bradley 1998; Lewis et al. 1998; Trigger 1990). The *rehuekuel* mound complexes are not so much a matter of exclusivity but of inclusivity and feasting by all social levels, operating a complex set of interlineage relations whose development might more fruitfully be related to the formation of the topographic pathways and nodalities discussed in Chapter 6, where ceremonial participation occurred. These relations and pathways formed part of the public awareness of the organizational power that I believe was already partly Andean before contact with the Inka and later partly emulated from the latter prior to the arrival of the Spanish. The *ayllarehue* political and religious institutions comprising the ceremonies at these localities, by contrast, were involved in the transfer of ideas, objects, and people from the enclosed domains of local patrilineages, in which they had previously participated, to restructure the plural *rehuekuel* audiences and to progressively open more public feasting areas where they formed vehicles for inscribing and showcasing the ideas and visions of the new order being formed throughout the Araucanian society.

This organization was reinforced by two different sets of religious institutions and their accompanying knowledge/power relations in the *rehuekuel* complexes, whose histories, in these respects, ran in opposing temporal directions, albeit intersecting in public ceremony. One was the mound literacy, or *nauchi*, of individual lineage members with the past reflecting on the future (i.e., knowing how to conduct oneself in ceremony and especially to read *kuel* behavior to protect and benefit society, as was the case in the *TrenTrenkuel* and *Hualonkokuel* rituals), and the other was the *nguillatun* ceremony with the future reflecting on the past. Yet they are also parallel histories. These institutions brought together a multitude of spaces and histories. In doing so, they translated these spaces and histories into special religio-political settings, which, when negotiated by actions of leaders and lineage members, in simultaneously ordering lineages for recruitment and ordering the public that participated in them, were to have a profound and lasting influence on the subsequent development of political structure, public ceremony, and social harmony.

In many ways, mound literacy was based on a sense of belonging to a stable patrilineage and of becoming a dutiful compatriot (and almost citizen) of the newly restructured society: in this case, the "imagined community," or imagined polity, was the idealized utopic one that was believed to be developing, or whose incipient rise was celebrated and fostered even more in the form of an ethnic identity and regionalized, if not nationalized, Araucanian resistance. As Leiva states again:

> Los araucanos de ese tiempo nos parecen también un caso de desen-volvimiento de la cultura a partir del espíritu nacional: la resistencia a la dominación y la autosuficiencia. Vemos además que entre los araucanos se despertaron intereses crecientemente nacionales de una manera intensa y desconocida antes. Tenemos así una prueba de la tenacidad del vínculo, de las cualidades los rasgos culturales con el suelo la tierra, de lo que llama Kroeber, "la facultad a un mismo tiempo absorbente y resistente de una cultura" que, durante muchos años, por más que se difunden préstamos culturales a su interior, logra conversarse como algo propio. Por último, los araucanos logran encon-trar la norma dinámica para organizar su sociedad: la guerra. (Leiva 1977:160)

> The Araucanians of that time appear to us as a case of the development of a culture beginning with a national spirit: resistance to domina-tion and self-sufficiency. Moreover, we see that there arose among the Araucanians an increasingly intense and previously unknown national interests. Thus we have proof of the tenacity of the link, of the nature of cultural traits with the land, of what Kroeber calls, "the capacity of a culture to absorb and resist at the same time." Which, over many years, for all that cultural borrowings diffuse into its interior, succeeds in finding the dynamic principle to organize their society: warfare. (Leiva 1977:160)

In particular, mound literacy perfected the public acts associated with var-ious forms of multilineage movement, recruitment, and adoption that came to suffice the Purén, Lumaco, and other populations with a new identity and power during this early period of tension. Set within this framework, the *rehuekuel* complexes were the materialized responses (*sensu* DeMarrais et al. 1996) to the need for politico–religious order by exhibiting different *kuel* behaviors, such as the different negotiated circumstances seen in the two ritual narratives presented in Chapter 5, and thus by forcing old and new lineage members to learn about and learn from these behaviors, but one which also worked to transform the Araucanian culture – it became a matter of winning the hearts and minds of different groups as well as the discipline and training of the members comprising newly formed corporate bodies. As such, public ceremony rendered the forces and principles of order visible to the populace – transformed, here, into an Araucanian ethnicity, territory, and compatriotism. Through the provision of object lessons in the shamanic ritual discourses with local *kuel*, the military actions with outsiders, and the political organizational power of *ayllarehue* – the agency (and power) of *toqui*, *machi*, and other leaders to command and arrange people required a greater public awareness and participation – they sought to allow the people to know and regulate themselves, which gave agency to people; to become both the subjects and the objects of ancestral knowledge and power. I envision this process having unfolded in the following manner.

First was the tendency for the mid-sixteenth-century Purén and Lumaco society to begin to reorganize itself in response to increased conflict with the Spanish. This is especially clear in attempts to sponsor larger feasts, to reorganize and build new *rehuekuel* complexes, and to make them visible from various landscape points, and hence knowable, as a wider ceremonial network. While local patrilineage life was penetrated by developing networks of fragmented groups, local communities increasingly opened up their lives and their lands to public participation in multiple ceremonies across the valley. Second was the increased involvement of certain lineage agents in the provision of public ceremonies. Here I am speaking of the individual achievements of rulers like Lautaro, Lientur, Anganamón, Pelantaro, Butapichón, and so on (see Chapters 3 and 7). This was effective because these leaders could retain direction over policy by virtue of their control over public gatherings and especially the *rehuekuel* settings where they occurred. Third was that the *rehuekuel* complexes provided a context for the permanent but alternating display of both shamanic and secular authority. Ceremonies formed part of a system of growing religious and political power, which recharged itself in the rotation of ritual display from community to community, as it does today in the valley through a network of *nguillatun* ceremonies. The recursiveness of ceremonies ensured this display and provided opportunities for the display of leader's tactical and organizational power (*sensu* Wolf 1999), which manifested itself in sponsoring events and in administering objects, space, and the relations between the living and the dead.

Such practices consisted not just in a staging of power that positioned recruited lineages on the other side of leader's power as its potential recipients but sought rather to place them – as compatriots-in-the-making within the expanding polity – on the growing side of organizational power as its subject and its beneficiary. There was an identity with leader's organizational power, which was a force regulated and channeled by society's ruling patrilineages but for the good of all: this was the rhetoric of the tactical and oratory power of *toqui*, *ülmen*, and *weupin* embodied in public ceremony – power that was manifested not only in its ability to relate to the ancestors, to the deities, and to the *Nag Mapu* land but also to its ability to organize and coordinate a structural order of things and to produce a place for multiple lineages in relation to ancestral time–space orders (see Chapter 4). The ideological politics of the Araucanian principles of cosmological organization transformed *rehuekuel* into the aesthetic material signifiers of the utopic progress, a progress also reminiscent of the past Inka – but of progress as a collective "ethnic" achievement with *kuel*, *rehuekuel*, mountains, and volcanoes as the great topo-coordinators of this movement. This tactical and organizational power of leaders thus subjugated fragmented groups by public feasting and by placing itself on the side of the people by affording them a place within its workings – a power which placed the people behind it, ritually invited into complicity with it rather than coerced into submission before it.

In retrospect, one problem faced by all societies that attempt to build large-scale organizations is how to integrate local activity into higher levels of organization (e.g., Agnew 1999; Allen 1999; Johnson 1982; Yoffee 2005). Identification of the local with the regional took place only through the use of symbols that identified the one with the other. With the spread of the Araucanian polity, organizational problems arose that had never before been confronted on such a vast geographic scale. What was it that made a patrilineal community in one part of the early "*estado*" a loyal participating member rather than an autonomous political unit? How were local lineages encouraged to think of themselves as part of such nebulous and distant concepts as the *ayllarehue* and the *butanmapu*, when all they may have seen from time to time were occasional visiting leaders and warriors, the latter often outsiders themselves? Part of the solution was to construct standardized public monuments and to repeat large-scale public ceremonies that served as perpetual reminders of regional ties and pan-Araucanian principles of organization and beliefs. This use of ritual ceremony to tie local communities to a pan-Araucanian sense of compatriotism assumed urgency when new *ayllarehue* were established. Establishing local ceremonies in all areas did this. Regular ceremonies were held in each community in order to foster a sense of unity with the larger *ayllarehue* and *butanmapu* organizations and thus make individual communities believe that they were becoming part of and belonging to a larger entity. These common public displays, with their standardized presentations at local ceremonies, not only related the local people to the broader polity, but also provided a symbolic means for the local people to identify with Araucanians living elsewhere in the new order. Prior to the arrival of the Spanish, many of these people had been considered non-kinsmen and, in some cases, enemies; but now, as they were all busily performing the same rituals and learning how to interact through ritually enacted mound literacy, they have been redefined as fellow Araucanians, as becoming compatriots of the same indigenous movement.

In summary, little scholarly work has focused on the internal social dynamics of lineage groups that were forced to live shared lives during the early wars with the Spanish. As stated previously, I believe that an objective of both secular and sacred leaders was to reduce the social variation or diversity that the political centralizing tendency of multiple *ayllarehue* and the *butanmapu* was creating. That is, the parallel processes of population nucleation and centralization were much more manageable if the variation across multiple lineages could be more standardized and diminished – that is reducing ambiguity and unknowns – which was done by spatially, socially, and temporally compressing history, by reascribing lineage identities, and thus by controlling the immediate social "destiny" by making everyone more common. When incorporating too many different lineage voices and experiences, it probably was much more difficult for leaders to direct diversity, but this was done by taking vulnerable groups and redefining their histories, which already was partially linked via prior exchange of women in the virilocal patrilineal system. Too many lineage histories and too many different voices could lead to congested social memories and thus to an unmanageable ceremony and restructuring of kinship relations. Leaders needed to fuse local and nonlocal social memories and genealogies. This was done through repetitive participation in ceremony, which established interlineage communalities of social memory and identity.

These remarks make clear where situation-defining strategies of leader's agency were focused and what their limitations were. This agency was not about patterns that might be discerned in the flow of Araucanian history, except insofar as they impacted upon everyday lives. Nor did it have to do with the outcome of grand designs directed toward planned changes. But these patterns came alive in the actions of leaders such as Anaganamón, Lientur, Butapichón, and *machi* or other ritual specialists who experienced, categorized, and adapted to them by redefining their social order and by employing ancestral knowledge to achieve their goals. To put it another way, agency, authority, and religious power were functions of knowledge of the past and how it could be employed to direct the present and future. Agency also laid in the pragmatic and political approach to the use of various identities and symbolism and in deciding which of these were contextually acceptable or more appropriate. It was these creative and interpretative strategies in different military, political, and religious settings, employed tactically by *toqui* war leaders, *ülmen*, *machi*, and other leaders, which offered new understandings of the processes by which identities and compatriotism were produced.

IDENTITIES, COMPATRIOTS, AND *AYLLAREHUE*

One purpose of this book has been to establish the existence of certain patterns in the history of the Araucanians, patterns that would appear to be cyclical in their order of emergence and disappearance, following the dynamics of expansion and contraction of patrilineage, *ayllarehue*, and *butanmapu* political organizations. The clash of different social forces in the 1500s drew together a heterogeneous cluster of histories and identities: that of indigenous movements seeking to form an identity against the forces of Spanish contact and threats of territorial and cultural dispossession; that of several generations of patrilineages removed from their original homelands and seeking new identities in new places; and that of a traditional indigenous social order and identity, rooted in despair and in defense of its existence. There are numerous variations of these themes that can be documented in the ethnographic, textual, and archaeological records, from forced adoption to less stringent recruitment tactics (see Chapters 3, 4, 5, 7). But these variations are not just examples of the way lineages interacted. They also are part of the changing identity structure of the Araucanian population and the way in which identity and compatriotism were constituted.

Contact with the Spanish implied a heightening of Araucanian social activity – of seeking, of finding, of opposing – and a frenetic creativity in the adaptation to changing political conditions. In the mid-1500s, I think that this created an identity crisis at the core of local patrilineage communities – one related to ethnic and spatial repositioning. Yet, the crisis of identity in the center was expressive of a more general crisis. This crisis consisted in the weakening of former local identities in the patrilocal and patrilineal society and the emergence of new regional identities – especially the emergence of a kind of suprapatrilocal membership or "compatriot." I see this specifically related to what the Araucanians called *ayllarehue*. In the abstract meaning of membership in regional *ayllarehue* communities, each is defined as a nine patrilineal or *rehue*-governed society identified with primordial loyalties to the *Araucanian cause*, ethnicity, local community, language, and other culturally concrete forms. As noted throughout this study, a centralized state never formed but an Araucanian confederation of supralineage *ayllarehue* or a regional polity did form.

As is the case with many primary or secondary polity formations (cf. Yoffee 2005), the constituent *ayllarehue* groups were never successfully assimilated to a central imperial identity. Thus, the dissolution of local patrilineages and the constant emergence of new *ayllarehue* territorialities were two aspects of the same phenomenon. In this case, the disorder was related to the dissolution of more encompassing local structures and the outcome was the increasing integration of lower-order patrilineages through fragmentation, recruitment, and annexation, the emergence of new solidarities and new political units and, as a result, a new and increasing scope for solidarities and conflicts (see Bengoa 1985, 2003, and

Villalobos et al. 1982 for excellent discussions of these relations). In order to reorganize the society, there must have been sufficient and necessary conditions for this, which socially revolved around the *ayllarehue* and spatially and ceremonially around the *rehuekuel*.

Whereas members of newly formed *ayllarehue* communities were often culturally heterogenous and likely drawn from various areas (see Krumm 1971), at the same time, there were certain overall cultural understandings concerning what a community member, or compatriot, should value, believe, and think. The *ayllarehue* displayed a certain distinct religious and civic style in this respect – a certain *esprit de corps* or corporate culture. Its esprit de corps was a function of the negotiated new religio-political order produced by the interaction between the different patrilineages for which it could be regarded as a political meeting place. As a negotiated social order, the *ayllarehue* comprising the polity or *estado* did not necessarily correspond in their geographical boundaries to the many patrilineages which made them up, but still they produced an espirit de corps, which affected the understandings and values of social relations and the way in which they functioned. This interaction mainly concerned the development of Araucanian values and norms, which reduced demands and pressures on some local groups. The internal differences with respect to basic orientations and values thus contributed to a reduction of the social conflict that was brought about by such drastic changes as contact with "others" and the population displacement and adoption of new groups. Increased public ceremonies, creation of a new warrior social category, and the consumption of Spanish and captive indigenous (those who sided with the Spanish) "others" alleviated some tensions by producing a heightened and new sense of self-identity – an Araucanian identity largely defined by opposition and increased interaction between multiple patrilineage communities (*rehue*) and single communities of multiple patrilineal families (*lov*).

In other words, social identities during this period must have been individual and patrilineal tugs-of-war between different forces. Every patrilineage, if not nearly every compatriot, must have sensed a kind of push and pull, an inevitable ever-increasing conflict between, on the one hand, their affiliation to their home lineage and, on the other, their allegiance to new social and political forms that were in the process of forming. But these groups also must have derived their identities from particular features and understandings of the landscape in much the way that people do today in the valley. They have a "*topophilia*" for the *kuel*, *rehuekuel*, and other sacred places, an attachment they feel for these places.

My understanding of these transformations is similar in some ways to Boccara's thesis (1999; cf. Leiva 1977), who believes that Araucanian society formed a warrior membership and self-identity that greatly altered the relationships between different social units in the late sixteenth century when warfare with the Spanish sporadically intensified (see discussion in Chapter 3). However, warfare also produced a new identity that formed across the society and was associated with the *ayllarehue* and with the construction of a civic society. The more profound affective dimensions of these developments were expressed in symbolic form in which various events, material objects, and aesthetically effective landscapes communicated the common structures that linked people together and integrated their activities within different *ayllarehue* units. One such symbolic form was the *rehuekuel*, which was used to create and sustain patrilineal community identities. Other forms were human sacrifice and trophy head exchange. As implied by Boccara, the *ayllarehue* collectivities were situationally induced and determined and therefore ultimately definable only in subjective terms. Multilineage identities were apparently crystallized fairly quickly by the situational pressures of the frontier in the late 1500s and early 1600s, vested interests of individual secular and sacred lineage agents, and the myriad other forces that operated to differentiate yet aggregate political entities. The realities of the shifting power structures, as well as the variable military policies and practices of the Spanish, made it necessary for the Araucanians to seek unification and independence within the larger political unit in which fate had placed them, and this consisted of the *ayllarehue* subterritories composed of individual patrilineages which made up the *estado* and later the *butanmapu* organization. It was this sheer practical necessity to maintain independence when faced with increased contact with the Spanish which eventually made the larger multi–*ayllarehue butanmapu* territory the focus in the 1600s and 1700s. The growth of this larger territorial unit over the traditional patrilineal *rehue* and *ayllarehue* groups was further strengthened by the far greater opportunity it presented for rapid social mobility, pronounced leader agency, political ascendancy of a rising warrior and later merchant elites (see Jones 1999; Mandrini 1992), and shifting identities.

Identity requires difference in order to have meaning, and it converts difference into otherness in order to secure its own self-certainty (Connolly 1991). Identity also is relational and collectible. These relational processes are tied to who has the power to construct the social identity of others. As pointed out in the last chapter, the tasks for secular leaders (*toqui* and *ülmen*) in the late 1500s and early 1600s was to erase the identity of, or to *disidentify* (the process of changing or subordinating an old identity and making a new one), recruited lineages with their original or homeland identities and to adopt local ones. Thus, it was not just establishing alliances but also of modifying the identity of these incoming recruited or annexed groups. Disidentity thus must have become a strategic power of leaders that was grounded in the setting of public ceremony where genealogies and local histories were recognized and then reidentified for outsiders. The mutual dependence derived from these processes was the basis for articulating recursive nodal points at standardized *rehuekuel* that were reworked through the continuous disidentification and reidentification of displaced lineages adopted into local ones. Recognizing these manipulated identities as partly tied to leadership agency and to the situational constructs of warfare, recruitment, and public ceremony directs us to the patrilineal hegemony of *toqui* leaders and others, as to how their hegemonic social power fixed identities around geographic pathways and nodal points in the Purén and Lumaco Valley or in other places where identity was deconstructed, reconstructed, and regulated by these agents. The maintenance of identity and its public material expression took the form of *kuel* and *rehuekuel* construction and the spread of the Mapudungun language, religion, and legal codes throughout south-central Chile and large areas of Argentina in the seventeenth and eighteenth centuries.

The new Araucanian social order of the early contact period liberated some people from their local lineage loyalties and fused them into larger civic-political *ayllarehue* communities, which provided a sense of belonging and security to uprooted lineages joining stable ones. This order must have elevated the public domain of political and religious union over the private sphere of individual family lineages and economic life and signaled membership within the wider cause. It transformed the need to subsist economically to a need to survive politically, with a rationalized collective deliberation over a common destiny, usually through a political process of attempted increased centralization of multiple lineages within *rehuekuel*, *ayllarehue*, and later *butanmapu* structures that replaced fragmented and overlapping leadership authority with uniform practices within its wider territorial boundaries. These new systems of boundaries were inscribed around diverse groups made up of different lineage populations.

A necessary response of stable or powerful lineages such as those in Purén and Lumaco must have been to redefine the social boundaries within them to realign with the growing diversity of stable and fragmented identities within it. There also must have been cases when there was resistance to dominant lineages (see Chapters 3 and 7). And there must have been increased fragmentation of evermore complex social categories of warrior groups, secular and sacred leaders, and marriage groupings, as a result of the increased mixing of local and regional populations. And because these newly defined categories were in essence existing categories, I suggest that they left intact the traditional system of social and cultural boundaries used to collect diversity in the first place (see Bengoa [2003:393–518] for descriptions of the disruptive nature of the war in the late 1500s and early 1600s).

All of these new relations were not just about forming a polity but also creating a sense of community and compatriotism. There were certain duties that all lineage and *ayllarehue* members had to perform, and, when called upon, defending political alliances and frontiers which, because they created order, made the achievement of other purposes and goals possible. The argument is therefore that if the new order created productive compatriots, including warriors, support agriculturalists, craft specialists, leaders, laborers at large, and so on, it also at the same time, created a multilineage religious and political community intimately linked with local and regional ancestors. If the conditions for the religious practice of compatriotism were met, then so, too, were those for the existence of the *rehuekuel* cosmological communities. So, the idea of community also had to do with formal organization and with a sense of belonging and commitment to the new polity order and to Araucanian cosmology.

Thus, the Araucanian polity of the late 1500s and early 1600s was not only premised on new social organizations but on a new consciousness of interlineage membership and compatriotism. The elimination of some lineage divisions through recruitment and annexation must have been crucial for allowing the free association and solidarity on which communities of mixed interlineage members were formed. In the Araucanian polity, with the exception of Spanish and *yanacona* (other "*indios*") slaves and captives, all lineage members had compatriot privileges and responsibilities. Individuals became members of social units larger than themselves, and one of these larger units was the political community formed by *ayllarehue*. Politics and territorial defense thus became a communal affair, and it was an enduring political attachment that provided compatriots – those loyal to the Araucanian cause – with new identities. Compatriots were who they were by virtue of participating in the life of the political and religious community and by identifying with its identity. Pursuing the common goal of territorial defense was the core of the compatriot's political virtue. Individuals and patrilineages were regarded as beholden to their *ayllarehue* and were required to demonstrate an ever-growing loyalty to leaders and to the emerging polity. If not, they were often executed or exiled as revealed in quotes presented in Chapters 3 and 7.

Membership and compatriotism were guided by publicly recognized *admapu* rules and procedures that those who were cooperating had to accept and regard as properly regulating their conduct. Fair terms of cooperation specified ideas of kinship reciprocity or mutuality. A conception of political justice characterized the fair terms of social cooperation between rulers and kinsmen, as was demonstrated in the case of the leader's and warrior's wives who lost husbands in battle and who demanded customary compensation from the *toqui* who were responsible for their loss (see Chapter 7). In particular, individuals recognized that they had rights and duties, which extended further than the minimally civic respect for others, and which were associated with the fact that they identified themselves socially as leaders, nonleaders, warriors, and so on; as members of a religion, as slaves, captives, or recruited allies. Some of these social identities were no doubt chosen by individuals, but most were the "givens" of their patrilineal existence and place of residence. These identities were expressive of many changing forms of collective life, and many carried explicit duties with them. If one of the social identities to which duties were attached was that of a responsible member or compatriot of the lineage or *ayllarehue*, then one of the forms of collective life was the political and religious community. In a political community what was shared was identity, determined largely by patrilineal descent and in part from a common history, or continued occupancy of the same territory.

In order to empower lineage members with compatriotism and with duties and rights, the institutional setting also had to be appropriate (Goldfarb 1998; Lefort 1988; Maalouf 1996). There had to be places where potentially everyone could take part, where everyone could do something and to share publicly. That place in Araucanian society was the *rehuekuel*. Yet even empowerment and opportunity together were not sufficient for the practice of compatriotism. What was further required was a particular ideology, which not only prompted individuals to recognize what their duties were as compatriots but also motivated them to perform them as well. This ideology was practiced in "prescriptive" public ceremony and other communal gatherings. Compatriots were learners, and enculturation and indoctrination in the sense of the building of the appropriate religious character for willing engagement in the practice of compatriotism never ceased, as clearly revealed in the two ritual narratives reported in Chapter 5, where the *machi* shamans constantly remind people of their duty to be obedient, respectful, and proper of ritual acts and of the *kuel*, ancestors, and deities. These narrative rituals and others reflect what Sahlins (1985:28) defines as prescriptive rituals "with bounded groups and compelling rules that prescribe in advance much of the way people act and interact." In these groups, "nothing is new, or at least happenings are valued for their similarity to the system as constituted. What happens then is the projection of the existing order." To me, the prescriptive rituals performed in public ceremony at *rehuekuel* and *nguillatun* fields were part of a utopically engineered order guided by existing Araucanian values.

There are many questions raised by the issues presented for which I have no answers. For example, how long was it possible to avert the danger of diverse patrilineage's members being forced to endorse a collective interest that they did not necessarily view as their own? When would such communities come to exist outside, and therefore above, the individual families who originally constituted them and came to resemble a closed, hierarchical society? What was the social status of different recruited groups? Did the admission of diversity into the patrilineal community allow its communal compatriotism to take precedence over local identities? I raise these questions to point out the many possible outcomes that must have resulted from these historical processes and also to suggest topics for future study.

Memory and Perpetuity

I have discussed in previous publications how the present-day Araucanians draw upon historical ceremonial forms and social memories in the bonding of communities (Dillehay 1985, 1990c, 1999, 2003). Selected aspects of a previous religious and social organization have been organizationally transformed and have become the focus of the contemporary *nguillatun* and *rehuekuel* ceremonial form. Yet, history and social memory in the Araucanian case are more than simply histories repeating themselves ceremonially. It is the use of history, identity, and memory for a purpose. The continued use of ancient monuments and ceremonial fields, as generational and relational monuments, that emerged in times of conflict with the outside world in the early historic period is congruent with the current Mapuche struggle for culture survival in the Chilean world. Through the twentieth century, there has been a continual practice of regional ceremonies at ancient *nguillatun* and *rehuekuel* and of the maintenance of sacred monuments.

While many monuments are still preserved today, the Mapuche or Araucanian communities around them are changing, and so are their histories. These changes have lead to several alternatives in the perceived meaning of monuments. First, the interpretation of Araucanian history has generally remained the same but has been enriched with new knowledge, and symbolic meaning in memory has been enhanced. Second, historical events and interpretations of them have changed the course of history, and the Araucanians have reinterpreted the dedicated meanings used in memory for past events. These additional interpretations of history can also be contradictory, and thus memories are seen as having conflicting meanings. Finally, certain events are considered less important, and they are largely forgotten as a result – meaning that monuments simply fade away (Dillehay 1990a, 2002) as in the case of authentic ancestors changing to mythic ones.

Understanding these issues benefits from the direct historical approach gained from moving back and forth between written texts, live informants, and archaeological records, for over time ancestral traditions were secured as the seal of destiny, the desirable culmination of the past and the present, laden with future promise. Whether deployed as a pre-articulated policy so weighted in the present that its fulfillment was destined to arrive, or presented *ex post facto* as a selective ordering of past events that demonstrated the present as a casual link in a past/future cycle – ancestral cosmology was used by *machi* and others to support the *toqui* who were the heirs of those who came before them.

Araucanian cosmology was a system of representations which served to sustain existing relations of patrilineage domination and prestige by orienting local level individuals toward the future through the past and to build new relations of dominance and cooperation with outsiders by orienting them toward the past of others (e.g., Inka) as well for survivability. All of this was materially oriented toward images and ideas that revealed relations and guided them more toward a collective pursuit of social connectedness and survivability. This is not a continuum of Araucanian past-present-future but future-present-past-future. It was a material record of mounds, other sacred sites, and domestic localities that expanded in forward-flowing time and became indistinguishable from one collapsing in backward-flowing time. This is best represented in the time–space compaction in the *nguillatun* ceremony. This also is somewhat similar to what Rappaport (1985) observed among the Cumbales of Colombia. Historical events happened in the past, but because the Cumbales live their consequences today, the past is present for the future. Hence the abuses of the past can be corrected and history can serve as a moral of the future (cf. Faron 1964). For the Cumbales, then, historical knowledge (or what is *admapu* traditional knowledge to the Araucanians) is a political strategy and a potential source of power that is continually deployed in the past and present. As Lillios (2003:146) related in her study of social memory: "Memories are not primarily about revisiting the past but about defining the present and managing the future of individuals and groups within meaningful, yet shifting, contexts. Thus, the control of memory and the objects of memory is an important component of power."

What is important in all of this is that on the one hand, *admapu* (traditional law) is a concrete representation of the Araucanian's theoretical beliefs, which dramatically reenacts the central principles of life in expanded space and time. On the other hand, the traveling spirit of *machi* (and *kuel*) is a visible temporal capsule that links the afterlife with the past and through the present. It points out, and constantly reminds people of, a radically different conception of reality in which time and space are condensed into one form in ceremony, and are not the restraining barriers they seem to be. Lastly, as if to underscore this point, the *nguillatun* ceremony concretely affirms the principle of patrilineage cohesiveness by validating the belief in ancestors, and in life after death.

Further, the Araucanians have developed a view of time in which they are connected to their ancestors by a seamless genealogical web of mythical and authentic ancestors and to a network of kinsmen *kuel*, and therefore to deified features of the landscape, and finally to forces of the cosmos itself. Such time-related behavior cannot be told alone from the sizes and shapes of mounds and other material expressions, but may be conjectured from other cultural furnishings. I give an example. Still located in a few places are the *chemamüll*, which depict human-like ancestral figures sculpted of wood (see Chapter 4). By imitating the image of authentic ancestors, including their life and death, it is believed that the future may be influenced and the success of battle and other endeavors assured. Sculptures like mounds have mastered time to the Araucanians. They sculpture a sense of time in the people responsible for rituals held at them. Their existence is an outcome of time's arrow – an event in the history of the steady coalescence of the Araucanians and also a confirmation of the continuities of time cycles – a material manifestation of the Araucanian's surviability, with memory, identity, power, and compatriotism all accessed through a sculptured landscape.

Important to this landscape are contexts and processes that ensured social memory. Public ritual repetitively channeled through standardized fields, the display of symbolic objects, repetitive song and dance, and naming and tying local kinsmen to specific dates, places and events, and kin groups coordinated the recollection of kinship relations and alliances by successive generations by using these objects in ceremonies of social healing and of uniting the deal and the living. The old visual roads (*kuifirupu*) between *rehuekuel* and other sacred places in the valley also created and channeled social memory by establishing tangible and symbolic connections with ancestral histories and belief. As Joyce (2003:112) has stated for Maya ritual spaces: "channeled movement was a means through which memory could be rehearsed and, through recall, strengthened." Memory can also be manipulated, erased, and reconstituted as reflected in informant's comments on dismantling one *kuel* in order to mix its "social soil" with the social layers of another *kuel* and on placing soil from distant habitational sites in mounds (see Chapters 5 and 6), which are acts of appropriating the social memory representative of old mounds and existing habitation sites and redefining/reidentifying it with new mounds in the valley-wide network of kin relations. (When we excavated *TrenTrenkuel*, we recovered a portion of a horse skeleton [which usually is the horse of the defunct leader buried inside the mound] that was understood by the local Mapuche to be a secondary burial – one brought from another *kuel* only to be reidentified with *TrenTrenkuel*, they told us.) Redeposited or secondary social soil taken from old mounds and domestic sites, if identified in location with a particular lineage, is a powerful mnemonic device for redefining the genealogy of the dead and thus the living and for metaphorically changing the social memory of local groups and probably adopted ones as well.

But the Araucanian acts and mound spaces were not constituted just to rehearse, recall, and negotiate common memories. Memories and the identities they produced also created rules of compatriotism and how to belong to the society and to conduct proper public ceremony. Again, as shown in the two narratives at the *kuel*, the *machi* constantly chided the ritual audience to conduct themselves properly as members of the society. In this characterization of remembering and learning to be good persons, ceremonial and social education, learning how to belong, and how to conduct proper ritual meant the construction of experience and proper behavior from ancestral knowledge and from the ethereal world of the deities. The memory of historical events, special leaders, and achievements made this knowledge into a useful experience. The memory of these experiences were organized into strategies, ideas, and models which became people's choices and judgments (see Carruthers 1990) in forming the Araucanian polity.

BACK TO THE FUTURE: THE CONFEDERATED UTOPIC LOCALITY – A HETEROTOPIC ENTITY

The elements that formed the ends, priorities, and identifications of the Araucanians and their eventual ethnic shift to Mapuche in the mid-1800s have never fitted neatly together. They have never formed a smooth, harmonious group of mutually sustaining ethnic and political parts. Rather, they are best represented historically as a constellation of constantly shifting conjunctions and disjunctions joined by links of interdependence and disrupted by local and regional obstructions, frictions, and contingencies built into these interdependencies. If one reads closely the early chroniclers and interacts closely with Mapuche communities today, the same forces are in operation – there exists a collective cultural and political identity that was and still is a set of interlocking elements in strife and tension (see Dillehay 1990b:121–41; Faron 1964; Saavedra 2002; Stuchlik 1976), a set periodically scrambled, reorganized, blocked, and gridlocked by contingencies from within and without. But Araucanian/Mapuche society has always tended to represent itself to itself as a relatively harmonious set of geographical parts that functioned smoothly together unless outsiders or forces – inside or outside its boundaries – disrupted this harmony (see Dillehay 1990c, 2003; Stuchlik 1976). Nonetheless, in the Araucanian polity of the sixteenth and seventeenth centuries, the politics of this "imagined" collective identity organized the utopic idealisms of its members into a viable and surviving collective identity. This has always been made up of diverse responses to a general set of pressures and perceptions – responses to pressures of the present linked to perceptions of the past and future among a growing number of political constituencies.

I stated earlier that within sixteenth- and seventeenth-century Araucanian society, there was a mosaic of patrilineages and *ayllarehue* in different developmental stages of unification and/or fragmentation. I wish to emphasize the interconnection or flow of people, ideas, and objects across the boundaries of these social groupings, in contexts in which the polity shaped and contained lineages and their movements. In some ways, it was an imagined polity but a utopic one too that realized many of its objectives. Here is where appropriation of some Inka ideas and the spatial location, distribution, and internal form of *kuel* (as *huacas* or shrines) perhaps came to play.

To reiterate briefly what I described in Chapter 1, utopics does not refer to the establishment of small utopia communities but to broader social practices whereby the utopic ideals that a society has are expressed spatially. Marín (1984) calls this "spatial play." He views utopics implemented as a practice whereby designs for a future order and development are reflected through specific types of planned social spaces and the events associated with them. That is, the utopic engineering of social space produces a network of certain places and nodes that have a degree of centrality and influence within a set of relations. Marín also characterizes these spaces or sites as *heterotopia* (*sensu* Foucault 1984), or "other places," which are viewed as localities of different orders. That is, within a society and the social and spatial order through which it represents itself, certain new sites, or newly interpreted sites, will emerge that offer an alternative expression of social ordering to that which currently exists. Within modern societies, that alternate ordering can be a utopic one that looks to how society might be improved in the future. There is, therefore, a distinct temporal frame that is associated with such sites – they are oriented to the future, or to some sense of the new, rather than to the present or past. It is this temporal frame – newness, and the uncertainty that it brings – that gives it its alternate "other" status or a new direction. Within the practice of utopics, only certain sites, certain nodes within the network, can attain such a status. Following Callon (1986) and Latour (1986), it is only those sites that came to act as obligatory points of passage within a network of social spaces that should be viewed as successful heterotopic sites.

In the Araucanian case, whether it was warfare, increased population size and greater pressure placed on resources, or whatever, the uncertainty and stress of the 1500s and 1600s led to a heightening of tensions. I contend that the *rehuekuel* as multifunctional localities of burial, ceremonial, memorabilia, and social change, gave the Araucanians a sense of other alternatives, other directions. *Rehuekuel* were the obligatory heterotopic points within a framework of religious and political spaces through which the society had to pass and experienced in order to achieve its goals. These places were the material metaphors for the Araucanian cosmology and for shared ideas, histories, and visions. They collectively became a landscape charged with the identity of a utopic vision for the future; they materially and spatially reordered it into a fresh memory network. I further argue that the inter-linked *rehuekuel* came to be seen as a way in which Purén and Lumaco society, represented in these particular places, could be improved not only in terms of the use of natural and social resources or in comparison with other places but also in comparison with its own past. Public gatherings at *rehuekuel* and their focus on the memory of and identity with ancestral knowledge served this purpose. However, the *rehuekuel* were and are also significant in another way too. They helped to order something else – something much more fundamental to the idea of interpatrilineage and *ayllarehue* solidarity. They provided a sense of how public ceremony and political discourse should be organized, and they expressed a new sense of intergroup social spacing that came into acceptance in the latter half of the sixteenth century. These special sites moved or, in Marin's terms, engineered the society forward in cyclical ancestral time, whereby the past worked for the future.

An important aspect of Araucanian engineering was (and still is) the public healing ritual (*dahatun*), which is designed to socially remedy and therapeutically solace the society of its suffering and loss as much as it was to continually link the living and the dead. Healing forms, of which the ancestor spirit is one, function(ed) as philosophical tools for traversing the conditions of temporality the Araucanians know as past, present, and future. The references to *Wenumapu* ancestral spirit-space and the conception of *kuel* as sacred kinsmen are grasped only if we listen closely to the shaman's discourses on healing, and their rationale for choosing their respective themes in the *Hualonkokuel* and *TrenTrenkuel* narratives. In the case of *Hualonkokuel*, healing and ritual were seen as an invocation of ancestral spirits through giving concrete form or body to them before they can enter into the human world. In this view, ritual enabled the shamans to treat the present as a point of transition to and from the past into the future, and to and from the future into the past. Since the present moment, or "the here-and-now," is not actually extended in three-dimensional space, ritual becomes the vehicle for extending it, reminding us that the present finds extension in future states. In the *Tren Trenkuel* ritual, the ethereal planes of the good and evil worlds of the Mapuche were collapsed into a single ritual time–space frame, within which locals and outsiders (the archaeologists) constantly moved back and forth from the past through the present to the future and the reverse. Further, ritual in this case was a medium for shifting identities, manipulating memories, and aligning fictive and real kinsmen, including the *kuel* to whom the ritual was directed. Time was forgotten in this ritual as reference was made to insiders and outsiders, Spanish and Chileans, upper worlds and lower worlds, and proper and improper ways to conduct oneself, all of which is reminiscent of the political and demographic experiences of the Araucanians living in these same lands four hundred years ago. Both rituals reflect multitudes of disorders, disjunctions, and reorderings and conjunctions. But, in essence, all of this was for the future not the past or the present.

In the two ritual narratives, the ritual audiences knew they could not see into the future because the future is not available, but one of the goals of the *machi's* visions (*perimontun*) was to recognize past social principles and the successful ones of others, then compare social orderings for time and change as they looked prior to an event, and metaphorically deconstructing them during the process, and afterward when restructured in response to them. The proposed utopic future presented at the two *kuel* was in a sense an Araucanian social logic in dialogue of memory, identity, and history with events; understanding and deconstructing it helped the *machi* and the audience to make *admapu* sense of otherwise vague actions and unforeseeable time frames. To speak of the past or the future was not a matter of linear time but of mapping out successful events and sacredness and tracing their cause and effect through ancestral and living history. All of this history gives weight to agency and social action in the present (sixteenth century or today), which is informed by knowledge of past times that are similar to the present. Past and present thus inform each other reciprocally for the future. Continued warfare in the past and continued conflicts today over land have built up a continuity of action and infused action with meaning and with what Carruthers (1990) called recollective memory over time (see Chapter 2). Irrespective of the century under study, *kuel* and *rehuekuel* have continuously been perceived as active kinsmen and places to ritually meet to contemplate history then and now.

NINE:

EPILOGUE

By combining different sources of information, I have attempted to locate Araucanian mounds within the broader social history that constituted them and was partly constructed by them. Much of this history is related to culture contact, empire building, resistance, utopic vision, knowledge systems, secular and sacred agency, identity and memory, population movement, compatriotism, and polity formation. It might be that almost all specific forms of economic, social, and cultural organization that are documented for the Araucanians in the sixteenth and seventeenth centuries need to be understood primarily as transformations within a unitary field of population displacement and ethnic polity development. If so, it is necessary to pay closer attention to the interconnections between lineages and other groups, such as ceremonial exchanges, alliances and conflicts, and patterns of recruitment. A working hypothesis has been that patterns of lineage expansion and contraction changed markedly between the late pre-Hispanic and early to middle Hispanic period and that a single dynamic process of resistance to outsiders characterized many of the shifting social structures and residential patterns associated with *kuel* and *rehuekuel* as religious and political centers and with the exchange of people and materials.

In an attempt to relocate Araucanian history, a purpose of this book has been to challenge the notion that the southern Araucanians were primarily hunters and gatherers, with some knowledge of agriculture, prior to contact with the Spanish and that as a result of this contact they amalgamated and semicentralized to defend themselves against the intruders. According to previous scholarly accounts, this amalgamation developed rapidly into the politically complex and bellicose *estado* society described by the early chroniclers and especially for the historically known center of political resistance in the Purén and Lumaco Valley and, to a lesser extent, in the neighboring areas of Arauco, Catiray, and Tucapel, for instance. But there is a reason why this valley was the primary center to respond to the Spanish. It was one of the most politically and economically advanced areas in late pre-Hispanic times in south-central Chile and thus already had the organizational condition and population density in place not only to resist but to lead other groups to defeat and expel the Spanish. The patrilineal dynasties of this valley not only left behind their political legacies in oral traditions and written records but in the mounded geography they built and dominated. As any anthropologist and historian know, this type of geography signals social complexity well beyond the level of hunters and gatherers. It indicates corporate labor, wealth, hierarchy, population density, a rational ideological base, and other features typical of more complex societies. The Araucanians have encoded all of these features as well as their history of struggle and change in their geography, so that past meets present in the sacred terrain of the valley. But their geography does more than carry important historical referents: it also organizes the manner in which these acts were conceptualized, remembered, organized, and transformed into a temporal framework. *Kuel* and *rehuekuel* were and still are the framework for a symbolic organization that revealed itself through human agency, in this case primarily through interlineage recruitment and adoption of displaced refugees and alliance-building and through movement from one ceremonial feast to another in the study valley. Human activity within the valley (and others) was directed by these architectural arrangements, but the architecture was itself a product of the spatialities and temporalities of indigenous cosmology and history. It was precisely when indigenous cosmology and history coalesced with norms, knowledges, values, and ancestors to create a new conceptual and ritual landscape that the Araucanian polity began to form in this area and altered through time to sustain and expand itself. Although the landscape of this polity may appear to have been static after its initial formation in the middle to late 1500s, it expanded from the multipatrilineal *lov* community to the multi-*lov rehue* level to the multi-*rehue ayllarehue* and the multi-*ayllarehue butanmapu* levels and constantly repositioned itself by creating new social values and meanings (e.g., warrior or champion mentality, various leadership roles formed around a warfare culture). In effect, it is what Thomas (1991:32) calls an "inscribed landscape," which conveyed a variety of meanings that were constantly being altered and interpreted. But it was more than this – it was a landscape that was utopically and socially constructed with ascriptive duties, rights, and expectations of compatriotism within the newly ordered polity, which extended beyond the local-level kinship structure of the patrilineage to ever increasingly higher levels of religio-political organization and outwardly to other places in the Araucania. That is, social practices within which immediate future-oriented models of order and improvement were given expression through new spatial and aesthetic arrangements – a constant works in progress. Primary among these new arrangements were the *rehuekuel* complexes which were necessary nodes of intercurrence in a wider framework of interlineage communication, interaction, and socialization often revolving around sporadic armed conflict and the continual threat of warfare. Yet the importance of this framework is not simply that it provided for a new utopics of Araucanian resistance and survival. Rather it is that the social practices emerging through the complex sacred geography of the Araucanians centered on the design, construction, and conceptualization of the *ayllarehue* and *butanmapu* units, which organized ever increasingly larger territories for defense of the ethnic nation.

I have learned from study of the Araucanian polity that we should not only examine polities as institutional practices and organizations that unify societies but also as ideological constructs giving unity, morality (*sensu* Faron 1964), and autonomy to previously fragmented groups. Although some communities remained intact during the Araucanian wars, others were socially differentiated by the nature of people's locations based on age, gender, proximity to the frontier, and so forth. In many areas, including Purén and Lumaco, there were overlapping and superimposed communities, paisley designs within which formed a multitude of smaller patterns, weaving groups together, ultimately making up a single design and overarching Araucanian identity. Also resulting from the restructuring and commingling of different social units were different types of ritual and political leaders who shared a diffused political structure. Not understood are the ideological forms in which communities became conscious of these conditions, and within which they struggled, and in which they unconsciously absorbed certain beliefs. Yet, I believe that it was the construction of resistance and the polity that formed the Araucanian's compatriotism, national character, and ethnic identity. The polity was rendered real through an iconic reorganizing of public social space that transformed what was once the land of local and regional autonomous patrilineages into more homogenized and nationalized Araucanian domains, where an objectified official history made the presence of the polity palpable in everyday life. Tactical strategies of mound building and mound literacy, at once material and symbolic, produced the idea of the polity while concretizing the utopic or idealized community of the broader Araucanian ethnicity by articulating spatial and temporal matrixes through the routines, rituals, and policies of the ever expanding polity system. Moreover, the transformation of patrilineal social space into sacred landscape that was central to the emerging Araucanian compatriotism and nationalism relied on the conceptualization of people (mixed, stable, and displaced groups) as living within a single shared spatial frame and history. Thus, an identity between Araucanians and territory or landscape was created through the pragmatic visual devices of mounded landscapes and pathways, which represented local political and religious alliances.

Set in this context, the *kuel* and *rehuekuel* became repetitious generations of ancestral monuments, the key signifiers of the grandeur and glory of their identity and memory. The idiom of ancestry had a special potency as a basis of community because it drew upon the past not simply to posit a common origin but also to claim identity in the present, which was achieved through the practice of building alliances, recruiting displaced populations, breaking and making identities, and making memory in spatially and historically uniform and replicated *rehuekuel* monuments. Thus, memory making mediated the identity of people and heritage in space, just as the replication, representation, and organization of sacred space mediated the identity of people and heritage through time. This is not to say that the Araucanian polity never approached a permanent centralized political organization or a real state formation, because it did produce an "imagined" sense of centralized political community in the form of the *ayllarehue* and *butanmapu* organizations that often conflated peoplehood, territory, and polity. These organizations were associated with sequential, situational, simultaneous, and centralized social, religious, and political practices at special places like *rehuekuel*, but they were not centralized political structures with permanent hierarchical networks of leaders and followers. In this sense, centralized social practices did not necessarily constitute hierarchically centralized political organizations.

In a sense, the Araucanian *kuel* and *rehuekuel* can be seen as a tactic of stable and displaced populations – a mobile and temporary set of meanings that inserted themselves into the interstices of the formal spatial organization of Purén, Lumaco, and other places. The style of mound building – its form and aesthetic effectiveness – symbolized both the immobile and mobile nature of those who practiced it and who worshipped at *kuel* and *rehuekuel*. The visual effect and replication of these places became fixed places that allowed the moving rotational sets of participants in the Purén and Lumaco Valley. It was an aesthetic signboard effect that transacted the fixed, static environment of sanctioned meanings, created by the dominant notions of public *rehuekuel* places. To these places, *toqui* leaders added their personal marks and their deathbeds. These beds were later inhabited by the kindred spirits of priestly shamans and by performative rituals fixed on mound literacy, public healing, and commensal politics. The Purén and Lumaco Valley in some sense was thus appropriated by those who lived and died in it. Under these circumstances, the sacred landscapes of the Araucanians transformed and were transformed by newly constituted social relations and by political resistance.

I have emphasized mound worship and mound literacy in order to study how performative and oral traditions, specifically public healing rituals, encompass the cosmological knowledge and history of the Araucanians. Rituals constitute a highly consistent body of information in which history and knowledge are metaphorically expressed in special acts, words, phrases, and places. For instance, in Araucanian cosmology, in the beginning, out of the floodwaters of chaos emerged the primordial mounds – *TrenTrenkuel* – to help humankind. These mounds express the conviction that the universe is dependent on the supreme deities *Ngenechen* and *Pillan* and that their cause was sanctified by these deities. Thus, human action, spiritual sanctity, and the natural environment formed parts of a symbolic framework in which each affects and reflects the other. Because rituals embody the whole complex of cosmological ideas that frame the way of life of the Araucanians in the study area, they can be used as guidelines to reconstruct certain aspects of the past, for we have found that the sacred metaphors consistently exhibited in sixteenth- to eighteenth-century mound uses are similar to the concepts that manage contemporaneous mound rituals today. Also important is the performance of ritual on and around the *kuel*, which includes digging pits representing life and death and tunnels joining them, burying the dead in graves, recapping mounds annually, and other acts. Each act follows a planned spatial and temporal structure, each part of which carried both local and pan-Araucanian symbolic and historical meaning, as revealed in the ritual narratives at the living mounds and in the historical records.

I also have attempted to reveal how the ritual narratives and the metaphors they contain are important sources of information about the coherent and consistent body of thought and the changing principles of organization that have sustained the Araucanians for centuries. Contained within the rituals are messages that define the responsibilities and benefits of ascriptive compatriotism and of belonging to a newly ordered polity and of the culturally defined reciprocal relationships between the living and the spiritual worlds of deities, ancestors, and mounds. I have mapped out a broad understanding of the early historic Araucanian society and culture and especially the changing morphologies of social spaces: the spatialized contexts of polity formation, the construction of landscape as ritual, therapeutic, symbolic, and aesthetic spaces, and the effects of political policies on the physical shape of mounded landscapes and domestic settlements. In short, both the spatial and material records of the Araucanians represent what a newly reorganized polity looks like in responding to outside pressures and in restructuring itself inside. Also discussed are the pre-Hispanic Andean and Inka influences in the Araucanian society, and how old indigenous institutions were telescopically transformed into new and larger geopolitical and religious institutions. That is, these institutions were made larger and more effective by extending overlapping and legible principles of Andean organization one inside another.

A WIDE-ANGLE VIEW OF MOUNDS

A number of prehistoric societies that appear to have had historical conditions, genealogically based status, power, and wealth, varying heterarchical and hierarchical organizations, expansionistic tendencies, and mounded landscapes similar to the Araucanians are in Europe, Mesoamerica, North America, Asia, and most of South America. Archaeologists generally see mounds in these areas representing a wide array of activities and meanings about spatial and social order and about patterned symmetries or designs that have repetition and represent reflections of larger or smaller entities. Often studies of mound societies are based on limited data, which leads to guesswork. I am not saying that there is no guesswork in this study, but in the case of the Araucanians, we know the cultural, social, and historical contexts in which people experienced mounds through the textual, ethnographic, and archaeological records. To date, the dialogues and continuities in these records are unparalleled in other mound studies, suggesting that the accessibility and remembrance of the past 400 years lend an extra measure of validity to social memory and reliability of the direct historical approach employed here. The archaeological record reveals that the general meaning and design of Araucanian mounds has pre-Hispanic time depth. This is not to say that there were no major changes in the organization and meaning of Araucanian ritual and sacred landscape. It is just that the indigenous names of places, people, and events in Purén and Lumaco still correspond with many names and communities today. This correspondence suggests that names are like cultural artifacts distributed over the landscape and that they reflect meaningful continuities and changes.

In this book, I have presented a different approach to thinking about mound-building cultures, with emphasis given to political, religious, spiritual, and geographic processes and to the material and spatial correlates of those processes. I also have tried to investigate the mechanisms, resources, and meanings that allowed mound worship and mound literacy to emerge within the geographical and historical contexts of the south Andes. In this regard, it has been possible to address the past and present in a distinctive way that acknowledges the contingency of both the material and cognitive worlds within which the Araucanians have found themselves. But it has been primarily through the medium of material culture and sacred geographies that I have been able to investigate the forms and sources of mound building, the kinds of experiences that were available to past Araucanians, and the kinds of aesthetic and political adjustments in which they faced their surroundings. Much of the inspiration for this approach has come from my long anthropological experience with the Mapuche in the field and specifically from observing first-hand the metaphysical significance of ritual healing and other ceremonies to a society undergoing change. This is most clearly demonstrated in the ritual narratives of the living mounds studied in Chapter 5. Yet, different kinds of rituals served other purposes too, those being venues for commensal politics as shown repeatedly in the chroniclers and ethnographies and inferred from the organization and content of the archaeological record of *kuel* and *rehuekuel*. These issues are far from being completely understood, and what I have stressed in this book represents the perspective that I have constructed.

I also have emphasized that Araucanian monumentality and sacred architecture are not just *kuel* and *rehuekuel* and the activities on and the spaces between and around them; they are collectively the mounds, the modified *ñichi* platforms on which mounds sit, the open spaces and plazas between mounds where ritual ceremonies take place, and the visual contacts distant participants have with ceremonies in these spaces. As Kidder (2004:69) has noted for the North American southeast, plazas and open spaces must be understood as architecture and monuments too. They are not just empty spaces that developed because architecture enclosed them. They are centrally designed elements of communal planning, intrasite regularity, and local mindspaces. The same is true of the *ñichi* platforms and beveled hillsides that were chosen for their prominent locations, their commanding views of the Purén and Lumaco Valley, and the views toward them from other locations in the valley.

In recent years, much has been made of the idea of a sense of place in the social sciences, and how specific places provide density, memory, security, and understanding. In addition to being political and religious gathering places, the Araucanian mounded landscapes were therapeutic places that alleviated anxiety, suffering, disease, and fear. Health and suffering had and still have places in the active *rehuekuel* and *nguillatun* fields, along with ritual objects and gestures. It is not only a landscape in motion but one full of spiritual powers. Similar to the Inka *ceque* system, the sight lines, radially configured in the distinct *rehuekuel* and other sacred features, which organized multiple patrilineages in the Purén and Lumaco Valley, were integral to Araucanian conceptions of newly ordered utopic spaces and religio-political authority. I also have suggested that *rehuekuel* and their associated domestic settlements were the center points of both the horizontal and vertical dimensions of Araucanian space and time. The organization of cosmic space–time exemplified by the layout of *rehuekuel* and their spatial and elevational references to domestic and other sites – the cosmunities – embodied the integrated form of the everyday processes of social production and reproduction through which the social life of the community, the human life cycle, and the developmental cycles of lineages and families were reproduced. Although some of these notions must seem vague and too ethereal to hard empiricists, they best fit the reality of the way these people perceive(ed) these spaces and their lives in them. The Araucanians simply do not demarcate a single locality or place, as archaeologists do in the field. Everything is related visibly and invisibly in ideological and pragmatic ways in their society.

Anthropologists have argued that pragmatic and ideological agendas are tightly related to cosmological ideas, beliefs, and metaphors, which are expressed in architecture and space. For example, some Mayanists view the spatial order of ancient settlements related to the role of cosmology in the aesthetic design of the structure and layout of towns and cities. Ashmore and Sabloff (2002), in particular, argue that the position and arrangement of civic construction was anything but random and that the spatial expressions of Maya cosmology and of Maya politics constituted the most prominent ideational foundations for planning, with some site designs mimicking specific celestial configurations. Mayanists refer to these designs as "cosmograms." In the eastern United States, Buikstra and Charles (1999) view burial mounds as three-dimensional representations of Hopewellian cosmography, which was defined by air, land, and water imagery. They suggest that this arrangement provided a forum for power relations whereby monuments recreated a vertically and horizontally differentiated cosmos, just as they provided a forum for the negotiation of power relations among the living.

In some ways, the *nguillatun* and *rehuekuel* fields are similar in that their layout is a microcosm of multilineage community patterns, which also incorporates elements of the sacred ancestral and cosmological world above and represents power relations between lineages, deities, and ancestors. This model also extends to the relative elevation of *rehuekuel*, *kuel*, domestic, and cemetery sites, which are positioned from the top to the bottom of hills, respectively, to reflect the hierarchical and spatialized ranking of deities and ancestors in the upper world and the living below them. The Araucanian model differs somewhat from Mayan localities, however, in that few parts of any site are intentionally designed to reflect celestial figures and that the relative layout of sites forming communities are positioned to reflect social order, sacred geographies, and ancestral identity. Another element is the form of *kuel* and *rehuekuel*, which represents a continuous horizon of conical shapes on high ground, so that the form of the mounds provides an aesthetic microcosm of the distant volcanoes and irregular landscapes from one *rehuekuel* to another. For these reasons, I prefer to call the Araucanian sites cosmunities rather than cosmograms.

The Inka also produced sacred geographies – the *huacas* (shrines) and *ceque* lines that were associated with an underlying cognition of identity and social order embedded in these places and in the mindscapes of the people (Guchte 2000). I see the visual lifelines of the Araucanians in Purén and Lumaco being similar. The lifelines are part of a landscape of the Araucanian's mind that they see in physically sacred places and that frame the social, religious, and political relationships in the valley. Ritual procession and rotation take place along these lines or pathways at special topographic locations. The location and size of *kuel* and *rehuekuel* along the pathways relate to the number of times people gathered in them and gazed at them, thus involving two forms of participation directly in the ceremony and indirectly by gazing at ceremony, both of which provide a sense of intergoup solidarity. Too, the aesthetic effectiveness of the combined and recursive arrangement of *kuel*, *rehuekuel*, and their allocation along the pathways (*sensu* Pollard 2001) symbolized the ideal community of the future – a utopic gaze toward what was and what is to come. This effectiveness is not at one site but at the inter-*rehuekuel* and whole valley level and includes the vertical cosmological world. Almost like the citizenship level in a state system, at the multi-*rehuekuel* valley level it unites at an esoteric level with deities and ancestors.

In turning to a different matter, I have not provided an in-depth archaeological analysis of the architecture of mounds, the settlement and artifact patterns of these and other sites, and the paleoecological studies of the valley. I also have not considered in depth that the mounded landscapes of Purén and Lumaco were changing over time in ways not conceived here, although I am not particularly concerned about this issue, given the rather short time frame of analysis (ca. 1500 and 1700) and the strong correspondence between causal variables inferred from the multiple databases. Further discussion of the meaning of intergroup war games to religious practice and polity formation also is needed. The Araucanian ritual game of *palin* between lineages was and still is essential to defining and reassuring intergroup social duties and to linking them with the ancestral world. Another topic not discussed is a greater understanding of the relations between mounds and astronomical features, which is important for ascertaining the historical relations between cultural landscapes and principles of cosmological organizations. I also have not detailed the political economy and particularly craft specialization, trade and exchange, and agricultural intensification. I deal with these and other issues in a forthcoming volume given to the archaeological data.

EFFECTIVE RECURSIVENESS

Many of the above notions might be expanded to a larger Andean and Amazonian time and space frame to understand increased contact between largely autonomous communities, uncertainty and risk, population movement, expansion and aggregation at fairly uniform ceremonial centers, the appearance of new ideological constructs and principles of organization, intensified agricultural economies, and regional polities in various Formative Period cultures emerging between 4,500 and 1,000 years ago. I envision many Andean and other American Formative societies and many other early complex societies worldwide organizing and transforming themselves in many of the political and religious ways described in Chapters 7 and 8 and having utopic visions focused on certain goals. In the Central Andes, there was an early development of powerful ideological constructs adopted by regional communities, which led to the construction of public monumental architecture in small and large ceremonial centers. Many Andeanists view this period characterized by a kinship-based community organization related to the fluctuating dominance of political organization, by the presence of several local paramount chiefdoms, if not pre-state polities, each controlling an irrigation system and related by marriage exchange and shared ideology, and by greater regional interaction (see Burger 1992), but with none achieving dominant status over others (Bawden 1996). Although each polity may have had a hierarchically centralized political structure, they probably had heterarchical organizations among themselves that were characterized by situationally constructed political alliances and religious gatherings similar to the *ayllarehue*, *butanmapu*, *rehuekuel*, and *nguillatun* settings, with power shifting from one group or center to another.

Not well understood in Formative South America are the relationships between ceremonial centers and the limits of the distance over which ceremonial communication operated effectively beyond the location of each individual center and between neighboring centers. In the Araucanian area, the technical media of *rehuekuel* centers and their topographical and architectural uniformity enable individual communities to interact with one another across spatial and temporal distances. This gets us back to the uniformity or recursiveness of these centers, which is crucial to the institutional and social memory that groups rely upon to break up and regroup across time and space. That is, recursiveness in the design and location of these centers allows for time and space sharing in multiple contexts; it is, in essence, institutional familiarity that facilitates solidarity and different levels of heterarchical and hierarchical organizations.

Although the Araucanian polity never became a true centralized state, it nonetheless developed a high and effective level of political integration similar to that described for the Formative societies of other regions of South America cultures. The existence of parallel Araucanian power structures within and between lineages (notably *toqui* war leaders and *machi* priestly shamans) is reminiscent of the concept of heterarchy. The Araucanian case also provides relevant insights into the functional variability among *rehuekuel* centers and how hierarchies operated independently and interdependently within and between lineages and within and between multilineage organizations such as the *rehue, ayllarehue*, and *butanmapu*. Political organization was strictly hierarchical within the smaller kinship-based lineage and within the larger *butanmapu*, but it was heterarchical on the intermediate and lower levels of the *ayllarehue* and *rehue* units, respectively, where greater interaction occurred between regional groups at *rehuekuel* and other gathering places. Thus, heterarchy is related to scale, to distance, and to repetitive places and situations such as commensal feasting at *rehuekuel* and armed conflict on the battlefield. A critical threshold was crossed when these kinds of societies started to move beyond the patrilineal sphere and into some formalized and structured public life at ceremonial centers and when these centers were planned and constructed in conjunction with domestic and other nonceremonial localities.

For many decades, archeologists have focused their attention on the standardized or repetitive monumental architecture of early complex or Formative societies in pre-Hispanic America, such as Chavin, Olmec, Anazazi, Adena, and Hopewell, which have led many scholars to posit early polity or even proto-urban state systems. The idea is that the recursiveness of the size and form of ceremonial edifices and the repetitive practices at them equate with centralized political authority and polity development. There is no doubt that many early societies possessed a set of collective institutional structures and ritual practices that framed social groups as polity-like structures. Societies of this type generally formed duplicated social and material structures in which each level of organization embodied the structure of the process, through which it was produced and reproduced, which the productive form of this process was projected outside the realm of the social as the organization of cosmic time and space. These organizations include the structure of society at all levels as recursive organizations based on the replication of the modular pattern of relations exemplified by the cosmology (or ideology) and the system of collective institutions. However, I think some Andean and other archeologists have confused this type of uniformity in structure, its varying material expression of replicated building forms, and centralized practices at them as representative of centralized political structures such as paramount chiefdoms and incipient states. In the Araucanian case, recursive hierarchies are largely based on the appropriation of nonmaterial forms of surplus — that is, the social construction of relations and linkages rather than the production of economic material surplus. To date, most scholarly explanations of the movements of people and goods within local and regional Andean contexts have relied primarily on different versions of the concept of verticality (cf. ecological complementarity: Murra 1975), which refers to groups sending colonies to neighboring and distant ecological zones to maximize the control and exploitation of a wide range of resources, including humans. Derivative models postulate diaspora settlements expanding on their own accord and maintaining variable relations with a home base (e.g., Owen 2005). However, similar goals in the Andes may have been accomplished by dominant or stable groups recruiting and annexing other groups through religious proselytizing, intergroup marriage, alliance building, and/or public feasting, all managed through integrated sets of recursive to semirecursive political and religious centers, which may or may not have led to polity formation.

TIMELESSNESS OF MAPUCHE LANDSCAPES

Today, the Araucanians or Mapuche and the Chileans live in and have created quite different social landscapes, memories, and identities. The Chilean landscape has been created through a process that involved a change in land use and a break with the previous indigenous history of the land, amounting almost to a denial that the land had a previous history and identity until Europeans arrived, and that the Mapuche had ever attained a complex level of cultural development. European colonizers in the sixteenth through nineteenth centuries moved into what (to them) was a previously unutilized environment, their objective being to release its economic potential (Dillehay 2003). To them, the past had little history and no memory except as it was reflected through military battles of the moment with the Mapuche. But the Spanish colonists and their descendants, the Chileans, brought with them a concept of indigenous development that was part of distant landscapes that they had experienced with the well-developed Inka state and that partly influenced their conceptualization and prospect of the "simple but bellicose" Mapuche — an image and identity that continues into the present century.

The Mapuche, on the other hand, created a social landscape with places, memories, boundaries, and directions that had an effect on the pattern of Chilean colonization, which in turn had more obvious consequences on the continued Mapuche uses of space. For instance, to the Mapuche, sacred places are integrated within a process that often acts to freeze time; that makes the past a referent for the present and future. Set in this context, the present is not so much produced by the past, but reproduces itself in the form of the past, making land and its socially shaped dimension imbued with deep history, memory, and ethnic identity. Traditional Mapuche identity is achieved through memorial songs, tales, practices, and sacred places by which life is phrased in terms of movement along nodal pathways constituted by residential dwellings, cemeteries, memorial places such as *kuel*, *rehuekuel*, and *nguillatun* fields, and other places. In this regard, memories are selective reconstructions of past events that complement a present collective need. Memories also provide the framework that individuals use to locate themselves in time and space, but they also are used for political purposes to negotiate communal objectives. To realize a political community (e.g., past *rehue*, *ayllarehue*, *butanmapu*, modern *reduccion*) as a salient group identity, political leaders must act to inscribe and codify the social memory of that entity in architecture, ritual, and other media.

The new and changing Chilean laws of the past century have occasionally brought these two different concepts of history, memory, landscape, and identity into open conflict as part of the contemporary Mapuche political process. It is through this process and through a thirty-year archaeological, ethnohistorical, and ethnographical study that I have come to partially understand the Mapuche concepts of social landscape, memory, and identity as part of a historical process that is characterized by timeless continuity. Hence, although Mapuche concepts of landscape and memory are temporally prior to those of Chileans, they are also subsequent to, if not consequent on, the colonial and modern-day process. It is the Mapuche ideology of timeless continuity as an ethnic group occupying the land that has proved conceptually difficult for some Chilean officials and scholars, particularly historians, to grasp and has proved frustrating for Chilean objectors to Mapuche land claims and resource rights.

In 1978, when I first began doing research in Lumaco and Purén, there were seven *rehuekuel* in active use. Today, three are in a process of fading use; many fewer traditional ceremonies are carried out there each year. Sacred shrines in some areas are being appropriated by evangelists and small churches are appearing in the Mapuche countryside. In other areas, mounds and other sacred sites are being used less and are becoming commodities of a traditional past. While mounds are dying as sacred ritual places, they also are emerging in a few places as new living symbols of a remembered glorified past of political autonomy and resistance. In Purén and Lumaco, the reuse and rethinking of ancient mounds today, partly through our research presence, for contemporary ritual involve a contemporary set of political and historical meanings that does not always include the original use or understanding of those places. There also is a social disjunction between the living Mapuche and the mounds whereby their maintenance is not related to the meaning and memory of all living in the area. This is due to the demographic mixture of some local lineages that have social continuity with the landscape and others who are inmarried and have none. At stake is an understanding of the Mapuche's historic culture and the formulation of its social future, because whether put into practice through continued live ritual with mounds or through the memory of dying live ritual, these sacred landscapes mediate between the past and future not only by giving the people a sense of *admapu* tradition but also by providing some continuities into the future.

APPENDIX ONE:

ETHNOGRAPHIC RITUAL

NARRATIVES AT *HUALONKOKUEL*

AND *TRENTRENKUEL*

The two narratives are structured differently with the *Hualonkokuel* dialogue presented in short separate verses, which reflect the ritual speaking style of *machi* Juanita, and with the *TrenTrenkuel* recording given in long continuous verses by *machi* Lucinda. Maria Catrileo transcribed both rituals from Mapundungun to Spanish. The Spanish in the *Hualonkokuel* was translated to English by Patricia Netherly; the *TrenTrenkuel* dialogue was translated to English by Ricardo Fernandéz. The author aided in the transcription of Mapundungun to Spanish and Spanish to English in both narratives. Only the Mapundungun and English versions are provided below. The selected English passages presented in Chapter 5 are numbered by verse segments in Roman numerals. Pauses in the *machi's* presentations are noted as pauses in the narratives. Also referenced are places where the tape recordings are illegible and where the transcribers could not understand the language. Words in brackets identify the subject of action or clarify the meaning of a behavior. Ritual audience refers to the local indigenous communities participating in ceremony. The *Wenumapu* and *Nag Mapu* are capitalized in the English translations, because they were given special voice inflexions in Mapundungun by the shamans. Finally, both *machi* often speak in the third person.

HUALONKOKUEL NARRATIVE

This narrative relates to healing ritual dialogues (*llaimatun*) and healing rites (*dahatun*) focusing on curing a sick *kuel* that threatens to harm the local community, because it is not giving him prayers and offerings. The *machi* has been summoned by the community to cure him. In the dialogue, the *machi* shaman switches back and forth between speaking (1) with the *kuel*, whom she variably refers to as her brother, her son, the son of the deity *Chaw* or *Ngenechen*, or the great deity and father of all, (2) with the ritual audience, who she calls brothers and sisters or friends, (3) with ancient or mythical *machi* (*fileu*), and (4) with *Chaw* or *Ngenechen* and ancient ancestors. The Mapundungun is spoken in an archaic ritual language that is difficult to understand. Postceremonial conversations with the *machi* Juanita clarified many nouns, pronouns, and subject matters in the narrative. The *machi* narrates and begins by describing her opening dialogue with the *kuel* who feels that he has been mistreated by the local community.

I. *Fey kiñe may trananagalu*
Thus someone [?] is going to fall

wenche piwmaenew kuel.
something the *kuel* [mound] told me.

Feylle ta amukey ta machi mew
This is why it [*kuel*] goes to the *machi*

awükan dungu mew
because of a tribulation affair [mistreatment]

Chaw en, awem!
Father [*Ngenechen*], wow!

II. *Poyen nienulu, poyen nienulu, eluketufiñ*
One who does not have love, I give it back to him

felelu mew awükangey,
because it [*kuel*] has been mistreated,

utrüfentu ngümakey may,
it thus cries a lot,

ütrüfentu lladkükey ka,
it thus has a great sorrow,

ngümakey ka,
it thus cries,

feymaew may tiew ngillatuñmangey.
thus, this is why they [ritual audience] hold a supplication.

Amukalngey, tuwkey; mongelüway, puen,
It [*kuel*] is directed, it goes; it is going to be saved.

III. *Inangepulley ka, pengelayam dungu ka.*
Thus, he [*kuel*] has been followed, so that this is not seen [?].

Koylanukam. Eymi ta kimnielleymi,
This is not a lie. Thus you know it,

feyti pu chaw em am amulkey tañi chaw em.
thus those ancestors guide his [*kuel*] father [*Chaw, Ngenechen*].

–¡Marichi wew!–
Victory, ten times over!

Küdawngey, pewmangey dungu kam,
It is hard [conducting the ritual], one has to dream this affair,

ngümangey, ngümangey dungu ka, we!
thus, this affair is something to cry about!

Ütrüfentu arofün pikey ta,
My sweat flows, he [*kuel*] thus says,

longkongelu ka. Perimontun mew....
he who is at the head [the leader?]. For having visions . . .

–¡Marichi wew!–
Victory, ten times over!

IV. *Ka felepuy kuñifall femika,*
And so it is that a poor bereft one [*kuel*] is also there,

kiñe fillakantun mew ta niellefiñ piwey.
because of an evil deed I have him here, he [*kuel*] says.

Mütrümtuafulu,
He [*kuel*] should make a request,

afkentu anülepuyñi,
for a long time he has been seated there,

felen ñi ra kiduam ta,
his [*kuel*] thoughts so being,

konangepuy ta üyeu ta Wenumapu.
he [*kuel*] is an assistant there, in the [*Wenumapu*] land above.

Afkentu nieñmaeymew ta wenu mapu ta,
For a long time the land above has had
him [kuel],

ütrir longko chi we,
this [leader?] is the one who put envy in
his head,

rakiduàm mew ta femngeke fuluka pofre yem,
for having that in his thoughts, this poor
bereft one [kuel],

kom lipümtupan mew,
for fixing it all, here,

nienmew may ñi milla lelfün mew,
for having him [kuel] in his golden land,

¡pofre yem, kuel!
poor kuel!

Fürenengen mew, fürenengen maw may, kuel,
For doing you a favor, thus, kuel,

kisutun ta ñukeluwlu kay eymi,
thus for setting up roots alone, you [kuel],

kisu kayta ñukeluwlu.
for setting up roots.

Fey ta liwen may ta fürenefiñ
This is why in the morning I have done it
[kuel] a favor

pofre kuñifall ka,
to that poor unprotected one [kuel],

femngenam perimontun may,
thus I [machi] have had visions,

inche kay ta puwüluwün kay, kuel,
thus, I am also capable, kuel,

iñche may ta wechulenew ta Chaw wenu.
thus I have been lifted by the father
[Ngenechen] above.

¿Chemew am ta mallfawafun kay, kuel?
Why should I feel arrogant, kuel?

Mongenpefiñ ta ka fillem kay.
Thus, I have life above all things.

Inche may akun, treka mapupen,
I have arrived, I have stepped on the
ground [earth's surface],

küpan em ka lelfün,
I come, poor me! from another [nguillatun]
field,

perimontun nierkelu engün faw.
because here they [ritual audience] had
visions.

Llownagpan kimün.
I have received the news.

Wellimtuy che. Wewmuntuyngün,
They [ritual audience] have cleared out.
The people have encouraged, themselves
[ritual audience],

fey ramay engün, kom muñkupuy,
they [ritual audience] have made ramadas
(ritual wooden structures), they have
congregated,

inangen küpay, law, law küleyngün,
they are following each other, dispersed
through the [nguillatun] fields,

iñey may ñi waria mew ka ñi. . . . [pause],
each [lineage] in his community and
his. . . . . [pause],

V. Inaleyu ka,
We two [?] are following,

kiñe ngillañ may üngümtuayu,
thus, we are going to wait for a relative
[ancestor],

inaleyu kom,
we are following them all [ancestors],

kisu mayñi üngümkan mew,
for his [Ngenechen] own will to
wait,

ümültukuy ñi kuñifall lawen mew,
he lets his bereft one [kuel] roll in, looking
for a cure,

lawen elüfi fey.
thus he [Ngenechen] gave her [machi] a
remedy.

Anülepufuy ñi lawen ngelu,
She [machi] who possesses the medicine
was seated,

ñochi ñochi umültukufuy em, puen.
little by little she made him [*kuel*] roll
inside [?], my friends.

IV. *¡Chem duamngefuy dungu ka!*
Alas! What is one to think, then?

Ngümanngefuy dungu ka,
Is something to cry about,

perimontuy may chem dungu en chey,
what kind of visions he [*kuel*] may have
had perhaps,

puy may weku yem, weku yem,
he arrived there our poor uncle [ancestor],

piyu. Lawentun kutran rume may
we [*machi* and her assistants] have said. A
sick one [*kuel*] also with medicines

fente weya kela fuy, puen.
never had it so bad, my friends [ritual
audience].

VII. *Inche may rupalewen fill dungu mew,*
I have been through so many things,

inche may repalewen dungu mew.
I have been through so many things.

Ew – Ew. . . . [pause]
Whew! Whew!

¡Marichi wew!
Victory ten times over!

XVIII. *¡Feley fel, feley em ka!*
Thus it is, poor ones that we are [ritual
audience]!

¡Marichi wew!
Victory ten times over!

¡Yallemay, yallemay!
So be it, so be it!

Chaña künudungu nga elupefi.
She [ancestral *machi*] gave him [*kuel*] the
naked truth.

¿Amutuy am ta, amutuy am ta?
Are they [ancestors] gone, are they?

Epu yem ta wente lelfün mew miawlu ka?
Two of those poor ones [the two *kuel* in
the *Hualonkokuel* field] who walked this
earth?

Mülefule mew ta kuden mew ka.
Thus, for being involved in a race.

Mülefule kuell muday,
If there was some *muday* [corn beer] for
the *kuel*,

fürenmeafun ka kiñe femngen mew,
please, be so kind as to give me some,

*tüfa may miawülün epu wecheke koña ñi
kuel.*
thus it is, that I am here with two young
assistants [apprentice *machi*] of the *kuel*.

Mülefule pichin may wingka we kulperu,
If there was some drink instead of the
wingka [non-Mapuche],

iñche may, iñche may ya fütu la fiñ,
I would thus reinvigorate them [the two
kuel] with it,

fewla ñi ulael dungu mew pu fotüm ka.
thus it is only now that these sons are
going to hand over the affairs [?].

Yafkakilpe yengu, ya fütu pe ka feyengu.
Be it that they not come to misfortune
[*kuel*], that they both become
reinvigorated.

¡Ew – Ew!
Whew! Whew!

Fey may müten lle, feymay müten lle
This is only what

piyawlleiñ ka, chaw em, awem!
we are saying, father [*Ngenechen*], alas!

IX. *¡Marichi wew!*
Victory ten times over!

¡Yallemay, yallemay!
So be it, so be it!

¡Marichi wew!
Victory ten times over!

Firküpay mu mapu em kay.
The ground [ceremonial field] that used to
belong to you two [*kuel*] has turned cold.

Firküpay mu wingkul em kay,
The hill [*ñichi* platform] that use to belong
to you two has turned cold,

fotüm em kay, krasia may,
children of bygone days [ancestors], thus,
thanks,

mülepe ta küme wenüy.
may there be good friendships.

¡*Marichi wew!*
Victory ten times over!

Feyllemay ta ngen,
This is thus the owner [*Ngenechen*],

feyllemay ta witralepay lawenngelu.
so it is that she [*machi*] who possesses the
medicine is standing up.

¿*Chemew em am ta kelluaenew ta?*
Why, then, has he [*Ngenechen?*] not helped
me?

chem dungu mew?
in this matter?

Wicha fimün ta laenngelu,
You [ritual audience] have asked for the
services of she [*machi*] who possesses the
medicine,

feyllemay, feyllemay.
thus, this is it.

¿*Chemew em ta, chemew am ta kellumulan?*
Why, then, do you not help me?

Pikeymün ka,
Thus you tell me,

tüfa llemay, tüfallemay, milla kalera mew.
thus here, thus here, on the golden ladder
[*rehue* pole].

X. K*om i tamün elumekeel,*
All of those who were served have eaten
[ritual audience],

weku yem kay ta angküy em ka,
thus our poor uncle [ancestor] has dried
out,

lawenngelu ka,
for thus having a cure,

fey ta wenu kutran em kay dungu
because this is a matter of disease from
above [*Wenumapu*]

machi müten pimün.
only the *machi* can solve it, you [ritual
audience] have said.

¡*Hu . . . ¡Marichi wew!*
Victory ten times over!

XI. *Feymay feypilekeymün,*
Thus, you go on saying,

eymünngen mew ta kimdungukelay mün.
because you're here, you [ritual audience]
do not know about these things.

Welu ta wenu mapu,
But, thus the land above,

fewla may tamün peafiel,
it is only now that you are going to see,

küme mapu mew lawenngelu ka.
somebody [*machi*] who possesses the
medicines that come from the good
ground.

Kellu nagümkefimi Chaw,
You, Father [*Ngenechen*], are helping me to
bring it down,

Küme lawenngelu, awem, awem!
To the one who has the positive medicine,
alas! Alas!

Kellu nagümkefimi,
You [*Ngenechen*] have always helped to
bring it down,

lawenngelu, eymikay, peñi.
to the one who has the medicine, you too,
brother [*kuel*].

¡*Ihi! ¡Marichi wew!*
Victory ten times over!

XII. ¡*Mari, kimlaymi pikeymi wenu mapu ka!*
Ten times, you do not know thus you say,
oh land above!

Kimünngela fuy wenu_mapu fotüm ka,
But the son [*kuel*] of the land above did
not have the knowledge either

we longkoyenielu ñi lawenngelu kay,
for he was just learning about the
medicine, too,

feymew may kellunagümkarkea fulu kay.
this is why it would be better if he [*kuel*], too, was helping in bringing it [medicine] down.

¡Yallemay! ¡Kiñemür rupa iñ ka!
So be it! Let's go forward in pairs [addressed to ritual audience]!

¡Yallemay! Puruleaiñ.
So be it! Let's proceed with the dance.

Allküfi tañi milla bandera,
He [*kuel*] has listened to his golden flag,

kafey tañi kuel kawell ta,
thus, the horse from the *kuel* too,

kafey ta kudenngelley.
is also ready for the race.

Unelgepe ta tripawe_antü konay,
First you [ritual audience] start toward the sunrise (east),

ka amu tuay ta waywen püra.
and then you come back through the south.

¿Fewla amta mün koun ta dungu mew, puen?
Have you never participated in this affair, my friends [ritual audience]?

Eluaenew ta, eluaenew dungu machi,
May the *machi* [ancestral] give me the news (matters),

Pikeymün, puen.
so you say, my friends.

Kisu müten küdawlnuwlu machi mew, puen,
One person [the *machi*] alone does not advance much in the *machi's* matters, my friends,

piyawlleiñ ka.
thus we say.

¡Ya!
Ya!

Ngam chumekemuli am fey may,
If you do all kinds of things for me [ritual audience], then,

ngam chumekemuli am fey, puen,
if you do all kinds of things for me, my friends,

feyula yean ñi duamchen tüfachi
until that moment I will carry the thoughts of

pu fotüm, puen,
these children [the two *kuel*], my friends,

fey ula yeyaiñ,
until then we will carry them,

kelluaeneu machi pikeymün.
may the *machi* help me you say [ritual audience].

XIII. *Femeken mew pu peñi, puen,*
Because of the brothers [another community at other *kuel* in the valley] doing this, my friends,

femeken mew em kay pu lamngen,
because of the brothers doing this in general,

¡yaka! piaetew dungu mew,
so that they support me in this matter,

mütu femngen mew wicha mekeenew pu fotüm.
because I have this [power], and this is so, the children [lineages] are going to request my services.

Machi pi pu fotüm, puen.
The children request the *machi's* services.

Awen ta lawenngenule kay,
Alas! If, by misfortune, there is no cure,

lawenngenule. ¿Chempiafuyngün kay?
if it [sick *kuel*] has no cure. What could they say?

Milla kalera mew trupefküley ñi perimo, apuen.
On the golden ladder [*rehue*] my vision gets scared, my friends.

¡Marichi wew!
Victory ten times over!

Pürapeyüm dungu pipingelika,
The reasons to climb [to *Wenumapu*] if I
were to divulge them,

dew künu a lu ñi dungu yengün.
to settle the matter in their [*kuel*] name.

XIV. *Kulpalayay ta kuyü te (?) ka,*
the *kuyü te* [?] will not be to blame,

kangelu lleta füreneen ka.
do me the favor for the other [?].

Fureneen tañi konün em ka.
Thus, do me the favor for the one [the
machi] that entered [the *kuel*], poor
one.

Kutran kan ñi piwke,
My heart is suffering,

kutran lle may.
thus it is a disease.

Aliman ka piwkeniepay ñi lawen ngelu kay.
The heart of she [*machi*] who possesses the
medicine gets warmer.

Dunqunen tukünuy tañi. . . .
First it [*kuel*] revealed its [recording is
illegible]. . . .

¡Ya llemay? ¡Nenqümüwllenge!
So be it?! Get moving [ritual audience]!

Piwlleiñ ka, apuen.
Thus I am telling you, my friends.

¿Chemew am trü rümtu dunquley? pimun ka.
Why does she [*machi*] make up things?
thus they say about me, my friends.

¿Chemew am welu entuay ñi nütram?
How is she going to go err in her
report?

Pikeymün, puen.
So you say, my friends.

Eymün ta kelluafulu,
You [ritual audience] should all help,

konpalelu müten ta, fey müten em,
may the closest ones [*machi's* relatives] help,

pipiyengetu key.
they then say.

Müley ta dungu llemay, apuen.
Thus there are events [?], my friends.

¡Ya llemay!. Weñangküy.
So be it! He [*kuel*] is sad.

¿Welu trutruka küpalay, am?
Have you not brought any *trutrukas*?
[drums: musical instruments]

We lawenngelu.
He [*Ngenechen*] who has new medicines.

¿Chum wechiam ta ünutualu we?
How, thus, will he [*Ngenechen*] spread his
wings here?

Pipiengepeyu.
So we have been told.

¿Kimlaymi am ta ürkütuwe? Pipiengen.
Do you not know the resting place? They
[ritual audience] ask me.

¡Fey dungu, fey dungu!
That is the issue, that is the issue!

We lawenkimpe.
You should learn about the new
medicine.

Awem, awem kay. Fotüm awem, awem kay,
Alas, alas! Alas, my son [*kuel*]!

Pingetuy em kay.
Thus one tells him [*kuel*].

¿Chumngechi amkay, ünutualu eymi kay, we?
How is he [*Ngenechen*] going to spread his
wings? Alas!

–¡Uhu! . . . ¡Ya! ¡Ya! (kefafan)
Uh! Ya! Ya! (cheer up)

XV. *Adnagküley fotüm wen.*
Down they [ritual audience] walk, parents
and children, in the right direction.

Püramlongkowela tüfachi fotümwen.
They no longer raise their heads these
parents and their children.

¿Chemew am . . . ?
Why . . . ?

−¡*Marichi wew!*
Victory ten times over!

E malon wiñon mew niey ñi fill filew newen,
Only when returning from a *malon* [raid]
she [*machi*] would have her different *filew*
[ancient *machi*] strengths,

piay.
she would say.

−¡*Uhu! ¡Ya, Ya!*
Uh! Ya! Ya!

Maneluwpafule kay lawen ngelu.
If he [*Ngenechen*] with the medicine were
to stay here.

¿*Chem piafuy mün kay? piyawlleiñ, puen.*
What could you then say? we say, my
friends [ritual audience].

Maneluwoafule lawen ngelu nga,
If he [*Ngenechen*] who has the medicine
were to stay here, then,

inche may ta kulpangelleafun.
I could also be guilty.

Feymew lle ta kulpangeymün, apuen.
This is why you are guilty, too, my friends
[ritual audience].

Feley ta dunga ka.
Thus this is established.

Mülekey dungu ka, puen.
Thus, things often happen, my friends.

Tüfachi pürapürawe mew püralayan,
On this ladder [*rehue*] I will not climb,

pipingelley chi, ¡we!
she [*machi*] is saying, alas!

Feymew lle ta tripay, puen.
This is why she [*machi*] went out, my
friends.

−¡*Uhu!* . . . *ew.* . . . [pause]
Uh! [pause]

Iñche yem ta nagüm lawengayaiñ,
Thus, poor me, I am not going to bring
you any medicine down here,

kellu nagüm nuaiñ,
she [the *machi* herself] has to help us bring
it down,

kafey ta pipingelley ta wenumapu.
this is also being said in the land above.

¡*Ewem! dungudungungelu yem nga,*
Alas! the poor one [*kuel*] who spoke,

kalkuluwma mapu, kuel ka.
the one who bewitched the ground, this
kuel, that is.

Ka femngekey. ¿*Ngüneduamürkelaymi ama
fotüm?*
It [*kuel*] is also treated like that. Did you
not notice, son?

Kiñe taiñ dungu, ka,
One of our affairs,

wente taiñ dungu müley.
is above our thing.

XVI. *Müle fule rume dew milla kalera,*
If there was, perhaps, a golden-ladder
[*rehue*] that was already made,

aretunge fotüm em.
borrow it, son [*kuel*].

Elelngen fotüm nga,
They [?] left me, children [ritual
audience],

pifiñ may fotüm nga.
thus I said, to the son [*kuel*].

*Ngillange. Ngillange mealu nga petu mülen
nga,*
Buy it [*rehue*]. They [ritual audience] are
going to buy it, some will still be there,

petu wa lünglu, pieyew may kuel.
when the summer comes, thus said the
kuel.

Mü lea lu may nga lelfün mew.
Thus it [the sick *kuel*] is going to stay in
the [*nguillatun*] field.

XVII. *Akulu ula may fey ula kutranngey
pi.*
On arrival, he [*kuel*] told her that it was
sick.

Piwümlu kay lipang em
Thus the poor arm [of the *kuel*] dried
out

are piwke lipang em.
the poor arm that got sick with the heat.

*Tu kulpaafulu. Füta kulpa küdaw nien
miñchemapu.*
He [*kuel*] could have said it. I have a great
deal of work because of the sins [of the
ritual audience] in the land below.

¡Ew! . . . [pause]
Whew! . . . [pause]

−¡Marichi wew!
Victory ten times over!

Femngerkeel, machingen, kuel.
It is for this reason that I am a *machi*,
kuel.

Feyñi kutran kawün mew, fem iawürkelu.
Because of its [*kuel*] feelings, it is going
like this.

Ka kiñe machi lawenngerke lu,
Another *machi* who possesses the
medicines,

a mu mapu lawenngey, mia wün.
all over the land she [various *machi*] has
medicines, when walking.

−¡Marichi wew!
Victory ten times over!

XVIII. *Piwün ruka mew nga.*
In the dry house [?] . . . [illegible
recording].

XIX. *A mu piwkeyengu nga*
His [*kuel*] heart is gone

lawen ngelu mew,
to where the person [*machi*] who has the
medicine is,

rangi filu miawün (?),
among snakes I walk (?),

femnge chi nga, femeken, puen.
thus this is what is happening to me, my
friends.

¿Chemew am ta femekengen nay?
Why do you [*Ngenechen*] do this to me?

−¡Uhu! −¡Marichi wew!
Uh! Victory ten times over!

¡Ya! ¡Ya!
Ya! Ya!

Mari pian nga pipingeymün.
I am going to say ten you say.

−¡Marichi wew!
Victory ten times over!

Mari pinge, pu wali ka.
Listen for ten, for as long as I am capable.

Falefuy em ta ka fill we ka.
There are other places [other
communities], too.

Feyentulu reke mekengen.
That only pretend to obey me.

¿Falefu am ta ka fill küyen?
Do you think this is how it is on other
moons?

Mülefuy Wenumapu ka.
Thus, the land above [*Wenumapu*] does
exist.

Kom dapiñ mew niefekefuy laen ngelu, puen.
Someone who [*machi* and *kuel*] possesses
the medicine's gift deserves all the
attentions, my friends.

Iñche rumeltu anümniengen ka.
You [ritual audience] have had me here
for so long.

[pause] . . . *¡Hi! ¡Marichi wew!*
Victory ten times over!

Rangimapu lawen ngelu.
Someone who possesses the medicine is
the center of the Earth.

¿Chemew nga femeke mulu
Why do you [*Ngenechen*] behave like that
toward me

tüfachi lukutuwün mew, apueñ?
in this kneeling ceremony, my friends?

Ew. . . . [pause]
Whew. . . . [pause]

Feymew tüngümkünu ngeken
This is why you [*Ngenechen*] leave me in peace

milla pütra mew, ina awarelwe mew.
on the golden *pitra* (tree), on the lima beans field.

Tüfachi fotüm fewla may ñi femekeetew ka nga,
This son [*kuel*], it is only now that he does this to me,

kuel, piawüñ kom.
that he [*kuel*] behaves like this toward me, *kuel*, we are all saying.

Dew ken tu may, ayetu etew femngechi
For such a long time, for laughing at me, that one [*kuel*]

nielu may aye kawe, tüfachi fotüm em.
who has laughter objects, this poor son.

Kake kona rumeenew,
Other brave ones [*kuel*] have surpassed me,

Ka femnegechi ñi feme tew nga.
This is also how they [*kuel*] behaved toward me.

¡Ihi! . . . ew . . . ew. . . . [pause]
Hi . . . whew . . . whew . . . [pause]

Feypifenew may, feypifenew may,
Thus I had been told,

lawen ngelu werküy.
he [*Ngenechen*] sent she [*machi*] who possesses the medicine.

Kutran kaw puay mi,
You [ritual audience] will suffer,

ayütu fupni mapu em,
you go back to loving your beloved land,

kintuapni pife new nga.
you will look for it, he [*Ngenechen*] had told me.

Ella pu ka pülla mew, kuel.
Already close, close, *kuel*.

–¡Eu! . . . ¡Ya, Ya!
–Eu! . . . ¡Ya, Ya!

Kutrani tañi neyen.
My breath has become sick.

Kisu yawülngekilchi, puen.
May I not be left alone, my friends.

Fali tañi neyen pifun.
My breath is brave so I think.

–¡Ya, ya!
Ya, Ya!

¡Marichi wew!
Victory ten times over!

Femkünumu fuli,
If they [ritual audience] left me like this,

ka fey ta maneliüw fuy em ka, puen!
I also had hopes, my friends!

Pipingelley ta Wenumapa ka, puen.
So is saying the land above [*Wenumapu*], my friends.

Ramtu nagümngekey machi ka,
Thus one goes down to ask the *machi*,

wichangemey, puen.
they [ritual audience] went to request her services, my friends.

Ramtu nagümngekey machi ka.
Thus one goes down to ask the *machi*

Ramtu nagümdungu.
It is a matter of going down to ask her.

Metanielle lacnew tüfachi wentru?
Do you not see that this man [*Ngenechen?*] has me in his lap?

¡Ya, Ya!.
Ya! Ya!.

¡Feyllemay! Feyllemay!
So be it! So be it!

Lipümtufimün maychi,
Clean it [?] up, then,

kiñe milla saku mew, ewem!
with a golden cloak, alas!

Lipüm lipüm tumuchi, puen.
Try cleaning me up, my friends.

Furenemuchi, piyawllen may.
Do me this favor, thus I am saying.

Lipüm lipüm tuafimün müten ka.
Just clean it up, that is all.

Rulpa rulpa künua fimün.
Pass it on, quick.

–¡Hi!... [pause]
Hi... [pause]

XX. *Küme pewmangeay chaw em, awem!*
May you [ritual audience] have sweet
dreams of the father [*Ngenechen*], alas!

Purupale nga machi. Rupale kellungeay.
When the *machi* comes to dance. When
she passes by, one must help her.

Küme pewmangeay, chaw em, awem!
May you have sweet dreams of the Father,
alas!

Epu antü yafka leaymün ka.
You [ritual audience] are going to suffer
two days of misfortune.

Epu antü yafka leaymün ka.
For two days, you will suffer misfortune.

Feypifenew tüfachi fotüm em ka, puen.
Thus this son [*kuel*] had told me, my
friends.

Pewma mew ñi fey pietew.
He [*kuel*] told me in a dream.

Akun em may, nieke laymi ta pütrem.
When, poor me, I arrive and you [*kuel*]
have no tobacco.

Akun em may, nieke laymi lawen.
When, poor me, I arrive and you [*kuel*]
have no medicines.

Püllo püllowe mew may ngillañmawam,
I am going to hold supplications with the
püllo püllowe (ancient *machi* spirits),

pikey.
he [*kuel*] says.

Fey feypienew may tüfa.
Thus he [*kuel*] told me.

Kiñeke meliñma mew,
among four.... [illegible recording],

en tu menge mi ruka mew, puen.
go take them [?] from your houses, my
friends.

Feyem nga ñi piwkeyellen nga machi ka,
Thus because a *machi* feels compassion,

kuel nga wefkey ñi dungu ka.
so the affairs of the *kuel* begin to appear.

Mane lüwfule machi ka,
If the *machi* [ancient?] were to realize her
hopes,

yaf machi pitua fenew,
she is also a *machi* she would say about me,

mallmawi nga lawenngelu,
she [other *machi*] boasts of possessing
medicines,

lef tripatuy pitua fenew engün ka.
thus, she left in a rush, they could say
about me.

Yafkaniepefiñ dungu new engün.
Maybe I have caused them [ritual
audience] some affliction.

–¡Ew, Ew!... [pause]
Whew!...Whew!... [pause]

¡Ya may! lu kunagaymün.
So be it! kneel down [ritual audience].

Ngillañmawaymün, kangeluwpuan, kafey,
Hold supplications for yourselves, I will
also behave differently,

Entuluwlayaiñ dungu, femekemuli.
If you [ritual audience] behave like this, I
would not solve your affairs.

Pentukumeaiñ ko, pipingey ta wenu.
Let us go visit the waters [inside the *kuel*]
say those [ancestors] from above.

¡Yamay, yamay!
So be it, so be it!

Longkolelu. ¿Chew am müley ta longkolelu?
He [*Ngenechen*] who is chief. Where is the chief?

Allkütripamün, kay.
Listen, too.

¿Chem dungu amta nieymi?
What is the matter with you [*Ngenechen*]?

Entulen tu dungu.
Let me know about things.

Füreneen ka chaw em nga.
Thus, do me the favor, beloved Father.

Müna kutran kawün.
I have suffered much.

¿Lukutun müten anchi?
Is this just a genuflection?

¿Chem dungu anchi?
What is this?

Fey ta kim dunguay, tati. Awem, awem ta.
May this one [*kuel*] learn to talk, this one. Alas! Alas!

Nagümeleyu, milla dunguwe mew.
I have brought it [*kuel*] down for you, to the place of golden speech.

Feymew ula yamün ka, pipielleymew wenu mapu ka.
Only now have I decided to do it, the land above is telling them.

¡Ihi!. . . [pause]
Ihi!. .[pause]

Kom lladken mew mülepan.
Among many sorrows, here I am.

Dallula fimün ta machi ka.
Tell the *machi* everything, then.

Feymew ta maychitulaymü mew ta kona ka.
Thus, the brave one [*kuel*] will give you [ritual audience] a signal.

Dallul fimün ka.
Tell them, then.

¿Dungu nag femay mün am?
Or are you [*kuel*] going to speak immediately?

Pipiewlleiñ ka.
We are telling ourselves.

¡Ya! ¡Ya!.. . [pause]
Ya! Ya!. . . [pause]

XXI. *En tu niew keiñ lepün mew.*
I have you [*Ngenechen*] present in space.

Entu niew keiñ witran mew.
I have you present whenever I rise.

¿Chemew am femmuken?
Why do you do this to me?

Tañi lepün mew mayta,
To my [ritual] space, then, this way,

ngillapay ta fey ka püra pürawe.
he [*kuel*] too, came to buy a ladder.

¡Uhu!. . . [pause]
Uh!. . . [pause]

Fürenemuan pingelleymi chaw em am.
You will do us a favor, thus they are telling you, Father [*Ngenechen*].

Pütrüntu fürenemukeyu.
You have helped us for so long.

¿Chemew am yafkakenta?
In which way have I caused you displeasure?

Pikelleeyu, ka eymi ta.
Thus, I tell you.

Nielleymi ta dungu yem pipiyelleeyu.
Thus, you have the past affairs, I am telling you.

Kakelu kam, eymi mew yafkalemi ka.
The others [ritual audience], before you [*Ngenechen*] they have also made mistakes.

Mülen mew dungu, yafkangeymika.
Thus, they have somehow mortified you.

Kom ngünen mew yafkangen ka.
Through deception they have mortified
me, too.

¡Ey!... [pause]
Ey!... [pause]

XXII. *Epuchi ngümakefuy kiñe ka.*
One [*kuel*] has thus cried twice.

Epuchi antü nag witra ngemey müten.
In just two days they [ritual audience] will
go looking for him.

Eludungungemey.
They are going to leave messages for
him.

¿Chumngey am ta mi ngillañmawün ka?
How do you [ritual audience] hold your
supplications?

Pingekellefuy ta machi, apuen, filew.
They used to ask the *machi*, the *filew*
(ancestral *machi*), my friends.

Yamniengey chi filew ka.
Thus they [ancestral ritual audiences]
addressed the *filew* with much
respect.

Yamniengey machi may.
Thus the *machi* was shown respect.

Feymew lle ta fey konküleken mew,
This is why I always participate,

kom lladkün mew felepan kuel mew.
I am inside here, in the *kuel*, with all the
mortifications.

Feymew felepan. Ütrufentu a rofün,
This is why I am here. My sweat flows,

yañchüley ñi piwke,
my heart is trembling,

küpan em feychi dungu mew.
I have come because of these affairs [sick
kuel and lack of offerings to it by the ritual
audience].

Trupefküley ñi piwke pütrün dungu mew.
My heart is afraid of so many things.

Uya müten ñi l of mew ka,
Only yesterday, in my community, too,

piñuf nag mekey ñi kawell ka.
my horse breathed downwards, too.

¡Feyürke ta dungu tiey!
This is the issue!

Newnmapaley ñi kawell ka.
There was some [spiritual] force in my
horse, too.

¡Ihi!... [pause]
Ihi!... [pause]

XXIII. *Uya ngillañmawün mew inche, puen,*
For holding a supplication yesterday, my
friends,

mari füda epuyawün.
ten knots in pairs [refers to the *quipu* here]
I am carrying.

Felepurken ñi dungu mapu ñi pewma.
Those were in my dreams the affairs of the
land.

Kinechi may ñi piwka fel tüfey,
Once you [ritual audience] have come to
agreement there,

wewpi ley ngilla tun mew.
give the speech in the supplication.

Weda pewma fun pimi ka.
Thus, you [?] said, I had a bad dream.

¿Chum lepu tuan tüfey kay?
Under what conditions will I be back,
then?

Chaw em, apuen,
Dear Father, all of you,

eymi kay chaw,
you too, Father,

katrül dungu lefuymi ka.
are thus mediating in these affairs.

Kiñe epu, kiñe meli dungu trananagün ela fiñ
Two, four issues I will drop

ñi longkolechi lawen ngelu" pifuymi ka.
on she [*machi*] who possesses the
medicine, who is acting like a chief, thus
you said.

We lu kay üftule lawenngwlu kay,
But just in case she who possesses the
medicine were to become mute,

trekapuwtule ñi milla ruka mew.
and arrived to her golden house on foot.

¿Chum lepu tuay kay?
Under which conditions is she going to
be there?

¿Chem kastiku niepu tuay kay?
What punishment is she going to receive?

Fewla pimi em kay.
Thus have you [ritual audience] now said.

¡Ihi!... [pause]
Ihi!... [pause]

Femngechi, femngechi añchi?
So, is it so?

Ina fill kangelu mew puwan ka.
Close to all the others I will thus reach.

Rangiñma lelu mew, puan ka.
I will reach to where the mediator is.

Tu te fiñ eymün pu fotüm.
I have pleased you, children [ritual
audience].

¡Kümey ka!
Thus it is good!

Doy ka müle a fulu kiñe, epu,
There should be more than one, two [the
two *kuel* in the *Hualonkokuel* field],

küla nga aguardiente tüfey.
three liquors there.

¿Che mew am afnaqtuymün?
Why have you [ritual audience] ran out
of it?

Iñche ta kellewaiñ pipiengeymu, puen.
I will help you, they are telling you, my
friends.

Afnagmuken milla pütren mew.
The golden tobacco is coming to an end
for me.

Afnagmuken aguardiente mew.
The liquor is coming to an end for me.

Ka trekapan dedetemu (?) em.
And I have stepped here on... [illegible
recording].

Ka ayüntulu femngelu, femekemuken,
You [ritual audience] consider me
someone who takes whatever she
likes,

pipiwlleiñ ka.
I am thus telling you.

Inatra pümkay pu fotüm.
You all gather the children.

Chumwechi kuñifallngey rume
Even if it is someone helpless

en tu key dungu, puen,
he would come to a happy ending, my
friends,

en tu key dungu.
he [*kuel*] would come to a happy
ending.

Iñchiw nga yu kuñifallngen em,
We two [*machi* and the *kuel*], because we
are helpless,

kellun tukungelayu reke nga iñchiw.
receive almost no help from the others
[other *machi* and *kuel*].

¿Chemew am amule tuaiñ afkadel?
And how are we supposed to go back?

Pikelleyu.
We often say.

Füreneaeyu pipiyengen.
I will do you a favor, they [ritual
audience] are telling me.

Feyñi fe mekengen wenu mapu ka.
This they are doing to the land above,
too.

Ew.... [pause]

Ew!.... [pause]

XXIV. *Femngechi miawülngepetun ka.*
Thus, this is how they [ritual audience] bring me here.

Pu llang kay miaw la.
Because the *llang* [*llangi, rehue* or *axis mundi*] goes.

Ka tripache kutran ka.
A sick one [*kuel*] from another kind of people.

Fay ta yaf tukuel femngechi.
Thus they [ritual audience] threw him [*kuel*].

Ta fey aguardiente nga llaglu.
The one [*Ngenechen*] who served the liquor.

Kisu ñi mülen mew elupay pu kuñifall.
On his own [*Ngenechen*], he gave it to the helpless ones.

Faw wingkul inayawuli ñi kawell mew.
Here on the hill [*ñichi* platform] a horse wanders.

Afkadilepay ñi fotün, apuen.
To his [*Ngenechen*] side is his son [*kuel*], my friends.

Kisu may ta füta amun mapu ta.
On his own [*kuel*], alone on a great expanse of land.

Rupay ta pu.... [illegible recording].
Thus they go, ... [illegible recording].

Re ngümayeñmangey am ka fey, puen.
Not only have they cried for him [*kuel*], too, my friends,

Müley ñi kawiñ.
Here is his meeting.

¿Chumkünu peafuiñ yewün em ka?
How could we leave the beloved offerings around [the *kuel*]?

Akuy ta fachantü.... [pause].
Today's day has come.... [pause].

Fey mew em ta küpaiñ. Angkadüwpaiñ.
Thus, this is why we [ritual audience] have come. On the back of that horse we have come.

XXV. *¡Ew!....* [pause].
Ew!.... [pause]

¡Ya, ya apuen kefafallemün!
So be it! Breathe harder!

¿Chew am müley chi milla kuchillu?
Where is the golden knife?

¡Awem mamuchi ka, awem!
Help me [ritual audience] with the shouting!

¡Marichi wew!
Victory ten times over!

Feley may ka. Feley may dungu yem.
Thus it is. So are the things of the past.

Epeyantü. Awüy iñ kawellu.
The day is racing. Our horses have raced.

Wenu lüw puan fütake kuyfi we.
I am going to rise to the huge ancient places [where the ancestors live].

¡Ew!... [pause]
Ew!... [pause]

Yafkangenymi chaw em, awem!
They have mortified you, father [*Ngenechen*], alas!

¡Ew!... [pause] *¡Marichi wew!*
Ew!... [pause]Victory ten times over!

Lladken wenru, lladkenpay may lawen.
A sad man [*Ngenechen*], thus makes the medicines sad.

XXVI. *Kom nün ñi antü piwke, femngelle,*
In all his heart, if this is how it is,

tüfachi fotün fewla noy,
this son [*kuel*] now crossed,

ñi femaetew fill dingu mew ketronagi.
because he [*kuel*] caused me all of this, he has become silent.

We laentuwe, we laentuay,
In the place [tomb] where one puts away
that which has just died, put away that
which has just died,

arofün mew.
in the sweat.

Epuyawingu we filew, kafey ka.
There are two new *filew* [two ancient
machi present], this is also so.

*¿Chumngechi am ta ungümpua lu dungu kay,
puen?*
How are you going to wait for the new
things, my friends [ritual audience]?

¡Ew!... [pause]
Ew!... [pause]

Feley dungu ka. Feley nütram ka.
This is how things are. Thus it is said.

Piwaylley ñi dungu ka kuel.
So they [ritual audience] say the things of
the *kuel*.

Feypi, feypi. Awem, awem!
It [*kuel*] has said so: Alas, alas!

Welu may manelüwpuan,
But I will keep hope alive,

Femtukukey, tienmew pi.
So it places it there, he [*kuel*] says.

*Inche may trana künu puken ñi milla lelfün,
kuel.*
Thus I toss aside my golden [*nguillatun*]
field, *kuel*.

Epu kuñifall ngilla tuy, kuel.
Two helpless [*machi* and her assistant] ones
hold a supplication, *kuel*.

Fey tripapa key. Nen tu paya fel dungu mew.
Then is comes here. That should be said.

En tu paya fel nütram mew, pu peñi.
It should be told, brothers and sisters
[ritual audience].

Fe meke putu enew, engkaña pu tu kelu,
It [*kuel*] often treats me like that, there, it
deceives me, there,

kiñe manel, kuel.
that one which one trusts, *kuel*.

Kutran dungu nielu kiñekeltu,
Some [*kuel*] who have issues of disease,

kisu amulelu nütua fenew yengün, pikuel.
If we were to go alone, they [ritual
audience] could grab me, says the *kuel*.

Nütu a fenew yengün ka.
Thus they could grab me again.

Nge ngen ta dañumun,
Because they [ritual audience] are the
owners, they have harmed me [*kuel*],

piel mew dungu ka, piawlleiñ.
because there is agreement, we say.

Kiñe lefkentu lleta,
Thus, once and quickly,

amulelley ta purun. Amulelley.
the dancing continues. Thus it keeps
going.

Aponieymün feychi dungu mew dew
You have it in the things, already

pipingelleymün ta wenu kon.
you [*Ngenechen*] are saying above.

Feley ta, feley tamün femken.
So it is, it is true that you often do this.

Feypikelleymün may.
So it has been said.

Wichamella fiñ may, laenngelu.
Let us request the services of she [*machi*]
who has the medicine

pikeymün eymün, kom.
you say, all of you [ritual audience].

Wichameafiñ machi pikey mün.
We are going to go request the services of
the *machi*, you say.

Welu may ta, engkaña tuke fimün
Yet, soon you [ritual audience] deceive her

angka-pun mew ta lawen ngelu mew.
with someone [another power] who has
midnight remedies.

¡Ihu! ... [pause]
Ihu! ... [pause]

¡Feyllemay! ¡Feyllemay!
This is how it is! This is how
it is!

Eymi nieymi nga mi wiritu paliwe,
You have your palin field drawn [*palin*: ball
game],

eymille, chaw em, awem.
thus, you Father, alas!

¿Chemew am aretunaküm kawimi?
Why have you [*Ngenechen*] borrowed it
[the field]?

Eymi nga longkoleymi, chaw em ko mew,
You [present *Ngenechen*], thus are playing
chief in the ancient father's [father of the
present *Ngenechen*] waters,

mapu mew, eymi nga allkünie paymi.
on the ground, you [*Ngenechen*] are here,
listening.

Feypikeeyu, chaw em, awem!
I have told you so, dear father, alas!

Epuchi pewmay, külachi pewman:
He has dreamed twice, I have dreamed
thrice:

Femngechi may witra konpay nga
This way he [*Ngenechen*] entered

pütrün lawenngelu.
he who has many medicines for
you.

Amufulu ruka mew, kintur paymu mu dungu.
When going to the house, they [?] picked
up their affairs.

¡Femllemay! Fey wenu wungelu,
This is so! The one [*Ngenechen*] who
speaks from above,

epuchi witra konkey.
he enters twice.

Eymi mayta aretu paliwe wenu kelleymi nga,
Thus, you were asking for a *palin* field
high above,

aretu lu kay mi dungu,
the same way you borrowed a thing,

aretu neyenmew fele purkelleymi,
for a borrowed breath you are thus there,

ka fotün mew, pillee yu, pillee yu.
in the hands of another son [*kuel*], I have
told you [*Ngenechen*], I have told you.

Ingkayam dungu mew, ulechi antü mew,
To mediate in this issue, tomorrow,

kawingkul mew,
on another hill [*kuel*],

ka yafkan elkaan ka, pifuy em kuel.
I am going to leave another mortification,
the poor *kuel* had said.

Pipielleeyu fotüm em, puen.
I am telling you, my children, my friends
[ritual audience].

¿Küme dungu am ta tüfey kay?
Do you not think that this may be wrong?

Lawen ngelu mew, puen?
Do you not think that this should not be
done in front of a person [*Ngenechen*] who
possesses the medicine?

Aretu falafiñ tüfachi wingkul mapu.
I am going to borrow this hill [*kuel*].

¿Chem may, luku machilu wün
What would be the effect of the *machi*
kneeling down

tüfachi wingkul mapu mew
on this hill

kalawen ngelu mew?
in front of somebody [*Ngenechen*] who has
another kind of medicine?

Niey milla may tüfachi pürapürawe mew.
Someone who [*Ngenechen*] has gold in this
[*rehue*] ladder.

Iñche am witra künuen tüfey.
Look how you have left me on foot.

¿Chumken dungu lamgen em?
What do I do with these things, my dear
brother [*kuel*]?

Awem, apuen. ¡Pipielleeyu kay we!
Alas! My friends [ritual audience], I am
telling you, alas!

Anokefimi lawen ngelu ka.
You [*Ngenechen*] are competing with she
who possesses the medicines.

Noke fimi lawen ngelu eymille ta.
Thus you defeat she [*machi*] who possesses
the medicines.

Yafka nie puke fimi dungu mew ka.
Thus you are mortifying her on some
issue.

En tu la feyu dungu müchay nga.
I could clarify things for you [*Ngenechen*],
later.

En tu la feyu nütram nga.
I could clarify a conversation (tale).

Kutran tu le we tu a fuymi welu ka.
But you could feel bad afterwards.

–¡Ihi! . . . [pause]
–Ihi! . . . [pause]

XXVII. *Kisu em, kisu em.*
Alone, the poor one [*kuel*], alone, the
poor one.

Nielay lelfün tüfachi fotüm ka,
Thus, this son [*kuel*] has no place,

Kisu em nielay milla paliwe tüfachi fotüm ka.
Thus, on his own this son has no place
in this golden *palin* field.

Tu palu dungu pipiefeyu.
This was his fate I have told you.

Piluam nielay.
Because this is how he [*kuel*] wanted it, he
does not have it.

Milla lelfün trefküpaymi
To a golden space you [*kuel*] have arrived
by sheer chance

millalelfün ka wingkul mew.
in a golden space located on another hill
[*kuel*].

¡Ihi! . . . [pause].
Ihi! . . . . [pause].

XVIII. *¿Chumwechi am ta lu ku nagan?*
How could I kneel down?

¿Chumwechi am ta lle llipulafiñ,
How am I going to pray for him [*kuel*],

tüfeychi fotüm iñche kay, puen?
for that son [*kuel*], my friends?

Ramtu nagnieeyew fotüm ka.
This is what the son [*kuel*] from above also
asks himself.

¿Chumwechi am ta lle llepuyea fiñ
How am I going to supplicate before

tüfachi wingkul mapu Kisunu ñi mapu.
these hills [other *kuel* in the Butarincón
complex]? This soil does not belong to
him.

¿Chumwechi am ta kellua eyew ta Wenumapu chi?
How is he [*kuel*] going to obtain help
from the land above?

Chemew rume lladkütu würkey chaw em, awem!
The fathers [*Ngenechen*] are upset for any
issue, alas!

pütrün dungu mew llad kütuwi.
for many things he [*kuel*] has got in
conflict.

¡Ehy! . . . [pause].
Ehy! . . . [pause].

Feymew may, wente may,
This is why, there, high up,

wente may rupakefiñ lawenngelu, puen.
above he [*Ngenechen*] who has the
medicine I pass, my friends [ritual
audience].

Pipielleelu ta, awem, awem.
I am telling you, alas, alas!

¿Chemew llikan mew niengefuy kay
Why would one be afraid to be

tüfachi milla kalera mew?
on this golden ladder [*rehue*]?

Iñche may pürapuafun kay.
I could climb it, too.

Iñche nga wente rupa mekefiñ tüfeychi,
I have gone over all this,

mülew ma lawenngelu nga, kuel.
where the one [*Ngenechen*] who had the
medicine was.

Chem ütrirkan mew niekelaenew tüfey ka,
I don't think he [*kuel*] was envious of me,

iñche ka feypifiñ nga.
I told him that, too.

Püra pürawe mew pürayan, puen.
I am going to climb the [*rehue*] ladder, my
friends.

¿Eymün am ta nierke laymün longko kay?
Do you [*kuel*] not have a chief, too?

¿Nierke laymün am ta ka lül longko kay?
Do you not have a higher chief, too?

Iñche nga en tu nie pa keeyu dungu mew.
I have always come to resolve their issues
[*kuel*].

Tunte pu ütrirkakelan tüfey, puen.
I have never felt envy, my friends [ritual
audience].

Mandakü nulge palufikay,
If they [deities of upper world] sent me
here, by chance,

mandakünulngepafuli newen.
if they sent me a power (forces).

¿Chumletuafin iñche kay?
How would I feel?

Pipiekefeyu kay. ¡Awem, awem!
Thus, I have told them. Alas, alas!

Feymew lle ta, ketronagüm ela feyu.
Because of this, I could leave him [*kuel*]
mute.

Iñche ta ngilañ mawel.
I am related to the *mawel* (*kuel*?).

¡*Ihi!* . . . [pause].
Ihi!. . . . [pause]

XXIX. *Fotüm may, fotüm may,*
So, son [*kuel*], so, son,

felekellefuy, ¿feymew pe may chawem am,
that is how it was, maybe this is why, my
dear father [*Ngenechen*],

kiñeke laynqün em machi, puen.
some *machi* died, my friends.

¿Chumngeymün eymün dungu mew?
What happened to you [*kuel*] in this affair?

Kiñe lay tamun ngünen ka fey.
One of your guides also died.

Ka felerkelley ta lawenngelu ta
And there is also people who have
medicines

Wenumapu ta. Allkütripange chaw em, apuen.
in the land above. Listen, fathers, friends
[ritual audience].

Kisu ka fey ñi perimontun.
And my visions are different.

Chaw em am, ¿Chumwechi am ta tüfey kay?
My dear father [*Ngenechen*], how is this
possible?

Pipielleyu ka.
I am telling you.

XXX. *Ngillatuñmangey ka. Ngillatuley
fotüm engu.*
They [ritual audience] held a supplication,
too. Both sons [two *kuel* in the
Hualonkokuel field] are supplicating.

Feleke fuy may ngillatun mew kom mapu,
This is how things were in a supplication,
everywhere,

welliy may ta mülewe, pipiyaw welu,
now the place [field] is empty, somebody
is saying,

muntuñmangen mülewe pipiyawita, ¡we!
they have taken my space away, he [*kuel*] is
saying, well!

Pipiyewlleiñ, dungu yewün.
I am telling you, in our conversation.

¡Ew!... [pause].
Ew!... [pause]

XXXI. *Feydungu. Fey nütram am ta tu kulparkeymün.*
This is the issue. But now they [ritual audience] have not remembered this story.

¿Chemew am ta?, lladkülüwun dungu mew mülelaymi.
Why? You are not in a sorrowful meeting.

Eymi lle Amunge pimi.
You [ritual audience] went looking for me.

Eymi may, eymi may tüfeychi dungu feypimeen.
Thus, you went looking for me because of this issue [problem of sick *kuel*].

Kom ñi rakitun mayni küdawken
Considering all of my work

feymay mu pin mew
and because of your [ritual audience] own decision

küpatun ñi küdawelüwün mew.
I forced myself to come.

Pin müten ta en tu ngeke lleymi, chae em am.
Things are done when you decide it, dear Father [*Ngenechen*].

Engkañake la ya fimi lawenngelu.
Do not deceive she [*machi*] who possesses the medicine.

¿Chumwechi am ta kellungea fuymi tüfeychi dungu mew?
How do you [ritual audience] want me to help you in this affair?

¿Chumal am ngunenka ke fimün machi, puen?
What is the reason that you deceive the *machi*, my friends [ritual audience]?

¿Chumal am ngüneneka ke fimün lawen-ngelu?
What is the reason that you deceive she who possesses the medicine?

¿Chumwelu dallu ke la fimün chi dungu?
Why had you not revealed this [problem with the sick *kuel*] before?

Eymi mew ula nga, kon pa püllüle ula,
Just because of you, when the spirits come in, only

eluke fimün dungu.
then they reveal things to him [*kuel*].

¡Yah!.... [pause].
Yah!... [pause]

Allkütripange, pipielleeyu.
Listen, I tell you.

Kisuley may tüfeu. Ngünen ngey may ta tüfa.
Ah, she [*machi*] is alone. Thus she possesses something.

Ngüneniewaiñ, kisu ñi ngünenkan nien mew.
I will take care of you [ritual audience], because I have the gift of governance, too.

Pütrüntu kamañ kawellün,
For the longest time I took care of the horses,

mülelu Wenumapu kam
that are in the land above,

kawellngelu Wenumapu.
because the land above has its horses.

Iñche may ñikawell em, mapu kawel,
But my dear horse is the one from the *mapu* (earth's surface),

ulngey ta Wenumapu, puen.
it was given in the *Wenumapu* (land above), my friends.

XXXII. *Pipielleeyu, awem, awem, pipielleeyu fotüm.*
I am telling you, alas, alas!, I am telling you, son [*kuel*].

Iñche may rakiduamün,
This is why, I think,

kom kutran nieel Wenumapu well,
I experienced all the diseases somewhere in the *Wenumapu*

milla rayen ngen,
I was a golden flower,

milla realmu ngen,
I was a golden rainbow,

Wenumapu well
some place in the *Wenumapu*,

milla perkin wenu ngen,
I was a golden tuft (*pañache*) of the land above,

Wenu ka fill puen,
and of everything above, my friends,

milla puchi yungen ka,
the golden edges, too,

Wenumapu millarafe,
the *millarafe* [golden?] of the *Wenumapu*

rume fun Wenumapu pu yall.
I passed among the offspring of the *Wenumapu*.

Pipielleyu. Munale layu.
I am telling you. Look at how deft we are (*machi* and the *kuel*).

Misaw weda yaymi.
You [ritual audience] will share everything at your entire satisfaction.

Welu ka kamay engkaña ngela yan nga.
But then, may they not deceive me.

Kisuleayu. Engkaña ngela yayu, welu ka,
We are going to be alone [*machi* and the *kuel*]. But then, may the [ritual audience] not deceive us,

Pipielleyu. Wimbalayaymi ka,
I am telling you. And neither should you [*kuel*] get used to this,

pipielleyu, fotüm em.
I am telling you, my dear son [*kuel*].

Tamew ka nieymi lawenngelu, pipingellen.
Here, too, you have someone who possesses the medicines, I am telling you.

Anoka nieymi we filew, pimi,
But you too, have a new filew [*machi*], so you say,

welu ta kisu mandawlay we filew.
but the new *filew* does not rule herself.

Fey machi Wenumapu longko nien mew ka,
Then the *machi* also has a *longko* (chief) in the *Wenumapu*,

müley longko ta Wenumapu, puen.
there is a *longko* in the *Wenumapu*, my friends [ritual audience].

Witranagüm ngünen el pa eliyu ta,
Thus if it were to cast a power (onto us),

Wenumapu, feymew lle ta en tu key
the *Wenumapu*, this is how [*machi*] she comes to a good

ñi dungu lle ta machi, puen.
end, the *machi*, my friends.

¡Uhu! ... [pause].
Uhu! ... [pause].

XXXIII. *Feleyale, feleay dungu ka,*
Thus, if this is how it is going to be, so be it,

feleay nütram ka.
so be the narrative.

Fürene ya yu may chi.
The *machi* will do a favor.

¿Anüley am ta fotüm ka?
Is the son [*kuel*] seated?

¿Anüley am ta peñi ka?
Is the brother [*kuel*] seated?

Felepay. Fütake ka wingkul kü pay mün.
So it is, here. You come from high hills [ancient *kuel*].

Kama pu kü pay mün, puen,
You [ritual audience] come from afar, my friends,

all kütu dungua lu. All kütu nütrama lu,
to listen to these things. To listen to the tale,

karü lawenngele lu mew, puen.
to listen to her, she who possesses the
green medicine, my friends.

Fey mew em ta küpa key ngün ka, apuen.
This is the reason why you come, my
friends.

Mane lüwfule nga lawenngelu.
If she who possesses the medicine were to
grant your [ritual audience] wishes.

¿Chem pitulla fuymi kay chaw em, awem?
What could you then say, my dear father
[Ngenechen]? Alas!

Eymi nga longko leymi tüfachi dungu mew,
You [Ngenechen] are the chief in this
matter,

longko leymi ka.
thus you are the chief.

Longko yem elimi lawenngelu,
You left an ancient chief with the
medicine gift,

eymi lle ta ola llungeymi nütram ka,
you, then have been informed about the
tale,

pipielleeyu, fotüm ka.
thus I am telling you, son [kuel].

¿Feyngeley añchi dungu ka?
Is it not true what I am saying?

¡Uhu!. . . . [pause].
Uhu!. . . . [pause]

XXXIV. *¡Feley may, felea le may, feleay,
puen!*
This is so, if this is how it is going to be,
so be it, my friends!

Kuel mew ka ayün ka,
so I wish it for the *kuel,*

kom füta küda wun mew mülelu ka,
since it is the product of an enormous
effort [congregational ritual],

welu ka ¿chum le putu a lu chey,
but then, in which condition is it [kuel]
going to be when I come back,

pikey ñi kuñifall kuel.
says the helpless *kuel.*

XXV. *Kellu lu may, wenu lu way ka may.*
Thus, the one who helps him will also
rise.

Ngillñ ma waiñ, ka.
We [ritual audience] will pray for
ourselves, too.

Konle may dungu, nagaiñ,
When the ceremony begins we will go
down,

yenieaymün kuel muday,
take *muday* for the *kuel,*

Pew künieaymün kuel muday,
And scatter this *muday,*

pewkülleñ mua ymi kuel mapu,
and scatter soil from the *kuel,*

¿chume kelley mün am ta?
and thus, what are you doing?

XXXVI. *Ka pülle le pay pichiken miawul lu,*
Those [ritual audience] who carry
something are already approaching,

pingey ta kuel.
they say to the *kuel.*

Tüfachi wün mew em, elua eyu dungu kay,
In this especial dawn, I will tell you
something, too,

eluaye nütram ka, kuel:
I will tell you something, *kuel:*

Kúmel kaya fimün wenu ta lawenngelu.
You will have to be in good terms with
someone [Ngenechen] who possesses the
medicine from above.

Püro piwke pallechi. Are piwke pallechi.
Let me tie the links. Let me cheer myself.

¡Weñangkúpallechi, we!
Let me feel nostalgia, alas!

XXXVII. *Mülerke lley ta kiñe ta, uldungu
alu ta,*
Thus, there is one [machi] here who will
deliver the message,

eluafi lu ta traf nieyelu.
who is going to deliver the message to the one who goes beside her.

Machi nge kelley, wentrungekelley ka,
It is a *machi*, certainly, it is also often a man

all kütu nie kelay dungu. Yam ka piwke niey.
who rarely keeps listening. He is discreet, too.

Füre nemuchi. Kudaw tumuchi.
Do me a favor. Do what you [?] can to help me.

Ka feyem. Feyem mew ta elua fiñ dungu ka.
This is why, alas! This is why I am going to deliver a message to him.

¡Ew!... [pause].
Ew!... [pause].

XXXVIII. *Mane luw key ñi chaw lawen.*
My father [*Ngenechen*] often trusts the medicine.

Mane luw key ñi chaw lawen ngelu mew.
My father trusts she who possesses the medicine.

Ayiwkey, ka fey.
He rejoices, too.

Mane luw key ñi lamngen may, pikeymi.
Thus trust me, brother [*kuel*], you say.

Kafey, kafey. Welu may pekan kaw kelayan pien fey.
So, so. But then you [*Ngenechen*] told me that I am not going to become distracted.

Eymün nga küme küne mun pi.
You have pleased me he said.

Ka mün dungu ta ka küme künuay ta ka fey.
And your ceremony will also cause pleasure.

Kom ad amuli, iñche ka fey manelu wan,
If everything goes well, I [*Ngenechen*], too, will trust,

Pipingelley ta Wenumapu, pueñ.
so says the *Wenumapu*, my friends.

Küpa kisu mandaw küle lle lan,
I do not want to rule myself,

pipielleeyu chaw em, awem.
I am telling you, my dear father, alas!

Füre neen Wenumapu ka pipielleeyu.
Thus, favor me, *Wenumapu*, I am telling you.

Iñche may niellen ta, Wenumapu ngey ñi milla stipu,
Thus I have, by the way, a golden stirrup that comes from *Wenumapu*,

¡chaw em, awem!
my dear father, alas!

¡Ihi!... [pause].
Ihi!... [pause].

Pipielleeyu, pipelleeyu, chaw em, awem!
I am telling you, telling you, my dear father [*Ngenechen*], alas!

Füre nekayseyu ka. Füre neka ya eyu ka,
Yes, I will help you. Yes, I will help you,

kom iñkañpea eyu ka.
I will defend you in everything.

Welu may iñche, nütram ka nielu dungu mew eymika,
But then I, who have you in my conversations,

yafka lleiñ, yafka lleiñ dungu mew,
yes, we [ritual audience] have caused mortifications; yes, we have made mistakes,

chaw em, awem!
my dear father, alas!

¿Chum ngea fuyam? Felerken tüfa.
What can one do about that? This is how things stand.

Une yafül dungu lüw key,
First seek to convince,

feyta kiñeke mew lleta fotüm ka
then, sometimes the son [*kuel*]

fey ula meke putuy ñi trürüm dungu ka,
even there he [*kuel*] seeks for the link among things,

trürüm tu nütram ka.
he thus creates the facts.

XXXIX. *Eymi em ta fem laymi,*
You, poor one [*kuel*], you are not the one doing it,

wüyü longko laymi ka,
thus you do not suffer dizziness,

welu ta ule lle ta, pielleeyu ta:
but then, tomorrow, I am telling you:

¿Chemew am ta pekan ka mekey tami dungu ka?
What is the reason why you are careless in the things that you are doing?

Ram tu nagüm ngekey lawenngelu, puen,
It is asked to she who possesses the medicine, my friends [ritual audience],

Amüm tuku femnge kelay milla foye, puen.
You must not arrive and plant the golden cinnamon (sacred tree), my friends.

Akuy ula lawenngelu, fey ula lle ta
Only when she who possesses the medicine arrives it is time

anüm nge key milla foye, puen.
to plant the golden cinnamon, my friends.

¿Chem lawenngelu che kay?
Who of those [*Ngenechen*] who possess the medicine?

Püra a fulu milla kalera mew ta
could climb the golden ladder [*rehue*]

dew fele fule lawen?
if the remedy was not there?

Fey akulu ñi lawenngelu küdawfe,
Then, upon the arrival of the worker [*machi?*] who has the medicines,

fey kisu niekey, piwlu niekey,
then only she holds the thread,

füta kimün niekey.
she has a great knowledge.

Fayta udakey mün, kümel
From that you retreat, in good manner

ngilla fuy em ta lawenngelu llemay.
thus, the poor owner [*machi*] of the medicine supplicates.

¿Chem lawenngelu, chey,
What kind of owner of the medicines

chem lawenngelu, chey
what kind of owner of the medicines

ngü nen ma nieey mün new?
would be deceiving you [*Ngenechen*]?

Piñ mangen, fey ta Wenumapu lawen.
You make me notice, that is the medicine from above.

Felerke lay dungu. Felerke lay nütram faw.
Things are not so. The tale here is different.

Anüm ngekelay petu ñi akunun lawenngelu.
One does not plant when she [*machi*] who possesses the medicine has yet to arrive.

Rayün kay nierke lay tüfey kay.
Look at this, it has no flowers.

Ina kon pule kangelu kawell mew,
If she [*machi*] were to leave with another one and on another horse,

nagpale lawenngelu,
the owner [*Ngenechen*] of the medicine would go down,

¿Utrüfun tuafuy kay chaw em, puen?
Do you think the Father [*Ngenechen*] could unsaddle her?

Winaf nienge kelay milla kalera, apuen.
The golden ladder [*rehue*] is not held like this, my friends.

Ngam fillem niekelay milla kalera.
One does not place all kinds of things on the golden ladder.

Akuy ula ta lawenngelu,
Only when she who possesses the medicine arrives,

fey ule lleta nünagüm ngekey,
then and only then, one grabs it [*rehue*],
firmly,

kom ram tu nagün mew,
after consulting,

ñi mülen ta lawenngelu, puen.
with she who possesses the medicine, my
friends.

Kisu ulkey ñi ngüne leam,
Only she would deliver the standards,

chum kunul ngel mün milla bandera,
about the design of the golden emblem [of
the lineages participating in the ritual],

fill engün ñi pipielleeyu may,
thus, with all this that I am telling
you,

chaw em, apuen.
parents, friends [ritual audience].

Few la nu mi konal dungu mew, we,
This is not the first time that you
participate in this, alas!

fey llemay, fey añchi?,
thus, this is so, is it not?

Ka lawenngelu nieymi, ka fey ka dungu ka.
You have another one [deity from the
upper world] who possesses the medicine,
this is another matter.

XXXX. *¿Chumuechi nga ka wicha ngemen?*
How is it that you [ritual audience] went
asking for my services?

Kiñe lefkentu tukulmeaen nga dungu pingen.
At once and fast you will go start the
ceremony, I was told.

Kom ngünen mew küpal ngen.
I was brought in with many a deception.

Ka epe felekatu llefun ka, dungulle fun:
I almost stayed as I was, thus I spoke:

Kiñe mayño man namun kon küley
Well, my right foot has

may kutran trüfey, pipean may.
thus a disease I might say.

Iñka tuenew feychi kutran mew, puen.
Because of this disease my services were
requested, my friends.

Lef ye ngemen.
All of a sudden I was summoned.

Trülmur nagi ñi man namun em.
My poor right foot ended up sore.

Kude fe kawell doy fali fun.
I am worth more than a race horse [*machi's*
pay for performing the ritual].

Mane lüw kü le tuy, faw rupa fulu
I had high hopes, since it went through
here

tüfey chi kawell kay, we, pipilleeyu chaw em.
that horse, thus, alas!, I am telling you, my
dear father.

Descansa nie fimün machi ka,
Make the *machi* rest, too,

trem machi, lawenngelu ka,
thus an adult *machi* [ancient *machi*], she has
remedies,

mane lüw fule lawenngelu, piam machi.
may they trust she who possesses the
medicine, it is said that the *machi* said.

Uya filew, pinge tu key ka, puen.
She is a filew [ancestral *machi*] from the
past, they also say about her, my friends.

Fay mew ta mün yafka puke llel machi mew,
This is why you mortify the *machi*, there,

tu te pu kelay mün.
you do not cause pleasure, there.

*Fey mew lle ta mane lüw pukey mün machi
mew ka.*
Thus, this is why you have some hope in
the *machi*, there.

¡Ihi! . . . [pause].
Ihi! . . . [pause].

XXXXI. *Eymün may ano ka niefiñ, pikey
mün,*
You [*kuel*] believe that you can govern the
machi,

welu ta Wenumapu feypilay.
but *Wenumapu* does not believe this

Machi ta kisu mandawlay, puen.
The *machi* does not govern alone, friends [ritual audience]

kiñe welu che kay, kiñe welu pünon niey,
a different person [*machi*] takes a different path,

pünon tu key ka machi ka, apuen.
a different *machi* who follows the paths of others can be harmed.

Fey mew lle ta fente puken ta machi, apuen.
For this reason each *machi* has to go a long way, friends

Fey mew lle ta ñi ka ram tu ken ta lawenngelu, puen.
For this, for certain, one must consult with the owner [*Ngenechen*] of the medicine [in *Wenumapu*].

Küy daw tu ke lay ka tuwun mapu, puen.
One from the same *mapu* [place on earth] does not have so many problems, friends

Rume anoka me ke layan, piaw lley ngu tüfa. . . .
These two [*kuel*] are asking that we not be competitive with them. . . .

iñche am ta uya ta fachantü muten ka
not only yesterday but today, no longer

tukulan ñi ngilla tun ta wenu nga.
[the *kuel*] that I don't initiate my prayer ceremony on top of them [*kuel*].

Ye me fun ta ngünen. Ye me fun ta dungu ka,
I was gone in search of dominance. Thus I had gone in search of knowledge,

pipielleeyu chaw.
I am telling you, father.

Ngüneyen, puen. Ngünewun ta dungu yewün.
Willingly, my friends. for wanting it like this, the other is criticized.

Fey engkaña muken, ey mün ka, apuen.
Thus, you too are deceiving me, my friends [ritual audience].

Iñche may amuli rangi wun,
If I go there in the midst of dawn,

Iñche may ñi kulpa pa mew nu
it is not my fault

feleiñ tüfey, puen.
that we are all in this situation, my friends.

Eymün tamün kulpa mewlle, puen.
It is the fault of you all, my friends

küme nepe fule tüfa dungu ka,
if this ceremony were to have a good waking up,

küme ne pe fu le nütram.
if the report were to have a good waking up (one wishes).

Newentu amuy iñ dungu ka,
Thus, our invocation would go strongly.

Mane luwaiñ. En tu we ñang künpay,
We will keep the hopes. She [*machi*] came to remove the sorrows,

utrü fen tu ngüman pay machi.
she came to cast away the weeping, the *machi* did.

Fey may ta ayüy mün küme tripan dungu ka.
You have been pleased with the good end given to these matters.

Rangiñ konpa key wedange lu feyngelu mew.
Yet, the curse [of the *kuel*] often intervenes.

Futran mew küme machi pinge fuy mün ka.
A good *machi* so as to confront disease, thus they had been told,

Rangiñ mew wir kükey machi,
A *machi* does not become tired half-way through [ceremony],

pipingelay kiñeke mew, apuen.
she is not telling you, sometimes, my friends.

Pipiewlleiñ ka.
I am telling you, then, you all.

¡Ew! . . . [pause]
Ew! . . . [pause].

XXXXII. *Pe tu, pe tu may malli tu leyngün
ka wing kul pmapu.*
And they [other ritual audiences in other
rehuekuel] are still, still alert in another
rehuekuel [in the valley] before.

Ka pe kar kean em dungu.
There is, other work awaits me there [in
the other *nguillatun* field].

Iñche ta lawenngen.
I have the power.

Kiñe nana trana nagküley em.
There is a *nana* [another *machi*] who has
died and been buried there [in the
Hualonko field] before.

Ka fey, ka fey ka,
She [other *machi*] too, she

ka wingkul mew, ka feyem kuel.
too is in another *kuel* and this too is a poor
kuel,

Peri montul ngey kla fey em kuel.
There also are visions coming from this
kuel, hay.

Amu le perkean may ñi küdawelu wün ka,
I believe that I have to continue working
with them [the *kuel*], well

feymew, ring kün mawün do mo mew,
Hay, I passed over that woman [the other
machi?],

pipingey, kuel.
says the kuel.

Pew kentu presu nieñma fiñ ñi milla may,
In my presence I have gold, well,

tañi milla oriñ [sic] em,
your past orin [sic] of gold,

milla foye mew kisu kaw küley . . . . .
and from the golden cinnamon tree I take
favors. . . .

*Mule yüm ta, müle yüm ta, pipielleyu, dungu
kay,*
It is because there is some event, I am
telling you [ritual audience],

fotüm em, puen.
my dear son [*kuel*], my friends [ritual
audience].

XXXXIII. *Faw ule kay füre neae new,*
And she [other *machi* in other field] would
also do me a favor tomorrow,

iñkañ pe yanew dungu mew, pifeliyu,
she will defend me from those events, if I
told you,

treka yawimi,
you are walking,

iñche ta mapu kay mane lüw tu layan.
but I, for sure, will not trust the earth's
surface.

Kiñeke mew nga pu fotüm,
Sometimes the children [ritual audiences],

kellungeal dungu mew müten em ayü keyngün.
want me to help them and only them.

Faw fem key, pingey em, kangelu fem key ka.
This is how it is done it is said, the other
one does it like this, too.

Ka fem liem, ka kiñe nana lle kam,
If I do it, too, it is because it is another
nana [another *machi*],

fürene künu pu fiñ may fewla,
I went and I did a favor, there, now,

lawenmüten em, küñifall.
remedies, thus nothing more,
helpless.

Fey chi nana fey, küpa lelel tu eyu ka.
That *nana*, I have brought it back
again.

Weñe ngeymu, perimon tun kuñifall, feley.
They [?] were robbed, a victim of the
vision, that is.

Amulerpu perkeayu may ñi dungu,
And our existence will continue,

kiñe chaw ta tüfa piw lu.
those who consider themselves sons [all *kuel*] of a father [*Ngenechen*].

Tüfa ñi dungu ngen may chi ¡we!,
And so it is that they [all *kuel*] speak to me, alas!,

Kiñe may ta une may en tu pualu,
One must go first remove this [?],

fey ula may kangelu, pipingefuy Wenumapu.
then, afterwards the other, the *Wenumapu* is saying.

¡Chem duam welu montu luwiñi dungu ka, apuen!
Thus, why are things going to get confused, my friends!

¡Ihi! . . . [pause].
Ihi! . . . [pause].

XXXXIV. *Newen nge perkey may ta mawün ka fey.*
Apparently here, too, the rain has strength.

Newen nge perkey may ta mawünlu ka ülmen key.
Thus it would seem as if another lord's rain would also have strength.

¿Chemew am ngülam mapu yawün?
Why do you [*Ngenechen*] give advice in this land?

Ka rü pü mew kon küler key,
I have seen that he [the *kuel*] is on another road,

piwütuy ñi nana kay kuel.
the *nana* [*machi*] of the other *kuel* has dried up [died].

¿Che mew em ñi akun?
How did she arrive here?

Inche ñi lelfün mapu mew,
In the space of my own *mapu*.

mia wu lün kay we,
she brings something too.

Petu küda wi Wenumapu.
The *Wenumapu* is working.

XXXXV. *¡Marichi wew!*
Victory ten times over!

Fey lle may ti we filew,
Thus, then, the new *filew* [another *machi*],

ta ki duam llay may. Ya fentu ke eli.
she would have to think. Do not take me from here.

Fay pifey pingen ta, mia wül ngen mew ka.
Thus, I am saying this because you are carrying something on.

XXXXVI. *Neyen, neyen, neyen.*
Breath, breath, breath. (cheering).

Chong ka tun amuley, fey ngey, fey ngey neyen.
It goes on leaping, this is so, the breath.

¡Fey lle, fey lle, fey lle! ¡Awem, awem!
This is so! This is so! This is so! Alas, alas, alas!

XXXXVII. *Amu anay. Amu kon küle pe.*
Go, listen. May he [*kuel*] go that way.

Fey mew lle ta, witra nie mun ta milla joye mew.
This is why, this is so, that you [ritual audience] have me standing on the [*rehue*] golden cinnamon.

¡Ihi! . . . [pause].
Ihi! . . . . [pause]

Ngüne mapuy pipingey Wenumapu, puen.
The *mapu* [earth's surface] already rules, says the *Wenumapu*, my friends [ritual audience].

Fey may, müñam müñam künu kefuy dungu.
Thus, it it there that matters are quickly woven.

Welu my yaf kange fule ka fey piay:
but just in case we were to displease them [deities in upper world] they could also say:

en tu layay ñi dungu,
this one would not come to a good end,

trantu puñ maya fiñ ni milla rayen ka,
I am going to fell her [other *machi*] golden flower too,

pipingelley ta Wenumapu.
thus, is saying the *Wenumapu*.

Ka fey ta müley ka, apuen.
Thus, this is how this stands, my friends (one has to respect it).

¡Ya!... [pause].
Ya!.... [pause].

XXXXVIII. *Küpay, küparkey, epu küpan we,*
They come, they have come, two [the *kuel* in the *Hualonkokuel* field] who are coming,

müle pay, chaw em, awem!
here they are, my dear father [*Ngenechen*], alas!

¡Ya pile mün!
Say ya! (do cheer and give support)!

Epu am pell kelen pimun.
Because there are two of them, you might think that I am afraid.

¿Che mew am ta, ngelay tami pu peñi?
Where are the other brothers [other *kuel* in the valley] not here?

¡Uhu!... [pause].
Uhu!... [pause].

XXXXIX. *All küley kenge lu kay.*
The other one [another *kuel*?] is also listening.

Welu may ta aretu pangi wingkul,
But on a borrowed hill [*kuel*] of the puma,

fey mew em ta mane lüw pay ta lawen ngelu.
there she [*machi*] who possesses the medicine has set her hopes.

Eymi em ta wimpar keymi,
You, poor one [sick *kuel*], you have grown familiar with being here,

fay mew am mia wimi tüfachi lelfün mapu mew.
this is why you walk here, in this space of the *mapu*.

Eymi, eymi. Müleay dungu ka.
You, you. Thus, something is going to happen.

Ngilla nierkey mi fey chi dungu ka.
You have acquired this affair, too.

Ngillatumey peñi wen ngelu,
Those who are brothers who went to supplicate,

kiñe küme lamngen wen ngelu lu kunagi.
those who are good brothers [*kuel*] kneeled down,

kom lu ku tuay mün, pipiewlleiñ, fotüm, ewem!
all of you [ritual audience], kneel down, I am telling you, son, alas!

Femay, fele chi dungu mew.
This is how it is going to be, it is a matter that has been so settled.

Kompuan pilafun, puen,
I never thought that I would enter here, my friends.

Küpan ñi ngilla tu ael.
And I came to hold the supplication.

L. *Une may, una may anüm tu pay ñi lepütun,*
First they came [ritual audience] to tidy up their place,

mü pütu laenew lawenngelu pimun ka.
*t*hus you [*Ngenechen*] have said that I should bring the remedies, immediately.

Elueiñ kiñe lawen, pifen ka.
Give me a remedy for all, you had thus said.

Müler key mi chaw. Müler ke yu.
Look that you are here, father. We are thus here.

Feleay may. Feleay taiñ piw keye wün.
So be it. Let us all [ritual audience] stay in affection and friendship.

LI. *Müle le kay rüwelwi dungu ka.*
Since there is a matter of [illegible recording] . . . , too.

Rel mapu machitu wa lo, feypi yawpay.
He [?] who is beside this space will perform a *machitun*, it is being said around.

Wenumapu, ayiw maluy, ngüm elngey karü lawen.
The *Wenumapu*, getting happy, hands down the green medicine.

Amuley mün may, amuley. . . .
All of you [ritual audience] are going, thus all of this is going like this. . . .

Ngenngelu, ngenngelu, rüf künuaen.
He [*Ngenechen*] who dominates, he who dominates, may he do me a favor.

¡Ya lle may! ¡ya lle may! Milla pütrem füreneen,
So be it, so be it! Would you please bring me the golden tobacco.

Milla fotüm, pipiengeymi may fotüm,
Golden son [*kuel*] thus they are telling you, son,

neyen ma llaen, fey lle ka.
cover me with your breath (cheers), thus this is it.

(trutruka, kultrun)
(flute and drum beats)

LII *¿Chew, chew am müley fill fotüm em kay?*
And where are all the beloved children [all *kuel*]?

¿Chew, chew am müley?
Where, where are they?

Weri, pingen ka fey. Ka fem ngen mew.
They also say that I have felt contempt. And for doing this to me.

LIII. *Ürku newen mew ka. Ngillatun chi dingu.*
In a strength out of weariness, too. In a supplication ceremony.

(trutruka)
(flute play)

¡Ihu! . . . [pause].
Ihi! . . . [pause].

Felen em kay eymün ka. Felen tañi dungu tañi chaw.
Thus, so are you all. So has my father [*Ngenechen*] established it.

LIV. *Welu mayta ketro kela yay mün ka, we!,*
But, then, do not become silent, alas!

Welu may ta kim kaw key mün.
But if you do endeavor to know it [truth].

Welu kon ta tüfa ta dungu, tüfa tañi chaw
Each and everyone of you say: this is the truth this is my father

piw ke mün tüfa.
you tell each other here.

Iñkaw key mün neyen mew.
You defend yourselves with your breath.

En tuw key mün neyen mew, pu fotüm ka.
You [*kuel*] also cast away somebody with your breath, my children [*kuel*].

¿Chemew am lawenngelu, pütrüntu küdaw pay,
Why has the one [*machi*] who has the medicine worked so hard here,

tüfa yem?
this one who is worth of affection?

Chum kaw tu may ta ye pa yay ku tran,
It is not possible that she [*machi*] comes and takes diseases away,

tüfachi kuñifall, awüngelu.
this helpless, poor little one [sick *kuel*].

¡Ihi! . . . ¡Marichi wew!
Ihi!. . . . Victory ten times over!

LV. *All kütripa, all kütripa.*
Listen, listen.

Feler key may ta tüfa, weda we,
This is how this place of evil [under world] thus is,

weya may, yafen tu pafiñ,
thus the evil, I took from here,

tüfa ñi dungu, kom.
this is my business, all of it.

Feyem, küparkey pipingey ta Wenumapu ta we.
So it is that she [the *machi*] has come, thus is saying the space of the *Wenumapu.*

¡Marichu wew!, piaymün ta!
Thus, say it, victory ten times over!

Feley ta dungu lle. Feley ta nütram em
This is how things stand. So says the past tale

kuel mew ka tüfa may.
about the *kuel*, here, too.

Faw pi nagpay moll füñ em.
Here, the [sacrificial blood of animals] blood has pointed out from above.

Kisu may, kisu ñi mulewe.
Only his, this is his [*Ngenechen*] abode.

Wenu em, re ngünen, puen,
Above, thus only one guide, my friends.

Kisu am ñi nielu lawenengün,
As they [*Ngenechen* and his followers] have the medicine on their own,

küpa tu fuy ta mapu mew engün,
they had decided to go back to the *mapu,*

wiri wiri künu pafi lle küm engün ka,
and quickly they twined the plants, too,

müle lu am newen dungu luwam kimün.
because there is a force to divulge knowledge.

Tuy may kim papellu ula pi.
It came to them when they learned of paper [?] it says.

Fuyfi may kim wela fuy papel,
Before, paper was not known [refers to pre-Hispanic times],

pipingey fotüm, puen.
the son [*kuel*] is saying, my friends.

Kiñeke may, kim wingka nielu rume
Some, even when they had the good knowledge of the *wingka* [non-Mapuche]

en tu la fuy, wiñolla fuy engün em we.
did not make it known, neither did they make the space return.

¡Marichi wew!
Victory ten times over!

Kim la fuy may ñi wingka nieel pu fotüm.
But the children [*kuel* and ancestors] were not aware of the *wingka's* belongings.

Amuletuy ngün. Marichi may, marichi kyu ku ngey ngün.
And they [ancestors] keep coming back. Surprisingly, they have scores of grandmothers.

Marichi may fill mawida niey ngün, piyeelu
Surprisingly, they have all kinds of mountains, others

ka ke lu mwe yengün.
said about them.

Ke trange fuy wingka ngen mew ka,
They had decided to plow the *wingka's* [Spaniards] land,

lle küm ka.
other plants.

Fey may fülu ka eyew wingka yengün.
But then the *wingka* dispersed them [during the Araucanian wars].

Fill may piwüd ka eyew wingka yengün.
In all areas they cornered the *wingka* [Spanish and Chilean armies].

Kim we tu lay tañi dungu yengün, apuen.
Today people don't remember these successes, friends.

Few la may, few la may,
Thus, now, thus, now,

fem iaw welay fotüm ka, few la may,
thus the children do not go like this, now,

fem ngewelay choyüm ka,
the new generations no longer do these things,

fem ngewelay fotüm em,
they no longer do this with the poor son
[*kuel*].

Pie le yu weycha we mew.
I have said this for all of you in the *palin* of
war.

Piele yu, chaw em . . . .
I have said it for you, beloved *Chaw*
[*Ngenechen*]. . . .

Ka tripal karkey, tripal karkey
It also came to light, came to light

faw nielel. Dungul pay pu fotüm ka.
what is kept here. Thus the children made
it speak.

Iñkañpefuymi moll fün ka, kuel.
You want to defend your bloodline, well,
kuel.

Ina kin tu tuy ñi pu moll fün may,
But you returned your gaze toward your
kinsmen [living communities and other
kuel], well

Ka tripa nütram mew, ka tripa nien mew.
In other types of matters in order to do
something different.

Alün pilu dungu yengün ka,
Thus they [ancestors] narrated many
things,

alün pilu nütram yengün kisu yengün.
they told many tales on their own.

Fey pipiyeeyu chaw engün.
I am telling you, my parents [*Ngenechen*].

Feler kelley dungu, wera may.
This is how things stand, mostly like
this.

Wera may machi tuwle, pi.
If a great *machitun* [shaman's ritual] were
to be performed, it is said.

Fem lay.
It is not going to happen like this.

Fey pile fuy ta Wenumapu.
The *Wenumapu* does not think so.

Engkaña pe en welu ka kiñe milla may,
But thus you deceived me for a gold,

Pipiyelleeyu.
I am telling you.

Dungu puan. Feymew lle ta mane lüw pan.
I will speak there. This is why, by the way,
I have kept the hope here.

Feylle ta ka well ngen.
By the way, I am riding a horse.

¡Marichi wew!
Victory ten times over!

Fente tu wün mew, fente tu wün mew,
In this expanse, in this expanse of space
[ritual field],

ñagkin tuniey Wenumapu ñi pu.
the *Wenumapu* looks from above.

Fey mew ula en tu parkey yea lu kiñe kawell llemay.
Only then it took a horse to take.

Feley tamün dungu ka.
Thus this is how things stand.

Feley tamün nütram ka pu wenüy.
Thus this is how events stand, my friends.

Nor pewma ngey mün ka, nor pewma ngey mün ka,
Thus, you have a correct dream,

küme ta dungu leñ muay mün.
try to speak right, for your [ritual
audience] own sake.

Kiñe küme ngillatun. Kiñe küme rangilwe.
A good supplication. A good
intermediary.

Kiñe kümel welun mew nga piaymi,
Because one [*kuel*] erred you will say,

fem ngen nga piaymi.
this is why this happened to me, you will
say.

LIV. *Feler key may, feler key may, feler key may dungu lle.*
Well, well, well, this is the way things are.

Few la ula, few la ula, küdaw tu pay mün.
Now, only now, you [ritual audience] have
worked hard.

Faw fey küdaw pay ñi kuñifall rewall.
Here you have come to work on the
needy [kuel].

Küla, epu, mapuche kay eymün.
Two, three, you people are mapuche for
certain.

Kiñe mür, kiñe mür wingkul pamu mew,
A pair, in a pair of kuel [in the
Hualonkokuel field],

*kiñe mür wingkul mapu mew trawuw küley
mün,*
in a pair of kuel you have come together,

kiñe rangi pu n kom, kiñe rangi pu n kom,
at midnight, at midnight, well,

afkentu may pi domo, ¡we!
for a long time the woman [machi] has
said, alas!

Iñche may mür kia wülün kompañ em,
Thus, I go with a couple of companions
[other machi],

ka feyem ka,
thus, that too.

Machi may ñi faw ulel, ñidol filew may,
Because what the machi left here, thus a
chief filew [powerful old machi],

faw, kisu mew, kisu yawi may ka.
here, on her own, she goes around alone,
too.

Küla kafül (?) ka neyen miawi.
Three [illegible recording] . . . of another
breath are going around here.

Inayawi ñi longko layew lu mew,
I am following the head of that one [the
powerful dead machi] whose relative died,

mekey ñi wuyün ñi longko,
the head that suffers from dizziness,

kü pa key ñi neyen .
and its breath comes.

Ina kintu mea fiñ pipingey ta pifiengün.
I will go observe her, she [?] said, they [?]
said.

Ina ya wülngey ta la.
They [dead machi?] are following the dead
[ancestors].

Eluyengey ngün.
They all received.

*Welu may ta aku key ta pu feyem, ka pu
fotüm ka.*
But then the dead often come, and their
children [the living], too.

Iñche may ñi lawentupeel fey llemay,
but then, to those that I give medicines,

ina yawul maenew ñi kay kawell pingun ka.
they say that I am after their horses.

¿Chem pin amta niepea fun ta iñche yem?
What other advice can I give you, my
poor one [sick kuel]?

Rüf utuñ muay mün ta,
You take care,

iña muay mün ta mün feyel kawün
for your sake, follow what is right.

Dew man ta ka trüntukun mawün,
I made the rain that produces the break,

feman ta, kiman em, ¿pipingea fun?,
I will do it, may I know it, how could I
say it?

Pipinge pay Wenumapu.
The Wenumapu is saying, here.

Wera ula may elu wingwün.
Long afterwards they readied themselves.

*Rulpa ke la yaey mün mew, rulpa ke laya
eymün mew,*
May this son [kuel] not convince you, may
this male,

fachi fotüm wentru may.
son [male kuel] not convince you.

Fachi antümew may akukefun pinga.
On a day like this, I used to arrive, he/she
said.

443

Anületu pun nga faw.
Sit here in the night.

Amule kayay mün tiew pi.
You will always go there, she said.

Tie may kompañ künuw kelayay mün,
Do not let that one [*kuel*] accompany you,

mütrüm ngelmün may, ka ¡we!
thus if you are summoned, alas!

Kiñe mew, fey mew llada kon key.
Somewhere, it gets bogged down, there.

Kangelu nga inalelu kay,
And the one [*kuel*?] who trails you,

ütruf puw tualu nga ñi peñi em mew.
should fall there, by his dead brother [*kuel*?].

LVII. *Awem, awem, kiñe kechu, kiñe meli, kompañ kinol nge.*
Alas, alas!, do not accompany five or four of them [*kuel*].

Laftra kon key, layay mün.
They [*kuel*] are falling through and through, they are going to die.

Wingka ngey ngün, ¡ewem!
And they are strangers [?], alas!

Feychi fücha kuyfi ñi mülen mew,
For having been there [?] for a long time,

amun mew ula may ñi mapu, pingey
because their *mapu* [earth's surface] is gone, so they say

ta felepulu, longko yemelu ka.
for being there, for having gone looking for a leader.

Re amuleiñ, kom küdawtun mew müle keay mün.
Let us go like this, with great effort you [ritual audience] will continue.

Kom küdaw tungelu kay,
Thus thanks to all the efforts,

amukange pilayay mün ka.
just go, thus you will not say.

Ütrir kawkey pimi nga.
They [*kuel*] are envious you [*Ngenechen*] said.

Felepule, longko ngelu. . . . [pause]
If this is how he is, he who is chief. . . . [pause]

LVIII. *Küme rüpütu lewñ mul mün,*
If you [ritual audience] keep to a good path,

küme amuleñ mulu ka,
thus he [*kuel*] who goes right,

amuñ muay mün pipingen ka.
go for your [ritual audience] own sake, I am telling you.

Ka trütu rüpüluw layaiñ pipiyewiiñ.
I am not going to block your path, I am telling you.

Kom kelluñ muniewaiñ ka.
I will thus help you in everything.

LIX. *Chem piwün mew tüfachi wün mew,*
In what we tell to each other [*machi, kuel,* deities, and ritual audience] this sunrise,

ulechi antu mew, puñ püleay nütram ka, puen.
tomorrow I will thus match the knowledge, my friends.

Kimiyu ta mawel . . . [illegible recording]
We know the . . . [illegible recording]

Küme may, küme may,
In good manner, in good manner

eputuleñ muay mün fotüm, ewem!
they [two *kuel* in the field] will be paired, son, alas!

Nor pew mangen kom nieñ muay mün.
For your [*kuel*] own sake, have a correct dream.

Fey ta küme dungu ay üy füta chaw Dios.
These are the good news that please the great Father God [*Ngenechen*].

Küme rüpu mew amuñ muay mün ta,
For your [*kuel*] own sake, follow a good path,

kümeleñ muay mün ta, küdaw nien mew,
may you be relaxed, because you have a job,

piley, pikon küley.
he [*kuel*] says, he says, and he says.

Dew malan ta, kümelelay dungu piafun kay?
I did not come to a good end, things do not go well, how could I say that?

Piaw muken.
I am saying, for my own sake.

Dew malan ta, ka küdaw tungey küdaw pimun.
I have not finished, it is hard to finish the job [healing ceremony], you have told me.

Ngüma yawaiñ ka, ngüna yewaiñ ka,
We will go on crying, I will thus be considerate toward you [*kuel*],

Wenumapu yem ta meme küwam tañi dungu llekay.
so that the orders [principles] of the *Wenumapu* are thus put into practice.

Tachi ngümatuwe ta ka ungkü akuay pu Nag Mapu.
This place of tears will also arrive in a vertical fashion in this *Nag Mapu*.

Fey kisu mayta witrale pan tüfachi milla paliwe mew.
Then I am alone, standing in this place of the golden *paliwe* [*palin* field].

Feyti ta mawe, . . . [illegible recording] *küme amuleñ muay mün ka,*
This is . . . [illegible recording] may they go in peace,

küme peñi ngenngelu ka,
those who are good brothers and sisters [ritual audience],

kiñe küme nütram mew ka,
in a good report, too,

kiñe küme lamngen mew ka.
for a good brother [*kuel*], too.

Fem ngechi antü mew, ayeka leñ mutuay mün ka,
On a day like that, they [*kuel*] would laugh again,

rüf dungu tuay mün ka.
they would have to tell the truth, too.

¡Hi! . . . [pause] *¡Marichi wew!*
Hi! . . . Victory ten times over!

¡Marichi wew! piay mün ka,
Victory ten times over!, thus you will say,

pu fotüm ewem em ka, ¡marichi wew! piay mün ka.
you all, children [ancestors] of the past too, victory ten times over!, you will say.

Tüfa ta niepan ñi kuñifall kawell, apuen.
Here I have my poor horse, friends.

Trari konay tüfachi wingkul mapu yem mew.
It will remain tied up in this space of the kuel of the past.

Fay may ta ka müleyey ta dungu llemay.
Then, also, there are other successes, for certain.

Afma tu pafiñ wente wingkul, kiñe fotüm kay.
I admire one son [*kuel*] that is on top of the *ñichi* hill [*rehuekuel* platform].

Kiñe fotüm kay ¿chem am müley?
This son [*kuel*] that is one. Where are you?

Chi kuel em ka mapun mew pifiñ.
This *kuel* of the past that is in the other *mapu*, I ask you.

Kama pu küpalu kay, kamapu küpala kay.
He who comes a long way, he who comes a long way.

Mülerkey ka, feymew ta kangelu ka ¿iñey pingey?
Also present is the other [second *kuel* in the Hualonko field]. What is your name?

Fey llemay, fey llemay, ¿chew am müley mi fotüm em ka?
This is, this is. Where are the sons [other *kuel*] from the past?

¿Chew wamun kay?, pipiyefiiñ.
Where have you gone? We are
asking.

¿Kom punt a ngüneltuniey rangi rayen am?
Who is vigilating among the flowers?

¿Chew am müley mi chaw?
Where are you, *Chaw* [*Ngenechen*]?

LX. *¿Iñey am ta dungu kerkey?*
Who then is speaking?

¿Ka ngilla nieñma eymew ku wü?
Who also has bought the hands?

Küme amuñmuyaymi ta,
That follows well.

Ka müleymu chaw.
Also there are the two of you [two *kuel*].

Wenu rüpu kimaymi ka.
Do you [*kuel*] know the road above?

LXI. *Wenumapu ta ngen ngeymi ka.*
You [*Ngenechen*] are thus the owner of the
Wenumapu.

Witra nie paymi lawenngelu.
And you [*Ngenechen*] have here, standing,
she who possesses the medicine.

LXII. *Ulechi küpachi antü mew kay,*
When tomorrow arrives,

eluw tuaiñ kiñe küme mapu pi
I will give you [kinsmen] good land, he
[*Ngenechen*] says,

fill mapu pi.
all over the land, he says.

Fill mapu tremün lamngen.
To all the brothers [different lineages]
from diverse lands.

Tiew may iñ eletew nga.
There, the one [?] who left us here.

LXIII. *¡Ihi!...* [pause].
LXIV. Ihi!.... [pause].

Ka kiñe lele tüfachi nagküle lu mew?
Is there another one [*kuel*] in this
mapu?

Püra pape yüm faw, tüfa mew feyta füreya fiñ,
Here where one climbs [into the upper
world], here, well, I will do you [*kuel*] a
favor,

pipiyengey feymew em ta . . . [pause].
I am telling you, well . . . [pause].

¿Chem ngünen mew eymi yem kay?
What gives you strength, you, poor you
[*kuel*]?

Chem dungu nuam, llangkü nagün mew.
It's nothing bad that you have fallen here.

Fey llemay ta dungu.
This is the matter?

All küwaiñ epu peñi.
Let us hear from you two [*kuel*], brothers.

Külangey mün chey, melingey mün,
Are there three or four of you [*kuel*],

pi ngillañ mapu.
says the parent of the earth [the deity
Pillan].

Ka kintul muan nga ñi pekan,
And look for my mistakes, too,

epu neyen ta lawenngelu.
two breaths that possess the power,

witra künu ta dungu tua fimün,
standing up, thus they [*kuel*] would
speak,

pipiefiñ ta kom eymün,
I am telling you all [ritual audience],

pipiewlleiñ. Kimüwlaiñ ka chaw em awem!
us all. Thus we do not know you, father
[*Ngenechen*], alas!

LXIV. *Küme amuñ müllay mün ka.*
Thus, have a safe trip [*kuel*].

Pew kelaya ey mün mew ka moll füñ.
May no one see you [*kuel*], someone from
another blood [another line of *kuel*].

*Diw mapu kelayay mün. Chewüd mapu
kelayay mün,*
Do not try to emulate each other. Do not
wander over the land,

pipiefiñ Nag Mapu.
I am saying to the [living] *Nag Mapu* below.

Eymün em kay ta ingkaw muay mün,
You, too, have to defend themselves,

küme neyen mew wele lu.
with somebody who has a new breath [another *machi*].

Ayüm fimün ta wingka neyen.
They make the Spaniard's breath endearing.

Eymün nu kay ta weya fotüm ñu.
But you too, are not bad children [*kuel*], either.

Echa fe üdefe fotüm yem nga,
A son [sick *kuel*] that makes himself loathed, he was,

rupa kelu ta dungu mew ka.
sombody [*kuel*] who was involved in a certain affair.

¡Marichi wew!... [pause].
Victory ten times over!

Tüfa wingkul mew,
Here on this hill [*kuel*],

witra künu ta dungu kelu ta,
those who speak while standing up,

epu fotüm, pipiyewün.
two sons [two *kuel* in the field], I am telling myself.

¿Chem am kay ta tripakelay tamün neyen kay?
And for what reason do they not exhale their breath?

Ta eymu ka.
You two [*kuel*].

Few la trür akuy mün mülen mew am kay,
Thus you now arrive together for being there [?].

Pipiewlleiñ.
I am saying to us all [ritual audience].

Kom kellun mew, kom kellun mew,
With everybody's help, with everybody's help,

pipiewlleiñ, fotüm apuen.
we are telling ourselves, all of my children [ancestors and *kuel*].

Küme tripaleñ muay mün ka,
may everything go well, then,

nor pewma ngelmün,
if you have a correct dream

pwemayaymi ta machi mew ka,
thus you will dream of the *machi*,

pewmayafimün Wenumapu
you will dream of the *Wenumapu*.

¡Konpa llenge may ta mawel!
Thus, enter... [illegible recording]!

TREN TRENKUEL NARRATIVE BY MACHI LUCINDA

Unlike the *Hualonkokuel* narrative, this one involves conversation between the *kuel*, deities and ancestors, *machi*, her assistant the *dungumachifi*, and the local secular *lonko*. The difference between the two ceremonies is that the first was a healing ritual administered by the shaman. The second involves both sacred and secular issues related to soliciting permission from the *Tren Trenkuel*, the deities, and the local community to carry out limited excavations in and around the mound.

The ritual begins with the participants facing the *rehue* in a *nguillatun* field located about 500 m north of *Tren Trenkuel*. Several persons are playing musical instruments. *Machi*, *dungunmachifu*, and *longko* (*lonko*) speakers are indicated at the beginning of each

447

verse. Different pronunciations of some words are spoken by the *machi* in this narrative, thus the slightly different spellings of words. For instance, *lonko* or leader is spelled *longko* and *Ngenechen* or supreme deity is *Ngunechen* here.

MACHI AND RITUAL AUDIENCE: ¡*Marichiwew!*, ¡*Marichiwew!*
MACHI AND RITUAL AUDIENCE: Victory ten times over! Victory ten times over!

LONGKO: *Fawpüle, fawpüle*. . . .
LONGKO: [giving directions] . . . this way, on this side. . . .

MACHI: *Faw may mülepan, witralepan chaw ngünechen, llellipuwe mew. Tüfamew nga re-huekuel newenpemun, ngünechen nga eluenew newen. Mülepan tüfachi rangi wingkulmapu mew, lukutulen, llellipulen. . . . Ngünechen ñi pin mew mülepan. Fey küme ngünekonaiñ, küme llellipun mew, dungutun mew. Feymew ngünechen fürenemuan, kellumuan, newenpe-muan, witrañpemuan dungu mew. Lukutuleiñ küme rakiduam mew tüfachi wellin mew. Kom kümekechi trawüley nga ñi pu lamngen. Kom kümekechi amuay nga iñ dungu, fey eluaen newen rangiñ wenu chaw ngünechen. Eymi ngünechen, witrañpüramniemuan tüfachi dungu mew fewla. Witrantunieen kom dungu mew. Iñchiñ nga llellipuleiñ, ka kom müley nga ñi pu Nag Mapu lamngen. Welu may kellunmayaen, üdelayaeiñ mew nga ngen trengtreng kuel. Welu may allkütuñmayaen nga ñi luku-tulen. Nielay may mediñ nga mi lukutu-niefiel nga iñ küme rakiduam mew, eymi, rangiñ Wenumapu ngünechen. Eymi may elen dungu mew, witrañpenieaen kom dungu mew, allkütuñmayaen ñi pin. Eymi nga witranieen, feymew nga lukutulen. Iñche müten nga llel-lipulelan, eymi nga tukuen dungu mew. Re iñche ñi pin mew mülepalan. Eymi nga mi pin mew mülepan. Eymi nga feychi dungu mew witrakünuen, welu may allkütuñmayaen nga ñi lukutulen. Fey may eluen newen, llikantunieen kom dungu mew küme triapayawaiñ. Kom pewmangeaiñ tüfachi llellipun mew. Adkintu-niemuaiñ, allkütuñmamuaiñ nga iñ dungutulen.*
MACHI: Here I am standing in this place of supplication [old *nguillatun* field]. Here in this *rehuekuel* of supplication that gave me strength, *Ngünechen* [the Father Guide] gave it to me. And today in the midst of these mounds I am beseeching, kneeling, praying. . . . And this is happening because *Ngünechen* makes it possible. And I beg of you, that we enter into the place of ceremony [*Tren Trenkul*] with respect and good order. Father Guide, and all you up there, aid me in this ceremony in which we are praying on our knees, only with the good thought we have at this moment, We wish to begin everything in good form, for this reason, grant me the necessary strength. Father of *Rangiñ Wenu* [the mid-dle world above], oh thou *Ngünechen*, aid me and help me to stand and raise me up in this special matter of this moment. Also all [of] you behold my brothers and sisters [ritual audience] here in *Nag Mapu* [the Earth's surface], we are all attentive in this ceremony taking place in this place. But, indeed, please hear them. May the guardians of this *Trengtrengkuel* not frighten us away. Protect us. We are going to pray in good faith on our knees, Oh *Ngünechen* of *Rangiñ Wenumapu* [deity who is in the upper and middle world above]. Thou hast left me to stand here, thou hast allowed me to be here in this ceremony, I beseech thee to hear this entreaty on my knees, what I say. Thou hast left me here stand-ing for this purpose, thou hast put me here in this matter. And so I beseech thee to give me the great strength to rise and defend myself against anything that might happen. Help us in these things, in these pleas and in these journeys. May we have a *peuma* [dream] all of us together in this supplication. Listen to our pleas and what we are saying here in this moment. All together we are going to pray with our best feelings, kneeling. . . . And you all, pray as well, look at us and listen to what we are saying.

They continue to play musical instruments and there are shouts of solidarity, fellowship and support of the ceremony.

II. *Dungumachife*: *Fawpüle, fawpüle.* . . .
Kom, kom amulepe. . . .
Dungumachife: Here, here, over here. [The music and encouragement continue] Keep on, keep on. . . .

Machi: *¡Oh . . . ¡ ¡Ellangey, ellangey trawün! Müley nga iñ kuyfikeche may. Wingkulmapu mew nga pünonagkiawi kom che. Petu may perimontun mew, ngünemapun ñi pin mew mülepay pu che.*

Machi: Oooooooh . . . ! Oh . . . ! What a beautiful meeting we have! Here lie our forefathers. On this hill many people walk across or around this mound. But we are here because of a *perimontun* [dream] and because the *Ngünemapun* [he who rules this space] desires it so.

Good day to all the sons and daughters!
Ritual Audience: Good day!

III. *Machi*: *Feymew may müley ñi ül, ñi kintun püno Nag Mapu mew. Ngünechen adkintunieeiñ mew tüfachi püno Nag Mapu mew. Kiñe kuel mülerkey tüfachi puno Nag Mapu mew. Tüfamew elngerkeymi, lukutuwe, llellipuwe mapu. Femngechi llellipungekey, amul trufürpelu milla ngillatuwe. Feymew may kiñe ngillatun niepayaiñ. Petu may müleay ngillatun ñi pin mew che Nag Mapu mew. Kom witralen amuaymün. Une amuley pu longko, piwke rakiduam nielu, fey lukutuay tiemew. Amuley, amuley, une perimontuy ta pu kuñifall. Fey may küpalngen, püraiñ lukutuwe mapu mew. Fey may pu kona trekakonay, lukutuay ilo Nag Mapu mew, pin may niepaiñ. "Awem, awem, awem, awem" pin may iñche püraiñ. Feley may ilo Nag Mapu, chumafel ta duamngey dungu mew. Umalepan, femngey ta ellangey ta ilo Nag Mapu püchü müna duamngey dungu mew. Amumün fey may, witrapüramün, lukutualu. Amuy nga iñ longkolüw piwkelu may. Mongelen mew mülepaiñ faw. Fey may mülerkey kiñe perimontun kongilwe mew, kiñe millariku ñi nieel ka. Pin may faw niepaiñ, fachikintulepaiñ, kom pin niepaiñ fachi kuel mapu mew,* *lukutuwe mew, pin may iñche mülepan. Welu may, welu may pin may niepan.*

Machi: Thus this is how my song and my gaze are in this *Nag Mapu*. *Ngünechen* gazes upon us here where we are in this place below. There is a *kuel* here in this place below. Here they left thee a space to kneel, to make supplications. And thus supplication is made, a golden [sacred] *Ngillatun* is made which raises dust. Then each one will come into this place of supplication. This *Ngillatun* shall be held because someone [people of the community] call [on me] and intend to carry out a [ceremonial] act in this place, here in the world below [*Nag Mapu* is below *Wenumapu*]. There they go, standing. There go the *longko* [chiefs], those who truly think with their hearts, they are going to kneel in this place of supplication.

There they go . . . first there is a *perimontun* [a ritual vision]. They brought me there on a path, and there we climbed up to this place of entreaty. All the warriors [*kona*] are going to march and pray. They shall also kneel in this place of ceremony in the *Ilo Nag Mapu* [the earth that pulls people down into it]. I am suffering as I go upward, for this place which is a sacred space of prayer is being invaded.

I lodged here, and thus the *Ilo Nag Mapu* is very favorably disposed in this moment in which he is needed for an important matter. Go and ascend in order to kneel, in this fashion all of us who think with our hearts. We are here because we are alive. And this has come about thus through a *perimontun* [a vision] in the space which has been cleared [cut over] by a *millariku* [a person with gold or money]. And all this matter engages us now in this moment. All of us are gathered here in a single purpose here in this *kuel*, in this place of supplication. This is what I am saying. But, but, but here speech is my perogative. . . .

RITUAL AUDIENCE: ¡*Marichiwew!*
RITUAL AUDIENCE: Victory ten times over!

IV. MACHI: *Müley ta tüfachi mapu. Fey ta ñamkelay. Pülom Nag Mapu ñamkelay, lukutuwe, llellipuwe turpu ñamkelay, pin may. Welu may, welu may koyagwe elngey may pülom Nag Mapu, pin may iñche, puen. Fey may witralüwpan, longkolüwpan, lukulüwpan pülom Nag Mapu mew. Ilo Nag Mapu nga, chew nga Wenumapu ñi lüpülüwpan, afünngey nga iñ kuñilall perimontun. Tüfamew nga llellipuley nga che ka, lukutuleymew koyagwe mew, fentren fotüm, pin may ta niepaiñ. Mülepaiñ kom koyagwe mew, pin may iñche pu peñi. Chem duam nieymi, kompüle püchün fotüm mülepay.*

MACHI: Yes, [this] is the ground we walk on. This is never lost. The place below [*mapu* space], a place of ceremony, a place of gathering is never lost. But, I say, this is a place of speeches. Here I am standing, thinking on my knees on this ground below. Here is the *Ilo Nag Mapu* where the *Wenumapu* [the World Above] inclined [unto us] according to the *perimontun* [vision] which we have had, [we] the *kuñifall* [orphans in this place]. And here in this place, the people are praying on their knees, thus all the sons and daughters together. This is how we have gathered here in this *koyagwe* [place of speeches] say I, brothers and sisters. What dost thou think? There are many people from everywhere. I think there must be an explanation. Thou hast brought many sons and daughters here.

DUNGUMACHIFE: *Fey may ta fentren fotüm mülepay tati. . . .*

DUNGUMACHIFE [spokesman for the *machi*]: Yes, there are very many sons and daughters here attending this ceremony.

V. MACHI: *Welu reche trekakontuay lukutuwe, amulniefiñ tüfachi ül, pin may niepan. . . .*

MACHI: But none but the true people should come into this place of gathering where I am guiding the ritual by means of this song, say I. . . .

DUNGUMACHIFE: *Mülepay may ta che, ka femngechi may ta ayiwi tüfachi nütram mew. Femngechi may tachi pu wingka, kakeñpüle may tuwingün, küfküleyngün may, pu mapu reke may kim mapulerkey fanten mew, ka femngechi may ta lefkentu reke, kakeñpüle may mülefuy lawenngelu küpalael koyagwe mew, fey ta femingün. Re femngechi müten may mülepay ta wentru. . . .*

DUNGUMACHIFE: It is true that there are non-Mapuche people here, but in like fashion they also want to hear the discourse. Yes, it is true that these *wingka* [archeologists] come from another place. But they are silent and respectful in this place. They want to see and learn what is happening in this place of prayer. There is no disorder or actions which can disrupt the ceremony. They [the *wingka*] thought that this place of discourse and decision-making [*nguillatun* field and *kuel*] had other histories, this is why they wish to witness all this. Moreover, they are familiar with this land and know that in another place there was a person of power [ancestral *machi*] who could come to this place of discourse. And in that they worked together. This is why they [the ritual audience] are here as well. [Translator not sure of this latter interpretation, since the *dungumachife's* speech was barely understood.]

MACHI: *Pin may niepaiñ tüfaew . . . ew.ew . . . ew. . . .*

MACHI: For this matter we are here . . . ew . . . ew . . ew . . . ew. . . .

VI. DUNGUMACHIFE: *Ka femngechi may ta . . . feymew may ta fentrelepaiñ. Kiñeke may tiechi wingkul mew triparkeiñ. Fey may kom inal wingkul müley püñeñ. Fey may "permiso" piaiñ tüfachi ngen mapu mew. Pekan dungu mew miawlaiñ, kiñe mapu mew mülerkeymün t üfa. Femngechi may ta pilen, tüfachi mapu mew kom trawülepaiñ. Küme trawün mew mülepay ta pu che. Küme piwke mew kom adkintuleiñ. Chaw dios adkintunieeiñ mew. ¡Re femngechi mulelay ta mapu maychi, wentru!*

DUNGUMACHIFE: Yes, we are here in this ceremony in great numbers. Some of us are native to this place in this area of the mound. And thus many come from the parts corresponding to the sides of the mound [off mound areas and outlying lineage lands]. We wish to beg permission here from the guardian of this place. We are not going to gather here for any kind of amusement, for this is a sacred ground. This is what I say here in the midst of a perfectly united group. The people are here in a gathering which has positive traits. All are focused on the same objective, a desire which fills this [sacred] space. God the Father is gazing on us. This place has not been abandoned at all!

VII. *MACHI*: *Fey may iñ koyag kom niepaiñ fachi mapu mew miawiiñ ka wingka, kom peñi. Kom may mülepaiñ ilonagwingkulmalon mapu mew ka. Fey may witrakonküleparken ka fachi mapu mew. Feyürkelle ta fochüm, feyürkelle ta pu peñi, pin may iñche. . . . Welu llemay t üfayengün amulerkey, allkütuam . . . feyllemay ta amulerkey, amulerkey tañi rüngakolen. Fenteñma may ta mawida wingkul mapungey, wingkulmawidawi, wingkulmawida, wingkul mapu. Tüfeychi may ta mawida relelay ka, fey may ta müley mapu kürüf. Welu may, welu may peñi yengün rumel, machi, machi mew may ta dungungeymün, llellipuwe mew ka tukungeymün. Machi, machi mew ñi koyag mew reke may witrañpüramdungunngerkeymün, ka kiñe llellipun mew, antiku em mew ka. Iñche may nien nga ñi llellipun, nieiñ nga iñ newenngelu, ngenulu nga eymün mew. Welu anta fantepu mew ka tripan miawi ka. Tüfa ngaiñ koyag pin nga müley ka fantepu mew, pin may niepaiñ tüfamew. Pin may niepaiñ nga, welu may chem pi nga piafuiñ ka. Welu nagpay lawenngelu taiñ püñeñ mew faw, feymew may ta mülepay, dungulepay ka. Feymew may taiñ lawenngelu ka femngechi mew trekakonaiñ, welu nga pekantulayan ngañi lukutuwe, llellipuwe. Lukutrekantulayan ngañi millarewe, chew nga kutrankawün, chew nga awükawken dungu mew, chew nga entuken ngañi pu peñi lawenngelu, feymew may ta mülekey koyag.*

MACHI: Here is a discourse [ceremony] which we are all holding today including the totality of our brothers and sisters, the *wingka* as well. We are all gathered here in this *Ilo Nag Wingkul Malon Mapu* [Land of the mound that draws people down below the earth's surface and encircled by people [the participants].] [Translator not sure of the meaning] And I am standing here in this place. So it is, sons and daughters, brothers and sisters, say I. . . . But I am moved by what all are going to hear. . . . They [archeologists] go and come to excavate the water [refers to history] of the mound in this range of hills. . . . Until today when it has become a height on the mountain, a mound, a height on the mountain in the land of hills [mounds]. But this mound does not exist by chance. There is a spirit of the land there. Oh brothers and sisters for always!! They [archaeologists] have been spoken to through a *machi*. They have been brought to the place of supplication. In a discourse similar to that of a *machi* they have been encouraged and directed in the matter present here, in a ceremony of prayer and according to the order of the ancestors. I have my own ceremony of prayer. We have someone with power here with us, although you [*Ngenechen* or *Newenngelu* the supreme deity who gives power] do not have it here in your land. But in this moment you have someone from another place. Now we can say, "Here is our *koyag* [discourse]," we can say now. This is what we can say now. Someone [*Newenngelu*] of power has come down to replace [the mound, his son] among our sons and daughters, he is here, he is speaking. Just as she who posseses the power, we are also going to enter. But the *Newenngelu* [the power that has the resolution] has come down to this place among his sons and daughters and is standing here, speaking. . . . In like fashion we are going to enter together with the one who holds the power [the *machi*], but I swear that I shall not use this place of prayer and meeting wrongly. I shall not profane the *millarewe* [the golden *rehue*] where I have suffered, where I have undergone much affliction for many things, where I have ordered others who also possess the power. We are praying and we are holding this discourse for all these reasons.

IX. RITUAL AUDIENCE: ¡*Marichiwew*!
RITUAL AUDIENCE: ¡*Marichiwew*! Victory ten times over.
[Music and cries of encouragement]

MACHI: *Chem pin am miawiiñ ka, chaw. Chem pin am miawiiñ chaw fotüm. Amuleaiñ ka. Küpaley may kimün wentru ka. Feynudungu pin anta miawiiñ, longkolüwpalu, piwkekonpaiñ. Feymew ta mülepaiñ. Feley ta dungu pu fotüm, peñi yengün. Welu ta tukungerkeymün dungu mew pu kona, welu ta ngelay une trekalelu trawün mew.*
MACHI: These are the things in which we are engaged, Father. This is what we are doing, sons and daughters. And so we shall continue. Here comes the one who holds wisdom. We are concerned in this matter, we are praying with our heads and our hearts. This is the way it is, sons and daughters, brothers and sisters. But all of you participants hold this matter and are bound up in something special. But there is no one who can truly direct this ceremony.

DUNGUMACHIFE: *Feymewllemay ta pelom eluaeiñmew pi may ta pu longko.*
DUNGUMACHIFE: This is why the *longko* and all of us beseech thee to illumine us in this ceremony.

X. MACHI: *Müley may nielu, kuñifallngelu ngaiñ lawenngelu tüfachi füta wingkul mamüll mew, puñma ko mew. Witrakünungey, kuñifallngey dungu mew, poyengekelay, trürümngekelay dungu mew ka. Kiñe llellipun nga entuaiñ pipingey lawenngelu tachi Nag Mapu mew pünonagmekepaiñ ka. Llellipuleiñ . . . welu may ta afkadiñmangekey lawenngelu, feymew ta newenngelu kiñeke kona, peñi, feymew ta reke, ayiwkey ta dungu ka, chempin am nieafuiñ fotüm, fey ta ka llellipuaiñ.*
MACHI: There is the *kuñifall* [person alone] who holds the power next to a wooded

mound and the waters before it. Thus he was left standing for this matter, now he is alone, no one extends affection, no one offers him respect. "But this is how we are going to make a petition," says the holder of the power in this *Nag Mapu* where we are standing. And here we are praying. And thus we are . . . [we] must sit down beside the one [*kuel*] who holds the power, thus affection is shown, thus happiness is created and the results are favorable . . . and we have to adapt ourselves to this way of doing things, my sons and daughters, and so we will continue praying.

RITUAL AUDIENCE: ¡*Marichiwew*!
RITUAL AUDIENCE: Victory ten times over!

XI. DUNGUMACHIFE: *May, petu llellipulleiñ may.*
DUNGUMACHIFE: Yes, here we are praying.

MACHI: *Welu may, welu may, pin may ta niepaiñ. Welu may kom mün adpin, femürkeay ka, wenu ad, ¿chumley ama llellipuwe?, ¿müley nga ta milla muday, milla kako, we kofke kom.*
MACHI: But . . . this is what we are saying in this moment. If all are agreed in this [ceremony of] prayer, certain requirements must be met according to the custom of [the land] above. In what condition is the place of prayer? Are there the [special] foods like the golden *chicha*, the golden hominy, fresh-baked bread, and all the rest.

DUNGUMACHIFE: *Müleay, müleay. Ka fey, ka fey kom müleay. . . .*
DUNGUMACHIFE: Yes, yes . . . all that will be here.

XII. MACHI: *Fey may fotüm, fey may. Kom femnieymün, femürkelley may. Fey ta faw llellipulmün ta . . . llellipule taiñ lawenngelu, fey ula ta trekamapuaymün, wingkulaymün. Witrapuwaymün ta chew ta mün lukutuael, chew ta mün llellipuael. Ka femngechi ta welu may, une may ta petu ta man kontunufiel ta trengtreng kuel, feymew ta pin ta lawenngelu pin ta llellipuay. Niefuy chey kimay, niele, rüfngele küme, fey ula trekakonaymün, anümafimün anta milla reke nga, re anükünuafimün nga. . . .*

MACHI: That's right, sons and daughters. Everything is ready among you. This is what you have. But first you must pray here [*Nguillatun*] field, you have to listen to the person with the power [*machi*] who will make the prayer and then you can walk and go to the mound. Thus you will be able to continue the prayer and reach the place of prayer and supplication. Before standing on the right of the *Trengtreng kuel*, the person with the power must pray and say what must be said in her prayer. If she is successful and something positive results, once she has finished and has good results, you shall also enter carrying something like gold [Translator does not fully understand this expression.] which you shall place just there.

DUNGUMACHIFE: *May, kom may ta rewall mülefuy. . . .*

DUNGUMACHIFE: Yes, that is all good and everything is ready. . . .

XIII. MACHI: *Femngechi may ta niey taiñ lawenngelu pe, feymew chemay ta duamlaymün ta dungu mew ka. Feymew ta mülepaiñ ka. Feymew ta llellipulngeay ta trengtreng kuel . . . welu ta . . . amulniengerkelley tañi rüngape l eniengen ta trengtreng kuel ka. Feymew may, rengelay ta wingkul mapu ka, rengelay ta trengtreng kuel ka. Niey tañi newen, niey tañi chillan kawell. . . . Fey may ta mülepaiñ ta fotüm, peñi engün. Ka femngelu mew ta milla renü niey ta wingkul ka mawidantu . . . niey tañi fütron, niey ta newen ka. .trufkenküley ta trarikon mapu kom wingkulmawida mew ka, fey ta müley tañi piwke, mülekey ta fey tañi . . . fey tañi piwke mülen . . . feyta witrün konpay ta . . . wiwün konpay ta wingkul, wingkul ka . . . fey ta kom wingkul mapu may ta kom feley ta trengtreng kuel lle. Müley ta llellipun, müley ta kimün, müley ta witranewen. Fey may piay fotüm ka, kake pin am nieafuiñ peñi. . . . Fey may ta llellipuaymün ka. Kiñe milla muday mew, kofke mew, kelükünuwaymün ka fotüm . . . Fey*

may fotüm, ngen dungu, fey ula may longkontukun amuay ta lawenngelu, llellipumeaymün kay, elmeaymün tamün millaseña ka, kümekechi ka, fotüm engün. ¿Müley anta kawell fotum . . . ?, milla banderangelu, peñi . . . ngelay bandera milla kuel mew, fey anta müleay . . . allkütumün . . . ¿Mufüley anta kuel bandera, peñi?. . . .

MACHI: That is, according to my understanding, what he [*Ngunechen*] who holds the power says and has. He knows all this and because of that has agreed to participate in this matter. And this is why we are here. And thus, supplication will be made to the *Trengtreng kuel*. I see that they are carrying out their work and excavating earth in the *Trengtreng kuel*, indeed. But I tell them that the *Wingkulmapu* [mound] is not thus alone. The *Trengtreng kuel* is not alone. He has his power there, he has his saddled horse. . . . And here we are sons and daughters, brothers and sisters. . . . Thus he also has his *millarenü* [the golden cave [tomb] of the forefathers] in the mound and mountain. It has its *fumarole* [?] and its power. The earth on all the mountain mounds seems like ashes. There his heart is, there his thought is wont to be. . . . Then the mounds come together in rows and thus there surely is *Trengtreng kuel* in all the mounds. There are the *llellipun* [supplication], the *kimün* [wisdom], the *witranewen* [the power or force that attracts]. Everything appears as a place of ashes here in all the mounds and on the mountains. His heart has entered these places and settled [there]. So he is to be found bound thus to all these mounds of *Trengtreng kuel*. In this way we come to recognize our being. All you are going to participate in this supplication as masters of the ceremony. And thus, you will have to make the supplications. You will have to prepare yourselves with the *millamuday*, [the golden drink, *chicha*], the bread and some marks of color, my dear sons and daughters. Once she [*machi*] who holds the power has prayed, then you shall go to make a supplication to the mound, leaving there your *millaseña* [golden sign], in a very orderly and respectful way, my dear sons and daughters. Thus it is ... let him go who has the *millabandera* [the golden banner]. There has never been a *kuelbandera* [banner of the *kuel*] in this place. Is there a horse?.... He who has the *kuel* banner. Then, listen, there should be a banner. How many *kuel* banners are there, brother?

DUNGUMACHIFE: *Epu mari mülewefuy ta bandera....*
DUNGUMACHIFE: There remain about twenty banners....

XIV. *MACHI*: *Kiñe melileafulullenu ka.... Epu ta mülewealu faw*
MACHI: There should be about four. Two should remain in this place.

DUNGUMACHIFE: *Epu müley rewe mew.*
DUNGUMACHIFE: There are two in the *rehue* [at the foot of the mound]

MACHI: *Welu ta tüfey ka nagümngeay, yengeay ka, fey ta kom meli ta amuay, epu ta wiño-meay, epu ta elmengeay ka fotüm ... pin may ta niepaiñ, peñi ka.... Feyllemay fotüm, allkütumün, peñi engün: ¿Chumi anta ngen külelu wingkulmawida mew kay? Chum-leafel. Kimeltufimün ka, rangiantü mün lukukonpuael ka, pin ta niepaiñ peñi, kom .... Küfkülelu, kimkülelu, ngen mawidan-gelu, witranmawidangelu. Fey may ta nie-paiñ ta dungu ka ... niepaiñ ka ... pin may ta nieiñ ka ... yallemay, puen ... amulea-fuymün, pürafuy ta angkatraru, kuel muday ka ... kuel kako, kuel kofke kiñe pichiken ..., femngechi llellipukelleymün am.... Ka femngelu mew, feyta, katrüna-gümaymün tamün katrüpeye, kenü ta mün kuel mollfüñ ka, peñi engün, welu may pin mew miawpaiñ....*
MACHI: Good, they should take them down to carry them away, but two banners should be brought back and the other two should stay there [on the mound], my brother and sons and daughters. This is what we are agreeing to in this moment. Now, listen all of you, my brothers and sisters, What has

occurred with the *ngen külelu* [he who acts as guardian] on *wingkulmawida* [the mound on the mountain]? We shall see what happens. Let him know that all of you are going to go there to pray at midday. This is our concern now. Tell him that this is the intention, brothers and sisters. The *ngenmawida* [guardian of the mound] is there in silence with all his wisdom. Let him know that you are going to make supplication there. This is our concern and we have to carry out the ceremony in a very respectful way. Go then, friends. Go up now with the *angka-traru* [sacred pottery pieces broken on the mound]. As you go up, you should take the *kuel muday* [the *kuel* chicha], the *kuel kako* [the *kuel* hominy], also the *kuel kofke* [*kuel* bread].... I tell you all this, because you are not accustomed to make this kind of prayer. Then you will have to cut [sacrifice] that which you bring for this purpose, Thus you will have the *kuel mollfüñ* [the blood animals sacrificed to the *kuel*]. This is what we are doing here.

DUNGUMACHIFE: *Fey may ta allkütuniewiiñ. Fey may ta iñ chumael. Fey may ta ngenngelu tañi pin, adkintunietulu.... Fey may tati.*
DUNGUMACHIFE: Yes, we are listening. This is what we have to do. This is an order which the *ngengelu* [the lord of all this] has always maintained here. This is the way things are.

XV. *MACHI*: *Feyürke may peñi, felerkey ka pin may niepaiñ, fotüm.... Fey ta ka katrüpeye ... fotüm, une may ta rul-pafimün.... femngechi müten ... ngenukü-nuafilu anta eymün ka.... Kiñe epu rul-pafimün ka, fey ta rulpangekeaymün ka fotüm, feleaymün. Feymew wüdamtukufemngellelay nga tüfey em....*
MACHI: This is the order established in antiquity and which we are now following in this place, sons and daughters [the ritual audience]. Then, son [the mound], the *katrüpeye* [the animal for sacrifice] should go first. It cannot be that you are going to leave it as it is. Make two circuits [around

the mound] with him [male animal], praying thus all the while, son. And from there one leaves right away.

[music and ceremony]

XIV. MACHI: *Yallemay, küpalmün milla-wangku, kuel muday ka, angkacharu ka, pin may ta nieiñ ta tüfa. ¡Ya . . . ! Neyüleaymün ka, pu peñi . . . küpaley ta degiñ, re wü nmew may ta witrakonaiñ ka, peñi. Müley manga che, laku awelu nga wenu fotüm, yagngey ta koy-agwe mew ka, ellangey ka. . . . Fey may, fey may kuel, fey may, fey may kuel . . . ngenoleafuymün anta charu mew kuel, kom mongeleafuymün ka milla angkacharu mew. Fey ta rakitungeafuy. Fey ta llellipuaymün. Inaye katrünagümafimün ta katrüpeye ka famngelu mew ka. Inaye, ka femngelu mew katrüafimün katrüpeye . . . dew ta llellipulen milla muday mew, kuel kako mew, fey ta kuel mollfüñ mew ka femngechi. Fey ta . . . yengeay ta kuel mollfüñ ka, ka femngechi yekentungeay kom kuel mollfüñ, miaw ta llel-lipungeay kiñe chemkün mew kom ta yenken-tungeay ka. Müley ta küme wenu anay fotüm, ellaley ta küme wenu anay, peñi. ¡Ewem, anay fotüm! . . . witrakintulerkey tami küme wenu, peñi, feymew em lle ka awüngey ta küme wenu. Ellangefuy taiñ küme wenu anay fotüm. Küme amukelaymi, fanewkeymi kiñeke mew weda fotüm, welu ta fill mongen küme wenu mew ta witranpepuwley.*

MACHI: Now, bring the *millawangku* [the golden seat] and the *kuel muday* [the *kuel* drink [*chicha*] and the *angkacharu* [the cere-monial [pottery] vessel]. We are in this cere-mony and we are carrying it out thus. Now! You have to pay attention, the volcano is coming. The volcano rises upward and we are going to enter [it] only with words. The grandfather and the youth, they are two in the place of discourse. They look very well. Now, you *kuel*. You could not remain out-side the ceremonial sherds. All should be alive within the golden vessel [containing the *chicha*]. That should be considered. And you will have to pray thus. So also you will have to cut the animal [to be] sacri-ficed and do it in the same way. There you

will have to cut and make the sacrifice. . . . I am already praying with the golden *muday* [*chicha*], with the *kuel* hominy, and the *kuel* blood. Now . . . you must take the blood [for the] *kuel* and you have to beseech him for all that is needed. The *küme wenu* [good world above], my son, is very beautiful, my brother [*kuel*]. Take care, for the *küme wenu* can be angered, sons and daughters [the rit-ual audience]. But it can feel sorrow, since it gazes upon you from above. Sometimes you [*kuel*] do not walk rightly, you are stub-born like a bad son. There is the *küme wenu* in its majesty and beauty, my son. But all the forms of life depend on the kindness from above.

[Shouts of support and encouragement]

XVII. MACHI: *Müley ta küme wenu . . . ellangey ta küme wenu ka. . . . Fey may dituaymün ka . . . füta wingkul llellipuwe. Dipuafimün ta trengtreng kuel ka, inakontuaiñ trengtreng kuel, welu ta sentimulayaiñ, llel-lipulüwaiñ. Iñche ta kürüfkülellen, kiñengey tañi kürüfkülen, tüfachi medilwe mew, pari-ente kuel. Fürenemuaiñ, fürenemuaiñ, piwke-tumuaiñ dungu mew. Lladkülayaymi trengtreng kuel, nieymi tami newen, lladkülayaymi, wirarnielu amuaiñ. Infitangellefuluaiñ müten, witrakünulüwaiñ ta millaseña. Welu ta fürenemuaiñ trengtreng kuel, pillaymün ka. Nütramtu kuel, femngechi kuel, payllan-gen wingkul, fey may ta mülepaymün ka. Fey may kuel, rakiduamimün angkacharu. Kiñepüleley tamün angkacharu, awem anay, fotüm, ngüneduamlaymün ka, awem . . . awem, pin may ta nieiñ ka. Rangiñpüle elkünungekey ta angkacharu, dipualu. . . . Fey may pin may ta nieaiñ ka, welu may kom llellipuay, kom lukutuaymün ka. . . . Ka femngelu mew, chafkonkülepalu, millawingka peñi ka, kom lukutuayngün, kisu tañi neyen mew ka fey nen-tuay tañi neyen engün. Iñchiñ ta witrantuküleiñ ta küdaw mew.*

MACHI: Yes, the *küme wenu* exists . . . it is very beautiful. Now you are going to reach that immense mound where the prayers are offered. You are going to arrive where the *Trengtreng kuel* is, surely. . . . We are going inside the *Trengtreng kuel*, but do not feel badly, I am going to pray to him. I am like the wind, I have the capacity to behave like the wind in this place, kinsman *kuel*. Grant us this favor, decide with compassion in this matter. . . . Do not be angry, *Trengtreng kuel*, thou hast the *newen* [power], do not be angry because we are making noise. Yes, we are going to go as guests but we are only going to leave standing a *millaseña* [a golden marker]. But, please, grant us the favor *Trengtreng kuel*, give us an affirmative answer. *Kuel* of spoken history, *payllangen wingkul* [sacred guardians of the mounds], you [all] are here. Now you have already reflected with the *angkacharu* [sacred vessel]. Brothers and sisters, the *angkacharu* is not correctly placed. You are not paying attention to this. Alas! That [the sacred sherds] has to be placed near the center to offer the supplication so that it reaches its goal. This is our ceremony. Indeed, all have to kneel. The outsiders as well who have been permitted to be here. The *millawingka* [the non-Mapuche in the sacred place] have to kneel and thus, in their own breath . . . and they must follow their own breath. We are standing and very involved in this task.

XVIII. *MACHI: Petu ta llellipuiñ rangiñwenu chaw Ngünechen.* . . .

MACHI: We are beseeching thee *rangiñwenu* chaw *ngünechen* [Father Guide from the center of the world above].

DUNGUMACHIFE: Pataka epu mari puwi. . . .

DUNGUMACHIFE: It comes to one hundred twenty. . . . [Translator does not understand the rest of the sentence.]

XIX. *MACHI: Femi may, femi ka.* . . . *Petu ta witrantukuleiñ ka, llellipuwe rangiñ may, rangiñ wenu chaw ngünechen, fürenemuaiñ. Welu may ta "permiso" piaiñ ka, trengtreng mawida kuel mew, feymew ta wüdaley taiñ küdaw, pin ta nieiñ ta katripachi.* . . .

MACHI: That's right, yes, that's right. Here we are standing, indeed, in the middle of this place of prayer, *rangiñ wenu chaw Ngünechen* [Father and guide from the mid-

dle of the land above]. We continually beseech you to help us. But we want to ask "permission" for this, to be on the mound where the *Trengtreng kuel* is. Yes, here we are standing. This is our word on this matter. . . .

DUNGUMACHIFE: [Speaks in Spanish]: permiso, vamos entrar entrar en trengtreng kuel. Permiso mi nuestro señor, . . . *Pero hablen en castellano, igual no más.* .

DUNGUMACHIFE: [Speaks in Spanish]: with permission, we are going to enter, enter [sic] the *Trengtreng kuel*. With your permission, my, our lord [sic], . . . but speak in Spanish, just the same.

RITUAL AUDIENCE: *Ya.* . . .
RITUAL AUDIENCE: Yes. . . .

XX. *MACHI: Püñeñ mew ta lukutumuaiñ . . . ngen muday kom nielu. Fey ta lukukonaiñ, pin ta niey ta katripa ka . . . kom pu peñi ka . . . kom pu peñi ka . . . kom lukutuaymün ka. Pin may ta nieiñ ka.* . . .

MACHI: You are going to pray for the sons and daughters [ritual audience] . . . with all who have *muday* [chicha]. We are going to kneel like this. This says she who comes from another place . . . also all the brothers and sisters . . . All the sons and daughters are going to kneel and are going to pray. That is our word in this moment.

[shouts of encouragement and music]

XXI. *MACHI: Ka wente kawellngelu, tüfapüle kakünuway pu fotüm.* . . .

MACHI: Those who are on horseback have to get in place, sons and daughters. . . .

LONGKO: Kawellngelu, fawpüle. . . .

LONGKO: Those on horseback, go take [your] place on this side.

MACHI: Kom tami peñi bandera . . . nagpape ka. Ka epu wütrulniepe ka, ka epu ngenule ta wentekawellngealu ka, fey ta lukuleaymün. Fey ta yeaymün tamün kuel bandera ka. Kimay ta peñi ka. Kiñe yeniemün kiñe kuel bandera une, peñi. allfe, kañpüle, ka yeniemün kiñe kurü, ka femngechi. Yenielleaymün may fotüm.

Ka femngechi, katrünagümaymün inaye tamün katrüpeye yengepelu wenu. . . . [Translator does not understand this phrase.] Ka femngechi welukonüwam, peñi engün. . . .

MACHI: Have them gather all the banners here. And the other two which are waving. And leave two more in case the horseman is not [there]. And so, all have to kneel. Take the *kuel* banner and carry it. Remember that this is our brother [*kuel*]. In the first place, carry the *kuel* banner, brothers and sisters. Since you are going to be in another place, in like fashion, carry a black banner also. Carry all this, sons and daughters. In the same way, cut also the sacrifice [animals], which should be brought up [to the top of the mound?] All this in order to occupy the place of the other [sacred space of the mound], brothers and sisters. . . .

[Cries and shouts of encouragement]

XXII. MACHI: *Yallemay, peñi, yallemay, fotüm. Llakope ka pichintu nga wenu müley, fotüm. Awem anay fotüm, ellangepelu nga iñ küme wenu, anay peñi, konkelu anta eymi mew, fantepulekelu anta ñi kümen. Pin may ta nieiñ ka. Welu may ta . . . ngelayay turpu, chem ayentun rume, küme dunguafuy tañi dungu ta kom che küme. Chem ayentun rume ngelayafuy, rüf küme rakiduam mew. Chew may ta yom rakiduam mew ta, nütuafuymün tamün dungu. Trafdunguleymün, püno Nag Mapullenu anta pin may ta niepaiñ. ¡EEE ww . . . ! Yallemay fotüm, ngaiñ lawenngelu, nielay tañi . . . miawül-lay tañi . . . may tañi llellipuwe ta fotüm. Feyllemay, peñi, muyüpelu pe kam, fente may nga iñ lawenngelu, reke nga, molliwmaletuy nga ñi dungu mew ka. . . .*

Kiñe kuel muday may, yallemay, yallemay puen. ¡Yallemay!. Witrapüramün ka . . . kom lukutuaymün, llellipuaymün ka, ngen wenu chaw ngünechen. Kiñe kurü may ta nana mülele, nentuay tañi neye n ka, kiñe nana. Yallemay, puen, kom lukutuaymün ka. . . .

MACHI: Now then, brothers and sisters! Now then, sons and daughters! Let us warm the place above a little, sons and daughters. Ay, sons and daughters! Our good land above has always been beautiful, my brothers and sisters. It is within you, because its goodness is so great. This is our word, here. But everyone should have an attitude of respect. No one should joke or laugh. All thoughts should be concentrated on our present endeavor so that we may have the desired results. Any contrary thought can go against you. You are sharing the word. And here we are standing on this space below offering our prayer. . . . Eeww! . . . Now, brothers and sisters, this person with power has not brought her *llellipuwe* [what is used in the supplication]. Perhaps she forgot it. This person [*machi*] who has the power seems to have become drunk [in trance] in the course of our ceremony. Bring the *kuel muday* [gloss], right away, friends. Right now! Stand up and then all will have to kneel and pray. Thus is *Ngen Wenu Chaw Ngünechen* [Father Guide, master of the world above]. If there is a sister in black, may she blow out her breath and make it circulate . . . yes, a sister. Well now, friends, everyone has to kneel.

[music, ritual encouragement]

XXIII. RITUAL AUDIENCE: ¡*Marichiwew*! RITUAL AUDIENCE: Victory ten times over!

MACHI: *Yallemay, feymay, ina rewe, kom iñchiñ fotüm, miawpaiñ, inalkawellngetuaiñ ka milla rewe mew fotüm. . . .*

MACHI: Well, now. We are all here now, sons and daughters. Then we will guide the horses toward the millarewe [golden *rehue*], sons and daughters. . . .

[Music and ritual encouragement]

DUNGUMACHIFE: *Femlley may. . . .*
DUNGUMACHIFE: This is the way it is. . . .

MACHI: *Dew may dungupaayngün, ka dew may llellipupalleymün ka, dew may küme tripapaymün ka, fotüm engün. . . .*

MACHI: Now you have spoken, now you have prayed and you have been successful in this prayer. . . .

RITUAL AUDIENCE: ¡*Marichiwew!*
RITUAL AUDIENCE: Victory ten times over!
[Demonstration and shout of joy]

MACHI: Feymay, chageltun may, pin may nieputulleaymün ka. . . .
MACHI: Now, on return, there you will also give thanks through ritual and speech. . . .

LONGKO: Los peñi para este lado. . . .
LONGKO: [The banners?] brothers and sisters to this side. . . .

MACHI: Pin may nieputuaymün, peñi. Fey may nieputuaymün. Feymay, fotüm. Feymay . . . amuaiñ ka peñi. . . . Feymay.
MACHI: Brothers and sisters, you have to carry out this ritual. Yes, you have to do it. That is it, sons and daughters. That is . . . now we are going, brothers and sisters.

[Music and shouts of encouragement]

LONGKO: [in Spanish] Ahora vamos continuar la ceremonia. . . .

La bandera . . . , la camioneta . . . do bandera aquí . . . hijo . . . , do bandera ahí: alláhta la negra. . . . Una negra y una blanca. . . . Ahíhtan loh caballoh. . . .
LONGKO: Now we are going to continue the ceremony. . . . The banner . . . , the pick-up . . . son . . . , [do] banner there: there's the black one. . . . A black one and a white. . . . There're the horses. . . .

[The music continues. . . . I note the accordion and the ritual music]

XXIV. *MACHI: Welu may ta, welu may ta dewmay ta küdaw. Dew may ta nagkawelluy ka longlüwpiwkelu, mülekey nga iñ perimontun mew. Welu may ta kutrankawiiñ ta iñ kuñifall kawellngelu ka. Awüngefuy dungu mew ka, chaw. Welu nga chem kanakey fey fotüm. Kom kutrankawün mew rulpay.*
MACHI: Well now, well now, he [*kuel*] has done his work. He has come down from that horse which was imagined with feeling, that one which was in our vision. Well now, indeed, we have suffered for our

lone horseman. Look, now, he has suffered because of this matter. But, then, What has he gained with all this, son [*kuel*]. He experienced all kinds of misfortune.

RITUAL AUDIENCE: ¡*Iiihuuu!* . . . .
RITUAL AUDIENCE: Iiihuuuuu!

DUNGUMACHIFE: Eymi ta müleymi ta tüfa. . . .
DUNGUMACHIFE: Here you have. . . .

MACHI: ¡Eeeeuuuuh . . . !. Dew may ta kimay ta dungutun, llellipun. Dew may ta müley nütramtun. Alofi may ñi rayen. . . .
MACHI: Eeeeuuuuh! Now he [*kuel*] shall know about the celebration of the *dungutun* [ritual oration] and the *llellipun* [prayer]. Now comes the *nütramtun* [ceremonial discourse invited from the participants]. I see its flowering brilliance . . . . . . [Translator does not understand the rest of this sentence].

DUNGUMACHIFE: Felelley may. Mülefule may ta nütram, fey ta kümeafuy. . . .
DUNGUMACHIFE: That is the way it is, then. May the ceremonial conversation be welcome.

MACHI: Fey may ta kümekünuymün, kümekünuymün. . . .
MACHI: Now then, you have done it well. . . .

XXV. RITUAL AUDIENCE ¡*Marichiwew!*. . . .
RITUAL AUDIENCE: Ten times the victory!

[Music and shouts of affirmation of identity]

MACHI: Ka femngelu mew ta millawingka femngelu, kom mantay, ka kisu nielay dungu ka.
MACHI: And in this process the *millawingka* [the golden or sacred outsider, non-Mapuche] has ordered everything, but he does not carry out this matter alone.

DUNGUMACHIFE: Femi ka. Iñchiñ may ta kom mantalelleiñ ta ka.
DUNGUMACHIFE: That's right. But all of us are also ordering everything. . . .

MACHI: *Dew may, dew may kuntrankaw-longkolüw, piwkelu, peñi may iñ kuñifallngen. Awüngey, awüngey nga ñi kuñifall perimontun. Illkutungewelay, illkutungewelay.*

MACHI: Now, then, we who have made an effort and suffered, my dear brother [*kuel*]. We the defenseless [*machi* and ritual audience], here we are. Welladay, we [*machi* alone] who have had these visions! But for now, they no longer reprove us [*machi* and her assistants], they are not angry with us any more.

DUNGUMACHIFE: *¡Feyllemay!*
DUNGUMACHIFE: That is the way it is.

XXVI. MACHI: *Wentekawellküley nga dungu mew. Kom kutrantuwün mew, kom awükawün mew müley may dungu mew. Welu may, welu may, welu may, welu may iñfitungerkey ka. Feychi dungu may niepaiñ fotüm. Feymew ta ka fentren mew may ta, ka nentutuaymün ta mün katrüpeye ka fotüm, kümekechi peñi puwaymün. Yamafimün ta katripa ka, yamafimün ta dungu mew ka, anolayafimün dungu mew ka. Mufültukuafimün ka, küme dunguafimün kuel mew ka. . . . Küme llellipun nieaymün ka . . . pin may ta nieiñ peñi engün. . . . Kiñechi mew ta lukulelayaymün, feymew tañi dungu mew ta llellipuleymün tüfachi trayen mew, tüfachi wingkul mew . . . welu may yamafimün, pin may niepaiñ peñi engün. . . .*

MACHI: He [*kuel*] is aware of all these matters. He is here with great sacrifice, with great suffering in all this. But they have also wronged him. This is why we are here, my son [*kuel*]. Then, and after a prudent wait, you [the assembled group] will bring out the sacrificial animal, my son [*kuel*]. And do this with great respect. You should respect someone with a different status. You must respect him in these things. Be prudent in your dealings. Speak with him with great respect, with the right words, there in the *kuel.* . . . Seek to have a good ceremony of prayer. . . . this is our word, dear brothers and sisters. Do not remain kneeling in one place. This is why you are gathered here on these different levels, on this hill [*kuel*]. . . . [Translator does not understand the last sentence.]

DUNGUMACHIFE: *¡Feyllemay epu rütru!*
DUNGUMACHIFE: That is the way it is on both sides!

XXVII. MACHI: *Fey may, rangiñ akurkeafuymün am fotüm. Re femngen ayekatun mew feleaymün ka, femngechi ta mün femkentun miawün ka. Allkütunge fotüm ka, allkütunge peñi ka. Iñchiñ taiñ lawenngelu wente kawell miawi ka. Ka femngelu mew ka, witrakonküley dungu mew tüfachi degiñ mew ka, fotüm. Fey ta rüfkentu müleñmuay faw, pin ta niepaiñ ka fotüm. Petu ta müley tañi wechulüwael, pepilüwael taiñ kuñifall lawenngelu. Petu ta ngünel kawellngean pipingey tañi werañ ka, tañi elpaetew meli mew ka witran. . . . Fey may, peñi. Tuntepu ta mün dew rupamum tamün trawütuwe, lukutuwe, datuleafuymün ta mün llellipuwe ka. Dew ta wewimün dungu mew, dew ta wechuymün. . . .*

MACHI: Then, it cannot be that only half the people [ritual audience] have arrived here. They are used to amusing themselves; that is your custom in these parts. But listen, my son! Listen, brother! Our holder [*machi*] of the power is paying attention. In like fashion, my son [*kuel*], he is following this ceremony here on this volcano. We are saying that in effect he [*kuel*] should remain in this [statement oriented toward *Pillan*] place, that is our plea, my son [*kuel*]. Our holder of the power must still gather her power to attain the goal, she must prepare herself. Get my horse ready for me, she is telling her agrieved companion and those four assistants [visiting *machi* helpers] who came to leave me here for a visit. . . . That is it, brother. Once this ceremony here in this place of gathering and adoration is over, you could hold a curing ceremony in this place of adoration, you could hold a curing ceremony in this field of prayer. You have been successful with this ceremony. You have reached the goal now. . . .

RITUAL AUDIENCE: *¡Marichiwew . . . !*
RITUAL AUDIENCE: Victory ten times over!

DUNGUMACHIFE: *Dew ta feleay ta dungu. . . .*
DUNGUMACHIFE: This is the way things will be. . . .

MACHI: *Fey may, puen . Fey may ta fentepuleaiñ may pin nieiñ. Feley ka feley. . . .*
MACHI: This is [it], friends. We are nearing the end of this gathering is the word we have now. Thus, then, thus. . . .

DUNGUMACHIFE: *Felerkeay puw nütram. . . .*
DUNGUMACHIFE: This is how this conversation will end. . . .

MACHI: *Ffeley ka fotüm pin may nieiñ, fotüm. Welu may fotüm, welu may peñi, tüfachi katripa felepayngün, tüfayengün. Küdaw mew ka femngechi miawingün, kamapun mew küdawingün ka. . . .*
MACHI: Thus, my son [*kuel*] is our saying here, my son. But also, my son, but also brother, these outsiders who are here have come to take part in this work. They have come from other places [other communities] to work with us here.

DUNGUMACHIFE: *Feley may, küdawingün.*
DUNGUMACHIFE: That's right. They have collaborated.

XXVIII. MACHI: *Petu may wentru . . . welu may peñi, pin may nieiñ ka. Kisuyengün ta dullipay engün ka. Feymew ta yamafi lawenngelu ka. . . . Felerkey nga ñi dungu. Felerkey nga ñi kimün, pin may ta nietullaymün fantepumew eymün ka fotüm, fey dungu niepaiñ. . . .*
MACHI: Nevertheless, man [*kuel*] . . . nevertheless, my brother [*kuel*], we have to add something more. They [the ritual audience], themselves have chosen this, and thus they will have to respect the holder of the power. . . . You, my sons and daughters, will have to remember the following afterwards, thus is her word established, thus is her [of the *machi*] wisdom. Since, for this we have gathered here.

DUNGUMACHIFE: *Felelley may.*
DUNGUMACHIFE: Thus it is.

MACHI: *Katripallemay, ayekawrumelu ka, ngünenkay tañi lawenngelu ka. "üllamenew" piafuymün rume. Kisu may ñi wingkul mew llellipuñmualu nga iñ lawenngelu. Kisu nga iñ wingkulngenmapu mew ka fotüm. Ka feymew miawkefuy, feyrume nga ka welltun mapu mew lukukonkiakey, ¡peñi!*
MACHI: And those who are not part of this group and those who suddenly burst out laughing, deceive her who holds the power. You can think that I am scolding you. If only our holder of the power were praying on her own mountain [mound], in the space of our father [*Ngenechen*], of the mound that sits on the surface of the earth, now, my son [*kuel*]. And he [*Ngenechen*] usually walks there. He himself usually goes kneeling in other lands, [my] brothers and sisters!

RITUAL AUDIENCE: *¡Huihuuuuuuuu!*
RITUAL AUDIENCE: Huihuuuuuuuu!

XXIX. MACHI: *¡Eeww . . . ! Welu may ta yamfi lawenngelu ka, longkotripalu, chafkonkülepalu ka fotüm. ampiley engün, lamngenkechiley ka dungu mew ka femngechi. Welu may fotüm, kisu engün ta kimniey fotüm, peñi. Ano ta kimi ka, dew mañumfile tañi lawenngelu engün, piay may ta fotüm. Kutrankawün mew llemay, awükawün mew llemay dungukey lawenngelu. Longkolüwküley, piwkelüwküley, feymew nga tripakey nga dungu mew, kisu kimün tripakey nga fotüm. Tüfachi machi nga kutrankawi ulüw ka, fotüm. . . .*
MACHI: Eeww . . . ! But yes, those who are related, those who have come from the other side, they show respect for the holder of the power, now [my] son [*kuel*]. But yes, [my] son, they know it, [my] son, my brothers and sisters. In any case they know it. Once they have thanked the holder of the power, this son [the son of *Ngenechen*] will say it. The holder of the power expresses her wisdom after a process of suffering and much painful effort, surely. She trusts her mind, her heart. This is how those who lead us who create knowledge are formed, this unique wisdom, son [*kuel*]. This *machi*

has undergone a period of sacrifice, then, [my] son.... [Translator: I cannot understand the last sentence]

RITUAL AUDIENCE: ¡*Iiiiihhuuuu* !
RITUAL AUDIENCE: Iiiiihhuuuu!

MACHI: *Kkuñifallngey ta trengtreng kuel pipingey ta kiñeke che purun mew ta ka. Inatudungumekeyngün. Welu taiñ lawenngelu pekan dungu mew ta dukukelay. Kisu ta longkolüwküley, piwkelüwküley dungu mew.*
MACHI: Some people in the dance are saying that *Trengtreng kuel* [the most sacred mound] is unprotected. They are talking about this matter. But I should tell them that our *lawenngelu* [holder of the power, the supreme deity, *Ngenechen*]

DUNGUMACHIFE: *Fey ta Nag Mapu feychi....*
DUNGUMACHIFE: In *Nag Mapu* [the world below *Wenumapu*] those....

MACHI: *Pekan dungu mew, pekan dungu mew ta lukukonkelay taiñ lawenngelu. Feymew taaa, longkolüwküleiñ, piwlelüwküleiñ ta ... lukulüwküleiñ trengtreng kuel mew kaaa, ka fotüm, peñi.*
MACHI: Our *lawenngelu* does not come in to kneel in an unimportant act. That is why, well then, we are here kneeling on the *Trengtreng kuel* with our minds and with our feelings, my son [*kuel*], my brother [*kuel*].

DUNGUMACHIFE: ¡*Feyllemay* ... !
DUNGUMACHIFE: That's right ... !

XXX. MACHI: *Welu may taaa ... llowünngekelay trengtreng kuel pingeymün ta. Yamünngekeyngün, kütraldungungey pipingey ta nierkeyngün. Welu ta felen ta dungu may welu Nag Mapu mew tañi felen ka. Fey ta iñche nien kimün pileyngün wente awelu ta. Welu ta ka awülchekelay tañi kimün engün ka.*
MACHI: All the same ... it is said that you all [the ritual congregation] do not receive the message from this *Trengtreng kuel*. You all are respected [by *Ngenechen*], but at the same time, it seems that you all say that this is a burning issue. But things are estab-

lished thusly here in *Nag Mapu* [on the surface of the earth]. Some think they hold power over the [ancestors], but, surely, their [the ancestors'] wisdom does not reach the people.

RITUAL AUDIENCE: ¡*Iihuuww*!....
RITUAL AUDIENCE: Iihuuww!....

MACHI: *Fey may fotüm, amuaiñ peñi ka, fentepuiñ may fotüm ...*
MACHI: That is [thus], my son [*kuel*]. Now, brothers and sisters, we are leaving. We have come together so far, my son.

DUNGUMACHIFE: *Yallemay, fentepuy peñi. Fentepuy may pu longko. Chageltu may piafimi pu longko ka, pu peñi ka. Trawülepaiñ tüfamew....*
DUNGUMACHIFE: That's right, then. This is ended, brothers and sisters. Chiefs [*longko*] this thing [the ceremony] is ended. Thanks as well to the chiefs and the brothers and sisters. We have gathered here....

MACHI: *Dew kümelkaymün, dew lifretripaymün, kümekünuael müten tamün.... Ayekantuleael, küme nentuael, fey ula ta putuaymün ka, pipingeiñ ta küme femkentun. Peñilüwaymün, lamngenüwaymün, eluwaymün. Chumwechi nga kuñifallngeaymün rume dungu mew, welu ta Chaw Ngünechen adkintunieafeymün mew engün ka, kümelkanieiñ ka.*
MACHI: You all [the ritual congregation] have done it well now. You all have come out unharmred. Now you all have to keep on playing the musical instruments, so that all may come out well, and afterward you can make an offering [of *chicha* to the *kuel*]. This is what we say with a good will. You all have to behave as brothers and sisters toward each other, and share with each other. Although you may feel defenseless in the face of an event, *Chaw Ngünechen* [the Great Father] will continually watch over you. And we are doing it well here.

RITUAL AUDIENCE: ¡*Marichiwew*!
RITUAL AUDIENCE: Victory ten times over!

461

MACHI: ¡Yaah . . . ! Kuñifallngelu am ta ü
lu Nag Mapu. Kuñifallngelu am ta iñ
newenngelu dungu mew, pin may ta niepaiñ
femngen kay, fey may ta niepaiñ, fotüm
engün.

MACHI: Yaaah . . . ! As the ü lu Nag Mapu
[healing in Nag Mapu, the World Below
Wenumapu] is alone and our holder of the
power is alone, then we tell it, all of you
kuel I can see [all the kuel within view of
the ritual audience].

DUNGUMACHIFE: ¡Feyllemay!
DUNGUMACHIFE: That's right!

XXXI. MACHI: Feyreke taa . . . kiñekeche ta
duamkününiengelay ta newenngelu. Feylle taa
. . . poyengelay dungu mew. Adkintungelay
dungu mew, feyentungelay dungu mew ka. Welu
taaa . . . küpaley ta perimo. Wenu taa . . . uneley
ta kastiku. Wenu taa . . . trürküley ta perimo, trürküley ta kastiko. Fantepalle, fey
ula ta dunguay ta rümü mapu. Feymew
müley, kutrankaeiñmew nga chaw ngünechen
pin nga nielüwaymün. Fantepale, fey ula ta
küpalrutupiwkeleyengün, fey ula ta kimüway
kisu engün. Feyentukelay perimontun mew
engün, feyentukelay ñi chumwechi entuael
dungu, feyentukelay ñi llellipuael, trürüwkelay
dungu mew. Ngelay trürüwün, ngelay kiñe wün,
ngelay lukutun, ngelay pürakintun newenngelu
mew. Kisu may ñi feleael, feleiñ, pikeyngün ka.
Kisu may iñ ngümayewküleael ngümayewküleiñ
pikeyngün ka. Welu ta . . . welu ta . . . falele,
küpaley ta trürümnieel, perimontun ta Nag
Mapu ka, pipingepuay kay perimo. Filu ta konpuay, mülewe mew ta konpuay, kom ta konpuay ka perimo. Llellipuntu mew, ngenmapu ñi
nagümün mew konpuay ta perimo. Welu ta chaw
ngünechen kintuay ula ta püran mapu, fantepale ta kintun. Ka femngelu mew kake mapu
ka trürküley, tamün wingkul mapu ka rume ta
awükawkey ta ngünen mapu, poyen mapu mew.
Fantepu mew may ta, fantepa newen tañi nien
ta ngenmapu ka. Welu ta trürnielu ka, fantepa
newenkontupayay.

MACHI: Thus, I understand . . . some people
do not pay a lot of attention to the person who holds the power. And thus she

is not taken into consideration when an
event occurs. But yes, . . . now the perimontun [vision] comes. From above one can see
how the punishment comes in first place.
Up there the vision and the punishment
are together. When this measure comes
about, then there the the world below [Nag
Mapu, the surface of the earth] will speak.
And there is the reason for which Chaw
Ngünechen [the Great Father]. And you all
[ritual congregation] will say this. Until
then, when you all will have reflected, then,
thus you all will know each other better. For those [in the ritual congregation]
who do not believe in visions, who do
not follow the steps they should to solve
a problem, who do not believe in prayer,
and who do not agree, there is no agreement among all [of them], there is no union
around a single problem, there is no lukutun
[ceremony of prayer], no looking upward,
toward the one who has the power [Chaw
Ngünechen]. They say they would rather
remain as they are. They think that they
can continue weeping alone. But yes, but
yes, if they remain thus, they shall see the
vision come nearer and this [the vision]
thus will be seen in Nag Mapu and thus
will remain a vision. A serpent shall come
in which shall enter the dwellings. The
whole vision shall enter there. It shall also
also enter the field of prayer and around
the Ngenmapu [the steward of the land].
But Chaw Ngünechen shall seek the earth
that rises up when his gaze is turned here.
And thus, also, other spaces are grouped
together. And in this mountain [kuel] of
yours [Chaw Ngünechen], the Ngünenmapu
[the Great Father who controls the space]
makes sacrifices on this beloved earth. Until
this time, in reality, this is the power
which the Ngenmapu has. Then, he has
all these spaces together until now, it
will be he [Chaw Ngünechen] who gives
power.

RITUAL AUDIENCE: ¡Wihuuuuu!
RITUAL AUDIENCE: Wihuuuuu!

XXXII. MACHI: *Feymew kaaaa . . . lukutuaiñ, llellipuaiñ ka ngünechen mew pipingelu am ka pu Nag Mapu ka. Feyentukenulu kay perimontun mew, mupitukenulu kay perimontun mew. Lukuaiñ, llellipuaiñ, peñilüwaiñ pikenulu am ü lu Nag Mapu. Kisu nga ñi mongelpiwkengen, kisu nga ngünewkülen dungu mew, kisu nga ngümayewkülen pikey ta ngünayewkülelu ka. Welu ta . . . kimlay tañi . . . kimlay tañi rangiwenu chaw ngünechen, kom ta wüsakünukey. Rangiñwenu chaw ngünechen ta femi, feymew ta kom ta felekeiñ kom che feyta rume kom mülekey, kiñeley ta rume mülekey kiñe rüna mülewe. Chaw ngünechen ta ul-lay chemrume ta ngekelay. . . .*

MACHI: This is why . . . that we may kneel, and we are going to pray to *Ngünechen*. This is what the people of *Nag Mapu* [the World Below *Wenumapu*] are saying. There are people who do not believe in the *perimontun* [visions], and the people who do not tell the truth about a *perimontun*. This happens because the *ülumapu* [healer] [*machi*] does not invite [people] to pray, beseech, and treat each other as brothers. "You [*Ngünechen*], alone, have left only me to live, thus I take care of my own proper task. Thus, all alone, I feel affliction around me," says the proud person. But . . . they [the misguided people] do not know . . . they do not know that *Rangiñwenu Chaw Ngünechen* [Father Guide of this world of the space between *Nag Mapu* and *Wenumapu*] orders everything thus. *Rangiñwenu Chaw Ngünechen* behaved thus, this is why we are all in this way, all the people are placed thus in their dwellings of *rüna* [the roots of herbs]. If *Chaw Ngünechen* does not give it, nothing exists.

RITUAL AUDIENCE: ¡*Wiihuuwwww*!
RITUAL AUDIENCE: Wiihuuwwww!

MACHI: *Fotüm, fotüm, wentekawellngetuaiñ. Fentepuleaiñ, peñi engün. Dew rumepaiñ. . . .*
MACHI: My sons, my sons, now we are going to go back. Our time together ends here. Now we have won. . . .

RITUAL AUDIENCE: Ya, ya, yaaaaaa. . . .
RITUAL AUDIENCE: Ya, ya, yaaaaaa. . . .

MACHI: *Dew may ta kutrankapaiñ taiñ lawenngelu, nü Nag Mapu mew. Welu may ta kümey may ta mün trafüwkülen. Wesake konangeymün, peñilüwkeymün dungu mew ka. Welu may, pekan dungu mew ta witranpa lukukelaymün tüfachi ngillatuwe llellipuwe antiku mew ka, peñi engün. . . .*
MACHI: Now we have sacrificed her to our holder of the power in this *NüNag Mapu* [in this land below which someone holds]. But the fact that you all are gathered here is somewhat beneficial. You all are the poor inhabitants who gather as brothers and sisters. But you all have not come here by a simple accident to stand and kneel in this ceremonial space of prayer of the ancestors, [my] brothers and sisters. . . .

DUNGUMACHIFE: *Feley may pu longko. . . .*
DUNGUMACHIFE: That is the way it is, chiefs [*longko*].

XXXIII. MACHI: *Welu may, nopewmangewen müten, tuntepuafuymün chey tamün felen. Yepuafun chey ta llellipun, welu nag ta felen ta epu neyen chey, pin may ta niepaiñ. Yalle may fotüm, femaymi tami kümewenu ka peñi. Pelaymi tami miawken wenu. Nütramkaniefiñ taaa. . . . wellin mew ta kümewenu ka fotüm, peñi kom. Eymi am fotüm, fey may niepaiñ, peñi. Niepan ta inalu kümewenu. Iney am ta inayeñmaaetew tami kümewenu ta eymi. Iñchin am ta mangelüwaiñ, fotüm. Iñchiñ ta mülelu Nag Mapu mew, ngünekulliñken. feymew may ta feleafuy chi pu kawell ka, ti pu kawellu nga kom, pipingeiñ luku mew. . . .*
MACHI: But nevertheless, only my dreams are here. It isn't known how long you [*kuel*] can sustain this situation [the excavation and the present ceremony]. Perhaps the ritual congregation can continue successfully with the prayer below, perhaps there are two *neyen* [winds] here. This is what we are saying here. Now, my son [*kuel*], pay attention to *kümewenu* [the good world above], now, brother [*kuel*]. You cannot realize the true feeling of walking above. I am

speaking, surely, in the space of the *kümewenu*, now my son [*kuel*], brothers all [all the other *kuel* in sight]. This is what I say to you, my son [*kuel*]. This is what we are doing here, brothers and sisters. Here I have a follower [the *kuel*] of the affairs of *kümewenu*. Who else [the *machi*] could follow you [*kuel*] to *kümewenu*? We invite you, my son [*kuel*]. We [the ritual congregation], who are in *Nag Mapu* [the land below], have the knowledge to guide the animals. And it is for this reason that the horses can maintain a certain form, and thus all the horses [?]. This is what we are saying here as we kneel.

RITUAL AUDIENCE: *¡Iiiiihuuw . . . !*
RITUAL AUDIENCE: Iiiiihuuw . . . !

MACHI: *Yalle may . . . fey may amuaiñ, peñi engün.*
MACHI: Now then . . . now it is time to go, my brothers and sisters.

DUNGUMACHIFE: *Yalle may, chageltu may pu longko. . . .*
DUNGUMACHIFE: Thus it is, now. Thank you chiefs [*longko*]. . . .

MACHI: *Amuaiñ peñi engün, amuaiñ peñi engün. . . .*

MACHI: Now we are going, brothers and sisters. Now we are going, brothers and sisters.

RITUAL AUDIENCE: *Ya, ya, ya, ya . . . !*
RITUAL AUDIENCE: Now, now, now, now . . . !
[Music and ritual encouragement]

MACHI: *Yalle may, femkonpapen üluwenu mew. . . .*
MACHI: Now then, this is how I have come from entering the *üluwenu* [the space for curing above].

RITUAL AUDIENCE: *Uah . . uah . . uah. . . .*
RITUAL AUDIENCE: Utterances.

[Ritual encouragement]

MACHI: *Eymi witran kaaaa, munulongkolean pilayaymi. . . .*
MACHI: Well, you, as a visitor [Tom Dillehay], do not ask him to put a handkerchief [an emblem of identity] on his head. . . . [Translator does not understand the rest of the sentence]

RITUAL AUDIENCE: *Marichiwew!*
RITUAL AUDIENCE: Victory ten times over!

Music . . . and the ceremony ends.

APPENDIX TWO

RADIOCARBON DATES*#

Site No./Lab No.	Provenience	Conventional 14C-Age ± STD [B.P.]	CalAge p(95%) [calB.C./A.D.]	CalAge p(95%) [calB.P.(0 = A.D.1950]	$\delta^{13}C\%_0$
Domestic 9 Beta 169771	Hearth in upper living surface	560 ± 50	1250–1450 calA.D.	700–500 calB.P.	−23.2
Domestic 11 Beta 168999	Hearth in deeper living surface	1100 ± 80	720–1080 calA.D.	1230–870 calB.P.	−26.1
Maicoyakuel Beta 167558	Hearth in upper floor of mound	160 ± 40	1590–1990 calA.D.	360–40 calB.P.	−25.7
Maicoyakuel Beta 167559	Hearth in upper floor of mound	250 ± 60	1400–1920 calA.D.	550–30 calB.P.	−25.2
Maicoyakuel Beta 167557	Hearth on lower floor of mound	2520 ± 40	840–480 calB.C.	2790–2430 calB.P.	−24.7
Domestic 23 Beta 68999	Charcoal from burned floor in middle level of site	1100 ± 80	720–1080 calA.D.	1230–870 calB.P.	−27.0
Rapahuekuel Beta 167559	Hearth in middle floor of mound	550 ± 40	1260–1460 calA.D.	690–490 calB.P.	−25.2
Tren Trenkuel AA64643	Burned area on upper floor of mound	125 ± 40	1590–1990 calA.D.	360–40 calB.P.	−21.3
Tren Trenkuel AA64642	Burned area on middle floor of mound	1780 ± 35	90–370 calA.D.	1860–1580 calB.P.	−27.3
Tren Trenkuel AA64653	Charcoal from middle floor of mound	1730 ± 40	200–400 calA.D.	1750–1550 calB.P.	−26.1

(continued)

(continued)

Site No./Lab No.	Provenience	Conventional 14C-Age ± STD [B.P.]	CalAge p(95%) [calB.C./A.D.]	CalAge p(95%) [calB.P.(0 = A.D.1950]	$\delta^{13}C‰$
Tren Trenkuel AA64977	Charcoal from lower use floor of mound	1850 ± 35	50–250 calA.D.	1900–1700 calB.P.	−27.5
Tren Trenkuel AA64641	Burned area on lower floor of mound	1930 ± 40	40 calB.C.–160 calA.D.	1990–1790 calB.P.	−26.0
Tren Trenkuel AA64644	Burned domestic sediment under mound	7625 ± 55	6590–6390 calB.C.	8540–8340 calB.P.	−25.9
Kuel 36 Beta 191662	Living surface under mound	6140 ± 40	5270–4950 calB.C.	7220–6900 calB.P.	−24.2
Domestic 39 Beta 191668	Hearth in lower living surface	600 ± 20	1260–1420 calA.D.	690–530 calB.P.	−24.6
Domestic 165 AA203868	Burned corn from upper house floor	430 ± 40	1380–1540 calA.D.	570–410 calB.P.	−11.0
Domestic 165 AA64654	Charcoal from upper floor	660 ± 40	1220–1420 calA.D.	730–0530 calB.P.	−25.7
Domestic 165 AA13772	Hearth in middle living surface	1315 ± 50	600–800 calA.D.	1350–1150 calB.P.	−25.0
Domestic 165 AA64657	Charcoal from middle floor	1615 ± 40	330–570 calA.D.	1620–1380 calB.P.	−26.2
Domestic 165 AA64651	Charcoal from hearth in middle level floor	1680 ± 40	210–450 calA.D.	1740–1500 calB.P.	−25.3
Domestic 165 AA64645	Charcoal from middle level floor	1735 ± 40	190–390 calA.D.	1760–1560 calB.P.	−26.1
Domestic 165 AA64655	Charcoal from hearth in lower living surface	1740 ± 35	190–390 calA.D.	1760–1560 calB.P.	−25.0
Domestic 165 AA64980	Charcoal from hearth in middle level	1715 ± 60	170–450 calA.D.	1780–1500 calB.P.	−25.9
Domestic 165 AA64979	Burned area on middle use surface	1780 ± 40	90–370 calA.D.	1860–1580 calB.P.	−26.4
Domestic 165 AA64647	Charcoal from hearth in lower living surface	1800 ± 40	70–350 calA.D.	1880–1600 calB.P.	−25.3
Domestic 165 AA-13780	Hearth in lower living surface	1810 ± 90	20 calB.C.–420 calA.D.	1970–1530 calB.P.	−25.0

Site No./Lab No.	Provenience	Conventional 14C-Age ± STD [B.P.]	CalAge p(95%) [calB.C./A.D.]	CalAge p(95%) [calB.P.(0 = A.D.1950]	$\delta^{13}C$‰
Domestic 165 AA64652	Charcoal from burned feature in lower use floor	1845 ± 40	50–250 calA.D.	1900–1700 calB.P.	−24.1
Domestic 165 AA64646	Charcoal from hearth in lower living surface	2010 ± 40	120 calB.C.–80 calA.D.	2070–1870 calB.P.	−26.0
Domestic 165 AA64658	Charcoal from middle use floor	2530 ± 40	850–490 calB.C.	2800–2440 calB.P.	−27.0
Kuifilkuel AA64978	Charcoal from middle use floor	2080 ± 55	250 calB.C.–30 calA.D.	2200–1920 calA.D.	−27.5
Kuifilkuel AA64656	Charcoal from middle use floor	2175 ± 40	420–100 calB.C.	2370–2050 calB.P.	−24.7
Kuifilkuel AA64649	Charcoal from hearth in lower use floor	2200 ± 40	420–140 calB.C.	2370–2090 calB.P.	−26.2
Kuifilkuel AA64648	Charcoal from lower use surface	2735 ± 55	1020–780 calB.C.	2970–2730 calB.P.	−26.6
Kuifilkuel AA64650	Charcoal from lower use surface	2720 ± 40	950–790 calB.C.	2900–2740 calB.P.	−25.9
Kuel 19 Beta 69000	Charcoal from middle floor	250 ± 60	1400–1920 calA.D.	550–30 calB.P.	−27.2
Deume Raised Fields	Organic use floor	670 ± 40	1210–1320 calA.D.	820–930 calB.P.	−25.8

* Radiocarbon dates from the University of Arizona calculated by Christopher Eastoe, Ph.D. at the University of Arizona and additional calibration with *CalPal: The Köln Radiocarbon Calibration & Paleoclimate Research Package*.
# All dates are on wood charcoal.

THERMOLUMINESCENCE DATES

Site No./ Lab No.	Provenience	Conventional Age	Calendar Age	P(Gy)	D(Gy/yr)
Domestic 13 UCTL 1557	Hearth in upper living floor	300 ± 60 B.P.	A.D. 1700	1.55 ± 0.16	$5.15 * 10^{-3}$
Domestic 13 UCTL 1556	Hearth in lower living floor	1540 ± 160 B.P.	A.D. 460	6.38 ± 0.65	$4.14 * 10^{-3}$
Maicoyakuel UCTL 1555	Hearth in upper floor	425 ± 40 B.P.	A.D. 1575	2.03 ± 0.21	$4.76 * 10^{-3}$
Maicoyakuel UCTL 1554	Hearth in lower floor	2535 ± 230 B.P.	A.D. 535	12.50 ± 1.25	$4.93 * 10^{-3}$
Maicoyakuel UCTL 1552	Hearth in middle floor	1670 ± 170 B.P.	A.D. 330	5.80 ± 0.58	$3.47 * 10^{-3}$
Maicoyakuel UCTL 1553	Hearth in lower floor	2065 ± 200 B.P.	A.D. 65	7.50 ± 0.73	$3.47 * 10^{-3}$
Domestic 41 UCTL 1558	Hearth in upper living floor	405 ± 35 B.P.	A.D. 1595	1.76 ± 0.12	$4.33 * 10^{-3}$
Domestic 41 UCTL 1559	Hearth in middle living floor	665 ± 40 B.P.	A.D. 1335	2.23 ± 0.13	$3.36 * 10^{-3}$

REFERENCES CITED

Abercrombie, N. and B. Longhurst 1998 *Audiences*. Sage, London.

Acosta, J. [1590] 1894 *Historia natural y moral de las Indias*. R. Anglés, Impresiones, Madrid.

Acuña, M. P., L. Eaton, N. R. Ramírez, L. Cifuentes, and E. Llop 2003 Genetic Variants of Serum *Butyrylcholinesterase* in Chilean Mapuche Indians. *American Journal of Physical Anthropology* 121(1):81–85.

Adam, B. 1991 *Time and Social Theory*. Polity Press, London.

Adán L. and M. Alvarado 1999 Análisis de colecciones alfareras pertenecientes al complejo Pitrén: Una aproximación desde la arqueología y la estética. In *Actas de las II Jornadas de Arqueología de la Patagonia*. Bariloche.

Adán, L. and R. Mera 1997 Acerca de la distribución espacial y temporal del complejo Pitrén. Una reevaluación a partir del estudio sistemático de colecciones. *Boletín Sociedad Chilena de Arqueología*. Santiago.

Agnew, J. 1999 New Geopolitics of Power. In *Human Geography Today*, edited by D. Massey, J. Allen, and P. Sarre, pp. 173–193. Polity Press, London.

Alcock, S. E., T. N. D'Altroy, K. D. Morrison, and S. M. Sinopoli (editors) 2001 *Empires: Perspectives from Archaeology and History*. Cambridge University Press, Cambridge.

Alconini, S. 2004 The Southeastern Inka Frontier against the Chiriguanos: Structure and Dynamics of the Inka Imperial Borderlands. *Latin American Antiquity* 15:389–418.

Aldunate, C. 1989 Estadio alfarero en el sur de Chile. *Culturas de Chile Prehistórica*. Editorial Andrés Bello, Santiago, Chile.

Aldunate, C. 1996 Mapuche: Gente de la tierra. In *Etnografía: Sociedades Indígenas Contemporáneas y su Ideología*. Editorial Andrés Bello, Santiago, Chile, pp. 111–134.

Allen, J. 1999 Spatial Assemblages of Power: From Domination to Empowerment. In *Human Geography Today*, edited by D. Massey, J. Allen, and P. Sarre, pp. 194–217. Polity Press, London.

Alonqueo, M. 1979 *Instituciones Religiosas del Pueble Mapuche*. Ediciones Nueva Universidad, Santiago, Chile.

Alvaro, J. 1971 *Guerra y Sociedad en Chile*. Editorial Universitaria, Santiago.

Amunategui Solar, D. 1909 *Las encomiendas de indígenas en Chile*. 2 Tomos. Santiago.

Anderson, B. 1983 *Imagined Community: Reflections on the Origin and Spread of Nationalism*. Verso, London.

Anderson, D. A. 1994 *Savannah River Chiefdoms: Political Change in the Late Prehistoric Southeast*. University of Alabama.

Anderson, D. A. 1996 Fluctuations between Simple and Complex Chiefdoms in the Late Prehistoric Southeast. In *Political Structure and Change in the Prehistoric Southeastern United States*, edited by J. F. Scarry, pp. 231–252. University Press of Florida, Gainesville.

Anonymous 1993 Presas del Bio-Bio: La base para desaparicion de los Mapuches y para la destrucción del ecosistema. *América Latina* 11:23–29.

Araya Espinosa, A. 1999 *Ociosos, vagaboundos y malentretenidos en Chile colonial*. LOM Ediciones, Santiago.

Archer, M. 1988 *Culture and Agency: The Place of Culture in Social Theory*. Cambridge University Press, Cambridge.

Archivo Nacional de Chile, M.V.M., Vol. 279, Santiago.

Arnold, J. E. 1996 *Emergent Complexity: The Evolution of Intermediate Societies*, edited by J. E. Arnold. International Monographs in Prehistory, Ann Arbor, Michigan.

Ashmore, W. and A. B. Knapp (editors) 1999 *Archaeologies of Landscape: Contemporary Perspectives*. Blackwell, Oxford.

Ashmore, W. and J. Sabloff 2002 Spatial Orders in Maya Civic Plans. *Latin American Antiquity* 13:201–216.

Atkinson, J. 1992 Shamanism Today. *Annual Review of Anthropology* 21:307–30.

Augusta, Felix José de 1934 *Lecturas Araucanas*. Editorial San Francisco, Padre de las Casas, Chile.

Augustinians [1560] 1865 Relación de la religión y ritos del Perú, hecha por los primeros religiosos agustinos que allí pasaron para la conversión de los naturales. *Colección de Documentos Inéditos Relativos al Descubrimiento, Conquista y Colonización de las Posesiones Españolas en América y Oceanía* 3:5–58.

Bacigalupo, A. M. 1995 Renouncing Shamanistic Practice: The Conflict on Individual and Culture Experienced by a Mapuche Machi. *Anthropology of Consciousness* 6(3): 1–16.

Bacigalupo, A. M. 1996 Identidad, Espacio y Dualidad en los Perimontum (Visiones) de Machi Mapuche. *Scripta Ethnológica* 18:37–63.

Bacigalupo, A. M. 1998 The Exorcising Sounds of Warfare: Shamanic Healing and the Struggle to Remain Mapuche. *Anthropology of Consciousness* 9(5):1–16.

Bacigalupo, A. M. 1999 Studying Mapuche Shaman/Healers in Chile from an Experimental Perspective: Ethical and Methodological Problems. *Anthropology of Consciousness* 10(2–3):35–40.

Bacigalupo, A. M. 2001 *La voz del kultrun en la modernidad: Tradición y cambio en la terapéutica de siete Machi Mapuche.* Editorial Universidad Católica de Chile, Santiago, Chile.

Bacigalupo, A. M. 2002 Mapuche Shamanic Bodies and the Chilean State: Polemic Gendered Representations and Indigenous Responses. In *Violence and the Body: Race, Gender and the State,* edited by A. Aldama, pp. 322–46. Indiana University Press, Bloomington.

Bacigalupo, A. M. 2004a Ritual, Gendered Relationships, Kinship, Marriage, Mastery, and Machi Modes of Personhood. *Journal of Anthropological Research* 60:203–229.

Bacigalupo, A. M. 2004b The Struggle for Mapuche Shamans's Masculinity: Colonial Politics of Gender, Sexuality, and Power in Southern Chile. *Ethnohistory* 51(3):489–533.

Bacigalupo, A. M. 2004c The Mapuche Man Who Became a Woman Shaman: Selfhood, Gender Transgression, and Competing Cultural Norms. *American Ethnologist* 31(3):440–457.

Bacigalupo, A. M. 2004d Local Shamanic Knowledge: A Response to Guillaume Boccara. *L'Homme* 169:219–223.

Bacigalupo, A. M. 2005 Gendered Rituals for Cosmic Order: Mapuche Shamanic Struggles for Wholeness. *Journal of Ritual Studies* 19(2):53–69.

Balandier, G. 1970 *Political Anthropology.* Pantheon Books, New York.

Balzer, M. M. 1990 *Shamanism: Soviet Studies of Traditional Religion in Siberia and Central Asia.* Sharpe, New York.

Barnes, B. 1988 *The Nature of Power.* Polity Press, London.

Barrett, J. 1990 Monumentality of Death: The Character of Early Bronze Age Mortuary Mounds in Southern Britain. *World Archaeology* 22:179–189.

Barrett, J. 2000 A Thesis on Agency. In *Agency in Archaeology,* edited by M. A. Dobres and J. Robb, pp. 61–68. Routledge Press, London and New York.

Barrett, J. 2001 Agency, the Duality of Structure, and the Problem of the Archaeological Record. In *Archaeological Theory Today,* edited by I. Hodder, pp. 141–164. Polity Press, Cambridge.

Barros Arana, D. 1884 *Historia General de Chile.* Santiago.

Barros Arana, D. 1909 *Estudios Históricos.* Obras Completas T. VII. Santiago.

Bawden, G. 1996 *The Moche.* Blackwell, Oxford.

Bengoa, J. 1985 *Historia del Pueblo Mapuche.* Editorial Andrés Bello. Santiago.

Bengoa, J. 1998 *Boletín Pueblos Indígenas.* Santiago.

Bengoa, J. 2003 *Historia de Los Antiquos Mapuches del Sur.* Imprenta Catalonia. Santiago.

Benko, G. and U. Strohmayer (editors) 1997 *Space and; Social Theory: Interpreting Modernity and Postmodernity.* Blackwell Publishers.

Berdichewsky, B. and M. Calvo 1973 *Excavaciones en Cementerios Indígenas de la Región de Calafquen.* Actas del VI Congreso de Arqueología Chilena, Santiago.

Bernard, V. C. 1994 *Descubrimiento, conquista y colonización de América a quinientos años.* Fondo de Cultura Económica, Mexico.

Bibar, G. De [1555] 1966 *Crónica y Relación Copiosa y Verdadera de los Reinos de Chile [1555].* Fondo Histórico y Bibliográfico José Toribio Medina, Santiago.

Blagg, T. 1986 Roman Religious Sites in the British Landscape. *Landscape History* 8:15–26.

Blake, M. 1991 Emerging Early Formative Chiefdom at Paso de la Amada, Chiapas, Mexico. *Formation of Complex Society in Southeastern Mesoamerica,* edited by W. R. Fowler, pp. 27–46. CRC Press, Boca Raton, Florida.

Blanton, R. E. 2001 Beyond Centralization: Steps Toward a Theory of Egalitarian Behavior in Archaic States. In *Archaic States,* edited by G. Feinman and J. Marcus, pp. 135–172. School of American Research Press, Santa Fe, New Mexico.

Blanton, R. E., G. M. Feinman, S. A. Kowalewski, and P. N. Peregrine 1996 A Dual-Process Theory for the Evolution of Mesoamerican Civilization. *Current Anthropology* 37(1):1–14, 73–86.

Blitz, J. H. 1999 Mississippian Chiefdoms and the Fission Fusion-Process. *American Antiquity* 64.

Blumer, H. 1969 *Symbolic Interactionism: Perspective and Method.* Prentice-Hall, Englewood Cliffs, New Jersey.

Boccara, G. 1998 *Guerre et ethnogenese Mapuche dans le Chili colonial: L'invention du Soi.* L'Harmattan, Paris.

Boccara, G. 1999 Etnogénesis mapuche: resistencia y reestructuración entre los indígenas del centro-sur de Chile (siglos X–XVIII). *Hispanic American Historical Review* 79(3):425–461. L'Harmattan, Paris.

Boccara, G. 2000 Colonización, resistencia y etnogénesis en las fronteras Americanas. In *Colonización, Resistencia y Mestizaje en las Américas, Siglos XVIXX,* pp. 47–82. Ediciones Abya-Yala, Ecuador.

Bondi, L. 1993 Locating Identity Politics. In *Place and the Politics of Identity,* edited by M. Keith and J. Pile. Routledge Press, London and New York.

Bourdieu, P. 1977 *Outline of a Theory of Practice.* Cambridge University Press, Cambridge.

Bourdieu, P. 1994 Structure, Habitus, Power: Basis for a Theory of Symbolic Power. In *Culture/Power/History: A Reader in Contemporary Theory,* edited by N. B. Dirks,

G. Eley, and S. Ortner, pp. 155–199. Princeton University Press, Princeton, New Jersey.

Bradley, R. 1991 Ritual, Time and History. *World Archaeology* 23, pp. 209–219.

Bradley, R. 1998 *The Significance of Monuments: On the Shaping of Human Experiences in Neolithic and Bronze Age Europe*. Routledge Press, London and New York.

Bradley, R. 2000 *An Archaeology of Natural Places*. Routledge Press, London and New York.

Brody, H. 1987 *Stories of Sickness*. Yale University Press, New Haven, Connecticut.

Brumfiel, E. 1994 Factional Competition and Political Development in the New World: An Introduction. In *Factional Competition and Political Development in the New World*, edited by E. M. Brumfiel and J. W. Fox, pp. 3–13. Cambridge University Press, Cambridge.

Buikstra, J. and D. Charles 1999 Centering the Ancestors: Cemeteries, Mounds, and Sacred Landscapes of the Ancient North American Midcontinent. In *Archaeologies of Landscape: Contemporary Perspectivas*, edited by W. Ashmore and A. Knapp, pp. 201–228. Blackwell, Oxford.

Bullock, D. 1955 Urnas funerarias prehistóricas de la región de Angol. *Boletín de Museo Nacional de Historia Natural* 26:73–157.

Burger, R. 1992 *Chavin and the Origins of Andean Civilization*. Thames and Hudson, London.

Callon, M. 1986 *Mapping the Dynamics of Science and Technology: Sociology of Science in the Real World*. Macmillan, Basingstoke.

Canals, F. S. 1946 The Argentina Araucanians. In *Handbook of South American Indians*, edited by J. Stewart, Smithsonian Institution, Bureau of American Ethnology, Bulletin 143(2):761–766.

Caravallo y Goyeneche, V. [1796] 1876 Descripción histórica-geográfica del reino de Chile. *Colección de Historia de Chile, Vol. X*. Santiago.

Carneiro, R. 1970 A Theory of the Origin of the State. *Science* 169:733–739.

Carneiro, R. 1971 The Chiefdom: Precursors of the State. In *The Transition to Statehood in the New World*, edited by G. Jones and R. Kautz, pp. 39–70. Cambridge University Press, Cambridge.

Carnese, F. R. 1996 Demography and Blood Genetics of Argentinian Mapuche Indians. *International Journal of Anthropology* 11(2–4):33–42.

Carr, C. and D. T. Case, (editors) 2004 *Gathering Hopewell: Society, Ritual, and Ritual Interaction*. Springer, New York.

Carruthers, M. J. 1990 *The Book of Memory: A Study of Memory in Medieval Culture*. Cambridge University Press, New York.

Casamiquela, R. 1960 *El nguillatun o kamaritun araucano (Kamaruco)*. Misiones Culturales, Dirección General de Educación y Cultura, Viedma, Río Negro, Argentina, No. 4.

Casanova, H. 1989 *Las rebeliones araucanas del siglo XVIII*. Temuco, Ediciones Universidad de la Frontera.

Castro, V. and L. Adán 2001 Abriendo Diálogos. Una mirada entre la etnohistoria y la arqueología del área centro-sur de Chile: asentamientos en la zona Mapuche. *Werken* 2:5–36.

Catrileo, M. 1998 *Diccionario Lingüístico-Etnográfico de la Lengua Mapuche*. Editorial Andrés Bello, Santiago, Chile.

Cecil, L. and M. D. Glasscock 2005 Instrumental Neutron Activation Analysis of Ceramics and Clays from the Araucanian Polity in the Puren-Lumaco Region. Report in possession of the author.

Cieza de Leon, P. 1945 *La Crónica del Perú*. Buenos Aires.

Citarella, L. (editor) 1995 *Mediciones y Culturas en la Araucanía*. Editorial Sudamericana. Santiago, Chile.

Claessen, H. J. 2000 *War and State Formation – Is There a Connection ?* Paper Presented at the War and Society Seminars, Aarhus University, Denmark, October 5, 2000.

Clark, J. and M. Blake 1994 The Power of Prestige: Competitive Generosity and the Emergence of Rank Societies in Lowland Mesoamerica. In *Factional Competition and Political Development in the New World*, edited by E. Brumfiel and J. Fox, pp. 17–30. Cambridge University Press, Cambridge.

Cohen, A. 1981 *The Politics of Elite Culture: Explorations in the Dramaturgy of Power in a Modern African Society*. University of California Press, Berkeley.

Cohen, R. 1979 Political Symbolism. *Annual Reviews of Anthropology* 8:87–113.

Comaroff, J. L. 1998 Reflections of the Colonial State in South Africa and Elsewhere: Factions, Fragments, Facts and Fiction. *Social Identities* 4(3):321–61.

Coña, P. 1973 *Memorias de un Cacique Mapuche*. Imprenta Cervantes, Santiago, Chile.

Connerton, P. 1989 *How Societies Remember*. Cambridge University Press, Cambridge.

Connolly, W. E. 1991 *Identity/Difference*. University of Minnesota Press, Minneapolis.

Cooper, F. 2005 *Colonialism in Question: Theory, Knowledge, History*. University of California Press, Berkeley.

Cooper, J. 1946 The Araucanians. In *Handbook of South American Indians*, edited by J. H. Steward, Vol. 2:687–760. Smithsonian Institution, Washington, D.C.

Cordero, M. de Jesus 2001 *The Transformations of Araucania from Valdivia's Letters to Vivar's Chronicle*. Peter Lang Publishing Group, Inc., New York.

Córdoba y Figueroa, P. de [1861] 1942 *Historia de Chile*. Colección de Historiadores de Chile. T. II. Santiago.

Cornely, F. L. 1956 The El Molle Culture of Chile. *Archaeology* 9(3):200–205. Archaeological Institute of America, New Haven, Connecticut.

Croese, R. 1985 Mapuche Dialect Survey. In *South American Indian Languages: Retrospect and Prospect*, edited by H. Klein and L. Stark, pp. 784. University of Texas Press, Austin.

Crumley, C. 1995 Heterarchy and the Analysis of Complex Societies. In *Heterarchy and the Analysis of Complex*

Societies, edited by R. Ehrenreich, C. L. Crumley, and J. E. Levy, pp. 1–6. Archaeological Papers of the American Anthropological Association No. 6, Washington, D.C.

Czarniawska-Joerges, B. 1990 *Exploring Complex Organizations*. Macmillan, New York.

D'Altroy, T. 2003 *The Incas*. Blackwell Publishing, Oxford.

DeMarrais, E., L. J. Castillo and T. K. Earle 1996 Ideology, Materialism, and Power Strategies, *Current Anthropology* 37:15–32.

Dietler, M. 1996 Feasts and Commensal Politics in the Political Economy: Food, Power, and Status in Prehistoric Europe. In *Food and the Status Quest*, edited by P. Wiessner and W. Schiefenhövel, pp. 87–125. Berghahn Books, Oxford.

Dietler, M. and B. Hayden 2001 Digesting the Feast: Good to Eat, Good to Drink, Good to Think. In *Feasts: Archaeological and Ethnographic Perspectives on Food, Politics, and Power*, edited by M. Dietler and B. Hayden, pp. 1–20. Smithsonian Institution Press, Washington, D.C.

Dillehay, T. 1976 Observacisones y consideraciones sobre la adaptación humana en el centro-sur de Chile durante el período temprano histórico. In *Estudios Antropológicos Sobre los Mapuche del Sur de Chile*, edited by T. D. Dillehay, pp. 13–56. Universidad Católica de Chile, Temuco.

Dillehay, T. 1978 *Acercamiento metodológico: El comportamiento del jaquar y la organización socio-espacial humana*, pp. 38–48. Actas del V Congreso Nacional de Arqueología Argentina. San Juán, Argentina.

Dillehay, T. 1980 *Felinization of the Andes: Animal Iconography, Human Behavior and Societal Development*. Paper read at the Latin American Heritage Conference, Cornell University, Ithaca.

Dillehay, T. 1981 Una visión actual de estudios de Araucanía pre-hispánica. *Boletín del Museo Nacional de Historia Natural* 23:21–34. Santiago.

Dillehay, T. 1985a Cuel: observaciones y comentarios sobre los túmulos en la cultura Mapuche. *Revista Chungará* 16–17:181–93.

Dillehay, T. 1985b La Influencia Política de los (Las) Chamanes Mapuches. *Cultura, Hombre, Sociedad* 2(2): 141–157. Pontífica Universidad Católica de Chile, Temuco.

Dillehay, T. 1988 Rol de conocimiento ancestral y las ceremonias en la continuidad y persistencia de la cultura mapuche. In *Rituales y Fiestas de las Americas*. Ediciones Uniandes, Bogotá.

Dillehay, T. 1990a Mapuche Ceremonial Landscape, Social Recruitment and Resource Rights. *World Archaeology* 22(2):223–41. England.

Dillehay, T. 1990b El formativo del extremo sur de Chile. *Gaceta Arqueológica Andina* 17:101–114. Lima.

Dillehay, T. 1990c *Los Araucanos: El Pasado y Presente*. Editorial Andrés Bello, Santiago, Chile.

Dillehay, T. 1992a Keeping Outsiders Out: Public Ceremony, Resource Rights, and Hierarchy in Historic and Contemporary Mapuche Society. In *Wealth and Hierarchy in the Intermediate Area*, edited by F. W. Lange, pp. 379–422. Dumbarton Oaks, Washington, D.C.

Dillehay, T. 1992b Identificación de grupos sociales y límites entre los Mapuche de Chile: Implicaciones para la arqueología. In *Arqueología en América Latina Hoy*, edited by G. Politis, pp. 144–57. Colección Textos Universitarios, Bogotá.

Dillehay, T. 1992c Araucanía presente y pasado. Respuesta a los comentarios del Señor Parentini sobre mi libro. *Boletín de Historia y Geografía* 9:251–57. Santiago.

Dillehay, T. 1995 Mounds of Social Death: Araucanian Funerary Rites and Political Succession. In *Tombs for the Living: Andean Mortuary Practices*, edited by T. Dillehay. Dumbarton Oaks, Washington, D.C.

Dillehay, T. 1998 Felines, Patronyms, and History of the Araucanians in the Southern Andes. In *Icons of Power: Feline Symbolism in the Americas*, edited by N. Saunders, pp. 203–224. Routledge Press, London and New York.

Dillehay, T. 1999 El paisaje cultural y público: el monumentalismo holístico, circunscripto de las comunidades Araucanas. In *Arqueología de las Tierras Bajas*, edited by A. Durán and R. Bracco, pp. 451–68. Ministerio de Educación y Cultura, Comisión Nacional de Arqueología, Montevideo.

Dillehay, T. 2001 *Informe Preliminar de 1996–2004 del Proyecto Purén y Lumaco*. Submitted to the Consejo Nacional de Monumentos Nacionales, Santiago.

Dillehay, T. 2002 Una historia incompleta y una identidad cultural sesgada de los Mapuche. In *Colonización, Resistencia y Mestizaje en las Américas*, Siglos XVIXX, edited by G. Bocarra, pp. 163–184. Ediciones Abya-Yala, Ecuador.

Dillehay, T. 2003 *Informe Técnico sobre el Proyecto Purén y Lumaco: 2002*. Report submitted to the Consejo Nacional de Monumentos. Santiago.

Dillehay, T. 2004 *Informe Preliminar de 1996–2004 del Proyecto Purén y Lumaco*. Submitted to the Consejo Nacional de Monumentos Nacionales, Santiago.

Dillehay, T. 2005 *Informe Preliminar de 2005 del Proyecto Purén y Lumaco*. Submitted to the Consejo Nacional de Monumentos Nacionales, Santiago.

Dillehay, T. 2006 *Informe Preliminar de 2006 del Proyecto Purén y Lumaco*. Submitted to the Consejo Nacional de Monumentos Nacionales, Santiago.

Dillehay, T. n.d. Local Family Histories in Purén Valley, Chile. Manuscript in possession of the author.

Dillehay, T. D. and A. Gordon 1979 El simbolismo en el ornitomorfismo Mapuche: La mujer casada y el *ketru* metawe. In *Actas del VII Congreso de Arqueología de Chile*, pp. 303–316. Santiago.

Dillehay, T. D. and A. Gordon 1988 La actividad prehispánica de los Incas y su influencia en la Araucanía. In *La Frontera del Estado Inca*, edited by T. D. Dillehay and P. Netherly, pp. 215–234. BAR International Series 442, Oxford.

Dillehay, T. D. and P. Kaulicke 1985 Aproximación Metodológico: El Comportamiento del Jaquar y la Organización Socio-Espacial Humana. *Relaciones* 26:27–36. Buenos Aires.

Dillehay, T. D. and P. Netherly (editors) 1988 *La Frontera del Estado Inca*. BAR International Series 442, Oxford.

Dobres, M. A. and Robb, J. E. (editors) 2000 *Agency in Archaeology*. Routledge Press, London and New York.

Dobyns, H. F. 1983 *Their Number Become Thinned: Native American Population Dynamics in Eastern North America*. University of Tennessee Press, Knoxville.

Doyle, M. E. 1988 *The Ancestor Cult and Burial Ritual in Seventeenth and Eighteenth Century Central Peru*. Dissertation submitted for the degree Doctor of Philosophy in History at the University of California, Los Angeles.

Duviols, P. 1967 Un inedito de Cristobal de Albornoz: la instrucción para descubrir todas las guacas del Peru y sus camayos u haziendas. *Journal de la Societe des Americanistes* 65:7–39.

Earle, T. K. (editor) 1991 *Chiefdoms: Power, Economy, and Ideology*. Cambridge University Press, Cambridge.

Earle, T. K. 1997 *How Chiefs Come to Power: The Political Economy in Prehistory*. Stanford University Press, Stanford California.

Eliade, M. 1959 *The Sacred and the Profane: The Nature of Religion*. Translated by W. Trask. Harcourt Brace, San Diego, New York, and London.

Eliade, M. 1961 *The Sacred and the Profane*. Harper & Row, New York.

Eliade, M. 1972 *Shamanism: Archaic Techniques of Ecstasy*. Princeton University Press, Princeton, New Jersey.

Encina, F. A. 1950 *Historia de Chile*. Santiago.

Ensalaco, M. 2000 *Chile Under Pinochet: Recovering the Truth*. University of Pennsylvannia Press, Philadelphia.

Ercilla y Zuñiga, Alonso de [1569] 1982 *La Araucana*. Editorial Universitaria, Santiago.

Errazuriz, C. 1912 *Historia de Chile. Pedro de Valdivia*. Santiago, Chile.

Espejo, J. L. 1967 *Nobiliario de la Capitanía General de Chile*. Santiago, Chile.

Eulogio, R. R. 1911 Costumbres y creencias Araucanas: neigurehuen baile de machi. *Revista de Folklore Chileno* 3:113–16.

Eulogio, R. R. 1912 Costumbres y creencias Araucanas: machiluhun iniciación de machi. *Revista de Folklore Chileno* 4:155–81.

Faiola, A. 1999 Chilean Reawakening: Democracy Emboldens Natives to Fight for Land, Better Lives. *Washington Post*, June 6, pp. A19–21.

Faron, L. 1964 *Hawks of the Sun: Mapuche Morality and its Ritual Attributes*. University of Pittsburgh Press, Pittsburgh.

Febres, A. [1765] 1882 *Diccionario Araucano-Español*. Juan A. Alsina, Buenos Aires.

Feierman, S. and J. M. Janzen 1992 Preface and Introduction. In *The Social Basis of Health and Healing in Africa*, edited by S. Feierman and J. M. Janzen, pp. xv–xvii, 1–23. University of California Press, Berkeley.

Feinman, G. 2000 Corporate/Network: New Perspectives on Models of Political Action and the Puebloan Southwest. In *Social Theory in Archaeology*, edited by M.

Schiffer, pp. 31–51. University of Utah Press, Salt Lake City.

Feinman, G. and L. Nicholas (editors) 2004 *Archaeological Perspectives on Political Economies*. University Utah Press, Salt Lake City.

Fine, G. 1984 Negotiated Orders and Organizational Cultures. *Annual Review of Sociology* 10:239–62.

Finnegan, R. 1984 Note on Oral Tradition and Historical Evidence. In *Oral History: An Interdisciplinary Anthology*, edited by D. Dunaway and W. Baum, pp. 107–115. American Association for State and Local History, Nashville.

Flannery, K. 1999 Process and Agency in Early State Formation. *Cambridge Archaeological Journal* 9:3–21.

Foerster, R. 1993 *Introducción a la Religiosidad Mapuche*. Editorial Universitaria, Santiago.

Foerster, R. and H. Gundermann K. 1996 Religiosidad Mapuche contemporánea: elementos introductorios. In *Etnografía: Sociedades Indígenas Contemporáneas y su Ideología*, edited by J. Hildalgo, V. Schiappacasse, H. Niemeyer, C. Aldanate, and P. Mege, pp. 189–240. Editorial Andrés Bello, Santiago, pp. 189–240.

Foucault, M. 1984 Space, Knowledge, and Power. In *The Foucault Reader*, edited by R. Rabinow, pp. 239–256. Penguin Books, New York.

Fuerst, D. 2002 *Social and Environmental Circumscription Theory*. Manuscript in possession of the author.

Fuerst, P. 1974 The Roots and Continuities of Shamanism. *Arts Canada* 184(7):33–50.

Gallagher, W. 1993 *Power of Place: How Our Surroundings Shape Our Thoughts, Emotions and Actions*. Poseidon Press, New York.

Gay, C. 1852 *Historia Física y Política de Chile*. Documentos. Vols. I and II, Paris.

Geertz, Clifford 1983 *Local Knowledge: Further Essays in Interpretive Anthropology*. Basic Books, New York.

Giddens, A. 1976 *New Rules of Sociological Method*. Basic Books, New York.

Giddens, A. 1984 *The Constitution of Society: Outline of the Theory of Structuration*. Polity Press, Cambridge.

Goicoechea, A., et al. 2000 Demography, Genetic Diversity, and Population Relationships among Argentinean Mapuche Indians. *Genetic and Molecular Biology* 23(3). Sao Paulo.

Golden, C. 2005 Where Does Memory Reside and Why Isn't It History? *American Anthropologist* 107:270–274.

Goldfarb, J. C. 1998 *Civility & Subversion: The Intellectual in Democratic Society*. Cambridge University Press, London.

Góngora Marmolejo, A. [1575] 1960 *Historia de Chile desde su Descubrimiento hasta el Año 1575*. Biblioteca de Autores Españoles 131, Madrid.

González, A. R. 1998 *Cultura la Aguada: Arqueología y Disenos*. Film Ediciones Valero. Buenos Aires.

González de Nájera, A. [1614] 1971 *Desengaño y Reparo de la Guerra del Reino de Chile*, Vol. 16. Colección de Historiadores de Chile, Santiago.

Gopal, B. 1988 Holy Mother Ganges. *Geographical Magazine*, May:38–43.

Gordon, A. 1975 Excavación de una sepultura in LonCoche, provincia de Cautín, Novena Región, Chile. *Boletín del Museo Nacional de Historia Natural de Chile* 34:63–68.

Gordon, A. 1978 Urna y canoa funeraries. Una sepultura doble excavada ed Padre Las Casa, Provincia de Cautín, IX Región, Chile. *Revista de Antropología* 1:61–80.

Gordon, A. 1984 Huimpil: Un cementerio agroalfarero temprano en el centro-sur de Chile. *Cultura Hombre y Sociedad* 2: 86–112.

Gordon, A. 1992 *Informe Técnico sobre la Cerámica Indígena y Español de Santa Silvia, Pucón, Chile*. Report submitted to FONDICYT, Santiago.

Gosden, C. 2004 *Archaeology and Colonialism: Cultural Contact from 5000 BC to the Present*. Cambridge University Press, Cambridge.

Grebe, M. E., S. Pacheco, and J. Segura 1972 Cosmovisión Mapuche. *Cuadernos de la Realidad Nacional* 14:46–73. Universidad Católica de Chile, Santiago.

Grove, D. 1981 Olmec Monuments: Mutilation as a Clue to Meaning. *The Olmec and Their Neighbors. Essays in Honor of Matthew W. Stirling*, edited by E. P. Benson, pp. 49–68. Dumbarton Oaks, Washington, D.C.

Guarda, H. C. 1986 El rol del jefe en la sociedad Mapuche prehispánica. In *Araucanía, Temas de Historia Fronteriza*, edited by S. Villalobos R. and J. Pinto R. Universidad de la Frontera, Temuco, Chile.

Guchte, M. 2000 The Inca Cognition of Landscape: Archaeology, Ethnohistory, and the Aesthetic of Alterity. In *Archaeologies of Landscape: Contemporary Perspectivas*, edited by W. Ashmore and A. B. Knapp, 149–168. Blackwell, Oxford.

Guevara, T. 1908 *Psicología del Pueblo Araucano*. Imprenta Cervantes, Santiago, Chile.

Guevara, T. 1913 *Las Últimas Familias y Costumbres Araucanas*. Imprenta Cervantes, Santiago, Chile.

Guevara, T. 1925 *Historia de Chile: Chile Prehispánico*. Balcells & Co., Santiago, Chile.

Guevara, T. 1929 *Historia de Chile. Chile Prehispánico*. Vols. I and II, Imprenta Cervantes, Santiago, Chile.

Haas, E. J. C. 1985 HLA Antigens and Other Genetic Markers in the Mapuche Indians of Argentina. *Human Heredity* 35(5):306–313.

Haas, J., W. Creamer, and A. Ruiz 2005 Power and the Emergence of Complex Society in the Peruvian Preceramic. *Foundations of Power in the Ancient Andes*, edited by K. Vaughn, D. Ogburn, and C. Conlee, pp. 37–52. American Anthropological Association, Arlington, Virginia.

Hajduk, A. 1978 Excepcionales Ceramios de la Provincia del Neuquen. *Revista del Museo Provincial* 1:103–119.

Hajduk, A. 1986 *Arqueología del Montículo Angostura. Primer Fechado Radiocarbonico de la Provincia del Neuquen*. Vol. 1. Museo Histórico Provincial. Ediciones Culturales Neuquinas. Neuquen, Argentina.

Hally, D. 1996 Platform-Mound Construction and the Instability of Mississippian Chiefdoms. In *Political Structure and Change in the Prehistoric Southeastern United States*, pp. 92–127. University Press of Florida, Gainesville.

Hammond, N. (editor) 1991 *Cuello: An Early Maya Community in Belize*. Cambridge University Press, Cambridge.

Handlin, O. 1951 *The Uprooted*. Little Brown & Co., New York.

Harcha, L. 1977 *El Concepto de Historia Mapuche*. Tésis de Maestría. Universidad Pontificia Católica de Chile, Temuco.

Hayden, B. 1995 Pathways to Power: Principles for Creating Socioeconomic Inequality. In *Foundations of Social Inequality*, edited by D. Price and G. Feinman, pp. 15–86. Plenum Press, New York.

Helman, C. G. 1994 Doctor-Patient Interactions. In *Culture, Health and Illness*. 3rd ed., pp. 101–145. Butterworth Heinemann, Oxford.

Helms, M. W. 1979 *Ancient Panama: Chiefs in Search of Power*. University of Texas Press, Austin.

Hetherington, K. 1997 *The Badlands of Modernity: Heterotopia and Social Ordering*. Routledge Press, London and New York.

Hirsch, E. and M. O'Hanlon 1995 *The Anthropology of Landscape*. Clarendon Press, Oxford.

Hodder, I. 1999 *The Archaeological Process: An Introduction*. Blackwell Press, Oxford.

Housse, R. E. 1939 *Une Épopée Indienne: Les Araucand du Chile*. Zig-Zag Press, Paris.

Hyslop, J. 1984 *Inka Road System*. Academic Press, Orlando, Florida.

Inostroza, I. 1991 La población Araucana en la segunda mitad del Siglo XVII. *Revista Frontera* 9:31–41.

Iribarren, C. J. 1964 Decoración con pintura negative y la cultura de El Molle. In *Arqueología de Chile Central y Areas Vecinas*, Publicación de los Trabajos Presentados al Tercer Congreso Internacional del Arqueologiá Chilena, pp. 29–51, Imprenta Los Andes, Santiago.

Isbell, B. J. 1978 *To Defend Ourselves: Ecology and Ritual in an Andean Village*. University of Texas Press, Austin.

Janusek, J. W. 2004 *Identity and Power in the Ancient Andes: Tiwanaku Cities Through Time*. Routledge Press, London and New York.

Jara, A. 1971 *Guerra y Sociedad en Chile*. Editorial Universitaria, Santiago, Chile.

Johnson, G. A. 1973 *Local Exchange and Early State Development in Southwestern Iran*. Anthropological Paper 51. Museum of Anthropology, University of Michigan, Ann Arbor.

Johnson, G. A. 1982 Organizational Structure and Scalar Stress. In *Theory and Explanation in Archaeology*, edited by C. Renfrew, M. Rowlands, and B. Seagrave, pp. 389–421. Academic Press, New York.

Johnson, A. W. and T. Earle 1987 *The Evolution of Human Societies: From Foraging Group to Agrarian States*. Stanford University Press, Stanford, California.

Jones, K. L. 1999 Warfare, Reorganization, and Readaptation at the Margins of Spanish Rule: The Southern Margin (1573–1882). In *South America* (Vol. 2), edited by F. Salomon and S. B. Schwartz, pp. 139–187.

Cambridge University Press, London and New York.

Joseph, C. F. 1930 Las ceremonias araucanas. *Boletín del Museo Nacional* XXXIV. Santiago, Chile.

Joyce, R. 2003 Concrete Memories: Fragments of the Past in the Classic Maya Present (500–1000 AD). In *Archaeologies of Memory*, edited by R. M. Van Dyke and S. E. Alcock, pp 104–126. Blackwell Publishing, Massachusetts.

Jufre del Aguila, M. 1896 *Compendio Histórico del Descubrimiento, Conquista y Guerra del Reino de Chile*. Anales de la Universidad de Chile Vol. XCIII, Santiago.

Kalipeni, E. and P. T. Zeleza (editors) 1999 *Sacred Spaces and Public Quarrels: African Cultural and Economic Landscapes*. Africa World Press, New Jersey.

Kaufman, L., et al. 1998 Beta-Globin Gene Cluster Haplotypes in the Mapuche Indians of Argentina. *Genetic and Molecular Biology* 21(4). Sao Paulo.

Kaulicke, P. 2001 *Memoria y Muerte en el Perú Antiguo*. Pontificia Universidad Católica del Perú, Fondo Editorial, Lima, Perú.

Keeley, L. 1996 *War Before Civilization: The Myth of the Peaceful Savage*. Oxford University Press.

Keith, M. and S. Pile (editors) 1993 *Place and the Politics of Identity*. Routledge Press, London and New York.

Kertzer, D. 1988 *Ritual, Politics, and Power*. Yale University Press, New Haven, Connecticut.

Key, M. R. 1978 Linguistica comparativa Araucana. *Vicus Cuadernos Linguistica* 2:46–54.

Key, M. R. 1979 *The Grouping of South American Indian Languages*. Gunter Narr Verlas Tübingen.

Kicza, J. E. (editor) 1993 *The Indian in Latin American History: Resistance, Resilience, and Acculturation*. Scholarly Resources, Wilmington, Delaware.

Kidder, T. R. 2004 Plazas as Architecture: An Example from the Raffman Site, Northeast Louisiana. *American Antiquity* 69:514–533.

King, A. and J. Freer 1994 Mississippian Southeast: A World-Systems Perspective. In *Native American Interaction: Multiscalar Analyses and Interpretations in the Eastern Woodlands*, edited by M. S. Nassaney and K. E. Sassaman, pp. 266–288. University of Tennessee Press, Knoxville.

Kleinman, A. 1988 *The Illness Narratives: Suffering, Healing, and the Human Condition*. Basic Books, New York.

Knight, V. J. 1989 Symbolism of Mississippian Mounds. In *Powhatan's Mantle: Indians in the Colonial Southeast*, edited by T. M. Hatley, pp. 279–291. University of Nebraska Press, Lincoln.

Koss-Chioino, J. and P. Hefner 2006 *Spritual Transformations and Healing: Anthropological, Theological, Neurological, and Clinical Perspectives*. Altamira Press, Walnut Creek, California.

Kroskrity, P. 2000 *Regimes of Language: Ideologies, Polities, and Identities*. SAR Press, Santa Fe, New Mexico.

Krumm, G. S. 1971 División territorial de la Araucanía. *Revista Chilena de Historia y Geografía* 139:87–104. Santiago, Chile.

Kus, S. 1989 Sensuous human activity and the state: towards an archaeology of bread and circuses. In *Domination and Resistance*, edited by D. Miller and M. Rowlands, pp. 140–54. Routledge Press, London.

Lane, B. C. 2001 *Landscapes of the Sacred: Geography and Narrative in American Spirituality*. Johns Hopkins University Press, Baltimore.

Latcham, R. E. 1924 *Organización social y las creencias religiosas de los antiguos araucanos*. Imprenta Cervantes, Santiago.

Latcham, R. E. 1928a *La Alfarera Indígena Chilena*. Sociedad Impresora Litográfica Universo, Santiago.

Latcham, R. E. 1928b *La Prehistoria de Chile*. Sociedad Impresora y Litográfica Universo, Santiago.

Lathrap, D. 1985 Jaws: The Control of Power in the Early Nuclear American Ceremonial Center. In *Early Ceremonial Architecture in the Andes*, edited by C. Donnan, pp. 241–267. Dumbarton Oaks, Washington, D.C.

Latour, B. 1986 The Powers of Association. In *Power, Action and Belief*, edited by J. Law, pp. 264–280. Routledge Press, London and New York.

Lefebvre, H. 1991 *The Production of Space*. Blackwell Publishing, Oxford, England.

Lefort, C. 1988 *Democracy and Political Theory*. University of Minnesota Press, Minneapolis.

Leiva, A. 1977 *Rechazo y Absorción de Elementos de la Cultura Española por los Araucanos en el Primer Siglo de la Conquista de Chile (1541–1655)*. Tésis de Licenciatura. Universidad de Chile, Santiago.

Leiva, A. 1984 *El Primer Avance a la Araucanía: Angol 1862*. Ediciones Universidad de la Frontera, Temuco, Chile.

León, L. 1986 La resistencia anti-Española y el rol de las fortalezas indígenas en Chile Central, 1536–1545. *CHUSO* 3(1):53–116, Temuco, Chile.

León, L. 1991 *Maloqueros y Conchavadores en Araucanía y las Pampas, 1700–1800*. Universidad de La Frontera, Temuco, Chile.

León, L. 1999 *Apogeo y Ocaso de Toqui Ayllapangui de Malleco, Chile. 1769–1776*. Dirección de Bibliotecas, Archivos y Museos, Chile.

Levine, R. 1997 *A Geography of Time*. Basic Books, New York.

Lewis, R. B., C. Stout, and C. B. Wesson 1998 Design of Mississippian Towns. In *Mississippian Towns and Sacred Spaces: Searching for an Architectural Grammar*, edited by R. B. Lewis and C. Stout, pp.56–78. The University of Alabama Press, Alabama.

Ley, D. 1981 Behavorial Geography and the Philosophies of Meaning. In *Behavorial Problems in Geography Revisited*, edited by K. R. Cox and R. C. Golledge, pp. 209–230. Methuen, New York.

Liendo, R. 2002 *The Organization of Agricultural Production at a Classic Maya Center: Settlement Patterns in the Palenque Region, Chiapas, Mexico*. Instituto Nacional de Antropología e Historia and University of Pittsburgh, Pittsburgh.

Lillios, K. 2003 Creating Memory in Prehistory: The Engraved Slate Plaques of Southwest Iberia. In *Archaeologies of Memory*, edited by R. M. Van Dyke and S. E.

Alcock, pp. 129–150. Blackwell Publishing, Oxford, England.

Loyola, I. [1620] 1908 *Constituciones de la Compañía de Jesús y sus Declaraciones*. Stablimento Danesi, Rome.

Luigi, J. de 1957 La Araucana. *Anales de la Universidad de Chile* No. 107–108.

Lumbreras, L. G. 1974 *The Peoples and Cultures of Ancient Peru*. Smithsonian Institution Press, Washington, D.C.

Lumbreras, L. G. 1985 *Chavín de Huántar en el nacimiento de la civilización Andina*. Instituto Nacional de Investigaciones Andinas, Lima.

Maalouf, A. 1996 *In the Name of Identity: Violence and the Need to Belong*. Arcade Publishing, New York.

MacCormack, S. 1991 *Religion in the Andes: Vision and Imagination in Early Colonial Peru*. Princeton University Press, Princeton, New Jersey.

Maítus, L. 1914 Instrucciones para el estudio de antropología araucana. In *Chile. Museo Nacional de Historia Natural*. Santiago.

Malkki, L. 1992 National Geographic: The Rooting of Peoples and the Territorialization of National Identity among Scholars and Refugees. *Cultural Anthropology* 7:24–44.

Mandrini, R. 1984 *Los Araucanos de las pampas en el Siglo XIX*. Centro Editorial de América Latina, Buenos Aires.

Mandrini, R. 1992 Indios y fronteras en el área Pampeana (s. XVI–XIX). Balance y Perspectivas. *Anuario del IEHS*, VII: 59–92.

Mandrini, R. and S. Ortelli 2002 Los "Araucanos" en las pampas (c. 1700–1850). In *Colonización, Resistencia y Mestizaje en las Américas*, Siglos XVI–XX, edited by G. Bocarra, pp. 201–236. Ediciones Abya-Yala, Ecuador.

Mann, M. 1984 The Autonomous Power of the State: Its Origins, Mechanisms and Results. *European Journal of Sociology* 25:185–213.

Marimán, J. 1998 *Lumaco y el movimiento Mapuche*. Electronic document. Available at http://www.xs4all.nl/~rehue/art/jmar6.html, accessed 30 March.

Marimán, J. 2003 Análisis político Mapuche: identidad fragmentada. *Azkintue: Periodico Nacional Mapuche*. Available at http://www.nodo50.org/azkintuwe/.

Marin, L. 1984 *Utopics: Spatial Play*. Macmillan, London.

Marin, L. 1992 *Lectures Traversières*. Bibliothèque du College International de Philosophie Paris.

Mariño de Lobera, P. [1594] 1960 *Crónica del Reino de Chile*. Vol. CXXXI, Biblioteca de Autores Españoles, Madrid.

Mason, J. A. 1961 *Ancient Civilizations of Peru*. Penguin Books, Baltimore.

Mason, R. J. 2000 Archaeology and Native North American Oral Traditions. *American Antiquity* 65:239–266.

Massey, D. 1993 Politics and Space/Time. In *Place and the Politics of Identity*, edited by M. Keith and S. Pile. Routledge Press, London and New York.

Massey, D. 2000 Talking of Space-Time. *Transactions of the Institute for British Geography* NS 26:257–261.

Medina, A. 1978 El Estado Araucano. *Boletín de Prehistoria* 7–8:23–50.

Medina, J. [1852] 1952 *Los Aborígenes de Chile*. Fondo Histórico y Bibliográfico J. T. Medina, Santiago.

Medina, J. 1953 *Cartas de Pedro de Váldivia*, edited by J. Medina. Fondo Histórico y Bibliografía José Torbidio Medina, Santiago.

Melville, T. 1976 Las Políticas de Poder Social de Mapuche Contemporanea. In *Estudios Anthropológicos sobre los Mapuches de Chile Sur-Central*, edited by T. D. Dillehay, pp: 101–144. Pontificia Universidad Católica de Chile, Temuco.

Menghin, O. 1962 Estudios de prehistoria Araucana. *Acta Praehistorica III–IV*. Buenos Aires.

Mera, R. and C. Garcia 2002 *Alero Marifilo-1. Ocupación Holoceno Temprana en la Costa de Lago Calafquen, X Región, Chile*. Actas V Jornadas de la Patagonia, Buenos Aires.

Métraux, A. 1942 El Chamanismo Araucano. *Revista del Instituto de Antropología de la Universidad Nacional de Tucumán* 2(10):309–62.

Millaman, R. 1993 Chile's Mapuches Organize Against NAFTA. *NACLA Report on the Americas* 29(5): 30–31. Washington, D.C.

Miller, J. H. 1995 *Topographies*. Stanford University Press, Stanford.

Milner, G. 2004 *The Moundbuilders: Ancient Peoples of Eastern North America*. Thames & Hudson, London.

Mitchell, W. J. T. 1994 Imperial Landscape. In *Landscape and Power*, edited by W. J. T. Mitchell, pp. 5–34. University of Chicago Press, Chicago.

Moesbach, W. 1936 *Vida y Costumbres de los Indígenas Araucanos en la Segunda Mitad del Siglo XIX*. Imprenta Universitaria, Santiago.

Molina, J. I. 1788 *Compendio de la Historia Civil de Reyno de Chile*. Parte Primera, Madrid.

Molina, J. I. 1795 *Compendio de la Historia Civil de Reyno de Chile*. Parte Segunda, Madrid.

Montecino, S. 1980 *La Sociedad Mapuche entre los Siglos XVI y XIX: su Transformación Estructural Tésis de Licenciatura*. Universidad de Chile, Santiago.

Moore, J. 1996 *Architecture and Power in the Ancient Andes: The Archaeology of Public Buildings*. Cambridge University Press, Cambridge.

Morris, C. 1972 State Settlements in Tawantinsuyu: A Strategy of Compulsory Urbanism. In *Contemporary Archaeology: A Guide to Theory and Contributions*, edited by M. Leone, pp. 393–401. Southern Illinois University Press, Carbondale.

Mostny, G. 1971 *Prehistoria de Chile*. Editorial Universitaria, Santiago de Chile.

Murra, J. 1975 El Control Vertical de una Máximo de Pisos Ecológicos en la Economia de las Sociedades Andinas. (1972). In *Formaciones Económias y Políticas del Mundo Andino*, edited by J. Murra, pp. 59–115. Instituto de Estudios Peruanos, Lima.

Nacuzzi, L. R. 1998 *Identidades impuestas: Tehuelches, aucas y pampas en el norte de la Patagonia*. Sociedad Argentina de Antropología, Buenos Aires.

Nanculef, J. 1990 La Autonomia y la Organización Social del Pueblo Mapuche. *Boletín Nutram* 2:9–22. Editorial Rehue, Santiago.

Navarro, X and L. Adán 1999 Experiencias tempranas de vida alfarera en el sector Lacustre Cordillerano de Villarrica. La ocupación del sitio Pucón VI. *Revista Chilena de Antropología*, 22:13–27. Santiago.

Núñez de Pineda y Bascuñán F. [1673] 1973 *Cautiverio Feliz y Razón de las Guerras Dilatadas de Chile*. Imprenta el Ferrocarril, Santiago.

Núñez de Pineda y Bascuñán F. [1673] 2003 *Cautiverio Feliz*. Colección Histórica Chilena. Santiago.

Olaverría, Miguel de [1594] 1852 Informe de don Miguel de Olaverría sobre el reyno de Chile, sus indios y sus guerras. In *Historia física y política de Chile*, edited by C. Gay. Paris.

Olivares, Miguel de [1594] 1864 Historia Militar, Civil, y Sagrada de Chile. *Colección de Historiadores de Chile*, Vol. 4. Imprenta del Ferrocarril, Santiago.

Oña, P. [1596] 1975 *Arauco Domado*. Editorial Universitaria, Santiago.

Ortiz, C. R. 2005a *Etnicidad en la Era de la Globalización: Estudio Comparativo sobre la Construcción de la Identidad Etnica en Comunidades Mapuche del Valle Purén y Lumaco*. Tésis de Licenciatura en Antropología. Universidad Austral de Chile, Valdivia.

Ortiz, C. R. 2005b *Cuaderno de Campo: Descripciones Etnográficas sobre Butarincón y sus Alrededores*. Technical report submitted to Proyecto Puren-Lumaco.

Ortiz, C. R. 2006 *Informe Etnográfico del Valle de Puren y Lumaco*. Manuscript in possession of author.

Otterbein, K. F. 1973 The Anthropology of War. In *Handbook of Social and Cultural Anthropology*, edited by J. J. Honigmann, pp. 923–958. Rand McNally, Chicago.

Ovalle, A. de [1646] 2003 *Histórica Relación del Reino de Chile*. Imprenta Pehuen, Santiago.

Oviedo, C. [1626] 1964 *Sínodo Diocesano de Santiago de Chile, 1626 (celebrado por) Francisco González de Salcedo*. Centro Intercultural de Documentación, Cuernavaca, Mexico.

Owen, B. 2005 Distant Colonies and Explosive Collapse: The Two Stages of the Tiwanaku Diaspora in the Osmore Drainage. *Latin American Antiquity* 16:45–80.

Padden, R. 1993 Cultural Adaptation and Militant Autonomy among the Araucanians of Chile. In *The Indian in Latin American History*, edited by J. Kicza, pp. 69–88. Scholarly Resources, Delaware.

Palermo, M. A. 1986 Reflexiones sobre el llamado 'complejo ecuestre' en la Argentina, en RUNA. *Archivo para las Ciencias del Hombre*, XVI (Buenos Aires): 157–178.

Parker, B. 2006 Toward an Understanding of Borderland Processes. *American Antiquity* 71:77–100.

Patterson, T. C. 1987 Tribes, Chiefdoms, and Kingdoms in the Inca Empire. In *Power Relations and State Formations*, edited by T. C. Patterson and C. W. Gailey, pp. 117–127. American Anthropological Association, Washington, D.C.

Patterson, T. C. 2004 Class Conflict, State Formation and Archaism. *Journal of Social Archaeology* 4(3):288–306.

Pauketat, T. R. 2004 The Economy of the Moment: Cultural Practices and Mississippian Chiefdoms. In *Archaeological Perspectives on Political Economies*, edited by G. Feinman and L. M. Nichols, pp. 25–40. University of Utah Press, Salt Lake City.

Payne, D. and R. Croese n.d. *On Mapugungun Linguistic Affiliations: An Evaluation of Previous Proposals and Evidence for an Arawakan Relationship*. Instituto Linguistico de Verano, Peru, and Universidad de la Frontera, Chile.

Pearson, M. P. 1994 Architecture and Order: Spatial Representation and Archaeology. In *Architecture and Order: Approaches to Social Space*, edited by M. P. Pearson and C. Richards, pp. 38–72. Routledge Press, London.

Pearson M. P. and C. Richards (editors) 1994 *Architecture and Order: Approaches to Social Space*. Routledge Press, London.

Pease, F. 1987 The Formation of Tawantinsuyu: Mechanisms of Colonization and Relationship with Ethnic Groups. In *The Inca and Aztec Status, 1400–1800*, edited by G. A. Collier, R. Rosaldo, and J. D. Wirth, pp. 173–198. Academia Press, New York.

Pentikainen, J. 1998 *Shamanism and Culture*. Etnika, Helsinki.

Pino, M. and O. Sequel 2004 *Informe del Estudio Paleocológico para el Proyecto Purén y Lumaco*. Manuscript in possession of the author. Vanderbilt University, Nashville, Tennessee.

Pino, M. 2004 Personal communication.

Pizarro, P. [1571] 1921 *Relation of the Discovery and Conquest of the Kingdoms of Peru*. Translated by Phillip Means. The Cortes Society of New York, New York.

Poblete, F. 2002 *Informe Etnográfica del Valle de Purén: Proyecto Purén-Lumaco*. Manuscript in possesion of author.

Pollard, J. 2001 The Aesthetics of Depositional Practice. *World Archaeology* 33:315–333.

Pollard, J. and C. Ruggles 2001 Shifting Perceptions: Spatial Order, Cosmology, and Patterns of Deposition of Stonehenge. *Cambridge Archaeological Journal* 11:68–90.

Prakash, G. 1995 *After Colonialism*. Princeton University Press, Princeton, New Jersey.

Pred, A. 1983 Structuration and Place: On Becoming of Sense and Place and Structure of Feeling. *Journal for the Theory of Social Behavior* 13:45–68.

Pred, A. 1990 *Making Histories and Constructing Human Geographies*. Westview Press, Boulder, Colorado.

Price, B. 1978 Secondary State Formation: An explanatory model. In *Origins of the State: The Anthropology of Political Evolution*, edited by R. Cohen and E. Service, pp. 161–186. Institute for the Study Human Issues, Philadelphia.

Price, N. 2001 An Archaeology of Altered States: Shamanism and Material Culture Studies. In *The Archeology of Shamanism*, edited by N. Price, pp. 3–16. Routledge Press, London and New York.

Quiroga, G. De [1690] 1979 *Memorias de los sucesos de la guerra de Chile*. Editorial Andrés Bello, Santiago.

Quiroz, D. and M. Sánchez 1997 *La isla de las palabras rotas.* Centro de Investigaciones. Barros Arana, Santiago.

Ramenofsky, A. F. 1987 *Vectors of Death: The Archaeology of European Contact.* University of New Mexico Press, Albuquerque.

Rappaport, J. 1985 History, Myth, and the Dynamics of Territorial Maintenance in Tierradentro, Colombia. *American Ethnologist* 12(1):27–45.

Rappaport, J. 1998 *The Politics of Memory: Native Historical Interpretation in the Colombian Andes.* Duke University Press, Durham, North Coralina

Redrado, R. 1775 Relación de los indios de las dos juridiciones de Chile y Valdivia y sus inclinaciones, errores y costumbres. *AFC, AS-VA:*Vol. 3. Santiago.

Ribeiro, D. 1973 *Fronteras Indígenas de la Civilización.* Siglo Veintiuno, México.

Robles, V. H. 1942 *Costumbre y Creencias Araucanas.* Ediciones Universidad de Chile, Santiago.

Rojas, A. 2005 *Informe etnográfico de la campana de terreno del Proyecto Purén-Lumaco.* Manuscript in possession of author.

Rojas, A. 2006 *Informe etnográfico de la campana de terreno del Proyecto Purén-Lumaco.* Manuscript in possession of author.

Rosales, D. de [1674] 1989 *Historia General del Reino de Chile,* Vol. 1. Editorial Andrés Bello, Santiago, Chile.

Rostworowski, de Díez Canseco, M. 1983 *Estructuras Andinas del poder. Ideologia religiosa y política.* Historia Andina 10. Instituto do Estudios Peruanos, Lima.

Rowe, J. H. 1967 Form and Meaning of Chavin Art. *Peruvian Archeology* :Selected Readings, edited by J. H. Rowe and Dorothy Menzel, pp. 72–103. Peek Publications, San Francisco.

Saavedra, A. 2002 *Los Mapuches en el Sociedad Chilena Actual.* LOM Ediciones, Santiago.

Saavedra, C. 1870 *Documentos Relativos a la Ocupación de Arauco,* Santiago.

Sahlins, M. 1985 *Islands of History.* Chicago University Press, Chicago.

Saitta, D. 1994 Agency, Class, and Archaeological Interpretation. *Journal of Anthropological Archaeology* 13(5):201–227.

San Martin, R. 1976 Machitun: Una Ceremonia Mapuche. In Las Políticas de Poder Social de Mapuche Contemporanea. In *Estudios Antropológicos sobre los Mapuches de Chile Sur-Central,* edited by T. D. Dillehay, pp. 164–209. Pontificia Universidad Católica de Chile, Temuco.

San Martín, R. 2002 *Informe etnográfico de la campana de terreno del Proyecto Purén-Lumaco.* Manuscript in possession of author.

Sans, M 2000 Admixture Studies in Latin America: From the 20th to the 21st Century. *Human Biology* 72(1):155–781.

Scarre, C. (editor) 2002a *Monuments and Landscape in Atlantic Europe: Perception and Society during the Neolithic and Early Bronze Age.* Routledge Press, London and New York.

Scarre, C. (editor) 2002b A Place of Special Meaning: Interpreting Pre-Historic Monuments in the Landscape. In *Inscribed Landscapes: Marking and Making Place,* edited

by B. David and M. Wilson. University of Hawaii Press, Honolulu.

Schama, S. 1996 *Landscape and Memory.* Vintage Books, New York.

Scott, J. C. 1985 *Weapons of the Weak: Everyday Forms of Peasant Resistance.* Yale University Press, New Haven, Conn.

Sekaquaptewa, E. and D. Washburn 2004 They Go Along Singing: Reconstructing the Hopi Past from Ritual Metaphors in Song and Images. *American Antiquity* 69:487–513.

Sepulveda, G. 1987 Personal communication.

Shady, R. and C. Leyva 2002 *La Ciudad Sagrada de Caral-Supe.* Instituto Nacional de Cultura, Lima.

Sheldrake, P. 2001 *Spaces for the Sacred: Place, Memory and Identity.* SCM Press, London.

Silva, C. 2006 *Informe sobre los Restos Arqueobotánicos del Proyecto de Purén-Lumaco.* Manuscript in possession of the author.

Silva, O. 1983 Detuvo la batalla de Maule le expansión Inca? *Cuadernos de Historia* 3:7–26.

Silva, O. 2001 Butanmapu Mapuche en el Parlamentos Pehuenche de Fuerte de San Carlos Mendoza, 1805. *Revista de Historia Indígena* 5:9–21.

Silva, O. and E. Téllez 1995 Los Pewenche: identidad y configuración de un mosaico étnico colonial. *Cuadernos de Historia* 13:23–44.

Silva, O. and E. Téllez 2001 Los Butalmapus de los Llanos en la Araucania. *Cuadernos de Historia* 21:12–23. Santiago.

Smith, A. 2000 Rendering the political aesthetic: political legitimacy in Uarrtian representations of the built environment. *Journal of Anthropological Archaeology* 19:131–63.

Smith, A. 2003 *The Political Landscape: Constellations of Authority in Early Complex Polities.* University of California Press, Berkeley.

Smith, B. D. 1990 *Mississippian Emergence.* Smithsonian Institution Press, Washington, D.C.

Soja, E. W. 1996 *Thirdspace.* Blackwell Publishers, Oxford, England.

Solís, L. 1990 *Maloqueros y Conchavadores en Araucanía y Las Pampas, 1700–1800.* Universidad de la Frontera, Temuco.

Spencer, C. 1993 Human Agency, Biased Transmission, and the Cultural Evolution of Chiefly Authority. *Journal of Anthropological Archaeology* 12:41–74.

Squire, E. G. and E. H. Davis 1997 *Ancient Mounuments of the Mississippi Valley.* Smithsonian Institution Press, Washington D.C.

Stanish, C. 2003 *Ancient Titicaca: The Evolution of Complex Society in Southern Society in Southern Peru and Northern Bolivia.* University of California Press, Berkeley.

Stehberg, R. L. 1976 *La Fortaleza de Chena y su Relación con la Ocupación Incaica de Chile Central.* Museo Nacional de Historia Natural, Santiago.

Stein, G. 2005 *The Archaeology of Colonial Encounters: Comparative Perspectives.* SAR Press, Santa Fe, New Maxico.

Stern, S. J. (editor) 1987 *Resistance, Rebellion, and Consciousness in the Andean Peasant World.* The University of Wisconsin Press, Madison, Wisconsin.

Stewart, P. and A. Strathern (editors) 2005 *Contesting Rituals: Islam and Practices of Identity-making*. Carolina Academic Press, Raleigh, North Carolina.

Stocking, Jr., G. W. (editor) 1987 *Colonial Situations: Essays on the Contextualization of Ethnographic Knowledge*. University of Wisconsin Press, Madison, Wisconsin.

Stuchlik, M. 1976 *Life on a Half Share: Mechanisms of Social Recruitment among the Mapuche of Southern Chile*. St. Martin's Press, New York.

Swan, J. A. 1990 *Sacred Places*. Bear & Co., Santa Fe, New Mexico.

Swan, J. A. 1991 *The Power of Place: Sacred Ground in Natural & Human Environments*, edited by Swan, J. A. Quest Books, Wheaton, Illinois.

Taussig, M. 1991 *Mimesis and Alterity: a Particular History of the Senses*. Routledge Press, London and New York.

Tellez, E. 2004 Evolución Historica de la Población Mapuche del Reino de Chile: 1536–1810. *Historia Indígena* 8:96–105.

Tesillo, S. De [1647] 1911 *Guerras de Chile: causas de su duración, advertencias para su fin*. Imprenta Ferrocarril, Santiago.

Thayer Ojeda, T. 1908 *Los Conquistadores de Chile*. Santiago

Thayer Ojeda, T. 1917 *Ensayo crítico sobre algunas obras históricas utilizables para el estudio de la Conquista de Chile*. Santiago

Thomas, J. 1991 *Rethinking the Neolithic*. Cambridge University Press, Cambridge.

Thomas, J. 1995 Politics of Vision and the Archaeologies of Landscape. In *Landscape: Politics and Perspectives*, edited by B. Bender, pp. 19–48. Berg, Oxford.

Thrift, N. 1988 Vicos Voco: Ringing the Changes in the Historical Geography Time Consciousness. In *The Rhythms of Society*, edited by M. Young and T. Schuller, pp. 53–94. Routledge Press, London, and New York.

Thrift, N. 1989 Images of Social Change. In *The Changing Social Structure*, edited by C. Hamnett, L. McDowell, and P. Sarre. Sage, London.

Thrift, N. 1998 Re-Imagining Places, Re-Imagining Identities. In *Consumption and Everday Life*, edited by H. Mackay, pp. 159–212. Sage, London.

Thrift, N. and A. Pred 1981 Time–Geography: A New Beginning. *Progress in Human Geography* 5:227–286.

Tierney, P. 1989 *The Highest Altar: The Story of Human Sacrifice*. Viking, New York.

Tilley, C. 1994 *Phenomenology of Landscape: Places, Paths and Monuments*. Berg, Oxford and Providence.

Titiev, M. 1951 *Araucanian Culture in Transition*. University of Michigan Press, Ann Arbor.

Treutler, P. 1958 *Andanzas de un Aleman en Chile: 1851–1863*. Editorial del Pacífico, Santiago.

Tuan, Y. F. 1974a Space and Place: Humanistic Perspective. *Progress in Geography* 6:211–252.

Tuan, Y. F. 1974b *Topophilia: A Study of Environmental Perception, Attitudes, and Values*. Prentice Hall, Englewood Cliffs, New Jersey.

Tuan, Y. F. 1976 Geopiety: A Theme in Man's Attachment to Nature and to Place. In *Geographies of the Mind: Essays in Historical Geography in Honor of John Kirtland Wright*, edited by D. Lowenthal and M. J. Bowden, pp. 13–14. Oxford University Press, New York.

Tuan, Y. F. 1977 *Space and Place: The Perspective of Experience*. University of Minnesota Press, Minneapolis.

Trigger, B. 1990 Monumental Architecture: A Thermo-dynamic Explanation of Symbolic Behavior. *World Archaeology* 22:119–132.

Turner, B. 1990 *Organizational Symbolism*. Routledge Press, London.

Turner, V. 1973 *Dramas, Fields, and Metaphors*. Cornell University Press, Ithaca, New York.

Uhle, M. 1909 La Esfera de Influencias del País de los Incas. *Revista Historica* 4:5–40. Lima.

Urton, G. 1981 *At the Crossroads of the Earth and the Sky: An Andean Cosmology*. University of Texas Press, Austin.

Urton, G. 1985 *Animal Myths and Metaphors in South America*. University of Utah Press, Salt Lake City.

Urton, G. 1990 *The History of a Myth*. The University of Austin Press, Austin, Texas.

Urton, G. 1999 *Inca Myths*. University of Texas Press, Austin.

Valderrama, J. 1927 *Diccionario Histórico-Geográfico de la Araucanía*. Santiago.

Valdivia, L. de [1606] 1887 *Arte, Vocabulario y Confesionario de la Lengua de Chile*. Teubner, Leipzig.

Valdivia, L. de [1612] 1887 *Relación de lo que secedio en la jornada que hicimos el señor Presidente Alonso de Rivera, Gobernador de este reino, y yo, desde Arauco a Paicavi, a concluir las paces de Elicura, ultima regua de Tucapel, y las de Purén y la Imperial (1612)*. Published in Volume II of the Biblioteca Hispano-Chilena by José Toribio Medina (1887), Santiago.

Valdivia, P. de [1555] 1960 *Cartas de Relación de la Conquista de Chile*, edited by Mario Ferreccio Podesta. Editorial Universitaria, Santiago.

Van Dyke, R. M. and S. E. Alcock (editors) 2003 *Archaeologies of Memory*. Blackwell Publishing, Oxford, England.

Villalobos, S. and J. Pinto (editors) 1985 *Araucanía: Temas de Historia Fronteriza*. Ediciones Universidad de la Frontera, Temuco, Chile.

Villalobos, S. C. Aldunte, H. Zapater, L. U. Méndez, and C. Bascuñán (editors) 1982 *Relaciones Fronterizas en la Araucania*. Ediciones Universidad Católica de Chile, Santiago.

Vitebsky, P. 1995 *The New Shamans: Psyche and Environment in an Age of Questioning*. Viking Penguin, New York.

Wachtel, N. 1971 Le dualisme Chipaya: compte-rendu du mission. *Boletín del Instituto Francés de Estudios Andinos* 3:55–65. Lima.

Washburn, D. 2003 *Religious Song Texts as Oral History*. Paper presented at the Fifth World Archaeological Congress, Washington, D.C., 23 June.

Whitehouse, H. and J. Laidlaw 2004 *Ritual and Memory: Toward a Comparative Anthropology of Religion*. AltaMira Press, Walnut Creek, Calif.

Wolf, E. 1984 Culture: Panacea or Problem. *American Antiquity* 49:393–400.

Wolf, E. 1999 *Envisioning Power: Ideologies of Dominance and Crisis.* University of California Press, Berkeley.

Wright, H. T. 1984 Primate Political Formations. In *On the Evolution of Complex Societies: Essays in Honor of Harry Hoifer*, edited T. K. Earle, pp. 43–77. Undena.

Wylie, A. 1982 Epistomological Issues raised by a structuralist archaeology. In *Symbolic and Structural Archaeology*, edited by I. Hodder, pp. 39–46. Cambridge University Press.

Yaeger, J. and M. A. Canuto 2002 Introducing an Archaeology of Communities. In *The Archaeology of Communities: A New World Perspective*, edited by J. Yaeger and M. A. Canuto, pp. 1–15. Routledge Press, London and New York.

Yoffee, N. 2005 *Myths of the Archaic State: Evolution of the Earliest Cities, States and Civilizations.* Cambridge University Press, New York.

Zapater, H. 1973 *Los Aborígenes Chilenos a través de Cronistas y Viajeros.* Editorial Andrés Bello, Santiago.

Zapater, H. 1974 Esbozo histórico del desarrollo de los pueblos Araucanos. *Estudios 89.* Instituto de Geografía, Universidad Católica de Chile, Santiago.

Zapater, H. 1978 Visión Araucana de la Conquista. *Revista Chilena de Antropología* 1:163–172.

Zapater, H. 1992 *La Busqueda de la Pax en la Guerra de Arauco: Padre Luis de Valdivia.* Editorial Andres Bello. Santiago.

Zavala, J. M. 2000 *Les Indiens Mapuche du Chili: Dynamiques Inter-Ethniques et Stratégies de Résistance.* L'Harmattan-IHEAL, Paris.

Zavala, J. M. 2005 *Informe Etnográfico del Valle de Purén y Lumaco.* Manuscript on file with author.

Zavala, J. M. 2006 *Informe Etnográfico del Valle de Purén y Lumaco.* Manuscript on file with author.

Zuidema, R. T. 1964 *The Ceque System of Cuzco: The Social Organization of the Capital of the Inca.* E.J. Brill, Leiden.

Zuidema, R. T. 1977 The Inca Kinship system: A New Theoretical View. *Special Publication of the American Anthropological Association*, no. 7: 240–292. Washington D.C.

Zuidema, R. T. 1985 The Lion in the City: Royal Symbols of Transition in Cuzco. In *Animal Myths and Metaphors in South America*, edited by G. Urton, pp. 183–250. University of Utah Press, Salt Lake City.

Zuidema, R. T. 1990 Dynastic Structures in Andean Cultures. In *The Northern Dynasties: Kingship and Statecraft in Chimor*, edited by M. Moseley and A. Cordy-Collins, pp. 489–505. Dumbarton Oaks Research Library and Collection, Washington, D.C.

INDEX